1978年海员培训、发证和值班标准国际公约马尼拉修正案

THE MANILA AMENDMENTS TO THE INTERNATIONAL CONVENTION ON STANDARDS OF TRAINING, CERTIFICATION AND WATCHKEEPING FOR SEAFARERS, 1978

中华人民共和国海事局　译

大连海事大学出版社

图书在版编目(CIP)数据

1978 年海员培训、发证和值班标准国际公约马尼拉修正案 : 汉英对照 / 中华人民共和国海事局译. —大连:大连海事大学出版社,2010.12(2013.4 重印)

ISBN 978-7-5632-2493-7

Ⅰ.①1… Ⅱ.①中… Ⅲ.①海员—管理—国际公约—汉、英 Ⅳ.①D998.2

中国版本图书馆 CIP 数据核字(2010)第 231131 号

大连海事大学出版社出版

地址:大连市凌海路 1 号　邮编:116026　电话:0411-84728394 传真:0411-84727996

http://www.dmupress.com　E-mail:cbs@dmupress.com

大连住友彩色印刷有限公司印装　大连海事大学出版社发行

2010 年 12 月第 1 版　2013 年 4 月第 2 次印刷

幅面尺寸:210 mm×297 mm　印张:53

字数:1200 千　印数:3001~5000 册

责任编辑:姚文兵　沈荣欣　封面设计:王　艳

责任校对:陈　亮　李继凯　史云霞

ISBN 978-7-5632-2493-7　定价:180.00 元

序

1978年7月，国际海事组织(IMO)通过了有史以来第一个《海员培训、发证和值班标准国际公约》(STCW公约)。1980年6月8日，我国政府向国际海事组织提交了批准STCW公约的文件，成为该公约的缔约国。公约于1984年4月生效。

1978年STCW公约通过和生效后，对促进包括我国在内的各缔约国海员素质的提高，在全球范围内保障海上人命、财产安全和保护海洋环境，有效控制人为因素对海上事故的影响，都起到了积极作用。

根据航海技术及航运业发展的需要，公约进行了多次修正。其中，1995年修正案对STCW公约的附则进行了全面修改，同时新制定了《海员培训、发证和值班规则》(STCW规则)，作为对STCW公约附则的补充。

随着全球经济一体化的进程，船舶正朝着大型化、快速化、专业化、现代化的方向发展，全球对海洋环境保护更严格，包括信息技术(IT)在内的新技术的应用越来越广泛与深入，对海员的培训与值班标准的要求越来越高。同时，由于海盗猖獗，海运安全受到严重的挑战，对海员的培训与值班标准又提出了新的保安要求。1995年修正案生效后，国际海事组织又对STCW公约和STCW规则进行了多次修正。1995年修正案通过10年后，国际海事组织认为需要对STCW公约和STCW规则进行全面回顾，从而对STCW公约与STCW规则进行系统的修正。

2006年，应STW分委会第37次会议的请求，海上安全委员会(MSC)第81次会议指示STW分委会在工作计划中加入“对STCW公约和规则全面回顾”的高优先权议题。2007年STW分委会第38次会议确定了对STCW公约和规则全面回顾的原则。经过4次STW分委会会议及2次特别会间会议的审议，2010年1月召开的STW分委会第41次会议基本完成对STCW公约和规则进行全面回顾的议题，形成STCW公约和规则的修正草案。该修正草案于2010年6月21日~25日在菲律宾马尼拉召开的STCW公约缔约国外交大会上获得通过，该修正案称为STCW公约马尼拉修正案。STCW公约马尼拉修正案将于2012年1月1日生效。

马尼拉修正案保留了STCW公约1995年修正案的结构与目标，不降低现有标准，不修改公约条款。其主要修正内容如下：

(1)理顺并规范了三种证书(适任证书、培训合格证书及书面证明)，规定适任证书及油船、化学品船、液化气船船长和高级船员的培训合格证应有海事主管机关签发。

(2)新增证书的签发和登记条款，对海上服务资历的认可、培训课程的确认、登记的电子查询、证书注册数据库的开发等都作了明确规定。

(3)明确了海员健康标准及健康证书的签发要求。要求海员健康检查均由缔约国认可的完全合格的有经验的从业医生完成。

(4)在控制近岸航行原则中新增缔约国应与相关国家就有关航区和其他相关条款的细节达成一致的条款。

(5)增加了独立评价报告内容的明确要求，对最初资料交流(履约报告)、后续报告(独立评价报告)及有资格人员的小组等作了明确规定。

(6)增加了公司的责任。公司应确保其指派到任一船上的海员均接受了本公约要求的知识更新的培训；任何时候都必须按SOLAS公约第V章第14条第3款的规定确保其在船上能进行有效的口头交流。

(7)修正了休息时间的量化标准，力求与《2006年海事劳工公约》的规定一致。

(8)调整了液货船船长、高级船员和普通船员培训和资格强制性最低要求。

(9)强调了团队精神、领导力和团队工作技能的要求，将BRM(驾驶台资源管理)、ERM(机舱资源管理)作为强制性要求。

(10)增加了提倡使用电子航海天文历和天文航海计算软件的内容。

(11)强调了对ECDIS、船用电子设备的知识、理解和熟练的要求。

(12)增加了电子员的培训与适任要求；增加了高级值班水手、高级值班机工与电子技工的培训与适任要求。

(13)加强了海洋环境保护意识方面的培训要求。

(14)强调与明确了保安要求。

为全面推进STCW公约马尼拉修正案的履约工作，中国政府对修正案的翻译工作高度重视。交通运输部海事局从2010年年初即开始组织专家对马尼拉修正案进行翻译，并先后召开了多次翻译和审定工作会议，包括：

2010年2月2日北京履约工作准备会议，会上对修正案的翻译进行了具体的分工布置；

2010年2月10日大连STCW公约有关术语翻译审定会，对公约中有关术语的翻译进行了规范，参会人员包括大连海事大学吴兆麟、刘正江、东昉、罗卫华、鲍君忠，上海海事大学阮巍，青岛远洋船员学院孟祥武、刘肖沛，广东海事局王伟奇，以及辽宁海事局和大连海事大学的其他人员；

2010年3月22日至28日东莞沙田翻译审定会，对公约修正草案进行了第一次翻译审定，会议由交通运输部海事局船员处李恩洪主持，参会人员包括大连海事大学吴兆麟、刘正江、孙培廷、东昉、罗卫华、鲍君忠、黄连忠，上海海事大学阮巍、李品友，青岛远洋船员学院张铎、卫桂荣、高兴斌，武汉理工大学付耀芳、杨志勇，集美大学黄志、李品芳，上海海事局王兴琦，上海海事职业技术学院潘艳萍，广东海事局毛洪鑫、王伟奇、陈悦、姜华、李隽枫；

2010年4月至7月间，大连海事大学在大连组织了两次对修正案的翻译审定会，STCW公约履约分委会在上海组织了一次对修正案的翻译审定会；

2010年8月9日至18日大连翻译审定会，对马尼拉缔约国大会通过的修正案进行翻译审定，形成正式的中文审定稿，参会人员包括交通运输部海事局郑和平、李大泽、石万里，大连海事大学东昉、鲍君忠、尚晓华、李冰冰，青岛远洋船员学院孟祥武、刘肖沛、张铎，集美大学翁跃宗，上海海事职业技术学院李勇，上海海事局王兴琦，上海远洋培训中心薛菁，广东海事局梁军、毛洪鑫、王伟奇、陈悦、姜华，以及大连海事大学出版社的部分人员。

2010年8月26日至27日在广州召开我国履约工作框架专家研讨会，成立STCW公约马尼拉修正案解读组，李恩洪为组长，成员包括韩杰祥、东昉、鲍君忠、戴达、孟祥武、阮巍、李勇、张铎、王伟奇。公约解读组负责马尼拉修正案中文译稿的最后审校工作。

部海事局又委托相关专家对马尼拉大会通过的最终文件正文和所附的19个决议进行翻译，最终形成了目前的《1978年海员培训、发证和值班标准国际公约马尼拉修正案》的中文译稿。

本次出版的中英文对照文本收录了《1978年海员培训、发证和值班标准国际公约》的正文和马尼拉缔约国大会通过的最终文件。为帮助读者全面正确理解STCW公约马尼拉修正案的内涵,促进履约工作的有效开展,马尼拉修正案解读组同时编写了《STCW公约马尼拉修正案履约指南》,另行出版。

由于时间的原因,马尼拉修正案的中文译本必然会存在许多不足,欢迎读者批评指正。

中华人民共和国海事局

2010年11月

Contents

目　录

Attachment 3 to the Final Act of the Conference

大会最终文件附件 3

International Convention on Standards of Training, Certification and Watchkeeping for Seafarers, 1978

THE PARTIES TO THIS CONVENTION,

DESIRING to promote safety of life and property at sea and the protection of the marine environment by establishing in common agreement international standards of training, certification and watchkeeping for seafarers,

CONSIDERING that this end may best be achieved by the conclusion of an International Convention on Standards of Training, Certification and Watchkeeping for Seafarers,

HAVE AGREED as follows:

Article I
General obligations under the Convention

(1) The Parties undertake to give effect to the provisions of the Convention and the annex thereto, which shall constitute an integral part of the Convention. Every reference to the Convention constitutes at the same time a reference to the annex.

(2) The Parties undertake to promulgate all laws, decrees, orders and regulations and to take all other steps which may be necessary to give the Convention full and complete effect, so as to ensure that, from the point of view of safety of life and property at sea and the protection of the marine environment, seafarers on board ships are qualified and fit for their duties.

Article II
Definitions

For the purpose of the Convention, unless expressly provided otherwise:

(a) *Party* means a State for which the Convention has entered into force;

(b) *Administration* means the Government of the Party whose flag the ship is entitled to fly;

(c) *Certificate* means a valid document, by whatever name it may be known, issued by or under the authority of the Administration or recognized by the Administration authorizing the holder to serve as stated in this document or as authorized by national regulations;

(d) *Certificated* means properly holding a certificate;

(e) *Organization* means the Inter-Governmental Maritime Consultative Organization (IMCO);*

(f) *Secretary-General* means the Secretary-General of the Organization;

* The name of the Organization was changed to "International Maritime Organization (IMO)" by virtue of amendments to the Organization's Convention which entered into force on 22 May 1982.

1978 年海员培训、发证和值班标准国际公约

各缔约国，

本着制定一致同意的海员培训、发证和值班的国际标准，以增进海上人命与财产的安全和保护海洋环境的愿望，

考虑到达到这一目的的最好办法为缔结一项海员培训、发证和值班标准国际公约，

现经协议如下：

第 I 条　公约的一般义务

（1）　各缔约国承担义务实施本公约及其附则的各项规定，该附则为本公约的组成部分。凡引用本公约时，同时也就是引用该附则。

（2）　各缔约国承担义务颁布一切必要的法律、法令、命令和规则，并采取一切必要的其他措施，使本公约充分和完全生效，以便从海上人命与财产的安全和保护海洋环境的观点出发，保证船上的海员胜任其职责。

第 II 条　定 义

除另有明文规定者外，就本公约而言：

（a）　“缔约国”系指本公约已对之生效的国家；

（b）　“主管机关”系指船舶有权悬挂其国旗的缔约国政府；

（c）　“证书”系指由主管机关颁发或经主管机关授权颁发或为主管机关所认可的一种有效文件（不论其名称如何），该文件委派其持有人担任该文件中所指定的或国家规章所规定的职务；

（d）　“具有证书的”系指持有恰当的证书；

（e）　“组织”系指政府间海事协商组织（海协）；①

（f）　“秘书长”系指海协组织秘书长；

① 本组织的名称已由 1982 年 5 月 22 日生效的本组织公约的修正案更名为“国际海事组织（IMO）”。

(g) *Seagoing ship* means a ship other than those which navigate exclusively in inland waters or in waters within, or closely adjacent to, sheltered waters or areas where port regulation apply;

(h) *Fishing vessel* means a vessel used for catching fish, whales, seals, walrus or other living resources of the sea;

(i) *Radio Regulations* means the Radio Regulations annexed to, or regarded as being annexed to, the most recent International Telecommunication Convention which may be in force at any time.

Article III
Application

The Convention shall apply to seafarers serving on board seagoing ships entitled to fly the flag of a Party except to those serving on board;

(a) warships, naval auxiliaries or other ships owned or operated by a State and engaged only on governmental non-commercial service; however, each Party shall ensure, by the adoption of appropriate measures not impairing the operations or operational capabilities of such ships owned or operated by it, that the persons serving on board such ships meet the requirements of the Convention so far as is reasonable and practicable;

(b) fishing vessels;

(c) pleasure yachts not engaged in trade; or

(d) wooden ships of primitive build.

Article IV
Communication of information

(1) The Parties shall communicate as soon as practicable to the Secretary-General:

(a) the text oflaws, decrees, orders, regulations and instruments promulgated on the various matters within the scope of the Convention;

(b) full details, where appropriate, of contents and duration of study courses, together with their national examination and other requirements for each certificate issued in compliance with the Convention;

(c) a sufficient number of specimen certificates issued in compliance with the Convention.

(2) The Secretary-General shall notify all Parties of the receipt of any communication under paragraph (1) (a) and, *inter alia*, for the purposes of articles IX and X, shall, on request, provide them with any information communicated to him under paragraphs (1) (b) and (c).

(g) “海船”系指除了在内陆水域中或者遮蔽水域或港章所适用的区域以内或与此两者紧邻的水域中航行的船舶以外的船舶;

(h) “渔船”系指用于捕捞鱼类、鲸、海豹、海象或其他海洋生物资源的船舶;

(i) “无线电规则”系指附于或被视作附于随时有效的最新《国际电信公约》的《无线电规则》。

第 III 条 适用范围

本公约适用于在有权悬挂缔约国国旗的海船上工作的海员,但在下列船上工作的海员除外:

(a) 军舰、海军辅助舰船或者为国家拥有或营运而只从事于政府的非商业性服务的其他船舶;但是各缔约国应采取无损于其拥有或营运的此类船舶的作业或作业能力的适当措施以保证在此类船上工作的人员,在合理可行的范围内符合本公约的要求;

(b) 渔船;

(c) 非营业的游艇;或

(d) 构造简单的木船。

第 IV 条 资料交流

(1) 各缔约国应尽速将下述资料送交秘书长:

(a) 就本公约范围内各项事宜所颁布的法律、法令、规则及文件的文本;

(b) 为根据本公约规定所颁发的每一种证书而设置的学习课程内容和期限详细情况(如适当时)及其国家的考试和其他要求;

(c) 根据本公约规定所颁发的证书足够数量的样本。

(2) 秘书长应将本条第(1)(a)段所规定的任何资料的收到情况通知所有缔约国,同时为了第 IX 条和第 X 条的目的,在承索时,特别应将按本条第(1)(b)和(c)段所送交的资料提供给这些国家。

Article V
Other treaties and interpretation

(1) All prior treaties, conventions and arrangements relating to standards of training, certification and watchkeeping for seafarers in force between the Parties shall continue to have full and complete effect during the terms there of as regards:

(a) seafarers to whom this Convention does not apply;

(b) seafarers to whom this Convention applies, in respect of matters for which it has not expressly provided.

(2) To the extent, however, that such treaties, conventions or arrangements conflict with the provisions of the Convention, the Parties shall review their commitments under such treaties, conventions and arrangements with a view to ensuring that there is no conflict between these commitments and their obligations under the Convention.

(3) All matters which are not expressly provided for in the Convention remain subject to the legislation of Parties.

(4) Nothing in the Convention shall prejudice the codification and development of the law of the sea by the United Nations Conference on the Law of the Sea convened pursuant to resolution 2750 C (XXV) of the General Assembly of the United Nations, nor the present or future claims and legal views of any State concerning the law of the sea and the nature and extent of coastal and flag State jurisdiction.

Article VI
Certificates

(1) Certificates for masters, officers or ratings shall be issued to those candidate who, to the satisfaction of the Administration, meet the requirements for service, age, medical fitness, training, qualification and examinations in accordance with the appropriate provisions of the annex to the Convention.

(2) Certificates for masters and officers issued in compliance with this article shall be endorsed by the issuing Administration in the form as prescribed in regulation I/2 of the annex. If the language used is not English, the endorsement shall include a translation into that language.

Article VII
Transitional provisions

(1) A certificate of competency or of service in a capacity for which the Convention requires a certificate and which before entry into force of the Convention for a Party is issued in accordance with the laws of that Party of the Radio Regulations shall be recognized as valid for service after entry into force of the Convention for that Party.

(2) After the entry into force of the Convention for a Party, its Administration may continue to issue certificates of competency in accordance with its previous practices for a period not exceeding five years. Such certificates shall be recognized as valid for the purpose of the Convention. During this transitional period such certificates shall be issued only to seafarers who had

第 V 条　其他条约与解释

(1)　缔约国之间现行有效的一切以前的关于海员培训、发证和值班标准的条约、公约及协定，在其有效期间，对以下所述应继续完全和充分有效：

(a)　不适用于本公约的海员；

(b)　适用于本公约的海员但本公约未予明文规定的事项。

(2)　但是，在这些条约、公约或协定与本公约规定相抵触的方面，各缔约国应对其按这些条约、公约及协定所承担的义务重新予以审查，以保证这些义务与其根据本公约所承担的责任不相抵触。

(3)　凡本公约中未予明文规定的事项，仍受缔约国法律的约束。

(4)　本公约的任何规定，均不得损害根据联合国大会第 2750C(XXV)号决议召开的联合国海洋法会议对海洋法的编纂和发展，也不得损害任何国家目前和今后就海洋法以及沿海国和船旗国的管辖权的性质和范围所提出的要求和法律上的意见。

第 VI 条　证　书

(1)　船长、高级船员或普通船员的证书，应按照本公约附则的相应规定，签发给主管机关满意地认为在服务、年龄、健康、培训、资格和考试各方面都符合要求的证书申请人。

(2)　按本条规定签发给船长和高级船员的证书，应由发证的主管机关按规则第 I/2 条规定的形式予以签注。如所用文字不是英文，则该签注应包括有英文译文。

第 VII 条　过渡规定

(1)　在本公约对某一缔约国生效前，按缔约国法律或《无线电规则》，对本公约要求具有证书的职位所颁发的适任或职务证书，在本公约对该缔约国生效后，仍应被认为是有效的。

(2)　本公约对某一缔约国生效后，其主管机关可继续在不超过 5 年的期间内，按其过去的做法签发适任证书。就本公约而言，这种证书应被认为是有效的。在这一过渡期间内，这种

commenced their sea service before entry into force of the Convention for that Party within the specific ship department to which those certificates relate. The Administration shall ensure that all other candidates for certification shall be examined and certificated in accordance with the Convention.

(3) A Party may, within two years after entry into force of the Convention for that Party, issue a certificate of service to seafarers who hold neither an appropriate certificate under the Convention nor a certificate of competency issued under its laws before entry into force of the Convention for that Party but who have:

(a) served in the capacity for which they seek a certificate of service for not less than three years at sea within the last seven years preceding entry into force of the Convention for that Party;

(b) produced evidence that they have performed that service satisfactorily;

(c) satisfied the Administration as to medical fitness, including eyesight and hearing, taking into account their age at the time of application.

For the purpose of the Convention, a certificate of service issued under this paragraph shall be regarded as the equivalent of a certificate issued under the Convention.

Article VIII
Dispensation

(1) In circumstances of exceptional necessity, Administrations, if in their opinion this does not cause danger to persons, property or the environment, may issue a dispensation permitting a specified seafarer to serve in a specified ship for a specified period not exceeding six months in a capacity, other than that of the radio officer or radiotelephone operator, except as provided by the relevant Radio Regulations, for which he does not hold the appropriate certificate, provided that the person to whom the dispensation is issued shall be adequately qualified to fill the vacant post in a safe manner, to the satisfaction of the Administration. However, dispensations shall not be granted to a master or chief engineer officer except in circumstances *of force majeure* and then only for the shortest possible period.

(2) Any dispensation granted for a post shall be granted only to a person properly certificated to fill the post immediately below. Where certification of the post below is not required by the Convention, a dispensation may be issued to a person whose qualification and experience are, in the opinion of the Administration, of a clear equivalence to the requirements for the post to be filled, provided that, if such a person holds no appropriate certificate, he shall be required to pass a test accepted by the Administration as demonstrating that such a dispensation may safely be issued. In addition, Administrations shall ensure that the post in question is filled by the holder of an appropriate certificate as soon as possible.

(3) Parties shall, as soon as possible after 1 January of each year, send a report to the Secretary-General giving information of the total number of dispensations in respect of each capacity for which a certificate is required that have been issued during the year to seagoing ships, together with information as to the numbers of those ships above and below 1,600 gross register tons respectively.

证书只应签发给在本公约对该缔约国生效前业已开始在与这种证书有关的船上特定部门内从事海上工作的海员。主管机关应保证对所有其他要求取得证书的应试者均按本公约的规定进行考试和发证。

(3) 在本公约对某一缔约国生效后 2 年之内,该缔约国可对在本公约对该缔约国生效前既未持有本公约规定的适当证书,也未持有按该缔约国法律签发的适任证书的海员,签发职务证书,但这些海员应:

(a) 在本公约对该缔约国生效前的最近 7 年之内,至少在海上按其所要求取得的职务证书的职位已工作了 3 年;

(b) 已提出其令人满意地执行该项职务的证据;

(c) 已使主管机关参照其申请时的年龄认为健康状况(包括视力和听力)均合格。

就本公约而言,根据本款规定签发的职务证书,应视为等同于根据本公约规定所颁发的证书。

第 VIII 条 特 免

(1) 在特殊需要的情况下,主管机关如认为对人员、财产和环境不致造成危险时,可签发特免证明,允许某一指定的海员在某一指定的船上,在为期不超过 6 个月的指定期间内,担任他并未持有适当证书的职位,除非有关的无线电规则另有规定,无线电报务员和无线电话务员不在此列。但是,被发给这种特免证明的人员,应系主管机关满意地认为能安全地充分胜任其所补空缺者。然而,除在不可抗力的情况下外,对船长或轮机长不得给予特免证明,而在这种情况下所给予的这种证明其期限应尽可能地短。

(2) 凡给予某职位的特免证明,只应发给具有适当证书可充任仅比该职务低一级职务的人员。如本公约对该项低一级的职位并无证书要求,则可对主管机关认为其资格和经验显然相当于所要充任的职位的要求的人员颁发特免证明,但是,如果该人并未持有相应的证书,则应通过一个主管机关可接受的测试,以表明这种特免证明的颁发是安全的。此外,主管机关应保证尽速由持有相应证书的人员来充任该项职位。

(3) 各缔约国应于每年 1 月 1 日后,尽速向秘书长送交一份报告,说明一年中间对海船所签发的关于有证书要求的每项职位的特免证明的总数,以及分别说明 1 600 总登记吨以上和以下的这些船舶的艘数。

Article IX
Equivalents

(1) The Convention shall not prevent an Administration from retaining or adopting other educational and training arrangements, including those involving seagoing service and shipboard organization especially adapted to technical developments and to special types of ships and trades, provided that the level of seagoing service, knowledge and efficiency as regards navigational and technical handling of ship and cargo ensures a degree of safety at sea and has a preventive effect as regards pollution at least equivalent to the requirements of the Convention.

(2) Details of such arrangements shall be reported as early as practicable to the Secretary-General who shall circulate such particulars to all Parties.

Article X
Control

(1) Ships, except those excluded by article III, are subject, while in the ports of a Party, to control by officers duly authorized by that Party to verify that all seafarers serving on board who are required to be certificated by the Convention are so certificated or hold an appropriate dispensation. Such certificates shall be accepted unless there are clear grounds for believing that a certificate has been fraudulently obtained or that the holder of a certificate is not the person to whom that certificate was originally issued.

(2) In the event that any deficiencies are found under paragraph (1) or under the procedures specified in regulation I/4, "Control procedures", the officer carrying out the control shall forthwith inform, in writing, the master of the ship and the Consul or, in his absence, the nearest diplomatic representative or the maritime authority of the State whose flag the ship is entitled to fly, so that appropriate action may be taken. Such notification shall specify the details of the deficiencies found and the grounds on which the Party determines that these deficiencies pose a danger to persons, property or the environment.

(3) In exercising the control under paragraph (1), if, taking into account the size and type of the ship and the length and nature of the voyage, the deficiencies referred to in paragraph (3) of regulation I/4 are not corrected and it is determined that this fact poses a danger to persons, property or the environment, the Party carrying out the control shall take steps to ensure that the ship will not sail unless and until these requirements are met to the extent that the danger has been removed. The facts concerning the action taken shall be reported promptly to the Secretary-General.

(4) When exercising control under this article, all possible efforts shall be made to avoid a ship being unduly detained or delayed. If a ship is so detained or delayed it shall be entitled to compensation for any loss or damage resulting therefore.

(5) This article shall be applied as may be necessary to ensure that no more favourable treatment is given to ships entitled to fly the flag of a non-Party than is given to ships entitled to fly the flag of a Party.

第 IX 条　等 效

(1)　本公约的规定不应妨碍主管机关保留或采取其他教育和培训的安排,包括涉及专门适应技术上的发展和特种船舶及贸易的水上业务和船上组织的教育和培训的安排,但在船、货航行和技术操作方面,海上服务、知识与效率的水平,应保证并具有至少相当于本公约要求的海上安全程度和防污的效果。

(2)　应尽早将这种安排的详情报告秘书长,秘书长则应将这种详情通知所有缔约国。

第 X 条　监 督

(1)　除第 III 条所排除的船舶外,船舶在一缔约国的港口时,应受该缔约国正式授权的官员的监督,以核实船上凡公约要求具有证书的海员均持有证书或适当的特免证明。除非有明显的理由认为证书系骗取的或持证人不是该证书原来所发给的本人,否则此类证书应予承认。

(2)　在根据第(1)段或规则第 I/4 条"监督程序"的规定发现任何缺陷时,执行监督的官员应以书面形式通知该船船长及船旗国的领事或(在无领事时)最近的外交代表或海事管理当局,以便采取适当的措施。这种通知应说明所发现的缺陷的细节,以及该缔约国据以判定这些缺陷危及人员、财产和环境的理由。

(3)　在根据第(1)段的规定执行监督时,如果考虑到船舶的大小和类型以及航程的长短和性质,规则第 I/4 条第 3 段中所述的缺陷未能纠正,并经判定这将对人员、财产或环境构成危险时,执行监督的缔约国应采取措施,以保证船舶在消除危险并符合要求后才可开航。关于所采取的行动的实情,应立即报告秘书长。

(4)　在根据本条执行监督时,应尽量避免使船舶受到不适当的滞留或延误。如果船舶受到这种滞留或延误,则该船对于由此而引起的任何损失或损害,有权要求赔偿。

(5)　本条规定在必要时应予以施行,以保证不给予有权悬挂非缔约国国旗的船舶比有权悬挂缔约国国旗的船舶更为优惠的待遇。

Article XI
Promotion of technical co-operation

(1) Parties to the Convention shall promote, in consultation with, and with the assistance of, the Organization, support for those Parties which request technical assistance for:

(a) training of administrative and technical personnel;

(b) establishment of institutions for the training of seafarers;

(c) supply of equipment and facilities for training institutions;

(d) development of adequate training programmes, including practical training on seagoing ships; and

(e) facilitation of other measures and arrangements to enhance the qualifications of seafarers;

preferably on a national, sub-regional or regional basis, to further the aims and purposes of the Convention, taking into account the special needs of developing countries in this regard.

(2) On its part, the Organization shall pursue the aforesaid efforts, as appropriate, in consulation or association with other international organizations, particularly the International Labour Organization.

Article XII
Amendments

(1) The Convention may be amended by either of the following procedures:

(a) amendments after consideration within the Organization:

(i) any amendment proposed by a Party shall be submitted to the Secretary-General, who shall then circulate it to all Members of the Organization, all Parties and the Director-General of the International Labour Office at least six months prior to its consideration;

(ii) any amendment so proposed and circulated shall be referred to the Maritime Safety Committee of the Organization for consideration;

(iii) Parties, whether or not Members of the Organization, shall be entitled to participate in the proceedings of the Maritime Safety Committee for consideration and adoption of amendments;

(iv) amendments shall be adopted by a two-thirds majority of the Parties present and voting in the Maritime Safety Committee expanded as provided for in sub-paragraph (a) (iii) (hereinafter referred to as the "expanded Maritime Safety Committee") on condition that at least one third of the Parties shall be present at the time of voting;

(v) amendments so adopted shall be communicated by the Secretary-General to all Parties for acceptance;

第 XI 条　促进技术合作

(1)　本公约缔约国应与本组织协商并在本组织的协助下,促进并支持对下述有技术援助要求的缔约国:

(a)　培训行政管理和技术人员;

(b)　建立海员培训学校;

(c)　向培训学校提供设备与设施;

(d)　制定适当的培训计划,包括在海船上的实际培训;以及

(e)　促进提高海员资格的其他措施与安排;

考虑到发展中国家在这方面的特殊需要,这些援助宜以国家、分区或地区为基础,以促进实现本公约的目的和宗旨。

(2)　本组织方面,应根据情况与其他国际组织特别是国际劳工组织进行协商或联合,对以上所述作出努力。

第 XII 条　修正案

(1)　本公约可按下述的任一程序进行修正:

(a)　经本组织内审议后的修正:

(i)　一缔约国提议的任何修正案,应提交给秘书长,然后由秘书长至少在审议此修正案之前 6 个月分发给本组织所有成员、所有缔约国及国际劳工组织总干事;

(ii)　按上述规定提议和周知的任何修正案,应提交给本组织海上安全委员会审议;

(iii)　缔约国,不论其是否为本组织的成员,均有权参加海上安全委员会对修正案进行审议和通过的会议;

(iv)　修正案应在按第(a)(iii)分段所规定的扩大的海上安全委员会(以下简称为“海上安全委员会扩大会议”)上,以到会并投票的缔约国的 2/3 多数通过,但在表决时,至少应有 1/3 的缔约国出席;

(v)　这样通过的修正案,应由秘书长通知所有缔约国,以供接受;

(vi) an amendment to an article shall be deemed to have been accepted on the date on which it is accepted by two thirds of the Parties;

(vii)an amendment to the annex shall be deemed to have been accepted:

1 at the end of two years from the date on which it is communicated to the Parties for acceptance; or

2 at the end of a different period, which shall be not less than one year, if so determined at the time of its adoption by a two-thirds majority of the Parties present and voting in the expanded Maritime Safety Committee;

however, the amendments shall be deemed not to have been accepted if, within the specified period, either more than one third of Parties or Parties the combined merchant fleets of which constitute not less than 50% of the gross tonnage of the world's merchant shipping of ships of 100 gross register tons or more notify the Secretary-General that they object to the amendment;

(viii) an amendment to an article shall enter into force with respect to those Parties which have accepted it six months after the date on which it is deemed to have been accepted, and with with respect to each Party which accepts it after that date, six months after the date of that Party's acceptance;

(ix) an amendment to the annex shall enter into force with respect to all Parties, except those which have objected to the amendment under sub-paragraph (a) (vii) and which have not withdrawn such objections, six months after the date on which it is deemed to have been accepted. Before the date determined for entry into force, any Party may give notice to the Secretary-General that it exempts itself from giving effect to that amendment for a period not longer than one year from the date of its entry into force, or for such longer period as may be determined by a two-thirds majority of the Parties present and voting in the expanded Maritime Safety Committee at the time of the adoption of the amendment; or

(b) amendment by a conference:

(i) upon the request of a Party concurred in by at least one third of the Parties, the Organization shall convene, in association or consultation with the Director-General of the International Labour Office, a conference of Parties to consider amendments to the Convention;

(ii) every amendment adopted by such a conference by a two-thirds majority of the Parties present and voting shall be communicated by the Secretary-General to all Parties for acceptance;

(iii) unless the conference decides otherwise, the amendment shall be deemed to have been accepted and shall enter into force in accordance with the procedures specified in sub-paragraphs (a) (vi) and (a) (viii) or sub-paragraphs (a) (vii) and (a) (ix) respectively, provided that references in these sub-paragraphs to the expanded Maritime Safety Committee shall be taken to mean references to the conference.

(vi) 对于条款的修正案,在其为 2/3 的缔约国接受之日,即应视为已被接受;

(vii) 对于附则的修正案,在下列情况下,应视为已被接受:

(1) 自通知缔约国供其接受之日起满两年时;或

(2) 在海上安全委员会扩大会议上通过该修正案时经到会并投票的缔约国 2/3 多数所确定的另一期限届满时,但这一期限不得少于1 年;

但是,如果在规定的期间内,有 1/3 以上的缔约国,或其商船总和不少于世界 100 总登记吨或以上的商船总吨位的 50% 的缔约国,通知秘书长反对该修正案,则该修正案应视为未被接受;

(viii) 对条款的修正案,对已接受该修正案的各缔约国,应在其视为已被接受之后经过 6 个月生效;对在该修正案被视为接受之日后接受该修正案的每一缔约国,则应在该缔约国接受之日后经过 6 个月生效;

(ix) 对附则的修正案,应在其视为已被接受之日后过 6 个月对所有缔约国生效,但按第(a)(vii)分段的规定对该修正案提出过反对且未曾撤销该项反对的缔约国除外。在规定的生效日期之前,任何缔约国可通知秘书长,在该修正案生效之日起不超过 1 年的期间内,或在海上安全委员会扩大会议通过该修正案时经到会并投票的缔约国的 2/3 多数确定的较此为长的期间内,该缔约国免于实施该修正案;或

(b) 会议修正:

(i) 应一个缔约国的请求,并至少有 1/3 缔约国的同意,本组织应与国际劳工组织总干事联合或与之协商召开一次缔约国会议来审议对本公约的修正案;

(ii) 凡由这种会议以到会并投票的缔约国的 2/3 多数通过的修正案,应由秘书长通知所有缔约国,以供接受;

(iii) 除会议另有决定外,该修正案应分别按第(a)(vi)和第(a)(viii)分段或第(a)(vii)和第(a)(ix)分段中所规定的程序视为已被接受和生效,但这些项目中所提到的海上安全委员会扩大会议应被认为是指缔约国政府会议。

(2) Any declaration of acceptance of, or objection to, an amendment or any notice given under paragraph (1) (a) (ix) shall be submitted in writing to the Secretary-General, who shall inform all Parties of any such submission and the date of its receipt.

(3) The Secretary-General shall inform all Parties of any amendments which enter into force, together with the date on which each such amendment enters into force.

Article XIII
Signature, ratification, acceptance, approval and accession

(1) The Convention shall remain open for signature at the Headquarters of the Organization from 1 December 1978 until 30 November 1979 and shall thereafter remain open for accession. Any State may become a Party by:

(a) signature without reservation as to ratification, acceptance or approval; or

(b) signature subject to ratification, acceptance or approval, followed by ratification, acceptance or approval; or

(c) accession.

(2) Ratification, acceptance, approval or accession shall be effected by the deposit of an instrument to that effect with the Secretary-General.

(3) The Secretary-General shall inform all States that have signed the Convention or acceded to it and the Director-General of the International Labour Office of any signature or of the deposit of any instrument of ratification, acceptance, approval or accession and the date of its deposit.

Article XIV
Entry into force

(1) The Convention shall enter into force 12 months after the date on which not less than 25 States, the combined merchant fleets of which constitute not less than 50% of the gross tonnage of the world's merchant shipping of ships of 100 gross register tons or more, have either signed it without reservation as to ratification, acceptance or approval or deposited the requisite instruments of ratification, acceptance, approval or accession in accordance with article XIII.

(2) The Secretary-General shall inform all States that have signed the Convention or acceded to it of the date on which it enters into force.

(3) Any instrument of ratification, acceptance, approval or accession deposited during the 12 months referred to in paragraph (1) shall take effect on the coming into force of the Convention or three months after the deposit of such instrument, whichever is the later date.

(4) Any instrument of ratification, acceptance, approval or accession deposited after the date on which the Convention enters into force shall take effect three months after the date of deposit.

(5) After the date on which an amendment is deemed to have been accepted under article XII, any instrument of ratification, acceptance, approval or accession deposited shall apply to the Convention as amended.

(2) 对于一项修正案的任何接受或反对的声明,或根据第(1)(a)(ix)段所作的任何通知,均应以书面提交给秘书长。秘书长应将此类文件的提交及其收到日期通知所有缔约国。
(3) 秘书长应将任何生效的修正案连同每项这种修正案的生效日期通知所有缔约国。

第 XIII 条 签字、批准、接受、核准和加入

(1) 本公约自 1978 年 12 月 1 日起至 1979 年 11 月 30 日止,在本组织总部开放供签字,此后应继续开放供加入。任何国家可按下列方式参加本公约:

(a) 签字而对批准、接受或核准无保留;或

(b) 签字而有待批准、接受或核准,随后再予批准、接受或核准;或

(c) 加入。

(2) 批准、接受、核准或加入,应向秘书长交存一份相应的文件。
(3) 秘书长应将任何签字,或关于批准、接受、核准或加入的任何文件的交存及其交存日期,通知已签字或已加入本公约的所有国家和国际劳工组织总干事。

第 XIV 条 生 效

(1) 本公约应在至少有 25 个国家,其商船总和不少于全世界 100 总登记吨或以上的商船总吨的 50%,按第 XIII 条已签字而对批准、接受或核准无保留,或已交存所需的关于批准、接受、核准或加入的文件之后,经过 12 个月生效。
(2) 秘书长应将本公约的生效日期通知所有已签字或已加入本公约的国家。
(3) 凡在第(1)段所述的 12 个月的期间内交存的批准、接受、核准或加入的文件,应在本公约生效之日生效,或在交存上述文件之日起经过 3 个月生效,以较晚者为准。
(4) 凡在本公约生效之日后交存的批准、接受、核准或加入的文件,应在交存之日后经过 3 个月生效。
(5) 在修正案根据第 XII 条规定视为已被接受之日后交存的任何批准、接受、核准或加入的文件,应适用于修正后的公约。

Article XV
Denunciation

(1) The Convention may be denounced by any Party at any time after five years from the date on which the Convention entered into force for that Party.

(2) Denunciation shall be effected by notification in writing to the Secretary-General who shall inform all other Parties and the Director-General of the International Labour Office of any such notification received and of the date of its receipt as well as the date on which such denunciation takes effect.

(3) A denunciation shall take effect 12 months after receipt of the notification of denunciation by the Secretary-General or after any longer period which may be indicated in the notification.

Article XVI
Deposit and registration

(1) The Convention shall be deposited with the Secretary-General who shall transmit certified true copies thereof to all States that have signed the Convention or acceded to it.

(2) As soon as the Convention enters into force, the Secretary-General shall transmit the text to the Secretary-General of the United Nations for registration and publication, in accordance with Article 102 of the Charter of the United Nations.

Article XVII
Languages

The Convention is established in a single copy in the Chinese, English, French, Russian and Spanish languages, each text being equally authentic. Official translations in the Arabic and German languages shall be prepared and deposited with the signed original.

IN WITNESS WHEREOF the undersigned, being duly authorized by their respective Governments for that purpose, have signed the Convention.

DONE AT LONDON this seventh day of July, one thousand nine hundred and seventy-eight.

第 XV 条　退 出

(1)　任何缔约国,在本公约对其生效满 5 年后,可随时退出本公约。
(2)　退出本公约应以书面形式通知秘书长。秘书长应将收到的任何这种通知和收到日期以及退出的生效日期,通知所有其他缔约国和国际劳工组织总干事。
(3)　退出本公约应在秘书长收到退出通知 12 个月后,或该通知中所载明的任何较此为长的期限届满后生效。

第 XVI 条　保管和登记

(1)　本公约应交由秘书长保管,秘书长应将核证无误的本公约副本分发给所有已签字或已加入本公约的国家。
(2)　本公约一经生效,秘书长应即按照联合国宪章第 102 条的规定,将本公约文本送联合国秘书长登记并公布。

第 XVII 条　文 字

本公约正本一份,用中文、英文、法文、俄文和西班牙文写成,各种文本具有同等效力。应备有阿拉伯文、德文的正式译本,与签署的正本一并存放。
下列具名的经各国政府授权的代表,特签署本公约,以昭信守。
1978 年 7 月 7 日订于伦敦。

ADOPTION OF THE FINAL ACT AND ANY INSTRUMENTS, RESOLUTIONS AND RECOMMENDATIONS RESULTING FROM THE WORK OF THE CONFERENCE

Final Act of the Conference of Parties to the International Convention on Standards of Training, Certification and Watchkeeping for Seafarers (STCW), 1978

Text adopted by the Conference

1 Pursuant to the request of Parties to the International Convention on Standards of Training, Certification and Watchkeeping for Seafarers, 1978, (hereafter referred to as the 1978 STCW Convention) at the eighty-fourth session of the Maritime Safety Committee of the International Maritime Organization and subsequent decisions by the Council of the Organization at its one hundredth session and the Assembly of the Organization at its twenty-sixth session, and in accordance with article XII(1)(b) of the 1978 STCW Convention, a Conference of Parties to the 1978 STCW Convention was convened, in consultation with the Director-General of the International Labour Office, to consider amendments to the annex to the 1978 STCW Convention and the Seafarers' Training, Certification and Watchkeeping (STCW) Code.

2 The Conference was held at the Philippine International Convention Centre in Manila, the Philippines, from 21 to 25 June 2010.

3 Representatives of 85 States Parties to the 1978 STCW Convention participated in the Conference, namely the representatives of:

ANGOLA
ANTIGUA AND BARBUDA
ARGENTINA
AUSTRALIA
AZERBAIJAN
BAHAMAS
BANGLADESH
BELGIUM
BELIZE
BRAZIL
BRUNEI DARUSSALAM
CANADA
CHILE
CHINA
CONGO
COOK ISLANDS
CÔTE D'IVOIRE
CROATIA
CYPRUS
DEMOCRATIC PEOPLE'S REPUBLIC OF KOREA
DENMARK
ESTONIA
FIJI
FINLAND
FRANCE

《1978 年海员培训、发证和值班标准国际公约》缔约国大会最终文件

大会通过的文本

1 按照《1978 年海员培训、发证和值班标准国际公约》(下称《1978 年 STCW 公约》)缔约国在国际海事组织(IMO)海上安全委员会第 84 次会议上提出的要求和随后由国际海事组织理事会第 100 届会议和大会第 26 届会议做出的决定,以及根据上述公约第 XII(1)(b)条,并与国际劳工局秘书长协商,召开了《1978 年 STCW 公约》缔约国大会,审议该公约附则及《海员培训、发证和值班(STCW)规则》的修正案。

2 大会于 2010 年 6 月 21 日至 25 日在菲律宾马尼拉的国际公约中心举行。

3 《1978 年 STCW 公约》的 85 个缔约国的代表出席了大会,代表团列名如下:

安哥拉
安提瓜和巴布达
阿根廷
澳大利亚
阿塞拜疆
巴哈马
孟加拉国
比利时
伯利兹
巴西
文莱达鲁萨兰国
加拿大
智利
中国
刚果
库克群岛
科特迪瓦
克罗地亚
塞浦路斯
朝鲜民主主义人民共和国
丹麦
爱沙尼亚
斐济
芬兰
法国

GEORGIA
GERMANY
GHANA
GREECE
INDIA
INDONESIA
IRAN (ISLAMIC REPUBLIC OF)
IRAQ
IRELAND
ISRAEL
ITALY
JAMAICA
JAPAN
KENYA
LATVIA
LEBANON
LIBERIA
LIBYAN ARAB JAMAHIRIYA
LITHUANIA
LUXEMBOURG
MALAYSIA
MALTA
MARSHALL ISLANDS
MEXICO
MOROCCO
MOZAMBIQUE
MYANMAR
NETHERLANDS
NIGERIA
NORWAY
PANAMA
PAPUA NEW GUINEA
PHILIPPINES
POLAND
PORTUGAL
QATAR
REPUBLIC OF KOREA
ROMANIA
RUSSIAN FEDERATION
SAINT KITTS AND NEVIS
SAUDI ARABIA
SINGAPORE
SLOVENIA
SOUTH AFRICA
SPAIN
SRI LANKA
SWEDEN
SWITZERLAND
SYRIAN ARAB REPUBLIC
THAILAND
TUNISIA
TURKEY
TUVALU
UKRAINE
UNITED ARAB EMIRATES
UNITED KINGDOM OF GREAT BRITAIN AND NORTHERN IRELAND
UNITED REPUBLIC OF TANZANIA
UNITED STATES OF AMERICA
VANUATU
VIET NAM

4 The following State sent observers to the Conference:

SURINAME

5 The following Associate Members of the Organization sent observers to the Conference:

FAROES
HONG KONG, CHINA
MACAO, CHINA

6 The following organization of the United Nations system sent observers to the Conference:

INTERNATIONAL LABOUR ORGANIZATION (ILO)

格鲁吉亚
德国
加纳
希腊
印度
印度尼西亚
伊朗(伊斯兰共和国)
伊拉克
爱尔兰
以色列
意大利
牙买加
日本
肯尼亚
拉脱维亚
黎巴嫩
利比里亚
利比亚阿拉伯民众国
立陶宛
卢森堡
马来西亚
马耳他
马绍尔群岛
墨西哥
摩洛哥
莫桑比克
缅甸
荷兰
尼日利亚
挪威
巴拿马
巴布亚新几内亚
菲律宾
波兰
葡萄牙
卡塔尔
韩国
罗马尼亚
俄罗斯联邦
圣基茨和尼维斯
沙特阿拉伯
新加坡
斯洛文尼亚
南非
西班牙
斯里兰卡
瑞典
瑞士
叙利亚阿拉伯共和国
泰国
突尼斯
土耳其
图瓦卢
乌克兰
阿拉伯联合酋长国
大不列颠及北爱尔兰联合王国
坦桑尼亚共和国
美国
瓦努阿图
越南

4　下列国家向大会派出了观察员：

苏里南

5　下列国际海事组织的联系会员向大会派出了观察员：

法罗群岛
中国香港
中国澳门

6　联合国系统的下列组织向大会派出了观察员：

国际劳工组织(ILO)

7 The following intergovernmental organizations sent observers to the Conference:

EUROPEAN COMMISSION (EC)
LEAGUE OF ARAB STATES

8 The following non-governmental organizations sent observers to the Conference:

INTERNATIONAL CHAMBER OF SHIPPING (ICS)
INTERNATIONAL SHIPPING FEDERATION (ISF)
INTERNATIONAL TRANSPORT WORKERS' FEDERATION (ITF)
BIMCO
OIL COMPANIES INTERNATIONAL MARINE FORUM (OCIMF)
INTERNATIONAL ASSOCIATION OF DRILLING CONTRACTORS (IADC)
INTERNATIONAL FEDERATION OF SHIPMASTERS' ASSOCIATIONS (IFSMA)
INTERNATIONAL ASSOCIATION OF INDEPENDENT TANKER OWNERS (INTERTANKO)
CRUISE LINES INTERNATIONAL ASSOCIATION (CLIA)
INTERNATIONAL ASSOCIATION OF DRY CARGO SHIPOWNERS (INTERCARGO)
INTERNATIONAL MARITIME LECTURERS ASSOCIATION (IMLA)
THE INSTITUTE OF MARINE ENGINEERING, SCIENCE AND TECHNOLOGY (IMarEST)
INTERNATIONAL SHIP MANAGERS' ASSOCIATION (InterManager)
INTERFERRY
INTERNATIONAL MARITIME HEALTH ASSOCIATION (IMHA)
INTERNATIONAL ASSOCIATION OF MARITIME UNIVERSITIES (IAMU)
GLOBAL MARITIME EDUCATION AND TRAINING ASSOCIATION (GlobalMET)
THE NAUTICAL INSTITUTE (NI)

9 The Conference was opened by Mr. E.E. Mitropoulos, Secretary-General of the International Maritime Organization.

10 H.E. Mr. Noli de Castro, Vice President of the Republic of the Philippines, delivered a welcome address at the opening session of the Conference.

11 A message from Mr. Ban Ki-moon, Secretary-General of the United Nations, was read out at the opening session of the Conference.

12 The Conference elected Mr. Neil Frank R. Ferrer, of the Philippines, President of the Conference.

13 The Vice-Presidents elected by the Conference were:

H.E. Mr. Dwight C.R. Gardiner (Antigua and Barbuda)

Mr. Koffi Bertin Tano (Côte d'Ivoire)

Mr. Rajeev Gupta (India)

Rear Admiral Giancarlo Olimbo (Italy)

Mr. Abdel Hafiz El Kaissi (Lebanon)

7　下列政府间组织向大会派出了观察员：

欧盟委员会(EC)

阿拉伯国家联盟

8　下列非政府间组织向大会派出了观察员：

国际航运公会(ICS)

国际航运联合会(ISF)

国际运输工人联合会(ITF)

波罗的海及国际海事委员会(BIMCO)

石油公司国际海事论坛(OCIMF)

国际钻井承包商协会(IADC)

国际船长协会联合会(IFSMA)

国际独立油轮船东协会(INTERTANKO)

国际邮轮公司协会(CLIA)

国际干货船船东协会(INTERCARGO)

国际海事讲师协会(IMLA)

轮机工程、科学和技术学会(IMarEST)

国际船舶管理者协会(InterManager)

国际渡轮协会

国际海事健康协会(IMHA)

国际海事大学联合会(IAMU)

全球海事教育和培训联合会(GlobalMET)

航海学会(NI)

9　国际海事组织秘书长 Mitropoulos 先生宣布大会开幕。

10　菲律宾共和国副总统 Noli de Castro 先生阁下在大会开幕式上致欢迎辞。

11　联合国秘书长潘基文为大会发来了贺词,并在大会开幕式上宣读。

12　大会选举菲律宾的 Neil Frank R. Ferrer 先生为大会主席。

13　下列人员被选为大会的副主席：

Dwight C. R. Gardiner 先生阁下(安提瓜和巴布达)

Koffi Bertin Tano 先生(科特迪瓦)

Rajeev Gupta 先生(印度)

Giancarlo Olimbo 海军少将(意大利)

Abdel Hafiz El Kaissi 先生(黎巴嫩)

14 The Secretariat of the Conference consisted of the following officers:

Secretary-General:	Mr. E.E. Mitropoulos Secretary-General of the Organization
Executive Secretary:	Mr. K. Sekimizu Director, Maritime Safety Division
Deputy Executive Secretary:	Mr. H. Hesse Senior Deputy Director, Maritime Safety Division
Assistant Deputy Executive Secretary:	Mr. A. Mahapatra Head, Maritime Training and Human Element Section, Maritime Safety Division

15 The Conference established the following Committees and elected respective officers:

Committee of the Whole

Chairman:	Rear Admiral P. Brady (Jamaica)
First Vice-Chairman:	Mr. S. Hassing (Netherlands)
Second Vice-Chairman:	Mr. Zheng Heping (China)

Drafting Committee

Chairman:	Ms. M. Medina (United States)
First Vice-Chairman:	Mr. B. Groves (Australia)
Second Vice-Chairman:	Capt. M.A. Shahba (Islamic Republic of Iran)

Credentials Committee

Chairman:	Mr. L. Chichinadze (Georgia)

16 The Drafting Committee was composed of representatives of the following States:

ARGENTINA
AUSTRALIA
CHINA
FRANCE
IRAN (ISLAMIC REPUBLIC OF)
RUSSIAN FEDERATION
SPAIN
UNITED STATES

17 The Credentials Committee was composed of representatives of the following States:

GEORGIA
IRELAND
NIGERIA
PANAMA
THAILAND

14 大会秘书处由下列官员组成：

秘书长：	E. E. Mitropoulos 先生 国际海事组织秘书长
执行秘书：	K. Sekimizu 先生 海上安全司司长
副执行秘书：	H. Hesse 先生 海上安全司高级副司长
助理副执行秘书：	A. Mahapatra 先生 海上安全司海事培训和人为因素处处长

15 大会设立下列委员会并选举了各自的官员：

全体委员会

主席：	P. Brady 海军少将(牙买加)
第一副主席：	S. Hassing 先生(荷兰)
第二副主席：	郑和平先生(中国)

起草委员会

主席：	M. Medina 女士(美国)
第一副主席：	B. Groves 先生(澳大利亚)
第二副主席：	M. A. Shahba 船长(伊朗伊斯兰共和国)

资格审查委员会

主席：	L. Chichinadze 先生(格鲁吉亚)

16 起草委员会由下列国家的代表组成：

阿根廷
澳大利亚
中国
法国
伊朗(伊斯兰共和国)
俄罗斯联邦
西班牙
美国

17 资格审查委员会由下列国家的代表组成：

格鲁吉亚
爱尔兰
尼日利亚
巴拿马
泰国

18 The Conference used as the basis of its work the draft texts of amendments to the annex to the International Convention on Standards of Training, Certification and Watchkeeping for Seafarers, 1978 and the Seafarers' Training, Certification and Watchkeeping (STCW) Code prepared by the Sub-Committee on Standards of Training and Watchkeeping (STW), at its forty-first session, and endorsed by the Maritime Safety Committee, at its eighty-seventh session, of the Organization.

19 The Conference also considered proposals and comments submitted to the Conference by Parties to the 1978 STCW Convention and international organizations.

20 As a result of its deliberations, the Conference adopted:

- amendments to the annex to the International Convention on Standards of Training, Certification and Watchkeeping for Seafarers, 1978, together with resolution 1 on adoption of the amendments to the annex to the Convention, which constitute attachment 1 to this Final Act; and

- amendments to the Seafarers' Training, Certification and Watchkeeping (STCW) Code, together with resolution 2 on adoption of the amendments to the Code, which constitute attachment 2 to this Final Act.

21 The Conference also adopted the following resolutions set forth in attachment 3 to this Final Act:

Resolution 3: Expression of appreciation to the host Government;

Resolution 4: Transitional provisions and early implementation;

Resolution 5: Verification of certificates of competency and endorsements;

Resolution 6: Standards of training and certification and ships' manning levels;

Resolution 7: Promotion of technical knowledge, skills and professionalism of seafarers;

Resolution 8: Development of guidelines to implement international standards of medical fitness for seafarers;

Resolution 9: Revision of existing model courses published by the International Maritime Organization and development of new model courses;

Resolution 10: Promotion of technical co-operation;

Resolution 11: Measures to ensure the competency of masters and officers of ships operating in polar waters;

Resolution 12: Attracting new entrants to, and retaining seafarers in, the maritime profession;

Resolution 13: Accommodation for trainees;

18　大会将培训与值班标准分委会第 41 次会议准备的、由海上安全委员会第 87 次会议批准的《1978 年海员培训、发证和值班标准国际公约》附则及《海员培训、发证和值班（STCW）规则》的修正草案作为其工作的基础。

19　大会还考虑了 1978 年 STCW 公约缔约国和有关国际组织提交的提案和评论。

20　作为审议结果大会通过了：

–《1978 年海员培训、发证和值班标准国际公约》附则修正案，连同关于通过该修正案的决议 1，作为大会最终文件的附件 1；和

–《海员培训、发证和值班（STCW）规则》修正案，连同关于通过该修正案的决议 2，作为大会最终文件的附件 2。

21　大会还通过了载于本最终文件附件 3 的下列大会决议：

决议 3　对主办国政府表示感谢；

决议 4　过渡规定和及早实施；

决议 5　适任证书和签证的核实；

决议 6　培训、发证标准和船舶配员水平；

决议 7　提升海员的知识、技能和职业化水平；

决议 8　起草实施国际海员健康标准指南；

决议 9　修订国际海事组织出版的现有示范培训课程并制定新的示范培训课程；

决议 10　促进技术合作；

决议 11　确保在极区水域操作船舶的船长和高级船员适任的措施；

决议 12　吸引新人加入海员职业，留住现有海员；

决议 13　受训人员住宿；

Resolution 14: Promotion of the participation of women in the maritime industry;

Resolution 15: Future amendments and review of the STCW Convention and Code;

Resolution 16: Contribution of the International Labour Organization;

Resolution 17: Role of the World Maritime University, the IMO International Maritime Law Institute and the International Maritime Safety, Security and Environment Academy (IMSSEA) in promoting enhanced maritime standards;

Resolution 18: Year of the Seafarer; and

Resolution 19: Day of the Seafarer.

22 This Final Act is established in a single original text in the Arabic, Chinese, English, French, Russian and Spanish languages and is deposited with the Secretary-General of the International Maritime Organization.

23 The Secretary-General shall send:

(a) certified copies of this Final Act, with its attachments, to the Governments of the States invited to be represented at the Conference; and

(b) certified copies of the authentic texts of the amendments to the 1978 STCW Convention and the STCW Code, as referred to in paragraph 20 above, to all Parties to the 1978 STCW Convention, in conformity with article XII(1)(b)(ii) thereof.

DONE AT MANILA this twenty-fifth day of June, two thousand and ten.

IN WITNESS WHEREOF the undersigned have affixed their signatures to this Final Act.

决议 14　鼓励女性进入航海行业；

决议 15　对 STCW 公约和规则的后续修正和回顾；

决议 16　国际劳工组织的贡献；

决议 17　世界海事大学，IMO 国际海商法学院以及国际海上安全、保安及环境学会在倡议提高海事标准方面的作用；

决议 18　海员年；和

决议 19　海员日。

22　本最终文件用阿拉伯文、中文、英文、法文、俄文和西班牙文写成单一文本，并存放于国际海事组织秘书长处。

23　国际海事组织秘书长应：

(a)　将核证无误的最终文件的副本，包括其附件，寄送应邀出席本次大会的国家的政府；以及

(b)　将核证无误的 1978 年 STCW 公约和 STCW 规则修正案的正本，如上第 20 段述，遵照公约正文第 XII(1)(b)(ii)条，寄送《1978 STCW 公约》所有缔约国。

2010 年 6 月 25 日订于马尼拉。

以下署名者特签署本最终文件，以昭信守。

ADOPTION OF THE FINAL ACT AND ANY INSTRUMENTS, RESOLUTIONS AND RECOMMENDATIONS RESULTING FROM THE WORK OF THE CONFERENCE

Attachment 1 to the Final Act of the Conference

Resolution 1

Adoption of the Manila Amendments to the annex to the International Convention on Standards of Training, Certification and Watchkeeping for Seafarers (STCW), 1978

Text adopted by the Conference

THE 2010 MANILA CONFERENCE,

RECALLING Article XII(1)(b) of the International Convention on Standards of Training, Certification and Watchkeeping for Seafarers, 1978 (hereinafter referred to as "the Convention"), concerning the procedure for amendment by a Conference of Parties,

HAVING CONSIDERED the Manila amendments to the annex to the Convention proposed and circulated to the Members of the Organization and to all Parties to the Convention,

1. ADOPTS, in accordance with article XII(1)(b)(ii) of the Convention, amendments to the annex to the Convention, the text of which is set out in the annex to the present resolution;

2. DETERMINES, in accordance with article XII(1)(a)(vii) of the Convention, that the amendments annexed hereto shall be deemed to have been accepted on 1 July 2011, unless, prior to that date, more than one third of Parties to the Convention or Parties the combined merchant fleets of which constitute not less than 50% of the gross tonnage of the world's merchant shipping of ships of 100 gross register tons or more have notified the Secretary-General that they object to the amendments;

3. INVITES Parties to note that, in accordance with article XII(1)(a)(ix) of the Convention, the amendments annexed hereto shall enter into force on 1 January 2012 upon being deemed to have been accepted in accordance with paragraph 2 above;

4. REQUESTS the Secretary-General of the Organization to transmit certified copies of the present resolution and the text of the amendments contained in the annex to all Parties to the Convention;

5. FURTHER REQUESTS the Secretary-General to transmit copies of this resolution and its annex to all Members of the Organization which are not Parties to the Convention.

大会最终文件附件 1

决议 1
通过《1978 年海员培训、发证和值班标准国际公约》附则马尼拉修正案

大会通过的文本

2010 年马尼拉大会，

忆及《1978 年海员培训、发证和值班标准国际公约》（以下称为"本公约"）第 XII（1）（b）条关于缔约国大会通过修正案的程序，

审议了经提议的并散发给本组织各成员国及该公约各缔约国的本公约附则的马尼拉修正案，

1. 依据本公约第 XII（1）（b）（ii）条，**通过**本公约附则的修正案，该文本附在本决议之后；

2. 依据本公约第 XII（1）（a）（vii）条，**决定**所附的修正案应于 2011 年 7 月 1 日视为已被接受，除非在此日期之前，有 1/3 以上的缔约国，或其 100 总登记吨或以上的商船总吨位不少于世界商船总吨位的 50% 的缔约国通知秘书长反对该修正案；

3. **敦请**各缔约国注意，依据本公约第 XII（1）（a）（ix）条，附则的修正案在依据上述第 2 段被接受后，将于 2012 年 1 月 1 日生效；

4. **要求** IMO 秘书长将核证无误的决议副本及附件中修正案的文本分发给本公约各缔约国；

5. **进一步要求**秘书长将决议副本及附件分发给非本公约缔约国的该组织各成员国。

ANNEX

THE MANILA AMENDMENTS TO THE ANNEX TO THE INTERNATIONAL CONVENTION ON STANDARDS OF TRAINING, CERTIFICATION AND WATCHKEEPING FOR SEAFARERS, 1978

The annex to the International Convention on Standards of Training, Certification and Watchkeeping for Seafarers, 1978, is replaced by the following:

ANNEX

CHAPTER I

General provisions

Regulation I/1
Definitions and clarifications

1 For the purpose of the Convention, unless expressly provided otherwise:

.1 *Regulations* means regulations contained in the annex to the Convention;

.2 *Approved* means approved by the Party in accordance with these regulations;

.3 *Master* means the person having command of a ship;

.4 *Officer* means a member of the crew, other than the master, designated as such by national law or regulations or, in the absence of such designation, by collective agreement or custom;

.5 *Deck officer* means an officer qualified in accordance with the provisions of chapter II of the Convention;

.6 *Chief mate* means the officer next in rank to the master and upon whom the command of the ship will fall in the event of the incapacity of the master;

.7 *Engineer officer* means an officer qualified in accordance with the provisions of regulation III/1, III/2 or III/3 of the Convention;

.8 *Chief engineer officer* means the senior engineer officer responsible for the mechanical propulsion and the operation and maintenance of the mechanical and electrical installations of the ship;

.9 *Second engineer officer* means the engineer officer next in rank to the chief engineer officer and upon whom the responsibility for the mechanical propulsion and the operation and maintenance of the mechanical and electrical installations of the ship will fall in the event of the incapacity of the chief engineer officer;

.10 *Assistant engineer officer* means a person under training to become an engineer officer and designated as such by national law or regulations;

附则

《1978 年海员培训、发证和值班标准国际公约》附则
马尼拉修正案

《1978 年海员培训、发证和值班标准国际公约》附则由以下内容代替：

附则

第 I 章
总则

第 I/1 条
定义和说明

1 除另有明文规定外，就本公约而言：

.1 规则系指本公约附则中的规则；

.2 认可的系指缔约国按照本规则认可的；

.3 船长系指指挥船舶的人；

.4 高级船员系指除船长以外的，根据国家法律或法规指定，或在没有这种指定时根据集体协议或习惯做法指定为高级船员的船员；

.5 甲板部高级船员系指符合本公约附则第 II 章规定的合格的高级船员；

.6 大副系指级别仅低于船长并且在船长不能工作时替代船长指挥船舶的甲板部高级船员；

.7 轮机部高级船员系指符合本公约规则第 III/1 条、第 III/2 条或第 III/3 条规定的合格的高级船员；

.8 轮机长系指负责船舶机械推进以及机械和电气装置操作和维护的资深的轮机部高级船员；

.9 大管轮系指级别仅低于轮机长，并且在轮机长不能工作时替代轮机长负责船舶机械推进以及机械和电气装置操作和维护的轮机部高级船员；

.10 助理轮机员系指正在接受培训以成为轮机部高级船员并根据国家法律或法规指定为助理轮机员的人员；

.11 *Radio operator* means a person holding an appropriate certificate issued or recognized by the Administration under the provisions of the Radio Regulations;

.12 *GMDSS radio operator* means a person who is qualified in accordance with the provisions of chapter IV of the Convention;

.13 *Rating* means a member of the ship's crew other than the master or an officer;

.14 *Near-coastal voyages* means voyages in the vicinity of a Party as defined by that Party;

.15 *Propulsion power* means the total maximum continuous rated output power, in kilowatts, of all the ship's main propulsion machinery which appears on the ship's certificate of registry or other official document;

.16 *Radio duties* include, as appropriate, watchkeeping and technical maintenance and repairs conducted in accordance with the Radio Regulations, the International Convention for the Safety of Life at Sea, 1974 (SOLAS), as amended and, at the discretion of each Administration, the relevant recommendations of the Organization;

.17 *Oil tanker* means a ship constructed and used for the carriage of petroleum and petroleum products in bulk;

.18 *Chemical tanker* means a ship constructed or adapted and used for the carriage in bulk of any liquid product listed in chapter 17 of the International Bulk Chemical Code;

.19 *Liquefied gas tanker* means a ship constructed or adapted and used for the carriage in bulk of any liquefied gas or other product listed in chapter 19 of the International Gas Carrier Code;

.20 *Passenger ship* means a ship as defined in the International Convention for the Safety of Life at Sea, 1974, as amended;

.21 *Ro-ro passenger ship* means a passenger ship with ro-ro spaces or special category spaces as defined in the International Convention for the Safety of Life at Sea, 1974 (SOLAS), as amended;

.22 *Month* means a calendar month or 30 days made up of periods of less than one month;

.23 *STCW Code* means the Seafarers' Training, Certification and Watchkeeping (STCW) Code as adopted by the 1995 Conference resolution 2, as it may be amended by the Organization;

.24 *Function* means a group of tasks, duties and responsibilities, as specified in the STCW Code, necessary for ship operation, safety of life at sea or protection of the marine environment;

.11 无线电操作员系指持有主管机关根据《无线电规则》签发或承认的适当证书的人员；

.12 全球海上遇险与安全系统（GMDSS）无线电操作员系指符合本公约附则第IV章规定的合格的人员；

.13 普通船员系指除船长或高级船员以外的船员；

.14 近岸航行系指在缔约国划定的该国附近水域内的航行；

.15 推进功率系指在船舶登记证书或其他正式文件上标明的以千瓦计的船舶所有主推进机械的最大连续额定输出功率的总和；

.16 无线电职责包括按照相应的《无线电规则》、经修正的《1974年国际海上人命安全公约》（SOLAS）以及由主管机关自行决定采用的本组织有关建议案所进行的值班、技术维护和修理；

.17 油船系指建造并且用于载运散装石油和石油产品的船舶；

.18 化学品船系指建造或改建成并且用于散装载运《国际散装化学品规则》第17章所列的任何液体产品的船舶；

.19 液化气船系指建造或改建成并且用于散装载运《国际气体船舶规则》第19章所列的任何液化气体或其他产品的船舶；

.20 客船系指经修正的《1974年国际海上人命安全公约》所定义的船舶；

.21 滚装客船系指经修正的《1974年国际海上人命安全公约》（SOLAS）所定义的设有滚装处所或特种处所的客船；

.22 月系指日历月或由少于1个月的时间段所累积成的30天；

.23 《STCW规则》系指由1995年大会第2号决议通过，并可由本组织加以修正的《海员培训、发证和值班（STCW）规则》；

.24 职能系指《STCW规则》规定的船舶操作、海上人命安全或保护海洋环境所需的一组任务、职责和责任；

.25 *Company* means the owner of the ship or any other organization or person such as the manager, or the bareboat charterer, who has assumed the responsibility for operation of the ship from the shipowner and who, on assuming such responsibility, has agreed to take over all the duties and responsibilities imposed on the company by these regulations;

.26 *Seagoing service* means service on board a ship relevant to the issue or revalidation of a certificate or other qualification;

.27 *ISPS Code* means the International Ship and Port Facility Security (ISPS) Code adopted on 12 December 2002, by resolution 2 of the Conference of Contracting Governments to the International Convention for the Safety of Life at Sea (SOLAS), 1974, as may be amended by the Organization;

.28 *Ship security officer* means the person on board the ship, accountable to the master, designated by the Company as responsible for the security of the ship including implementation and maintenance of the ship security plan and liaison with the company security officer and port facility security officers;

.29 *Security duties* include all security tasks and duties on board ships as defined by chapter XI-2 of the International Convention for the Safety of Life at Sea (SOLAS 1974, as amended) and the International Ship and Port Facility Security (ISPS) Code;

.30 *Certificate of competency* means a certificate issued and endorsed for masters, officers and GMDSS radio operators in accordance with the provisions of chapters II, III, IV or VII of this annex and entitling the lawful holder thereof to serve in the capacity and perform the functions involved at the level of responsibility specified therein;

.31 *Certificate of proficiency* means a certificate, other than a certificate of competency issued to a seafarer, stating that the relevant requirements of training, competencies or seagoing service in the Convention have been met;

.32 *Documentary evidence* means documentation, other than a certificate of competency or certificate of proficiency, used to establish that the relevant requirements of the Convention have been met;

.33 *Electro-technical officer* means an officer qualified in accordance with the provisions of regulation III/6 of the Convention;

.34 *Able seafarer deck* means a rating qualified in accordance with the provisions of regulation II/5 of the Convention;

.35 *Able seafarer engine* means a rating qualified in accordance with the provisions of regulation III/5 of the Convention; and

.36 *Electro-technical rating* means a rating qualified in accordance with the provisions of regulation III/7 of the Convention.

.25 公司系指船舶所有人,或已承担船舶所有人的船舶营运责任并在承担此种责任时同意承担本规则规定的所有义务和责任的任何其他机构或人员,如管理人或光船承租人;

.26 海上服务资历系指与证书的签发、再有效或其他资格有关的船上服务;

.27 《ISPS 规则》系指 2002 年 12 月 12 日《1974 年国际海上人命安全公约》缔约国大会第 2 号决议通过,并可由本组织加以修正的《国际船舶和港口设施保安(ISPS)规则》;

.28 船舶保安员系指由公司指定的承担船舶保安责任并对船长负责的船上人员,其职责包括实施和维护船舶保安计划以及与公司保安员和港口设施保安员进行联络;

.29 保安职责包括经修正的《1974 年国际海上人命安全公约》(经修正的 SOLAS 1974) 第 XI-2 章以及《国际船舶和港口设施保安(ISPS)规则》所定义的所有船上保安任务及职责;

.30 适任证书系指依据本附则第 II 章、第 III 章、第 IV 章或第 VII 章的规定向船长、高级船员以及 GMDSS 无线电操作员签发和签注的使其合法持有人有资格按证书标明的责任等级担任职位和履行职能的证书;

.31 培训合格证书系指除适任证书以外向海员签发的,表明已符合本公约的有关培训、适任或海上服务资历相关要求的证书;

.32 书面证明系指除适任证书或培训合格证书以外的,用以证明已符合本公约的相关要求的文件;

.33 电子员系指符合本公约规则第 III/6 条规定的合格高级船员;

.34 高级值班水手系指符合本公约规则第 II/5 条规定的合格普通船员;

.35 高级值班机工系指符合本公约规则第 III/5 条规定的合格普通船员;以及

.36 电子技工系指符合本公约规则第 III/7 条规定的合格普通船员。

2 These regulations are supplemented by the mandatory provisions contained in part A of the STCW Code and:

.1 any reference to a requirement in a regulation also constitutes a reference to the corresponding section of part A of the STCW Code;

.2 in applying these regulations, the related guidance and explanatory material contained in part B of the STCW Code should be taken into account to the greatest degree possible in order to achieve a more uniform implementation of the Convention provisions on a global basis;

.3 amendments to part A of the STCW Code shall be adopted, brought into force and take effect in accordance with the provisions of article XII of the Convention concerning the amendment procedure applicable to the annex; and

.4 part B of the STCW Code shall be amended by the Maritime Safety Committee in accordance with its rules of procedure.

3 The references made in article VI of the Convention to "the Administration" and "the issuing Administration" shall not be construed as preventing any Party from issuing and endorsing certificates under the provisions of these regulations.

Regulation I/2
Certificates and endorsements

1 Certificates of competency shall be issued only by the Administration, following verification of the authenticity and validity of any necessary documentary evidence.

2 Certificates issued in accordance with the provisions of regulations V/1-1 and V/1-2 to masters and officers shall only be issued by an Administration.

3 Certificates shall be in the official language or languages of the issuing country. If the language used is not English, the text shall include a translation into that language.

4 In respect of radio operators, Parties may:

.1 include the additional knowledge required by the relevant regulations in the examination for the issue of a certificate complying with the Radio Regulations; or

.2 issue a separate certificate indicating that the holder has the additional knowledge required by the relevant regulations.

5 The endorsement required by article VI of the Convention to attest the issue of a certificate shall only be issued if all the requirements of the Convention have been complied with.

6 At the discretion of a Party, endorsements may be incorporated in the format of the certificates being issued as provided for in section A-I/2 of the STCW Code. If so incorporated, the form used shall be that set forth in section A-I/2, paragraph 1. If issued otherwise, the form of endorsements used shall be that set forth in paragraph 2 of that section.

2 本规则由《STCW 规则》A 部分的强制条款作为补充，并且：

.1 提及任何一条规则的要求时，也应提及《STCW 规则》A 部分中的对应章节；

.2 在应用本规则时，应最大限度地考虑《STCW 规则》B 部分中的有关指导和解释材料，以使本公约规定得以在全球更为统一地实施；

.3 对《STCW 规则》A 部分的修正应按照本公约第 XII 条关于适用于本附则的修正程序的规定予以通过、生效和实施；并且

.4 《STCW 规则》B 部分应由海上安全委员会按照其议事规则进行修正。

3 本公约第 VI 条所述及的"主管机关"和"发证的主管机关"不应解释为妨碍任何缔约国根据本规则规定进行证书的签发和签注。

第 I/2 条

证书和签证

1 在核实所有必要的书面证明的真实性和有效性后，适任证书仅应由主管机关签发。

2 根据规则第 V/1-1 条和第 V/1-2 条的规定签发给船长及高级船员的证书仅应由主管机关签发。

3 证书应使用发证国的一种或数种官方文字。如使用的文字不是英文，证书文本应包括英文译文。

4 关于无线电操作员，缔约国可以：

.1 在为签发符合《无线电规则》的证书所进行的考试中，包括有关规则所要求的附加知识；或

.2 签发一张单独的证书，指明持有人具有相关规则所要求的附加知识。

5 本公约第 VI 条所要求的用以证明签发证书的签证，仅应在公约全部要求得到遵守的情况下签发。

6 缔约国可自行决定将签证并入按《STCW 规则》第 A-I/2 节规定所签发证书的格式中。若并入，所用的格式应是第 A-I/2 节第 1 段规定的格式。若另行签发，签证所使用的格式应是该节第 2 段规定的格式。

7 An Administration which recognizes under regulation I/10:

.1 a certificate of competency; or

.2 a certificate of proficiency issued to masters and officers in accordance with the provisions of regulations V/1-1 and V/1-2 shall endorse such certificate to attest its recognition only after ensuring the authenticity and validity of the certificate.

The endorsement shall only be issued if all requirements of the Convention have been complied with. The form of the endorsement used shall be that set forth in paragraph 3 of section A-I/2 of the STCW Code.

8 The endorsements referred to in paragraphs 5, 6 and 7:

.1 may be issued as separate documents;

.2 shall be issued by the Administration only;

.3 shall each be assigned a unique number, except that endorsements attesting the issue of a certificate may be assigned the same number as the certificate concerned, provided that number is unique; and

.4 shall expire as soon as the certificate endorsed expires or is withdrawn, suspended or cancelled by the Party which issued it and, in any case, not more than five years after their date of issue.

9 The capacity in which the holder of a certificate is authorized to serve shall be identified in the form of endorsement in terms identical to those used in the applicable safe manning requirements of the Administration.

10 Administrations may use a format different from the format given in section A-I/2 of the STCW Code, provided that, as a minimum, the required information is provided in Roman characters and Arabic figures, taking into account the variations permitted under section A-I/2.

11 Subject to the provisions of regulation I/10, paragraph 5, any certificate required by the Convention must be kept available in its original form on board the ship on which the holder is serving.

12 Each Party shall ensure that certificates are issued only to candidates who comply with the requirements of this regulation.

13 Candidates for certification shall provide satisfactory proof:

.1 of their identity;

.2 that their age is not less than that prescribed in the regulation relevant to the certificate applied for;

.3 that they meet the standards of medical fitness specified in section A-I/9 of the STCW Code;

7 主管机关根据规则第 I/10 条承认：

.1 适任证书；或

.2 根据规则第 V/1-1 条和第 V/1-2 条的规定签发给船长及高级船员的培训合格证书，仅应在确保证书的真实性及有效性之后对该证书进行签注，以证明其认可。

签证仅应在公约全部要求得到遵守的情况下签发。签证所使用的格式应是《STCW 规则》第 A-I/2 节第 3 段所规定的格式。

8 第 5 段、第 6 段和第 7 段所述的签证：

.1 可作为单独的文件签发；

.2 仅应由主管机关签发；

.3 每份应给予唯一的编号，但证明签发证书的签证可与相关证书的编号相同，只要该编号也是唯一的；并且

.4 在所签注的证书到期或在签发证书的缔约国撤销、暂停有效或注销该证书时即应失效，并且在任何情况下，自签发之日起不得超过 5 年。

9 允许证书持有人担任的职位应在签证表格中载明，其用词应与主管机关适用的安全配员要求中的用词一致。

10 主管机关可以采用不同于《STCW 规则》第 A-I/2 节规定的格式，但最低限度是对需填写的项目使用罗马字母和阿拉伯数字，并考虑第 A-I/2 节所允许的不同形式。

11 以规则第 I/10 条第 5 段的规定为条件，本公约所要求的任何证书的原件必须保存在证书持有人服务的船上。

12 各缔约国应确保证书仅签发给符合本条规则要求的证书申请人。

13 证书申请人应提供下列符合要求的证明：

.1 身份；

.2 年龄不小于有关申请证书的规则中规定的年龄；

.3 达到《STCW 规则》第 A-I/9 节规定的健康标准；

.4 of having completed the seagoing service and any related compulsory training required by these regulations for the certificate applied for; and

.5 that they meet the standards of competence prescribed by these regulations for the capacities, functions and levels that are to be identified in the endorsement to the certificate.

14 Each Party undertakes to maintain a register or registers of all certificates and endorsements for masters, officers, and, as applicable, ratings which are issued, have expired or have been revalidated, suspended, cancelled or reported lost or destroyed and of dispensations issued.

15 Each Party undertakes to make available information on the status of such certificates of competency, endorsements and dispensations to other Parties and companies which request verification of the authenticity and validity of certificates produced to them by seafarers seeking recognition of their certificates under regulation I/10 or employment on board ship.

16 As of 1 January 2017, the information on the status of information required to be available in accordance with paragraph 15 of this regulation shall be made available, in the English language, through electronic means.

Regulation I/3
Principles governing near-coastal voyages

1 Any Party defining near-coastal voyages for the purpose of the Convention shall not impose training, experience or certification requirements on the seafarers serving on board the ships entitled to fly the flag of another Party and engaged on such voyages in a manner resulting in more stringent requirements for such seafarers than for seafarers serving on board ships entitled to fly its own flag. In no case shall any such Party impose requirements in respect of seafarers serving on board ships entitled to fly the flag of another Party in excess of those of the Convention in respect of ships not engaged on near-coastal voyages.

2 A Party that, for ships afforded the benefits of the near-coastal voyage provisions of the Convention, which includes voyages off the coast of other Parties within the limits of their near-coastal definition, shall enter into an undertaking with the Parties concerned specifying the details of both involved trading areas and other relevant conditions.

3 With respect to ships entitled to fly the flag of a Party regularly engaged on near-coastal voyages off the coast of another Party, the Party whose flag the ship is entitled to fly shall prescribe training, experience and certification requirements for seafarers serving on such ships at least equal to those of the Party off whose coast the ship is engaged, provided that they do not exceed the requirements of the Convention in respect of ships not engaged on near-coastal voyages. Seafarers serving on a ship which extends its voyage beyond what is defined as a near-coastal voyage by a Party and enters waters not covered by that definition shall fulfil the appropriate competency requirements of the Convention.

4 A Party may afford a ship which is entitled to fly its flag the benefits of the near-coastal voyage provisions of the Convention when it is regularly engaged off the coast of a non-Party on near-coastal voyages as defined by the Party.

.4 完成本规则对所申请证书要求的海上服务资历和相关强制性培训；并且

.5 达到本规则为在证书的签证中指明的职位、职能和级别所规定的适任标准。

14 各缔约国应保持对船长和高级船员，如可行，还包括普通船员的所有证书和签证的签发、到期或再有效、暂停有效、注销或报失或损毁以及签发特免证明的登记。

15 当海员向其他缔约国和公司呈交其证书以求根据规则第Ⅰ/10条得到承认或被雇用上船，而这些国家和公司需要核查证书的真实性和有效性时，各缔约国应向其提供适任证书、签证和特免证明情况的资料。

16 本条规则第15段要求的提供资料状况的信息应从2017年1月1日起，用英文以电子形式提供。

第Ⅰ/3条

控制近岸航行的原则

1 任何为实施本公约而规定近岸航行的缔约国不应将培训、资历或发证的要求强加于在悬挂另一缔约国国旗并从事此类航行的船舶上服务的海员，以免造成对这些海员的要求比在悬挂本国国旗的船舶上服务的海员更为严格的情况。在任何情况下，任何缔约国不应将超过公约中对从事非近岸航行船舶的要求，强加于在悬挂另一缔约国国旗的船舶上服务的海员。

2 一缔约国，当其定义的近岸航行区域包括其他缔约国的近岸航行区域时，针对其根据本公约有关近岸航行规定获得惠利的船舶，该缔约国应与相关缔约国就双方涉及的航区和其他相关条件等具体事宜达成一致。

3 对于悬挂一缔约国国旗，经常在另一缔约国海岸附近从事近岸航行的船舶，其船旗国应为在此种船舶上服务的海员规定至少相当于船舶所航经的缔约国的培训、资历和发证要求，但这些要求不得超出本公约对从事非近岸航行船舶所规定的要求。在航行超出一缔约国所规定的近岸航行范围并进入定义未包括的水域的船舶上服务的海员应满足本公约相应的适任要求。

4 缔约国对悬挂其国旗的船舶，当其经常在一非缔约国海岸附近从事该缔约国规定的近岸航行时，可给予本公约有关近岸航行规定的惠利。

5 The certificates of seafarers issued by a Party for its defined near-coastal voyages limits may be accepted by other Parties for service in their defined near-coastal voyages limits, provided the Parties concerned enter into an undertaking specifying the details of involved trading areas and other relevant conditions thereof.

6 Parties defining near-coastal voyages, in accordance with the requirements of this regulation, shall:

.1 meet the principles governing near-coastal voyages specified in section A-I/3;

.2 communicate to the Secretary-General, in conformity with the requirements of regulation I/7, the details of the provisions adopted; and

.3 incorporate the near-coastal voyages limits in the endorsements issued pursuant to regulation I/2, paragraphs 5, 6 or 7.

7 Nothing in this regulation shall, in any way, limit the jurisdiction of any State, whether or not a Party to the Convention.

Regulation I/4
Control procedures

1 Control exercised by a duly authorized control officer under article X shall be limited to the following:

.1 verification in accordance with article X(1) that all seafarers serving on board who are required to be certificated in accordance with the Convention hold an appropriate certificate or a valid dispensation, or provide documentary proof that an application for an endorsement has been submitted to the Administration in accordance with regulation I/10, paragraph 5;

.2 verification that the numbers and certificates of the seafarers serving on board are in conformity with the applicable safe manning requirements of the Administration; and

.3 assessment, in accordance with section A-I/4 of the STCW Code, of the ability of the seafarers of the ship to maintain watchkeeping and security standards, as appropriate, as required by the Convention if there are clear grounds for believing that such standards are not being maintained because any of the following have occurred:

.3.1 the ship has been involved in a collision, grounding or stranding, or

.3.2 there has been a discharge of substances from the ship when under way, at anchor or at berth which is illegal under any international convention, or

.3.3 the ship has been manoeuvred in an erratic or unsafe manner whereby routeing measures adopted by the Organization or safe navigation practices and procedures have not been followed, or

.3.4 the ship is otherwise being operated in such a manner as to pose a danger to persons, property, the environment, or a compromise to security.

5　若某一缔约国与有关缔约国就涉及的航区和其他相关条件等具体事宜达成一致，则该缔约国为海员在其规定的近岸航行区域签发的证书，有关缔约国在其规定的近岸航行区域内可予以接受。

6　根据本条规则的要求，规定近岸航行的缔约国应：

.1　符合第 A-I/3 节所规定的控制近岸航行的原则；

.2　遵照规则第 I/7 条的要求将所采用的规定的细节通知秘书长；并且

.3　在依据规则第 I/2 条第 5 段、第 6 段或第 7 段要求签发的签证中包含近岸航行区域的限制。

7　本条规则不应以任何方式限制任何国家的管辖权，不论其是否为本公约缔约国。

第 I/4 条

监督程序

1　经正式授权的监督官员按本公约第 X 条规定所行使的监督应限于下列各项：

.1　按照第 X(1)条核实所有在船上服务又要求按本公约规定发证的海员是否都持有适当的证书或有效的特免证明，或是否根据规则第 I/10 条第 5 段向主管机关提供了文件，证明已提交签证申请；

.2　核实在船上服务的海员的人数和证书是否符合主管机关适用的安全配员要求；并且

.3　如果因为发生了下列任一情况而有明显理由认为未能保持本公约要求的值班和保安标准时，如适用，则根据《STCW 规则》第 A-I/4 节，对船上海员保持值班和保安标准的能力进行评估：

.3.1　船舶发生碰撞、搁浅或触礁，或

.3.2　船舶在航、锚泊或靠泊时，违反任一国际公约而非法排放物质，或

.3.3　以不稳定或不安全方式操纵船舶，从而未遵循本组织采纳的定线措施或安全航行方法和程序，或

.3.4　以其他危及人员、财产或环境的方式或有损保安的方式操纵船舶。

2 Deficiencies which may be deemed to pose a danger to persons, property or the environment include the following:

.1 failure of seafarers to hold a certificate, to have an appropriate certificate, to have a valid dispensation or to provide documentary proof that an application for an endorsement has been submitted to the Administration in accordance with regulation I/10, paragraph 5;

.2 failure to comply with the applicable safe manning requirements of the Administration;

.3 failure of navigational or engineering watch arrangements to conform to the requirements specified for the ship by the Administration;

.4 absence in a watch of a person qualified to operate equipment essential to safe navigation, safety radiocommunications or the prevention of marine pollution; and

.5 inability to provide, for the first watch at the commencement of a voyage and for subsequent relieving watches, persons who are sufficiently rested and otherwise fit for duty.

3 Failure to correct any of the deficiencies referred to in paragraph 2, in so far as it has been determined by the Party carrying out the control that they pose a danger to persons, property or the environment, shall be the only grounds under article X on which a Party may detain a ship.

Regulation I/5
National provisions

1 Each Party shall establish processes and procedures for the impartial investigation of any reported incompetency, act, omission or compromise to security that may pose a direct threat to safety of life or property at sea or to the marine environment by the holders of certificates or endorsements issued by that Party in connection with their performance of duties related to their certificates and for the withdrawal, suspension and cancellation of such certificates for such cause and for the prevention of fraud.

2 Each Party shall take and enforce appropriate measures to prevent fraud and other unlawful practices involving certificates and endorsements issued.

3 Each Party shall prescribe penalties or disciplinary measures for cases in which the provisions of its national legislation giving effect to the Convention are not complied with in respect of ships entitled to fly its flag or of seafarers duly certificated by that Party.

4 In particular, such penalties or disciplinary measures shall be prescribed and enforced in cases in which:

.1 a company or a master has engaged a person not holding a certificate as required by the Convention;

.2 a master has allowed any function or service in any capacity required by these regulations to be performed by a person holding an appropriate certificate to be

2 可被认为危及人员、财产或环境的缺陷包括下列各项：

.1 海员未持有证书，未持有适当的证书或有效的特免证明，或未能依据规则第 I/10 条第 5 段向主管机关提供文件，证明已提交了签证申请；

.2 未符合主管机关适用的安全配员要求；

.3 未按主管机关为船舶规定的要求作出航行或轮机值班安排；

.4 没有专门负责操作安全航行、安全无线电通信或防止海洋污染必要设备的合格的人员值班；以及

.5 未能为航次开始第一个班次和其后的接班提供经过充分休息并在其他方面适于职责的人员。

3 只有未能纠正第 2 段所提及的任何缺陷，而且实施监督的缔约国确定这些缺陷危及人员、财产或环境，才构成缔约国按本公约第 X 条可以滞留船舶的唯一理由。

第 I/5 条

国家的规定

1 各缔约国应制定方法和程序，用于对缔约国签发的证书或签证的持有人在履行其与证书有关的职责时出现的可能对海上人命或财产安全或对海洋环境构成直接威胁的任何被举报的不适任表现、行为、不为或有损保安的行为进行公正的调查，和用于因此撤销、暂停有效或注销这种证书，以及用于预防欺诈。

2 各缔约国应采取并且实施适当的措施以防止与所签发的证书和签证有关的欺诈和其他非法行为。

3 各缔约国应对悬挂其国旗的船舶或由其正式发证的海员不遵守其为实施本公约而制定的国内法规规定的情况，规定处罚或纪律措施。

4 这种处罚或纪律措施应特别就下列情况作出规定并加以实施：

.1 公司或船长雇用了未持有本公约所要求的证书的人员；

.2 船长准许未持有所要求的证书、有效的特免证明或规则第 I/10 条第 5 段所要求的证明文件的人员，去承担按本规则规定应由持有适当证书的人员履行的职能或担任的职位；或

performed by a person not holding the required certificate, a valid dispensation or having the documentary proof required by regulation I/10, paragraph 5; or

.3 a person has obtained by fraud or forged documents an engagement to perform any function or serve in any capacity required by these regulations to be performed or filled by a person holding a certificate or dispensation.

5 A Party, within whose jurisdiction there is located any company which, or any person who, is believed on clear grounds to have been responsible for, or to have knowledge of, any apparent non-compliance with the Convention specified in paragraph 4, shall extend all co-operation possible to any Party which advises it of its intention to initiate proceedings under its jurisdiction.

Regulation I/6
Training and assessment

Each Party shall ensure that:

.1 the training and assessment of seafarers, as required under the Convention, are administered, supervised and monitored in accordance with the provisions of section A-I/6 of the STCW Code; and

.2 those responsible for the training and assessment of competence of seafarers, as required under the Convention, are appropriately qualified in accordance with the provisions of section A-I/6 of the STCW Code for the type and level of training or assessment involved.

Regulation I/7
Communication of information

1 In addition to the information required to be communicated by article IV, each Party shall provide to the Secretary-General, within the time periods prescribed and in the format specified in section A-I/7 of the STCW Code, such other information as may be required by the Code on other steps taken by the Party to give the Convention full and complete effect.

2 When complete information as prescribed in article IV and section A-I/7 of the STCW Code has been received and such information confirms that full and complete effect is given to the provisions of the Convention, the Secretary-General shall submit a report to this effect to the Maritime Safety Committee.

3 Following subsequent confirmation by the Maritime Safety Committee, in accordance with procedures adopted by the Committee, that the information which has been provided demonstrates that full and complete effect is given to the provisions of the Convention:

.1 the Maritime Safety Committee shall identify the Parties so concerned;

.2 shall review the list of Parties which communicated information that demonstrated that they give full and complete effect to the relevant provisions of the Convention, to retain in this list only the Parties so concerned; and

.3 个人利用欺骗或伪造文件的方式得到雇用，承担按本规则规定应由持有适当证书或特免证明的人员履行的职能或担任的职位。

5 当一缔约国有明显理由相信，在其管辖权范围内的任何公司或人员对第 4 段所规定的任何明显不符合本公约的情况负有责任或知情时，该缔约国应尽可能与告知有意向在其管辖权内采取行动的任何缔约国进行合作。

第 I/6 条

培训和评估

各缔约国应确保：

.1 本公约所要求的对海员的培训和评估是按照《STCW 规则》第 A-I/6 节规定进行管理、监督和检查的；并且

.2 按本公约要求负责海员培训和适任评估的人员，按照《STCW 规则》第 A-I/6 节规定，对所涉及培训或评估的种类和级别是充分合格的。

第 I/7 条

资料交流

1 除公约第 IV 条要求交流的资料外，各缔约国应将《STCW 规则》可能要求的关于缔约国为使本公约得以充分和完全实施而采取的其他步骤的有关资料，在规定时间内按照《STCW 规则》第 A-I/7 节规定的格式送交秘书长。

2 当公约第 IV 条和《STCW 规则》第 A-I/7 节规定的全部资料已经收到，并且这些资料确定本公约规定已得以充分和完全实施时，秘书长应就此事向海上安全委员会提交一份报告。

3 在海上安全委员会按其通过的程序确认所提供的资料表明本公约规定已得以充分和完全实施后：

.1 海上安全委员会应认定这些有关的缔约国；

.2 复查已交流资料且所提供资料表明其充分和完全实施了本公约相关规定的缔约国清单，仅将这些有关的缔约国保留在清单里；并且

.3 other Parties shall be entitled, subject to the provisions of regulations I/4 and I/10, to accept, in principle, that certificates issued by or on behalf of the Parties identified in paragraph 3.1 are in compliance with the Convention.

4 Amendments to the Convention and STCW Code, with dates of entry into force later than the date information has been, or will be, communicated to the Secretary-General in accordance with the provisions of paragraph 1, are not subject to the provisions of section A-I/7, paragraphs 1 and 2.

Regulation I/8
Quality standards

1 Each Party shall ensure that:

.1 in accordance with the provisions of section A-I/8 of the STCW Code, all training, assessment of competence, certification, including medical certification, endorsement and revalidation activities carried out by non-governmental agencies or entities under its authority are continuously monitored through a quality standards system to ensure achievement of defined objectives, including those concerning the qualifications and experience of instructors and assessors; and

.2 where governmental agencies or entities perform such activities, there shall be a quality standards system.

2 Each Party shall also ensure that an evaluation is periodically undertaken, in accordance with the provisions of section A-I/8 of the STCW Code, by qualified persons who are not themselves involved in the activities concerned. This evaluation shall include all changes to national regulations and procedures in compliance with the amendments to the Convention and STCW Code, with dates of entry into force later than the date information was communicated to the Secretary-General.

3 A report containing the results of the evaluation required by paragraph 2 shall be communicated to the Secretary-General in accordance with the format specified in section A-I/7 of the STCW Code.

Regulation I/9
Medical standards

1 Each Party shall establish standards of medical fitness for seafarers and procedures for the issue of a medical certificate in accordance with the provisions of this regulation and of section A-I/9 of the STCW Code.

2 Each Party shall ensure that those responsible for assessing the medical fitness of seafarers are medical practitioners recognized by the Party for the purpose of seafarer medical examinations, in accordance with the provisions of section A-I/9 of the STCW Code.

3 Every seafarer holding a certificate issued under the provisions of the Convention, who is serving at sea, shall also hold a valid medical certificate issued in accordance with the provisions of this regulation and of section A-I/9 of the STCW Code.

.3 其他缔约国应有权根据规则第I/4条和第I/10条的规定,原则上承认由第3.1段认定的缔约国所签发或代表其签发的证书是符合本公约规定的。

4 本公约及《STCW规则》的修正案,若其生效日期迟于第1段规定的资料已送交或将送交秘书长的日期,则不受第A-I/7节第1段和第2段规定的约束。

第I/8条
质量标准

1 各缔约国应确保:

.1 按照《STCW规则》第A-I/8节的规定,所有由其授权的非政府机构或组织所执行的培训、适任评估、发证(包括健康证书的发证)、签证和再有效,应通过质量标准体系进行连续监控,包括有关教员和评估员的资格和经历,以确保达到既定目标;并且

.2 如果政府机构或组织进行这种工作,应有一个质量标准体系。

2 各缔约国还应确保由不参与该项工作的合格的人员,按照《STCW规则》第A-I/8节的规定,进行定期评估。评估内容应包括按照在上次资料送交秘书长的日期之后生效的本公约和《STCW规则》的修正案对国家规定和程序所作的所有变更。

3 第2段要求的含有评估结果的报告应按照《STCW规则》第A-I/7节规定的格式送交秘书长。

第I/9条
健康标准

1 各缔约国应根据本条规则以及《STCW规则》第A-I/9节的规定制定海员健康标准和健康证书签发程序。

2 各缔约国应根据《STCW规则》第A-I/9节的规定确保由该缔约国认可的海员体检从业医生评估海员的健康状况。

3 持有按本公约规定签发的证书并正在海上服务的每个海员,也应持有按本条规则和《STCW规则》第A-I/9节的规定签发的有效健康证书。

4 Every candidate for certification shall:

.1 be not less than 16 years of age;

.2 provide satisfactory proof of his/her identity; and

.3 meet the applicable medical fitness standards established by the Party.

5 Medical certificates shall remain valid for a maximum period of two years unless the seafarer is under the age of 18, in which case the maximum period of validity shall be one year.

6 If the period of validity of a medical certificate expires in the course of a voyage, then the medical certificate shall continue in force until the next port of call where a medical practitioner recognized by the Party is available, provided that the period shall not exceed three months.

7 In urgent cases the Administration may permit a seafarer to work without a valid medical certificate until the next port of call where a medical practitioner recognized by the Party is available, provided that:

.1 the period of such permission does not exceed three months; and

.2 the seafarer concerned is in possession of an expired medical certificate of recent date.

Regulation I/10
Recognition of certificates

1 Each Administration shall ensure that the provisions of this regulation are complied with, in order to recognize, by endorsement in accordance with regulation I/2, paragraph 7, a certificate issued by or under the authority of another Party to a master, officer or radio operator and that:

.1 the Administration has confirmed, through an evaluation of that Party, which may include inspection of facilities and procedures, that the requirements of the Convention regarding standards of competence, training and certification and quality standards are fully complied with; and

.2 an undertaking is agreed with the Party concerned that prompt notification will be given of any significant change in the arrangements for training and certification provided in compliance with the Convention.

2 Measures shall be established to ensure that seafarers who present, for recognition, certificates issued under the provisions of regulations II/2, III/2 or III/3, or issued under regulation VII/1 at the management level, as defined in the STCW Code, have an appropriate knowledge of the maritime legislation of the Administration relevant to the functions they are permitted to perform.

3 Information provided and measures agreed upon under this regulation shall be communicated to the Secretary-General in conformity with the requirements of regulation I/7.

4 Certificates issued by or under the authority of a non-Party shall not be recognized.

4　每个证书申请人应：

.1　年龄不小于 16 周岁；

.2　提供满意的身份证明；并且

.3　达到该缔约国制定的适用的健康标准。

5　健康证书的有效期最长为两年，若海员年龄小于 18 周岁，则有效期最长为一年。

6　若在航行中健康证书有效期期满，则该健康证书在到达下一个有缔约国认可的从业医生的停靠港之前仍然有效，条件是为期不超过 3 个月。

7　在紧急情况下，主管机关可允许一个未持有效健康证书的海员工作至下一个有缔约国认可的从业医生的停靠港，条件是：

.1　这种许可的期限不超过 3 个月；并且

.2　该海员持有近日过期的健康证书。

第 I/10 条

证书的承认

1　各主管机关应确保本条规则的规定得以遵守，以便根据规则第 I/2 条第 7 段规定的签证来承认其他缔约国签发或授权签发给船长、高级船员或无线电操作员的证书，并应确保：

.1　主管机关通过对该缔约国的评价，其中可包括对设施和程序的检查，确认本公约有关适任标准、培训、发证以及质量标准的要求得以完全遵守；并且

.2　与有关缔约国约定，承诺迅速通知为遵守本公约而提供的培训和发证安排中的任何重大变化。

2　应采取措施以确保那些为了得到承认而提交按规则第 II/2 条、第 III/2 条或第 III/3 条签发的证书或按规则第 VII/1 条签发的《STCW 规则》规定的管理级证书的海员，具有与允许其履行的职能有关的主管机关海事法规的适当知识。

3　应按照规则第 I/7 条的要求向秘书长提交根据本条规则所提供的资料和所约定的措施。

4　对非缔约国签发或授权签发的证书应不予承认。

5 Notwithstanding the requirement of regulation I/2, paragraph 7, an Administration may, if circumstances require, subject to the provisions of paragraph 1, allow a seafarer to serve for a period not exceeding three months on board a ship entitled to fly its flag, while holding an appropriate and valid certificate issued and endorsed as required by another Party for use on board that Party's ships but which has not yet been endorsed so as to render it appropriate for service on board ships entitled to fly the flag of the Administration. Documentary proof shall be readily available that application for an endorsement has been submitted to the Administration.

6 Certificates and endorsements issued by an Administration under the provisions of this regulation in recognition of, or attesting the recognition of, a certificate issued by another Party shall not be used as the basis for further recognition by another Administration.

Regulation I/11
Revalidation of certificates

1 Every master, officer and radio operator holding a certificate issued or recognized under any chapter of the Convention other than chapter VI, who is serving at sea or intends to return to sea after a period ashore, shall, in order to continue to qualify for seagoing service, be required, at intervals not exceeding five years, to:

.1 meet the standards of medical fitness prescribed by regulation I/9; and

.2 establish continued professional competence in accordance with section A-I/11 of the STCW Code.

2 Every master, officer and radio operator shall, for continuing seagoing service on board ships for which special training requirements have been internationally agreed upon, successfully complete approved relevant training.

3 Every master and officer shall, for continuing seagoing service on board tankers, meet the requirements in paragraph 1 of this regulation and be required, at intervals not exceeding five years, to establish continued professional competence for tankers in accordance with section A-I/11, paragraph 3 of the STCW Code.

4 Each Party shall compare the standards of competence which it required of candidates for certificates issued before 1 January 2017 with those specified for the appropriate certificate in part A of the STCW Code, and shall determine the need for requiring the holders of such certificates to undergo appropriate refresher and updating training or assessment.

5 The Party shall, in consultation with those concerned, formulate or promote the formulation of a structure of refresher and updating courses as provided for in section A-I/11 of the STCW Code.

6 For the purpose of updating the knowledge of masters, officers and radio operators, each Administration shall ensure that the texts of recent changes in national and international regulations concerning the safety of life at sea, security and the protection of the marine environment are made available to ships entitled to fly its flag.

5 尽管规则第 I/2 条第 7 段已有要求,但主管机关在需要时,可根据第 1 段的规定,允许(持有按另一缔约国要求签发和签证而用于该缔约国船上的适当和有效证书,但该证书尚未经过签证,使其适于在悬挂该主管机关国旗的船上服务)的海员在悬挂主管机关国旗的船上的服务为期不超过 3 个月。应随时提供已向该主管机关提交签证申请的证明文件。

6 根据本条规则的规定,由一主管机关为承认或证明承认另一缔约国所发证书而签发的证书和签证,不应作为另一主管机关进一步承认的基础。

第 I/11 条

证书的再有效

1 每个在海上服务或在岸上一段时间后意欲重返海上服务的持有根据本公约除第 VI 章外的各章签发或承认的证书的船长、高级船员和无线电操作员,为了继续有资格从事海上服务,应按要求在不超过 5 年的间隔中:

.1 达到规则第 I/9 条规定的健康标准;并且

.2 按照《STCW 规则》第 A-I/11 节获得持续的专业适任能力。

2 为在国际上议定的有特殊培训要求的船上继续从事海上服务,每个船长、高级船员和无线电操作员应圆满完成认可的有关培训。

3 为在液货船上继续从事海上服务,每个船长和高级船员应符合本条规则第 1 段的要求,并按照《STCW 规则》第 A-I/11 节第 3 段,在不超过 5 年的间隔内获得持续的液货船专业适任能力。

4 各缔约国应对在 2017 年 1 月 1 日前签发证书的申请人所要求的适任标准,与《STCW 规则》A 部分中为取得适当证书所规定的适任标准进行比较,并应决定是否有必要要求这类证书的持有人接受适当的知识更新培训或评估。

5 缔约国应与有关方面协商,制定或促使制定一个《STCW 规则》第 A-I/11 节中所规定的知识更新课程大纲。

6 为了船长、高级船员和无线电操作员知识更新的目的,各主管机关应确保向悬挂其国旗的船舶提供有关海上人命安全、保安和海洋环境保护的国内和国际规则最新变动的文本。

Regulation I/12
Use of simulators

1 The performance standards and other provisions set forth in section A-I/12 and such other requirements as are prescribed in part A of the STCW Code for any certificate concerned shall be complied with in respect of:

.1 all mandatory simulator-based training;

.2 any assessment of competency required by part A of the STCW Code which is carried out by means of a simulator; and

.3 any demonstration, by means of a simulator, of continued proficiency required by part A of the STCW Code.

Regulation I/13
Conduct of trials

1 These regulations shall not prevent an Administration from authorizing ships entitled to fly its flag to participate in trials.

2 For the purposes of this regulation, the term *trial* means an experiment or series of experiments, conducted over a limited period, which may involve the use of automated or integrated systems in order to evaluate alternative methods of performing specific duties or satisfying particular arrangements prescribed by the Convention, which would provide at least the same degree of safety, security and pollution prevention as provided by these regulations.

3 The Administration authorizing ships to participate in trials shall be satisfied that such trials are conducted in a manner that provides at least the same degree of safety, security and pollution prevention as provided by these regulations. Such trials shall be conducted in accordance with guidelines adopted by the Organization.

4 Details of such trials shall be reported to the Organization as early as practicable but not less than six months before the date on which the trials are scheduled to commence. The Organization shall circulate such particulars to all Parties.

5 The results of trials authorized under paragraph 1, and any recommendations the Administration may have regarding those results, shall be reported to the Organization, which shall circulate such results and recommendations to all Parties.

6 Any Party having any objection to particular trials authorized in accordance with this regulation should communicate such objection to the Organization as early as practicable. The Organization shall circulate details of the objection to all Parties.

7 An Administration which has authorized a trial shall respect objections received from other Parties relating to such trial by directing ships entitled to fly its flag not to engage in a trial while navigating in the waters of a coastal State which has communicated its objection to the Organization.

8 An Administration which concludes, on the basis of a trial, that a particular system will provide at least the same degree of safety, security and pollution prevention as provided by these

第 I/12 条
模拟器的使用

1 下列各项应符合《STCW 规则》第 A-I/12 节规定的性能标准和其他规定，以及《STCW 规则》A 部分中为任何有关证书规定的其他要求：

.1 所有强制性的基于模拟器的培训；

.2 《STCW 规则》A 部分要求的、使用模拟器进行的任何适任评估；以及

.3 《STCW 规则》A 部分要求的、使用模拟器进行的任何持续熟练程度的演示。

第 I/13 条
试验的实施

1 本规则应不妨碍主管机关授权悬挂其国旗的船舶参与试验。

2 就本条规则而言，试验一词系指在一段有限的时间内实施的一项或一系列可能包括自动或综合系统的使用在内的试验，其目的在于评价执行具体任务或满足本公约规定的特定安排的可供选择的办法，这种办法所提供的安全、保安和防污染至少与本规则规定的程度相同。

3 授权船舶参与试验的主管机关应确信这种试验的安全和防污染至少与本规则规定的程度相同。这种试验应按照本组织通过的指南进行。

4 这类试验的详情应尽早报告本组织，不应晚于计划开始试验之日前 6 个月。本组织应将这些资料转发所有缔约国。

5 按照第 1 段授权的试验的结果和主管机关对这些结果可能提出的任何建议应报告本组织，本组织应将这些结果和建议转发所有缔约国。

6 任何缔约国如对按照本条规则批准的特定试验持反对意见，应尽早将反对意见通知本组织。本组织应将反对意见的详情转发所有缔约国。

7 授权进行试验的主管机关应尊重收到的其他缔约国对该项试验的反对意见，指示悬挂其国旗的船舶在航行于向本组织提出反对意见的沿海国水域时不进行试验。

8 当主管机关在试验的基础上断定，某一特定系统所提供的安全和防污染至少与本规则规定的程度相同时，则可授权悬挂其国旗的船舶不受限制地继续使用该系统进行试验，但应满足下列要求：

regulations may authorize ships entitled to fly its flag to continue to operate with such a system indefinitely, subject to the following requirements:

.1 the Administration shall, after results of the trial have been submitted in accordance with paragraph 5, provide details of any such authorization, including identification of the specific ships which may be subject to the authorization, to the Organization, which will circulate this information to all Parties;

.2 any operations authorized under this paragraph shall be conducted in accordance with any guidelines developed by the Organization, to the same extent as they apply during a trial;

.3 such operations shall respect any objections received from other Parties in accordance with paragraph 7, to the extent such objections have not been withdrawn; and

.4 an operation authorized under this paragraph shall only be permitted pending a determination by the Maritime Safety Committee as to whether an amendment to the Convention would be appropriate, and, if so, whether the operation should be suspended or permitted to continue before the amendment enters into force.

9 At the request of any Party, the Maritime Safety Committee shall establish a date for the consideration of the trial results and for the appropriate determinations.

Regulation I/14
Responsibilities of companies

1 Each Administration shall, in accordance with the provisions of section A-I/14, hold companies responsible for the assignment of seafarers for service on their ships in accordance with the provisions of the present Convention, and shall require every such company to ensure that:

.1 each seafarer assigned to any of its ships holds an appropriate certificate in accordance with the provisions of the Convention and as established by the Administration;

.2 its ships are manned in compliance with the applicable safe manning requirements of the Administration;

.3 seafarers assigned to any of its ships have received refresher and updating training as required by the Convention;

.4 documentation and data relevant to all seafarers employed on its ships are maintained and readily accessible, and include, without being limited to, documentation and data on their experience, training, medical fitness and competency in assigned duties;

.5 seafarers, on being assigned to any of its ships, are familiarized with their specific duties and with all ship arrangements, installations, equipment, procedures and ship characteristics that are relevant to their routine or emergency duties;

.1 在按照第 5 段提交了试验结果后，主管机关应向本组织提供任何这类授权的详情，包括指明可能获得该授权的具体船舶，本组织将把这些资料转发所有缔约国；

.2 根据本段授权的任何试验应按照本组织制定的任何有关指南来进行，并达到试验时同样的应用程度；

.3 这类试验应按第 7 段规定尊重收自其他缔约国的反对意见，只要这类反对意见还未撤回；并且

.4 在海上安全委员会对本公约的修正是否适当以及，如果适当，在修正生效以前对这类操作是否应暂停或继续进行作出决定期间，按照本段授权的试验才能被准许。

9 应任一缔约国的请求，海上安全委员会应确定审议试验结果并作出适当决定的日期。

第 I/14 条

公司的责任

1 各主管机关应按照第 A-I/14 节的规定责成各公司按照本公约的规定负责指派海员到其船上服务，并应要求各公司确保：

.1 每个指派到其任一船上的海员均按照本公约的规定和主管机关制定的规定持有适当的证书；

.2 其船舶是按照主管机关适用的安全配员要求进行船员配备的；

.3 指派到其任一船上的海员均接受了本公约要求的知识更新培训；

.4 保持并随时可查到其船上雇用的所有海员的有关文件和数据，包括但不限于海员的资历、培训、健康状况以及对所指派工作的适任情况的文件和数据；

.5 被指派到其任一船上的海员熟悉其具体职责以及与其日常或应急职责有关的所有船舶布置、装置、设备、程序和船舶特性；

.6 the ship's complement can effectively coordinate their activities in an emergency situation and in performing functions vital to safety, security and to the prevention or mitigation of pollution; and

.7 at all times on board its ships there shall be effective oral communication in accordance with chapter V, regulation 14, paragraphs 3 and 4 of the International Convention for the Safety of Life at Sea, 1974 (SOLAS), as amended.

Regulation I/15
Transitional provisions

1 Until 1 January 2017, a Party may continue to issue, recognize and endorse certificates in accordance with the provisions of the Convention which applied immediately prior to 1 January 2012 in respect of those seafarers who commenced approved seagoing service, an approved education and training programme or an approved training course before 1 July 2013.

2 Until 1 January 2017, a Party may continue to renew and revalidate certificates and endorsements in accordance with the provisions of the Convention which applied immediately prior to 1 January 2012.

.6 船舶在编人员在紧急情况下和履行与安全、保安和防止或减轻污染有关的关键职能时，能有效地协调其活动；并且

.7 按照经修正的《1974 年国际海上人命安全公约》(SOLAS)第 V 章第 14 条第 3 款及第 4 款的规定，在其船上任何时候都应能进行有效的口头沟通。

第 I/15 条

过渡规定

1 在 2017 年 1 月 1 日之前，缔约国可按照本公约 2012 年 1 月 1 日之前适用的规定，对在 2013 年 7 月 1 日之前开始了认可的海上服务资历、认可的教育和培训计划或认可的培训课程的海员，继续签发、承认和签注其证书。

2 在 2017 年 1 月 1 日之前，缔约国可按照本公约 2012 年 1 月 1 日之前适用的规定，继续进行证书和签证的更新和再有效。

CHAPTER II

Master and deck department

Regulation II/1
Mandatory minimum requirements for certification of officers in charge of a navigational watch on ships of 500 gross tonnage or more

1 Every officer in charge of a navigational watch serving on a seagoing ship of 500 gross tonnage or more shall hold a certificate of competency.

2 Every candidate for certification shall:

.1 be not less than 18 years of age;

.2 have approved seagoing service of not less than 12 months as part of an approved training programme which includes onboard training that meets the requirements of section A-II/1 of the STCW Code and is documented in an approved training record book, or otherwise have approved seagoing service of not less than 36 months;

.3 have performed, during the required seagoing service, bridge watchkeeping duties under the supervision of the master or a qualified officer for a period of not less than six months;

.4 meet the applicable requirements of the regulations in chapter IV, as appropriate, for performing designated radio duties in accordance with the Radio Regulations;

.5 have completed approved education and training and meet the standard of competence specified in section A-II/1 of the STCW Code; and

.6 meet the standard of competence specified in section A-VI/1, paragraph 2, section A-VI/2, paragraphs 1 to 4, section A-VI/3, paragraphs 1 to 4 and section A-VI/4, paragraphs 1 to 3 of the STCW Code.

Regulation II/2
Mandatory minimum requirements for certification of masters and chief mates on ships of 500 gross tonnage or more

Master and chief mate on ships of 3,000 gross tonnage or more

1 Every master and chief mate on a seagoing ship of 3,000 gross tonnage or more shall hold a certificate of competency.

2 Every candidate for certification shall:

.1 meet the requirements for certification as an officer in charge of a navigational watch on ships of 500 gross tonnage or more and have approved seagoing service in that capacity:

.1.1 for certification as chief mate, not less than 12 months, and

第 II 章
船长和甲板部

第 II/1 条
对 500 总吨或以上船舶的负责航行值班的高级船员发证的强制性最低要求

1 每个在 500 总吨或以上的海船上负责航行值班的高级船员,应持有适任证书。

2 每个证书申请人应:

.1 年龄不小于 18 周岁;

.2 具有不少于 12 个月的认可的海上服务资历,作为包括符合《STCW 规则》第 A-II/1 节要求的船上培训在内的认可的培训计划的组成部分,并在认可的培训记录簿中记载,或具有不少于 36 个月的认可的海上服务资历;

.3 在所要求的海上服务资历中,已在船长或合格的高级船员的监督下履行驾驶台值班职责不少于 6 个月;

.4 视情况符合第 IV 章有关规则的可适用的要求,以按照《无线电规则》履行指定的无线电职责;

.5 已完成认可的教育和培训,并且达到《STCW 规则》第 A-II/1 节规定的适任标准;并且

.6 达到《STCW 规则》第 A-VI/1 节第 2 段、第 A-VI/2 节第 1 段至第 4 段、第 A-VI/3 节第 1 段至第 4 段以及第 A-VI/4 节第 1 段至第 3 段规定的适任标准。

第 II/2 条
对 500 总吨或以上船舶的船长和大副发证的强制性最低要求

3 000 总吨或以上船舶的船长和大副

1 每个在 3 000 总吨或以上的海船上的船长和大副,应持有适任证书。

2 每个证书申请人应:

.1 符合对 500 总吨或以上船舶的负责航行值班的高级船员的发证要求,并在该职位上具有认可的海上服务资历:

.1.1 申请大副证书,不少于 12 个月,

.1.2 for certification as master, not less than 36 months; however, this period may be reduced to not less than 24 months if not less than 12 months of such seagoing service has been served as chief mate; and

.2 have completed approved education and training and meet the standard of competence specified in section A-II/2 of the STCW Code for masters and chief mates on ships of 3,000 gross tonnage or more.

Master and chief mate on ships of between 500 and 3,000 gross tonnage

3 Every master and chief mate on a seagoing ship of between 500 and 3,000 gross tonnage shall hold a certificate of competency.

4 Every candidate for certification shall:

.1 for certification as chief mate, meet the requirements of an officer in charge of a navigational watch on ships of 500 gross tonnage or more;

.2 for certification as master, meet the requirements of an officer in charge of a navigational watch on ships of 500 gross tonnage or more and have approved seagoing service of not less than 36 months in that capacity; however, this period may be reduced to not less than 24 months if not less than 12 months of such seagoing service has been served as chief mate; and

.3 have completed approved training and meet the standard of competence specified in section A-II/2 of the STCW Code for masters and chief mates on ships of between 500 and 3,000 gross tonnage.

Regulation II/3
Mandatory minimum requirements for certification of officers in charge of a navigational watch and of masters on ships of less than 500 gross tonnage

Ships not engaged on near-coastal voyages

1 Every officer in charge of a navigational watch serving on a seagoing ship of less than 500 gross tonnage not engaged on near-coastal voyages shall hold a certificate of competency for ships of 500 gross tonnage or more.

2 Every master serving on a seagoing ship of less than 500 gross tonnage not engaged on near-coastal voyages shall hold a certificate of competency for service as master on ships of between 500 and 3,000 gross tonnage.

Ships engaged on near-coastal voyages
Officer in charge of a navigational watch

3 Every officer in charge of a navigational watch on a seagoing ship of less than 500 gross tonnage engaged on near-coastal voyages shall hold a certificate of competency.

.1.2 申请船长证书,不少于 36 个月,但是,如果已具有不少于 12 个月的大副海上服务资历,则此段时间可缩短为不少于 24 个月;并且

.2 已完成认可的教育和培训,并且达到《STCW 规则》第 A-II/2 节为 3 000 总吨或以上船舶的船长和大副规定的适任标准。

500 至 3 000 总吨船舶的船长和大副

3 每个在 500 至 3 000 总吨海船上的船长和大副,应持有适任证书。

4 每个证书申请人应:

.1 申请大副证书,符合对 500 总吨或以上船舶的负责航行值班的高级船员的要求;

.2 申请船长证书,符合对 500 总吨或以上船舶的负责航行值班的高级船员的要求并在该职位上具有不少于 36 个月的认可的海上服务资历,但是,如果已具有不少于 12 个月的大副海上服务资历,则此段时间可缩短为不少于 24 个月;并且

.3 已完成认可的培训,并且达到《STCW 规则》第 A-II/2 节为 500 至 3 000 总吨船舶的船长和大副规定的适任标准。

第 II/3 条

对未满 500 总吨船舶的负责航行值班的高级船员和船长发证的强制性最低要求

不从事近岸航行的船舶

1 每个在不从事近岸航行的未满 500 总吨海船上负责航行值班的高级船员,应持有 500 总吨或以上船舶的适任证书。

2 每个在不从事近岸航行的未满 500 总吨海船上服务的船长,应持有 500 至 3 000 总吨船舶的船长的适任证书。

从事近岸航行的船舶

负责航行值班的高级船员

3 每个在从事近岸航行的未满 500 总吨海船上负责航行值班的高级船员,应持有适任证书。

4 Every candidate for certification as officer in charge of a navigational watch on a seagoing ship of less than 500 gross tonnage engaged on near-coastal voyages shall:

.1 be not less than 18 years of age;

.2 have completed:

.2.1 special training, including an adequate period of appropriate seagoing service as required by the Administration, or

.2.2 approved seagoing service in the deck department of not less than 36 months;

.3 meet the applicable requirements of the regulations in chapter IV, as appropriate, for performing designated radio duties in accordance with the Radio Regulations;

.4 have completed approved education and training and meet the standard of competence specified in section A-II/3 of the STCW Code for officers in charge of a navigational watch on ships of less than 500 gross tonnage engaged on near-coastal voyages; and

.5 meet the standard of competence specified in section A-VI/1, paragraph 2, section A-VI/2, paragraphs 1 to 4, section A-VI/3, paragraphs 1 to 4 and section A-VI/4, paragraphs 1 to 3 of the STCW Code.

Master

5 Every master serving on a seagoing ship of less than 500 gross tonnage engaged on near-coastal voyages shall hold a certificate of competency.

6 Every candidate for certification as master on a seagoing ship of less than 500 gross tonnage engaged on near-coastal voyages shall:

.1 be not less than 20 years of age;

.2 have approved seagoing service of not less than 12 months as officer in charge of a navigational watch;

.3 have completed approved education and training and meet the standard of competence specified in section A-II/3 of the STCW Code for masters on ships of less than 500 gross tonnage engaged on near-coastal voyages; and

.4 meet the standard of competence specified in section A-VI/1, paragraph 2, section A-VI/2, paragraphs 1 to 4, section A-VI/3, paragraphs 1 to 4 and section A-VI/4, paragraphs 1 to 3 of the STCW Code.

4 每个申请从事近岸航行的未满 500 总吨海船的负责航行值班的高级船员证书的申请人应：

.1 年龄不小于 18 周岁；

.2 已完成：

.2.1 专门的培训，包括主管机关要求的足够时间的相应海上服务资历，或

.2.2 不少于 36 个月在甲板部工作的认可的海上服务资历；

.3 视情况符合第 IV 章有关规则的可适用的要求，以按照《无线电规则》履行指定的无线电职责；

.4 已完成认可的教育和培训，并且达到《STCW 规则》第 A-II/3 节为从事近岸航行的未满 500 总吨船舶的负责航行值班的高级船员所规定的适任标准；并且

.5 达到《STCW 规则》第 A-VI/1 节第 2 段、第 A-VI/2 节第 1 段至第 4 段、第 A-VI/3 节第 1 段至第 4 段以及第 A-VI/4 节第 1 段至第 3 段规定的适任标准。

船长

5 每个在从事近岸航行的未满 500 总吨海船上服务的船长，应持有适任证书。

6 每个申请从事近岸航行的未满 500 总吨海船船长证书的申请人应：

.1 年龄不小于 20 周岁；

.2 具有不少于 12 个月的作为负责航行值班的高级船员的认可的海上服务资历；

.3 已完成认可的教育和培训，并且达到《STCW 规则》第 A-II/3 节为从事近岸航行的未满 500 总吨船舶的船长规定的适任标准；并且

.4 达到《STCW 规则》第 A-VI/1 节第 2 段、第 A-VI/2 节第 1 段至第 4 段、第 A-VI/3 节第 1 段至 4 段以及第 A-VI/4 节第 1 段至第 3 段规定的适任标准。

Exemptions

7 The Administration, if it considers that a ship's size and the conditions of its voyage are such as to render the application of the full requirements of this regulation and section A-II/3 of the STCW Code unreasonable or impracticable, may to that extent exempt the master and the officer in charge of a navigational watch on such a ship or class of ships from some of the requirements, bearing in mind the safety of all ships which may be operating in the same waters.

Regulation II/4
*Mandatory minimum requirements for certification of ratings forming part of a navigational watch**

1 Every rating forming part of a navigational watch on a seagoing ship of 500 gross tonnage or more, other than ratings under training and ratings whose duties while on watch are of an unskilled nature, shall be duly certificated to perform such duties.

2 Every candidate for certification shall:

.1 be not less than 16 years of age;

.2 have completed:

.2.1 approved seagoing service including not less than six months of training and experience, or

.2.2 special training, either pre-sea or on board ship, including an approved period of seagoing service which shall not be less than two months; and

.3 meet the standard of competence specified in section A-II/4 of the STCW Code.

3 The seagoing service, training and experience required by subparagraphs 2.2.1 and 2.2.2 shall be associated with navigational watchkeeping functions and involve the performance of duties carried out under the direct supervision of the master, the officer in charge of the navigational watch or a qualified rating.

Regulation II/5
Mandatory minimum requirements for certification of ratings as able seafarer deck

1 Every able seafarer deck serving on a seagoing ship of 500 gross tonnage or more shall be duly certificated.

2 Every candidate for certification shall:

.1 be not less than 18 years of age;

.2 meet the requirements for certification as a rating forming part of a navigational watch;

* These requirements are not those for certification of Able Seamen as contained in the ILO Certification of Able Seamen Convention, 1946, or any subsequent convention.

免除

7　主管机关如果认为某一船舶的尺度及航行条件会使适用本条和《STCW 规则》第 A-II/3 节的全部要求成为不合理或不切实可行时，则可适当免除对该船或该类船舶的船长和负责航行值班的高级船员的某些要求，但要注意可能在同一水域航行的所有船舶的安全。

第 II/4 条

对组成航行值班部分的普通船员发证的强制性最低要求①

1　对每个在 500 总吨或以上的海船上组成航行值班部分的普通船员，应适当发证以履行其职责，但培训中的普通船员和值班时其职责属非技术性的普通船员除外。

2　每个证书申请人应：

　.1　年龄不小于 16 周岁；

　.2　已完成：

　　.2.1　认可的海上服务资历，包括不少于 6 个月的培训和经验，或

　　.2.2　上船前的或船上的专门培训，包括不少于 2 个月的认可的海上服务资历；并且

　.3　达到《STCW 规则》第 A-II/4 节规定的适任标准。

3　第 2.2.1 段和第 2.2.2 段所要求的海上服务资历、培训和经验应与航行值班职能相关，并且涉及在船长、负责航行值班的高级船员或合格的普通船员的直接监督之下履行职责。

第 II/5 条

对作为高级值班水手的普通船员发证的强制性最低要求

1　对每个在 500 总吨或以上的海船上服务的高级值班水手，应适当发证。

2　每个证书申请人应：

　.1　年龄不小于 18 周岁；

　.2　符合对组成航行值班部分的普通船员的发证要求；

① 此要求并非 ILO《1946 年一等水手发证公约》或后续公约所述及的一等水手发证要求。

.3 while qualified to serve as a rating forming part of a navigational watch, have approved seagoing service in the deck department of:

.3.1 not less than 18 months, or

.3.2 not less than 12 months and have completed approved training; and

.4 meet the standard of competence specified in section A-II/5 of the STCW Code.

3 Every Party shall compare the standards of competence which it required of Able Seamen for certificates issued before 1 January 2012 with those specified for the certificate in section A-II/5 of the STCW Code, and shall determine the need, if any, for requiring these personnel to update their qualifications.

4 Until 1 January 2012, a Party which is also a Party to the International Labour Organization Certification of Able Seamen Convention, 1946 (No. 74) may continue to issue, recognize and endorse certificates in accordance with the provisions of the aforesaid convention.

5 Until 1 January 2017, a Party which is also a Party to the International Labour Organization Certification of Able Seamen Convention, 1946 (No. 74) may continue to renew and revalidate certificates and endorsements in accordance with the provisions of the aforesaid convention.

6 Seafarers may be considered by the Party to have met the requirements of this regulation if they have served in a relevant capacity in the deck department for a period of not less than 12 months within the last 60 months preceding the entry into force of this regulation for that Party.

.3 在取得组成航行值班部分的普通船员资格的同时，还具有认可的甲板部海上服务资历：

.3.1 不少于 18 个月，或

.3.2 不少于 12 个月，且已完成认可的培训；并且

.4 达到《STCW 规则》第 A-II/5 节规定的适任标准。

3 各缔约国应将在 2012 年 1 月 1 日前签发证书的值班水手所要求的适任标准与《STCW 规则》第 A-II/5 节对证书规定的适任标准进行比较，并决定是否有必要要求这些人员更新其资格。

4 在 2012 年 1 月 1 日之前，缔约国可按照在本规则生效之前适用的国际劳工组织《1946 年一等水手公约》(第 74 号)的规定，继续签发、承认和签注其证书。

5 在 2017 年 1 月 1 日之前，缔约国可按照在本规则生效之前适用的国际劳工组织《1946 年一等水手公约》(第 74 号)的规定，继续进行证书和签证的更新和再有效。

6 如果海员在本公约对该缔约国生效前的 60 个月内有不少于 12 个月的时间在甲板部相应的职位上服务，则该缔约国可以认为其已符合本条规则的要求。

CHAPTER III

Engine department

Regulation III/1
Mandatory minimum requirements for certification of officers in charge of an engineering watch in a manned engine-room or designated duty engineers in a periodically unmanned engine-room

1 Every officer in charge of an engineering watch in a manned engine-room or designated duty engineer officer in a periodically unmanned engine-room on a seagoing ship powered by main propulsion machinery of 750 kW propulsion power or more shall hold a certificate of competency.

2 Every candidate for certification shall:

.1 be not less than 18 years of age;

.2 have completed combined workshop skills training and an approved seagoing service of not less than 12 months as part of an approved training programme which includes onboard training that meets the requirements of section A-III/1 of the STCW Code and is documented in an approved training record book, or otherwise have completed combined workshop skills training and an approved seagoing service of not less than 36 months of which not less than 30 months shall be seagoing service in the engine department;

.3 have performed, during the required seagoing service, engine-room watchkeeping duties under the supervision of the chief engineer officer or a qualified engineer officer for a period of not less than six months;

.4 have completed approved education and training and meet the standard of competence specified in section A-III/1 of the STCW Code; and

.5 meet the standard of competence specified in section A-VI/1, paragraph 2, section A-VI/2, paragraphs 1 to 4, section A-VI/3, paragraphs 1 to 4 and section A-VI/4, paragraphs 1 to 3 of the STCW Code.

Regulation III/2
Mandatory minimum requirements for certification of chief engineer officers and second engineer officers on ships powered by main propulsion machinery of 3,000 kW propulsion power or more

1 Every chief engineer officer and second engineer officer on a seagoing ship powered by main propulsion machinery of 3,000 kW propulsion power or more shall hold a certificate of competency.

2 Every candidate for certification shall:

.1 meet the requirements for certification as an officer in charge of an engineering watch on seagoing ships powered by main propulsion machinery of 750 kW propulsion power or more and have approved seagoing service in that capacity:

第 III 章
轮机部

第 III/1 条
对有人值班机舱负责轮机值班的高级船员或周期性无人值班机舱指定值班的轮机员发证的强制性最低要求

1 每个在主推进装置为 750 kW 或以上海船上的有人值班机舱负责轮机值班的高级船员或周期性无人值班机舱指定值班的轮机部高级船员，应持有适任证书。

2 每个证书申请人应：

.1 年龄不小于 18 周岁；

.2 已完成不少于 12 个月的组合车间技能培训和认可的海上服务资历，作为包括符合《STCW 规则》第 A-III/1 节要求的船上培训在内的经认可的培训计划的组成部分，并在认可的培训记录簿中记载，或具有不少于 36 个月的组合车间技能培训和认可的海上服务资历，其中在轮机部的海上服务资历应不少于 30 个月；

.3 在所要求的海上服务资历中，已在轮机长或合格的轮机部高级船员的监督之下，履行机舱值班职责不少于 6 个月；

.4 已完成认可的教育和培训，并且达到《STCW 规则》第 A-III/1 节规定的适任标准；并且

.5 达到《STCW 规则》第 A-VI/1 节第 2 段、第 A-VI/2 节第 1 段至第 4 段、第 A-VI/3 节第 1 段至第 4 段及第 A-VI/4 节第 1 段至第 3 段规定的适任标准。

第 III/2 条
对主推进装置为 3 000 kW 或以上船舶的轮机长和大管轮发证的强制性最低要求

1 每个在主推进装置为 3 000 kW 或以上海船上的轮机长和大管轮应持有适任证书。

2 每个证书申请人应：

.1 符合对在主推进装置为 750 kW 或以上的海船上负责轮机值班的高级船员的发证要求，并在该职位上具有认可的海上服务资历：

.1.1 for certification as second engineer officer, have not less than 12 months as qualified engineer officer, and

.1.2 for certification as chief engineer officer, have not less than 36 months: however, this period may be reduced to not less than 24 months if not less than 12 months of such seagoing service has been served as second engineer officer; and

.2 have completed approved education and training and meet the standard of competence specified in section A-III/2 of the STCW Code.

Regulation III/3
Mandatory minimum requirements for certification of chief engineer officers and second engineer officers on ships powered by main propulsion machinery of between 750 kW and 3,000 kW propulsion power

1 Every chief engineer officer and second engineer officer on a seagoing ship powered by main propulsion machinery of between 750 kW and 3,000 kW propulsion power shall hold a certificate of competency.

2 Every candidate for certification shall:

.1 meet the requirements for certification as an officer in charge of an engineering watch and:

.1.1 for certification as second engineer officer, have not less than 12 months of approved seagoing service as assistant engineer officer or engineer officer, and

.1.2 for certification as chief engineer officer, have not less than 24 months of approved seagoing service of which not less than 12 months shall be served while qualified to serve as second engineer officer; and

.2 have completed approved education and training and meet the standard of competence specified in section A-III/3 of the STCW Code.

3 Every engineer officer who is qualified to serve as second engineer officer on ships powered by main propulsion machinery of 3,000 kW propulsion power or more, may serve as chief engineer officer on ships powered by main propulsion machinery of less than 3,000 kW propulsion power, provided the certificate is so endorsed.

Regulation III/4
Mandatory minimum requirements for certification of ratings forming part of a watch in a manned engine-room or designated to perform duties in a periodically unmanned engine-room

1 Every rating forming part of an engine-room watch or designated to perform duties in a periodically unmanned engine-room on a seagoing ship powered by main propulsion machinery of 750 kW propulsion power or more, other than ratings under training and ratings whose duties are of an unskilled nature, shall be duly certificated to perform such duties.

.1.1 申请大管轮证书，担任合格的轮机部高级船员不少于 12 个月，和

.1.2 申请轮机长证书，担任合格的轮机部高级船员不少于 36 个月，但若已具有不少于 12 个月的大管轮海上服务资历，则该资历可缩短为不少于 24 个月；并且

.2 已完成认可的教育和培训，并达到《STCW 规则》第 A-III/2 节规定的适任标准。

第 III/3 条

对主推进装置为 750 kW 至 3 000 kW 船舶上的轮机长和大管轮发证的强制性最低要求

1 每个在主推进装置为 750 kW 至 3 000 kW 海船上的轮机长和大管轮应持有适任证书。

2 每个证书申请人应：

.1 符合对负责轮机值班的高级船员的发证要求，并且：

.1.1 申请大管轮证书，具有不少于 12 个月的作为助理轮机员或轮机部高级船员的认可的海上服务资历，和

.1.2 申请轮机长证书，具有不少于 24 个月的认可的海上服务资历，其中具备大管轮资格并实际担任大管轮不少于 12 个月；并且

.2 已完成认可的教育和培训，并达到《STCW 规则》第 A-III/3 节规定的适任标准。

3 每个有资格担任主推进装置为 3 000 kW 或以上船舶大管轮的轮机部高级船员，只要其证书已如此签注，则可在主推进装置为 3 000 kW 以下的船舶上担任轮机长。

第 III/4 条

对组成有人值班机舱值班部分或指定在周期性无人值班机舱履行职责的普通船员发证的强制性最低要求

1 对每个在主推进装置为 750 kW 或以上的海船上组成机舱值班部分或指定在周期性无人值班机舱履行职责的普通船员，应适当发证以履行其职责，但培训中的普通船员和其职责属非技术性的普通船员除外。

2 Every candidate for certification shall:

.1 be not less than 16 years of age;

.2 have completed:

.2.1 approved seagoing service including not less than six months of training and experience, or

.2.2 special training, either pre-sea or on board ship, including an approved period of seagoing service which shall not be less than two months; and

.3 meet the standard of competence specified in section A-III/4 of the STCW Code.

3 The seagoing service, training and experience required by subparagraphs 2.2.1 and 2.2.2 shall be associated with engine-room watchkeeping functions and involve the performance of duties carried out under the direct supervision of a qualified engineer officer or a qualified rating.

Regulation III/5
Mandatory minimum requirements for certification of ratings as able seafarer engine in a manned engine-room or designated to perform duties in a periodically unmanned engine-room

1 Every able seafarer engine serving on a seagoing ship powered by main propulsion machinery of 750 kW propulsion power or more shall be duly certificated.

2 Every candidate for certification shall:

.1 be not less than 18 years of age;

.2 meet the requirements for certification as a rating forming part of a watch in a manned engine-room or designated to perform duties in a periodically unmanned engine-room;

.3 while qualified to serve as a rating forming part of an engineering watch, have approved seagoing service in the engine department of:

.3.1 not less than 12 months, or

.3.2 not less than 6 months and have completed approved training; and

.4 meet the standard of competence specified in section A-III/5 of the STCW Code.

3 Every Party shall compare the standard of competence which it required of ratings in the engine department for certificates issued before 1 January 2012 with those specified for the certificate in section A-III/5 of the STCW Code, and shall determine the need, if any, for requiring these personnel to update their qualifications.

4 Seafarers may be considered by the Party to have met the requirements of this regulation if they have served in a relevant capacity in the engine department for a period of not less

2 每个证书申请人应：

.1 年龄不小于 16 周岁；

.2 已完成：

.2.1 认可的海上服务资历，包括不少于 6 个月的培训和经验，或

.2.2 上船前或船上的专门培训，包括不少于 2 个月的认可的海上服务资历；并且

.3 达到《STCW 规则》第 A-III/4 节规定的适任标准。

3 第 2.2.1 段和第 2.2.2 段要求的海上服务资历、培训和经验应与机舱值班职能相关，并且涉及在合格的轮机部高级船员或合格的普通船员的直接监督之下履行职责。

第 III/5 条

对在有人值班机舱或指定在周期性无人值班机舱履行职责的作为高级值班机工的普通船员发证的强制性最低要求

1 对每个在主推进装置为 750 kW 或以上的海船上任职的高级值班机工应适当发证。

2 每个证书申请人应：

.1 年龄不小于 18 周岁；

.2 符合对组成有人值班机舱值班部分或指定在周期性无人值班机舱履行职责的普通船员的发证要求；

.3 在有资格担任组成轮机值班部分的普通船员时，具有认可的轮机部海上服务资历：

.3.1 不少于 12 个月，或

.3.2 不少于 6 个月且已完成认可的培训；并且

.4 达到《STCW 规则》第 A-III/5 节规定的适任标准。

3 各缔约国应对在 2012 年 1 月 1 日前签发轮机部普通船员证书所要求的适任标准与《STCW 规则》第 A-III/5 节规定的发证标准进行比较，并应决定是否有必要要求这些人员更新其资格。

4 如果海员在本公约对该缔约国生效前的 60 个月内有不少于 12 个月的时间在轮机部相应的职位上服务，则该缔约国可以认为其已符合本条规则的要求。

than 12 months within the last 60 months preceding the entry into force of this regulation for that Party.

Regulation III/6
Mandatory minimum requirements for certification of electro-technical officers

1 Every electro-technical officer serving on a seagoing ship powered by main propulsion machinery of 750 kW propulsion power or more shall hold a certificate of competency.

2 Every candidate for certification shall:

.1 be not less than 18 years of age;

.2 have completed not less than 12 months of combined workshop skills training and approved seagoing service of which not less than 6 months shall be seagoing service as part of an approved training programme which meets the requirements of section A-III/6 of the STCW Code and is documented in an approved training record book, or otherwise not less than 36 months of combined workshop skills training and approved seagoing service of which not less than 30 months shall be seagoing service in the engine department;

.3 have completed approved education and training and meet the standard of competence specified in section A-III/6 of the STCW Code; and

.4 meet the standard of competence specified in section A-VI/1, paragraph 2, section A-VI/2, paragraphs 1 to 4, section A-VI/3, paragraphs 1 to 4 and section A-VI/4, paragraphs 1 to 3 of the STCW Code.

3 Every Party shall compare the standard of competence which it required of electro-technical officers for certificates issued before 1 January 2012 with those specified for the certificate in section A-III/6 of the STCW Code, and shall determine the need for requiring those personnel to update their qualifications.

4 Seafarers may be considered by the Party to have met the requirements of this regulation if they have served in a relevant capacity on board a ship for a period of not less than 12 months within the last 60 months preceding the entry into force of this regulation for that Party and meet the standard of competence specified in section A-III/6 of the STCW Code.

5 Notwithstanding the above requirements of paragraph 1 to 4, a suitably qualified person may be considered by a Party to be able to perform certain functions of section A-III/6.

Regulation III/7
Mandatory minimum requirements for certification of electro-technical ratings

1 Every electro-technical rating serving on a seagoing ship powered by main propulsion machinery of 750 kW propulsion power or more shall be duly certificated.

第 III/6 条

对电子员发证的强制性最低要求

1 每个在主推进装置为 750 kW 或以上海船上任职的电子员应持有适任证书。

2 每个证书申请人应:

.1 年龄不小于 18 周岁;

.2 已完成不少于 12 个月的组合车间技能培训和认可的海上服务资历,其中有不少于 6 个月是作为包括符合《STCW 规则》第 A-III/6 节要求的船上培训在内的认可的培训计划的组成部分,并在认可的培训记录簿中记载,或具有不少于 36 个月的组合车间技能培训和认可的海上服务资历,其中有不少于 30 个月的轮机部海上服务资历;

.3 已完成认可的教育和培训,并达到《STCW 规则》第 A-III/6 节规定的适任标准;并且

.4 达到《STCW 规则》第 A-VI/1 节第 2 段、第 A-VI/2 节第 1 段至第 4 段、第 A-VI/3 节第 1 段至第 4 段及第 A-VI/4 节第 1 段至第 3 段规定的适任标准。

3 各缔约国应对在 2012 年 1 月 1 日前签发电子员证书所要求的适任标准与《STCW 规则》第 A-III/6 节规定的发证标准进行比较,并应决定是否有必要要求这些人员更新其资格。

4 如果海员在本公约对该缔约国生效前的 60 个月内有不少于 12 个月的时间在船上相应的职位上服务并达到《STCW 规则》第 A-III/6 节规定的适任标准,则该缔约国可以认为其已符合本条规则的要求。

5 尽管有以上第 1 段至第 4 段的要求,缔约国可以认为有适当资格的人员能够履行第 A-III/6节的某些职能。

第 III/7 条

对电子技工发证的强制性最低要求

1 对每个在主推进装置为 750 kW 或以上的海船上服务的电子技工应适当发证。

2 Every candidate for certification shall:

.1 be not less than 18 years of age;

.2 have:

.2.1 completed approved seagoing service including not less than 12 months training and experience, or

.2.2 completed approved training, including an approved period of seagoing service which shall not be less than 6 months, or

.2.3 qualifications that meet the technical competences in table A-III/7 and an approved period of seagoing service, which shall not be less than 3 months; and

.3 meet the standard of competence specified in section A-III/7 of the STCW Code.

3 Every Party shall compare the standard of competence which it required of electro-technical ratings for certificates issued before 1 January 2012 with those specified for the certificate in section A-III/7 of the STCW Code, and shall determine the need, if any, for requiring these personnel to update their qualifications.

4 Seafarers may be considered by the Party to have met the requirements of this regulation if they have served in a relevant capacity on board a ship for a period of not less than 12 months within the last 60 months preceding the entry into force of this regulation for that Party and meet the standard of competence specified in section A-III/7 of the STCW Code.

5 Notwithstanding the above requirements of paragraphs 1 to 4, a suitably qualified person may be considered by a Party to be able to perform certain functions of section A-III/7.

2 每个证书申请人应：

.1 年龄不小于 18 周岁；

.2 已经：

.2.1 完成认可的海上服务资历，包括不少于 12 个月的培训和经验，或

.2.2 完成认可的培训，包括不少于 6 个月的认可的海上服务资历，或

.2.3 具有符合表 A-III/7 规定的技术能力的资格，以及不少于 3 个月的认可的海上服务资历；并且

.3 达到《STCW 规则》第 A-III/7 节规定的适任标准。

3 各缔约国应对在 2012 年 1 月 1 日前签发电子技工证书所要求的适任标准与《STCW 规则》第A-III/7节规定的发证标准进行比较，并应决定是否有必要要求这些人员更新其资格。

4 如果海员在本公约对该缔约国生效前的 60 个月内有不少于 12 个月的时间在船上相应的职位上服务并达到《STCW 规则》第 A-III/7 节规定的适任标准，则该缔约国可认为其已符合本条规则的要求。

5 尽管有以上第 1 段至第 4 段的要求，缔约国可以认为有适当资格的人员能够履行第A-III/7节的某些职能。

CHAPTER IV

Radiocommunication and radio operators

Explanatory note

Mandatory provisions relating to radio watchkeeping are set forth in the Radio Regulations and in the International Convention for the Safety of Life at Sea, 1974, as amended. Provisions for radio maintenance are set forth in the International Convention for the Safety of Life at Sea, 1974 (SOLAS), as amended, and the guidelines adopted by the Organization*.

Regulation IV/1
Application

1 Except as provided in paragraph 2, the provisions of this chapter apply to radio operators on ships operating in the global maritime distress and safety system (GMDSS) as prescribed by the International Convention for the Safety of Life at Sea, 1974, as amended.

2 Radio operators on ships not required to comply with the provisions of the GMDSS in chapter IV of the SOLAS Convention are not required to meet the provisions of this chapter. Radio operators on these ships are, nevertheless, required to comply with the Radio Regulations. The Administration shall ensure that the appropriate certificates as prescribed by the Radio Regulations are issued to or recognized in respect of such radio operators.

Regulation IV/2
Mandatory minimum requirements for certification of GMDSS radio operators

1 Every person in charge of or performing radio duties on a ship required to participate in the GMDSS shall hold an appropriate certificate related to the GMDSS, issued or recognized by the Administration under the provisions of the Radio Regulations.

2 In addition, every candidate for certification of competency under this regulation for service on a ship, which is required by the International Convention for the Safety of Life at Sea, 1974, as amended, to have a radio installation, shall:

- .1 be not less than 18 years of age; and
- .2 have completed approved education and training and meet the standard of competence specified in section A-IV/2 of the STCW Code.

* Refer to the Radio Maintenance Guidelines for the Global Maritime Distress and Safety System (GMDSS) Related to Sea Areas A3 and A4 adopted by the Organization by resolution A.702(17), as amended.

第 IV 章
无线电通信和无线电操作员

说明

关于无线电值班的强制性规定,已在《无线电规则》和经修正的《1974 年国际海上人命安全公约》(SOLAS)中阐明。关于无线电维修的规定,已在经修正的《1974 年国际海上人命安全公约》和本组织通过的指南①中阐明。

第 IV/1 条
适用范围

1　除第 2 段规定外,本章的规定适用于在按经修正的《1974 年国际海上人命安全公约》规定的全球海上遇险与安全系统(GMDSS)的船舶上工作的无线电操作员。

2　无须符合《SOLAS 公约》第 IV 章关于 GMDSS 的规定的船舶无线电操作员,也无须符合本章的规定。但是,该类船舶的无线电操作员须符合《无线电规则》的规定。主管机关应确保对该类无线电操作员签发或承认《无线电规则》规定的适当的证书。

第 IV/2 条
对 GMDSS 无线电操作员发证的强制性最低要求

1　在已按要求加入 GMDSS 的船上负责或履行无线电职责的每个人员,应持有主管机关按《无线电规则》的规定签发或承认的与 GMDSS 相关的适当的证书。

2　此外,根据本条规则,每个申请在按经修正的《1974 年国际海上人命安全公约》要求配备无线电设备的船舶上工作的适任证书申请人应:

.1　年龄不小于 18 周岁;并且

.2　已完成认可的教育和培训,并且达到《STCW 规则》第 A-IV/2 节规定的适任标准。

① 参见本组织以大会 A.702(17)号决议通过的经修正的《关于 A3 和 A4 海区全球海上遇险与安全系统的无线电维修指南》。

CHAPTER V

Special training requirements for personnel on certain types of ships

Regulation V/1-1

Mandatory minimum requirements for the training and qualifications of masters, officers and ratings on oil and chemical tankers

1 Officers and ratings assigned specific duties and responsibilities related to cargo or cargo equipment on oil or chemical tankers shall hold a certificate in basic training for oil and chemical tanker cargo operations.

2 Every candidate for a certificate in basic training for oil and chemical tanker cargo operations shall have completed basic training in accordance with provisions of section A-VI/1 of the STCW Code and shall have completed:

.1 at least three months of approved seagoing service on oil or chemical tankers and meet the standard of competence specified in section A-V/1-1, paragraph 1 of the STCW Code; or

.2 an approved basic training for oil and chemical tanker cargo operations and meet the standard of competence specified in section A-V/1-1, paragraph 1 of the STCW Code.

3 Masters, chief engineer officers, chief mates, second engineer officers and any person with immediate responsibility for loading, discharging, care in transit, handling of cargo, tank cleaning or other cargo-related operations on oil tankers shall hold a certificate in advanced training for oil tanker cargo operations.

4 Every candidate for a certificate in advanced training for oil tanker cargo operations shall:

.1 meet the requirements for certification in basic training for oil and chemical tanker cargo operations; and

.2 while qualified for certification in basic training for oil and chemical tanker cargo operations, have:

.2.1 at least three months of approved seagoing service on oil tankers, or

.2.2 at least one month of approved onboard training on oil tankers, in a supernumerary capacity, which includes at least three loading and three unloading operations and is documented in an approved training record book taking into account guidance in section B-V/1; and

.3 have completed approved advanced training for oil tanker cargo operations and meet the standard of competence specified in section A-V/1-1, paragraph 2 of the STCW Code.

5 Masters, chief engineer officers, chief mates, second engineer officers and any person with immediate responsibility for loading, discharging, care in transit, handling of cargo, tank

第 V 章
特定类型船舶的人员特殊培训要求

第 V/1-1 条
对油船和化学品船船长、高级船员及普通船员的培训和资格的强制性最低要求

1 在油船或化学品船上承担特定的与货物或货物设备有关的职责和责任的高级船员和普通船员应持有油船或化学品船货物操作基本培训证书。

2 每个申请油船和化学品船货物操作基本培训证书的申请人,应完成《STCW 规则》第 A-VI/1节规定的基本培训,并应完成:

.1 至少 3 个月的认可的油船或化学品船海上服务资历,并且达到《STCW 规则》第 A-V/1-1节第 1 段规定的适任标准;或

.2 认可的油船和化学品船货物操作基本培训,并且达到《STCW 规则》第A-V/1-1节第 1 段规定的适任标准。

3 船长、轮机长、大副、大管轮和任何对油船上货物装卸、运输中照管货物、货物作业、洗舱或其他与货物相关的操作承担直接责任的人员,应持有油船货物操作高级培训证书。

4 每个申请油船货物操作高级培训证书的申请人应:

.1 符合油船和化学品船货物操作基本培训发证的要求;并且

.2 在有资格取得油船和化学品船货物操作基本培训证书时,具有:

.2.1 至少 3 个月的认可的油船海上服务资历,或

.2.2 至少 1 个月的作为编外人员的认可的油船船上培训,其中至少包括 3 次装货操作和 3 次卸货操作,并在认可的培训记录簿上记载,参考第 B-V/1 节中的指导;并且

.3 完成认可的油船货物操作高级培训,并且达到《STCW 规则》第 A-V/1-1 节第 2 段规定的适任标准。

5 船长、轮机长、大副、大管轮和任何对化学品船上货物装卸、运输中照管货物、货物作业、洗舱或其他与货物相关的操作承担直接责任的人员,应持有化学品船货物操作高级培训证书。

cleaning or other cargo-related operations on chemical tankers shall hold a certificate in advanced training for chemical tanker cargo operations.

6 Every candidate for a certificate in advanced training for chemical tanker cargo operations shall:

.1 meet the requirements for certification in basic training for oil and chemical tanker cargo operations; and

.2 while qualified for certification in basic training for oil and chemical tanker cargo operations, have:

.2.1 at least three months of approved seagoing service on chemical tankers, or

.2.2 at least one month of approved onboard training on chemical tankers, in a supernumerary capacity, which includes at least three loading and three unloading operations and is documented in an approved training record book taking into account guidance in section B-V/1; and

.3 have completed approved advanced training for chemical tanker cargo operations and meet the standard of competence specified in section A-V/1-1, paragraph 3 of the STCW Code.

7 Administrations shall ensure that a certificate of proficiency is issued to seafarers, who are qualified in accordance with paragraphs 2, 4 or 6 as appropriate, or that an existing certificate of competency or certificate of proficiency is duly endorsed.

Regulation V/1-2

Mandatory minimum requirements for the training and qualifications of masters, officers and ratings on liquefied gas tankers

1 Officers and ratings assigned specific duties and responsibilities related to cargo or cargo equipment on liquefied gas tankers shall hold a certificate in basic training for liquefied gas tanker cargo operations.

2 Every candidate for a certificate in basic training for liquefied gas tanker cargo operations shall have completed basic training in accordance with provisions of section A-VI/1 of the STCW Code and shall have completed:

.1 at least three months of approved seagoing service on liquefied gas tankers and meet the standard of competence specified in section A-V/1-2, paragraph 1 of the STCW Code; or

.2 an approved basic training for liquefied gas tanker cargo operations and meet the standard of competence specified in section A-V/1-2, paragraph 1 of the STCW Code.

6 每个申请化学品船货物操作高级培训证书的申请人应:

.1 符合油船和化学品船货物操作基本培训发证的要求;并且

.2 在有资格取得油船和化学品船货物操作基本培训证书时,具有:

.2.1 至少 3 个月的认可的化学品船海上服务资历,或

.2.2 至少 1 个月的作为编外人员的认可的化学品船船上培训,其中至少包括 3 次装货操作和 3 次卸货操作,并在认可的培训记录簿上记载,参考第 B-V/1 节中的指导;并且

.3 完成认可的化学品船货物操作高级培训,并且达到《STCW 规则》第 A-V/1-1 节第 3 段规定的适任标准。

7 主管机关应确保对符合第 2 段、第 4 段或第 6 段规定的船员相应地签发培训合格证书,或对现有的适任证书或培训合格证书进行适当签注。

第 V/1-2 条

对液化气船船长、高级船员和普通船员的培训和资格的强制性最低要求

1 在液化气船上承担特定的与货物或货物设备有关的职责和责任的高级船员和普通船员应持有液化气船货物操作基本培训证书。

2 每个申请液化气船货物操作基本培训证书的申请人,应完成《STCW 规则》第 A-VI/1 节规定的基本培训,并应完成:

.1 至少 3 个月的认可的液化气船海上服务资历,并且达到《STCW 规则》第 A-V/1-2 节第 1 段规定的适任标准;或

.2 认可的液化气船货物操作基本培训,并且达到《STCW 规则》第 A-V/1-2 节第 1 段规定的适任标准。

3 Masters, chief engineer officers, chief mates, second engineer officers and any person with immediate responsibility for loading, discharging, care in transit, handling of cargo, tank cleaning or other cargo-related operations on liquefied gas tankers shall hold a certificate in advanced training for liquefied gas tanker cargo operations.

4 Every candidate for a certificate in advanced training for liquefied gas tanker cargo operations shall:

.1 meet the requirements for certification in basic training for liquefied gas tanker cargo operations; and

.2 while qualified for certification in basic training for liquefied gas tanker cargo operations, have:

.2.1 at least three months of approved seagoing service on liquefied gas tankers, or

.2.2 at least one month of approved onboard training on liquefied gas tankers, in a supernumerary capacity, which includes at least three loading and three unloading operations and is documented in an approved training record book taking into account guidance in section B-V/1; and

.3 have completed approved advanced training for liquefied gas tanker cargo operations and meet the standard of competence specified in section A-V/1-2, paragraph 2 of the STCW Code.

5 Administrations shall ensure that a certificate of proficiency is issued to seafarers, who are qualified in accordance with paragraphs 2 or 4 as appropriate, or that an existing certificate of competency or certificate of proficiency is duly endorsed.

Regulation V/2
Mandatory minimum requirements for the training and qualifications of masters, officers, ratings and other personnel on passenger ships

1 This regulation applies to masters, officers, ratings and other personnel serving on board passenger ships engaged on international voyages. Administrations shall determine the applicability of these requirements to personnel serving on passenger ships engaged on domestic voyages.

2 Prior to being assigned shipboard duties on board passenger ships, seafarers shall have completed the training required by paragraphs 4 to 7 below in accordance with their capacity, duties and responsibilities.

3 Seafarers who are required to be trained in accordance with paragraphs 4, 6 and 7 below shall, at intervals not exceeding five years, undertake appropriate refresher training or be required to provide evidence of having achieved the required standard of competence within the previous five years.

4 Masters, officers and other personnel designated on muster lists to assist passengers in emergency situations on board passenger ships shall have completed training in crowd management as specified in section A-V/2, paragraph 1 of the STCW Code.

3 船长、轮机长、大副、大管轮和任何对液化气船上货物装卸、运输中照管货物、货物作业、洗舱或其他与货物相关的操作承担直接责任的人员，应持有液化气船货物操作高级培训证书。

4 每个申请液化气船货物操作高级培训证书的申请人应：

.1 符合液化气船货物操作基本培训发证的要求；并且

.2 在有资格取得液化气船货物操作基本培训证书时，具有：

.2.1 至少 3 个月的认可的液化气船海上服务资历，或

.2.2 至少 1 个月的作为编外人员的认可的液化气船船上培训，其中至少包括 3 次装货操作和 3 次卸货操作，并在认可的培训记录簿上记载，参考第 B-V/1 节中的指导；并且

.3 完成认可的液化气船货物操作高级培训，并且达到《STCW 规则》第 A-V/1-2 节第 2 段规定的适任标准。

5 主管机关应确保对符合第 2 段或第 4 段规定的船员相应地签发培训合格证书，或对现有的适任证书或培训合格证书进行适当签注。

第 V/2 条

对客船船长、高级船员、普通船员和其他人员的培训和资格的强制性最低要求

1 本条规则适用于在从事国际航行的客船上服务的船长、高级船员、普通船员和其他人员。主管机关应确定这些要求对在从事国内航行的客船上服务的人员的可适用性。

2 海员在被指定在客船上任职之前，应按照其职务、职责和责任完成以下第 4 段至第 7 段所要求的培训。

3 被要求按以下第 4 段、第 6 段和第 7 段进行培训的海员应以不超过 5 年的时间间隔接受适当的知识更新培训或需提供在最近 5 年内已达到规定的适任标准的证据。

4 客船上的船长、高级船员和应变部署表中指定在紧急情况下协助旅客的其他人员，应完成《STCW 规则》第 A-V/2 节第 1 段规定的有关密集人群管理的培训。

5 Personnel providing direct service to passengers in passenger spaces on board passenger ships shall have completed the safety training specified in section A-V/2, paragraph 2 of the STCW Code.

6 Masters, chief engineer officers, chief mates, second engineer officers and any person designated on muster lists of having responsibility for the safety of passengers in emergency situations on board passenger ships shall have completed approved training in crisis management and human behaviour as specified in section A-V/2, paragraph 3 of the STCW Code.

7 Masters, chief engineer officers, chief mates, second engineer officers and every person assigned immediate responsibility for embarking and disembarking passengers, loading, discharging or securing cargo, or closing hull openings on board ro-ro passenger ships shall have completed approved training in passenger safety, cargo safety and hull integrity as specified in section A-V/2, paragraph 4 of the STCW Code.

8 Administrations shall ensure that documentary evidence of the training which has been completed is issued to every person found qualified under the provisions of this regulation.

5　在客船旅客处所向旅客提供直接服务的人员，应完成《STCW 规则》第 A-V/2 节第 2 段规定的安全培训。

6　客船上的船长、轮机长、大副、大管轮和应变部署表中指定在紧急情况下负责旅客安全的任何人员，应完成《STCW 规则》第 A-V/2 节第 3 段规定的有关危机管理和人的行为的认可的培训。

7　滚装客船的船长、轮机长、大副、大管轮和直接负责旅客上下船、货物装卸或系固，或关闭船体开口的每一人员，应完成《STCW 规则》第 A-V/2 节第 4 段规定的关于旅客安全、货物安全和船体完整性的认可的培训。

8　主管机关应确保向根据本条规则经查合格的每一人员签发已完成培训的书面证明。

CHAPTER VI

Emergency, occupational safety, security, medical care and survival functions

Regulation VI/1
Mandatory minimum requirements for safety familiarization, basic training and instruction for all seafarers

1 Seafarers shall receive safety familiarization and basic training or instruction in accordance with section A-VI/1 of the STCW Code and shall meet the appropriate standard of competence specified therein.

2 Where basic training is not included in the qualification for the certificate to be issued, a certificate of proficiency shall be issued, indicating that the holder has attended the course in basic training.

Regulation VI/2
Mandatory minimum requirements for the issue of certificates of proficiency in survival craft, rescue boats and fast rescue boats

1 Every candidate for a certificate of proficiency in survival craft and rescue boats other than fast rescue boats shall:

.1 be not less than 18 years of age;

.2 have approved seagoing service of not less than 12 months or have attended an approved training course and have approved seagoing service of not less than six months; and

.3 meet the standard of competence for certificates of proficiency in survival craft and rescue boats, set out in section A-VI/2, paragraphs 1 to 4 of the STCW Code.

2 Every candidate for a certificate of proficiency in fast rescue boats shall:

.1 be the holder of a certificate of proficiency in survival craft and rescue boats other than fast rescue boats;

.2 have attended an approved training course; and

.3 meet the standard of competence for certificates of proficiency in fast rescue boats, set out in section A-VI/2, paragraphs 7 to 10 of the STCW Code.

Regulation VI/3
Mandatory minimum requirements for training in advanced fire fighting

1 Seafarers designated to control fire-fighting operations shall have successfully completed advanced training in techniques for fighting fire, with particular emphasis on organization, tactics and command, in accordance with the provisions of section A-VI/3, paragraphs 1 to 4 of the STCW Code and shall meet the standard of competence specified therein.

第 VI 章
应急、职业安全、保安、医护和求生职能

第 VI/1 条
对所有海员的安全熟悉、基本培训及训练的强制性最低要求

1 海员应按照《STCW 规则》第 A-VI/1 节的规定接受安全熟悉和基本培训或训练，并应达到该节所规定的相应适任标准。

2 在所发证书的资格中未包括基本培训时，应签发培训合格证书，以证明持证人已参加过基本培训课程。

第 VI/2 条
对签发救生艇筏、救助艇及快速救助艇培训合格证书的强制性最低要求

1 每个申请救生艇筏和除快速救助艇以外的救助艇培训合格证书的申请人应：

.1 年龄不小于 18 周岁；

.2 具有不少于 12 个月的认可的海上服务资历，或参加过认可的培训课程和具有不少于 6 个月的认可的海上服务资历；并且

.3 达到《STCW 规则》第 A-VI/2 节第 1 段至第 4 段规定的救生艇筏和救助艇培训合格证书的适任标准。

2 每个申请快速救助艇培训合格证书的申请人应：

.1 持有救生艇筏和除快速救助艇以外的救助艇培训合格证书；

.2 参加过认可的培训课程；并且

.3 达到《STCW 规则》第 A-VI/2 节第 7 段至第 10 段规定的快速救助艇培训合格证书的适任标准。

第 VI/3 条
对高级消防培训的强制性最低要求

1 指定为控制消防作业的海员应遵照《STCW 规则》第 A-VI/3 节第 1 段至第 4 段的规定，圆满完成着重于消防组织、战术及指挥方面的消防技术的高级培训，并应达到该节规定的适任标准。

2 Where training in advanced fire fighting is not included in the qualifications for the certificate to be issued, a certificate of proficiency shall be issued indicating that the holder has attended a course of training in advanced fire fighting.

Regulation VI/4
Mandatory minimum requirements relating to medical first aid and medical care

1 Seafarers designated to provide medical first aid on board ship shall meet the standard of competence in medical first aid specified in section A-VI/4, paragraphs 1 to 3 of the STCW Code.

2 Seafarers designated to take charge of medical care on board ship shall meet the standard of competence in medical care on board ships specified in section A-VI/4, paragraphs 4 to 6 of the STCW Code.

3 Where training in medical first aid or medical care is not included in the qualifications for the certificate to be issued, a certificate of proficiency shall be issued indicating that the holder has attended a course of training in medical first aid or in medical care.

Regulation VI/5
Mandatory minimum requirements for the issue of certificates of proficiency for ship security officers

1 Every candidate for a certificate of proficiency as ship security officer shall:

.1 have approved seagoing service of not less than 12 months or appropriate seagoing service and knowledge of ship operations; and

.2 meet the standard of competence for certification of proficiency as ship security officer, set out in section A-VI/5, paragraphs 1 to 4 of the STCW Code.

2 Administrations shall ensure that every person found qualified under the provisions of this regulation is issued with a certificate of proficiency.

Regulation VI/6
Mandatory minimum requirements for security-related training and instruction for all seafarers

1 Seafarers shall receive security-related familiarization and security-awareness training or instruction in accordance with section A-VI/6, paragraphs 1 to 4 of the STCW Code and shall meet the appropriate standard of competence specified therein.

2 Where security awareness is not included in the qualification for the certificate to be issued, a certificate of proficiency shall be issued indicating that the holder has attended a course in security awareness training.

3 Every Party shall compare the security-related training or instruction it requires of seafarers who hold or can document qualifications before the entry into force of this regulation with those specified in section A-VI/6, paragraph 4 of the STCW Code, and shall determine the need for requiring these seafarers to update their qualifications.

2　在所发证书的资格中未包括高级消防培训时，应签发培训合格证书，以证明持证人已参加过高级消防培训课程。

第 VI/4 条
关于医疗急救和医护的强制性最低要求

1　指定为在船上提供医疗急救的海员应达到《STCW 规则》第 A-VI/4 节第 1 段至第 3 段规定的医疗急救的适任标准。

2　指定为负责船上医护的海员应达到《STCW 规则》第 A-VI/4 节第 4 段至第 6 段规定的船上医护的适任标准。

3　在所发证书的资格中未包括医疗急救或医护的培训时，应签发培训合格证书，以证明持证人已参加过医疗急救或医护的培训课程。

第 VI/5 条
对签发船舶保安员培训合格证书的强制性最低要求

1　每个申请船舶保安员培训合格证书的申请人应：

.1　具有不少于 12 个月的认可的海上服务资历，或适当的海上服务资历和船舶运营的知识；并且

.2　达到《STCW 规则》第 A-VI/5 节第 1 段至第 4 段规定的船舶保安员培训合格证书的适任标准。

2　主管机关应确保向根据本条规则的规定经查合格的每一人员签发培训合格证书。

第 VI/6 条
对所有海员与保安有关的培训和训练的强制性最低要求

1　海员应根据《STCW 规则》第 A-VI/6 节第 1 段至第 4 段接受与保安有关的熟悉和保安意识培训或训练，并应达到该节规定的适当的适任标准。

2　在所发证书的资格中未包括保安意识时，应签发培训合格证书，以证明持证人已参加过保安意识培训课程。

3　每一缔约国应将在本条规则生效之前对海员获得或能够授予资格所要求的与保安有关的培训或训练与《STCW 规则》第 A-VI/6 节第 4 段所规定的培训或训练进行比较，并应决定是否有必要要求这些海员更新其资格。

Seafarers with designated security duties

4 Seafarers with designated security duties shall meet the standard of competence specified in section A-VI/6, paragraphs 6 to 8 of the STCW Code.

5 Where training in designated security duties is not included in the qualifications for the certificate to be issued, a certificate of proficiency shall be issued indicating that the holder has attended a course of training for designated security duties.

6 Every Party shall compare the security training standards required of seafarers with designated security duties who hold or can document qualifications before the entry into force of this regulation with those specified in section A-VI/6, paragraph 8 of the STCW Code, and shall determine the need for requiring these seafarers to update their qualifications.

承担指定保安职责的海员

4 承担指定保安职责的海员应达到《STCW 规则》第 A-VI/6 节第 6 段至第 8 段所规定的适任标准。

5 在所发证书的资格中未包括指定的保安职责的培训时,应签发培训合格证书,以证明持证人已参加过指定的保安职责的培训课程。

6 每一缔约国应将在本条规则生效之前对海员获得或能够授予资格所要求的保安培训标准与《STCW 规则》第 A-VI/6 节第 8 段所规定的标准进行比较,并应决定是否有必要要求这些海员更新其资格。

CHAPTER VII

Alternative certification

Regulation VII/1
Issue of alternative certificates

1 Notwithstanding the requirements for certification laid down in chapters II and III of this annex, Parties may elect to issue or authorize the issue of certificates other than those mentioned in the regulations of those chapters, provided that:

.1 the associated functions and levels of responsibility to be stated on the certificates and in the endorsements are selected from and identical to those appearing in sections A-II/1, A-II/2, A-II/3, A-II/4, A-II/5, A-III/1, A-III/2, A-III/3, A-III/4, A-III/5 and A-IV/2 of the STCW Code;

.2 the candidates have completed approved education and training and meet the requirements for standards of competence, prescribed in the relevant sections of the STCW Code and as set forth in section A-VII/1 of this Code, for the functions and levels that are to be stated in the certificates and in the endorsements;

.3 the candidates have completed approved seagoing service appropriate to the performance of the functions and levels that are to be stated on the certificate. The minimum duration of seagoing service shall be equivalent to the duration of seagoing service prescribed in chapters II and III of this annex. However, the minimum duration of seagoing service shall be not less than as prescribed in section A-VII/2 of the STCW Code;

.4 the candidates for certification who are to perform the function of navigation at the operational level shall meet the applicable requirements of the regulations in chapter IV, as appropriate, for performing designated radio duties in accordance with the Radio Regulations; and

.5 the certificates are issued in accordance with the requirements of regulation I/2 and the provisions set forth in chapter VII of the STCW Code.

2 No certificate shall be issued under this chapter unless the Party has communicated information to the Organization in accordance with article IV and regulation I/7.

Regulation VII/2
Certification of seafarers

1 Every seafarer who performs any function or group of functions specified in tables A-II/1, A-II/2, A-II/3, A-II/4 or A-II/5 of chapter II or in tables A-III/1, A-III/2, A-III/3, A-III/4 or A-III/5 of chapter III or A-IV/2 of chapter IV of the STCW Code shall hold a certificate of competency or certificate of proficiency, as applicable.

第 VII 章
可供选择的发证

第 VII/1 条
可供选择的证书的签发

1　尽管本公约附则第 II 章和第 III 章对发证作出要求,缔约国仍可选择签发或授权签发与这些章节提及的证书不同的证书,只要:

.1　此种证书和签证上载明的相关职能和责任级别是选自并等同于《STCW 规则》第 A-II/1 节、第 A-II/2 节、第 A-II/3 节、第 A-II/4 节、第 A-II/5 节、第 A-III/1 节、第 A-III/2节、第 A-III/3 节、第 A-III/4 节、第 A-III/5 节和第 A-Ⅳ/2 节中的相关规定;

.2　证书申请人已完成认可的教育和培训,并且符合《STCW 规则》有关章节所规定的以及在该规则第 A-VII/1 节提出的、对证书和签证上所载明的职能和级别的适任标准要求;

.3　证书申请人已具备与履行证书上所载明的职能和级别相适应的认可的海上服务资历,最短的海上服务时间应相当于本公约附则第 II 章和第 III 章所规定的时间,并不少于《STCW 规则》第 A-VII/2 节规定的时间;

.4　履行操作级航行职能的证书申请人应符合第 IV 章中各条规则规定的适用的要求,如适用,按照《无线电规则》履行指定的无线电职责;并且

.5　证书系根据规则第 I/2 条以及《STCW 规则》第 VII 章的规定签发。

2　除非缔约国根据本公约第 IV 条和规则第 I/7 条已向本组织提交资料,否则不得按本章规定签发证书。

第 VII/2 条
对海员的发证

1　每个履行《STCW 规则》第 II 章表 A-II/1、表 A-II/2、表 A-II/3、表 A-II/4 或表 A-II/5,或第 III 章表 A-III/1、表 A-III/2、表 A-III/3、表 A-III/4 或表 A-III/5,或第Ⅳ章表 A-IV/2 中规定的任何一种职能或一组职能的海员,应持有相应的适任证书或培训合格证书。

Regulation VII/3
Principles governing the issue of alternative certificates

1 Any Party which elects to issue or authorize the issue of alternative certificates shall ensure that the following principles are observed:

.1 no alternative certification system shall be implemented unless it ensures a degree of safety at sea and has a preventive effect as regards pollution at least equivalent to that provided by the other chapters; and

.2 any arrangement for alternative certification issued under this chapter shall provide for the interchangeability of certificates with those issued under the other chapters.

2 The principle of interchangeability in paragraph 1 shall ensure that:

.1 seafarers certificated under the arrangements of chapters II and/or III and those certificated under chapter VII are able to serve on ships which have either traditional or other forms of shipboard organization; and

.2 seafarers are not trained for specific shipboard arrangements in such a way as would impair their ability to take their skills elsewhere.

3 In issuing any certificate under the provisions of this chapter, the following principles shall be taken into account:

.1 the issue of alternative certificates shall not be used in itself:

.1.1 to reduce the number of crew on board,

.1.2 to lower the integrity of the profession or "de-skill" seafarers, or

.1.3 to justify the assignment of the combined duties of the engine and deck watchkeeping officers to a single certificate holder during any particular watch; and

.2 the person in command shall be designated as the master; and the legal position and authority of the master and others shall not be adversely affected by the implementation of any arrangement for alternative certification.

4 The principles contained in paragraphs 1 and 2 of this regulation shall ensure that the competency of both deck and engineer officers is maintained.

第 VII/3 条
控制签发可供选择的证书的原则

1 任何选择签发或授权签发可供选择的证书的缔约国应确保以下原则:

.1 除非确保海上安全的程度和防污染的效果至少相当于其他各章的规定,否则不应实施可供选择的发证制度;并且

.2 按本章规定签发可供选择的证书的任何安排应能使该证书与按其他章节规定签发的证书互相通用。

2 第 1 段中所述的互相通用原则应确保:

.1 按第 II 章和/或第 III 章的安排取得证书的海员和那些按第 VII 章规定取得证书的海员可以在传统的组织形式或其他组织形式的船上服务;并且

.2 对海员进行特定的船上安排的培训以不影响他们发挥其他岗位能力的方式进行。

3 按本章规定签发任何证书,应考虑以下原则:

.1 签发可供选择的证书本身并非用于:

.1.1 减少船上的船员人数,

.1.2 削弱专业的完整性或降低海员的技能,或

.1.3 证明在任何特定的值班时,由一名证书持有人担任轮机值班和航行值班高级船员的结合的职责是正当的;以及

.2 负责指挥的人应被指定为船长;船长和其他人员的法律地位和权限不应因实施可供选择的发证安排而受到负面影响。

4 本条规则第 1 段和第 2 段中的原则应确保甲板部和轮机部高级船员都保持适任。

CHAPTER VIII

Watchkeeping

Regulation VIII/1
Fitness for duty

1 Each Administration shall, for the purpose of preventing fatigue:

.1 establish and enforce rest periods for watchkeeping personnel and those whose duties involve designated safety, security and prevention of pollution duties in accordance with the provisions of section A-VIII/1 of the STCW Code; and

.2 require that watch systems are so arranged that the efficiency of all watchkeeping personnel is not impaired by fatigue and that duties are so organized that the first watch at the commencement of a voyage and subsequent relieving watches are sufficiently rested and otherwise fit for duty.

2 Each Administration shall, for the purpose of preventing drug and alcohol abuse, ensure that adequate measures are established in accordance with the provisions of section A-VIII/1 while taking into account the guidance given in section B-VIII/1 of the STCW Code.

Regulation VIII/2
Watchkeeping arrangements and principles to be observed

1 Administrations shall direct the attention of companies, masters, chief engineer officers and all watchkeeping personnel to the requirements, principles and guidance set out in the STCW Code which shall be observed to ensure that a safe continuous watch or watches appropriate to the prevailing circumstances and conditions are maintained on all seagoing ships at all times.

2 Administrations shall require the master of every ship to ensure that watchkeeping arrangements are adequate for maintaining a safe watch or watches, taking into account the prevailing circumstances and conditions and that, under the master's general direction:

.1 officers in charge of the navigational watch are responsible for navigating the ship safely during their periods of duty, when they shall be physically present on the navigating bridge or in a directly associated location such as the chartroom or bridge control room at all times;

.2 radio operators are responsible for maintaining a continuous radio watch on appropriate frequencies during their periods of duty;

.3 officers in charge of an engineering watch, as defined in the STCW Code, under the direction of the chief engineer officer, shall be immediately available and on call to attend the machinery spaces and, when required, shall be physically present in the machinery space during their periods of responsibility;

第 VIII 章
值班

第 VIII/1 条
适于值班

1 为防止疲劳,各主管机关应:

.1 依据《STCW 规则》第 A-VIII/1 节的规定,制定和实施值班人员以及被指定安全、防污染和保安职责的人员的休息时间制度;并且

.2 要求值班制度的安排能使所有值班人员的效率不致因疲劳而受到影响,并且班次的组织能使航次开始的第一个班次及其后各班次人员均已充分休息,并在其他方面适于值班。

2 为防止滥用药物和酗酒,各主管机关应确保依据第 A-VIII/1 节的规定制定适当的措施,并考虑《STCW 规则》第 B-VIII/1 节中的指导。

第 VIII/2 条
值班安排和应遵循的原则

1 主管机关应使公司、船长、轮机长和全体值班人员注意到《STCW 规则》中规定的要求、原则和指导,以确保在所有海船上始终保持安全、连续并适合当时环境和条件的值班。

2 主管机关应要求每船船长考虑船舶当时环境和条件,确保其值班安排足以保持安全值班,并且在船长全面指导下:

.1 负责航行值班的高级船员在值班时间内始终在驾驶台或与之直接相连的场所,如海图室或驾驶台控制室,对船舶航行安全负责;

.2 无线电操作员在值班时间内,在适当的频率上负责保持连续值守;

.3 负责轮机值班的高级船员,根据《STCW 规则》的规定并在轮机长的指导下,应能立即就备并随时待命到达机器处所,并且在需要时应在其负责的时间内身在机器处所;

.4 an appropriate and effective watch or watches are maintained for the purpose of safety at all times, while the ship is at anchor or moored and, if the ship is carrying hazardous cargo, the organization of such watch or watches takes full account of the nature, quantity, packing and stowage of the hazardous cargo and of any special conditions prevailing on board, afloat or ashore; and

.5 as applicable, an appropriate and effective watch or watches are maintained for the purposes of security.

.4 当船舶锚泊或系泊时,为安全起见,随时保持适当和有效的值班。如果船上载有危险货物,值班安排充分考虑到危险货物的性质、数量、包装和积载,以及当时船上、水上或岸上的任何特殊情况;以及

.5 如适用,为保安起见,保持适当和有效的值班。

ADOPTION OF THE FINAL ACT AND ANY INSTRUMENTS, RESOLUTIONS AND RECOMMENDATIONS RESULTING FROM THE WORK OF THE CONFERENCE

Attachment 2 to the Final Act of the Conference

Resolution 2

Adoption of the Manila Amendments to the Seafarers' Training, Certification and Watchkeeping (STCW) Code

Text adopted by the Conference

THE 2010 MANILA CONFERENCE,

HAVING ADOPTED resolution 1 on Adoption of the Manila amendments to the annex to the International Convention on Standards of Training, Certification and Watchkeeping for Seafarers (STCW), 1978,

RECOGNIZING the importance of establishing detailed mandatory standards of competence and other mandatory provisions necessary to ensure that all seafarers shall be properly educated and trained, adequately experienced, skilled and competent to perform their duties in a manner which provides for the safety of life, property and security at sea and the protection of the marine environment,

ALSO RECOGNIZING the need to allow for the timely amendment of such mandatory standards and provisions in order to effectively respond to changes in technology, operations, practices and procedures used on board ships,

RECALLING that a large percentage of maritime casualties and pollution incidents are caused by human error,

APPRECIATING that one effective means of reducing the risks associated with human error in the operation of seagoing ships is to ensure that the highest practicable standards of training, certification and competence are maintained in respect of the seafarers who are or will be employed on such ships,

DESIRING to achieve and maintain the highest practicable standards for the safety of life, property and security at sea and in port and for the protection of the environment,

HAVING CONSIDERED amendments to the Seafarers' Training, Certification and Watchkeeping (STCW) Code, comprised in part A – Mandatory standards regarding provisions

大会最终文件附件 2

决议 2
通过《海员培训、发证和值班规则》马尼拉修正案

大会通过的文本

2010 年马尼拉大会，

通过了决议 1——通过《1978 年海员培训、发证和值班标准国际公约》附则马尼拉修正案，

认识到建立详细的强制性适任标准及其他必要的强制性条款，对确保所有海员能够接受合适的教育的培训，拥有适当的资历，熟练并且胜任其保证海上人命及财产安全、保安和保护海洋环境的工作的重要性，

还认识到允许对此类强制性标准及条款进行及时修订的必要性，以便有效反映船上技术、操作、做法及程序上的变化，

忆及大多数海上事故及污染事件是由人为过失造成，

意识到减少由于人操船失误造成的风险的一种有效方法是确保培训、发证及适任的最高可行标准在此类船上服务的海员中得以保持，

希望达成及保持最高可行标准，以保证海上、港口人命及财产安全、保安和保护海洋环境，

审议了 STCW 规则修正案，经修订的有关 1978 年 STCW 公约附则条款的强制性标准包含在本规则的 A 部分，经修订的有关 1978 年 STCW 公约附则条款的建议性指南包含在 B 部分，散发给该组织各成员国及本公约各缔约国，

of the annex to the 1978 STCW Convention, as amended, and part B – Recommended guidance regarding provisions of the 1978 STCW Convention, as amended, proposed and circulated to all Members of the Organization and all Parties to the Convention,

NOTING that regulation I/1, paragraph 2, of the annex to the 1978 STCW Convention provides that amendments to part A of the STCW Code shall be adopted, brought into force and take effect in accordance with the provisions of article XII of the Convention concerning the amendment procedure applicable to the annex,

HAVING CONSIDERED amendments to the STCW Code proposed and circulated to the Members of the Organization and to all Parties to the Convention,

1. ADOPTS amendments to the Seafarers' Training, Certification and Watchkeeping (STCW) Code, set out in annex to the present resolution;

2. DETERMINES, in accordance with article XII(1)(a)(vii) of the Convention, that the amendments to part A of the STCW Code shall be deemed to have been accepted on 1 July 2011, unless, prior to that date, more than one third of Parties or Parties the combined merchant fleets of which constitute not less than 50% of the gross tonnage of the world's merchant shipping of ships of 100 gross register tons or more have notified the Secretary-General that they object to the amendments;

3. INVITES Parties to note that, in accordance with article XII(1)(a)(ix) of the Convention, the amendments to part A of the STCW Code annexed hereto shall enter into force on 1 January 2012 upon being deemed to have been accepted in accordance with paragraph 2 above;

4. RECOMMENDS that the guidance contained in part B of the STCW Code, as amended, should be taken into account by all Parties to the 1978 STCW Convention as from the date of entry into force of the amendments to part A of the STCW Code;

5. REQUESTS the Maritime Safety Committee to keep the STCW Code under review and amend it, as appropriate;

6. ALSO REQUESTS the Secretary-General of the Organization to transmit certified copies of the present resolution and the text of amendments to the STCW Code contained in the annex to all Parties to the Convention;

7. FURTHER REQUESTS the Secretary-General to transmit copies of this resolution and its annex to all Members of the Organization which are not Parties to the Convention.

注意到 1978 年 STCW 公约附则的第 I/1 条第 2 段关于对 STCW 规则 A 部分的任何修正均应按照本公约第 XII 条关于适用于附则的修正程序的规定予以通过、生效和实施的规定；

审议了拟定的 STCW 规则修正案并散发给该组织的成员国及本公约的各缔约国，

1. **通过** STCW 规则的修正案，该文本附在本决议后；

2. 依据本公约第 XII(1)(a)(vii)条，**决定** STCW 规则 A 部分的修正案应于 2011 年 7 月 1 日视为已被接受，除非在此日期之前，有 1/3 以上的缔约国，或其 100 总登记吨或以上的商船总吨位不少于世界商船总吨位的 50% 的缔约国通知秘书长反对该修正案；

3. **敦请**各缔约国注意，依据本公约第 XII(1)(a)(ix)条，附件中的 STCW 规则 A 部分的修正案在依据上述第 2 段被接受后，将于 2012 年 1 月 1 日生效；

4. **建议** 1978 年 STCW 公约的各缔约国从 STCW 规则 A 部分的修正案生效之日起，应考虑经修订的 STCW 规则 B 部分中包含的指南；

5. **要求**海上安全委员会对 STCW 规则进行回顾并予以适当修订；

6. **还要求**该组织的秘书长将核证无误的决议副本及附件中 STCW 规则修正案的文本分发给本公约的各缔约国；

7. **进一步要求**秘书长将决议副本及附件分发给非本公约缔约国的该组织各成员国。

ANNEX

THE MANILA AMENDMENTS TO THE SEAFARERS' TRAINING, CERTIFICATION AND WATCHKEEPING (STCW) CODE

1 The part A of the Seafarers' Training, Certification and Watchkeeping (STCW) Code is replaced by the following:

PART A

Mandatory standards regarding provisions of the annex to the STCW Convention

Introduction

1 This part of the STCW Code contains mandatory provisions to which specific reference is made in the annex to the International Convention on Standards of Training, Certification and Watchkeeping for Seafarers, 1978, as amended, hereinafter referred to as the STCW Convention. These provisions give in detail the minimum standards required to be maintained by Parties in order to give full and complete effect to the Convention.

2 Also contained in this part are standards of competence required to be demonstrated by candidates for the issue and revalidation of certificates of competency under the provisions of the STCW Convention. To clarify the linkage between the alternative certification provisions of chapter VII and the certification provisions of chapters II, III and IV, the abilities specified in the standards of competence are grouped, as appropriate, under the following seven functions:

.1 Navigation
.2 Cargo handling and stowage
.3 Controlling the operation of the ship and care for persons on board
.4 Marine engineering
.5 Electrical, electronic and control engineering
.6 Maintenance and repair
.7 Radiocommunications

at the following levels of responsibility:

.1 Management level
.2 Operational level
.3 Support level

Functions and levels of responsibility are identified by subtitle in the tables of standards of competence given in chapters II, III and IV of this part. The scope of the function at the level of responsibility stated in a subtitle is defined by the abilities listed under it in column 1 of the table. The meaning of "function" and "level of responsibility" is defined in general terms in section A-I/1 below.

3 The numbering of the sections of this part corresponds with the numbering of the regulations contained in the annex to the STCW Convention. The text of the sections may be divided into numbered parts and paragraphs, but such numbering is unique to that text alone.

附则

《海员培训、发证和值班规则》马尼拉修正案

1 《海员培训、发证和值班规则》(《STCW 规则》)A 部分由以下内容代替:

A 部分
关于《STCW 公约》附则的强制性标准

引言

1 《STCW 规则》的本部分包含经修正的《1978 年海员培训、发证和值班标准国际公约》(以下称《STCW 公约》)附则中专门提及的强制性规定。这些规定详细列出要求各缔约国为充分和完全地实施该公约所需保持的最低标准。

2 本部分还包含依据《STCW 公约》的规定申请签发适任证书和使适任证书再有效的申请人所需表明的适任标准。为了阐明第 VII 章可供选择的发证规定与第 II 章、第 III 章和第 IV 章发证规定之间的联系,现将在适任标准中规定的能力适当地归纳为以下 7 项职能:

.1 航行

.2 货物装卸和积载

.3 船舶作业管理和船上人员管理

.4 船舶轮机

.5 电气、电子和控制工程

.6 维护和修理

.7 无线电通信

和以下责任级别:

.1 管理级

.2 操作级

.3 支持级

职能和责任级别在本部分的第 II 章、第 III 章和第 IV 章的适任标准表中由分标题予以明确。分标题中所述的责任级别的职能范围由该表的第 1 栏中列明的各种能力予以限定。“职能”和“责任级别”的含义在以下第 A-I/1 节中以一般性术语予以定义。

3 本部分章节的编号与《STCW 公约》附则中各条规则的编号是相对应的。有些章节的内容可能又分为若干带编号的部分和段落,但这种编号仅用于该部分内容。

CHAPTER I

Standards regarding general provisions

Section A-I/1
Definitions and clarifications

1 The definitions and clarifications contained in article II and regulation I/1 apply equally to the terms used in parts A and B of this Code. In addition, the following supplementary definitions apply only to this Code:

.1 *Standard of competence* means the level of proficiency to be achieved for the proper performance of functions on board ship in accordance with the internationally agreed criteria as set forth herein and incorporating prescribed standards or levels of knowledge, understanding and demonstrated skill;

.2 *Management level* means the level of responsibility associated with:

.2.1 serving as master, chief mate, chief engineer officer or second engineer officer on board a seagoing ship, and

.2.2 ensuring that all functions within the designated area of responsibility are properly performed;

.3 *Operational level* means the level of responsibility associated with:

.3.1 serving as officer in charge of a navigational or engineering watch or as designated duty engineer for periodically unmanned machinery spaces or as radio operator on board a seagoing ship, and

.3.2 maintaining direct control over the performance of all functions within the designated area of responsibility in accordance with proper procedures and under the direction of an individual serving in the management level for that area of responsibility;

.4 *Support level* means the level of responsibility associated with performing assigned tasks, duties or responsibilities on board a seagoing ship under the direction of an individual serving in the operational or management level;

.5 *Evaluation criteria* are the entries appearing in column 4 of the "Specification of Minimum Standard of Competence" tables in part A and provide the means for an assessor to judge whether or not a candidate can perform the related tasks, duties and responsibilities; and

.6 *Independent evaluation* means an evaluation by suitably qualified persons, independent of, or external to, the unit or activity being evaluated, to verify that the administrative and operational procedures at all levels are managed, organized, undertaken and monitored internally in order to ensure their fitness for purpose and achievement of stated objectives.

第 I 章
关于总则的标准

第 A-I/1 节
定义和说明

1 本公约第 II 条和规则第 I/1 条中的定义和说明同样适用于本规则 A 部分和 B 部分所使用的术语。此外,以下补充的定义仅适用于本规则:

.1 适任标准系指按照本部分所列的国际上公认的标准并结合所规定的知识、理解和所表明的技能的标准或水平,为正确履行船上的有关职能应达到的熟练程度;

.2 管理级系指与下列内容有关的责任级别:

.2.1 作为船长、大副、轮机长或大管轮在海船上服务,并

.2.2 确保正确履行指定职责范围内的所有职能;

.3 操作级系指与下列内容有关的责任级别:

.3.1 作为负责航行或轮机值班的高级船员或被指定为周期性无人值班机舱的轮机部值班高级船员或作为无线电操作员在海船上服务,以及

.3.2 在相同责任范围的管理级人员的指导下,按照正规的程序,对指定责任范围内的所有职能的履行保持直接的控制;

.4 支持级系指在操作级或管理级人员的指导下,在海船上与履行指定的任务、职责或责任有关的责任等级;

.5 评价标准是 A 部分中"最低适任标准表"第 4 栏的记载内容,为评估人员提供判定申请人能否履行有关的任务、职责和责任的方法;以及

.6 独立评价系指由独立于被评价的单位或工作或被评价的单位或工作以外的有适当资格的人员所作的评价,审核各个层次的管理和操作程序是否在内部得到管理、组织、实施和监控,以确保适合其用途并达到既定的目标。

Section A-I/2
Certificates and endorsements

1 Where, as provided in regulation I/2, paragraph 6, the endorsement required by article VI of the Convention is incorporated in the wording of the certificate itself, the certificate shall be issued in the format shown hereunder, provided that the words "or until the date of expiry of any extension of the validity of this certificate as may be shown overleaf" appearing on the front of the form and the provisions for recording extension of the validity appearing on the back of the form shall be omitted where the certificate is required to be replaced upon its expiry. Guidance on completion of the form is contained in section B-I/2 of this Code.

第 A-I/2 节

证书和签证

1　如果按照本公约规则第 I/2 条第 6 段的规定，将本公约第 VI 条要求的签证并入证书本身的文字中，则该证书应以如下所示的格式签发，如果要求该证书在有效期届满时换新证书，则应删除格式正面的“或至可能在背面载明的此证书有效期的任何延期届满之日止”一段文字以及格式背面有关记录有效期延长的内容。对填写本格式的指导见本规则第 B-I/2 节。

(Official Seal)

(COUNTRY)

CERTIFICATE ISSUED UNDER THE PROVISIONS OF THE INTERNATIONAL CONVENTION ON STANDARDS OF TRAINING, CERTIFICATION AND WATCHKEEPING FOR SEAFARERS, 1978, AS AMENDED

The Government of .... certifies that .... has been found duly qualified in accordance with the provisions of regulation .... of the above Convention, as amended, and has been found competent to perform the following functions, at the levels specified, subject to any limitations indicated until .... or until the date of expiry of any extension of the validity of this certificate as may be shown overleaf:

FUNCTION	LEVEL	LIMITATIONS APPLYING (IF ANY)

The lawful holder of this certificate may serve in the following capacity or capacities specified in the applicable safe manning requirements of the Administration:

CAPACIT	LIMITATIONS APPLYING (IF ANY)

Certificate No. .... issued on ....

(Official Seal)

....
Signature of duly authorized official

....
Name of duly authorized official

The original of this certificate must be kept available in accordance with regulation I/2, paragraph 11 of the Convention while its holder is serving on a ship.

Date of birth of the holder of the certificate ....

Signature of the holder of the certificate ....

Photograph of the holder of the certificate

（公章）

（国家）

根据经修正的《1978 年海员培训、发证和值班标准国际公约》的规定签发的证书

____________________政府证明____________________按照经修正的上述公约的规则____________________的规定完全合格，有资格履行规定级别的下列职能，但受载明的任何限制的制约，有效期至____________________或至可能在背面载明的此证书有效期的任何延期届满之日止：

职能	级别	适用的限制（如有）

本证书的合法持有人可担任主管机关在相应的安全配员要求中规定的下列一种或几种职位：

职位	适用的限制（如有）

证书编号____________________签发日期____________________

（公章）

____

经正式授权的官员签名

____

经正式授权的官员姓名

按照本公约规则第 I/2 条第 11 段规定，当持证人在船上服务时，本证书原件必须保持随时可用。

持证人出生日期____________________

持证人签名____________________

持证人照片

The validity of this certificate is hereby extended until .... *(Official Seal)* .... *Signature of duly authorized official* Date of revalidation .... *Name of duly authorized official*
The validity of this certificate is hereby extended until .... *(Official Seal)* .... *Signature of the authorized official* Date of revalidation .... *Name of duly authorized official*

2 Except as provided in paragraph 1, the form used to attest the issue of a certificate shall be as shown hereunder, provided that the words "or until the date of expiry of any extension of the validity of this endorsement as may be shown overleaf" appearing on the front of the form and the provisions for recording extension of the validity appearing on the back of the form shall be omitted where the endorsement is required to be replaced upon its expiry. Guidance on completion of the form is contained in section B-I/2 of this Code.

本证书的有效期特此延至________________________________ （公章）　　　　　　　　　　　　　　　　　　________________ 　　　　　　　　　　　　　　　　　　　　　　经正式授权的官员签名 再有效日期____________　　　　　　　　　　　________________ 　　　　　　　　　　　　　　　　　　　　　　经正式授权的官员姓名
本证书的有效期特此延至________________________________ （公章）　　　　　　　　　　　　　　　　　　________________ 　　　　　　　　　　　　　　　　　　　　　　经正式授权的官员签名 再有效日期____________　　　　　　　　　　　________________ 　　　　　　　　　　　　　　　　　　　　　　经正式授权的官员姓名

2　除第 1 段规定外，用于证明签发证书的格式应是如下所示的格式，如果该签证有效期届满需要换新签证，则应删除格式正面的“或至可能在背面载明的此签证有效期的任何延期届满之日止”一段文字以及格式背面有关记录有效期延长的内容。对填写本格式的指导见本规则第 B-Ⅰ/2 节。

(Official Seal)

(COUNTRY)

ENDORSEMENT ATTESTING THE ISSUE OF A CERTIFICATE UNDER THE PROVISIONS OF THE INTERNATIONAL CONVENTION ON STANDARDS OF TRAINING, CERTIFICATION AND WATCHKEEPING FOR SEAFARERS, 1978, AS AMENDED

The Government of ……….………………… certifies that certificate No. ……..…. has been issued to …………………………………….. who has been found duly qualified in accordance with the provisions of regulation …………………………….. of the above Convention, as amended, and has been found competent to perform the following functions, at the levels specified, subject to any limitations indicated until ……………………… or until the date of expiry of any extension of the validity of this endorsement as may be shown overleaf:

FUNCTION	LEVEL	LIMITATIONS APPLYING (IF ANY)

The lawful holder of this endorsement may serve in the following capacity or capacities specified in the applicable safe manning requirements of the Administration:

CAPACITY	LIMITATIONS APPLYING (IF ANY)

Endorsement No. .... issued on ....

(Official Seal)

....
Signature of duly authorized official

....
Name of duly authorized official

The original of this endorsement must be kept available in accordance with regulation I/2, paragraph 11 of the Convention while its holder is serving on a ship.

Date of birth of the holder of the certificate ....

Signature of the holder of the certificate ....

Photograph of the holder of the certificate

（公章）

（国家）

证明根据经修正的《1978 年海员培训、发证和值班标准国际公约》的规定签发证书的签证

__________政府证明编号为__________的证书已签发给__________，该持证人按照经修正的上述公约的规则__________的规定完全合格，有资格履行规定级别的下列职能，但受载明的任何限制的制约，有效期至____________或至可能在背面载明的此签证有效期的任何延期届满之日止：

职能	级别	适用的限制（如有）

本签证的合法持有人可担任主管机关在相应的安全配员要求中规定的下列一种或几种职位：

职位	适用的限制（如有）

签证编号______________签发日期______________

（公章）

____
经正式授权的官员签名

____
经正式授权的官员姓名

按照本公约规则第 I/2 条第 11 段规定，当持证人在船上服务时，本签证原件必须保持随时可用。

持证人出生日期______________

持证人签名______________

持证人照片

The validity of this endorsement is hereby extended until ....

(Official Seal) ....
Signature of duly authorized official

Date of revalidation ....
Name of duly authorized official

The validity of this endorsement is hereby extended until ....

(Official Seal) ....
Signature of the authorized official

Date of revalidation ....
Name of duly authorized official

---

3 The form used to attest the recognition of a certificate shall be as shown hereunder, except that the words "or until the date of expiry of any extension of the validity of this endorsement as may be shown overleaf" appearing on the front of the form and the provisions for recording extension of the validity appearing on the back of the form shall be omitted where the endorsement is required to be replaced upon its expiry. Guidance on completion of the form is contained in section B-I/2 of this Code.

本签证的有效期特此延至______________________________

（公章）

____

经正式授权的官员签名

再有效日期____________________

____

经正式授权的官员姓名

本签证的有效期特此延至______________________________

（公章）

____

经正式授权的官员签名

再有效日期____________________

____

经正式授权的官员姓名

3　用于证明承认证书的签证格式应是如下所示的格式，如果该签证有效期届满需要换新签证，则应删除格式正面的“或至可能在背面载明的此签证有效期的任何延期届满之日止”一段文字以及格式背面有关记录有效期延长的内容。对填写本格式的指导见本规则第 B-I/2 节。

(Official Seal)

(COUNTRY)

ENDORSEMENT ATTESTING THE RECOGNITION OF A CERTIFICATE UNDER THE PROVISIONS OF THE INTERNATIONAL CONVENTION ON STANDARDS OF TRAINING, CERTIFICATION AND WATCHKEEPING FOR SEAFARERS, 1978, AS AMENDED

The Government of ………..…….…………………… certifies that certificate No. .... issued to ……………………………………….. by or on behalf of the Government of ....…...... is duly recognized in accordance with the provisions of regulation I/10 of the above Convention, as amended, and the lawful holder is authorized to perform the following functions, at the levels specified, subject to any limitations indicated until ……………………… or until the date of expiry of any extension of the validity of this endorsement as may be shown overleaf:

FUNCTION	LEVEL	LIMITATIONS APPLYING (IF ANY)

The lawful holder of this endorsement may serve in the following capacity or capacities specified in the applicable safe manning requirements of the Administration:

CAPACITY	LIMITATIONS APPLYING (IF ANY)

Endorsement No. .... issued on ....

(Official Seal)

....
Signature of duly authorized official

....
Name of duly authorized official

The original of this endorsement must be kept available in accordance with regulation I/2, paragraph 11 of the Convention while its holder is serving on a ship.

Date of birth of the holder of the certificate ....

Signature of the holder of the certificate ....

Photograph of the holder of the certificate

（公章）

（国家）

证明根据经修正的《1978 年海员培训、发证和值班标准国际公约》的规定承认证书的签证

_____________政府证明，对由或者代表_______________政府签发给_______________的编号为_______________的证书，按照经修正的上述公约的规则第 I/10 条的规定予以正式承认，并且准许合法持证人履行规定级别的下列职能，但受载明的任何限制的制约，有效期至___________________或至可能在背面载明的此签证有效期的任何延期届满之日止：

职能	级别	适用的限制（如有）

本签证的合法持有人可担任主管机关在相应的安全配员要求中规定的下列一种或几种职位：

职位	适用的限制（如有）

签证编号___________________签发日期___________________

（公章）

____

经正式授权的官员签名

____

经正式授权的官员姓名

按照本公约规则第 I/2 条第 11 段规定，当持证人在船上服务时，本签证原件必须保持随时可用。

持证人出生日期___________________

持证人签名______________________

持证人照片

The validity of this endorsement is hereby extended until	
(Official Seal)	.... *Signature of duly authorized official*
Date of revalidation	.... *Name of duly authorized official*
The validity of this endorsement is hereby extended until	
(Official Seal)	.... *Signature of the authorized official*
Date of revalidation	.... *Name of duly authorized official*

4 In using formats which may be different from those set forth in this section, pursuant to regulation I/2, paragraph 10, Parties shall ensure that in all cases:

.1 all information relating to the identity and personal description of the holder, including name, date of birth, photograph and signature, along with the date on which the document was issued, shall be displayed on the same side of the documents; and

.2 all information relating to the capacity or capacities in which the holder is entitled to serve, in accordance with the applicable safe manning requirements of the Administration, as well as any limitations, shall be prominently displayed and easily identified.

ISSUE AND REGISTRATION OF CERTIFICATES

Approval of seagoing service

5 In approving seagoing service required by the Convention, Parties should ensure that the service concerned is relevant to the qualification being applied for, bearing in mind that, apart from the initial familiarization with service in seagoing ships, the purpose of such service is to allow the seafarer to be instructed in and to practice, under appropriate supervision, those safe and proper seagoing practices, procedures and routines which are relevant to the qualification applied for.

Approval of training courses

6 In approving training courses and programmes, Parties should take into account that the relevant IMO Model Courses can assist in the preparation of such courses and programmes and ensure that the detailed learning objectives recommended therein are suitably covered.

本签证的有效期特此延至________________________________

（公章）

____

经正式授权的官员签名

再有效日期________________

____

经正式授权的官员姓名

本签证的有效期特此延至________________________________

（公章）

____

经正式授权的官员签名

再有效日期________________

____

经正式授权的官员姓名

4 在采用可能不同于本节所规定的格式时，根据规则第 I/2 条第 10 段规定，缔约国应确保在任何情况下：

.1 有关持证人身份和个人情况的所有资料，包括姓名、出生日期、照片和签名以及该文件的签发日期，应在该文件的同一面上显示；并且

.2 关于按照主管机关适用的安全配员要求而授权持证人担任的一种或多种职位的资料和任何限制，应明显地列出并易于识别。

证书的签发和登记

海上服务资历的认可

5 在认可本公约要求的海上服务资历时，缔约国应确保所涉及的服务资历与所申请的资格是相关的，并切记除初步熟悉在海船上的工作外，这种服务的目的在于使海员在适当的指导下对与其申请的职位相关的那些海上实践、程序和日常工作进行那些训练与实习。

培训课程的认可

6 在认可培训课程和计划时，缔约国应考虑到相关 IMO 示范培训课程会帮助该类课程和计划的准备，并且确保适当涵盖所建议的详细学习目标。

Electronic access to registers

7 In the maintenance of the electronic register in accordance with paragraph 15 of regulation I/2, provisions shall be made to allow controlled electronic access to such register or registers to allow Parties and companies to confirm:

.1 the name of the seafarer to whom such certificate, endorsement or other qualification was issued, its relevant number, date of issue and date of expiry;

.2 the capacity in which the holder may serve and any limitations attaching thereto; and

.3 the functions the holder may perform, the levels authorized and any limitations attached thereto.

Development of a database for certificate registration

8 In implementing the requirement in paragraph 14 of regulation I/2 for the maintenance of a register of certificates and endorsements, a standard database is not necessary provided that all the relevant information is recorded and available in accordance with regulation I/2.

9 The following items of information should be recorded and available, either on paper or electronically, in accordance with regulation I/2:

.1 **Status of certificate**

Valid
Suspended
Cancelled
Reported lost
Destroyed

with a record of changes to status to be kept, including dates of changes.

.2 **Certificate details**

Seafarer's name
Date of birth
Nationality
Gender
Preferably a photograph
Relevant document number
Date of issue
Date of expiry
Last revalidation date
Details of dispensation(s)

登记的电子查询

7 在根据规则第 I/2 条第 15 段规定维护电子登记时,应制定规定使缔约国和公司能受控使用这一或这些电子登记,以便确认:

.1 已签发证书、签证或其他资格证明的海员的姓名,及其相应编号、签发日期和失效日期;

.2 持证人可担任的职务和附带的任何限制;以及

.3 持证人可履行的职能、所授级别和附带的任何限制。

证书注册数据库的开发

8 在履行规则第 I/2 条第 14 段中有关证书和签证登记的维护要求时,若所有相关信息已按照规则第 I/2 条记录并可供使用,则无须建立一个标准数据库。

9 下列各项信息应根据规则第 I/2 条以书面或电子方式记录并可供使用:

.1 证书状态

有效

暂停有效

注销

报失

损毁

保持证书状态更改记录,包括日期的更改。

.2 证书信息

海员姓名

出生日期

国籍

性别

照片(最好附有)

相关文件编号

签发日期

失效日期

前一再有效日期

特免证明

.3 **Competency details**

STCW standard of competence (e.g., regulation II/1)
Capacity
Function
Level of responsibility
Endorsements
Limitations

.4 **Medical details**

Date of issue of latest medical certificate relating to the issue or revalidation of the certificate of competency.

Section A-I/3
Principles governing near-coastal voyages

1 When a Party defines near-coastal voyages, *inter alia*, for the purpose of applying variations to the subjects listed in column 2 of the standard of competence tables contained in chapters II and III of part A of the Code, for the issue of certificates valid for service on ships entitled to fly the flag of that Party and engaged on such voyages, account shall be taken of the following factors, bearing in mind the effect on the safety and security of all ships and on the marine environment:

.1 type of ship and the trade in which it is engaged;

.2 gross tonnage of the ship and the propulsion power in kilowatts of the main machinery;

.3 nature and length of the voyages;

.4 maximum distance from a port of refuge;

.5 adequacy of the coverage and accuracy of navigational position-fixing devices;

.6 weather conditions normally prevailing in the near-coastal voyages area;

.7 provision of shipboard and coastal communication facilities for search and rescue; and

.8 the availability of shore-based support, regarding especially technical maintenance on board.

2 It is not intended that ships engaged on near-coastal voyages extend their voyages worldwide, under the excuse that they are navigating constantly within the limits of designated near-coastal voyages of neighbouring Parties.

Section A-I/4
Control procedures

1 The assessment procedure provided for in regulation I/4, paragraph 1.3, resulting from any of the occurrences mentioned therein shall take the form of a verification that members of the crew who are required to be competent do in fact possess the necessary skills related to the occurrence.

.3 适任信息

STCW 适任标准(例如规则第 II/1 条)

职位

职能

责任等级

签证

限制

.4 健康信息

与适任证书签发或再有效相关的最新的健康证书的签发日期。

第 A-I/3 节

控制近岸航行的原则

1 当一缔约国对近岸航行进行定义,特别是为在悬挂其国旗并从事近岸航行的船上服务的海员签发证书而改动本规则 A 部分第 II 章和第 III 章适任标准表第 2 栏内所列科目时,应考虑到下列因素,并切记对所有船舶的安全、保安和海洋环境的影响:

.1 船舶种类及其航区;

.2 船舶总吨位和主推进功率(以千瓦计);

.3 航次性质和长短;

.4 距避风港的最远距离;

.5 导航定位设备的覆盖范围和定位精度;

.6 近岸航行区域通常的天气状况;

.7 提供用于搜救的船上和岸上通信设施;以及

.8 岸基支持的可用性,特别是有关船上技术保养的岸基支持。

2 本原则无意使从事近岸航行的船舶以其始终在相邻国家指定的近岸航行区内航行为理由而将其航行扩展到全球。

第 A-I/4 节

监督程序

1 因发生规则第 I/4 条第 1.3 段所列任一情况而引起的评估程序应采用一种核实的方式,即核实按要求应适任的船员是否确实具备与所发生的情况有关的必要技能。

2 It shall be borne in mind when making this assessment that onboard procedures are relevant to the International Safety Management (ISM) Code and that the provisions of this Convention are confined to the competence to safely execute those procedures.

3 Control procedures under this Convention shall be confined to the standards of competence of the individual seafarers on board and their skills related to watchkeeping as defined in part A of this Code. Onboard assessment of competency shall commence with verification of the certificates of the seafarers.

4 Notwithstanding verification of the certificate, the assessment under regulation I/4, paragraph 1.3 can require the seafarer to demonstrate the related competency at the place of duty. Such demonstration may include verification that operational requirements in respect of watchkeeping standards have been met and that there is a proper response to emergency situations within the seafarer's level of competence.

5 In the assessment, only the methods for demonstrating competence together with the criteria for its evaluation and the scope of the standards given in part A of this Code shall be used.

6 Assessment of competency related to security shall be conducted for those seafarers with specific security duties only in case of clear grounds, as provided for in chapter XI/2 of the International Convention for the Safety of Life at Sea (SOLAS). In all other cases, it shall be confined to the verification of the certificates and/or endorsements of the seafarers.

Section A-I/5
National provisions

The provisions of regulation I/5 shall not be interpreted as preventing the allocation of tasks for training under supervision or in cases of *force majeure*.

Section A-I/6
Training and assessment

1 Each Party shall ensure that all training and assessment of seafarers for certification under the Convention is:

.1 structured in accordance with written programmes, including such methods and media of delivery, procedures, and course material as are necessary to achieve the prescribed standard of competence; and

.2 conducted, monitored, evaluated and supported by persons qualified in accordance with paragraphs 4, 5 and 6.

2 Persons conducting in-service training or assessment on board ship shall only do so when such training or assessment will not adversely affect the normal operation of the ship and they can dedicate their time and attention to training or assessment.

2　进行此类评估时应切记，船上的程序与《国际安全管理(ISM)规则》有关，而本公约的规定只限于安全实施那些程序的适任能力。

3　本公约的监督程序应限于船上海员个人的适任标准，以及本规则 A 部分规定的与海员值班有关的技能。在船上对适任能力进行评估应从核实海员的证书开始。

4　尽管核实了证书，在按规则第 I/4 条第 1.3 段进行评估时，可以要求海员在其岗位上表明其有关的适任能力。这种能力的表明可包括核查是否符合值班标准方面的操作要求，以及该海员对紧急情况是否能作出其适任级别范围内的适当反应。

5　在评估时，只应采用本规则 A 部分中的表明适任能力的方法以及评价标准和适任标准的范围。

6　有关保安的适任能力的评估，仅应在有明显理由的情况下，依照《国际海上人命安全公约》(SOLAS)第 XI-2 章的规定，对承担特定保安职责的海员实施。在其他情况下，该项评估仅限于对海员证书和/或签证的核实。

第 A-I/5 节

国家的规定

规则第 I/5 条的规定不应解释为妨碍在监督下以培训为目的的任务分派，或在不可抗力情况下的任务分派。

第 A-I/6 节

培训和评估

1　各缔约国应确保对按本公约申请发证的海员的所有培训和评估是：

- .1　按照书面计划来组织进行的，该计划中包括为达到规定的适任标准所必需的授课方法与手段、程序和教材；以及
- .2　按照第 4 段、第 5 段和第 6 段的规定由具备资格的人员来实施、监督、评价并予以支持的。

2　在船上进行在职培训或评估的人员，仅应在该培训或评估不会影响船舶的正常操作以及在他们能集中时间和精力时进行培训或评估。

Qualifications of instructors, supervisors and assessors*

3 Each Party shall ensure that instructors, supervisors and assessors are appropriately qualified for the particular types and levels of training or assessment of competence of seafarers either on board or ashore, as required under the Convention, in accordance with the provisions of this section.

In-service training

4 Any person conducting in-service training of a seafarer, either on board or ashore, which is intended to be used in qualifying for certification under the Convention, shall:

.1 have an appreciation of the training programme and an understanding of the specific training objectives for the particular type of training being conducted;

.2 be qualified in the task for which training is being conducted; and

.3 if conducting training using a simulator:

.3.1 have received appropriate guidance in instructional techniques involving the use of simulators; and

.3.2 have gained practical operational experience on the particular type of simulator being used.

5 Any person responsible for the supervision of in-service training of a seafarer intended to be used in qualifying for certification under the Convention shall have a full understanding of the training programme and the specific objectives for each type of training being conducted.

Assessment of competence

6 Any person conducting in-service assessment of competence of a seafarer, either on board or ashore, which is intended to be used in qualifying for certification under the Convention, shall:

.1 have an appropriate level of knowledge and understanding of the competence to be assessed;

.2 be qualified in the task for which the assessment is being made;

.3 have received appropriate guidance in assessment methods and practice;

.4 have gained practical assessment experience; and

.5 if conducting assessment involving the use of simulators, have gained practical assessment experience on the particular type of simulator under the supervision and to the satisfaction of an experienced assessor.

---

* The relevant IMO Model Course(s) may be of assistance in the preparation of courses.

教员、监督人员和评估人员的资格①

3 各缔约国应按照本节的规定确保教员、监督人员和评估人员完全胜任公约要求的船上或岸上特定种类和级别的培训或对海员适任能力的评估。

在职培训

4 在船上或岸上对海员进行旨在用于根据本公约取得发证资格的在职培训的任何人员应:

.1 对培训计划有正确认识并对所进行的特定种类的培训的具体目标有充分了解;

.2 胜任所进行的培训工作;并且

.3 如果使用模拟器进行培训:

.3.1 接受过有关使用模拟器的教学技术的适当指导,并且

.3.2 已获得对所使用的特定种类模拟器的实际操作经验。

5 负责对海员旨在用于根据本公约取得发证资格的在职培训进行监督的任何人员,应对培训计划和正在进行的各种培训的具体目标有充分的了解。

适任评估

6 在船上或岸上对海员进行旨在用于根据本公约取得发证资格的在职适任评估的任何人员应:

.1 对所评估的适任能力具有适当水平的知识和理解;

.2 胜任所执行的评估任务;

.3 接受过有关评估方法和实践的适当指导;

.4 已获得评估的实际经验;并且

.5 如果所进行的评估涉及模拟器的使用,已获得在有经验的评估人员监督下并使其满意的特定种类模拟器的实际评估经验。

① 相关 IMO 示范培训课程可有助于准备课程。

Training and assessment within an institution

7 Each Party which recognizes a course of training, a training institution, or a qualification granted by a training institution, as part of its requirements for the issue of a certificate required under the Convention, shall ensure that the qualifications and experience of instructors and assessors are covered in the application of the quality standard provisions of section A-I/8. Such qualification, experience and application of quality standards shall incorporate appropriate training in instructional techniques, and training and assessment methods and practice, and shall comply with all applicable requirements of paragraphs 4 to 6.

Section A-I/7

Communication of information

1 The information required by regulation I/7, paragraph 1 shall be communicated to the Secretary-General in the formats prescribed in the paragraphs hereunder.

PART 1 – INITIAL COMMUNICATION OF INFORMATION

2 Within one calendar year of entry into force of regulation I/7, each Party shall report on the steps it has taken to give the Convention full and complete effect, which report shall include the following:

.1 contact details and organization chart of the ministry, department or governmental agency responsible for administering the Convention;

.2 a concise explanation of the legal and administrative measures provided and taken to ensure compliance, particularly with regulations I/2, I/6 and I/9;

.3 a clear statement of the education, training, examination, competency assessment and certification policies adopted;

.4 a concise summary of the courses, training programmes, examinations and assessments provided for each certificate issued pursuant to the Convention;

.5 a concise outline of the procedures followed to authorize, accredit or approve training and examinations, medical fitness and competency assessments required by the Convention, the conditions attached thereto, and a list of the authorizations, accreditations and approvals granted;

.6 a concise summary of the procedures followed in granting any dispensation under article VIII of the Convention; and

.7 the results of the comparison carried out pursuant to regulation I/11 and a concise outline of the refresher and upgrading training mandated.

培训机构内的培训和评估

7　将认可培训课程、培训机构或培训机构所核准的资格作为其按本公约签发证书的部分要求的各缔约国应确保,将教员和评估人员的资格和经历纳入第 A-I/8 节的质量标准条款的适用范围。该资格、经历和质量标准的运用应纳入适当的教学技术培训以及培训和评估方法与实践,并应符合第 4 段至第 6 段所有适用的要求。

第 A-I/7 节

资料交流

1　规则第 I/7 条第 1 段要求的资料应按以下段落规定的格式提交秘书长。

第 1 部分　初始资料交流

2　在规则第 I/7 条生效后的一个日历年内,各缔约国应就其采取的使本公约充分和完全实施的有关措施提交报告,该报告应包括下列内容:

.1　负责主管本公约的部委、司局或政府机构的联系方式和组织机构图;

.2　为确保遵守,特别是遵守规则第 I/2 条、第 I/6 条和第 I/9 条而制定并采取的法律和行政措施的简明介绍;

.3　对所采取的教育、培训、考试、适任评估以及发证政策的明确说明;

.4　对按本公约签发的每种证书规定的课程、培训计划、考试及评估的简要总结;

.5　对授权、认可或批准本公约要求的培训和考试、体检、适任评估所应遵循的程序及其附加条件的简要概述,以及一份授权、认可和批准清单;

.6　对依据本公约第 VIII 条规定核准任何特免证书所应遵循的程序的简要说明;和

.7　按照规则第 I/11 条所做的比较的结果以及对强制性知识更新培训的简要概述。

PART 2 – SUBSEQUENT REPORTS

3 Each Party shall, within six months of:

.1 retaining or adopting any equivalent education or training arrangements pursuant to article IX, provide a full description of such arrangements;

.2 recognizing certificates issued by another Party, provide a report summarizing the measures taken to ensure compliance with regulation I/10; and

.3 authorizing the employment of seafarers holding alternative certificates issued under regulation VII/1 on ships entitled to fly its flag, provide the Secretary-General with a specimen copy of the type of safe manning documents issued to such ships.

4 Each Party shall report the results of each evaluation carried out pursuant to regulation I/8, paragraph 2 within six months of its completion. The report of the evaluation shall include the following information:

.1 the qualifications and experience of those who conducted the evaluation; (e.g., certificates of competency held, experience as a seafarer and independent evaluator, experience in the field of maritime training and assessment, experience in the administration of certification systems, or any other relevant qualifications/experience);

.2 the terms of reference for the independent evaluation and those of the evaluators;

.3 a list of training institutions/centres covered by the independent evaluation; and

.4 the results of the independent evaluation, including:

.4.1 verification that:

.4.1.1 all applicable provisions of the Convention and STCW Code, including their amendments, are covered by the Party's quality standards system in accordance with section A-I/8, paragraph 3.1, and

.4.1.2 all internal management control and monitoring measures and follow-up actions comply with planned arrangements and documented procedures and are effective in ensuring achievement of defined objectives in accordance with section A-I/8, paragraph 3.2;

.4.2 a brief description of:

.4.2.1 the non-conformities found, if any, during the independent evaluation,

.4.2.2 the corrective measures recommended to address the identified non-conformities, and

.4.2.3 the corrective measures carried out to address the identified non-conformities.

第 2 部分　后续报告

3　各缔约国应：

.1　在按照公约第 IX 条规定保持或采取任何等效教育或培训安排 6 个月内，提交一份有关这种安排的全面说明；

.2　在承认由另一缔约国签发的证书的 6 个月内，提交一份为确保符合规则第 I/10 条所采取措施的简要报告；并且

.3　在批准悬挂其国旗的船舶上雇用持有根据规则第 VII/1 条签发的可供选择证书的海员 6 个月内，向秘书长提供一份对此类船舶签发的安全配员文件的样本。

4　各缔约国应在按照规则第 I/8 条第 2 段的规定完成评价后 6 个月内，报告评价的结果。评价报告应包括下列资料：

.1　实施评价人员的资格和经历（如所持适任证书、作为海员以及独立评价人员的经历、在海事培训及评估领域的经历、发证体系管理经验或其他相关的资格/经历）；

.2　独立评价以及评价人员的职责范围；

.3　独立评价包含的培训机构/中心清单；以及

.4　独立评价的结果，包括：

.4.1　核实：

.4.1.1　本公约及《STCW 规则》所有适用条款，包括其修正案，都包括在缔约国符合第 A-I/8 节第 3.1 段的质量标准体系内，且

.4.1.2　所有内部的管理控制和监控措施以及后续行动符合计划安排和文件规定的程序，并有效地确保第 A-I/8 节第 3.2 段既定目标的实现；

.4.2　简明描述：

.4.2.1　独立评价中发现的不符合项（如有），

.4.2.2　解决已发现的不符合项的推荐纠正措施，以及

.4.2.3　用以解决已发现的不符合项的纠正措施。

5 Parties shall report the steps taken to implement any subsequent mandatory amendments to the Convention and STCW Code, not previously included in the report on the initial communication of information pursuant to regulation I/7 or any previous report pursuant to regulation I/8. The information shall be included in the next report pursuant to regulation I/8, paragraph 3, following the entry into force of the amendment.

6 The information on the steps taken to implement mandatory amendments to the Convention and STCW Code shall include the following, where applicable:

.1 a concise explanation of the legal and administrative measures provided and taken to ensure compliance with the amendment;

.2 a concise summary of any courses, training programmes, examinations and assessments provided to comply with the amendment;

.3 a concise outline of the procedures followed to authorize, accredit or approve training and examinations, medical fitness and competency assessments required under the amendment;

.4 a concise outline of any refresher training and upgrading training required to meet the amendments; and

.5 a comparison between the measures to implement the amendment and existing measures contained in previous reports pursuant to regulation I/7, paragraph 1 and/or regulation I/8, paragraph 2 where applicable.

PART 3 – PANEL OF COMPETENT PERSONS

7 The Secretary-General shall maintain a list of competent persons approved by the Maritime Safety Committee, including competent persons made available or recommended by the Parties, who may be called upon to evaluate the reports submitted pursuant to regulation I/7 and regulation I/8 and may be called to assist in the preparation of the report required by regulation I/7, paragraph 2. These persons shall ordinarily be available during relevant sessions of the Maritime Safety Committee or its subsidiary bodies, but need not conduct their work solely during such sessions.

8 In relation to regulation I/7, paragraph 2, the competent persons shall be knowledgeable of the requirements of the Convention and at least one of them shall have knowledge of the system of training and certification of the Party concerned.

9 When a report is received from any Party under regulation I/8, paragraph 3, the Secretary-General will designate competent persons from the list maintained in accordance with paragraph 7 above, to consider the report and provide their views on whether:

.1 the report is complete and demonstrates that the Party has carried out an independent evaluation of the knowledge, understanding, skills and competence acquisition and assessment activities, and of the administration of the certification system (including endorsement and revalidation), in accordance with section A-I/8, paragraph 3;

.2 the report is sufficient to demonstrate that:

.2.1 the evaluators were qualified,

5 缔约国应报告实施任何本公约和《STCW 规则》后续强制性修正案所采取的措施，即没有包括在依据规则第 I/7 条所作的初始资料交流报告或任何依据规则第 I/8 条所作的先前报告中的措施。修正案生效后，资料应包括在依据规则第 I/8 条第 3 段所送交的下一个报告中。

6 有关实施本公约和《STCW 规则》强制性修正案所采取的措施的资料，如适用，应包括下列内容：

.1 为确保遵守修正案而制定并采取的法律和行政措施的简要说明；

.2 为遵守修正案而规定的课程、培训计划、考试及评估的简要总结；

.3 对授权、认可或批准修正案要求的培训和考试、体检和适任评估所应遵循的程序的概述；

.4 为符合修正案要求进行的知识更新培训和提高培训的概述；以及

.5 如适用，实施修正案的措施与按照规则第 I/7 条第 1 段及/或第 I/8 条第 2 段所采取的包括在以前报告中的现有措施间的比较。

第 3 部分　具有资格人员的小组

7 秘书长应保持一份经海上安全委员会批准的具有资格的人员的名单，其中包括由缔约国提供或推荐的具有资格的人员，这些人员可被召请评价按规则第 I/7 条和第 I/8 条提交的报告，还可被召请帮助准备规则第 I/7 条第 2 段所要求的报告。这些人员一般应在海上安全委员会或其下属机构召开有关会议时到会，但他们不必仅在这些会议期间进行工作。

8 与规则第 I/7 条第 2 段有关的具有资格的人员应了解本公约的要求，其中至少有 1 人应了解当事缔约国的培训和发证制度。

9 秘书长在收到任何缔约国依据规则第 I/8 条第 3 段规定提交的报告后，会从根据第 7 段保持的具有资格的人员名单中，指定具有资格的人员审议此报告并就下列各项表达意见：

.1 报告是否完整，并且是否表明该缔约国已根据第 A-I/8 节第 3 段对知识、理解、技能和适任能力的获得和评价活动以及对发证体系（包括签证和再有效）的管理进行了独立的评价；

.2 报告是否足以表明：

.2.1 评价人员是合格的，

.2.2 the terms of reference were clear enough to ensure that:

.2.2.1 all applicable provisions of the Convention and STCW Code, including their amendments, are covered by the Party's quality standards system; and

.2.2.2 the implementation of clearly defined objectives in accordance with regulation I/8, paragraph 1 could be verified over the full range of relevant activities,

.2.3 the procedures followed during the independent evaluation were appropriate to identify any significant non-conformities in the Party's system of training, assessment of competence, and certification of seafarers, as may be applicable to the Party concerned, and

.2.4 the actions being taken to correct any noted non-conformities are timely and appropriate.*

10 Any meeting of the competent persons shall:

.1 be held at the discretion of the Secretary-General;

.2 be comprised of an odd number of members, ordinarily not to exceed five persons;

.3 appoint its own chairman; and

.4 provide the Secretary-General with the agreed opinion of its members, or if no agreement is reached, with both the majority and minority views.

11 The competent persons shall, on a confidential basis, express their views in writing on:

.1 a comparison of the facts reported in the information communicated to the Secretary-General by the Party with all relevant requirements of the Convention;

.2 the report of any relevant evaluation submitted under regulation I/8, paragraph 3;

.3 the report of any steps taken to implement the amendments to the STCW Convention and Code submitted under paragraph 5; and

.4 any additional information provided by the Party.

---

* *Corrective actions must be timely and appropriate* means those actions must be focused on the underpinning/root causes of deficiencies and must be arranged to take place in a prescribed time schedule.

.2.2 职责范围明确,足以保证:

.2.2.1 本公约和《STCW 规则》的所有适用条款,包括其修正案,都纳入该缔约国的质量标准体系中,以及

.2.2.2 依据规则第 I/8 条第 1 段制定的明确目标的实施能够通过全面的相关活动得以证实,

.2.3 独立评价中所遵循的程序可适用于有关缔约国,以确认该缔约国的培训、适任能力评估以及海员发证体系中的任何重大不符合项,以及

.2.4 为纠正所发现的不符合项而采取的行动是及时的和适当的。①

10 具有资格的人员的任何会议应:

.1 由秘书长决定召开;

.2 由奇数人员组成,通常不超过 5 人;

.3 指定其会议主席;并且

.4 向秘书长提供与会成员的一致意见,如果达不成一致意见,则将多数意见和少数意见一并报告。

11 具有资格的人员应在保守秘密的基础上,就以下内容用书面形式表达他们的意见:

.1 对缔约国提交给秘书长的资料中所报告的事实与公约的所有有关要求进行比较;

.2 根据规则第 I/8 条第 3 段提交的任何有关的评价报告;

.3 根据第 5 段提交的任何为实施《STCW 公约》与《STCW 规则》修正案而采取的任何措施的报告;以及

.4 缔约国提供的任何附加资料。

① 纠正行动是及时的和适当的系指那些行动必须关注缺陷基础/根源和必须被安排在规定的日程表内进行。

PART 4 – REPORT TO THE MARITIME SAFETY COMMITTEE

12 In preparing the report to the Maritime Safety Committee required by regulation I/7, paragraph 2, the Secretary-General shall:

.1 solicit and take into account the views expressed by competent persons selected from the list established pursuant to paragraph 7;

.2 seek clarification, when necessary, from the Party of any matter related to the information provided under regulation I/7, paragraph 1; and

.3 identify any area in which the Party may have requested assistance to implement the Convention.

13 The Party concerned shall be informed of the arrangements for the meetings of competent persons, and its representatives shall be entitled to be present to clarify any matter related to the information provided pursuant to regulation I/7, paragraph 1.

14 If the Secretary-General is not in a position to submit the report called for by paragraph 2 of regulation I/7, the Party concerned may request the Maritime Safety Committee to take the action contemplated by paragraph 3 of regulation I/7, taking into account the information submitted pursuant to this section and the views expressed in accordance with paragraphs 10 and 11.

Section A-I/8
Quality standards

National objectives and quality standards

1 Each Party shall ensure that the education and training objectives and related standards of competence to be achieved are clearly defined and that the levels of knowledge, understanding and skills appropriate to the examinations and assessments required under the Convention are identified. The objectives and related quality standards may be specified separately for different courses and training programmes and shall cover the administration of the certification system.

2 The field of application of the quality standards shall cover the administration of the certification system, all training courses and programmes, examinations and assessments carried out by or under the authority of a Party and the qualifications and experience required of instructors and assessors, having regard to the policies, systems, controls and internal quality assurance reviews established to ensure achievement of the defined objectives.

3 Each Party shall ensure that an independent evaluation of the knowledge, understanding, skills and competence acquisition and assessment activities, and of the administration of the certification system, is conducted at intervals of not more than five years in order to verify that:

.1 all applicable provisions of the Convention and STCW Code, including their amendments, are covered by the quality standards system;

.2 all internal management control and monitoring measures and follow-up actions comply with planned arrangements and documented procedures and are effective in ensuring achievement of the defined objectives;

.3 the results of each independent evaluation are documented and brought to the attention of those responsible for the area evaluated; and

.4 timely action is taken to correct deficiencies.

第 4 部分　向海上安全委员会提交的报告

12　秘书长在根据规则第 I/7 条第 2 段起草向海上安全委员会提交的报告时应：

.1　向根据第 7 段确定的名单中所选出的具有资格的人员征询意见并考虑这些意见；

.2　必要时要求缔约国澄清其根据规则第 I/7 条第 1 段提供的资料中的任何有关事宜；并且

.3　确定缔约国为履约可能要求帮助的任何领域。

13 应通知当事缔约国关于具有资格人员会议的安排，同时，缔约国的代表应有权到会澄清根据规则第 I/7 条第 1 段所提供的资料的任何相关事宜。

14　如果秘书长未能提交规则第 I/7 条第 2 段所要求的报告，当事缔约国可要求海上安全委员会采取规则第 I/7 条第 3 段规定的行动，并考虑根据本节所提交的资料和根据本节第 10 段和第 11 段所表达的意见。

第 A-I/8 节
质量标准

国家的目标和质量标准

1　各缔约国应确保对其拟达到的教育和培训目标以及有关的适任标准作出明确规定，并对公约要求的适于考试和评估的知识、理解和技能水平予以确定。该目标和有关的适任标准可针对不同的课程和培训计划分别作出规定，并应包括对发证体系的管理。

2　质量标准的适用范围应覆盖发证体系的管理、所有的培训课程和计划、缔约国直接或授权进行的考试和评估以及教员和评估人员需要具备的资格和经历，并注意到为确保达到既定目标而制定的方针、制度、监督和内部质量保证审验。

3　各缔约国应确保每隔最多不超过 5 年，对知识、理解、技能和适任能力的获得和评估活动以及对发证体系的管理进行一次独立的评价，以核实：

.1　本公约及《STCW 规则》所有适用条款，包括其修正案，均包括在质量标准体系内；

.2　所有内部的管理控制和监控措施以及后续行动符合计划安排和文件规定的程序，并能有效地确保既定目标的实现；

.3　每次独立评价的结果形成文件并提请被评价部门的负责人注意；以及

.4　已及时采取纠正缺陷的行动。

Section A-I/9
Medical standards

1 Parties, when establishing standards of medical fitness for seafarers as required by regulation I/9, shall adhere to the minimum in-service eyesight standards set out in table A-I/9 and take into account the criteria for physical and medical fitness set out in paragraph 2. They should also take into account the guidance given in section B-I/9 of this Code and table B-I/9 regarding assessment of minimum physical abilities.

These standards may, to the extent determined by the Party without prejudice to the safety of the seafarers or the ship, differentiate between those persons seeking to start a career at sea and those seafarers already serving at sea and between different functions on board, bearing in mind the different duties of seafarers. They shall also take into account any impairment or disease that will limit the ability of the seafarer to effectively perform his/her duties during the validity period of the medical certificate.

2 The standards of physical and medical fitness established by the Party shall ensure that seafarers satisfy the following criteria:

.1 have the physical capability, taking into account paragraph 5 below, to fulfill all the requirements of the basic training as required by section A-VI/1, paragraph 2;

.2 demonstrate adequate hearing and speech to communicate effectively and detect any audible alarms;

.3 have no medical condition, disorder or impairment that will prevent the effective and safe conduct of their routine and emergency duties on board during the validity period of the medical certificate;

.4 are not suffering from any medical condition likely to be aggravated by service at sea or to render the seafarer unfit for such service or to endanger the health and safety of other persons on board; and

.5 are not taking any medication that has side effects that will impair judgment, balance, or any other requirements for effective and safe performance of routine and emergency duties on board.

3 Medical fitness examinations of seafarers shall be conducted by appropriately qualified and experienced medical practitioners recognized by the Party.

4 Each Party shall establish provisions for recognizing medical practitioners. A register of recognized medical practitioners shall be maintained by the Party and made available to other Parties, companies and seafarers on request.

5 Each Party shall provide guidance for the conduct of medical fitness examinations and issuing of medical certificates, taking into account provisions set out in section B-I/9 of this Code. Each Party shall determine the amount of discretion given to recognized medical practitioners on the application of the medical standards, bearing in mind the different duties of seafarers, except that there shall not be discretion with respect to the minimum eyesight standards for distance vision aided, near/immediate vision and colour vision in table A-I/9 for seafarers in the deck department required to undertake look-out duties. A Party may allow discretion on the application of these

第 A-I/9 节
健康标准

1　各缔约国在依据规则第 I/9 条制定海员的健康标准时，应按照表 A-I/9 中规定的在职视力最低标准，并考虑到第 2 段提出的体格和医疗适应性的标准，同时应考虑本规则第 B-I/9 节和表 B-I/9 最低体能评估表给出的指导。

在不损害船员或船舶的安全范围内，对那些准备从事海员职业的人和已经在海上服务的船员，同时考虑其不同的职能和职责，缔约国可以制定不同的标准。也应考虑在船员健康证书有效期内会限制其有效履行职责能力的任何损伤或疾病。

2　缔约国制定的体能和健康标准应保证海员符合以下条件：

.1　考虑到下面第 5 段，具备完成第 A-VI/1 节第 2 段所要求的基本训练的体能；

.2　具备足够的听觉和有效的语言沟通能力，并能听到任何声响警报；

.3　在健康证书有效期间，在船上不会出现影响有效地、安全地履行日常与应急职责的健康问题、不适或损伤状况；

.4　没有会因海上服务而导致病情加重、不再适合船上工作，或者会影响其他船员安全和健康的疾病；并且

.5　在船上没有采用任何导致阻碍判断、平衡或出现影响有效地、安全地履行日常与应急职责等有副作用的医疗。

3　海员的健康检查应由该缔约国认可的、合格的、有经验的从业医生执行。

4　各缔约国应制定认可从业医生的规则。缔约国应保持对认可的从业医生注册，并根据其他缔约国、公司及海员的请求提供。

5　各缔约国应为执行健康检查和签发健康证书提供指导，并考虑《STCW 规则》第 B-I/9 节规定的条款。各缔约国应切记海员的不同职责，并决定给予认可的从业医生运用健康标准的自行决定权的范围，由于甲板部船员承担瞭望职责，对表 A-I/9 所列的有关最低矫正远距视力、近距/直接视力及辨色力标准不应行使自行决定权。只要海员的综合视力符合表 A-I/9中规定的要求，缔约国可允许对轮机部船员适用这些标准的自行决定权。

standards with regard to seafarers in the engine department, on the condition that seafarers' combined vision fulfils the requirements set out in table A-I/9.

6 Each Party shall establish processes and procedures to enable seafarers who, after examination, do not meet the medical fitness standards or have had a limitation imposed on their ability to work, in particular with respect to time, field of work or trading area, to have their case reviewed in line with that Party's provisions for appeal.

7 The medical certificate provided for in regulation I/9, paragraph 3 shall include the following information as a minimum:

.1 **Authorizing authority** and the requirements under which the document is issued

.2 **Seafarer information**

.2.1 Name: *(Last, first, middle)*

.2.2 Date of birth: *(day/month/year)*

.2.3 Gender: *(Male/Female)*

.2.4 Nationality

.3 **Declaration of the recognized medical practitioner**

.3.1 Confirmation that identification documents were checked at the point of examination: *Y/N*

.3.2 Hearing meets the standards in section A-I/9: *Y/N*

.3.3 Unaided hearing satisfactory: *Y/N*

.3.4 Visual acuity meets standards in section A-I/9: *Y/N*

.3.5 Colour vision* meets standards in section A-I/9: *Y/N*

.3.5.1 Date of last colour vision test.

.3.6 Fit for look-out duties: *Y/N*

.3.7 No limitations or restrictions on fitness: *Y/N*
If "N", specify limitations or restrictions.

.3.8 Is the seafarer free from any medical condition likely to be aggravated by service at sea or to render the seafarer unfit for such service or to endanger the health of other persons on board: *Y/N*

.3.9 Date of examination: (*day/month/year*)

.3.10 Expiry date of certificate: (*day/month/year*)

* Note: Colour vision assessment only needs to be conducted every six years.

6 各缔约国应制定程序,使那些经健康检查后达不到健康标准或有工作能力限制,特别是有关时间、工作领域或航区的限制的海员,能够根据缔约国的申诉规定得到对其情况的复查。

7 规则第 I/9 条第 3 段提供的健康证书应至少包括下列信息:

.1 授权机关以及文件签发要求

.2 海员信息

.2.1 姓名:(姓、名、中间名)

.2.2 出生日期:(日/月/年)

.2.3 性别:(男/女)

.2.4 国籍

.3 认可的从业医生的声明

.3.1 身份证明文件在检查时经过确认:是/否

.3.2 听力达到第 A-I/9 节的标准:是/否

.3.3 裸耳听力符合要求:是/否

.3.4 视敏度达到第 A-I/9 节的标准:是/否

.3.5 辨色力①达到第 A-I/9 节的标准:是/否

.3.5.1 上一次辨色力测试日期。

.3.6 适合瞭望职责:是/否

.3.7 对适于职责无限制:是/否

若有限制,具体说明何种限制。

.3.8 海员无可能由于海上服务而使病情加重,或可能使海员不适合该服务,或可能使船上其他人员的健康受到危害的身体状况:是/否

.3.9 检查日期:(日/月/年)

.3.10 证书失效日期:(日/月/年)

① 注:辨色力测试仅需每 6 年作一次。

.4 Details of the issuing authority

.4.1 Official stamp (including name) of the issuing authority

.4.2 Signature of the authorized person

.5 Seafarer's signature – *confirming that the seafarer has been informed of the content of the certificate and of the right to a review in accordance with paragraph 6 of section A-I/9*

8 Medical certificates shall be in the official language of the issuing country. If the language used is not English, the text shall include a translation into that language.

.4 签发机关信息

.4.1 签发机关的官方印章(包括名称)

.4.2 被授权人的签名

.5 海员签名——确认已了解海员证书的内容以及依据第 A-I/9 节第 6 段享有的复查权利

8 健康证书应使用发证国的官方文字。如使用的文字不是英文,证书文本应包括英文译文。

Table A-I/9

Minimum in-service eyesight standards for seafarers

STCW Convention regulation	Category of seafarer	Distance vision Aided[1]		Near/immediate vision	Colour vision[3]	Visual fields[4]	Night blindness[4]	Diplopia (double vision)[4]
		One eye	Other eye	Both eyes together, aided or unaided				
I/11 II/1 II/2 II/3 II/4 II/5 VII/2	Masters, deck officers and ratings required to undertake look-out duties	0.5[2]	0.5	Vision required for ship's navigation (e.g., chart and nautical publication reference, use of bridge instrumentation and equipment, and identification of aids to navigation)	See Note 6	Normal Visual fields	Vision required to perform all necessary functions in darkness without compromise	No significant condition evident
I/11 III/1 III/2 III/3 III/4 III/5 III/6 III/7 VII/2	All engineer officers, electro-technical officers, electro-technical ratings and ratings or others forming part of an engine-room watch	0.4[5]	0.4 (see Note 5)	Vision required to read instruments in close proximity, to operate equipment, and to identify systems/ components as necessary	See Note 7	Sufficient visual fields	Vision required to perform all necessary functions in darkness without compromise	No significant condition evident
I/11 IV/2	GMDSS Radio operators	0.4	0.4	Vision required to read instruments in close proximity, to operate equipment, and to identify systems/ components as necessary	See Note 7	Sufficient visual fields	Vision required to perform all necessary functions in darkness without compromise	No significant condition evident

Notes:

1 Values given in Snellen decimal notation.

2 A value of at least 0.7 in one eye is recommended to reduce the risk of undetected underlying eye disease.

3 As defined in the *International Recommendations for Colour Vision Requirements for Transport* by the Commission Internationale de l'Eclairage (CIE-143-2001 including any subsequent versions).

4 Subject to assessment by a clinical vision specialist where indicated by initial examination findings.

5 Engine department personnel shall have a combined eyesight vision of at least 0.4.

6 CIE colour vision standard 1 or 2.

7 CIE colour vision standard 1, 2 or 3.

表 A-I/9
在职海员视力最低标准

<table>
<tr><th rowspan="2">《STCW 公约》规则</th><th rowspan="2">海员类别</th><th colspan="2">矫正远距视力[1]</th><th>近距/直接视力</th><th rowspan="2">辨色力[3]</th><th rowspan="2">视野[4]</th><th rowspan="2">暗适应[4]</th><th rowspan="2">复视（双影）[4]</th></tr>
<tr><th>一只眼</th><th>另一只眼</th><th>两眼都已矫正或未矫正</th></tr>
<tr><td>I/11
II/1
II/2
II/3
II/4
II/5
VII/2</td><td>船长、甲板部高级船员和履行瞭望职责的普通船员</td><td>0.5[2]</td><td>0.5</td><td>船舶航行所要求的视力（如查阅海图、航海出版物，使用驾驶台仪器设备和辨别航标）</td><td>参见注释 6</td><td>正常视野</td><td>在黑暗中履行所有必要职能所要求的视力（不得降低标准）</td><td>未显现明显状况</td></tr>
<tr><td>I/11
III/1
III/2
III/3
III/4
III/5
III/6
III/7
VII/2</td><td>所有轮机部高级船员、电子员、电子技工和组成机舱值班部分的普通船员或其他人员</td><td>0.4[5]</td><td>0.4（参见注释 5）</td><td>近距离读出仪器数据、操作设备和辨别必要的系统/部件所需要的视力</td><td>参见注释 7</td><td>足够的视野</td><td>在黑暗中履行所有必要职能所要求的视力（不得降低标准）</td><td>同上</td></tr>
<tr><td>I/11
IV/2</td><td>全球海上遇险与安全系统无线电操作员</td><td>0.4</td><td>0.4</td><td>近距离读出仪器数据、操作设备和辨别必要的系统/部件所需要的视力</td><td>参见注释 7</td><td>足够的视野</td><td>在黑暗中履行所有必要职能所要求的视力（不得降低标准）</td><td>同上</td></tr>
</table>

注：

1 斯内伦视力表中以十进制表示的数值。

2 建议一只眼的数值至少为 0.7，以减少未检查出的潜在眼疾的危险性。

3 按国际照明委员会（CIE）颁发的《运输领域辨色力要求国际建议案》（CIE-143-2001，包括其后续版本）中的规定。

4 如有最初检验结果，服从临床视力专家的评估。

5 轮机部人员综合视力不得小于 0.4。

6 CIE 辨色力标准 1 或 2。

7 CIE 辨色力标准 1、2 或 3。

Section A-I/10
Recognition of certificates

1 The provisions of regulation I/10, paragraph 4 regarding the non-recognition of certificates issued by a non-Party shall not be construed as preventing a Party, when issuing its own certificate, from accepting seagoing service, education and training acquired under the authority of a non-Party, provided the Party complies with regulation I/2 in issuing each such certificate and ensures that the requirements of the Convention relating to seagoing service, education, training and competence are complied with.

2 Where an Administration which has recognized a certificate withdraws its endorsement of recognition for disciplinary reasons, the Administration shall inform the Party that issued the certificate of the circumstances.

Section A-I/11
Revalidation of certificates

Professional competence

1 Continued professional competence as required under regulation I/11 shall be established by:

.1 approved seagoing service, performing functions appropriate to the certificate held, for a period of at least:

.1.1 twelve months in total during the preceding five years, or

.1.2 three months in total during the preceding six months immediately prior to revalidating; or

.2 having performed functions considered to be equivalent to the seagoing service required in paragraph 1.1; or

.3 passing an approved test; or

.4 successfully completing an approved training course or courses; or

.5 having completed approved seagoing service, performing functions appropriate to the certificate held, for a period of not less than three months in a supernumerary capacity, or in a lower officer rank than that for which the certificate held is valid immediately prior to taking up the rank for which it is valid.

2 The refresher and updating courses required by regulation I/11 shall be approved and include changes in relevant national and international regulations concerning the safety of life at sea, security and the protection of the marine environment and take account of any updating of the standard of competence concerned.

3 Continued professional competence for tankers as required under regulation I/11, paragraph 3 shall be established by:

.1 approved seagoing service, performing duties appropriate to the tanker certificate or endorsement held, for a period of at least 3 months in total during the preceding 5 years; or

第 A-I/10 节

证书的承认

1　规则第 I/10 条第 4 段关于不承认非缔约国签发的证书的规定，不应解释为妨碍一缔约国在签发自己的证书时对经非缔约国准许而取得的海上服务资历、教育和培训的承认，只要该缔约国在签发其证书时遵守了规则第 I/2 条的规定并确保遵守本公约关于海上服务资历、教育、培训和适任的要求。

2　如果承认证书的主管机关因处罚原因而撤销其承认证书的签证，则该主管机关应将有关情况通知签发证书的缔约国。

第 A-I/11 节

证书的再有效

专业适任能力

1　规则第 I/11 条要求的持续专业适任能力应通过以下方式确立：

　.1　履行了所持证书上相应职能的认可的海上服务资历至少：

　　.1.1　在前 5 年中累计 12 个月，或

　　.1.2　在再有效之前 6 个月中累计 3 个月；或

　.2　履行了被认为是等同于第 1.1 段要求的海上服务资历的职能；或

　.3　通过了认可的测试；或

　.4　圆满地完成了认可的一门或几门培训课程；或

　.5　在担任证书有效职务之前，作为一种编外职务或作为低于所持证书有效职务的高级船员职务不少于 3 个月，完成了履行所持证书上相应职能的认可的海上服务资历。

2　规则第 I/11 条要求的知识更新课程应经过认可，并包括涉及海上人命安全、保安和保护海洋环境的有关国内和国际规则的变动，同时考虑到有关适任标准的任何更新。

3　规则第 I/11 条第 3 段要求的液货船的持续专业适任能力应通过以下方式确立：

　.1　在前 5 年中累计不少于 3 个月履行所持液货船证书或签证相应职责的认可的海上服务资历；或

.2 successfully completing an approved relevant training course or courses.

Section A-I/12
Standards governing the use of simulators

PART 1 PERFORMANCE STANDARDS

General performance standards for simulators used in training

1 Each Party shall ensure that any simulator used for mandatory simulator-based training shall:

.1 be suitable for the selected objectives and training tasks;

.2 be capable of simulating the operating capabilities of shipboard equipment concerned, to a level of physical realism appropriate to training objectives, and include the capabilities, limitations and possible errors of such equipment;

.3 have sufficient behavioural realism to allow a trainee to acquire the skills appropriate to the training objectives;

.4 provide a controlled operating environment, capable of producing a variety of conditions, which may include emergency, hazardous or unusual situations relevant to the training objectives;

.5 provide an interface through which a trainee can interact with the equipment, the simulated environment and, as appropriate, the instructor; and

.6 permit an instructor to control, monitor and record exercises for the effective debriefing of trainees.

General performance standards for simulators used in assessment of competence

2 Each Party shall ensure that any simulator used for the assessment of competence required under the Convention or for any demonstration of continued proficiency so required shall:

.1 be capable of satisfying the specified assessment objectives;

.2 be capable of simulating the operational capabilities of the shipboard equipment concerned to a level of physical realism appropriate to the assessment objectives, and include the capabilities, limitations and possible errors of such equipment;

.3 have sufficient behavioural realism to allow a candidate to exhibit the skills appropriate to the assessment objectives;

.4 provide an interface through which a candidate can interact with the equipment and simulated environment;

.5 provide a controlled operating environment, capable of producing a variety of conditions, which may include emergency, hazardous or unusual situations relevant to assessment objectives; and

.2 圆满地完成了认可的一门或几门相关培训课程。

第 A-I/12 节

关于使用模拟器的标准

第 1 部分　性能标准

用于培训的模拟器的一般性能标准

1 各缔约国应确保任何用于基于模拟器的强制性培训的模拟器应:

.1 适于选定的目标和培训任务;

.2 能够模拟船上有关设备的操作性能,达到合乎培训目标的物理真实水平,并包括这种设备的性能、局限性和可能产生的误差;

.3 具有足够的行为真实性,使受培训者能够获得合乎培训目标的技能;

.4 提供一个可控制的操作环境,并能生成各种情况,其中可包括与培训目标有关的紧急、危险或异常情况;

.5 提供一个界面,受培训者可借此与设备、模拟的环境以及视情与教员相互作用;并且

.6 由教员控制、监控和记录训练情况,以便对受培训者作出有效的小结。

用于适任评估的模拟器的一般性能标准

2 各缔约国应确保任何用于评估本公约所要求的适任能力或用于表明公约所要求的持续熟练程度的模拟器应:

.1 能够达到规定的评估目标;

.2 能够模拟船上有关设备的操作性能,达到合乎评估目标的物理真实水平,并包括这种设备的性能、局限性和可能产生的误差;

.3 具有足够的行为真实性,使证书申请人能够表明合乎评估目标的技能;

.4 提供一个界面,证书申请人可借此与设备和模拟的环境相互作用;

.5 提供一个可控制的操作环境,并能生成各种情况,其中包括与评估目标有关的紧急、危险或异常状况;并且

.6 permit an assessor to control, monitor and record exercises for the effective assessment of the performance of candidates.

Additional performance standards

3 In addition to meeting the basic requirements set out in paragraphs 1 and 2, simulation equipment to which this section applies shall meet the performance standards given hereunder in accordance with their specific type.

Radar simulation

4 Radar simulation equipment shall be capable of simulating the operational capabilities of navigational radar equipment which meets all applicable performance standards adopted by the Organization* and incorporate facilities to:

.1 operate in the stabilized relative-motion mode and sea- and ground-stabilized true-motion modes;

.2 model weather, tidal streams, current, shadow sectors, spurious echoes and other propagation effects, and generate coastlines, navigational buoys and search and rescue transponders; and

.3 create a real-time operating environment incorporating at least two own-ship stations with ability to change own ship's course and speed, and include parameters for at least 20 target ships and appropriate communication facilities.

Automatic Radar Plotting Aid (ARPA) simulation

5 ARPA simulation equipment shall be capable of simulating the operational capabilities of ARPAs which meet all applicable performance standards adopted by the Organization*, and shall incorporate the facilities for:

.1 manual and automatic target acquisition;

.2 past track information;

.3 use of exclusion areas;

.4 vector/graphic time-scale and data display; and

.5 trial manoeuvres.

PART 2 OTHER PROVISIONS

Simulator training objectives

6 Each Party shall ensure that the aims and objectives of simulator-based training are defined within an overall training programme and that specific training objectives and tasks are selected so as to relate as closely as possible to shipboard tasks and practices.

* See relevant/appropriate performance standards adopted by the Organization.

.6 由评估人员控制、监控和记录训练情况,以便有效评估证书申请人的操作。

附加的性能标准

3 除符合第 1 段和第 2 段规定的基本要求外,本节所适用的模拟设备按其特定种类还应达到以下性能标准。

雷达模拟

4 雷达模拟设备应能够模拟达到本组织通过的所有适用的性能标准①的航海雷达设备的操作性能,并配有有关设施以便能:

.1 在稳定的相对运动模式和海、陆稳定的真运动模式上操作;

.2 模仿天气、潮流、海流、阴影扇形、假回波和其他电波传播影响,并产生岸线、导航浮标和搜救应答器;并且

.3 创造一个包括至少两个能够改变本船航向和航速的本船船台的实时操作环境,并包括至少 20 个目标船和相应的通信设备的参数。

自动雷达标绘仪(ARPA)模拟

5 ARPA 模拟设备应能够模拟达到本组织通过的所有适用的性能标准①的 ARPA 的操作性能,还应配有有关设施以便用于:

.1 手动和自动捕捉目标;

.2 航迹线信息;

.3 除外区域的应用;

.4 矢量/图解时间刻度和数据显示;以及

.5 试操纵。

第 2 部分 其他规定

模拟器培训目标

6 各缔约国应确保基于模拟器培训的目的和目标要在一个总体培训计划中加以规定,并应确保选择具体的培训目标和任务以使其尽可能接近船上的工作和实践。

① 参见国际海事组织通过的相关/适当的性能标准。

Training procedures

7 In conducting mandatory simulator-based training, instructors shall ensure that:

.1 trainees are adequately briefed beforehand on the exercise objectives and tasks and are given sufficient planning time before the exercise starts;

.2 trainees have adequate familiarization time on the simulator and with its equipment before any training or assessment exercise commences;

.3 guidance given and exercise stimuli are appropriate to the selected exercise objectives and tasks and to the level of trainee experience;

.4 exercises are effectively monitored, supported as appropriate by audio and visual observation of trainee activity and pre- and post-exercise evaluation reports;

.5 trainees are effectively debriefed to ensure that training objectives have been met and that operational skills demonstrated are of an acceptable standard;

.6 the use of peer assessment during debriefing is encouraged; and

.7 simulator exercises are designed and tested so as to ensure their suitability for the specified training objectives.

Assessment procedures

8 Where simulators are used to assess the ability of candidates to demonstrate levels of competency, assessors shall ensure that:

.1 performance criteria are identified clearly and explicitly and are valid and available to the candidates;

.2 assessment criteria are established clearly and are explicit to ensure reliability and uniformity of assessment and to optimize objective measurement and evaluation, so that subjective judgements are kept to the minimum;

.3 candidates are briefed clearly on the tasks and/or skills to be assessed and on the tasks and performance criteria by which their competency will be determined;

.4 assessment of performance takes into account normal operating procedures and any behavioural interaction with other candidates on the simulator or with simulator staff;

.5 scoring or grading methods to assess performance are used with caution until they have been validated; and

.6 the prime criterion is that a candidate demonstrates the ability to carry out a task safely and effectively to the satisfaction of the assessor.

培训程序

7 在进行基于模拟器的强制性培训时,教员应确保:

.1 事先对受培训者就训练目标和任务作充分的说明,并且在训练开始前给其足够的准备时间;

.2 受培训者在任何培训或评估训练开始前,有足够的时间熟悉模拟器及其设备;

.3 所给予的指导和训练的促进因素适于选定的训练目标和任务并适于受培训者的经验水平;

.4 通过听觉和视觉观察受培训者的活动并通过训练前后的评价报告,来有效地监控训练情况并在必要时给予支持;

.5 有效地对受培训者进行小结以确保达到培训目标,并使受培训者表明的操作技能达到认可的标准;

.6 在小结时,提倡受培训者相互评估;并且

.7 对模拟器训练进行设计和检验以确保其适于规定的培训目标。

评估程序

8 当使用模拟器来评估证书申请人的能力以表明其适任水平时,评估人员应确保:

.1 清楚、明确地确定操作标准,并且该操作标准对证书申请人而言是有效的和可获得的;

.2 清楚地确立评估标准,并做到详尽明晰,以确保评估的可靠性和统一性,并达到最佳的客观测定和评价,使主观判断保持在最低限度;

.3 向证书申请人清楚地说明拟进行评估的工作和/或技能,以及拟用于确定其适任能力的工作和操作标准;

.4 对操作的评估要考虑到正常的操作程序和在模拟器上与其他证书申请人或模拟器教员行为的相互影响;

.5 评估操作的评分或评级方法在被确认有效之前应慎用;并且

.6 首要的标准是证书申请人能够表明其安全有效地执行任务的能力并使评估人员满意。

Qualifications of instructors and assessors*

9 Each Party shall ensure that instructors and assessors are appropriately qualified and experienced for the particular types and levels of training and corresponding assessment of competence as specified in regulation I/6 and section A-I/6.

Section A-I/13
Conduct of trials

(No provisions)

Section A-I/14
Responsibilities of companies

1 Companies, masters and crew members each have responsibility for ensuring that the obligations set out in this section are given full and complete effect and that such other measures as may be necessary are taken to ensure that each crew member can make a knowledgeable and informed contribution to the safe operation of the ship.

2 The company shall provide written instructions to the master of each ship to which the Convention applies, setting forth the policies and the procedures to be followed to ensure that all seafarers who are newly employed on board the ship are given a reasonable opportunity to become familiar with the shipboard equipment, operating procedures and other arrangements needed for the proper performance of their duties, before being assigned to those duties. Such policies and procedures shall include:

.1 allocation of a reasonable period of time during which each newly employed seafarer will have an opportunity to become acquainted with:

.1.1 the specific equipment the seafarer will be using or operating;

.1.2 ship-specific watchkeeping, safety, environmental protection, security and emergency procedures and arrangements the seafarer needs to know to perform the assigned duties properly; and

.2 designation of a knowledgeable crew member who will be responsible for ensuring that an opportunity is provided to each newly employed seafarer to receive essential information in a language the seafarer understands.

3 Companies shall ensure that masters, officers and other personnel assigned specific duties and responsibilities on board their ro-ro passenger ships shall have completed familiarization training to attain the abilities that are appropriate to the capacity to be filled and duties and responsibilities to be taken up, taking into account the guidance given in section B-I/14 of this Code.

Section A-I/15
Transitional provisions

(No provisions)

* The relevant IMO Model Course(s) and resolution MSC.64(67), *Recommendations on new and amended performance standards*, may be of assistance in the preparation of courses.

教员和评估人员的资格①

9　各缔约国应确保教员和评估人员具备从事规则第 I/6 条和第 A-I/6 节规定的特定种类和等级的培训和相应的适任评估的适当资格和经验。

第 A-I/13 节

试验的实施

（无条文）

第 A-I/14 节

公司的责任

1　公司、船长和船员都有责任确保本节规定的义务得以充分和完全地履行，而且确保采取其他必要措施以确保每个船员均能利用其知识和经验为船舶的安全操作发挥作用。

2　公司应向所有适用于本公约的船舶的船长提供书面指示，规定应该遵循的政策和程序，以确保为新雇用到船上工作的每个海员提供一个合理的机会，使其在履行职责之前熟悉船上的设备、操作程序以及为正确履行其职责而需熟悉的其他安排。这些政策和程序应包括：

.1　给出一段合理的时间使每个新雇用的海员在此期间均有机会了解：

.1.1　该海员即将使用或操作的具体设备，

.1.2　船上具体的值班、安全、环境保护和应急程序以及海员需要知晓以正确履行指定职责的安排；以及

.2　指定一名熟悉业务的船员，让其负责确保向新雇用的每个海员提供以一种他懂得的语言获得基本信息的机会。

3　公司应确保滚装客船船长、高级船员以及其他承担特定职责及责任的人员已完成熟悉培训，获得适于所担任职务和所承担职责和责任的能力，并考虑本规则第 B-I/14 节所给予的指导。

第 A-I/15 节

过渡规定

（无条文）

①　相关 IMO 示范培训课程以及 MSC.64(67) 号决议《对新增及修正的操作标准建议案》可有助于准备课程。

CHAPTER II

Standards regarding the master and deck department

Section A-II/1
Mandatory minimum requirements for certification of officers in charge of a navigational watch on ships of 500 gross tonnage or more

Standard of competence

1 Every candidate for certification shall:

.1 be required to demonstrate the competence to undertake, at the operational level, the tasks, duties and responsibilities listed in column 1 of table A-II/1;

.2 at least hold the appropriate certificate for performing VHF radiocommunications in accordance with the requirements of the Radio Regulations; and

.3 if designated to have primary responsibility for radiocommunications during distress incidents, hold the appropriate certificate issued or recognized under the provisions of the Radio Regulations.

2 The minimum knowledge, understanding and proficiency required for certification is listed in column 2 of table A-II/1.

3 The level of knowledge of the subjects listed in column 2 of table A-II/1 shall be sufficient for officers of the watch to carry out their watchkeeping duties.*

4 Training and experience to achieve the necessary level of theoretical knowledge, understanding and proficiency shall be based on section A-VIII/2, part 4-1 – Principles to be observed in keeping a navigational watch – and shall also take into account the relevant requirements of this part and the guidance given in part B of this Code.

5 Every candidate for certification shall be required to provide evidence of having achieved the required standard of competence in accordance with the methods for demonstrating competence and the criteria for evaluating competence tabulated in columns 3 and 4 of table A-II/1.

Onboard training

6 Every candidate for certification as officer in charge of a navigational watch of ships of 500 gross tonnage or more whose seagoing service, in accordance with paragraph 2.2 of regulation II/1, forms part of a training programme approved as meeting the requirements of this section shall follow an approved programme of onboard training which:

.1 ensures that, during the required period of seagoing service, the candidate receives systematic practical training and experience in the tasks, duties and responsibilities of an officer in charge of a navigational watch, taking into account the guidance given in section B-II/1 of this Code;

* The relevant IMO Model Course(s) may be of assistance in the preparation of courses.

第 II 章
关于船长和甲板部的标准

第 A-II/1 节
对 500 总吨或以上船舶的负责航行值班的高级船员发证的强制性最低要求

适任标准

1 每个证书申请人应：

.1 按要求表明承担表 A-II/1 第 1 栏所列的操作级的任务、职责和责任的适任能力；

.2 至少持有按照《无线电规则》的要求进行甚高频无线电通信的适当证书；并且

.3 如果在遇险事件中被指定负有无线电通信的主要职责，则持有根据《无线电规则》的规定签发或承认的适当证书。

2 发证所要求的最低的知识、理解和熟练列于表 A-II/1 第 2 栏中。

3 表 A-II/1 第 2 栏所列各科目的知识水平，应足以能使值班的高级船员履行其值班职责。①

4 为获取所需水平的理论知识、理解和熟练的培训和经验，应以第 A-VIII/2 节第 4-1 部分——航行值班中应遵循的原则为基础，并也应考虑本规则本部分的有关要求和 B 部分给予的指导。

5 每个证书申请人应按照表 A-II/1 第 3 栏和第 4 栏所列的表明适任的方法和评价适任的标准，提供已达到所要求的适任标准的证据。

船上培训

6 每个申请 500 总吨或以上船舶的负责航行值班的高级船员证书的申请人，其海上服务资历按照规则第 II/1 条第 2.2 段构成经认可作为符合本节要求的培训计划的部分，则应参加一个认可的船上培训计划。该培训计划：

.1 确保证书申请人在要求的海上服务期间，受到关于在负责航行值班的高级船员的任务、职责和责任方面的系统而实际的培训并获得经验，同时考虑本规则第 B-II/1 节给予的指导；

① 相关 IMO 示范培训课程可有助于准备课程。

.2 is closely supervised and monitored by qualified officers aboard the ships in which the approved seagoing service is performed; and

.3 is adequately documented in a training record book or similar document.*

Near-coastal voyages

7 The following subjects may be omitted from those listed in column 2 of table A-II/1 for issue of restricted certificates for service on near-coastal voyages, bearing in mind the safety of all ships which may be operating in the same waters:

.1 celestial navigation; and

.2 those electronic systems of position fixing and navigation that do not cover the waters for which the certificate is to be valid.

* The relevant IMO Model Course(s) and a similar document produced by the International Shipping Federation may be of assistance in the preparation of training record books.

.2 在执行认可的海上服务中密切地受到船上合格的高级船员的监督和指导;并且

.3 在培训记录簿或类似的文件中予以充分记载。①

近岸航行

7 为签发限于近岸航行的证书,可从表 A-II/1 第 2 栏所列科目中删除下列科目,但应注意可能在同一水域航行的所有船舶的安全:

.1 天文航海;和

.2 不覆盖证书有效水域的电子定位和导航系统。

① 相关 IMO 示范培训课程和国际航运联合会(ISF)制定的一份类似文件可有助于编制培训记录簿。

Table A-II/1

Specification of minimum standard of competence for officers in charge of a navigational watch on ships of 500 gross tonnage or more

Function: Navigation at the operational level

Column 1	Column 2	Column 3	Column 4
Competence	**Knowledge, understanding and proficiency**	**Methods for demonstrating competence**	**Criteria for evaluating competence**
Plan and conduct a passage and determine position	*Celestial navigation* Ability to use celestial bodies to determine the ship's position *Terrestrial and coastal navigation* Ability to determine the ship's position by use of: .1 landmarks .2 aids to navigation, including lighthouses, beacons and buoys .3 dead reckoning, taking into account winds, tides, currents and estimated speed Thorough knowledge of and ability to use nautical charts, and publications, such as sailing directions, tide tables, notices to mariners, radio navigational warnings and ships' routeing information *Electronic systems of position fixing and navigation*	Examination and assessment of evidence obtained from one or more of the following: .1 approved in-service experience .2 approved training ship experience .3 approved simulator training, where appropriate .4 approved laboratory equipment training using chart catalogues, charts, nautical publications, radio navigational warnings, sextant, azimuth mirror, electronic navigation equipment, echo-sounding equipment, compass	The information obtained from nautical charts and publications is relevant, interpreted correctly and properly applied. All potential navigational hazards are accurately identified The primary method of fixing the ship's position is the most appropriate to the prevailing circumstances and conditions The position is determined within the limits of acceptable instrument/system errors The reliability of the information obtained from the primary method of position fixing is checked at appropriate intervals Calculations and measurements of navigational information are accurate The charts selected are the largest scale suitable for the area of navigation and charts and publications are corrected in accordance with the latest information available

表 A-II/1
500 总吨或以上船舶负责航行值班的高级船员的最低适任标准

职能:航行　操作级

第 1 栏	第 2 栏	第 3 栏	第 4 栏
适任	知识、理解和熟练	表明适任的方法	评价适任的标准
计划并引导航行和定位	天文航海 使用天体确定船位的能力 地文航海和沿海航行 使用下列各项确定船位的能力: .1 陆标 .2 灯塔、立标和浮标等助航标志 .3 考虑风、潮汐、流和推算船速进行航迹推算 使用海图和诸如航路指南、潮汐表、航海通告、无线电航行警告和船舶定线资料等航海出版物的全面知识和能力 电子定位和导航系统	考试并评估从下列一项或数项获取的证据: .1 认可的工作经历 .2 认可的培训船经历 .3 认可的模拟器培训,如适用 .4 认可的实验室设备培训 使用海图目录、海图、航海出版物、无线电航行警告、六分仪、方位镜、电子导航设备、回声测深仪、罗经	从海图和航海出版物获取的信息是相关的,并能正确地解释和正规地应用该信息,准确识别所有潜在的航行危险 主要定位方法最适合于当时环境和条件 确定的船位在可接受的仪器/系统误差限度内 以适当的时间间隔核查从主要定位方法获得的信息的可信性 航海信息的计算和测量是精确的 所选的海图是适合于航行区域的最大比例尺的并且海图和航海出版物已按可用的最新资料改正

Column 1	Column 2	Column 3	Column 4
Competence	**Knowledge, understanding and proficiency**	**Methods for demonstrating competence**	**Criteria for evaluating competence**
Plan and conduct a passage and determine position *(continued)*	Ability to determine the ship's position by use of electronic navigational aids *Echo-sounders* Ability to operate the equipment and apply the information correctly *Compass – magnetic and gyro* Knowledge of the principles of magnetic and gyro-compasses Ability to determine errors of the magnetic and gyro-compasses, using celestial and terrestrial means, and to allow for such errors *Steering control system* Knowledge of steering control systems, operational procedures and change-over from manual to automatic control and vice versa. Adjustment of controls for optimum performance *Meteorology* Ability to use and interpret information obtained from shipborne meteorological instruments Knowledge of the characteristics of the various weather systems, reporting procedures and recording systems		Performance checks and tests to navigation systems comply with manufacturer's recommendations and good navigational practice Errors in magnetic and gyro-compasses are determined and correctly applied to courses and bearings The selection of the mode of steering is the most suitable for the prevailing weather, sea and traffic conditions and intended manoeuvres Measurements and observations of weather conditions are accurate and appropriate to the passage

第 1 栏	第 2 栏	第 3 栏	第 4 栏
适任	知识、理解和熟练	表明适任的方法	评价适任的标准
计划并引导航行和定位(续)	使用电子助航仪器确定船位的能力 *回声测深仪* 正确操作该设备和应用所得信息的能力 *磁罗经和陀螺罗经* 磁罗经和陀螺罗经原理的知识 采用天文和地文方法确定磁罗经和陀螺罗经的误差的能力以及修正这种误差的能力 *操舵控制系统* 操舵控制系统、操作程序以及从手动转自动控制及相反操作的知识。调整控钮至最佳性能 *气象学* 使用和解释从船用气象仪器获取的信息的能力 各种天气系统的特性、报告程序和记录系统的知识 应用所获得的气象信息的能力		对导航系统的性能核对和测试符合制造商的建议和良好的航海习惯 测定磁罗经和陀螺罗经的误差并正确运用到航向和方位中 所选择的操舵方式,对于当时天气、海况和通航状况以及拟采取的操纵是最适合的 对天气情况的测量和观测是准确的并适于其航程 正确解释和运用气象资料

Column 1	Column 2	Column 3	Column 4
Competence	**Knowledge, understanding and proficiency**	**Methods for demonstrating competence**	**Criteria for evaluating competence**
Maintain a safe navigational watch	*Watchkeeping* Thorough knowledge of the content, application and intent of the International Regulations for Preventing Collisions at Sea, 1972, as amended Thorough knowledge of the Principles to be observed in keeping a navigational watch The use of routeing in accordance with the General Provisions on Ships' Routeing The use of information from navigational equipment for maintaining a safe navigational watch Knowledge of blind pilotage techniques The use of reporting in accordance with the General Principles for Ship Reporting Systems and with VTS procedures	Examination and assessment of evidence obtained from one or more of the following: .1 approved in-service experience; .2 approved training ship experience .3 approved simulator training, where appropriate .4 approved laboratory equipment training	The conduct, handover and relief of the watch conforms with accepted principles and procedures A proper look-out is maintained at all times and in such a way as to conform to accepted principles and procedures Lights, shapes and sound signals conform with the requirements contained in the International Regulations for Preventing Collisions at Sea, 1972, as amended, and are correctly recognized The frequency and extent of monitoring of traffic, the ship and the environment conform with accepted principles and procedures A proper record is maintained of the movements and activities relating to the navigation of the ship Responsibility for the safety of navigation is clearly defined at all times, including periods when the master is on the bridge and while under pilotage

第 1 栏	第 2 栏	第 3 栏	第 4 栏
适任	知识、理解和熟练	表明适任的方法	评价适任的标准
保持安全的航行值班(续)	值班 经修订的《1972 年国际海上避碰规则》的内容、应用和意图的全面知识 航行值班中应遵守的原则的全面知识 根据《船舶定线制的一般规定》使用定线制 使用来自导航设备的信息保持安全航行值班 依靠仪器引航的技术知识 根据《船舶报告制的一般原则》和 VTS 程序使用报告制	考试并评估从下列一项或数项获取的证据: .1 认可的工作经历 .2 认可的培训船经历 .3 认可的模拟器培训,如适用 .4 认可的实验室设备培训	值班、交班和接班符合公认的原则和程序 遵守公认的原则和程序,始终保持正规瞭望 号灯、号型和声号符合经修订的《1972 年国际海上避碰规则》中载明的要求并能正确辨认 监测交通、船舶和环境的频度和范围符合公认的原则和程序 对有关船舶航行的运动和活动保持正规记录 始终明确安全航行的责任,包括船长在驾驶台和船舶正在被引航期间

Column 1	Column 2	Column 3	Column 4
Competence	**Knowledge, understanding and proficiency**	**Methods for demonstrating competence**	**Criteria for evaluating competence**
Maintain a safe navigational watch *(continued)*	*Bridge resource management* Knowledge of bridge resource management principles, including: .1 allocation, assignment, and prioritization of resources .2 effective communication .3 assertiveness and leadership .4 obtaining and maintaining situational awareness .5 consideration of team experience	Assessment of evidence obtained from one or more of the following: .1 approved training .2 approved in-service experience .3 approved simulator training	Resources are allocated and assigned as needed in correct priority to perform necessary tasks Communication is clearly and unambiguously given and received Questionable decisions and/or actions result in appropriate challenge and response Effective leadership behaviours are identified Team member(s) share accurate understanding of current and predicted vessel state, navigation path, and external environment
Use of radar and ARPA to maintain safety of navigation *Note*: Training and assessment in the use of ARPA is not required for those who serve exclusively on ships not fitted with ARPA. This limitation shall be reflected in the endorsement issued to the seafarer concerned	*Radar navigation* Knowledge of the fundamentals of radar and automatic radar plotting aids (ARPA) Ability to operate and to interpret and analyse information obtained from radar, including the following: Performance, including: .1 factors affecting performance and accuracy .2 setting up and maintaining displays .3 detection of misrepresentation of information, false echoes, sea return, etc., racons and SARTs	Assessment of evidence obtained from approved radar simulator and ARPA simulator plus in-service experience	Information obtained from radar and ARPA is correctly interpreted and analysed, taking into account the limitations of the equipment and prevailing circumstances and conditions

第 1 栏	第 2 栏	第 3 栏	第 4 栏
适任	**知识、理解和熟练**	**表明适任的方法**	**评价适任的标准**
保持安全的航行值班(续)	驾驶台资源管理 驾驶台资源管理原则的知识,包括: .1 资源的分配、分派和优先排序 .2 有效的交流 .3 决断力和领导力 .4 情景意识的获得和保持 .5 考虑团队的经验	评估从下列一项或数项获取的证据: .1 认可的培训 .2 认可的工作经历 .3 认可的模拟器培训	根据需要,按正确的优先顺序分配和分派资源,以执行必要任务 交流清楚、无歧义 有疑问的决定和/或行动受到适当质疑和反应 认同有效的领导行为 团队成员对当前和预测的船舶状态、航路和外部环境有着共同的准确理解
使用雷达和自动雷达标绘仪保持航行安全 注:对仅在未配备自动雷达标绘仪(ARPA)的船上工作的人员不要求进行该设备使用方面的培训和评估。该限制应反映在给当事海员签发的签证中	雷达导航 雷达和自动雷达标绘仪(ARPA)的基本知识 操作雷达以及解释和分析雷达信息的能力,包括下列各项: 性能方面包括: .1 影响性能和精度的因素 .2 设定和保持显示 .3 探测信息错误显示、假回波和海浪杂波等,以及雷达应答器和搜救应答器	评估从认可的雷达模拟器和自动雷达标绘仪模拟器培训加上从工作经历中获取的证据	正确地解释和分析从雷达和自动雷达标绘仪获取的信息,并考虑设备的局限性以及当时环境和条件

Column 1	Column 2	Column 3	Column 4
Competence	**Knowledge, understanding and proficiency**	**Methods for demonstrating competence**	**Criteria for evaluating competence**
Use of radar and ARPA to maintain safety of navigation *(continued)* *Note*: Training and assessment in the use of ARPA is not required for those who serve exclusively on ships not fitted with ARPA. This limitation shall be reflected in the endorsement issued to the seafarer concerned	Use, including: .1 range and bearing; course and speed of other ships; time and distance of closest approach of crossing, meeting overtaking ships .2 identification of critical echoes; detecting course and speed changes of other ships; effect of changes in own ship's course or speed or both .3 application of the International Regulations for Preventing Collisions at Sea, 1972, as amended .4 plotting techniques and relative- and true-motion concepts .5 parallel indexing		Action taken to avoid a close encounter or collision with other vessels is in accordance with the International Regulations for Preventing Collisions at Sea, 1972, as amended Decisions to amend course and/or speed are both timely and in accordance with accepted navigation practice Adjustments made to the ship's course and speed maintain safety of navigation Communication is clear, concise and acknowledged at all times in a seamanlike manner Manoeuvring signals are made at the appropriate time and are in accordance with the International Regulations for Preventing Collisions at Sea, 1972, as amended

第1栏	第2栏	第3栏	第4栏
适任	知识、理解和熟练	表明适任的方法	评价适任的标准
使用雷达和自动雷达标绘仪保持航行安全(续) 注:对仅在不要求配备 ARPA 的船上的工作人员不要求进行该设备使用方面的培训和评估。该限制规定应反映在给当事海员签发的签证中	使用方面包括: .1 距离和方位;他船航向和航速;船舶交叉相遇、对遇或追越时到达最接近点的时间和距离 .2 识别重要回波;探测他船航向和航速的变化;本船航向或航速或两者都变化的影响 .3 经修订的《1972 年国际海上避碰规则》的应用 .4 标绘技术以及相对运动和真运动概念 .5 平行标线法		为避免和他船在很近距离上会遇或碰撞而采取的行动符合经修订的《1972 年国际海上避碰规则》 作出调整航向和/或航速的决定均是及时的,并遵照公认的航海习惯 调整航向和航速保持航行安全 在任何时候都清楚、简要地交流并以海员的方式确认 在适当的时刻发出操纵信号,并符合经修订的《1972 年国际海上避碰规则》

Column 1	Column 2	Column 3	Column 4
Competence	**Knowledge, understanding and proficiency**	**Methods for demonstrating competence**	**Criteria for evaluating competence**
Use of radar and ARPA to maintain safety of navigation (*continued*) *Note*: Training and assessment in the use of ARPA is not required for those who serve exclusively on ships not fitted with ARPA. This limitation shall be reflected in the endorsement issued to the seafarer concerned	Principal types of ARPA, their display characteristics, performance standards and the dangers of over-reliance on ARPA Ability to operate and to interpret and analyse information obtained from ARPA, including: .1 system performance and accuracy, tracking capabilities and limitations, and processing delays .2 use of operational warnings and system tests .3 methods of target acquisition and their limitations .4 true and relative vectors, graphic representation of target information and danger areas .5 deriving and analysing information, critical echoes, exclusion areas and trial manoeuvres		
Use of ECDIS to maintain the safety of navigation Note: Training and assessment in the use of ECDIS is not required for those who serve exclusively on ships not fitted with ECDIS These limitations shall be reflected in the endorsements issued to the seafarer concerned	*Navigation using ECDIS* Knowledge of the capability and limitations of ECDIS operations, including: .1 a thorough understanding of Electronic Navigational Chart (ENC) data, data accuracy, presentation rules, display options and other chart data formats .2 the dangers of over-reliance .3 familiarity with the functions of ECDIS	Examination and assessment of evidence obtained from one or more of the following: .1 approved training ship experience .2 approved ECDIS simulator training	Monitors information on ECDIS in a manner that contributes to safe navigation Information obtained from ECDIS (including radar overlay and/or radar tracking functions, when fitted) is correctly interpreted and analysed, taking into account the limitations of the equipment, all connected sensors (including radar and AIS where interfaced), and prevailing circumstances and conditions

第 1 栏	第 2 栏	第 3 栏	第 4 栏
适任	知识、理解和熟练	表明适任的方法	评价适任的标准
使用雷达和自动雷达标绘仪保持航行安全(续) 注:对仅在不要求配备 ARPA 的船上的工作人员不要求进行该设备使用方面的培训和评估。该限制规定应反映在给当事海员签发的签证中	自动雷达标绘仪的主要类型,其显示特点和性能标准,以及过分依赖自动雷达标绘仪的危险性 操作自动雷达标绘仪及解释和分析从该设备获取的信息的能力,包括: .1 系统性能和精度,跟踪能力和局限性,以及处理延迟 .2 工作报警和系统测试的使用 .3 录取目标的方法及其局限性 .4 真运动和相对运动矢量,目标信息和危险区域的图形显示 .5 导出和分析信息,重要回波、排除区和试操纵		
使用 ECDIS 保持航行安全 注:对仅在未配备 ECDIS 的船上工作的人员不要求进行该设备使用方面的培训和评估 该限制应反映在给当事海员签发的签证中	使用 ECDIS 导航 ECDIS 运行的性能和限制的知识,包括: .1 全面理解电子导航图(ENC)数据、数据精度、呈现规则、显示选择和其他海图数据格式 .2 过分依赖的危险性 .3 熟悉有效的性能标准所要求的 ECDIS 功能	考试并评估从下列一项或数项获取的证据: .1 认可的培训船经历 .2 认可的 ECDIS 模拟器培训	以有助于安全航行的方式监控 ECDIS 信息 正确地解释和分析从 ECDIS(包括雷达叠加和/或雷达跟踪功能,如装有)获取的信息,并考虑设备的局限性、所有相连的传感器(包括雷达和 AIS,如连接)以及当时的环境和条件

Column 1	Column 2	Column 3	Column 4
Competence	**Knowledge, understanding and proficiency**	**Methods for demonstrating competence**	**Criteria for evaluating competence**
Use of ECDIS to maintain the safety of navigation *(continued)*	required by performance standards in force Proficiency in operation, interpretation, and analysis of information obtained from ECDIS, including: .1 use of functions that are integrated with other navigation systems in various installations, including proper functioning and adjustment to desired settings .2 safe monitoring and adjustment of information, including own position, sea area display, mode and orientation, chart data displayed, route monitoring, user-created information layers, contacts (when interfaced with AIS and/or radar tracking) and radar overlay functions (when interfaced) .3 confirmation of vessel position by alternative means .4 efficient use of settings to ensure conformance to operational procedures, including alarm parameters for anti-grounding, proximity to contacts and special areas, completeness of chart data and chart update status, and backup arrangements .5 adjustment of settings and values to suit the present conditions		Safety of navigation is maintained through adjustments made to the ship's course and speed through ECDIS-controlled track-keeping functions (when fitted) Communication is clear, concise and acknowledged at all times in a seamanlike manner

第 1 栏	第 2 栏	第 3 栏	第 4 栏
适任	知识、理解和熟练	表明适任的方法	评价适任的标准
	熟练地操作、解释和分析从 ECDIS 获取的信息,包括: .1 ECDIS 与各类装置中其他导航系统集成功能的使用,包括正确使用功能和调整到所需设置 .2 安全地监视和调整信息,包括本船位置、海区显示、模式和定向、显示的海图数据、航路监视、用户创建的信息层、目标(当接入 AIS 和/或雷达跟踪时)和雷达叠加功能(当接入时) .3 使用不同方式确认船位 .4 充分使用参数设置以确保符合操作程序,包括预防搁浅、临近物标和特殊区域的报警参数,海图数据的完整性,海图更新状态和备用方案 .5 调整设置和数值以适合当前情况		通过 ECDIS 控制的航迹保持功能(如装有)调节船舶航向和航速,使船舶的航行安全得以保持 在任何时候都清楚、简要地交流并以海员的方式确认

Column 1	Column 2	Column 3	Column 4
Competence	**Knowledge, understanding and proficiency**	**Methods for demonstrating competence**	**Criteria for evaluating competence**
Use of ECDIS to maintain the safety of navigation *(continued)*	.6 situational awareness while using ECDIS including safe water and proximity of hazards, set and drift, chart data and scale selection, suitability of route, contact detection and management, and integrity of sensors		
Respond to emergencies	*Emergency procedures* Precautions for the protection and safety of passengers in emergency situations Initial action to be taken following a collision or a grounding; initial damage assessment and control Appreciation of the procedures to be followed for rescuing persons from the sea, assisting a ship in distress, responding to emergencies which arise in port	Examination and assessment of evidence obtained from one or more of the following: .1 approved in-service experience .2 approved training ship experience .3 approved simulator training, where appropriate .4 practical training	The type and scale of the emergency is promptly identified Initial actions and, if appropriate, manoeuvring of the ship are in accordance with contingency plans and are appropriate to the urgency of the situation and nature of the emergency
Respond to a distress signal at sea	*Search and rescue* Knowledge of the contents of the International Aeronautical and Maritime Search and Rescue (IAMSAR) Manual	Examination and assessment of evidence obtained from practical instruction or approved simulator training, where appropriate	The distress or emergency signal is immediately recognized Contingency plans and instructions in standing orders are implemented and complied with

第1栏	第2栏	第3栏	第4栏
适任	知识、理解和熟练	表明适任的方法	评价适任的标准
使用 ECDIS 保持安全航行(续)	.6 使用 ECDIS 时的情景意识,包括安全水域和对危险的临近程度、流向和流速、海图数据和比例尺选择、航路的适合性、物标探测和管理,以及传感器的集成性		
应急反应	*应急程序* 在紧急情况下的旅客保护和安全预防措施 碰撞或搁浅后应采取的初步措施;损害的初步评估和控制 救助落水人员、协助遇险船舶、港内应急反应应遵循的程序的了解	考试并评估从下列一项或数项获取的证据: .1 认可的工作经历 .2 认可的培训船经历 .3 认可的模拟器培训,如适用 .4 实际培训	迅速确认紧急情况的类型和范围 初始行动和船舶的操纵(如适合)符合应急计划并适合于形势的急迫性和紧急情况的性质
对海上遇险信号的反应	*搜寻和救助* 《国际航空和海上搜寻救助手册》内容的知识	考试并评估从实际训练或认可的模拟器培训(如适用)中获取的证据	立即判明遇险和应急信号 实施并遵守应急计划和常规命令中的指示

Column 1	Column 2	Column 3	Column 4
Competence	**Knowledge, understanding and proficiency**	**Methods for demonstrating competence**	**Criteria for evaluating competence**
Use the IMO Standard Marine Communication Phrases and use English in written and oral form	*English language* Adequate knowledge of the English language to enable the officer to use charts and other nautical publications, to understand meteorological information and messages concerning ship's safety and operation, to communicate with other ships, coast stations and VTS centres and to perform the officer's duties also with a multilingual crew, including the ability to use and understand the IMO Standard Marine Communication Phrases (IMO SMCP)	Examination and assessment of evidence obtained from practical instruction	English language nautical publications and messages relevant to the safety of the ship are correctly interpreted or drafted Communications are clear and understood
Transmit and receive information by visual signalling	*Visual signalling* Ability to use the International Code of Signals Ability to transmit and receive, by Morse light, distress signal SOS as specified in Annex IV of the International Regulations for Preventing Collisions at Sea, 1972, as amended, and appendix 1 of the International Code of Signals, and visual signalling of single-letter signals as also specified in the International Code of Signals	Assessment of evidence obtained from practical instruction and/or simulation	Communications within the operator's area of responsibility are consistently successful

第 1 栏	第 2 栏	第 3 栏	第 4 栏
适任	知识、理解和熟练	表明适任的方法	评价适任的标准
使用 IMO《标准航海通信用语》，以书面和口头形式使用英语	英语 足够的英语知识，使高级船员能使用海图和其他航海出版物，理解气象资料和有关船舶安全和操作的信息，并能与他船、岸台和 VTS 中心通信，以及同使用多种语言的船员一起工作时履行高级船员职责，其中包括使用并理解《IMO 标准航海通信用语》(IMO SMCP)的能力	考试并评估从实际训练中获取的证据	正确解释或起草英版航海出版物和有关船舶安全的信息 交流清楚易懂
用视觉信号发出和接收信息	视觉信号通信 使用《国际信号规则》的能力 用莫尔斯灯收发经修订的《1972 年国际海上避碰规则》附录 4 和《国际信号规则》附则 1 规定的遇险信号 SOS 以及同样在《国际信号规则》中规定的单字母信号的视觉信号的能力	评估从实际训练和/或模拟训练中获取的证据	在操作者职责范围内始终保持成功的交流

Column 1	Column 2	Column 3	Column 4
Competence	**Knowledge, understanding and proficiency**	**Methods for demonstrating competence**	**Criteria for evaluating competence**
Manoeuvre the ship	*Ship manoeuvring and handling* Knowledge of: .1 the effects of deadweight, draught, trim, speed and under-keel clearance on turning circles and stopping distances .2 the effects of wind and current on ship handling .3 manoeuvres and procedures for the rescue of person overboard .4 squat, shallow-water and similar effects .5 proper procedures for anchoring and mooring	Examination and assessment of evidence obtained from one or more of the following: .1 approved in-service experience .2 approved training ship experience .3 approved simulator training, where appropriate .4 approved training on a manned scale ship model, where appropriate	Safe operating limits of ship propulsion, steering and power systems are not exceeded in normal manoeuvres Adjustments made to the ship's course and speed to maintain safety of navigation

第 1 栏	第 2 栏	第 3 栏	第 4 栏
适任	知识、理解和熟练	表明适任的方法	评价适任的标准
操纵船舶	船舶操纵和操作 具有下列知识： .1 载重量、吃水、纵倾、航速和龙骨下水深对旋回圈和冲程的影响 .2 风、流对船舶操作的影响 .3 救助落水人员的操纵和程序 .4 船体下坐、浅水和类似影响 .5 锚泊和系泊的正确程序	考试并评估从下列一项或数项获取的证据： .1 认可的工作经历 .2 认可的培训船经历 .3 认可的模拟器培训，如适用 .4 认可的有人操纵船模的培训，如适用	在正常的操纵中，船舶推进、操舵和动力系统不超出安全操作的限度 调整船舶航向和航速保持航行安全

Function: Cargo handling and stowage at the operational level

Column 1	Column 2	Column 3	Column 4
Competence	**Knowledge, understanding and proficiency**	**Methods for demonstrating competence**	**Criteria for evaluating competence**
Monitor the loading, stowage, securing, care during the voyage and the unloading of cargoes	*Cargo handling, stowage and securing* Knowledge of the effect of cargo, including heavy lifts, on the seaworthiness and stability of the ship Knowledge of safe handling, stowage and securing of cargoes, including dangerous, hazardous and harmful cargoes, and their effect on the safety of life and of the ship Ability to establish and maintain effective communications during loading and unloading	Examination and assessment of evidence obtained from one or more of the following: .1 approved in-service experience .2 approved training ship experience .3 approved simulator training, where appropriate	Cargo operations are carried out in accordance with the cargo plan or other documents and established safety rules/regulations, equipment operating instructions and shipboard stowage limitations The handling of dangerous, hazardous and harmful cargoes complies with international regulations and recognized standards and codes of safe practice Communications are clear, understood and consistently successful
Inspect and report defects and damage to cargo spaces, hatch covers and ballast tanks	Knowledge* and ability to explain where to look for damage and defects most commonly encountered due to: .1 loading and unloading operations .2 corrosion .3 severe weather conditions Ability to state which parts of the ship shall be inspected each time in order to cover all parts within a given period of time Identify those elements of the ship structure which are critical to the safety of the ship	Examination and assessment of evidence obtained from one or more of the following: .1 approved in-service experience .2 approved training ship experience .3 approved simulator training, where appropriate	The inspections are carried out in accordance with laid-down procedures, and defects and damage are detected and properly reported Where no defects or damage are detected, the evidence from testing and examination clearly indicates adequate competence in adhering to procedures and ability to distinguish between normal and defective or damaged parts of the ship

* It should be understood that deck officers need not be qualified in the survey of ships.

职能:货物装卸和积载　操作级

第 1 栏	第 2 栏	第 3 栏	第 4 栏
适任	**知识、理解和熟练**	**表明适任的方法**	**评价适任的标准**
监控装货、积载、系固、航行中货物照管和卸货	货物装卸、积载和系固 货物(包括大件货)对船舶适航性和稳性的影响的知识 货物(包括危险和有害货物)安全装卸、积载和系固及其对人命和船舶安全的影响的知识 建立和保持装卸货期间有效交流的能力	考试并评估从下列一项或数项获取的证据: .1　认可的工作经历 .2　认可的培训船经历 .3　认可的模拟器培训,如适用	按照配载图或其他文件、所制定的安全规则、设备操作规程和船舶积载限制进行货物操作 按照国际规则和公认的安全操作标准和规则装卸危险和有害货物 交流清楚、易懂且持续有效
检查和报告货舱、舱盖和压载舱的缺陷和损坏	解释何处寻找下列情况引起的最常遇到的损坏和缺陷的知识①和能力: .1　装卸操作 .2　腐蚀 .3　恶劣天气条件 陈述为在给定期限内检查完所有部件每次应检查哪些部件的能力 确认对船舶安全至关重要的船舶结构部件	考试并评估从下列一项或数项获取的证据: .1　认可的工作经历 .2　认可的培训船经历 .3　认可的模拟器培训,如适用	按照规定的程序进行检查,探查到缺陷和损坏并正确报告 如未探查到缺陷或损坏,从测试和考试中获取的证据清楚地显示出在区别正常的、有缺陷的或损坏的船舶部件的程序和能力方面充分适任

① 应该理解为甲板部高级船员不必具有船舶检验的资格。

Column 1	Column 2	Column 3	Column 4
Competence	**Knowledge, understanding and proficiency**	**Methods for demonstrating competence**	**Criteria for evaluating competence**
Inspect and report defects and damage to cargo spaces, hatch covers and ballast tanks (*continued*)	State the causes of corrosion in cargo spaces and ballast tanks and how corrosion can be identified and prevented Knowledge of procedures on how the inspections shall be carried out Ability to explain how to ensure reliable detection of defects and damages Understanding of the purpose of the "enhanced survey programme"		

第 1 栏	第 2 栏	第 3 栏	第 4 栏
适任	知识、理解和熟练	表明适任的方法	评价适任的标准
检查和报告货舱、舱盖和压载舱的缺陷和损坏(续)	陈述货舱和压载舱腐蚀的原因及如何识别和防止腐蚀 如何实施检查程序的知识 解释如何确保可靠地探查缺陷和损坏的能力 理解“加强检验计划”的用途		

Function: Controlling the operation of the ship and care for persons on board at the operational level

Column 1	Column 2	Column 3	Column 4
Competence	**Knowledge, understanding and proficiency**	**Methods for demonstrating competence**	**Criteria for evaluating competence**
Ensure compliance with pollution-prevention requirements	*Prevention of pollution of the marine environment and anti-pollution procedures* Knowledge of the precautions to be taken to prevent pollution of the marine environment Anti-pollution procedures and all associated equipment Importance of proactive measures to protect the marine environment	Examination and assessment of evidence obtained from one or more of the following: .1 approved in-service experience .2 approved training ship experience .3 approved training	Procedures for monitoring shipboard operations and ensuring compliance with MARPOL requirements are fully observed Actions to ensure that a positive environmental reputation is maintained
Maintain seaworthiness of the ship	*Ship stability* Working knowledge and application of stability, trim and stress tables, diagrams and stress-calculating equipment Understanding of fundamental actions to be taken in the event of partial loss of intact buoyancy Understanding of the fundamentals of watertight integrity *Ship construction* General knowledge of the principal structural members of a ship and the proper names for the various parts	Examination and assessment of evidence obtained from one or more of the following: .1 approved in-service experience .2 approved training ship experience .3 approved simulator training, where appropriate .4 approved laboratory equipment training	The stability conditions comply with the IMO intact stability criteria under all conditions of loading Actions to ensure and maintain the watertight integrity of the ship are in accordance with accepted practice
Prevent, control and fight fires on board	*Fire prevention and fire-fighting appliances* Ability to organize fire drills Knowledge of classes and chemistry of fire Knowledge of fire-fighting systems	Assessment of evidence obtained from approved fire-fighting training and experience as set out in section A-VI/3	The type and scale of the problem is promptly identified and initial actions conform with the emergency procedure and contingency plans for the ship Evacuation, emergency shutdown and isolation

职能:船舶作业管理和人员管理　操作级

第 1 栏	第 2 栏	第 3 栏	第 4 栏
适任	**知识、理解和熟练**	**表明适任的方法**	**评价适任的标准**
确保遵守防污染要求	防止海洋环境污染和防污染程序 为防止海洋环境污染采取的预防措施的知识 防污染程序和所有附属设备 采取积极措施保护海洋环境的重要性	考试并评估从下列一项或数项获取的证据: .1 认可的工作经历 .2 认可的培训船经历 .3 认可的培训	完全遵守有关船上操作监控及确保符合《MARPOL 公约》要求的程序 采取行动旨在确保保持良好的环保声誉
保持船舶的适航性	船舶稳性 稳性、吃水差、强度图表和强度计算仪器的实用知识和应用 了解一旦丧失部分完整浮力时应采取的基本行动 了解水密完整性的基本知识 船舶构造 船舶主要构件和各种部件的正确名称的一般知识	考试并评估从下列一项或数项获取的证据: .1 认可的工作经历 .2 认可的培训船经历 .3 认可的模拟器培训,如适用 .4 认可的实验室设备培训	在各种装载条件下稳性状况达到 IMO 完整稳性标准 按照公认的做法采取保证和维持船舶水密完整性的行动
船上防火、控制火灾和灭火	防火和灭火设备 组织消防演习的能力 火的种类和化学性质的知识 灭火系统的知识	评估从第 A-VI/3 节规定的认可的消防培训和经历中获取的证据	迅速确定问题的类型和范围,初始行动符合船舶应急程序和意外事故应急计划 撤离、应急关闭和隔离程序适合紧急情况的性质,并迅速实施

Column 1	Column 2	Column 3	Column 4
Competence	**Knowledge, understanding and proficiency**	**Methods for demonstrating competence**	**Criteria for evaluating competence**
	Knowledge of action to be taken in the event of fire, including fires involving oil systems		procedures are appropriate to the nature of the emergency and are implemented promptly The order of priority and the levels and time-scales of making reports and informing personnel on board are relevant to the nature of the emergency and reflect the urgency of the problem
Operate life-saving appliances	*Life-saving* Ability to organize abandon ship drills and knowledge of the operation of survival craft and rescue boats, their launching appliances and arrangements, and their equipment, including radio life-saving appliances, satellite EPIRBs, SARTs, immersion suits and thermal protective aids	Assessment of evidence obtained from approved training and experience as set out in section A-VI/2, paragraphs 1 to 4	Actions in responding to abandon ship and survival situations are appropriate to the prevailing circumstances and conditions and comply with accepted safety practices and standards
Apply medical first aid on board ship	*Medical aid* Practical application of medical guides and advice by radio, including the ability to take effective action based on such knowledge in the case of accidents or illnesses that are likely to occur on board ship	Assessment of evidence obtained from approved training as set out in section A-VI/4, paragraphs 1 to 3	The identification of probable cause, nature and extent of injuries or conditions is prompt and treatment minimizes immediate threat to life
Monitor compliance with legislative requirements	Basic working knowledge of the relevant IMO conventions concerning safety of life at sea, security and protection of the marine environment	Assessment of evidence obtained from examination or approved training	Legislative requirements relating to safety of life at sea, security and protection of the marine environment are correctly identified

第1栏	第2栏	第3栏	第4栏
适任	知识、理解和熟练	表明适任的方法	评价适任的标准
	一旦失火，包括涉及油类系统的火灾，应采取的行动的知识		作出报告和通知船上人员的优先顺序、级别和时限与紧急情况的性质相关，并反映事态的紧急程度
操作救生设备	救生 组织弃船演习的能力和操作救生艇筏、救助艇及其释放装置和设备，包括无线电救生设备、卫星应急无线电示位标、搜救应答器、救生服和保暖用具在内的知识	评估从 A-VI/2 节第 1 段至第 4 段规定的认可的培训和经历中获取的证据	弃船和求生情况下的应急行动适合于当时的环境和条件，并符合公认的安全做法和标准
在船上应用医疗急救	医护 医疗指南和无线电咨询的实际应用，包括根据这种知识对船上可能发生的事故或疾病采取有效行动的能力	评估从 A-VI/4 节第 1 段至第 3 段规定的认可的培训中获取的证据	迅速确认伤病的可能原因、性质和程度，采取治疗以尽量减少对生命的直接威胁
监督遵守法定要求	涉及海上人命安全和保护海洋环境的 IMO 有关公约的基本实用知识	评估从考试或认可的培训中获取的证据	正确确认有关海上人命安全、保安和保护海洋环境的法定要求

Column 1	Column 2	Column 3	Column 4
Competence	**Knowledge, understanding and proficiency**	**Methods for demonstrating competence**	**Criteria for evaluating competence**
Application of leadership and teamworking skills	Working knowledge of shipboard personnel management and training A knowledge of related international maritime conventions and recommendations, and national legislation Ability to apply task and workload management, including: .1 planning and co-ordination .2 personnel assignment .3 time and resource constraints .4 prioritization	Assessment of evidence obtained from one or more of the following: .1 approved training .2 approved in-service experience .3 practical demonstration	The crew are allocated duties and informed of expected standards of work and behaviour in a manner appropriate to the individuals concerned Training objectives and activities are based on assessment of current competence and capabilities and operational requirements Operations are demonstrated to be in accordance with applicable rules
	Knowledge and ability to apply effective resource management: .1 allocation, assignment, and prioritization of resources .2 effective communication onboard and ashore .3 decisions reflect consideration of team experiences .4 assertiveness and leadership, including motivation .5 obtaining and maintaining situational awareness		Operations are planned and resources are allocated as needed in correct priority to perform necessary tasks Communication is clearly and unambiguously given and received Effective leadership behaviours are demonstrated Necessary team member(s) share accurate understanding of current and predicted vessel status and operational status and external environment Decisions are most effective for the situation

第 1 栏	第 2 栏	第 3 栏	第 4 栏
适任	知识、理解和熟练	表明适任的方法	评价适任的标准
领导力和团队工作技能的运用	船上人员管理和培训的实用知识 有关国际海事公约和建议案以及国内法规的知识 运用任务和工作量管理的能力,包括: .1 计划和协调 .2 人员分派 .3 时间和资源的限制 .4 优先排序 运用有效资源管理的知识和能力: .1 资源的分配、分派和优先排序 .2 船上和岸上的有效沟通 .3 决策反映出对团队经验的考虑 .4 决断力和领导力,包括激励 .5 具有并保持情景意识	评估从下列一项或数项获取的证据: .1 认可的培训 .2 认可的工作经历 .3 实际演示	分配船员工作,并以适合相关个人的方式告知所要求的工作标准和行为准则 培训目标和培训活动基于对目前适任性和能力的评估和操作要求 表明操作符合适用的规则 操作有计划并根据需要按正确的优先顺序分配资源,以执行必要的任务 交流清楚、无歧义 表明有效的领导行为 必要的团队成员对当前和预测的船舶和操作的状态及外部环境有共同的准确的理解 决策对于局面最有效

Column 1	Column 2	Column 3	Column 4
Competence	**Knowledge, understanding and proficiency**	**Methods for demonstrating competence**	**Criteria for evaluating competence**
Application of leadership and teamworking skills *(continued)*	Knowledge and ability to apply decision-making techniques: .1 situation and risk assessment .2 identify and consider generated options .3 selecting course of action .4 evaluation of outcome effectiveness		
Contribute to the safety of personnel and ship	Knowledge of personal survival techniques Knowledge of fire prevention and ability to fight and extinguish fires Knowledge of elementary first aid Knowledge of personal safety and social responsibilities	Assessment of evidence obtained from approved training and experience as set out in section A-VI/1, paragraph 2	Appropriate safety and protective equipment is correctly used Procedures and safe working practices designed to safeguard personnel and the ship are observed at all times Procedures designed to safeguard the environment are observed at all times Initial and follow-up action on becoming aware of an emergency conforms with established emergency response procedures

第 1 栏	第 2 栏	第 3 栏	第 4 栏
适任	知识、理解和熟练	表明适任的方法	评价适任的标准
领导力和团队工作技能的运用(续)	运用决策技能的知识和能力: .1 局面和风险评估 .2 识别并考虑形成的选项 .3 选择行动过程 .4 评价结果的有效性		
有助于人员和船舶的安全	个人求生技能的知识 防火知识和灭火能力 基本急救的知识 个人安全和社会责任的知识	评估从第 A-VI/1 节第 2 段规定的认可的培训和经历中获取的证据	正确使用适当的安全和防护设备 始终遵守为保护人员和船舶而制定的程序和安全工作做法 始终遵守为保护环境而制定的程序 意识到紧急情况时的初始和后续行动符合既定的应急反应程序

Section A-II/2

Mandatory minimum requirements for certification of masters and chief mates on ships of 500 gross tonnage or more

Standard of competence

1 Every candidate for certification as master or chief mate of ships of 500 gross tonnage or more shall be required to demonstrate the competence to undertake, at the management level, the tasks, duties and responsibilities listed in column 1 of table A-II/2.

2 The minimum knowledge, understanding and proficiency required for certification is listed in column 2 of table A-II/2. This incorporates, expands and extends in depth the subjects listed in column 2 of table A-II/1 for officers in charge of a navigational watch.

3 Bearing in mind that the master has ultimate responsibility for the safety and security of the ship, its passengers, crew and cargo, and for the protection of the marine environment against pollution by the ship, and that a chief mate shall be in a position to assume that responsibility at any time, assessment in these subjects shall be designed to test their ability to assimilate all available information that affects the safety and security of the ship, its passengers, crew or cargo, or the protection of the marine environment.

4 The level of knowledge of the subjects listed in column 2 of table A-II/2 shall be sufficient to enable the candidate to serve in the capacity of master or chief mate*.

5 The level of theoretical knowledge, understanding and proficiency required under the different sections in column 2 of table A-II/2 may be varied according to whether the certificate is to be valid for ships of 3,000 gross tonnage or more or for ships of between 500 gross tonnage and 3,000 gross tonnage.

6 Training and experience to achieve the necessary level of theoretical knowledge, understanding and proficiency shall take into account the relevant requirements of this part and the guidance given in part B of this Code.

7 Every candidate for certification shall be required to provide evidence of having achieved the required standard of competence in accordance with the methods for demonstrating competence and criteria for evaluating competence tabulated in columns 3 and 4 of table A-II/2.

Near-coastal voyages

8 An Administration may issue a certificate restricted to service on ships engaged exclusively on near-coastal voyages and, for the issue of such a certificate, may exclude such subjects as are not applicable to the waters or ships concerned, bearing in mind the effect on the safety of all ships which may be operating in the same waters.

* The relevant IMO Model Course(s) may be of assistance in the preparation of courses.

第 A-II/2 节

对 500 总吨或以上船舶的船长和大副发证的强制性最低要求

适任标准

1　每个申请500总吨或以上船舶的船长和大副证书的申请人，应按要求表明承担表 A-II/2 第1栏所列的管理级的任务、职责和责任的适任能力。

2　发证所要求的最低的知识、理解和熟练列于表 A-II/2 第2栏中。其内容包括、扩大和加深了表 A-II/1 第2栏所列的对负责航行值班的高级船员的科目。

3　切记船长对船舶、旅客、船员和货物的安全和保安以及保护海洋环境免受船舶污染负有最高责任，而大副则应处于随时承担这种责任的地位；因此，对这些科目的评估应旨在考查他们从影响船舶、旅客、船员或货物安全和保安或保护海洋环境的一切可用的资料中吸收知识的能力。

4　表 A-II/2 第2栏所列各科目的知识水平，应足以能使证书申请人在船长或大副职位上服务①。

5　表 A-II/2 第2栏不同部分所要求的理论知识、理解和熟练的水平，可按照证书对3 000总吨或以上船舶和对500至3 000总吨船舶的有效与否而有所不同。

6　为获取所需水平的理论知识、理解和熟练的培训和经验，应考虑本规则本部分的有关要求和 B 部分给予的指导。

7　每个证书申请人应依照表 A-II/2 第3栏和第4栏所列的表明适任的方法和评价适任的标准，提供已达到所要求的适任标准的证据。

近岸航行

8　主管机关可签发一种从事近岸航行船舶上服务的证书。签发该类证书，可删去不适用于当事水域或当事船舶的那些科目，但要注意对可能在同一水域航行的所有船舶的安全的影响。

① 相关 IMO 示范培训课程可有助于准备课程。

Table A-II/2

Specification of minimum standard of competence for masters and chief mates on ships of 500 gross tonnage or more

Function: Navigation at the management level

Column 1	Column 2	Column 3	Column 4
Competence	**Knowledge, understanding and proficiency**	**Methods for demonstrating competence**	**Criteria for evaluating competence**
Plan a voyage and conduct navigation	Voyage planning and navigation for all conditions by acceptable methods of plotting ocean tracks, taking into account, e.g.: .1 restricted waters .2 meteorological conditions .3 ice .4 restricted visibility .5 traffic separation schemes .6 vessel traffic service (VTS) areas .7 areas of extensive tidal effects Routeing in accordance with the General Provisions on Ships' Routeing Reporting in accordance with the General principles for Ship Reporting Systems and with VTS procedures	Examination and assessment of evidence obtained from one or more of the following: .1 approved in-service experience .2 approved simulator training, where appropriate .3 approved laboratory equipment training using: chart catalogues, charts, nautical publications and ship particulars	The equipment, charts and nautical publications required for the voyage are enumerated and appropriate to the safe conduct of the voyage The reasons for the planned route are supported by facts and statistical data obtained from relevant sources and publications Positions, courses, distances and time calculations are correct within accepted accuracy standards for navigational equipment All potential navigational hazards are accurately identified
Determine position and the accuracy of resultant position fix by any means	Position determination in all conditions: .1 by celestial observations .2 by terrestrial observations, including the ability to use appropriate charts, notices to mariners and other publications to assess the accuracy of the resulting position fix .3 using modern electronic	Examination and assessment of evidence obtained from one or more of the following: .1 approved in-service experience .2 approved simulator training, where appropriate .3 approved laboratory equipment training	The primary method chosen for fixing the ship's position is the most appropriate to the prevailing circumstances and conditions The fix obtained by celestial observations is within accepted accuracy levels The fix obtained by terrestrial observations is

表 A-II/2
500 总吨或以上船舶的船长和大副的最低适任标准

职能:航行 管理级

第 1 栏	第 2 栏	第 3 栏	第 4 栏
适任	知识、理解和熟练	表明适任的方法	评价适任的标准
制定航次计划并引导航行	通过可接受的标绘远洋航线的方法制定航次计划和各种条件下的航行,并考虑: .1 受限水域 .2 气象条件 .3 冰况 .4 能见度不良 .5 分道通航制 .6 船舶交通管理(VTS)区域 .7 潮汐影响大的区域 按照《船舶定线制的一般规定》确定航线 按照《船舶报告制的一般原则》和 VTS 程序进行报告	考试并评估从下列一项或数项获取的证据: .1 认可的工作经历 .2 认可的模拟器培训,如适用 .3 认可的实验室设备培训 使用海图目录、海图、航海出版物和船舶资料	列举航次所需的设备、海图和航海出版物,并与安全地引导航行相适应 用从有关资料和出版物获取的事实和统计数据来支持所计划的航线的依据 正确计算船位、航向、航程和时间,并处于公认的助航设备精度标准之内 准确地判明所有潜在的航行危险
定位和确定各种定位方法获取的最终船位的精度	在各种条件下定位: .1 利用天文观测 .2 利用地文观测,包括使用适当的海图、航海通告和其他航海出版物,以判断最终所得船位的精度的能力 .3 使用现代电子助航仪器,具有其操作原理、局限性、误差源、错误信息的检测和获得准确船位的纠正方法等专门知识	考试并评估从下列一项或数项获取的证据: .1 认可的工作经历 .2 认可的模拟器培训,如适用 .3 认可的实验室设备培训	所选的主要船舶定位方法最适合于当时环境和条件 利用天文观测获得的船位在公认的精度范围内 利用地文观测获得的船位在公认的精度范围内

Column 1	Column 2	Column 3	Column 4
Competence	**Knowledge, understanding and proficiency**	**Methods for demonstrating competence**	**Criteria for evaluating competence**
	navigational aids, with specific knowledge of their operating principles, limitations, sources of error, detection of misrepresentation of information and methods of correction to obtain accurate position fixing	using: .1 charts, nautical almanac, plotting sheets, chronometer, sextant and a calculator .2 charts, nautical publications and navigational instruments (azimuth mirror, sextant, log, sounding equipment, compass) and manufacturers' manuals .3 radar, terrestrial electronic position-fixing systems, satellite navigation systems and appropriate nautical charts and publications	within accepted accuracy levels The accuracy of the resulting fix is properly assessed The fix obtained by the use of electronic navigational aids is within the accuracy standards of the systems in use. The possible errors affecting the accuracy of the resulting position are stated and methods of minimizing the effects of system errors on the resulting position are properly applied
Determine and allow for compass errors	Ability to determine and allow for errors of the magnetic and gyro-compasses Knowledge of the principles of magnetic and gyro-compasses An understanding of systems under the control of the master gyro and a knowledge of the operation and care of the main types of gyro-compass	Examination and assessment of evidence obtained from one or more of the following: .1 approved in-service experience .2 approved simulator training, where appropriate .3 approved laboratory equipment training using: celestial observations, terrestrial bearings and comparison between magnetic and gyro-compasses	The method and frequency of checks for errors of magnetic and gyro-compasses ensures accuracy of information

第 1 栏	第 2 栏	第 3 栏	第 4 栏
适任	知识、理解和熟练	表明适任的方法	评价适任的标准
		使用: .1 海图、航海天文历、雷达作图纸、天文钟、六分仪和计算器 .2 海图、航海出版物、航海仪器(方位镜、六分仪、计程仪、测深设备、罗经)和厂家手册 .3 雷达、地面电子定位系统、卫星导航系统和有关海图和出版物	正确地评估最终船位的精度 使用电子助航设备获得的船位在所用系统的精度标准内。说明影响最终船位精度的可能误差,以及正确应用减少影响最终船位的系统误差的方法
测定和修正罗经差	测定和修正磁罗经和陀螺罗经误差的能力 磁罗经和陀螺罗经原理的知识 了解主罗经控制下的系统和主要类型陀螺罗经的操作和保养知识	考试并评估从下列一项或数项获取的证据: .1 认可的工作经历 .2 认可的模拟器培训,如适用 .3 认可的实验室设备培训 使用天文观测、陆标方位以及磁罗经和陀螺罗经之间的比较	测定磁罗经和陀螺罗经误差的方法和频度能保证有关信息的精度

Column 1	Column 2	Column 3	Column 4
Competence	**Knowledge, understanding and proficiency**	**Methods for demonstrating competence**	**Criteria for evaluating competence**
Coordinate search and rescue operations	A thorough knowledge of and ability to apply the procedures contained in the International Aeronautical and Maritime Search and Rescue (IAMSAR) Manual	Examination and assessment of evidence obtained from one or more of the following: .1 approved in-service experience .2 approved simulator training, where appropriate .3 approved laboratory equipment training using: relevant publications, charts, meteorological data, particulars of ships involved, radiocommunication equipment and other available facilities and one or more of the following: .1 approved SAR training course .2 approved simulator training, where appropriate .3 approved laboratory equipment training	The plan for coordinating search and rescue operations is in accordance with international guidelines and standards Radiocommunications are established and correct communication procedures are followed at all stages of the search and rescue operations
Establish watchkeeping arrangements and procedures	Thorough knowledge of content, application and intent of the International Regulations for Preventing Collisions at Sea, 1972, as amended Thorough knowledge of the content, application and intent of the Principles to be observed in keeping a navigational watch	Examination and assessment of evidence obtained from one or more of the following: .1 approved in-service experience .2 approved simulator training, where appropriate	Watchkeeping arrangements and procedures are established and maintained in compliance with international regulations and guidelines so as to ensure the safety of navigation, protection of the marine environment and safety of the ship and persons on board

第 1 栏	第 2 栏	第 3 栏	第 4 栏
适任	知识、理解和熟练	表明适任的方法	评价适任的标准
协调搜寻和救助作业	IMO《国际航空和海上搜寻救助手册》中程序的全面知识和应用该程序的能力	考试并评估从下列一项或数项获取的证据： .1 认可的工作经历 .2 认可的模拟器培训，如适用 .3 认可的实验室设备培训 使用有关的出版物、海图、气象数据、当事船舶的技术资料、无线电通信设备和其他可用的设施以及下列一项或数项： .1 认可的搜救培训课程 .2 认可的模拟器培训，如适用 .3 认可的实验室设备培训	协调搜救作业计划符合国际指南和标准 建立无线电通信，并在搜救作业所有阶段遵循正确的通信程序
制定值班安排和程序	经修订的《1972 年国际海上避碰规则》的内容、应用和意图的全面的知识 航行值班中应遵守的基本原则的内容、应用和意图的全面的知识	考试并评估从下列一项或数项获取的证据： .1 认可的工作经历 .2 认可的模拟器培训，如适用	按照国际规则和指南制定并保持值班安排和程序，从而保证航行安全，保护海洋环境以及船舶和船上人员的安全

Column 1	Column 2	Column 3	Column 4
Competence	**Knowledge, understanding and proficiency**	**Methods for demonstrating competence**	**Criteria for evaluating competence**
Maintain safe navigation through the use of information from navigation equipment and systems to assist command decision making *Note*: Training and assessment in the use of ARPA is not required for those who serve exclusively on ships not fitted with ARPA. This limitation shall be reflected in the endorsement issued to the seafarer concerned	An appreciation of system errors and thorough understanding of the operational aspects of navigational systems Blind pilotage planning Evaluation of navigational information derived from all sources, including radar and ARPA, in order to make and implement command decisions for collision avoidance and for directing the safe navigation of the ship The interrelationship and optimum use of all navigational data available for conducting navigation	Examination and assessment of evidence obtained from approved ARPA simulator and one or more of the following: .1 approved in-service experience .2 approved simulator training, where appropriate .3 approved laboratory equipment training	Information obtained from navigation equipment and systems is correctly interpreted and analysed, taking into account the limitations of the equipment and prevailing circumstances and conditions Action taken to avoid a close encounter or collision with another vessel is in accordance with the International Regulations for Preventing Collisions at Sea, 1972, as amended
Maintain the safety of navigation through the use of ECDIS and associated navigation systems to assist command decision making Note: Training and assessment in the use of ECDIS is not required for those who serve exclusively on ships not fitted with ECDIS. This limitation shall be reflected in the endorsement issued to the seafarer concerned	Management of operational procedures, system files and data, including: .1 manage procurement, licensing and updating of chart data and system software to conform to established procedures .2 system and information updating, including the ability to update ECDIS system version in accordance with vendor's product development .3 create and maintain system configuration and backup files .4 create and maintain log files in accordance with established procedures .5 create and maintain route plan files in accordance with established procedures	Assessment of evidence obtained from one of the following: .1 approved in-service experience .2 approved training ship experience .3 approved ECDIS simulator training	Operational procedures for using ECDIS are established, applied, and monitored Actions taken to minimize risk to safety of navigation

第 1 栏	第 2 栏	第 3 栏	第 4 栏
适任	知识、理解和熟练	表明适任的方法	评价适任的标准
通过使用协助指挥决策的从导航设备和系统获得的信息,保持航行安全 注:对仅在未配备 ARPA 的船上工作人员的不要求进行该设备使用方面的培训和评估。该限制应反映在给当事海员签发的签证中	懂得系统的误差,全面了解导航系统的操作原理 依靠仪器引航计划 为了作出并实施避碰指挥决策和指挥船舶安全航行,评价从所有来源(包括雷达和自动雷达标绘仪)获取的导航信息 引导航行可用的所有导航数据的内在关系和最佳运用	考试并评估从认可的自动雷达标绘仪模拟器以及下列一项或数项获取的证据: .1 认可的工作经历 .2 认可的模拟器培训,如适用 .3 认可的实验室设备培训	正确解释和分析从导航设备和系统中获得的信息,并考虑到该设备的局限性和当时的环境和条件 为避免和他船在很近距离上会遇或碰撞而采取的行动符合经修订的《1972 年国际海上避碰规则》
通过使用协助指挥决策的 ECDIS 和关联导航系统,保持航行安全 注:对仅在未配备 ECDIS 的船上工作人员的不要求进行该设备使用方面的培训和评估。该限制应反映在给当事海员签发的签证中	操作程序、系统文件和数据的管理,包括: .1 管理海图数据和系统软件的采购、许可和更新,以符合既定的程序 .2 系统和信息更新,包括依据厂商产品开发更新 ECDIS 系统版本的能力 .3 创建和维护系统配置和备份文件 .4 依据既定的程序创建和维护运行记录文件 .5 依据既定的程序创建和维护航线计划文件	评估从下列一项获取的证据: .1 认可的工作经历 .2 认可的培训船经历 .3 认可的 ECDIS 模拟器培训	使用 ECDIS 的操作程序得以建立、应用和监控 采取尽量减少航行安全风险的行动

Column 1	Column 2	Column 3	Column 4
Competence	**Knowledge, understanding and proficiency**	**Methods for demonstrating competence**	**Criteria for evaluating competence**
	.6 use ECDIS log-book and track history functions for inspection of system functions, alarm settings and user responses Use ECDIS playback functionality for passage review, route planning and review of system functions		
Forecast weather and oceanographic conditions	Ability to understand and interpret a synoptic chart and to forecast area weather, taking into account local weather conditions and information received by weather fax Knowledge of the characteristics of various weather systems, including tropical revolving storms and avoidance of storm centres and the dangerous quadrants Knowledge of ocean current systems Ability to calculate tidal conditions Use all appropriate nautical publications on tides and currents	Examination and assessment of evidence obtained from one or more of the following: .1 approved in-service experience .2 approved laboratory equipment training	The likely weather conditions predicted for a determined period are based on all available information Actions taken to maintain safety of navigation minimize any risk to safety of the ship Reasons for intended action are backed by statistical data and observations of the actual weather conditions
Respond to navigational emergencies	Precautions when beaching a ship Action to be taken if grounding is imminent, and after grounding Refloating a grounded ship with and without assistance Action to be taken if collision is imminent and following a collision or impairment of the watertight integrity of the hull by any cause	Examination and assessment of evidence obtained from practical instruction, in-service experience and practical drills in emergency procedures	The type and scale of any problem is promptly identified and decisions and actions minimize the effects of any malfunction of the ship's systems Communications are effective and comply with established procedures Decisions and actions maximize safety of persons on board

第 1 栏	第 2 栏	第 3 栏	第 4 栏
适任	知识、理解和熟练	表明适任的方法	评价适任的标准
	.6 使用 ECDIS 日志和航迹历史功能，检查系统功能、警报设定和用户反应 使用 ECDIS 回放功能进行航行审查、航线设计和系统功能的审查		
预报天气和海洋水文状况	考虑到当地天气条件和用气象传真收到的信息，理解和解释天气图并预报地区天气的能力 各种天气系统特性的知识，包括热带风暴及避开风暴中心和危险象限的知识 洋流系统的知识 计算潮汐状况的能力 使用所有适当的关于潮汐和流的航海出版物	考试并评估从下列一项或数项获取的证据： .1 认可的工作经历 .2 认可的实验室设备培训	基于所有可用的信息，预测给定时间段的可能的天气状况 采取保持航行安全的行动，减少对船舶安全的任何风险 拟采取行动的理由基于统计数据和对实际天气状况的观测
航行中的应急反应	船舶抢滩时的注意事项 搁浅前后应采取的措施 在有或无外来协助情况下使搁浅船脱浅 在碰撞前后或无论何种原因造成船体的水密完整性受损时应采取的措施	考试并评估从实际训练、工作经历和应急程序的实际演习中获取的证据	迅速确定紧急情况的种类和范围，作出决定并采取行动以减小船舶系统任何故障的影响 通信有效且遵守规定的程序 作出的决定和采取的行动能最大限度地保证船上人员的安全

Column 1	Column 2	Column 3	Column 4
Competence	**Knowledge, understanding and proficiency**	**Methods for demonstrating competence**	**Criteria for evaluating competence**
	Assessment of damage control Emergency steering Emergency towing arrangements and towing procedure		
Manoeuvre and handle a ship in all conditions	Manoeuvring and handling a ship in all conditions, including: .1 manoeuvres when approaching pilot stations and embarking or disembarking pilots, with due regard to weather, tide, headreach and stopping distances .2 handling ship in rivers, estuaries and restricted waters, having regard to the effects of current, wind and restricted water on helm response .3 application of constant-rate-of-turn techniques .4 manoeuvring in shallow water, including the reduction in under-keel clearance caused by squat, rolling and pitching .5 interaction between passing ships and between own ship and nearby banks (canal effect) .6 berthing and unberthing under various conditions of wind, tide and current with and without tugs .7 ship and tug interaction .8 use of propulsion and manoeuvring systems	Examination and assessment of evidence obtained from one or more of the following: .1 approved in-service experience .2 approved simulator training, where appropriate .3 approved manned scale ship model, where appropriate	All decisions concerning berthing and anchoring are based on a proper assessment of the ship's manoeuvring and engine characteristics and the forces to be expected while berthed alongside or lying at anchor While under way, a full assessment is made of possible effects of shallow and restricted waters, ice, banks, tidal conditions, passing ships and own ship's bow and stern wave so that the ship can be safely manoeuvred under various conditions of loading and weather

第 1 栏	第 2 栏	第 3 栏	第 4 栏
适任	知识、理解和熟练	表明适任的方法	评价适任的标准
	损害控制的评估 应急操舵 应急拖带安排和拖带程序		
在各种条件下操纵和操作船舶	在各种条件下操纵和操作船舶,包括: .1 在接近引航站和引航员登、离船时的船舶操纵,特别注意天气、潮汐、淌航距离和冲程 .2 在河道、江河口和受限水域操作船舶,注意流、风和受限水域对舵效的影响 .3 恒定旋回速率技术的运用 .4 浅水中的船舶操纵,包括由于船体下坐、横摇和纵摇的影响而造成龙骨下富余水深的减少 .5 会船时船与船之间以及本船与附近岸边之间的相互作用(运河效应) .6 在各种不同的风、潮汐和水流条件下,使用或不使用拖船靠离泊位 .7 船与拖船的相互作用 .8 推进和操纵系统的使用	考试并评估从下列一项或数项获取的证据: .1 认可的工作经历 .2 认可的模拟器培训,如适用 .3 认可的有人操纵的船模培训,如适用	基于对船舶操纵和主机特性的正确评估,以及对靠泊或锚泊时可能产生的力的估算,作出有关系泊和锚泊的决定 在航时,全面评估浅水和受限水域、浮冰、浅滩、潮汐情况、过往船只以及本船的首波和尾波的可能影响,以使该船在各种装载和天气条件下能够安全地操纵

Column 1	Column 2	Column 3	Column 4
Competence	**Knowledge, understanding and proficiency**	**Methods for demonstrating competence**	**Criteria for evaluating competence**
Manoeuvre and handle a ship in all conditions *(continued)*	.9 choice of anchorage; anchoring with one or two anchors in limited anchorages and factors involved in determining the length of anchor cable to be used .10 dragging anchor; clearing fouled anchors .11 dry-docking, both with and without damage .12 management and handling of ships in heavy weather, including assisting a ship or aircraft in distress; towing operations; means of keeping an unmanageable ship out of trough of the sea, lessening drift and use of oil .13 precautions in manoeuvring to launch rescue boats or survival craft in bad weather .14 methods of taking on board survivors from rescue boats and survival craft .15 ability to determine the manoeuvring and propulsion characteristics of common types of ships, with special reference to stopping distances and turning circles at various draughts and speeds .16 importance of navigating at reduced speed to avoid damage caused by own ship's bow wave and stern wave		

第 1 栏	第 2 栏	第 3 栏	第 4 栏
适任	知识、理解和熟练	表明适任的方法	评价适任的标准
在各种条件下操纵和操作船舶(续)	.9 锚地选择,在受限锚地内使用单锚和双锚锚泊,确定使用的锚链长度的有关因素 .10 走锚,清解缠锚 .11 在船舶有损坏或无损坏的状态下进出干船坞 .12 在恶劣天气下管理和操纵船舶,包括援助遇险船或飞机,拖带作业,使失去控制船舶脱离浪谷、减少漂流和使用镇浪油的方法 .13 在恶劣天气下释放救助艇或救生艇筏的操纵注意事项 .14 从救助艇或救生艇筏上把幸存人员救上船的方法 .15 确定普通种类船舶的操纵和推进特性的能力,特别是对船舶在各种吃水和速度下的冲程和旋回圈的确定 .16 减速航行以避免因本船的首波和尾波造成浪损的重要性		

Column 1	Column 2	Column 3	Column 4
Competence	**Knowledge, understanding and proficiency**	**Methods for demonstrating competence**	**Criteria for evaluating competence**
Manoeuvre and handle a ship in all conditions (*continued*)	.17 practical measures to be taken when navigating in or near ice or in conditions of ice accumulation on board .18 use of, and manoeuvring in and near, traffic separation schemes and in vessel traffic service (VTS) areas		
Operate remote controls of propulsion plant and engineering systems and services	Operating principles of marine power plants Ships' auxiliary machinery General knowledge of marine engineering terms	Examination and assessment of evidence obtained from one or more of the following: .1 approved in-service experience .2 approved simulator training, where appropriate	Plant, auxiliary machinery and equipment is operated in accordance with technical specifications and within safe operating limits at all times

Function: Cargo handling and stowage at the management level

Column 1	Column 2	Column 3	Column 4
Competence	**Knowledge, understanding and proficiency**	**Methods for demonstrating competence**	**Criteria for evaluating competence**
Plan and ensure safe loading, stowage, securing, care during the voyage and unloading of cargoes	Knowledge of and ability to apply relevant international regulations, codes and standards concerning the safe handling, stowage, securing and transport of cargoes Knowledge of the effect on trim and stability of cargoes and cargo operations Use of stability and trim diagrams and stress-calculating equipment, including automatic data-based (ADB) equipment, and knowledge of loading cargoes and ballasting in order to keep hull stress within acceptable limits	Examination and assessment of evidence obtained from one or more of the following: .1 approved in-service experience .2 approved simulator training, where appropriate using: stability, trim and stress tables, diagrams and stress-calculating equipment	The frequency and extent of cargo condition monitoring is appropriate to its nature and prevailing conditions Unacceptable or unforeseen variations in the condition or specification of the cargo are promptly recognized and remedial action is immediately taken and designed to safeguard the safety of the ship and those on board Cargo operations are planned and executed in accordance with

第 1 栏	第 2 栏	第 3 栏	第 4 栏
适任	知识、理解和熟练	表明适任的方法	评价适任的标准
在各种条件下操纵和操作船舶(续)	.17 当航行在或接近冰区,或在船上积冰的情况下应采取的实际措施 .18 使用分道通航制和船舶交通管理(VTS)区域,以及在和临近该类区域时的操纵		
遥控操作推进装置和轮机系统与设施	船舶动力装置的工作原理 船舶辅机 船舶轮机术语的一般知识	考试并评估从下列一项或数项获取的证据: .1 认可的工作经历 .2 认可的模拟器培训,如适用	随时按照技术规程并在安全操作的限制内,操作动力装置、辅机和设备

职能:货物装卸和积载 管理级

第 1 栏	第 2 栏	第 3 栏	第 4 栏
适任	知识、理解和熟练	表明适任的方法	评价适任的标准
计划并确保安全地装货、积载、系固、航行中照管货物和卸货	运用有关货物的安全装卸、积载、系固和运输的相关国际规定、规则和标准的知识和能力 货物和货物装卸对吃水差和稳性的影响的知识 使用稳性和吃水差图表和强度计算仪器,包括自动化数据(ADB)仪器,为保持船体强度在可接受的限度以内的装货和压载的知识	考试并评估从下列一项或数项获取的证据: .1 认可的工作经历 .2 认可的模拟器培训,如适用 使用稳性、吃水差和强度图表及强度计算仪器	监测货物情况的频度和程度适合于货物特性和当时情况 迅速确认货物条件或规格上的不可接受或未料到的变化,并立即采取保证船舶和船上人员安全的补救措施 按照规定的程序和法定的要求计划并进行货物作业

Column 1	Column 2	Column 3	Column 4
Competence	**Knowledge, understanding and proficiency**	**Methods for demonstrating competence**	**Criteria for evaluating competence**
Plan and ensure safe loading, stowage, securing, care during the voyage and unloading of cargoes (*continued*)	Stowage and securing of cargoes on board ships, including cargo-handling gear and securing and lashing equipment Loading and unloading operations, with special regard to the transport of cargoes identified in the Code of Safe Practice for Cargo Stowage and Securing General knowledge of tankers and tanker operations Knowledge of the operational and design limitations of bulk carriers Ability to use all available shipboard data related to loading, care and unloading of bulk cargoes Ability to establish procedures for safe cargo handling in accordance with the provisions of the relevant instruments such as IMDG Code, IMSBC Code, MARPOL 73/78 Annexes III and V and other relevant information Ability to explain the basic principles for establishing effective communications and improving working relationship between ship and terminal personnel		established procedures and legislative requirements Stowage and securing of cargoes ensures that stability and stress conditions remain within safe limits at all times during the voyage

第 1 栏	第 2 栏	第 3 栏	第 4 栏
适任	**知识、理解和熟练**	**表明适任的方法**	**评价适任的标准**
计划并确保安全地装货、积载、系固、航行中照管货物和卸货(续)	在船上积载和系固货物，包括货物装卸设备和系固与绑扎设备 装卸作业，特别注意《货物积载和系固安全操作规则》中指明的货物的运输 液货船和液货船操作的一般知识 散货船操作和设计局限性的知识 使用与散装货物装载、照管和卸载有关的所有可用的船上数据的能力 根据诸如《国际海运危险货物(IMDG)规则》、《国际海运散装固体货物(IMSBC)规则》、《MARPOL 73/78》附则 III 和附则 V 等相关文件的规定以及其他相关信息建立安全货物操作的程序的能力 解释在船舶与码头人员之间建立有效沟通并改善工作关系的基本原则的能力		货物的积载和系固保证整个航次中稳性和强度状况始终处在安全限度之内

Column 1	Column 2	Column 3	Column 4
Competence	**Knowledge, understanding and proficiency**	**Methods for demonstrating competence**	**Criteria for evaluating competence**
Assess reported defects and damage to cargo spaces, hatch covers and ballast tanks and take appropriate action	Knowledge of the limitations on strength of the vital constructional parts of a standard bulk carrier and ability to interpret given figures for bending moments and shear forces Ability to explain how to avoid the detrimental effects on bulk carriers of corrosion, fatigue and inadequate cargo handling	Examination and assessment of evidence obtained from one or more of the following: .1 approved in-service experience .2 approved simulator training, where appropriate using: stability, trim and stress tables, diagrams and stress-calculating equipment	Evaluations are based on accepted principles, well-founded arguments and correctly carried out. The decisions taken are acceptable, taking into consideration the safety of the ship and the prevailing conditions
Carriage of dangerous goods	International regulations, standards, codes and recommendations on the carriage of dangerous cargoes, including the International Maritime Dangerous Goods (IMDG) Code and the International Maritime Solid Bulk Cargoes (IMSBC) Code Carriage of dangerous, hazardous and harmful cargoes; precautions during loading and unloading and care during the voyage	Examination and assessment of evidence obtained from one or more of the following: .1 approved in-service experience .2 approved simulator training, where appropriate .3 approved specialist training	Planned distribution of cargo is based on reliable information and is in accordance with established guidelines and legislative requirements Information on dangers, hazards and special requirements is recorded in a format suitable for easy reference in the event of an incident

第 1 栏	第 2 栏	第 3 栏	第 4 栏
适任	**知识、理解和熟练**	**表明适任的方法**	**评价适任的标准**
评估报告的货舱、舱盖和压载舱的缺陷和损坏并采取适当的行动	标准散货船关键构件强度的限制的知识以及解释弯曲力矩和剪力的给定数值的能力 解释如何避免腐蚀、疲劳和不适当的货物装卸对散货船的不利影响的能力	考试并评估从下列一项或数项获取的证据: .1 认可的工作经历 .2 认可的模拟器培训,如适用 使用稳性、吃水差和强度图表及强度计算仪器	评价基于公认的原则和依据充分的理由并得到正确实施。采取的决策可接受并考虑到船舶安全和当前情况
危险货物运输	有关危险货物运输的国际规定、标准、规则和建议案,包括《国际海运危险货物(IMDG)规则》和《国际海运固体散装货物(IMSBC)规则》 危险和有害货物的运输;装卸货物期间的预防措施和运输途中对货物的照管	考试并评估从下列一项或数项获取的证据: .1 认可的工作经历 .2 认可的模拟器培训,如适用 .3 认可的专业培训	货物的配载计划基于可信的资料,并按确定的指南和法定要求进行 有关危险性和有害性及特殊要求的资料以适当的格式记载,以便于发生事故时查询

Function: Controlling the operation of the ship and care for persons on board at the management level

Column 1	Column 2	Column 3	Column 4
Competence	**Knowledge, understanding and proficiency**	**Methods for demonstrating competence**	**Criteria for evaluating competence**
Control trim, stability and stress	Understanding of fundamental principles of ship construction and the theories and factors affecting trim and stability and measures necessary to preserve trim and stability Knowledge of the effect on trim and stability of a ship in the event of damage to and consequent flooding of a compartment and countermeasures to be taken Knowledge of IMO recommendations concerning ship stability	Examination and assessment of evidence obtained from one or more of the following: .1 approved in-service experience .2 approved training ship experience .3 approved simulator training, where appropriate	Stability and stress conditions are maintained within safe limits at all times

职能：船舶作业管理和人员管理　管理级

第 1 栏	第 2 栏	第 3 栏	第 4 栏
适任	**知识、理解和熟练**	**表明适任的方法**	**评价适任的标准**
控制吃水差、稳性和强度	了解船舶构造的基本原理和影响吃水差与稳性的理论和因素以及保持吃水差和稳性的必要措施 因一舱受损进水而影响船舶吃水差和稳性以及应采取的对策的知识 IMO 有关船舶稳性的建议案的知识	考试并评估从下列一项或数项获取的证据： .1　认可的工作经历 .2　认可的培训船经历 .3　认可的模拟器培训，如适用	稳性和强度状况始终保持在安全限度之内

Column 1	Column 2	Column 3	Column 4
Competence	**Knowledge, understanding and proficiency**	**Methods for demonstrating competence**	**Criteria for evaluating competence**
Monitor and control compliance with legislative requirements and measures to ensure safety of life at sea, security and the protection of the marine environment	Knowledge of international maritime law embodied in international agreements and conventions Regard shall be paid especially to the following subjects: .1 certificates and other documents required to be carried on board ships by international conventions, how they may be obtained and their period of validity .2 responsibilities under the relevant requirements of the International Convention on Load Lines, 1966, as amended .3 responsibilities under the relevant requirements of the International Convention for the Safety of Life at Sea, 1974, as amended .4 responsibilities under the International Convention for the Prevention of Pollution from Ships, as amended .5 maritime declarations of health and the requirements of the International Health Regulations .6 responsibilities under international instruments affecting the safety of the ship, passengers, crew and cargo .7 methods and aids to prevent pollution of the marine environment by ships .8 national legislation for implementing international agreements and conventions	Examination and assessment of evidence obtained from one or more of the following: .1 approved in-service experience .2 approved training ship experience .3 approved simulator training, where appropriate	Procedures for monitoring operations and maintenance comply with legislative requirements Potential non-compliance is promptly and fully identified Planned renewal and extension of certificates ensures continued validity of surveyed items and equipment

第 1 栏	第 2 栏	第 3 栏	第 4 栏
适任	知识、理解和熟练	表明适任的方法	评价适任的标准
监督和控制法定要求的遵守以及保证海上人命安全与保护海洋环境的措施	国际协定和公约中包括的国际海事法律的知识 应特别注意下列各项: .1 国际公约要求随船携带的证书和其他文件,如何取得这些文件以及这些文件的有效期 .2 经修正的《1966 年国际载重线公约》有关要求规定的责任 .3 经修正的《1974 年国际海上人命安全公约》有关要求规定的责任 .4 经修正的《国际防止船舶造成污染公约》规定的责任 .5 《船员健康声明》和《国际卫生条例》的要求 .6 影响船舶、旅客、船员和货物安全的国际文件所规定的责任 .7 防止船舶污染海洋环境的方法和设备 .8 为实施国际协定和公约的国内法规	考试并评估从下列一项或数项获取的证据: .1 认可的工作经历 .2 认可的培训船经历 .3 认可的模拟器培训,如适用	监督操作和维护保养的程序符合法定要求 迅速和全面确认潜在的不符合法定要求的情况 按计划换新证书和给证书延期以保证经检验的项目和设备继续有效

Column 1	Column 2	Column 3	Column 4
Competence	**Knowledge, understanding and proficiency**	**Methods for demonstrating competence**	**Criteria for evaluating competence**
Maintain safety and security of the ship's crew and passengers and the operational condition of life-saving, fire-fighting and other safety systems	Thorough knowledge of life-saving appliance regulations (International Convention for the Safety of Life at Sea) Organization of fire drills and abandon ship drills Maintenance of operational condition of life-saving, fire-fighting and other safety systems Actions to be taken to protect and safeguard all persons on board in emergencies Actions to limit damage and salve the ship following a fire, explosion, collision or grounding	Examination and assessment of evidence obtained from practical instruction and approved in-service training and experience	Procedures for monitoring fire-detection and safety systems ensure that all alarms are detected promptly and acted upon in accordance with established emergency procedures
Develop emergency and damage control plans and handle emergency situations	Preparation of contingency plans for response to emergencies Ship construction, including damage control Methods and aids for fire prevention, detection and extinction Functions and use of life-saving appliances	Examination and assessment of evidence obtained from approved in-service training and experience	Emergency procedures are in accordance with the established plans for emergency situations

第1栏	第2栏	第3栏	第4栏
适任	**知识、理解和熟练**	**表明适任的方法**	**评价适任的标准**
保持船上船员和旅客的安全和保安以及救生、消防和其他安全系统的工作状态	救生设备有关规则(《国际海上人命安全公约》)的全面知识 组织消防和弃船演习 保持救生、消防及其他安全系统的工作状态 在紧急情况下保护和保卫船上所有人员安全应采取的行动 在失火、爆炸、碰撞或搁浅时限制损害和救助船舶的行动	考试并评估从实际训练和认可的在职培训和经历中获取的证据	监测探火和安全系统的程序保证迅速探测到所有报警,并按既定的应急程序采取行动
制定应急和损害控制计划并处置紧急情况	制定应急反应计划 船舶构造,包括损害控制 防火、探火和灭火的方法和设备 救生设备的功能和使用	考试并评估从认可的在职培训和经历中获取的证据	应急程序符合为紧急情况制定的计划

Column 1	Column 2	Column 3	Column 4
Competence	**Knowledge, understanding and proficiency**	**Methods for demonstrating competence**	**Criteria for evaluating competence**
Use of leadership and managerial skill	Knowledge of shipboard personnel management and training A knowledge of related international maritime conventions and recommendations, and national legislation Ability to apply task and workload management, including: .1 planning and co-ordination .2 personnel assignment .3 time and resource constraints .4 prioritization Knowledge and ability to apply effective resource management: .1 allocation, assignment, and prioritization of resources .2 effective communication on board and ashore .3 decisions reflect consideration of team experiences .4 assertiveness and leadership, including motivation .5 obtaining and maintaining situation awareness Knowledge and ability to apply decision-making techniques: .1 situation and risk assessment .2 identify and generate options .3 selecting course of action	Assessment of evidence obtained from one or more of the following: .1 approved training .2 approved in-service experience .3 approved simulator training	The crew are allocated duties and informed of expected standards of work and behaviour in a manner appropriate to the individuals concerned Training objectives and activities are based on assessment of current competence and capabilities and operational requirements Operations are demonstrated to be in accordance with applicable rules Operations are planned and resources are allocated as needed in correct priority to perform necessary tasks Communication is clearly and unambiguously given and received Effective leadership behaviours are demonstrated Necessary team member(s) share accurate understanding of current and predicted vessel state and

第 1 栏	第 2 栏	第 3 栏	第 4 栏
适任	**知识、理解和熟练**	**表明适任的方法**	**评价适任的标准**
领导力和管理技能的运用	船上人员管理和培训的知识 有关国际海事公约和建议案以及国内法规的知识 运用任务和工作量管理的能力,包括: .1 计划和协调 .2 人员分派 .3 时间和资源的限制 .4 优先排序 运用有效资源管理的知识和能力: .1 资源的分配、分派和优先排序 .2 船上和岸上的有效沟通 .3 决策反映出对团队经验的考虑 .4 决断力和领导力,包括激励 .5 具有并保持情景意识 运用决策技能的知识和能力: .1 局面和风险评估 .2 识别并形成选项 .3 选择行动过程	评估从下列一项或数项获取的证据: .1 认可的培训 .2 认可的工作经历 .3 认可的模拟器培训	分配船员工作,并以适合相关个人的方式告知所要求的工作标准和行为准则 培训目标和培训活动基于对目前适任性和能力的评估和操作要求 表明操作符合适用的规则 操作有计划并根据需要按正确的优先顺序分配资源,以执行必要的任务 交流清楚、无歧义 表明有效的领导行为 必要的团队成员对当前和预测的船舶和操作状态以及外部环境有共同的准确的理解

Column 1	Column 2	Column 3	Column 4
Competence	**Knowledge, understanding and proficiency**	**Methods for demonstrating competence**	**Criteria for evaluating competence**
Use of leadership and managerial skill (*continued*)	.4 evaluation of outcome effectiveness Development, implementation, and oversight of standard operating procedures		operational status and external environment Decisions are most effective for the situation Operations are demonstrated to be effective and in accordance with applicable rules
Organize and manage the provision of medical care on board	A thorough knowledge* of the use and contents of the following publications: .1 International Medical Guide for Ships or equivalent national publications .2 medical section of the International Code of Signals .3 Medical First Aid Guide for Use in Accidents Involving Dangerous Goods	Examination and assessment of evidence obtained from approved training	Actions taken and procedures followed correctly apply and make full use of advice available

* The relevant IMO Model Course(s) may be of assistance in the preparation of courses.

第 1 栏	第 2 栏	第 3 栏	第 4 栏
适任	知识、理解和熟练	表明适任的方法	评价适任的标准
	.4 评价结果的有效性 制定、实施和监督标准操作程序		决策对于局面最有效 表明操作是有效的并符合适用的规则
组织和管理船上医疗的提供	下列出版物的使用和内容的全面知识①： .1 《国际船舶医疗指南》或等效的国内出版物 .2 《国际信号规则》的医疗部分 .3 《危险货物事故医疗急救指南》	考试并评估从认可的培训中获取的证据	所采取的行动和所遵循的程序正确运用并充分使用所得到的建议

① 相关 IMO 示范培训课程可有助于准备课程。

Section A-II/3

Mandatory minimum requirements for certification of officers in charge of a navigational watch and of masters on ships of less than 500 gross tonnage, engaged on near-coastal voyages

OFFICER IN CHARGE OF A NAVIGATIONAL WATCH

Standard of competence

1 Every candidate for certification shall:

.1 be required to demonstrate the competence to undertake, at operational level, the tasks, duties and responsibilities listed in column 1 of table A-II/3;

.2 at least hold the appropriate certificate for performing VHF radiocommunications in accordance with the requirements of the Radio Regulations; and

.3 if designated to have primary responsibility for radiocommunications during distress incidents, hold the appropriate certificate issued or recognized under the provisions of the Radio Regulations.

2 The minimum knowledge, understanding and proficiency required for certification is listed in column 2 of table A-II/3.

3 The level of knowledge of the subjects listed in column 2 of table A-II/3 shall be sufficient to enable the candidate to serve in the capacity of officer in charge of a navigational watch.

4 Training and experience to achieve the necessary level of theoretical knowledge, understanding and proficiency shall be based on section A-VIII/2, part 4-1 – Principles to be observed in keeping a navigational watch, and shall also take into account the relevant requirements of this part and the guidance given in part B of this Code.

5 Every candidate for certification shall be required to provide evidence of having achieved the required standard of competence in accordance with the methods for demonstrating competence and the criteria for evaluating competence tabulated in columns 3 and 4 of table A-II/3.

Special training

6 Every candidate for certification as officer in charge of a navigational watch on ships of less than 500 gross tonnage, engaged on near-coastal voyages, who, in accordance with paragraph 4.2.1 of regulation II/3, is required to have completed special training, shall follow an approved programme of onboard training which:

.1 ensures that, during the required period of seagoing service, the candidate receives systematic practical training and experience in the tasks, duties and responsibilities of an officer in charge of a navigational watch, taking into account the guidance given in section B-II/1 of this Code;

.2 is closely supervised and monitored by qualified officers on board the ships in which the approved seagoing service is performed; and

.3 is adequately documented in a training record book or similar document[*].

---

[*] The relevant IMO Model Course(s) and a similar document produced by the International Shipping Federation may be of assistance in the preparation of training record books.

第 A-II/3 节
对从事近岸航行未满 500 总吨船舶的船长和负责航行值班的高级船员发证的强制性最低要求

负责航行值班的高级船员

适任标准

1 每个证书申请人应:

.1 按要求表明承担表 A-II/3 第 1 栏所列的操作级的任务、职责和责任的适任能力;

.2 至少持有按照《无线电规则》的要求进行甚高频无线电通信的适当证书;并且

.3 如果在遇险事件中被指定负有无线电通信的主要职责,则持有根据《无线电规则》的规定签发或承认的适当证书。

2 发证所要求的最低的知识、理解和熟练列于表 A-II/3 第 2 栏中。

3 表 A-II/3 第 2 栏所列各科目的知识水平,应足以能使证书申请人在负责航行值班的高级船员职位上服务。

4 为获取所需水平的理论知识、理解和熟练的培训和经验,应以第 A-VIII/2 节第 4-1 部分——航行值班中应遵循的原则为基础,并也应考虑本规则本部分的有关要求和 B 部分给予的指导。

5 每个证书申请人应按照表 A-II/3 第 3 栏和第 4 栏所列的表明适任的方法和评价适任的标准,提供已达到所要求的适任标准的证据。

特殊培训

6 每个申请从事近岸航行未满 500 总吨船舶的负责航行值班的高级船员证书的申请人,按照规则第 II/3 条第 4.2.1 段已完成特殊培训的,应参加认可的船上培训计划,该培训计划:

.1 确保证书申请人在要求的海上服务期间,受到关于在负责航行值班的高级船员的任务、职责和责任方面的系统而实际的培训并获得经验,同时考虑本规则第 B-II/1 节给予的指导;

.2 在执行认可的海上服务中密切地受到船上合格的高级船员的监督和指导;并且

.3 在培训记录簿或类似的文件中予以充分记载①。

① 相关 IMO 示范培训课程和国际航运联合会(ISF)制定的一份类似文件可有助于编制培训记录簿。

MASTER

7 Every candidate for certification as master on ships of less than 500 gross tonnage, engaged on near-coastal voyages, shall meet the requirements for an officer in charge of a navigational watch set out below and, in addition, shall be required to provide evidence of knowledge and ability to carry out all the duties of such a master.

船长

7　每个申请从事近岸航行未满 500 总吨船舶的船长证书的申请人,应符合以下规定的对负责航行值班的高级船员的要求。此外,还应提供有关履行该类船长所有职责的知识和能力的证据。

Table A-II/3

Specification of minimum standard of competence for officers in charge of a navigational watch and for masters on ships of less than 500 gross tonnage engaged on near-coastal voyages

Function: Navigation at the operational level

Column 1	Column 2	Column 3	Column 4
Competence	**Knowledge, understanding and proficiency**	**Methods for demonstrating competence**	**Criteria for evaluating competence**
Plan and conduct a coastal passage and determine position Note: Training and assessment in the use of ECDIS is not required for those who serve exclusively on ships not fitted with ECDIS. These limitations shall be reflected in the endorsement issued to the seafarer concerned	*Navigation* Ability to determine the ship's position by the use of: .1 landmarks .2 aids to navigation, including lighthouses, beacons and buoys .3 dead reckoning, taking into account winds, tides, currents and estimated speed Thorough knowledge of and ability to use nautical charts and publications, such as sailing directions, tide tables, notices to mariners, radio navigational warnings and ships' routeing information Reporting in accordance with General Principles for Ship Reporting Systems and with VTS procedures *Note*: This item is only required for certification as master	Examination and assessment of evidence obtained from one or more of the following: .1 approved in-service experience .2 approved training ship experience .3 approved simulator training, where appropriate .4 approved laboratory equipment training using: chart catalogues, charts, nautical publications, radio navigational warnings, sextant, azimuth mirror, electronic navigation equipment, echo-sounding equipment, compass	Information obtained from nautical charts and publications is relevant, interpreted correctly and properly applied The primary method of fixing the ship's position is the most appropriate to the prevailing circumstances and conditions The position is determined within the limits of acceptable instrument/system errors The reliability of the information obtained from the primary method of position fixing is checked at appropriate intervals Calculations and measurements of navigational information are accurate Charts and publications selected are the largest scale on board suitable for the area of navigation and charts are corrected in accordance with the latest information available

表 A-II/3
从事近岸航行未满 500 总吨船舶的船长和负责航行值班的高级船员的最低适任标准

职能:航行　操作级

第 1 栏	第 2 栏	第 3 栏	第 4 栏
适任	知识、理解和熟练	表明适任的方法	评价适任的标准
计划并引导沿海航行和定位 注:对仅在未配备 ECDIS 的船上工作人员的不要求进行该设备使用方面的培训和评估。该限制应反映在给当事海员签发的签证中	航行 使用下列各项确定船位的能力: .1 陆标 .2 灯塔、立标和浮标等助航标志 .3 考虑风、潮汐、流和推算航速来进行航迹推算 使用海图和诸如航路指南、潮汐表、航行通告、无线电航行警告和船舶定线资料等航海出版物的全面知识和能力 按照《船舶报告制的一般原则》和 VTS 程序进行报告 注:本项目仅对船长证书的申请人提出要求	考试并评估从下列一项或数项获取的证据: .1 认可的工作经历 .2 认可的培训船经历 .3 认可的模拟器培训,如适用 .4 认可的实验室设备培训 使用海图目录、海图、航海出版物、无线电航行警告、六分仪、方位镜、电子导航设备、回声测深仪、罗经	从海图和航海出版物获取的信息是相关的,解释正确,应用恰当 主要定位方法最适合于当时环境和条件 确定的船位在可接受的仪器/系统误差限度内 以适当的时间间隔核查从基本定位方法获得的信息的可靠性 航海信息的计算和测量精确 所选的海图是船上适合于航行区域的最大比例尺的,并且海图和出版物已按可用的最新资料进行改正

Column 1	Column 2	Column 3	Column 4
Competence	**Knowledge, understanding and proficiency**	**Methods for demonstrating competence**	**Criteria for evaluating competence**
Plan and conduct a coastal passage and determine position (*continued*)	Voyage planning and navigation for all conditions by acceptable methods of plotting coastal tracks, taking into account, e.g.: .1 restricted waters .2 meteorological conditions .3 ice .4 restricted visibility .5 traffic separation schemes .6 vessel traffic service (VTS) areas .7 areas of extensive tidal effects *Note*: This item is only required for certification as master		
	Thorough knowledge of and ability to use ECDIS	Examination and assessment of evidence obtained from one or more of the following: .1 approved training ship experience .2 approved ECDIS simulator training	

第 1 栏	第 2 栏	第 3 栏	第 4 栏
适任	知识、理解和熟练	表明适任的方法	评价适任的标准
计划并引导沿海航行和定位(续)	通过可接受的标绘沿海航线的方法制定航次计划和各种条件下的航行,并考虑例如以下的情形: .1 受限水域 .2 气象条件 .3 冰况 .4 能见度不良 .5 分道通航制 .6 船舶交通管理(VTS)区域 .7 潮汐影响大的区域 注:本项目仅对船长证书的申请人提出要求		
	使用 ECDIS 的全面知识和能力	考试并评估从下列一项或数项获取的证据: .1 认可的培训船经历 .2 认可的 ECDIS 模拟器培训	

Column 1	Column 2	Column 3	Column 4
Competence	**Knowledge, understanding and proficiency**	**Methods for demonstrating competence**	**Criteria for evaluating competence**
Plan and conduct a coastal passage and determine position (*continued*)	*Navigational aids and equipment* Ability to operate safely and determine the ship's position by use of all navigational aids and equipment commonly fitted on board the ships concerned	Assessment of evidence obtained from approved radar simulator	Performance checks and tests of navigation systems comply with manufacturer's recommendations, good navigational practice and IMO resolutions on performance standards for navigational equipment Interpretation and analysis of information obtained from radar is in accordance with accepted navigational practice and takes account of the limits and accuracy levels of radar
	Compasses Knowledge of the errors and corrections of magnetic compasses Ability to determine errors of the compass, using terrestrial means, and to allow for such errors		Errors in magnetic compasses are determined and applied correctly to courses and bearings
	Automatic pilot Knowledge of automatic pilot systems and procedures; change-over from manual to automatic control and vice versa; adjustment of controls for optimum performance		Selection of the mode of steering is the most suitable for prevailing weather, sea and traffic conditions and intended manoeuvres
	Meteorology Ability to use and interpret information obtained from shipborne meteorological instruments Knowledge of the characteristics of the various weather systems, reporting procedures and recording systems		Measurements and observations of weather conditions are accurate and appropriate to the passage
	Ability to apply the meteorological information available		Meteorological information is evaluated and applied to maintain the safe passage of the vessel

第 1 栏	第 2 栏	第 3 栏	第 4 栏
适任	知识、理解和熟练	表明适任的方法	评价适任的标准
计划并引导沿海航行和定位(续)	*导航仪器和设备* 使用当事船舶上通常安装的一切导航仪器和设备安全地操作并确定船位的能力	评估从认可的雷达模拟器中获取的证据	导航系统性能的核对和测试符合厂家的建议和良好的航海习惯以及 IMO 关于导航设备性能标准的决议 按照公认的航海习惯解释和分析从雷达上获取的信息,并考虑雷达的局限性和精度水平
	罗经 磁罗经误差及校正的知识 使用地文航海手段确定罗经误差和修正这种误差的能力		测定磁罗经的误差并正确运用到航向和方位上
	自动操舵 自动操舵系统和程序、从手动到自动舵的相互转换、调整控钮至最佳性能的知识		操舵方式的选择最适合于当时的天气、海况、交通状况和拟采取的操纵
	气象学 应用和解释从船用气象仪器上获取的信息的能力 各种天气系统的特性、报告程序和记录系统的知识 运用可用的气象信息的能力		对天气情况的测定和观测精确并适合航行 评价和运用气象信息以保持船舶安全航行

Column 1	Column 2	Column 3	Column 4
Competence	**Knowledge, understanding and proficiency**	**Methods for demonstrating competence**	**Criteria for evaluating competence**
Maintain a safe navigational watch	*Watchkeeping* Thorough knowledge of content, application and intent of the International Regulations for Preventing Collisions at Sea, 1972, as amended Knowledge of content of the Principles to be observed in keeping a navigational watch Use of routeing in accordance with the General Provisions on Ships' Routeing Use of reporting in accordance with the General Principles for Ship Reporting Systems and with VTS procedures	Examination and assessment of evidence obtained from one or more of the following: .1 approved in-service experience .2 approved training ship experience .3 approved simulator training, where appropriate .4 approved laboratory equipment training	The conduct, handover and relief of the watch conforms with accepted principles and procedures A proper look-out is maintained at all times and in conformity with accepted principles and procedures Lights, shapes and sound signals conform with the requirements contained in the International Regulations for Preventing Collisions at Sea, 1972, as amended and are correctly recognized The frequency and extent of monitoring of traffic, the ship and the environment conform with accepted principles and procedures Action to avoid close encounters and collision with other vessels is in accordance with the International Regulations for Preventing Collisions at Sea, 1972, as amended Decisions to adjust course and/or speed are both timely and in accordance with accepted navigation procedures A proper record is maintained of movements and activities relating to the navigation of the ship Responsibility for safe navigation is clearly defined at all times, including periods when the master is on the bridge and when under pilotage

第 1 栏	第 2 栏	第 3 栏	第 4 栏
适任	知识、理解和熟练	表明适任的方法	评价适任的标准
保持安全航行值班	值班 经修订的《1972 年国际海上避碰规则》的内容、应用和意图的全面知识 航行值班中应遵守的原则的内容的知识 根据《船舶定线制的一般规定》使用定线制 根据《船舶报告制的一般原则》和 VTS 程序使用报告制	考试并评估从下列一项或数项获取的证据: .1 认可的工作经历 .2 认可的培训船经历 .3 认可的模拟器培训,如适用 .4 认可的实验室设备培训	按照公认的原则和程序进行值班、交班和接班 随时保持正规的瞭望,并符合公认的原则和程序 号灯、号型和声号符合经修订的《1972 年国际海上避碰规则》中的有关要求,并能被正确辨认 监测交通、船舶和环境的频度和范围符合公认的原则和程序 为避免和他船在很近距离上会遇或碰撞而采取的行动符合经修订的《1972 年国际海上避碰规则》 作出调整航向和/或航速的决定均是及时的,并符合公认的航海习惯 对有关船舶航行的运动和活动保持正规的记录 始终明确安全航行的责任,包括船长在驾驶台和船舶正在被引航期间

Column 1	Column 2	Column 3	Column 4
Competence	**Knowledge, understanding and proficiency**	**Methods for demonstrating competence**	**Criteria for evaluating competence**
Respond to emergencies	Emergency procedures, including: .1 precautions for the protection and safety of passengers in emergency situations .2 initial assessment of damage and damage control .3 action to be taken following a collision .4 action to be taken following a grounding In addition, the following material should be included for certification as master: .1 emergency steering .2 arrangements for towing and for being taken in tow .3 rescuing persons from the sea .4 assisting a vessel in distress .5 appreciation of the action to be taken when emergencies arise in port	Examination and assessment of evidence obtained from one or more of the following: .1 approved in-service experience .2 approved training ship experience .3 approved simulator training, where appropriate .4 practical instruction	The type and scale of the emergency is promptly identified Initial actions and, if appropriate, manoeuvring are in accordance with contingency plans and are appropriate to the urgency of the situation and the nature of the emergency
Respond to a distress signal at sea	*Search and rescue* Knowledge of the contents of the International Aeronautical and Maritime Search and Rescue (IAMSAR) Manual	Examination and assessment of evidence obtained from practical instruction or approved simulator training, where appropriate	The distress or emergency signal is immediately recognized Contingency plans and instructions in standing orders are implemented and complied with

第 1 栏	第 2 栏	第 3 栏	第 4 栏
适任	**知识、理解和熟练**	**表明适任的方法**	**评价适任的标准**
应急反应	应急程序包括： .1 在紧急情况下的旅客保护和安全预防措施 .2 初始损害评估和损害控制 .3 碰撞后应采取的行动 .4 搁浅后应采取的行动 此外，对船长证书的申请人，还应包括下列内容： .1 应急操舵 .2 拖带和被拖带的安排 .3 从海中救助人员 .4 援助遇险中的船舶 .5 了解在港内发生紧急情况下应采取的行动	考试并评估从下列一项或数项获取的证据： .1 认可的工作经历 .2 认可的培训船经历 .3 认可的模拟器培训，如适用 .4 实际训练	迅速确定紧急情况的类型和范围 初始行动和操纵（如适用）符合应急计划并适合于局面的紧迫性和紧急情况的性质
对海上遇险信号的反应	*搜寻和救助* 《国际航空和海上搜寻救助（IAMSAR）手册》中内容的知识	考试并评估从实际训练或认可的模拟器培训（如适用）中获取的证据	立即判明遇险或应急信号 实施并遵守应急计划和常规命令中的指示

Column 1	Column 2	Column 3	Column 4
Competence	**Knowledge, understanding and proficiency**	**Methods for demonstrating competence**	**Criteria for evaluating competence**
Manoeuvre the ship and operate small ship power plants	*Ship manoeuvring and handling* Knowledge of factors affecting safe manoeuvring and handling The operation of small ship power plants and auxiliaries Proper procedures for anchoring and mooring	Examination and assessment of evidence obtained from one or more of the following: .1 approved in-service experience .2 approved training ship experience .3 approved simulator training, where appropriate	Safe operating limits of ship propulsion, steering and power systems are not exceeded in normal manoeuvres Adjustments made to the ship's course and speed maintain safety of navigation Plant, auxiliary machinery and equipment is operated in accordance with technical specifications and within safe operating limits at all times

第1栏	第2栏	第3栏	第4栏
适任	知识、理解和熟练	表明适任的方法	评价适任的标准
操纵船舶和操作小型船舶动力装置	船舶操纵和操作 影响安全操纵和操作的因素的知识 小型船舶动力装置和辅机的操作 锚泊和系泊的正确程序	考试并评估从下列一项或数项获取的证据： .1 认可的工作经历 .2 认可的培训船经历 .3 认可的模拟器培训，如适用	在正常的操纵中，船舶推进、操舵和动力系统不超出安全操作的限度 调整船舶航向和航速，保持航行安全 按照技术规程并始终在安全操作的限度内操作动力装置、辅机和设备

Function: Cargo handling and stowage at the operational level

Column 1	Column 2	Column 3	Column 4
Competence	**Knowledge, understanding and proficiency**	**Methods for demonstrating competence**	**Criteria for evaluating competence**
Monitor the loading, stowage, securing and unloading of cargoes and their care during the voyage	*Cargo handling, stowage and securing* Knowledge of safe handling, stowage and securing of cargoes, including dangerous, hazardous and harmful cargoes, and their effect on the safety of life and of the ship Use of the International Maritime Dangerous Goods (IMDG) Code	Examination and assessment of evidence obtained from one or more of the following: .1 approved in-service experience .2 approved training ship experience .3 approved simulator training, where appropriate	Cargo operations are carried out in accordance with the cargo plan or other documents and established safety rules/regulations, equipment operating instructions and shipboard stowage limitations The handling of dangerous, hazardous and harmful cargoes complies with international regulations and recognized standards and codes of safe practice

Function: Controlling the operation of the ship and care for persons on board at the operational level

Column 1	Column 2	Column 3	Column 4
Competence	**Knowledge, understanding and proficiency**	**Methods for demonstrating competence**	**Criteria for evaluating competence**
Ensure compliance with pollution-prevention requirements	*Prevention of pollution of the marine environment and anti-pollution procedures* Knowledge of the precautions to be taken to prevent pollution of the marine environment Anti-pollution procedures and all associated equipment	Examination and assessment of evidence obtained from one or more of the following: .1 approved in-service experience .2 approved training ship experience	Procedures for monitoring shipboard operations and ensuring compliance with MARPOL requirements are fully observed

职能:货物装卸和积载　操作级

第 1 栏	第 2 栏	第 3 栏	第 4 栏
适任	知识、理解和熟练	表明适任的方法	评价适任的标准
监控装货、积载、系固和卸货,以及航行中货物照管	货物装卸、积载和系固 货物(包括危险和有害货物)安全装卸、积载和系固的知识,及其对人命和船舶安全影响的知识 《国际海运危险货物(IMDG)规则》的使用	考试并评估从下列一项或数项获取的证据: .1 认可的工作经历 .2 认可的培训船经历 .3 认可的模拟器培训,如适用	按照配载图或其他文件、所制定的安全规则、设备操作规程和船舶积载限制进行货物操作 按照国际规则和公认的安全操作标准和规则装卸危险和有害货物

职能:船舶作业管理和人员管理　操作级

第 1 栏	第 2 栏	第 3 栏	第 4 栏
适任	知识、理解和熟练	表明适任的方法	评价适任的标准
确保遵守防污染要求	防止海洋环境污染和防污染程序 防止海洋环境污染应采取的预防措施的知识 防污染程序和所有附属设备	考试并评估从下列一项或数项获取的证据: .1 认可的工作经历 .2 认可的培训船经历	全面遵守关于监控船上操作和保证符合《MARPOL 公约》要求的程序

Column 1	Column 2	Column 3	Column 4
Competence	**Knowledge, understanding and proficiency**	**Methods for demonstrating competence**	**Criteria for evaluating competence**
Maintain seaworthiness of the ship	*Ship stability* Working knowledge and application of stability, trim and stress tables, diagrams and stress-calculating equipment Understanding of fundamental actions to be taken in the event of partial loss of intact buoyancy Understanding of the fundamentals of watertight integrity *Ship construction* General knowledge of the principal structural members of a ship and the proper names for the various parts	Examination and assessment of evidence obtained from one or more of the following: .1 approved in-service experience .2 approved training ship experience .3 approved simulator training, where appropriate .4 approved laboratory equipment training	The stability conditions comply with the IMO intact stability criteria under all conditions of loading Actions to ensure and maintain the watertight integrity of the ship are in accordance with accepted practice
Prevent, control and fight fires on board	*Fire prevention and fire-fighting appliances* Ability to organize fire drills Knowledge of classes and chemistry of fire Knowledge of fire-fighting systems Understanding of action to be taken in the event of fire, including fires involving oil systems	Assessment of evidence obtained from approved fire-fighting training and experience as set out in section A-VI/3	The type and scale of the problem is promptly identified and initial actions conform with the emergency procedure and contingency plans for the ship Evacuation, emergency shutdown and isolation procedures are appropriate to the nature of the emergency and are implemented promptly The order of priority, and the levels and time-scales of making reports and informing personnel on board, are relevant to the nature of the emergency and reflect the urgency of the problem

第 1 栏	第 2 栏	第 3 栏	第 4 栏
适任	知识、理解和熟练	表明适任的方法	评价适任的标准
保持船舶的适航性	*船舶稳性* 稳性、吃水差、强度图表和强度计算仪器的实用知识和应用 了解一旦丧失部分完整浮力时应采取的基本行动 了解水密完整性的基本知识 *船舶构造* 船舶主要构件和各种部件的正确名称的一般知识	考试并评估从下列一项或数项获取的证据： .1 认可的工作经历 .2 认可的培训船经历 .3 认可的模拟器培训，如适用 .4 认可的实验室设备培训	在各种装载条件下，稳性状况达到 IMO 完整稳性的标准 按照公认的做法采取保证和维持船舶水密完整性的行动
船上防火、控制火灾和灭火	*防火和灭火设备* 组织消防演习的能力 火的种类及其化学性质的知识 灭火系统的知识 了解一旦失火时，包括涉及油类系统着火时应采取的行动	评估从第 A-VI/3 节规定的认可的消防培训和经历中获取的证据	迅速确定问题的种类和范围，初始行动符合船舶的应急程序和应急计划 撤离、应急关闭和隔离程序与紧急情况的性质相适应，并迅速实施 作出报告和通知船上人员的优先顺序、级别和时限与紧急情况的性质相关，并反映事态的紧急程度

Column 1	Column 2	Column 3	Column 4
Competence	**Knowledge, understanding and proficiency**	**Methods for demonstrating competence**	**Criteria for evaluating competence**
Operate life-saving appliances	*Life-saving* Ability to organize abandon ship drills and knowledge of the operation of survival craft and rescue boats, their launching appliances and arrangements, and their equipment, including radio life-saving appliances, satellite EPIRBs, SARTs, immersion suits and thermal protective aids	Assessment of evidence obtained from approved training and experience as set out in section A-VI/2, paragraphs 1 to 4	Actions in responding to abandon ship and survival situations are appropriate to the prevailing circumstances and conditions and comply with accepted safety practices and standards
Apply medical first aid on board ship	*Medical aid* Practical application of medical guides and advice by radio, including the ability to take effective action based on such knowledge in the case of accidents or illnesses that are likely to occur on board ship	Assessment of evidence obtained from approved training as set out in section A-VI/4, paragraphs 1 to 3	The identification of probable cause, nature and extent of injuries or conditions is prompt and treatment minimizes immediate threat to life
Monitor compliance with legislative requirements	Basic working knowledge of the relevant IMO conventions concerning safety of life at sea, security and protection of the marine environment	Assessment of evidence obtained from examination or approved training	Legislative requirements relating to safety of life at sea, security and protection of the marine environment are correctly identified
Contribute to the safety of personnel and ship	Knowledge of personal survival techniques Knowledge of fire prevention and ability to fight and extinguish fires Knowledge of elementary first aid Knowledge of personal safety and social responsibilities	Assessment of evidence obtained from approved training and experiences as set out in section A-VI/1, paragraph 2	Appropriate safety and protective equipment is correctly used Procedures and safe working practices designed to safeguard personnel and the ship are observed at all times Procedures designed to safeguard the environment are observed at all times Initial and follow-up actions on becoming aware of an emergency conform with established emergency response procedures

第 1 栏	第 2 栏	第 3 栏	第 4 栏
适任	知识、理解和熟练	表明适任的方法	评价适任的标准
操作救生设备	救生 组织弃船演习的能力和救生艇筏、救助艇及其释放装置、布置和设备的操作知识，设备包括无线电救生设备、卫星应急无线电示位标、搜救应答器、救生服和保温用具	评估从第 A-VI/2 节第 1 段至第 4 段规定的认可的培训和经历中获取的证据	弃船和求生情况下的应急行动适合于当时环境和条件，并符合公认的安全做法和标准
在船上应用医疗急救	医护 医疗指南和无线电咨询的实际应用，包括根据这种知识对船上可能发生的事故或疾病采取有效行动的能力	评估从第 A-VI/4 节第 1 段至第 3 段规定的认可的培训中获取的证据	迅速确认伤病的可能原因、性质和程度，采取治疗以减少对生命的直接威胁
监督遵守法定要求	涉及海上人命安全、保安和保护海洋环境的 IMO 有关公约的基本实用知识	评估从考试或认可的培训中获取的证据	正确确认有关海上人命安全和保护海洋环境的法定要求
有助于人员和船舶的安全	个人求生技能的知识 防火知识和灭火能力 基本急救的知识 个人安全和社会责任的知识	评估从第 A-VI/1 节 2 段规定的认可的培训和经历中获取的证据	正确使用合适的安全和防护设备 始终遵守为保护人员和船舶而制定的程序和安全工作做法 始终遵守为保护环境而制定的程序 意识到紧急情况时的初始和后续行动符合既定的应急反应程序

Section A-II/4

Mandatory minimum requirements for certification of ratings forming part of a navigational watch

Standard of competence

1 Every rating forming part of a navigational watch on a seagoing ship of 500 gross tonnage or more shall be required to demonstrate the competence to perform the navigation function at the support level, as specified in column 1 of table A-II/4.

2 The minimum knowledge, understanding and proficiency required of ratings forming part of a navigational watch on a seagoing ship of 500 gross tonnage or more is listed in column 2 of table A-II/4.

3 Every candidate for certification shall be required to provide evidence of having achieved the required standard of competence in accordance with the methods for demonstrating competence and the criteria for evaluating competence specified in columns 3 and 4 of table A-II/4. The reference to "practical test" in column 3 may include approved shore-based training in which the trainees undergo practical testing.

4 Where there are no tables of competence for the support level in respect to certain functions, it remains the responsibility of the Administration to determine the appropriate training, assessment and certification requirements to be applied to personnel designated to perform those functions at the support level.

第 A-II/4 节

对组成航行值班部分的普通船员发证的强制性最低要求

适任标准

1 每个在 500 总吨或以上的海船上组成航行值班部分的普通船员应按要求表明履行表 A-II/4 第 1 栏规定的支持级航行职能的适任能力。

2 对在 500 总吨或以上的海船上组成航行值班部分的普通船员所要求的最低的知识、理解和熟练列于表 A-II/4 第 2 栏中。

3 每个证书申请人应按照表 A-II/4 第 3 栏和第 4 栏所列的表明适任的方法和评价适任的标准，提供已达到所要求的适任标准的证据。第 3 栏中提及的“实操测试”可包括能够对学员进行实操测试的认可的岸基培训。

4 对于未用适任表列出的某些支持级职能，主管机关有责任对指定履行那些支持级职能的人员确定适当的培训、评估和发证要求。

Table A-II/4

Specification of minimum standard of competence for ratings forming part of a navigational watch

Function: Navigation at the support level

Column 1	Column 2	Column 3	Column 4
Competence	**Knowledge, understanding and proficiency**	**Methods for demonstrating competence**	**Criteria for evaluating competence**
Steer the ship and also comply with helm orders in the English language	Use of magnetic and gyro-compasses Helm orders Change-over from automatic pilot to hand steering and vice versa	Assessment of evidence obtained from: .1 practical test, or .2 approved in-service experience, or .3 approved training ship experience	A steady course is steered within acceptable limits, having regard to the area of navigation and prevailing sea state. Alterations of course are smooth and controlled Communications are clear and concise at all times and orders are acknowledged in a seamanlike manner
Keep a proper look-out by sight and hearing	Responsibilities of a look-out, including reporting the approximate bearing of a sound signal, light or other object in degrees or points	Assessment of evidence obtained from: .1 practical test, or .2 approved in-service experience, or .3 approved training ship experience	Sound signals, lights and other objects are promptly detected and their approximate bearing, in degrees or points, is reported to the officer of the watch
Contribute to monitoring and controlling a safe watch	Shipboard terms and definitions Use of appropriate internal communication and alarm systems Ability to understand orders and to communicate with the officer of the watch on matters relevant to watchkeeping duties Procedures for the relief, maintenance and handover of a watch Information required to maintain a safe watch Basic environmental protection procedures	Assessment of evidence obtained from approved in-service experience or approved training ship experience	Communications are clear and concise and advice/clarification is sought from the officer on watch where watch information or instructions are not clearly understood Maintenance, handover and relief of the watch is in conformity with accepted practices and procedures

表 A-II/4
组成航行值班部分的普通船员的最低适任标准

职能:航行　支持级

第 1 栏	第 2 栏	第 3 栏	第 4 栏
适任	知识、理解和熟练	表明适任的方法	评价适任的标准
按照舵令(包括英语舵令)操舵	使用磁罗经和陀螺罗经舵令 自动舵与手动操舵的互换	评估从下列各项中获取的证据: .1 实操测试,或 .2 认可的工作经历,或 .3 认可的培训船经历	在可接受的限度内稳定地操舵以保持航向,注意航行区域和当时海况,平稳地控制航向的改变 在任何时候交流清楚简明,并以海员的方式确认有关指令
用视觉和听觉保持正规的瞭望	瞭望人员的责任,包括用度或罗经点报告声号、灯号或其他目标的大致方位	评估从下列各项中获取的证据: .1 实操测试,或 .2 认可的工作经历,或 .3 认可的培训船经历	迅速地探测到声号、灯号和其他目标,并以度或罗经点向值班高级船员报告其大致方位
有助于监测和控制安全值班	船上术语和定义 使用相应的船上内部通信和报警系统 理解舵令并能就有关值班职责的事宜与值班高级船员进行沟通的能力 接班、值班和交班程序 保持安全值班所需的信息 基本的保护环境程序	评估从认可的工作经历或认可的培训船经历中获取的证据	交流清楚简明,在未能清楚地理解值班信息或指示时,能从值班高级船员处求得建议/说明 值班、交班和接班符合公认的原则和程序

Column 1	Column 2	Column 3	Column 4
Competence	**Knowledge, understanding and proficiency**	**Methods for demonstrating competence**	**Criteria for evaluating competence**
Operate emergency equipment and apply emergency procedures	Knowledge of emergency duties and alarm signals Knowledge of pyrotechnic distress signals; satellite EPIRBs and SARTs Avoidance of false distress alerts and action to be taken in event of accidental activation	Assessment of evidence obtained from demonstration and approved in-service experience or approved training ship experience	Initial action on becoming aware of an emergency or abnormal situation is in conformity with established practices and procedures Communications are clear and concise at all times and orders are acknowledged in a seamanlike manner The integrity of emergency and distress alerting systems is maintained at all times

第 1 栏	第 2 栏	第 3 栏	第 4 栏
适任	知识、理解和熟练	表明适任的方法	评价适任的标准
操作应急设备和应用应急程序	应急职责和报警信号的知识 烟火遇险信号、卫星应急无线电示位标和搜救应答器的知识 误遇险报警的避免和偶然触发警报时应采取的行动	评估从演示和认可的工作经历或认可的培训船经历中获取的证据	意识到紧急或异常情况时的初始行动符合既定的做法和程序 在任何时候交流清楚简明,并以海员的方式确认有关指令 始终保持紧急和遇险报警系统的完整性

Section A-II/5
Mandatory minimum requirements for certification of ratings as able seafarer deck

Standard of competence

1 Every able seafarer deck serving on a seagoing ship of 500 gross tonnage or more shall be required to demonstrate the competence to perform the functions at the support level, as specified in column 1 of table A-II/5.

2 The minimum knowledge, understanding and proficiency required of an able seafarer deck serving on a seagoing ship of 500 gross tonnage or more is listed in column 2 of table A-II/5.

3 Every candidate for certification shall be required to provide evidence of having achieved the required standard of competence in accordance with the methods for demonstrating competence and the criteria for evaluating competence specified in columns 3 and 4 of table A-II/5.

第 A-II/5 节

对作为高级值班水手的普通船员发证的强制性最低要求

适任标准

1　每个在 500 总吨或以上的海船上服务的高级值班水手应按要求表明履行表 A-II/5 第 1 栏规定的支持级职能的适任能力。

2　对在 500 总吨或以上的海船上服务的高级值班水手所要求最低的知识、理解和熟练列于表 A-II/5 第 2 栏中。

3　每个证书申请人应按照表 A-II/5 第 3 栏和第 4 栏所列的表明适任的方法和评价适任的标准,提供已达到所要求的适任标准的证据。

Table A-II/5

Specification of minimum standards of competence of ratings as able seafarer deck

Function: Navigation at the support level

Column 1	Column 2	Column 3	Column 4
Competence	**Knowledge, understanding and proficiency**	**Methods for demonstrating competence**	**Criteria for evaluating competence**
Contribute to a safe navigational watch	Ability to understand orders and to communicate with the officer of the watch on matters relevant to watchkeeping duties Procedures for the relief, maintenance and handover of a watch Information required to maintain a safe watch	Assessment of evidence obtained from in-service experience or practical test	Communications are clear and concise Maintenance, handover and relief of the watch is in conformity with acceptable practices and procedures
Contribute to berthing, anchoring and other mooring operations	Working knowledge of the mooring system and related procedures, including: .1 the function of mooring and tug lines and how each line functions as part of an overall system .2 the capacities, safe working loads, and breaking strengths of mooring equipment, including mooring wires, synthetic and fibre lines, winches, anchor windlasses, capstans, bitts, chocks and bollards .3 the procedures and order of events for making fast and letting go mooring and tug lines and wires, including towing lines .4 the procedures and order of events for the use of anchors in various operations Working knowledge of the procedures and order of events associated with mooring to a buoy or buoys	Assessment of evidence obtained from one or more of the following: .1 approved in-service experience .2 practical training .3 examination .4 approved training ship experience .5 approved simulator training, where appropriate	Operations are carried out in accordance with established safety practices and equipment operating instructions

表 A-II/5
作为高级值班水手的普通船员的最低适任标准

职能:航行　支持级

第 1 栏	第 2 栏	第 3 栏	第 4 栏
适任	知识、理解和熟练	表明适任的方法	评价适任的标准
有助于安全航行值班	理解舵令并就有关值班职责的事宜与值班高级船员进行沟通的能力 接班、值班和交班程序 保持安全值班所需的信息	评估从工作经历或实操测试中获取的证据	交流清楚简明 值班、交班和接班符合可接受的做法和程序
有助于靠泊、锚泊和其他系泊操作	系泊系统和相关程序的实用知识,包括: .1　系缆和拖缆的功能以及每根缆绳作为整体系统一部分的功能 .2　系泊设备的承载能力、安全工作负荷和破断强度,包括系泊钢丝缆、合成纤维缆、绞车、锚机、绞盘、缆柱、导缆钳和缆桩 .3　系住和解掉系缆、拖船缆、钢丝绳(包括拖缆)的程序和顺序 .4　各种操作中用锚的程序和顺序 有关系泊单浮筒或多浮筒的程序和顺序的实用知识	评估从下列一项或数项获取的证据: .1　认可的工作经历 .2　实操培训 .3　考试 .4　认可的培训船经历 .5　认可的模拟器培训,如适用	按照既定的安全做法和设备操作规程进行操作

Function: Cargo handling and stowage at the support level

Column 1	Column 2	Column 3	Column 4
Competence	**Knowledge, understanding and proficiency**	**Methods for demonstrating competence**	**Criteria for evaluating competence**
Contribute to the handling of cargo and stores	Knowledge of procedures for safe handling, stowage and securing of cargoes and stores, including dangerous, hazardous and harmful substances and liquids Basic knowledge of and precautions to observe in connection with particular types of cargo and identification of IMDG labelling	Assessment of evidence obtained from one or more of the following: .1 approved in-service experience .2 practical training .3 examination .4 approved training ship experience .5 approved simulator training, where appropriate	Cargo and stores operations are carried out in accordance with established safety procedures and equipment operating instructions The handling of dangerous, hazardous and harmful cargoes or stores complies with established safety practices

Function: Controlling the operation of the ship and care for persons on board at the support level

Column 1	Column 2	Column 3	Column 4
Competence	**Knowledge, understanding and proficiency**	**Methods for demonstrating competence**	**Criteria for evaluating competence**
Contribute to the safe operation of deck equipment and machinery	Knowledge of deck equipment, including: .1 function and uses of valves and pumps, hoists, cranes, booms, and related equipment .2 function and uses of winches, windlasses, capstans and related equipment .3 hatches, watertight doors, ports, and related equipment	Assessment of evidence obtained from one or more of the following: .1 approved in-service experience .2 practical training .3 examination .4 approved training ship experience	Operations are carried out in accordance with established safety practices and equipment operating instructions

职能:货物装卸和积载　支持级

第 1 栏	第 2 栏	第 3 栏	第 4 栏
适任	**知识、理解和熟练**	**表明适任的方法**	**评价适任的标准**
有助于货物和物料的装卸	安全装卸、积载和系固货物和物料的程序的知识,包括危险、有害固体和液体 与特定种类货物和识别 IMDG 标签有关的基本知识和要遵循的预防措施	评估从下列一项或数项获取的证据: .1 认可的工作经历 .2 实操培训 .3 考试 .4 认可的培训船经历 .5 认可的模拟器培训,如适用	按照既定的安全程序和设备操作规程进行货物和物料操作 危险和有害货物或物料的装卸符合既定的安全做法

职能:船舶作业管理和人员管理　支持级

第 1 栏	第 2 栏	第 3 栏	第 4 栏
适任	**知识、理解和熟练**	**表明适任的方法**	**评价适任的标准**
有助于甲板设备和机械的安全操作	甲板设备的知识,包括: .1 阀和泵、升降机、克令吊、吊臂和相关设备的功能和使用 .2 绞车、锚机、绞盘和相关设备的功能和使用 .3 舱口、水密门、驳门和相关设备	评估从下列一项或数项获取的证据: .1 认可的工作经历 .2 实操培训 .3 考试 .4 认可的培训船经历	按照既定的安全做法和设备操作规程进行操作

Column 1	Column 2	Column 3	Column 4
Competence	**Knowledge, understanding and proficiency**	**Methods for demonstrating competence**	**Criteria for evaluating competence**
Contribute to the safe operation of deck equipment and machinery (*continued*)	.4 fibre and wire ropes, cables and chains, including their construction, use, markings, maintenance and proper stowage		
	.5 ability to use and understand basic signals for the operation of equipment, including winches, windlasses, cranes, and hoists	Assessment of evidence obtained from practical demonstration	Communications within the operator's area of responsibility are consistently successful
	.6 ability to operate anchoring equipment under various conditions, such as anchoring, weighing anchor, securing for sea, and in emergencies	Assessment of evidence obtained from practical demonstration	Equipment operation is safely carried out in accordance with established procedures
	Knowledge of the following procedures and ability to:		
	.1 rig and unrig bosun's chairs and staging .2 rig and unrig pilot ladders, hoists, rat-guards and gangways	Assessment of evidence obtained from practical demonstration	Demonstrate the proper methods for rigging and unrigging in accordance with safe industry practice
	.3 use marlin spike seamanship skills, including the proper use of knots, splices and stoppers		Demonstrate the proper creation and use of knots, splices, stoppers, whippings, servings as well as proper canvas handling
	Use and handling of deck and cargo-handling gear and equipment:		
	.1 access arrangements, hatches and hatch covers, ramps, side/bow/stern doors or elevators		
	.2 pipeline systems – bilge and ballast suctions and wells		

第 1 栏	第 2 栏	第 3 栏	第 4 栏
适任	知识、理解和熟练	表明适任的方法	评价适任的标准
有助于甲板设备和机械的安全操作(续)	.4 纤维和钢丝绳、绳索和链索，包括其构造、使用、标志、保养和正确堆存		
	.5 使用和理解操作设备的基本信号的能力，包括绞车、锚机、克令吊和升降机	评估从实际演示中获取的证据	在操作者责任范围内的交流持续有效
	.6 在各种情况下操作锚设备的能力，例如锚泊、起锚、开航前固定以及紧急情况	评估从实际演示中获取的证据	设备操作按照既定的程序安全地进行
	下列程序和能力的知识： .1 安装和拆卸坐板和架板 .2 安装和拆卸引航梯、升降机、鼠挡和舷梯 .3 使用扩索锥的水手技能，包括适当使用绳结、插接和制缆索	评估从实际演示中获取的证据	表明安装和拆卸的适当方法符合安全的行业做法 表明绳结、插接、制缆索、绳头缠扎、卷缠的制作和使用以及帆布的操作适当
	使用和操作甲板和货物装卸装置和设备： .1 登船装置、舱口和舱口盖、登陆舌门、舷侧/船首/船尾门或升降梯 .2 管系——污水和压载水、吸入口和污水井		

Column 1	Column 2	Column 3	Column 4
Competence	**Knowledge, understanding and proficiency**	**Methods for demonstrating competence**	**Criteria for evaluating competence**
Contribute to the safe operation of deck equipment and machinery (*continued*)	.3 cranes, derricks, winches Knowledge of hoisting and dipping flags and the main single-flag signals (A, B, G, H, O, P, Q)		Demonstrate the proper use of blocks and tackle Demonstrate the proper methods for handling lines, wires, cables and chains
Apply occupational health and safety precautions	Working knowledge of safe working practices and personal shipboard safety including: .1 working aloft .2 working over the side .3 working in enclosed spaces .4 permit to work systems .5 line handling .6 lifting techniques and methods of preventing back injury .7 electrical safety .8 mechanical safety .9 chemical and biohazard safety .10 personal safety equipment	Assessment of evidence obtained from one or more of the following: .1 approved in-service experience .2 practical training .3 examination .4 approved training ship experience	Procedures designed to safeguard personnel and the ship are observed at all times Safe working practices are observed and appropriate safety and protective equipment is correctly used at all times
Apply precautions and contribute to the prevention of pollution of the marine environment	Knowledge of the precautions to be taken to prevent pollution of the marine environment Knowledge of the use and operation of anti-pollution equipment Knowledge of the approved methods for disposal of marine pollutants	Assessment of evidence obtained from one or more of the following: .1 approved in-service experience .2 practical training .3 examination .4 approved training ship experience	Procedures designed to safeguard the marine environment are observed at all times

第 1 栏	第 2 栏	第 3 栏	第 4 栏
适任	知识、理解和熟练	表明适任的方法	评价适任的标准
有助于甲板设备和机械的安全操作（续）	.3 克令吊、吊杆、绞车 升旗和行点旗礼以及主要单旗信号（A,B,G,H,O,P,Q）的知识		表明滑车和绞辘的使用适当 表明操作缆绳、钢丝绳、绳索和链索的方法适当
采取职业健康和安全预防措施	安全工作做法和人员在船安全的实用知识，包括： .1 高空作业 .2 舷外作业 .3 封闭场所作业 .4 作业许可制度 .5 缆索操作 .6 吊装技术和防止后背受伤的方法 .7 电气安全 .8 机械安全 .9 化学品和生物危害的安全 .10 个人安全设备	评估从下列一项或数项获取的证据： .1 认可的工作经历 .2 实操培训 .3 考试 .4 认可的培训船经历	始终遵守为保护人员和船舶而制定的程序 始终遵守安全工作做法并正确使用适合的安全和防护设备
采取预防措施和有助于防止海洋环境污染	采取措施防止海洋环境污染的知识 防污染设备的使用和操作的知识 处置海洋污染物的认可的方法的知识	评估从下列一项或数项获取的证据： .1 认可的工作经历 .2 实操培训 .3 考试 .4 认可的培训船经历	始终遵循保护海洋环境的程序

Column 1	Column 2	Column 3	Column 4
Competence	**Knowledge, understanding and proficiency**	**Methods for demonstrating competence**	**Criteria for evaluating competence**
Operate survival craft and rescue boats	Knowledge of the operation of survival craft and rescue boats, their launching appliances and arrangements, and their equipment Knowledge of survival at sea techniques	Assessment of evidence obtained from approved training and experience as set out in section A-VI/2, paragraphs 1 to 4	Actions in responding to abandon ship and survival situations are appropriate to the prevailing circumstances and conditions and comply with accepted safety practices and standards

Function: Maintenance and repair at the support level

Column 1	Column 2	Column 3	Column 4
Competence	**Knowledge, understanding and proficiency**	**Methods for demonstrating competence**	**Criteria for evaluating competence**
Contribute to shipboard maintenance and repair	Ability to use painting, lubrication and cleaning materials and equipment Ability to understand and execute routine maintenance and repair procedures Knowledge of surface preparation techniques	Assessment of evidence obtained from practical demonstration	Maintenance and repair activities are carried out in accordance with technical, safety and procedural specifications
	Understanding manufacturer's safety guidelines and shipboard instructions Knowledge of safe disposal of waste materials Knowledge of the application, maintenance and use of hand and power tools	Assessment of evidence obtained from one or more of the following: .1 approved in-service experience .2 practical training .3 examination .4 approved training ship experience	

第 1 栏	第 2 栏	第 3 栏	第 4 栏
适任	**知识、理解和熟练**	**表明适任的方法**	**评价适任的标准**
操作救生艇筏和救助艇	操作救生艇筏和救助艇及其释放装置和布置以及设备的知识 海上求生技能的知识	评估从第 A-VI/2 节第 1 段至第 4 段规定的认可的培训和经历中获取的证据	弃船和求生情况下的应急行动适合于当时的环境和条件，并符合公认的安全做法和标准

职能：维护和修理　支持级

第 1 栏	第 2 栏	第 3 栏	第 4 栏
适任	**知识、理解和熟练**	**表明适任的方法**	**评价适任的标准**
有助于船上维护和修理	使用油漆、润滑和清洁材料和设备的能力 理解和执行常规维护和修理程序的能力 表面清理技能的知识 了解制造商安全准则和船上规程 安全处置废料的知识 应用、维护和使用手动和电动工具的知识	评估从实操演示中获取的证据 评估从下列一项或数项获取的证据： .1　认可的工作经历 .2　实操培训 .3　考试 .4　认可的培训船经历	按照技术、安全和程序规范进行维护和修理活动

CHAPTER III

Standards regarding engine department

Section A-III/1

Mandatory minimum requirements for certification of officers in charge of an engineering watch in a manned engine-room or as designated duty engineers in a periodically unmanned engine-room

Training

1 The education and training required by paragraph 2.4 of regulation III/1 shall include training in mechanical and electrical workshop skills relevant to the duties of an engineer officer.

Onboard training

2 Every candidate for certification as officer in charge of an engineering watch in a manned engine-room or as designated duty engineer in a periodically unmanned engine-room of ships powered by main propulsion machinery of 750 kW or more whose seagoing service, in accordance with paragraph 2.2 of regulation III/1, forms part of a training programme approved as meeting the requirements of this section shall follow an approved programme of onboard training which:

.1 ensures that, during the required period of seagoing service, the candidate receives systematic practical training and experience in the tasks, duties and responsibilities of an officer in charge of an engine-room watch, taking into account the guidance given in section B-III/1 of this Code;

.2 is closely supervised and monitored by a qualified and certificated engineer officer aboard the ships in which the approved seagoing service is performed; and

.3 is adequately documented in a training record book.

Standard of competence

3 Every candidate for certification as officer in charge of an engineering watch in a manned engine-room or as designated duty engineer in a periodically unmanned engine-room on a seagoing ship powered by main propulsion machinery of 750 kW propulsion power or more shall be required to demonstrate ability to undertake, at the operational level, the tasks, duties and responsibilities listed in column 1 of table A-III/1.

4 The minimum knowledge, understanding and proficiency required for certification is listed in column 2 of table A-III/1.

5 The level of knowledge of the material listed in column 2 of table A-III/1 shall be sufficient for engineer officers to carry out their watchkeeping duties.*

* The relevant IMO Model Course(s) may be of assistance in the preparation of courses.

第 III 章
关于轮机部的标准

第 A-III/1 节
对有人值班机舱负责轮机值班的高级船员或周期性无人值班机舱指定值班的轮机员发证的强制性最低要求

培训

1 规则第 III/1 条第 2.4 段要求的教育和培训,应包括有关轮机部高级船员职责的机械和电气车间技能的培训。

船上培训

2 每个申请在主推进装置为 750 kW 或以上海船上有人值班机舱负责轮机值班的高级船员或周期性无人值班机舱指定值班的轮机员证书的申请人,根据规则第 III/1 条第 2.2 段,其海上服务资历构成经认可符合本节要求的培训计划的一部分,应参加认可的船上培训计划,该培训计划:

.1 确保证书申请人在规定的海上服务期间,受到关于负责机舱值班高级船员的任务、职责和责任方面的系统而实际的培训并获得经验,同时考虑本规则第 B-III/1 节给予的指导;

.2 在执行认可的海上服务中受到船上合格并持证的轮机部高级船员的密切监督和指导;并且

.3 在培训记录簿中充分记载。

适任标准

3 每个申请在主推进装置为 750 kW 或以上海船上有人值班机舱负责轮机值班的高级船员或周期性无人值班机舱指定值班的轮机员证书的申请人,应表明承担表 A-III/1 第 1 栏所列操作级的任务、职责和责任的能力。

4 发证要求的最低的知识、理解和熟练列于表 A-III/1 第 2 栏中。

5 表 A-III/1 第 2 栏所列内容的知识水平,应足以能使轮机部高级船员履行其值班职责。①

① 相关 IMO 示范培训课程可有助于准备课程。

6 Training and experience to achieve the necessary theoretical knowledge, understanding and proficiency shall be based on section A-VIII/2, part 4-2 Principles to be observed in keeping an engineering watch, and shall take into account the relevant requirements of this part and the guidance given in part B of this Code.

7 Candidates for certification for service in ships in which steam boilers do not form part of their machinery may omit the relevant requirements of table A-III/1. A certificate awarded on such a basis shall not be valid for service on ships in which steam boilers form part of a ship's machinery until the engineer officer meets the standard of competence in the items omitted from table A-III/1. Any such limitation shall be stated on the certificate and in the endorsement.

8 The Administration may omit knowledge requirements for types of propulsion machinery other than those machinery installations for which the certificate to be awarded shall be valid. A certificate awarded on such a basis shall not be valid for any category of machinery installation which has been omitted until the engineer officer proves to be competent in these knowledge requirements. Any such limitation shall be stated on the certificate and in the endorsement.

9 Every candidate for certification shall be required to provide evidence of having achieved the required standard of competence in accordance with the methods for demonstrating competence and the criteria for evaluating competence tabulated in columns 3 and 4 of table A-III/1.

Near-coastal voyages

10 The requirements of paragraphs 2.2 to 2.5 of regulation III/1 relating to level of knowledge, understanding and proficiency required under the different sections listed in column 2 of table A-III/1 may be varied for engineer officers of ships powered by main propulsion machinery of less than 3,000 kW propulsion power engaged on near-coastal voyages, as considered necessary, bearing in mind the effect on the safety of all ships which may be operating in the same waters. Any such limitation shall be stated on the certificate and in the endorsement.

6 为获取所需的理论知识、理解和熟练的培训和经验,应以第 A-VIII/2 节第 4-2 部分——轮机值班中应遵循的原则为基础,并应考虑本规则本部分的有关要求和 B 部分给予的指导。
7 对在蒸汽锅炉不作为主动力装置部分的船上服务的证书申请人,可删除表 A-III/1 中的有关要求。据此所发的证书不应对蒸汽锅炉作为主动力装置部分的船舶上的服务有效,直至该轮机部高级船员达到了从表 A-III/1 中被删除项目的适任标准。任何这种限制应在证书和签证上载明。
8 主管机关可删除那些对所发证书有效的机械装置以外的其他类型的推进装置的知识要求。据此所发的证书不应对已被删除的任何种类的机械装置有效,直至该轮机部高级船员证明能符合这些知识要求。任何这种限制应在证书和签证上载明。
9 每个证书申请人应按照表 A-III/1 第 3 栏和第 4 栏所列的表明适任的方法和评价适任的标准,提供已达到所要求的适任标准的证据。

近岸航行

10 规则第 III/1 条第 2.2 段至第 2.5 段中与表 A-III/1 第 2 栏不同部分所列的对知识、理解和熟练水平的要求有关的规定,如认为必要,可对主推进装置为 3 000 kW 以下从事近岸航行的船舶的轮机部高级船员有所变动,但要切记对可能在同一水域航行的所有船舶安全的影响。任何这种限制应在证书和签证上载明。

Table A-III/1

Specification of minimum standard of competence for officers in charge of an engineering watch in a manned engine-room or designated duty engineers in a periodically unmanned engine-room

Function: Marine engineering at the operational level

Column 1	Column 2	Column 3	Column 4
Competence	**Knowledge, understanding and proficiency**	**Methods for demonstrating competence**	**Criteria for evaluating competence**
Maintain a safe engineering watch	Thorough knowledge of Principles to be observed in keeping an engineering watch, including: .1 duties associated with taking over and accepting a watch .2 routine duties undertaken during a watch .3 maintenance of the machinery space logs and the significance of the readings taken .4 duties associated with handing over a watch Safety and emergency procedures; change-over of remote/automatic to local control of all systems Safety precautions to be observed during a watch and immediate actions to be taken in the event of fire or accident, with particular reference to oil systems	Assessment of evidence obtained from one or more of the following: .1 approved in-service experience .2 approved training ship experience .3 approved simulator training, where appropriate .4 approved laboratory equipment training	The conduct, handover and relief of the watch conforms with accepted principles and procedures The frequency and extent of monitoring of engineering equipment and systems conforms to manufacturers' recommendations and accepted principles and procedures, including Principles to be observed in keeping an engineering watch A proper record is maintained of the movements and activities relating to the ship's engineering systems

表 A-III/1
有人值班机舱负责轮机值班的高级船员或周期性无人值班机舱指定值班的轮机员的最低适任标准

职能:轮机工程　操作级

第 1 栏	第 2 栏	第 3 栏	第 4 栏
适任	**知识、理解和熟练**	**表明适任的方法**	**评价适任的标准**
保持安全的轮机值班	轮机值班应遵守的原则的全面知识,包括: .1 与接班有关的职责 .2 值班期间履行的日常职责 .3 轮机日志的填写和所填读数的意义 .4 与交班有关的职责 安全和应急程序;将所有系统遥控/自控转换为现场控制 值班时应遵守的安全预防措施以及一旦发生火灾或事故(特别是油类系统火灾或事故)时应采取的紧急措施	评估从下列一项或数项获取的证据: .1 认可的工作经历 .2 认可的培训船经历 .3 认可的模拟器培训,如适用 .4 认可的实验室设备培训	值班和交接班符合公认的原则和程序 轮机设备和系统的检测频度和范围符合厂家的建议、公认的原则和程序,包括轮机值班应遵守的原则 对有关船舶轮机系统的动态和活动保持规范的记录

Column 1	Column 2	Column 3	Column 4
Competence	**Knowledge, understanding and proficiency**	**Methods for demonstrating competence**	**Criteria for evaluating competence**
Maintain a safe engineering watch (*continued*)	*Engine-room resource management* Knowledge of engine-room resource management principles, including: .1 allocation, assignment, and prioritization of resources .2 effective communication .3 assertiveness and leadership .4 obtaining and maintaining situational awareness .5 consideration of team experience	Assessment of evidence obtained from one or more of the following: .1 approved training .2 approved in-service experience .3 approved simulator training	Resources are allocated and assigned as needed in correct priority to perform necessary tasks Communication is clearly and unambiguously given and received Questionable decisions and/or actions result in appropriate challenge and response Effective leadership behaviours are identified Team member(s) share accurate understanding of current and predicted engine-room and associated systems state, and of external environment
Use English in written and oral form	Adequate knowledge of the English language to enable the officer to use engineering publications and to perform engineering duties	Examination and assessment of evidence obtained from practical instruction	English language publications relevant to engineering duties are correctly interpreted Communications are clear and understood
Use internal communication systems	Operation of all internal communication systems on board	Examination and assessment of evidence obtained from one or more of the following: .1 approved in-service experience .2 approved training ship experience .3 approved simulator training, where appropriate .4 approved laboratory equipment training	Transmission and reception of messages are consistently successful Communication records are complete, accurate and comply with statutory requirements

第 1 栏	第 2 栏	第 3 栏	第 4 栏
适任	知识、理解和熟练	表明适任的方法	评价适任的标准
保持安全的轮机值班(续)	机舱资源管理 机舱资源管理原则的知识,包括: .1 资源的分配、分派和优先排序 .2 有效的沟通 .3 决断力和领导力 .4 具有和保持情景意识 .5 考虑团队经验	评估从下列一项或数项获取的证据: .1 认可的培训 .2 认可的工作经历 .3 认可的模拟器培训	根据需要按正确的优先顺序分配和分派资源,以执行必要的任务 交流清楚、无歧义 对有疑问的决定和/或行动适当质疑和响应 确认有效的领导行为 团队成员对当前和预计的机舱及其关联系统的状态及外部环境有共同的准确理解
以书面和口语形式使用英语	使轮机部高级船员能够使用轮机出版物并能履行轮机职责的足够的英语知识	考试并评估从实际训练中获取的证据	正确解读与轮机职责有关的英语出版物 交流清楚、明白
使用内部通信系统	船上所有的内部通信系统的操作	考试并评估从下列一项或数项获取的证据: .1 认可的工作经历 .2 认可的培训船经历 .3 认可的模拟器培训,如适用 .4 认可的实验室设备培训	信息的发送和接收持续有效 通信记录完整、准确且符合法定要求

Column 1	Column 2	Column 3	Column 4
Competence	**Knowledge, understanding and proficiency**	**Methods for demonstrating competence**	**Criteria for evaluating competence**
Operate main and auxiliary machinery and associated control systems	Basic construction and operation principles of machinery systems, including: .1 marine diesel engine .2 marine steam turbine .3 marine gas turbine .4 marine boiler .5 shafting installations, including propeller .6 other auxiliaries, including various pumps, air compressor, purifier, fresh water generator, heat exchanger, refrigeration, air-conditioning and ventilation systems .7 steering gear .8 automatic control systems .9 fluid flow and characteristics of lubricating oil, fuel oil and cooling systems .10 deck machinery Safety and emergency procedures for operation of propulsion plant machinery, including control systems	Examination and assessment of evidence obtained from one or more of the following: .1 approved in-service experience .2 approved training ship experience .3 approved laboratory equipment training	Construction and operating mechanisms can be understood and explained with drawings/instructions

第 1 栏	第 2 栏	第 3 栏	第 4 栏
适任	**知识、理解和熟练**	**表明适任的方法**	**评价适任的标准**
操作主机和辅机以及相关的控制系统	机械系统的基本结构和工作原理,包括: .1 船用柴油机 .2 船用蒸汽轮机 .3 船用燃气轮机 .4 船用锅炉 .5 轴系,包括螺旋桨 .6 其他辅助机械,包括各种泵、空压机、分油机、造水机、热交换器、制冷装置、空调及通风系统 .7 舵机 .8 自动控制系统 .9 滑油系统、燃油系统和冷却系统的流体流动和特性 .10 甲板机械 推进装置机械的安全和应急操作程序,包括控制系统	考试并评估从下列一项或数项获取的证据: .1 认可的工作经历 .2 认可的培训船经历 .3 认可的实验室设备培训	利用图纸/说明书理解和解释结构及工作机理

Column 1	Column 2	Column 3	Column 4
Competence	**Knowledge, understanding and proficiency**	**Methods for demonstrating competence**	**Criteria for evaluating competence**
Operate main and auxiliary machinery and associated control systems *(continued)*	Preparation, operation, fault detection and necessary measures to prevent damage for the following machinery items and control systems: .1 main engine and associated auxiliaries .2 steam boiler and associated auxiliaries and steam systems .3 auxiliary prime movers and associated systems .4 other auxiliaries, including refrigeration, air-conditioning and ventilation systems	Examination and assessment of evidence obtained from one or more of the following: .1 approved in-service experience .2 approved training ship experience .3 approved simulator training, where appropriate .4 approved laboratory equipment training	Operations are planned and carried out in accordance with operating manuals, established rules and procedures to ensure safety of operations and avoid pollution of the marine environment Deviations from the norm are promptly identified The output of plant and engineering systems consistently meets requirements, including bridge orders relating to changes in speed and direction The causes of machinery malfunctions are promptly identified and actions are designed to ensure the overall safety of the ship and the plant, having regard to the prevailing circumstances and conditions
Operate fuel, lubrication, ballast and other pumping systems and associated control systems	Operational characteristics of pumps and piping systems, including control systems Operation of pumping systems: .1 routine pumping operations .2 operation of bilge, ballast and cargo pumping systems Oily-water separators (or similar equipment) requirements and operation	Examination and assessment of evidence obtained from one or more of the following: .1 approved in-service experience .2 approved training ship experience .3 approved simulator training, where appropriate .4 approved laboratory equipment training	Operations are planned and carried out in accordance with operating manuals, established rules and procedures to ensure safety of operations and avoid pollution of the marine environment Deviations from the norm are promptly identified and appropriate action is taken

第 1 栏	第 2 栏	第 3 栏	第 4 栏
适任	知识、理解和熟练	表明适任的方法	评价适任的标准
操作主机和辅机以及相关的控制系统(续)	为防止下列机械设备和控制系统的损坏的准备、操作、故障检测及必要的措施: .1 主机及相关辅助设备 .2 蒸汽锅炉和相关辅助设备及蒸汽系统 .3 副机原动机及相关系统 .4 其他辅助机械,包括制冷装置、空调和通风系统	考试并评估从下列一项或数项获取的证据: .1 认可的工作经历 .2 认可的培训船经历 .3 认可的模拟器培训,如适用 .4 认可的实验室设备培训	操作有计划,并按照操作手册、既定规则和程序进行,以确保操作安全和防止海洋环境污染 迅速发现异常情况 推进装置和轮机系统的输出功率持续符合要求,包括与变速和换向有关的驾驶台指令 迅速识别机械故障的原因,采取的措施旨在确保船舶和动力装置的总体安全,并考虑当前的环境和条件
燃油系统、滑油系统、压载水系统和其他泵系以及相关控制系统的操作	泵和管系的工作特性,包括控制系统 泵系操作: .1 泵的日常操作 .2 舱底水系统、压载水系统和货泵系统的操作 油水分离器(或类似设备)的要求和操作	考试并评估从下列一项或数项获取的证据: .1 认可的工作经历 .2 认可的培训船经历 .3 认可的模拟器培训,如适用 .4 认可的实验室设备培训	操作有计划,并按照操作手册、既定规则和程序进行,以确保操作安全和防止海洋环境污染 迅速发现异常情况,并采取适当的行动

Function: Electrical, electronic and control engineering at the operational level

Column 1	Column 2	Column 3	Column 4
Competence	**Knowledge, understanding and proficiency**	**Methods for demonstrating competence**	**Criteria for evaluating competence**
Operate electrical, electronic and control systems	Basic configuration and operation principles of the following electrical, electronic and control equipment: .1 electrical equipment: .a generator and distribution systems .b preparing, starting, paralleling and changing over generators .c electrical motors including starting methodologies .d high-voltage installations .e sequential control circuits and associated system devices .2 electronic equipment: .a characteristics of basic electronic circuit elements .b flowchart for automatic and control systems .c functions, characteristics and features of control systems for machinery items, including main propulsion plant operation control and steam boiler automatic controls .3 control systems: .a various automatic control methodologies and characteristics .b Proportional–Integral–Derivative (PID) control characteristics and associated system devices for process control	Examination and assessment of evidence obtained from one or more of the following: .1 approved in-service experience .2 approved training ship experience .3 approved simulator training, where appropriate .4 approved laboratory equipment training	Operations are planned and carried out in accordance with operating manuals, established rules and procedures to ensure safety of operations Electrical, electronic and control systems can be understood and explained with drawings/instructions

职能:电气、电子和控制工程　操作级

第 1 栏	第 2 栏	第 3 栏	第 4 栏
适任	知识、理解和熟练	表明适任的方法	评价适任的标准
操作电气、电子和控制系统	下列电气、电子和控制设备的基本配置和工作原理 .1 电气设备: .a 发电机和配电系统 .b 备车、启动、并车和发电机的切换 .c 电动马达,包括启动方式 .d 高压装置 .e 相序控制电路和相关系统设备 .2 电子设备: .a 基本电路元件的特性 .b 自动和控制系统的流程图 .c 机械设备控制系统的功能、特性和参数,包括主推进装置操作控制和蒸汽锅炉自动控制 .3 控制系统: .a 各种自动控制方式和特性 .b 比例—积分—微分(PID)的控制特性和用于程序控制的相关系统设备	考试并评估从下列一项或数项获取的证据: .1 认可的工作经历 .2 认可的培训船经历 .3 认可的模拟器培训,如适用 .4 认可的实验室设备培训	操作有计划,并按照操作手册、既定规则和程序进行,以确保操作安全 利用图纸/说明书理解和解释电气、电子及控制系统

Column 1	Column 2	Column 3	Column 4
Competence	**Knowledge, understanding and proficiency**	**Methods for demonstrating competence**	**Criteria for evaluating competence**
Maintenance and repair of electrical and electronic equipment	Safety requirements for working on shipboard electrical systems, including the safe isolation of electrical equipment required before personnel are permitted to work on such equipment Maintenance and repair of electrical system equipment, switchboards, electric motors, generator and DC electrical systems and equipment Detection of electric malfunction, location of faults and measures to prevent damage Construction and operation of electrical testing and measuring equipment Function and performance tests of the following equipment and their configuration: .1 monitoring systems .2 automatic control devices .3 protective devices The interpretation of electrical and simple electronic diagrams	Examination and assessment of evidence obtained from one or more of the following: .1 approved workshop skills training .2 approved practical experience and tests .3 approved in-service experience .4 approved training ship experience	Safety measures for working are appropriate Selection and use of hand tools, measuring instruments, and testing equipment are appropriate and interpretation of results is accurate Dismantling, inspecting, repairing and reassembling equipment are in accordance with manuals and good practice Reassembling and performance testing is in accordance with manuals and good practice

第 1 栏	第 2 栏	第 3 栏	第 4 栏
适任	知识、理解和熟练	表明适任的方法	评价适任的标准
电气和电子设备的维护与修理	船舶电气系统的工作安全要求,包括在允许人员检修该设备之前所要求的电气设备的安全隔离 电气系统设备、配电板、电动机、发电机和直流电气系统及设备的维护与修理 电气故障和故障位置的检测及防止损坏的措施 电气测试和测量设备的结构和操作 以下设备及其装置的功能和性能测试: .1 监控系统 .2 自动控制设备 .3 防护设备 电气和简单电子图的识读	考试并评估从下列一项或数项获取的证据: .1 认可的车间技能培训 .2 认可的实际经验和测试 .3 认可的工作经历 .4 认可的培训船经历	工作安全措施适当 手动工具、测量仪表、检测设备的选择和使用适当,且对结果的解释准确 设备的拆卸、检查、修理和装复符合操作手册及良好的做法 装复和性能测试符合操作手册及良好的做法

Function: Maintenance and repair at the operational level

Column 1	Column 2	Column 3	Column 4
Competence	**Knowledge, understanding and proficiency**	**Methods for demonstrating competence**	**Criteria for evaluating competence**
Appropriate use of hand tools, machine tools and measuring instruments for fabrication and repair on board	Characteristics and limitations of materials used in construction and repair of ships and equipment Characteristics and limitations of processes used for fabrication and repair Properties and parameters considered in the fabrication and repair of systems and components Methods for carrying out safe emergency/temporary repairs Safety measures to be taken to ensure a safe working environment and for using hand tools, machine tools and measuring instruments Use of hand tools, machine tools and measuring instruments Use of various types of sealants and packings	Assessment of evidence obtained from one or more of the following: .1 approved workshop skills training .2 approved practical experience and tests .3 approved in-service experience .4 approved training ship experience	Identification of important parameters for fabrication of typical ship-related components is appropriate Selection of materials is appropriate Fabrication is to designated tolerances Use of equipment and hand tools, machine tools and measuring instruments is appropriate and safe
Maintenance and repair of shipboard machinery and equipment	Safety measures to be taken for repair and maintenance, including the safe isolation of shipboard machinery and equipment required before personnel are permitted to work on such machinery or equipment Appropriate basic mechanical knowledge and skills	Examination and assessment of evidence obtained from one or more of the following: .1 approved workshop skills training .2 approved practical experience and tests .3 approved in-service experience	Safety procedures followed are appropriate Selection of tools and spare gear is appropriate

职能:维护和修理　操作级

<table>
<tr><th>第 1 栏</th><th>第 2 栏</th><th>第 3 栏</th><th>第 4 栏</th></tr>
<tr><th>适任</th><th>知识、理解和熟练</th><th>表明适任的方法</th><th>评价适任的标准</th></tr>
<tr><td>用于船上加工和修理的手动工具、机械工具及测量仪表的适当使用</td><td>船舶和设备建造和修理中使用的材料的特性和局限性
用于加工和修理的程序的特点和局限性
在系统和元器件的加工和修理中考虑的性质和参数
进行安全应急/临时修理的方法
为确保安全的工作环境和使用手动工具、机械工具及测量仪表而采取的安全措施
手动工具、机械工具及测量仪表的使用
各种类型的密封材料和填料的使用</td><td>评估从下列一项或数项获取的证据:
.1 认可的车间技能培训
.2 认可的实际经验和测试
.3 认可的工作经历
.4 认可的培训船经历</td><td>对用于典型船用元器件加工的重要参数的识别适当
材料的选择适当
加工满足指定的公差
设备、手动工具、机械工具及测量仪表的使用适当且安全</td></tr>
<tr><td>船上机械和设备的维护与修理</td><td>为修理和维护采取的安全措施,包括在允许人员进行船上机械或设备检修之前的安全隔离
适当的基础机械知识和技能</td><td>考试并评估从下列一项或数项获取的证据:
.1 认可的车间技能培训
.2 认可的实际经验和测试
.3 认可的工作经历</td><td>遵循的安全程序适当
工具和备件的选择适当</td></tr>
</table>

Column 1	Column 2	Column 3	Column 4
Competence	**Knowledge, understanding and proficiency**	**Methods for demonstrating competence**	**Criteria for evaluating competence**
Maintenance and repair of shipboard machinery and equipment *(continued)*	Maintenance and repair, such as dismantling, adjustment and reassembling of machinery and equipment The use of appropriate specialized tools and measuring instruments Design characteristics and selection of materials in construction of equipment Interpretation of machinery drawings and handbooks The interpretation of piping, hydraulic and pneumatic diagrams	.4 approved training ship experience	Dismantling, inspecting, repairing and reassembling equipment is in accordance with manuals and good practice Re-commissioning and performance testing is in accordance with manuals and good practice Selection of materials and parts is appropriate

Function: Controlling the operation of the ship and care for persons on board at the operational level

Column 1	Column 2	Column 3	Column 4
Competence	**Knowledge, understanding and proficiency**	**Methods for demonstrating competence**	**Criteria for evaluating competence**
Ensure compliance with pollution-prevention requirements	*Prevention of pollution of the marine environment* Knowledge of the precautions to be taken to prevent pollution of the marine environment Anti-pollution procedures and all associated equipment Importance of proactive measures to protect the marine environment	Examination and assessment of evidence obtained from one or more of the following: .1 approved in-service experience .2 approved training ship experience .3 approved training	Procedures for monitoring shipboard operations and ensuring compliance with MARPOL requirements are fully observed Actions to ensure that a positive environmental reputation is maintained

第 1 栏	第 2 栏	第 3 栏	第 4 栏
适任	知识、理解和熟练	表明适任的方法	评价适任的标准
船上机械和设备的维护与修理(续)	机械和设备的维护与修理,如拆卸、调整和装复 合适的专用工具及测量仪表的使用 设备制造中的设计特点和材料选择 机械图纸和手册的识读 管路、液压及气动图的识读	.4 认可的培训船经历	设备的拆卸、检测、修理和装复符合操作手册及良好的做法 重新调试和性能测试符合操作手册及良好的做法 材料和部件的选择适当

职能:船舶作业管理和人员管理　操作级

第 1 栏	第 2 栏	第 3 栏	第 4 栏
适任	知识、理解和熟练	表明适任的方法	评价适任的标准
确保遵守防污染要求	防止海洋环境污染 防止海洋环境污染应采取的预防措施的知识 防污染程序和所有相关设备 采取积极措施保护海洋环境的重要性	考试并评估从下列一项或数项获取的证据: .1 认可的工作经历 .2 认可的培训船经历 .3 认可的培训	监督船上操作和确保符合《MARPOL 公约》要求的程序得到全面遵守 采取的行动旨在确保维持良好的环保声誉

Column 1	Column 2	Column 3	Column 4
Competence	**Knowledge, understanding and proficiency**	**Methods for demonstrating competence**	**Criteria for evaluating competence**
Maintain seaworthiness of the ship	*Ship stability* Working knowledge and application of stability, trim and stress tables, diagrams and stress-calculating equipment Understanding of the fundamentals of watertight integrity Understanding of fundamental actions to be taken in the event of partial loss of intact buoyancy *Ship construction* General knowledge of the principal structural members of a ship and the proper names for the various parts	Examination and assessment of evidence obtained from one or more of the following: .1 approved in-service experience .2 approved training ship experience .3 approved simulator training, where appropriate .4 approved laboratory equipment training	The stability conditions comply with the IMO intact stability criteria under all conditions of loading Actions to ensure and maintain the watertight integrity of the ship are in accordance with accepted practice
Prevent, control and fight fires on board	*Fire prevention and fire-fighting appliances* Ability to organize fire drills Knowledge of classes and chemistry of fire Knowledge of fire-fighting systems Action to be taken in the event of fire, including fires involving oil systems	Assessment of evidence obtained from approved fire-fighting training and experience as set out in section A-VI/3, paragraphs 1 to 3	The type and scale of the problem is promptly identified and initial actions conform with the emergency procedure and contingency plans for the ship Evacuation, emergency shutdown and isolation procedures are appropriate to the nature of the emergency and are implemented promptly The order of priority, and the levels and time-scales of making reports and informing personnel on board, are relevant to the nature of the emergency and reflect the urgency of the problem

第 1 栏	第 2 栏	第 3 栏	第 4 栏
适任	知识、理解和熟练	表明适任的方法	评价适任的标准
保持船舶的适航性	船舶稳性 稳性、吃水差、强度图表和强度计算仪器的实用知识和应用 理解水密完整性的基本知识 理解一旦完整浮性部分丧失时应采取的基本行动 船舶构造 船舶主要构件和各部件的正确名称的一般知识	考试并评估从下列一项或数项获取的证据: .1 认可的工作经历 .2 认可的培训船经历 .3 认可的模拟器培训,如适用 .4 认可的实验室设备培训	各种装载条件下的稳性状况达到 IMO 完整稳性标准 为确保和维持船舶水密完整性而采取的行动符合公认的做法
船上防火、控制火灾和灭火	防火和灭火设备 组织消防演习的能力 火的种类和化学性质的知识 灭火系统的知识 失火(包括发生涉及油类系统的火灾)时应采取的行动	评估从第 A-VI/3 节第 1 段至第 3 段规定的认可的消防培训和经历中获取的证据	迅速确定问题的类型和范围,初始行动符合船舶应急程序和意外事故应急计划 撤离、应急关闭和隔离程序适合紧急情况的性质,并迅速实施 作出报告和通知船上人员的优先顺序、级别、时限与紧急情况的性质相关,并反映事态的紧急程度

Column 1	Column 2	Column 3	Column 4
Competence	**Knowledge, understanding and proficiency**	**Methods for demonstrating competence**	**Criteria for evaluating competence**
Operate life-saving appliances	*Life-saving* Ability to organize abandon ship drills and knowledge of the operation of survival craft and rescue boats, their launching appliances and arrangements, and their equipment, including radio life-saving appliances, satellite EPIRBs, SARTs, immersion suits and thermal protective aids	Assessment of evidence obtained from approved training and experience as set out in section A-VI/2, paragraphs 1 to 4	Actions in responding to abandon ship and survival situations are appropriate to the prevailing circumstances and conditions and comply with accepted safety practices and standards
Apply medical first aid on board ship	*Medical aid* Practical application of medical guides and advice by radio, including the ability to take effective action based on such knowledge in the case of accidents or illnesses that are likely to occur on board ship	Assessment of evidence obtained from approved training as set out in section A-VI/4, paragraphs 1 to 3	Identification of probable cause, nature and extent of injuries or conditions is prompt and treatment minimizes immediate threat to life
Monitor compliance with legislative requirements	Basic working knowledge of the relevant IMO conventions concerning safety of life at sea, security and protection of the marine environment	Assessment of evidence obtained from examination or approved training	Legislative requirements relating to safety of life at sea, security and protection of the marine environment are correctly identified
Application of leadership and teamworking skills	Working knowledge of shipboard personnel management and training A knowledge of related international maritime conventions and recommendations, and national legislation Ability to apply task and workload management, including: .1 planning and co-ordination .2 personnel assignment .3 time and resource constraints .4 prioritization	Assessment of evidence obtained from one or more of the following: .1 approved training .2 approved in-service experience .3 practical demonstration	The crew are allocated duties and informed of expected standards of work and behaviour in a manner appropriate to the individuals concerned Training objectives and activities are based on assessment of current competence and capabilities and operational requirements. Operations are demonstrated to be in accordance with applicable rules

第 1 栏	第 2 栏	第 3 栏	第 4 栏
适任	知识、理解和熟练	表明适任的方法	评价适任的标准
操作救生设备	救生 组织弃船演习的能力和操作救生艇筏、救助艇及其释放装置和设备，包括无线电救生设备、卫星应急无线电示位标、搜救应答器、救生服和保温用具在内的知识	评估从第 A-VI/2 节第 1 段至第 4 段规定的认可的培训和经历中获取的证据	在弃船求生情况下采取的行动适合当时的环境和条件，并符合公认的安全做法和标准
在船上应用医疗急救	医护 实际应用医疗指南和无线电咨询，包括根据这种知识对船上可能发生的事故和疾病采取有效行动的能力	评估从第 A-VI/4 节第 1 段至第 3 段规定的认可的培训中获取的证据	迅速确认伤病的可能原因、性质和程度，加以治疗以尽量减小对生命的直接威胁
监督遵守法定要求	涉及海上人命安全、保安和保护海洋环境的 IMO 有关公约的基本实用知识	评估从考试或认可的培训中获取的证据	正确确认有关海上人命安全、保安和保护海洋环境的法定要求
领导力和团队工作技能的运用	船上人员管理和培训的实用知识 相关国际海事公约和建议以及国内立法的知识 运用任务和工作量管理的能力，包括： .1 计划和协调 .2 人员指派 .3 时间和资源的限制 .4 优先排序	评估从下列一项或数项获取的证据： .1 认可的培训 .2 认可的工作经历 .3 实际演示	分配船员工作，并以适合相关人员的方式告知所要求的工作标准和行为准则 培训目标和活动以对目前适任性和能力的评估和操作要求为基础 表明操作符合适用的规则

Column 1	Column 2	Column 3	Column 4
Competence	**Knowledge, understanding and proficiency**	**Methods for demonstrating competence**	**Criteria for evaluating competence**
Application of leadership and teamworking skills *(continued)*	Knowledge and ability to apply effective resource management: .1 allocation, assignment, and prioritization of resources .2 effective communication on board and ashore .3 decisions reflect consideration of team experiences .4 assertiveness and leadership, including motivation .5 obtaining and maintaining situational awareness Knowledge and ability to apply decision-making techniques: .1 situation and risk assessment .2 identify and consider generated options .3 selecting course of action .4 evaluation of outcome effectiveness		Operations are planned and resources are allocated as needed in correct priority to perform necessary tasks Communication is clearly and unambiguously given and received Effective leadership behaviours are demonstrated Necessary team member(s) share accurate understanding of current and predicted vessel state and operational status and external environment Decisions are most effective for the situation

第 1 栏	第 2 栏	第 3 栏	第 4 栏
适任	知识、理解和熟练	表明适任的方法	评价适任的标准
领导力和团队工作技能的运用(续)	运用有效资源管理的知识和能力: .1 资源的分配、分派和优先排序 .2 船上和岸上的有效沟通 .3 决策反映出团队的经验 .4 决断力和领导力,包括激励 .5 获得并保持情景意识 运用决策技能的知识和能力: .1 局面和风险评估 .2 识别并考虑形成的选项 .3 选择行动方案 .4 评价结果的有效性		操作有计划,并根据需要按正确的优先顺序分配资源,以执行必要的任务 交流清楚、无歧义 表明有效的领导行为 相关团队成员对当前和预计的船舶与操作状态及外部环境有共同的准确理解 决策对于局面最有效

Column 1	Column 2	Column 3	Column 4
Competence	**Knowledge, understanding and proficiency**	**Methods for demonstrating competence**	**Criteria for evaluating competence**
Contribute to the safety of personnel and ship	Knowledge of personal survival techniques Knowledge of fire prevention and ability to fight and extinguish fires Knowledge of elementary first aid Knowledge of personal safety and social responsibilities	Assessment of evidence obtained from approved training and experience as set out in section A-VI/1, paragraph 2	Appropriate safety and protective equipment is correctly used Procedures and safe working practices designed to safeguard personnel and the ship are observed at all times Procedures designed to safeguard the environment are observed at all times Initial and follow-up actions on becoming aware of an emergency conform with established emergency response procedures

第 1 栏	第 2 栏	第 3 栏	第 4 栏
适任	知识、理解和熟练	表明适任的方法	评价适任的标准
有助于人员和船舶的安全	个人求生技能的知识 防火知识和灭火能力 基本急救的知识 个人安全和社会责任的知识	评估从第 A-VI/1 节第 2 段规定的认可的培训和经历中获取的证据	正确使用适当的安全和防护设备 始终遵循旨在保护人员和船舶的程序和安全工作做法 始终遵循旨在保护环境的程序 发觉紧急情况时的初始和后续行动符合既定的应急反应程序

Section A-III/2

Mandatory minimum requirements for certification of chief engineer officers and second engineer officers on ships powered by main propulsion machinery of 3,000 kW propulsion power or more

Standard of competence

1 Every candidate for certification as chief engineer officer and second engineer officer of seagoing ships powered by main propulsion machinery of 3,000 kW power or more shall be required to demonstrate ability to undertake, at the management level, the tasks, duties and responsibilities listed in column 1 of table A-III/2.

2 The minimum knowledge, understanding and proficiency required for certification is listed in column 2 of table A-III/2. This incorporates, expands and extends in depth the subjects listed in column 2 of table A-III/1 for officers in charge of an engineering watch.

3 Bearing in mind that a second engineer officer shall be in a position to assume the responsibilities of the chief engineer officer at any time, assessment in these subjects shall be designed to test the candidate's ability to assimilate all available information that affects the safe operation of the ship's machinery and the protection of the marine environment.

4 The level of knowledge of the subjects listed in column 2 of table A-III/2 shall be sufficient to enable the candidate to serve in the capacity of chief engineer officer or second engineer officer.*

5 Training and experience to achieve the necessary level of theoretical knowledge, understanding and proficiency shall take into account the relevant requirements of this part and the guidance given in part B of this Code.

6 The Administration may omit knowledge requirements for types of propulsion machinery other than those machinery installations for which the certificate to be awarded shall be valid. A certificate awarded on such a basis shall not be valid for any category of machinery installation which has been omitted until the engineer officer proves to be competent in these knowledge requirements. Any such limitation shall be stated on the certificate and in the endorsement.

7 Every candidate for certification shall be required to provide evidence of having achieved the required standard of competence in accordance with the methods for demonstrating competence and the criteria for evaluating competence tabulated in columns 3 and 4 of table A-III/2.

Near-coastal voyages

8 The level of knowledge, understanding and proficiency required under the different sections listed in column 2 of table A-III/2 may be varied for engineer officers of ships powered by main propulsion machinery with limited propulsion power engaged on near-coastal voyages, as considered necessary, bearing in mind the effect on the safety of all ships which may be operating in the same waters. Any such limitation shall be stated on the certificate and in the endorsement.

* The relevant IMO Model Course(s) may be of assistance in the preparation of courses.

第 A-III/2 节

对主推进装置为 3 000 kW 或以上船舶的轮机长和大管轮发证的强制性最低要求

适任标准

1 每个申请主推进装置为 3 000 kW 或以上海船轮机长和大管轮证书的申请人，应表明承担表 A-III/2 第 1 栏所列的管理级的任务、职责和责任的能力。

2 发证所要求的最低的知识、理解和熟练列于表 A-III/2 第 2 栏中。其内容包括、扩大和加深了表 A-III/1 第 2 栏所列的对负责轮机值班的高级船员要求的科目。

3 切记大管轮随时可能承担轮机长的责任，对这些科目的评估应旨在考查证书申请人从影响船舶机械安全操作和保护海洋环境的所有可用资料中吸收知识的能力。

4 表 A-III/2 第 2 栏所列科目的知识水平，应足以能使证书申请人在轮机长或大管轮职位上服务。①

5 为获取所需水平的理论知识、理解和熟练的培训和经验，应考虑本规则本部分的有关要求和 B 部分给予的指导。

6 主管机关可删除那些对所发证书有效的机械装置以外的其他类型的推进装置的知识要求。据此所发的证书不应对已被删除的任何种类的机械装置有效，直至该轮机部高级船员证明能符合这些知识要求。任何这种限制应在证书和签证上载明。

7 每个证书申请人应按照表 A-III/2 第 3 栏和第 4 栏所列的表明适任的方法和评价适任的标准，提供已达到所要求的适任标准的证据。

近岸航行

8 表 A-III/2 第 2 栏不同部分所列的对知识、理解和熟练水平的要求，如认为必要，可对主推进装置推进功率有限且从事近岸航行的船舶的轮机部高级船员有所变动，但要切记对可能在同一水域航行的所有船舶安全的影响。任何这种限制应在证书和签证上载明。

① 相关 IMO 的示范培训课程可有助于准备课程。

Table A-III/2

Specification of minimum standard of competence for chief engineer officers and second engineer officers on ships powered by main propulsion machinery of 3,000 kW propulsion power or more

Function: Marine engineering at the management level

Column 1	Column 2	Column 3	Column 4
Competence	**Knowledge, understanding and proficiency**	**Methods for demonstrating competence**	**Criteria for evaluating competence**
Manage the operation of propulsion plant machinery	Design features, and operative mechanism of the following machinery and associated auxiliaries: .1 marine diesel engine .2 marine steam turbine .3 marine gas turbine .4 marine steam boiler	Examination and assessment of evidence obtained from one or more of the following: .1 approved in-service experience .2 approved training ship experience .3 approved simulator training, where appropriate .4 approved laboratory equipment training	Explanation and understanding of design features and operating mechanisms are appropriate
Plan and schedule operations	*Theoretical knowledge* Thermodynamics and heat transmission Mechanics and hydromechanics Propulsive characteristics of diesel engines, steam and gas turbines, including speed, output and fuel consumption Heat cycle, thermal efficiency and heat balance of the following: .1 marine diesel engine .2 marine steam turbine .3 marine gas turbine .4 marine steam boiler	Examination and assessment of evidence obtained from one or more of the following: .1 approved in-service experience .2 approved training ship experience .3 approved simulator training, where appropriate .4 approved laboratory equipment training	The planning and preparation of operations is suited to the design parameters of the power installation and to the requirements of the voyage

表 A-III/2
主推进装置为 3 000 kW 或以上船舶的轮机长和大管轮的最低适任标准

职能:轮机工程　管理级

第 1 栏	第 2 栏	第 3 栏	第 4 栏
适任	知识、理解和熟练	表明适任的方法	评价适任的标准
推进装置机械的操作管理	下列机械和相关辅助设备的设计参数和工作机理: .1　船用柴油机 .2　船用蒸汽轮机 .3　船用燃气轮机 .4　船用蒸汽锅炉	考试并评估从下列一项或数项获取的证据: .1　认可的工作经历 .2　认可的培训船经历 .3　认可的模拟器培训,如适用 .4　认可的实验室设备培训	对设计参数和工作机理的解释和理解适当
操作的计划和安排	理论知识 热力学和热传导 力学和流体力学 柴油机、蒸汽轮机和燃气轮机的推进特性,包括速度、输出功率和燃油消耗 下列设备的热力循环、热效率和热平衡: .1　船用柴油机 .2　船用蒸汽轮机 .3　船用燃气轮机 .4　船用蒸汽锅炉	考试并评估从下列一项或数项获取的证据: .1　认可的工作经历 .2　认可的培训船经历 .3　认可的模拟器培训,如适用 .4　认可的实验室设备培训	操作计划和准备适于动力装置的设计参数和航次的要求

Column 1	Column 2	Column 3	Column 4
Competence	**Knowledge, understanding and proficiency**	**Methods for demonstrating competence**	**Criteria for evaluating competence**
Plan and schedule operations *(continued)*	Refrigerators and refrigeration cycle Physical and chemical properties of fuels and lubricants Technology of materials Naval architecture and ship construction, including damage control		
Operation, surveillance, performance assessment and maintaining safety of propulsion plant and auxiliary machinery	*Practical knowledge* Start up and shut down main propulsion and auxiliary machinery, including associated systems Operating limits of propulsion plant The efficient operation, surveillance, performance assessment and maintaining safety of propulsion plant and auxiliary machinery Functions and mechanism of automatic control for main engine Functions and mechanism of automatic control for auxiliary machinery including but not limited to: .1 generator distribution systems .2 steam boilers .3 oil purifier .4 refrigeration system .5 pumping and piping systems .6 steering gear system .7 cargo-handling equipment and deck machinery	Examination and assessment of evidence obtained from one or more of the following: .1 approved in-service experience .2 approved training ship experience .3 approved simulator training, where appropriate .4 approved laboratory equipment training	The methods of preparing for the start-up and of making available fuels, lubricants, cooling water and air are the most appropriate Checks of pressures, temperatures and revolutions during the start-up and warm-up period are in accordance with technical specifications and agreed work plans Surveillance of main propulsion plant and auxiliary systems is sufficient to maintain safe operating conditions The methods of preparing the shutdown, and of supervising the cooling down of the engine are the most appropriate The methods of measuring the load capacity of the engines are in accordance with technical specifications Performance is checked against bridge orders Performance levels are in accordance with technical specifications

第 1 栏	第 2 栏	第 3 栏	第 4 栏
适任	知识、理解和熟练	表明适任的方法	评价适任的标准
操作的计划和安排(续)	制冷装置和制冷循环 燃油和润滑油的物理和化学特性 材料技术 造船学和船舶构造,包括破损控制		
主推进装置和辅助机械的操纵、监控、性能评估及安全维护	实际知识 启动和关闭主推进装置和辅助机械,包括相关系统 推进装置的操作限制 有效操作、监测和性能评估以及保持主推进装置和辅助机械的安全 主机自动控制的功能和机理 辅助机械自动控制的功能和机理,辅助机械包括但不限于: .1 发电机配电系统 .2 蒸汽锅炉 .3 分油机 .4 制冷系统 .5 泵和管系 .6 操舵系统 .7 货物操作设备和甲板机械	考试并评估从下列一项或数项获取的证据: .1 认可的工作经历 .2 认可的培训船经历 .3 认可的模拟器培训,如适用 .4 认可的实验室设备培训	启动准备方法和燃油、润滑油、冷却水及压缩空气的备妥方式最合适 对启动和暖机期间的压力、温度和转速的检查符合技术规范和预定工作计划 对主推进装置和辅助系统的监视足以保持安全工作状态 准备停机和监管机器冷却的方法最合适 测定柴油机的负载能力的方法符合技术规范 按照驾驶台指令核查机器性能 机器性能等级符合技术规范

Column 1	Column 2	Column 3	Column 4
Competence	**Knowledge, understanding and proficiency**	**Methods for demonstrating competence**	**Criteria for evaluating competence**
Manage fuel, lubrication and ballast operations	Operation and maintenance of machinery, including pumps and piping systems	Examination and assessment of evidence obtained from one or more of the following: .1 approved in-service experience .2 approved training ship experience .3 approved simulator training, where appropriate	Fuel and ballast operations meet operational requirements and are carried out so as to prevent pollution of the marine environment

第 1 栏	第 2 栏	第 3 栏	第 4 栏
适任	知识、理解和熟练	表明适任的方法	评价适任的标准
燃油、润滑油和压载水的操作管理	机器的操作和维护，包括泵和管系	考试并评估从下列一项或数项获取的证据： .1 认可的工作经历 .2 认可的培训船经历 .3 认可的模拟器培训，如适用	燃油和压载水操作符合操作要求，并能防止海洋环境污染

Function: Electrical, electronic and control engineering at the management level

Column 1	Column 2	Column 3	Column 4
Competence	**Knowledge, understanding and proficiency**	**Methods for demonstrating competence**	**Criteria for evaluating competence**
Manage operation of electrical and electronic control equipment	*Theoretical knowledge* Marine electrotechnology, electronics, power electronics, automatic control engineering and safety devices Design features and system configurations of automatic control equipment and safety devices for the following: .1 main engine .2 generator and distribution system .3 steam boiler Design features and system configurations of operational control equipment for electrical motors Design features of high-voltage installations Features of hydraulic and pneumatic control equipment	Examination and assessment of evidence obtained from one or more of the following: .1 approved in-service experience .2 approved training ship experience .3 approved simulator training, where appropriate .4 approved laboratory equipment training	Operation of equipment and system is in accordance with operating manuals Performance levels are in accordance with technical specifications
Manage trouble-shooting, restoration of electrical and electronic control equipment to operating condition	*Practical knowledge* Troubleshooting of electrical and electronic control equipment Function test of electrical, electronic control equipment and safety devices Troubleshooting of monitoring systems Software version control	Examination and assessment of evidence obtained from one or more of the following: .1 approved in-service experience .2 approved training ship experience .3 approved simulator training, where appropriate .4 approved laboratory equipment training	Maintenance activities are correctly planned in accordance with technical, legislative, safety and procedural specifications Inspection, testing and troubleshooting of equipment are appropriate

职能:电气、电子和控制工程　管理级

第 1 栏	第 2 栏	第 3 栏	第 4 栏
适任	知识、理解和熟练	表明适任的方法	评价适任的标准
电气、电子控制设备的操作管理	理论知识 船舶电子技术、电子学、电力电子学、自动控制工程和安全设备 以下装置的自动控制设备和安全装置的设计参数和系统配置: .1 主机 .2 发电机和配电系统 .3 蒸汽锅炉 电动机操作控制设备的设计参数和系统配置 高压设备的设计参数 液压和气动控制设备的参数	考试并评估从下列一项或数项获取的证据: .1 认可的工作经历 .2 认可的培训船经历 .3 认可的模拟器培训,如适用 .4 认可的实验室设备培训	设备与系统的操作符合操作手册的要求 设备性能等级符合技术规范
电气和电子控制设备的故障诊断和恢复工况的管理	实际知识 电气和电子控制设备的故障诊断 电气和电子控制设备及安全设备的功能测试 监测系统的故障诊断 软件版本控制	考试并评估从下列一项或数项获取的证据: .1 认可的工作经历 .2 认可的培训船经历 .3 认可的模拟器培训,如适用 .4 认可的实验室设备培训	维护工作按照技术的、法定的、安全的和程序化的规范正确地计划 设备的检查、测试和故障诊断适当

Function: Maintenance and repair at the management level

Column 1	Column 2	Column 3	Column 4
Competence	**Knowledge, understanding and proficiency**	**Methods for demonstrating competence**	**Criteria for evaluating competence**
Manage safe and effective maintenance and repair procedures	*Theoretical knowledge* Marine engineering practice *Practical knowledge* Manage safe and effective maintenance and repair procedures Planning maintenance, including statutory and class verifications Planning repairs	Examination and assessment of evidence obtained from one or more of the following: .1 approved in-service experience .2 approved training ship experience .3 approved workshop training	Maintenance activities are correctly planned and carried out in accordance with technical, legislative, safety and procedural specifications Appropriate plans, specifications, materials and equipment are available for maintenance and repair Action taken leads to the restoration of plant by the most suitable method
Detect and identify the cause of machinery malfunctions and correct faults	*Practical knowledge* Detection of machinery malfunction, location of faults and action to prevent damage Inspection and adjustment of equipment Non-destructive examination	Examination and assessment of evidence obtained from one or more of the following: .1 approved in-service experience .2 approved training ship experience .3 approved simulator training, where appropriate .4 approved laboratory equipment training	The methods of comparing actual operating conditions are in accordance with recommended practices and procedures Actions and decisions are in accordance with recommended operating specifications and limitations
Ensure safe working practices	*Practical knowledge* Safe working practices	Examination and assessment of evidence obtained from one or more of the following: .1 approved in-service experience .2 approved training ship experience .3 approved laboratory equipment training	Working practices are in accordance with legislative requirements, codes of practice, permits to work and environmental concerns

职能:维护和修理　管理级

第 1 栏	第 2 栏	第 3 栏	第 4 栏
适任	知识、理解和熟练	表明适任的方法	评价适任的标准
安全有效的维护和修理程序的管理	理论知识 轮机工程实践 实际知识 安全有效的维护和修理程序的管理 编制维护计划,包括法定检验和船级检验 编制修理计划	考试并评估从下列一项或数项获取的证据: .1 认可的工作经历 .2 认可的培训船经历 .3 认可的车间培训	维护工作按照技术的、法定的、安全的和程序化的规范正确地计划和进行 维护和修理具有适当的计划、技术规范、材料和设备 采取最恰当的措施恢复装置功能
探测和识别机器故障原因并消除故障	实际知识 探测机器故障,确定故障点并采取防止损坏的措施 设备检查和调试 无损检测	考试并评估从下列一项或数项获取的证据: .1 认可的工作经历 .2 认可的培训船经历 .3 认可的模拟器培训,如适用 .4 认可的实验室设备培训	对实际工作状态的比较方法符合推荐做法和程序 按照推荐的操作规范和限制采取行动并作出决策
保证安全工作做法	实际知识 安全工作做法	考试并评估从下列一项或数项获取的证据: .1 认可的工作经历 .2 认可的培训船经历 .3 认可的实验室设备培训	工作做法符合法定要求、操作规程、作业许可和环保要求

Function: Controlling the operation of the ship and care for persons on board at the management level

Column 1	Column 2	Column 3	Column 4
Competence	**Knowledge, understanding and proficiency**	**Methods for demonstrating competence**	**Criteria for evaluating competence**
Control trim, stability and stress	Understanding of fundamental principles of ship construction and the theories and factors affecting trim and stability and measures necessary to preserve trim and stability Knowledge of the effect on trim and stability of a ship in the event of damage to, and consequent flooding of, a compartment and countermeasures to be taken Knowledge of IMO recommendations concerning ship stability	Examination and assessment of evidence obtained from one or more of the following: .1 approved in-service experience .2 approved training ship experience .3 approved simulator training, where appropriate	Stability and stress conditions are maintained within safety limits at all times
Monitor and control compliance with legislative requirements and measures to ensure safety of life at sea, security and protection of the marine environment	Knowledge of relevant international maritime law embodied in international agreements and conventions Regard shall be paid especially to the following subjects: .1 certificates and other documents required to be carried on board ships by international conventions, how they may be obtained and the period of their legal validity .2 responsibilities under the relevant requirements of the International Convention on Load Lines, 1966, as amended .3 responsibilities under the relevant requirements of the International Convention for the Safety of Life at Sea, 1974, as amended	Examination and assessment of evidence obtained from one or more of the following: .1 approved in-service experience .2 approved training ship experience .3 approved simulator training, where appropriate	Procedures for monitoring operations and maintenance comply with legislative requirements Potential non-compliance is promptly and fully identified Requirements for renewal and extension of certificates ensure continued validity of survey items and equipment

职能:船舶作业管理和人员管理　管理级

第 1 栏	第 2 栏	第 3 栏	第 4 栏
适任	知识、理解和熟练	表明适任的方法	评价适任的标准
控制吃水差、稳性和强度	理解船舶构造的基本原理、影响吃水差和稳性的理论和因素以及保持吃水差和稳性的必要措施 因舱室破损进水而影响吃水差和稳性的知识以及应采取的措施的知识 有关船舶稳性的 IMO 建议的知识	考试并评估从下列一项或数项获取的证据: .1 认可的工作经历 .2 认可的培训船经历 .3 认可的模拟器培训,如适用	稳性和强度状况始终保持在安全限度以内
监督和控制对法定要求的遵守及保证海上人命安全、保安与保护海洋环境的措施	国际协定和公约中体现的有关国际海事法律的知识 应特别注意下列各项: .1 国际公约要求随船携带的证书和其他文件,如何获得这些证书和文件及其法定有效期限 .2 经修正的《1966 年国际载重线公约》有关要求规定的职责 .3 经修正的《1974 年国际海上人命安全公约》有关要求规定的职责	考试并评估从下列一项或数项获取的证据: .1 认可的工作经历 .2 认可的培训船经历 .3 认可的模拟器培训,如适用	监督操作和保养的程序符合法定要求 迅速和全面确认潜在的不符合项 对证书更新和延期的要求,能保证检验项目和设备的继续有效

Column 1	Column 2	Column 3	Column 4
Competence	**Knowledge, understanding and proficiency**	**Methods for demonstrating competence**	**Criteria for evaluating competence**
Monitor and control compliance with legislative requirements and measures to ensure safety of life at sea, security and protection of the marine environment (*continued*)	.4 responsibilities under the International Convention for the Prevention of Pollution from Ships, as amended .5 maritime declarations of health and the requirements of the International Health Regulations .6 responsibilities under international instruments affecting the safety of the ships, passengers, crew or cargo .7 methods and aids to prevent pollution of the environment by ships .8 knowledge of national legislation for implementing international agreements and conventions		
Maintain safety and security of the vessel, crew and passengers and the operational condition of life-saving, fire-fighting and other safety systems	A thorough knowledge of life-saving appliance regulations (International Convention for the Safety of Life at Sea) Organization of fire and abandon ship drills Maintenance of operational condition of life-saving, fire-fighting and other safety systems Actions to be taken to protect and safeguard all persons on board in emergencies Actions to limit damage and salve the ship following fire, explosion, collision or grounding	Examination and assessment of evidence obtained from practical instruction and approved in-service training and experience	Procedures for monitoring fire-detection and safety systems ensure that all alarms are detected promptly and acted upon in accordance with established emergency procedures

第 1 栏	第 2 栏	第 3 栏	第 4 栏
适任	知识、理解和熟练	表明适任的方法	评价适任的标准
监督和控制对法定要求的遵守及保证海上人命安全、保安与保护海洋环境的措施(续)	.4 经修正的《国际防止船舶造成污染公约》规定的职责 .5 海员健康声明和《国际卫生条例》的要求 .6 影响船舶、旅客、船员或货物安全的国际文件规定的职责 .7 防止船舶污染环境的方法和设备 .8 为实施国际协定和公约的国内立法的知识		
保持船舶、船员和旅客的安全、保安及救生、消防和其他安全系统的工作状态	救生设备有关规则(《国际海上人命安全公约》)的全面知识 灭火和弃船演习的组织 救生、消防和其他安全系统的工作状态的保持 在紧急情况下保护船上所有人员安全应采取的行动 在失火、爆炸、碰撞或搁浅时限制损害与救助本船的行动	考试并评估从实际训练和认可的在职培训及实践中获取的证据	监测探火和安全系统的程序,保证迅速探测到所有报警,并按照所制定的应急程序采取行动

Column 1	Column 2	Column 3	Column 4
Competence	**Knowledge, understanding and proficiency**	**Methods for demonstrating competence**	**Criteria for evaluating competence**
Develop emergency and damage control plans and handle emergency situations	Ship construction, including damage control Methods and aids for fire prevention, detection and extinction Functions and use of life-saving appliances	Examination and assessment of evidence obtained from approved in-service training and experience	Emergency procedures are in accordance with the established plans for emergency situations
Use leadership and managerial skills	Knowledge of shipboard personnel management and training A knowledge of international maritime conventions and recommendations, and related national legislation Ability to apply task and workload management, including: .1 planning and coordination .2 personnel assignment .3 time and resource constraints .4 prioritization Knowledge and ability to apply effective resource management: .1 allocation, assignment, and prioritization of resources .2 effective communication on board and ashore .3 decisions reflect consideration of team experience	Assessment of evidence obtained from one or more of the following: .1 approved training .2 approved in-service experience .3 approved simulator training	The crew are allocated duties and informed of expected standards of work and behaviour in a manner appropriate to the individuals concerned Training objectives and activities are based on assessment of current competence and capabilities and operational requirements Operations are demonstrated to be in accordance with applicable rules Operations are planned and resources are allocated as needed in correct priority to perform necessary tasks Communication is clearly and unambiguously given and received

第 1 栏	第 2 栏	第 3 栏	第 4 栏
适任	知识、理解和熟练	表明适任的方法	评价适任的标准
制定应急与破损控制计划和处理紧急情况	船舶构造，包括破损控制 防火、探火和灭火的方法和设备 救生设备的功能和使用	考试并评估从认可的在职培训和实践中获取的证据	应急程序符合为紧急情况制定的计划
领导力和管理技能的运用	船上人员管理和培训的知识 国际海事公约和建议以及相关国内立法的知识 运用任务及工作量管理的能力，包括： .1 计划和协调 .2 人员分派 .3 时间和资源的限制 .4 优先排序 运用有效资源管理的知识和能力： .1 资源的分配、分派和优先排序 .2 船上和岸上的有效沟通 .3 决策反映出团队的经验	评估从下列一项或数项获取的证据： .1 认可的培训 .2 认可的工作经历 .3 认可的模拟器培训	分配船员工作，并以适合相关人员的方式告知所要求的工作标准和行为准则 培训目标和活动以对目前适任性和能力的评估和操作要求为基础 表明操作符合适用的规则 操作有计划，并根据需要按正确的优先顺序分配资源，以执行必要的任务 交流清楚、无歧义

Column 1	Column 2	Column 3	Column 4
Competence	**Knowledge, understanding and proficiency**	**Methods for demonstrating competence**	**Criteria for evaluating competence**
Use leadership and managerial skills (*continued*)	.4 assertiveness and leadership, including motivation .5 obtaining and maintaining situation awareness Knowledge and ability to apply decision-making techniques: .1 situation and risk assessment .2 identify and generate options .3 select course of action .4 evaluation of outcome effectiveness Development, implementation, and oversight of standard operating procedures		Effective leadership behaviours are demonstrated Necessary team member(s) share accurate understanding of current and predicted vessel state and operational status and external environment Decisions are most effective for the situation Operations are demonstrated to be effective and in accordance with applicable rules

第 1 栏	第 2 栏	第 3 栏	第 4 栏
适任	知识、理解和熟练	表明适任的方法	评价适任的标准
领导力和管理技能的运用(续)	.4 决断力和领导力,包括激励 .5 具有并保持情景意识 运用决策技能的知识和能力: .1 局面和风险评估 .2 确定并形成选项 .3 选择行动方案 .4 评价结果的有效性 制定、实施和监督标准操作程序		表明有效的领导行为 相关的团队成员对当前和预计的船舶与操作状态以及外部环境有共同的准确理解 决策对于局面最有效 表明操作有效且符合适用的规则

Section A-III/3

Mandatory minimum requirements for certification of chief engineer officers and second engineer officers on ships powered by main propulsion machinery of between 750 kW and 3,000 kW propulsion power

Standard of competence

1 Every candidate for certification as chief engineer officer and second engineer officer of seagoing ships powered by main propulsion machinery of between 750 kW and 3,000 kW power shall be required to demonstrate ability to undertake, at management level, the tasks, duties and responsibilities listed in column 1 of table A-III/2.

2 The minimum knowledge, understanding and proficiency required for certification is listed in column 2 of table A-III/2. This incorporates, expands and extends in depth the subjects listed in column 2 of table A-III/1 for officers in charge of an engineering watch in a manned engine-room or designated duty engineers in a periodically unmanned engine-room.

3 Bearing in mind that a second engineer officer shall be in a position to assume the responsibilities of the chief engineer officer at any time, assessment in these subjects shall be designed to test the candidate's ability to assimilate all available information that affects the safe operation of the ship's machinery and the protection of the marine environment.

4 The level of knowledge of the subjects listed in column 2 of table A-III/2 may be lowered but shall be sufficient to enable the candidate to serve in the capacity of chief engineer officer or second engineer officer at the range of propulsion power specified in this section.

5 Training and experience to achieve the necessary level of theoretical knowledge, understanding and proficiency shall take into account the relevant requirements of this part and the guidance given in part B of this Code.

6 The Administration may omit knowledge requirements for types of propulsion machinery other than those machinery installations for which the certificate to be awarded shall be valid. A certificate awarded on such a basis shall not be valid for any category of machinery installation which has been omitted until the engineer officer proves to be competent in these knowledge requirements. Any such limitation shall be stated on the certificate and in the endorsement.

7 Every candidate for certification shall be required to provide evidence of having achieved the required standard of competence in accordance with the methods for demonstrating competence and the criteria for evaluating competence tabulated in columns 3 and 4 of table A-III/2.

Near-coastal voyages

8 The level of knowledge, understanding and proficiency required under the different sections listed in column 2 of table A-III/2 and the requirements of paragraphs 2.1.1 and 2.1.2 of regulation III/3 may be varied for engineer officers of ships powered by main propulsion machinery of less than 3,000 kW main propulsion power engaged on near-coastal voyages, as considered necessary, bearing in mind the effect on the safety of all ships which may be operating in the same waters. Any such limitation shall be stated on the certificate and in the endorsement.

第 A-III/3 节

对主推进装置为 750 kW 至 3 000 kW 海船轮机长和大管轮发证的强制性最低要求

适任标准

1　每个申请主推进装置为 750 kW 至 3 000 kW 海船轮机长和大管轮证书的申请人，应表明承担表 A-III/2 第 1 栏所列的管理级的任务、职责和责任的能力。

2　发证所要求的最低的知识、理解和熟练列于表 A-III/2 第 2 栏中。其内容包括、扩大和加深了表 A-III/1 第 2 栏列出的对于有人值班机舱负责轮机值班的高级船员或周期性无人值班机舱指定值班的轮机员的科目。

3　切记大管轮随时可能承担轮机长的责任，对这些科目的评估应旨在考查证书申请人从影响船舶机械安全操作和保护海洋环境的所有可用资料中吸收知识的能力。

4　表 A-III/2 第 2 栏所列科目的知识水平可以降低，但应足以能使证书申请人在本节规定的推进功率范围的轮机长或大管轮的职位上服务。

5　为获取所需水平的理论知识、理解和熟练的培训和经验，应考虑本规则本部分的有关要求和 B 部分给予的指导。

6　主管机关可删除那些对所发证书有效的机械装置以外的其他类型的推进装置的知识要求。据此所发的证书不应对已被删除的任何种类的机械装置有效，直至该轮机部高级船员证明能符合这些知识要求。任何这种限制应在证书和签证上载明。

7　每个证书申请人应按照表 A-III/2 第 3 栏和第 4 栏所列的表明适任的方法和评价适任的标准，提供已达到所要求的适任标准的证据。

近岸航行

8　表 A-III/2 第 2 栏不同部分所列的对知识、理解和熟练水平的要求，以及规则第 III/3 条第 2.1.1 段和第 2.1.2 段的有关要求，如认为必要，对主推进装置 3 000 kW 以下且从事近岸航行的船舶的轮机部高级船员可有所变动，但要切记对可能在同一水域航行的所有船舶安全的影响。任何这种限制应在证书和签证上载明。

Section A-III/4

Mandatory minimum requirements for certification of ratings forming part of a watch in a manned engine-room or designated to perform duties in a periodically unmanned engine-room

Standard of competence

1 Every rating forming part of an engine-room watch on a seagoing ship shall be required to demonstrate the competence to perform the marine engineering function at the support level, as specified in column 1 of table A-III/4.

2 The minimum knowledge, understanding and proficiency required of ratings forming part of an engine-room watch is listed in column 2 of table A-III/4.

3 Every candidate for certification shall be required to provide evidence of having achieved the required standard of competence in accordance with the methods for demonstrating competence and the criteria for evaluating competence specified in columns 3 and 4 of table A-III/4. The reference to "practical test" in column 3 may include approved shore-based training in which the students undergo practical testing.

4 Where there are no tables of competence for the support level with respect to certain functions, it remains the responsibility of the Administration to determine the appropriate training, assessment and certification requirements to be applied to personnel designated to perform those functions at the support level.

第 A-III/4 节
对组成有人值班机舱值班部分的或周期性无人值班机舱指定履行职责的普通船员发证的强制性最低要求

适任标准

1 每个组成海船上机舱值班部分的普通船员,应表明履行表 A-III/4 第 1 栏所规定的支持级轮机工程职能的适任能力。

2 对组成机舱值班部分的普通船员要求的最低的知识、理解和熟练列于表 A-III/4 第 2 栏。

3 每个证书申请人应按照表 A-III/4 第 3 栏和第 4 栏所规定的表明适任的方法和评价适任的标准,提供已达到所要求的适任标准的证据。第 3 栏所提及的"实操测试"可包括对学员进行实操测试的认可的岸上培训。

4 对于未用适任表列出的某些支持级职能,主管机关有责任对指定履行那些承担支持级职能的人员确定适当的培训、评估和发证要求。

Table A-III/4

Specification of minimum standard of competence for ratings forming part of an engineering watch

Function: Marine engineering at the support level

Column 1	Column 2	Column 3	Column 4
Competence	**Knowledge, understanding and proficiency**	**Methods for demonstrating competence**	**Criteria for evaluating competence**
Carry out a watch routine appropriate to the duties of a rating forming part of an engine-room watch Understand orders and be understood in matters relevant to watchkeeping duties	Terms used in machinery spaces and names of machinery and equipment Engine-room watchkeeping procedures Safe working practices as related to engine-room operations Basic environmental protection procedures Use of appropriate internal communication system Engine-room alarm systems and ability to distinguish between the various alarms, with special reference to fire-extinguishing gas alarms	Assessment of evidence obtained from one or more of the following: .1 approved in-service experience; .2 approved training ship experience; or .3 practical test	Communications are clear and concise and advice or clarification is sought from the officer of the watch where watch information or instructions are not clearly understood Maintenance, handover and relief of the watch is in conformity with accepted principles and procedures
For keeping a boiler watch: Maintain the correct water levels and steam pressures	Safe operation of boilers	Assessment of evidence obtained from one or more of the following: .1 approved in-service experience; .2 approved training ship experience; .3 practical test; or .4 approved simulator training, where appropriate	Assessment of boiler condition is accurate and based on relevant information available from local and remote indicators and physical inspections The sequence and timing of adjustments maintains safety and optimum efficiency

表 A-III/4

组成机舱值班部分的普通船员的最低适任标准

职能:轮机工程　支持级

第 1 栏	第 2 栏	第 3 栏	第 4 栏
适任	**知识、理解和熟练**	**表明适任的方法**	**评价适任的标准**
执行适合于组成机舱值班部分的普通船员职责的日常值班任务 理解指令并能向其他人表述与值班职责有关的事宜	机器处所使用的术语及机器和设备名称 机舱值班程序 有关机舱操作的安全工作做法 基本的环境保护程序 相应的船上内部通信系统的使用 机舱报警系统和识别各种警报,特别是关于施放灭火气体的警报的能力	评估从下列一项或数项获取的证据: .1 认可的工作经历 .2 认可的培训船经历 .3 实操测试	交流清楚简明,在未能清楚地理解值班信息或指示时,能从值班高级船员处获得建议或说明 值班、交班和接班符合公认的原则和程序
值锅炉班 保持正确的水位和蒸汽压力	锅炉的安全操作	评估从下列一项或数项获取的证据: .1 认可的工作经历 .2 认可的培训船经历 .3 实操测试 .4 认可的模拟器培训,如适用	对锅炉状况的评估准确,并以从现场和遥测指示器以及实地检查获得的有关信息为基础 调节的顺序和时机能保持安全和最佳实效

Column 1	Column 2	Column 3	Column 4
Competence	**Knowledge, understanding and proficiency**	**Methods for demonstrating competence**	**Criteria for evaluating competence**
Operate emergency equipment and apply emergency procedures	Knowledge of emergency duties Escape routes from machinery spaces Familiarity with the location and use of fire-fighting equipment in the machinery spaces	Assessment of evidence obtained from demonstration and approved in-service experience or approved training ship experience	Initial action on becoming aware of an emergency or abnormal situation conforms with established procedures Communications are clear and concise at all times and orders are acknowledged in a seamanlike manner

第 1 栏	第 2 栏	第 3 栏	第 4 栏
适任	**知识、理解和熟练**	**表明适任的方法**	**评价适任的标准**
操作应急设备和应用应急程序	应急职责的知识 从机器处所逃生的路线 熟悉机器处所的灭火设备的位置及其使用	评估从演示和认可的工作经历或认可的培训船经历中获取的证据	发觉紧急或异常情况后采取的初始行动符合既定的程序 交流始终清楚简明并以海员的方式确认指令

Section A-III/5

Mandatory minimum requirements for certification of ratings as able seafarer engine in a manned engine-room or designated to perform duties in a periodically unmanned engine-room

Standard of competence

1 Every able seafarer engine serving on a seagoing ship powered by main propulsion machinery of 750 kW propulsion power or more shall be required to demonstrate the competence to perform the functions at the support level, as specified in column 1 of table A-III/5.

2 The minimum knowledge, understanding and proficiency required of an able seafarer engine serving on a seagoing ship powered by main propulsion machinery of 750 kW propulsion power or more is listed in column 2 of table A-III/5.

3 Every candidate for certification shall be required to provide evidence of having achieved the required standard of competence in accordance with the methods for demonstrating competence and the criteria for evaluating competence specified in columns 3 and 4 of table A-III/5.

第 A-III/5 节

对有人值班机舱或周期性无人值班机舱指定履行职责的高级值班机工发证的强制性最低要求

适任标准

1　每个在主推进装置为 750 kW 或以上的海船上服务的高级值班机工,应表明其履行表 A-III/5 第 1 栏所规定的支持级职能的适任能力。

2　对在主推进装置为 750 kW 或以上的海船上服务的高级值班机工所要求的最低的知识、理解和熟练列于表 A-III/5 第 2 栏。

3　每个证书申请人应按照表 A-III/5 第 3 栏和第 4 栏中规定的表明适任的方法和评价适任的标准,提供已达到所要求的适任标准的证据。

Table A-III/5

Specification of minimum standard of competence for ratings as able seafarer engine in a manned engine-room or designated to perform duties in a periodically unmanned engine-room

Function: Marine engineering at the support level

Column 1	Column 2	Column 3	Column 4
Competence	**Knowledge, understanding and proficiency**	**Methods for demonstrating competence**	**Criteria for evaluating competence**
Contribute to a safe engineering watch	Ability to understand orders and to communicate with the officer of the watch in matters relevant to watchkeeping duties Procedures for the relief, maintenance and handover of a watch Information required to maintain a safe watch	Assessment of evidence obtained from in-service experience or practical test	Communications are clear and concise Maintenance, handover and relief of the watch is in conformity with acceptable practices and procedures
Contribute to the monitoring and controlling of an engine-room watch	Basic knowledge of the function and operation of main propulsion and auxiliary machinery Basic understanding of main propulsion and auxiliary machinery control pressures, temperatures and levels	Assessment of evidence obtained from one or more of the following: .1 approved in-service experience; .2 approved training ship experience; or .3 practical test	The frequency and extent of monitoring of main propulsion and auxiliary machinery conforms with accepted principles and procedures Deviations from the norm are identified Unsafe conditions or potential hazards are promptly recognized, reported and rectified before work continues
Contribute to fuelling and oil transfer operations	Knowledge of the function and operation of fuel system and oil transfer operations, including: .1 preparations for fuelling and transfer operations .2 procedures for connecting and disconnecting fuelling and transfer hoses	Assessment of evidence obtained from one or more of the following: .1 approved in-service experience .2 practical training .3 examination .4 approved training ship experience	Transfer operations are carried out in accordance with established safety practices and equipment operating instructions The handling of dangerous, hazardous and harmful liquids complies with established safety practices Communications within the operator's area of responsibility are consistently successful

表 A-III/5
有人值班机舱或周期性无人值班机舱指定履行职责的高级值班机工的最低适任标准

职能:轮机工程　支持级

第 1 栏	第 2 栏	第 3 栏	第 4 栏
适任	知识、理解和熟练	表明适任的方法	评价适任的标准
有助于安全的轮机值班	理解值班指令以及与值班高级船员就值班职责相关事宜进行交流的能力 接班、值班和交班的程序 保持安全值班所需的信息	评估从工作经历或实操测试中获取的证据	交流清楚简明 值班和交接班符合可接受的做法和程序
有助于机舱值班的监控	主推进装置和辅助机械的功能和操作的基本知识 基本理解主推进装置和辅助机械的控制压力、温度和液位	评估从下列一项或数项获取的证据: .1　认可的工作经历 .2　认可的培训船经历 .3　实操测试	对主推进装置和辅助机械的监控频度和程度符合公认的原则和程序 发现异常情况 在工作继续进行之前能够立即察觉、报告并纠正不安全状况或潜在危险
有助于加燃油和驳油作业	燃油系统的功能和操作以及驳油作业的知识,包括: .1　加燃油和驳油作业的准备 .2　燃油管和驳油管的连接和拆开程序	评估从下列一项或数项获取的证据: .1　认可的工作经历 .2　实际培训 .3　考试 .4　认可的培训船经历	驳油作业符合既定的安全规程和设备操作说明 危险、有毒和有害液体的处理符合既定的安全规程 操作人员职责范围内的交流持续有效

Column 1	Column 2	Column 3	Column 4
Competence	**Knowledge, understanding and proficiency**	**Methods for demonstrating competence**	**Criteria for evaluating competence**
Contribute to fuelling and oil transfer operations (*continued*)	.3 procedures relating to incidents that may arise during fuelling or transferring operation .4 securing from fuelling and transfer operations .5 ability to correctly measure and report tank levels	Assessment of evidence obtained from practical demonstration	
Contribute to bilge and ballast operations	Knowledge of the safe function, operation and maintenance of the bilge and ballast systems, including: .1 reporting incidents associated with transfer operations .2 ability to correctly measure and report tank levels	Assessment of evidence obtained from one or more of the following: .1 approved in-service experience .2 practical training .3 examination .4 approved training ship experience Assessment of evidence obtained from practical demonstration	Operations and maintenance are carried out in accordance with established safety practices and equipment operating instructions and pollution of the marine environment is avoided Communications within the operator's area of responsibility are consistently successful
Contribute to the operation of equipment and machinery	Safe operation of equipment, including: .1 valves and pumps .2 hoists and lifting equipment .3 hatches, watertight doors, ports and related equipment Ability to use and understand basic crane, winch and hoist signals	Assessment of evidence obtained from one or more of the following: .1 approved in-service experience .2 practical training .3 examination .4 approved training ship experience Assessment of evidence obtained from practical demonstration	Operations are carried out in accordance with established safety practices and equipment operating instructions Communications within the operator's area of responsibility are consistently successful

第 1 栏	第 2 栏	第 3 栏	第 4 栏
适任	知识、理解和熟练	表明适任的方法	评价适任的标准
有助于加燃油和驳油作业(续)	.3 与在加燃油和驳油作业过程中可能出现的事故相关的程序 .4 安全进行加燃油和驳油作业 .5 正确测量和报告油舱液位的能力	评估从实际演示中获取的证据	
有助于舱底水和压载水作业	舱底水和压载水系统的安全功能、操作和维护的知识,包括: .1 报告与驳水操作有关的事故 .2 正确测量和报告液舱水位的能力	评估从下列一项或数项获取的证据: .1 认可的工作经历 .2 实际培训 .3 考试 .4 认可的培训船经历 评估从实际演示中获取的证据	操作符合既定的安全规程和设备操作说明,并防止海洋环境污染 操作人员职责范围内的交流持续有效
有助于设备和机械的操作	安全操作各种设备,包括: .1 阀和泵 .2 吊装设备 .3 舱盖、水密门、驳门和相关设备 使用和理解克令吊、绞车和升降机的基本信号的能力	评估从下列一项或数项获取的证据: .1 认可的工作经历 .2 实际培训 .3 考试 .4 认可的培训船经历 评估从实际演示中获取的证据	操作符合既定的安全规程和设备操作说明 操作人员职责范围内的交流持续有效

Function: Electrical, electronic and control engineering at the support level

Column 1	Column 2	Column 3	Column 4
Competence	**Knowledge, understanding and proficiency**	**Methods for demonstrating competence**	**Criteria for evaluating competence**
Safe use of electrical equipment	Safe use and operation of electrical equipment, including: .1 safety precautions before commencing work or repair .2 isolation procedures .3 emergency procedures .4 different voltages on board Knowledge of the causes of electric shock and precautions to be observed to prevent shock	Assessment of evidence obtained from one or more of the following: .1 approved in-service experience .2 practical training .3 examination .4 approved training ship experience	Recognizes and reports electrical hazards and unsafe equipment Understands safe voltages for hand-held equipment Understands risks associated with high-voltage equipment and onboard work

Function: Maintenance and repair at the support level

Column 1	Column 2	Column 3	Column 4
Competence	**Knowledge, understanding and proficiency**	**Methods for demonstrating competence**	**Criteria for evaluating competence**
Contribute to shipboard maintenance and repair	Ability to use painting, lubrication and cleaning materials and equipment Ability to understand and execute routine maintenance and repair procedures Knowledge of surface preparation techniques Knowledge of safe disposal of waste materials Understanding manufacturer's safety guidelines and shipboard instructions	Assessment of evidence obtained from practical demonstration Assessment of evidence obtained from one or more of the following: .1 approved in-service experience .2 practical training .3 examination .4 approved training ship experience	Maintenance activities are carried out in accordance with technical, safety and procedural specifications Selection and use of equipment and tools is appropriate

职能:电气、电子和控制工程　支持级

第 1 栏	第 2 栏	第 3 栏	第 4 栏
适任	知识、理解和熟练	表明适任的方法	评价适任的标准
电气设备的安全使用	电气设备的安全使用和操作,包括: .1 开始工作或修理前的安全预防措施 .2 隔离程序 .3 应急程序 .4 船上各种电压 触电的原因和防止触电应采取的预防措施的基本知识	评估从下列一项或数项获取的证据: .1 认可的工作经历 .2 实际培训 .3 考试 .4 认可的培训船经历	识别并报告电气危险和不安全的设备 了解手持设备的安全电压 了解与高压设备和船上工作有关的危险

职能:维护和修理　支持级

第 1 栏	第 2 栏	第 3 栏	第 4 栏
适任	知识、理解和熟练	表明适任的方法	评价适任的标准
有助于船上的维护和修理	使用油漆、润滑和清洁材料与设备的能力 理解并执行日常维护和修理程序的能力 表面清理技术的知识 安全处置废料的知识 理解制造商的安全指导和船上指令	评估从实际演示中获取的证据 评估从下列一项或数项获取的证据: .1 认可的工作经历 .2 实际培训 .3 考试 .4 认可的培训船经历	维护工作符合技术、安全和程序的规范 正确地选择和使用设备和工具

Column 1	Column 2	Column 3	Column 4
Competence	**Knowledge, understanding and proficiency**	**Methods for demonstrating competence**	**Criteria for evaluating competence**
Contribute to shipboard maintenance and repair (*continued*)	Knowledge of the application, maintenance and use of hand and power tools and measuring instruments and machine tools Knowledge of metalwork		

Function: Controlling the operation of the ship and care for persons on board at the support level

Column 1	Column 2	Column 3	Column 4
Competence	**Knowledge, understanding and proficiency**	**Methods for demonstrating competence**	**Criteria for evaluating competence**
Contribute to the handling of stores	Knowledge of procedures for safe handling, stowage and securing of stores	Assessment of evidence obtained from one or more of the following: .1 approved in-service experience .2 practical training .3 examination .4 approved training ship experience	Stores operations are carried out in accordance with established safety practices and equipment operating instructions The handling of dangerous, hazardous and harmful stores complies with established safety practices Communications within the operator's area of responsibility are consistently successful
Apply precautions and contribute to the prevention of pollution of the marine environment	Knowledge of the precautions to be taken to prevent pollution of the marine environment Knowledge of use and operation of anti-pollution equipment Knowledge of approved methods for disposal of marine pollutants	Assessment of evidence obtained from one or more of the following: .1 approved in-service experience .2 practical training .3 examination .4 approved training ship experience	Procedures designed to safeguard the marine environment are observed at all times

第 1 栏	第 2 栏	第 3 栏	第 4 栏
适任	知识、理解和熟练	表明适任的方法	评价适任的标准
有助于船上的维护和修理(续)	手持和电动工具、测量仪器和机械工具的应用、维护和使用的知识 金工工艺的知识		

职能:船舶操作控制和船上人员管理　支持级

第 1 栏	第 2 栏	第 3 栏	第 4 栏
适任	知识、理解和熟练	表明适任的方法	评价适任的标准
有助于物料管理	物料的安全管理、存放和系固程序的知识	评估从下列一项或数项获取的证据: .1 认可的工作经历 .2 实际培训 .3 考试 .4 认可的培训船经历	物料管理符合既定的安全做法和设备操作说明 危险、有毒和有害物料的处理符合既定的安全规程 操作人员职责范围内的交流持续有效
采取预防措施和有助于防止海洋环境污染	采取措施防止海洋环境污染的知识 防污染设备使用和操作的知识 处置海洋污染物的认可方法的知识	评估从下列一项或数项获取的证据: .1 认可的工作经历 .2 实际培训 .3 考试 .4 认可的培训船经历	始终遵循旨在保护海洋环境的程序

Column 1	Column 2	Column 3	Column 4
Competence	**Knowledge, understanding and proficiency**	**Methods for demonstrating competence**	**Criteria for evaluating competence**
Apply occupational health and safety procedures	Working knowledge of safe working practices and personal shipboard safety, including: .1 electrical safety .2 lockout/tag-out .3 mechanical safety .4 permit to work systems .5 working aloft .6 working in enclosed spaces .7 lifting techniques and methods of preventing back injury .8 chemical and biohazard safety .9 personal safety equipment	Assessment of evidence obtained from one or more of the following: .1 approved in-service experience .2 practical training .3 examination .4 approved training ship experience	Procedures designed to safeguard personnel and the ship are observed at all times Safe working practices are observed and appropriate safety and protective equipment is correctly used at all times

第 1 栏	第 2 栏	第 3 栏	第 4 栏
适任	**知识、理解和熟练**	**表明适任的方法**	**评价适任的标准**
应用职业健康和安全程序	安全工作做法和船上人身安全的实用知识,包括: .1 电气安全 .2 锁定/挂牌 .3 机械安全 .4 许可证制度 .5 高空作业 .6 封闭处所作业 .7 吊装技术和防止背部伤害的方法 .8 化学品和生物危害的安全 .9 个人安全设备	评估从下列一项或数项获取的证据: .1 认可的工作经历 .2 实际培训 .3 考试 .4 认可的培训船经历	始终遵循旨在保护人员和船舶安全的程序 始终遵循安全工作做法,始终正确使用合适的安全和防护设备

Section A-III/6

Mandatory minimum requirements for certification of electro-technical officers

Training

1 The education and training required by paragraph 2.3 of regulation III/6 shall include training in electronic and electrical workshop skills relevant to the duties of electro-technical officer.

Onboard training

2 Every candidate for certification as electro-technical officer shall follow an approved programme of onboard training which:

.1 ensures that, during the required period of seagoing service, the candidate receives systematic practical training and experience in the tasks, duties and responsibilities of an electro-technical officer;

.2 is closely supervised and monitored by qualified and certificated officers aboard the ships in which the approved seagoing service is performed; and

.3 is adequately documented in a training record book.

Standard of competence

3 Every candidate for certification as electro-technical officer shall be required to demonstrate the ability to undertake the tasks, duties and responsibilities listed in column 1 of table A-III/6.

4 The minimum knowledge, understanding and proficiency required for certification is listed in column 2 of table A-III/6 and it shall take into account the guidance given in part B of this Code.

5 Every candidate for certification shall be required to provide evidence of having achieved the required standard of competence tabulated in columns 3 and 4 of table A-III/6.

第 A-III/6 节

对电子员发证的强制性最低要求

培训

1 规则第 III/6 条第 2.3 段要求的教育和培训应包括对与电子员职责相关的电子和电气车间技能的培训。

船上培训

2 每个电子员证书申请人应完成认可的船上培训计划，该培训计划：

.1 确保申请人在规定的海上服务期间，受到在电子员应尽的任务、职责和责任方面的系统的实际培训并获得经验；

.2 在执行认可的海上服务中受到船上合格并持证的高级船员的密切监督和指导；且

.3 在培训记录簿中充分记载。

适任标准

3 每个电子员证书申请人应按要求表明其有能力承担表 A-III/6 第 1 栏所列的任务、职责和责任。

4 发证所要求的最低的知识、理解和熟练列于表 A-III/6 第 2 栏中，并应考虑本规则 B 部分给予的指导。

5 每个证书申请人应按要求提供已达到表 A-III/6 第 3 栏和第 4 栏中所列的适任标准的证据。

Table A-III/6

Specification of minimum standard of competence for electro-technical officers

Function: Electrical, electronic and control engineering at the operational level

Column 1	Column 2	Column 3	Column 4
Competence	**Knowledge, understanding and proficiency**	**Methods for demonstrating competence**	**Criteria for evaluating competence**
Monitor the operation of electrical, electronic and control systems	Basic understanding of the operation of mechanical engineering systems, including: .1 prime movers, including main propulsion plant .2 engine-room auxiliary machinery .3 steering systems .4 cargo handling systems .5 deck machinery .6 hotel systems Basic knowledge of heat transmission, mechanics and hydromechanics *Knowledge of:* Electro-technology and electrical machines theory Fundamentals of electronics and power electronics Electrical power distribution boards and electrical equipment Fundamentals of automation, automatic control systems and technology	Examination and assessment of evidence obtained from one or more of the following: .1 approved in-service experience .2 approved training ship experience .3 approved simulator training, where appropriate .4 approved laboratory equipment training	Operation of equipment and system is in accordance with operating manuals Performance levels are in accordance with technical specifications

表 A-III/6
电子员最低适任标准

职能:电气、电子和控制工程　操作级

第 1 栏	第 2 栏	第 3 栏	第 4 栏
适任	**知识、理解和熟练**	**表明适任的方法**	**评价适任的标准**
对电气、电子和控制系统运行的监控	基本理解机械工程系统的运行,包括: .1 原动机,包括主推进装置 .2 机舱辅助机械 .3 操舵系统 .4 装卸货系统 .5 甲板机械 .6 生活系统 有关传热、力学和流体力学的基本知识 下列知识: 电子技术和电气机械理论 电子学和电力电子学的基础 配电板和电气设备 自动化、自动控制系统及技术的基础 仪表、报警和监控系统 电力驱动 电气材料技术	考试并评估从下列一项或数项获取的证据: .1 认可的工作经历 .2 认可的培训船经历 .3 认可的模拟器培训,如适用 .4 认可的实验室设备培训	设备和系统的操作与操作手册一致 性能等级与技术规范一致

Column 1 Competence	Column 2 Knowledge, understanding and proficiency	Column 3 Methods for demonstrating competence	Column 4 Criteria for evaluating competence
Monitor the operation of electrical, electronic and control systems (*continued*)	Instrumentation, alarm and monitoring systems Electrical drives Technology of electrical materials Electro-hydraulic and electro-pneumatic control systems Appreciation of the hazards and precautions required for the operation of power systems above 1,000 volts		
Monitor the operation of automatic control systems of propulsion and auxiliary machinery	Preparation of control systems of propulsion and auxiliary machinery for operation	Examination and assessment of evidence obtained from one or more of the following: .1 approved in-service experience .2 approved training ship experience .3 approved simulator training, where appropriate .4 approved laboratory equipment training	Surveillance of main propulsion plant and auxiliary systems is sufficient to maintain safe operation condition
Operate generators and distribution systems	Coupling, load sharing and changing over generators Coupling and breaking connection between switchboards and distribution panels	Examination and assessment of evidence obtained from one or more of the following: .1 approved in-service experience .2 approved training ship experience .3 approved simulator training, where appropriate .4 approved laboratory equipment training	Operations are planned and carried out in accordance with operating manuals, established rules and procedures to ensure safety of operations Electrical distribution systems can be understood and explained with drawings/instructions

第 1 栏	第 2 栏	第 3 栏	第 4 栏
适任	知识、理解和熟练	表明适任的方法	评价适任的标准
对电气、电子和控制系统运行的监控(续)	电子—液压和电子—气动控制系统 理解 1 kV 以上供电系统操作的危险和所需的预防措施		
推进装置和辅助机械自动控制系统运行的监控	推进装置和辅助机械控制系统的操作准备	考试并评估从下列一项或数项获取的证据: .1 认可的工作经历 .2 认可的培训船经历 .3 认可的模拟器培训,如适用 .4 认可的实验室设备培训	对主推进装置和辅助系统的监控足以保持安全运行状态
发电机和配电系统的操作	发电机并车、负载分配和切换 配电板和配电屏之间的连接和切断	考试并评估从下列一项或数项获取的证据: .1 认可的工作经历 .2 认可的培训船经历 .3 认可的模拟器培训,如适用 .4 认可的实验室设备培训	按照操作手册、既定规则和程序计划和执行操作以确保操作安全 能用图纸/说明书理解和解释配电系统

Column 1	Column 2	Column 3	Column 4
Competence	**Knowledge, understanding and proficiency**	**Methods for demonstrating competence**	**Criteria for evaluating competence**
Operate and maintain power systems in excess of 1,000 volts	*Theoretical knowledge* High-voltage technology Safety precautions and procedures Electrical propulsion of the ships, electrical motors and control systems *Practical knowledge* Safe operation and maintenance of high-voltage systems, including knowledge of the special technical type of high-voltage systems and the danger resulting from operational voltage of more than 1,000 volts	Examination and assessment of evidence obtained from one or more of the following: .1 approved in-service experience .2 approved training ship experience .3 approved simulator training, where appropriate .4 approved laboratory equipment training	Operations are planned and carried out in accordance with operating manuals, established rules and procedures to ensure safety of operations
Operate computers and computer networks on ships	Understanding of: .1 main features of data processing .2 construction and use of computer networks on ships .3 bridge-based, engine-room-based and commercial computer use	Examination and assessment of evidence obtained from one or more of the following: .1 approved in-service experience .2 approved training ship experience .3 approved simulator training, where appropriate .4 approved laboratory equipment training	Computer networks and computers are correctly checked and handled
Use English in written and oral form	Adequate knowledge of the English language to enable the officer to use engineering publications and to perform the officer's duties	Examination and assessment of evidence obtained from practical instructions	English language publications relevant to the officer's duties are correctly interpreted Communications are clear and understood

第 1 栏	第 2 栏	第 3 栏	第 4 栏
适任	知识、理解和熟练	表明适任的方法	评价适任的标准
1 kV 以上供电系统的操作和维护	理论知识 高压电技术 安全预防措施和程序 电力推进船舶主电动机及控制系统 实际知识 高压电系统的安全操作和维护,包括了解特殊技术类型的高压电系统和操作1 kV以上高压电系统引起的危险	考试并评估从下列一项或数项获取的证据: .1 认可的工作经历 .2 认可的培训船经历 .3 认可的模拟器培训,如适用 .4 认可的实验室设备培训	按照操作手册、既定规则和程序计划和执行操作以确保操作安全
操作船上计算机及计算机网络	理解: .1 数据处理的主要特点 .2 船上计算机网络的构造和使用 .3 基于驾驶台的、基于机舱的和商用的计算机的使用	考试并评估从下列一项或数项获取的证据: .1 认可的工作经历 .2 认可的培训船经历 .3 认可的模拟器培训,如适用 .4 认可的实验室设备培训	正确检查和管理计算机网络和终端机
使用英语进行书面和口头表达	足够的英语语言知识以使电子员能使用工程出版物并履行其职责	考试并评估从实际训练中获取的证据	正确解读与电子员职责相关的英语出版物 交流清楚易懂

Column 1 **Competence**	Column 2 **Knowledge, understanding and proficiency**	Column 3 **Methods for demonstrating competence**	Column 4 **Criteria for evaluating competence**
Use internal communication systems	Operation of all internal communication systems on board	Examination and assessment of evidence obtained from one or more of the following: .1 approved in-service experience .2 approved training ship experience .3 approved simulator training, where appropriate .4 approved laboratory equipment training	Transmission and reception of messages are consistently successful Communication records are complete, accurate and comply with statutory requirements

第 1 栏	第 2 栏	第 3 栏	第 4 栏
适任	**知识、理解和熟练**	**表明适任的方法**	**评价适任的标准**
使用内部通信系统	船上所有内部通信系统的操作	考试并评估从下列一项或数项获取的证据： .1 认可的工作经历 .2 认可的培训船经历 .3 认可的模拟器培训，如适用 .4 认可的实验室设备培训	信息的发送和接收持续有效 通信记录完整、准确并符合法定的要求

Function: Maintenance and repair at the operational level

Column 1 Competence	Column 2 Knowledge, understanding and proficiency	Column 3 Methods for demonstrating competence	Column 4 Criteria for evaluating competence
Maintenance and repair of electrical and electronic equipment	Safety requirements for working on shipboard electrical systems, including the safe isolation of electrical equipment required before personnel are permitted to work on such equipment Maintenance and repair of electrical system equipment, switchboards, electric motors, generators and DC electrical systems and equipment Detection of electric malfunction, location of faults and measures to prevent damage Construction and operation of electrical testing and measuring equipment Function and performance tests of the following equipment and their configuration: .1 monitoring systems .2 automatic control devices .3 protective devices The interpretation of electrical and electronic diagrams	Examination and assessment of evidence obtained from one or more of the following: .1 approved workshop skills training .2 approved practical experience and tests .3 approved in-service experience .4 approved training ship experience	Safety measures for working are appropriate Selection and use of hand tools, measuring instruments, and testing equipment are appropriate and interpretation of results is accurate Dismantling, inspecting, repairing and reassembling equipment are in accordance with manuals and good practice Reassembling and performance testing is in accordance with manuals and good practice
Maintenance and repair of automation and control systems of main propulsion and auxiliary machinery	Appropriate electrical and mechanical knowledge and skills *Safety and emergency procedures*	Examination and assessment of evidence obtained from one or more of the following: .1 approved in-service experience	The effect of malfunctions on associated plant and systems is accurately identified, ship's technical drawings are correctly interpreted, measuring and calibrating instruments are correctly used and actions taken are justified

职能:维护和修理　操作级

第1栏	第2栏	第3栏	第4栏
适任	知识、理解和熟练	表明适任的方法	评价适任的标准
电气和电子设备的维护与修理	船上电气系统工作的安全要求,包括在允许人员检修该设备之前所要求的电气设备的安全隔离 电气系统设备、配电板、电动机、发电机和直流电气系统及设备的维护与修理 电气故障及故障位置的检测和防止损坏的措施 电气测试和测量设备的构造和操作 以下设备及其配置的功能和性能测试: .1　监控系统 .2　自动控制设备 .3　防护设备 电气和电子图的识读	考试并评估从下列一项或数项获取的证据: .1　认可的车间技能培训 .2　认可的实际经验和测试 .3　认可的工作经历 .4　认可的培训船经历	工作安全措施适当 选择和使用手动工具、测量仪表、检测设备适当,且对结果的解释准确 设备的拆卸、检测、修理和装复符合操作手册及良好的做法 装复和性能测试符合操作手册及良好的做法
维护和修理主推进装置和辅助机械的自动和控制系统	适当的电气和机械的知识和技能 安全和应急程序	考试并评估从下列一项或数项获取的证据: .1　认可的工作经历	准确识别相关装置和系统的故障的影响,正确解读船舶的技术图纸,正确使用测量和校准仪表并采取正确的方法

Column 1 **Competence**	Column 2 **Knowledge, understanding and proficiency**	Column 3 **Methods for demonstrating competence**	Column 4 **Criteria for evaluating competence**
	Safe isolation of equipment and associated systems required before personnel are permitted to work on such plant or equipment Practical knowledge for the testing, maintenance, fault finding and repair Test, detect faults and maintain and restore electrical and electronic control equipment to operating condition	.2 approved training ship experience .3 approved simulator training, where appropriate .4 approved laboratory equipment training	Isolation, dismantling and reassembly of plant and equipment are in accordance with manufacturer's safety guidelines and shipboard instructions and legislative and safety specifications. Action taken leads to the restoration of automation and control systems by the method most suitable and appropriate to the prevailing circumstances and conditions
Maintenance and repair of bridge navigation equipment and ship communication systems	Knowledge of the principles and maintenance procedures of navigation equipment, internal and external communication systems *Theoretical knowledge:* Electrical and electronic systems operating in flammable areas *Practical knowledge:* Carrying out safe maintenance and repair procedures Detection of machinery malfunction, location of faults and action to prevent damage		The effect of malfunctions on associated plant and systems is accurately identified, ship's technical drawings are correctly interpreted, measuring and calibrating instruments are correctly used and actions taken are justified Isolation, dismantling and re-assembly of plant and equipment are in accordance with manufacturer's safety guidelines and shipboard instructions, legislative and safety specifications. Action taken leads to the restoration of bridge navigation equipment and ship communication systems by the method most suitable and appropriate to the prevailing circumstances and conditions

第 1 栏	第 2 栏	第 3 栏	第 4 栏
适任	知识、理解和熟练	表明适任的方法	评价适任的标准
	允许人员检修该设备之前所要求的设备和相关系统的安全隔离 测试、维护、故障检查和修理的实际知识 电气和电子控制设备的测试、故障检查和维护并恢复运行状态	.2 认可的培训船经历 .3 认可的模拟器培训,如适用 .4 认可的实验室设备培训	装置和设备的隔离、拆卸和重装符合制造商的安全指导、船上指令、法规和安全规范。以最适合于当时的环境和状况的方法采取行动使自动和控制系统恢复原状
维护和修理驾驶台航行设备和船舶通信系统	航行设备和内外部通信系统的原理和维护程序的知识 理论知识: 易燃区域电气和电子系统的运行 实际知识: 执行安全的维护和修理程序 机械故障及故障位置的检测和防止损坏的措施		准确识别相关装置和系统的故障的影响,正确解读船舶的技术图纸,正确使用测量和校准仪表并采取正确的方法 装置和设备的隔离、拆卸和重装符合制造商的安全指导、船上指令、法规和安全规范。以最适合于当时的环境和状况的方法采取行动使驾驶台航行设备和船舶通信系统恢复原状

Column 1 Competence	Column 2 Knowledge, understanding and proficiency	Column 3 Methods for demonstrating competence	Column 4 Criteria for evaluating competence
Maintenance and repair of electrical, electronic and control systems of deck machinery and cargo-handling equipment	Appropriate electrical and mechanical knowledge and skills *Safety and emergency procedures* Safe isolation of equipment and associated systems required before personnel are permitted to work on such plant or equipment Practical knowledge for the testing, maintenance, fault finding and repair Test, detect faults and maintain and restore electrical and electronic control equipment to operating condition	Examination and assessment of evidence obtained from one or more of the following: .1 approved in-service experience .2 approved training ship experience .3 approved simulator training, where appropriate .4 approved laboratory equipment training	The effect of malfunctions on associated plant and systems is accurately identified, ship's technical drawings are correctly interpreted, measuring and calibrating instruments are correctly used and actions taken are justified Isolation, dismantling and re-assembly of plant and equipment are in accordance with manufacturer's safety guidelines and shipboard instructions, legislative and safety specifications. Action taken leads to the restoration of deck machinery and cargo-handling equipment by the method most suitable and appropriate to the prevailing circumstances and conditions
Maintenance and repair of control and safety systems of hotel equipment	*Theoretical knowledge:* Electrical and electronic systems operating in flammable areas *Practical knowledge:* Carrying out safe maintenance and repair procedures Detection of machinery malfunction, location of faults and action to prevent damage		The effect of malfunctions on associated plant and systems is accurately identified, ship's technical drawings are correctly interpreted, measuring and calibrating instruments are correctly used and actions taken are justified Isolation, dismantling and re-assembly of plant and equipment are in accordance with manufacturer's safety guidelines and shipboard instructions, legislative and safety specifications. Action taken leads to the restoration of control and safety systems of hotel equipment by the method most suitable and appropriate to the prevailing circumstances and conditions

第 1 栏	第 2 栏	第 3 栏	第 4 栏
适任	知识、理解和熟练	表明适任的方法	评价适任的标准
维护和修理甲板机械和装卸货设备的电气、电子和控制系统	适当的电气和机械的知识和技能 安全和应急程序 允许人员检修该设备之前所要求的设备和相关系统的安全隔离 测试、维护、故障检查和修理的实际知识 电气和电子控制设备的测试、故障检查和维护并恢复运行状态	考试并评估从下列一项或数项获取的证据： .1 认可的工作经历 .2 认可的培训船经历 .3 认可的模拟器培训，如适用 .4 认可的实验室设备培训	准确识别相关装置和系统的故障的影响，正确解读船舶的技术图纸，正确使用测量和校准仪表并采取正确的方法 装置和设备的隔离、拆卸和重装符合制造商的安全指导、船上指令、法规和安全规范。以最适合于当时的环境和状况的方法采取行动使甲板机械和装卸货设备恢复原状
维护和修理生活设备的控制和安全系统	理论知识： 易燃区域电气和电子系统的运行 实际知识： 执行安全的维护和修理程序 电气故障及故障位置的检测和防止损坏的措施		准确识别相关装置和系统的故障的影响，正确解读船舶的技术图纸，正确使用测量和校准仪表并采取正确的方法 装置和设备的隔离、拆卸和重装符合制造商的安全指导、船上指令、法规和安全规范。以最适合于当时的环境和状况的方法采取行动使生活设备的控制和安全系统恢复原状

Function: Controlling the operation of the ship and care for persons on board at operational level

Column 1	Column 2	Column 3	Column 4
Competence	**Knowledge, understanding and proficiency**	**Methods for demonstrating competence**	**Criteria for evaluating competence**
Ensure compliance with pollution-prevention requirements	*Prevention of pollution of the marine environment* Knowledge of the precautions to be taken to prevent pollution of the marine environment Anti-pollution procedures and all associated equipment Importance of proactive measures to protect the marine environment	Examination and assessment of evidence obtained from one or more of the following: .1 approved in-service experience .2 approved training ship experience .3 approved training	Procedures for monitoring shipboard operations and ensuring compliance with pollution-prevention requirements are fully observed Actions to ensure that a positive environmental reputation is maintained
Prevent, control and fight fire on board	*Fire prevention and fire-fighting appliances* Ability to organize fire drills Knowledge of classes and chemistry of fire Knowledge of fire-fighting systems Action to be taken in the event of fire, including fires involving oil systems	Assessment of evidence obtained from approved fire-fighting training and experience as set out in section A-VI/3, paragraphs 1 to 3	The type and scale of the problem is promptly identified and initial actions conform with the emergency procedure and contingency plans for the ship Evacuation, emergency shutdown and isolation procedures are appropriate to the nature of the emergency and are implemented promptly The order of priority, and the levels and time-scales of making reports and informing personnel on board, are relevant to the nature of the emergency and reflect the urgency of the problem

职能:船舶操作控制和船上人员管理　操作级

第 1 栏	第 2 栏	第 3 栏	第 4 栏
适任	知识、理解和熟练	表明适任的方法	评价适任的标准
确保符合防污染要求	防止海洋环境污染 采取预防措施防止海洋环境污染的知识 防污染程序和所有相关设备 采取积极措施保护海洋环境的重要性	考试并评估从下列一项或数项获取的证据: .1　认可的工作经历 .2　认可的培训船经历 .3　认可的培训	监督船上操作和确保符合《MARPOL 公约》要求的程序得到全面遵守 采取的行动旨在确保维持良好的环保声誉
船上防火、控制火灾和灭火	防火和灭火设备 组织消防演习的能力 火的分类和化学性质的知识 灭火系统的知识 失火(包括涉及油类系统火灾)时应采取的行动	评估从第 A-VI/3 节第 1 段至第 3 段规定的认可的消防培训中获取的证据	迅速确定问题的类型和范围,初始行动符合船舶应急程序和意外事故应急计划 撤离、应急关闭和隔离程序适合紧急情况的性质,并迅速实施 作出报告和通知船上人员的优先顺序、级别、时限与紧急情况的性质相关,并反映事态的紧急程度

Column 1	Column 2	Column 3	Column 4
Competence	**Knowledge, understanding and proficiency**	**Methods for demonstrating competence**	**Criteria for evaluating competence**
Operate life-saving appliances	*Life-saving* Ability to organize abandon ship drills and knowledge of the operation of survival craft and rescue boats, their launching appliances and arrangements, and their equipment, including radio life-saving appliances, satellite EPIRBs, SARTs, immersion suits and thermal protective aids	Assessment of evidence obtained from approved training and experience as set out in section A-VI/2, paragraphs 1 to 4	Actions in responding to abandon ship and survival situations are appropriate to the prevailing circumstances and conditions and comply with accepted safety practices and standards
Apply medical first aid on board ship	*Medical aid* Practical application of medical guides and advice by radio, including the ability to take effective action based on such knowledge in the case of accidents or illnesses that are likely to occur on board ship	Assessment of evidence obtained from approved training as set out in section A-VI/4, paragraphs 1 to 3	Identification of probable cause, nature and extent of injuries or conditions is prompt and treatment minimizes immediate threat to life
Application of leadership and teamworking skills	Working knowledge of shipboard personnel management and training Ability to apply task and workload management, including: .1 planning and co-ordination .2 personnel assignment .3 time and resource constraints .4 prioritization	Assessment of evidence obtained from one or more of the following: .1 approved training .2 approved in-service experience .3 practical demonstration	The crew are allocated duties and informed of expected standards of work and behaviour in a manner appropriate to the individuals concerned Training objectives and activities are based on assessment of current competence and capabilities and operational requirements

第1栏	第2栏	第3栏	第4栏
适任	知识、理解和熟练	表明适任的方法	评价适任的标准
操作救生设备	救生 组织弃船演习的能力和操作救生艇筏、救助艇及其释放装置、布置和设备,包括无线电救生装置、卫星应急无线电示位标、搜救应答器、救生服和保温用具在内的知识	评估从第 A-VI/2 节第1段至第4段规定的认可的培训和经历中获取的证据	在弃船求生情况下采取的行动适合于当时的环境和条件,并符合公认的安全做法和标准
在船上应用医疗急救	医护 实际应用医疗指南和无线电咨询,包括根据这种知识对船上可能发生的事故和疾病采取有效行动的能力	评估从第 A-VI/4 节第1段至第3段规定的认可的培训中获取的证据	迅速确认伤病的可能原因、性质和程度,并加以治疗以尽量减小对生命的直接威胁
领导力和团队工作技能的运用	船上人员管理和培训的实用知识 运用任务和工作量管理的能力,包括: .1 计划和协调 .2 人员分派 .3 时间和资源的限制 .4 优先排序	评估从下列一项或数项获取的证据: .1 认可的培训 .2 认可的工作经历 .3 实际演示	分配船员工作,并以适合相关人员的方式告知所要求的工作标准和行为准则 培训目标和活动以对目前适任性和能力的评估和操作要求为基础

Column 1	Column 2	Column 3	Column 4
Competence	**Knowledge, understanding and proficiency**	**Methods for demonstrating competence**	**Criteria for evaluating competence**
Application of leadership and teamworking skills *(continued)*	Knowledge and ability to apply effective resource management: .1 allocation, assignment, and prioritization of resources .2 effective communication on board and ashore .3 decisions reflect consideration of team experiences 4 assertiveness and leadership, including motivation .5 obtaining and maintaining situational awareness Knowledge and ability to apply decision-making techniques: .1 Situation and risk assessment .2 Identify and consider generated options .3 Selecting course of action .4 Evaluation of outcome effectiveness		Operations are planned and resources are allocated as needed in correct priority to perform necessary tasks Communication is clearly and unambiguously given and received Effective leadership behaviours are demonstrated Necessary team member(s) share accurate understanding of current and predicted vessel state and operational status and external environment Decisions are most effective for the situation
Contribute to the safety of personnel and ship	Knowledge of personal survival techniques Knowledge of fire prevention and ability to fight and extinguish fires Knowledge of elementary first aid Knowledge of personal safety and social responsibilities	Assessment of evidence obtained from approved training and experience as set out in section A-VI/1, paragraph 2	Appropriate safety and protective equipment is correctly used Procedures and safe working practices designed to safeguard personnel and the ship are observed at all times Procedures designed to safeguard the environment are observed at all times Initial and follow-up actions on becoming aware of an emergency conform with established emergency response procedures

第 1 栏	第 2 栏	第 3 栏	第 4 栏
适任	知识、理解和熟练	表明适任的方法	评价适任的标准
领导力和团队工作技能的运用(续)	运用有效资源管理的知识和能力: .1 资源的分配、分派和优先排序 .2 船上和岸上的有效沟通 .3 决策反映出团队的经验 .4 决断力和领导力,包括激励 .5 具有并保持情景意识 运用决策技能的知识和能力: .1 局面和风险评估 .2 识别并考虑形成的选项 .3 选择行动方案 .4 评价结果的有效性		操作有计划,并根据需要按正确的优先顺序分配资源,以执行必要的任务 交流清楚、无歧义 表明有效的领导行为 相关的团队成员对当前和预计的船舶及操作状态和外部环境有共同的准确理解 决策对于局面最有效
有助于人员和船舶的安全	个人求生技能的知识 防火知识和灭火能力 基本急救的知识 个人安全和社会责任的知识	评估从第 A-VI/1 节第 2 段规定的认可的培训和经历中获取的证据	正确使用适当的安全和防护设备 始终遵循旨在保护人员和船舶的程序和安全工作做法 始终遵循旨在保护环境的程序 发觉紧急情况时的初始和后续行动符合既定的应急反应程序

Section A-III/7

Mandatory minimum requirements for certification of electro-technical rating

Standard of Competence

1 Every electro-technical rating serving on a seagoing ship powered by main propulsion machinery of 750 kW propulsion power or more shall be required to demonstrate the competence to perform the functions at the support level, as specified in column 1 of table A-III/7.

2 The minimum knowledge, understanding and proficiency required of an electro-technical rating serving on a seagoing ship powered by main propulsion machinery of 750 kW propulsion power or more is listed in column 2 of table A-III/7.

3 Every candidate for certification shall be required to provide evidence of having achieved the required standard of competence in accordance with the methods for demonstrating competence and the criteria for evaluating competence specified in columns 3 and 4 of table A-III/7.

第 A-III/7 节

对电子技工发证的强制性最低要求

适任标准

1　每个在主推进装置为 750 kW 或以上的海船上服务的电子技工应表明其履行表 A-III/7 第 1 栏所规定的支持级职能的适任能力。

2　对在主推进装置为 750 kW 或以上的海船上服务的电子技工所要求的最低的知识、理解和熟练列于表 A-III/7 第 2 栏中。

3　每个证书申请人应按照表 A-III/7 第 3 栏和第 4 栏所规定的表明适任的方法和评价适任的标准,提供已达到所要求的适任标准的证据。

Table A-III/7

Specification of minimum standard of competence for electro-technical ratings

Function: Electrical, electronic and control engineering at the support level

Column 1	Column 2	Column 3	Column 4
Competence	**Knowledge, understanding and proficiency**	**Methods for demonstrating competence**	**Criteria for evaluating competence**
Safe use of electrical equipment	Safe use and operation of electrical equipment, including: .1 safety precautions before commencing work or repair .2 isolation procedures .3 emergency procedures .4 different voltages on board Knowledge of the causes of electric shock and precautions to be observed to prevent shock	Assessment of evidence obtained from one or more of the following: .1 approved in-service experience .2 practical training .3 examination .4 approved training ship experience	Understands and follows safety instructions of electrical equipment and machinery Recognizes and reports electrical hazards and unsafe equipment Understands safe voltages for hand-held equipment Understands risks associated with high-voltage equipment and onboard work
Contribute to monitoring the operation of electrical systems and machinery	Basic knowledge of the operation of mechanical engineering systems, including: .1 prime movers, including main propulsion plant .2 engine-room auxiliary machineries .3 steering systems .4 cargo-handling systems .5 deck machineries .6 hotel systems	Assessment of evidence obtained from one or more of the following: .1 approved in-service experience .2 practical training .3 examination .4 approved training ship experience	Knowledge that ensures: .1 operation of equipment and system is in accordance with operating manuals .2 performance levels are in accordance with technical specifications

表 A-III/7
电子技工的最低适任标准

职能:电气、电子和控制管理　支持级

第 1 栏	第 2 栏	第 3 栏	第 4 栏
适任	知识、理解和熟练	表明适任的方法	评价适任的标准
电气设备的安全使用	电气设备的安全使用和操作,包括: .1 开始工作或修理前的安全预防措施 .2 隔离程序 .3 应急程序 .4 船上各种电压 触电的原因和防止触电应遵循的预防措施的知识	评估从下列一项或数项获取的证据: .1 认可的工作经历 .2 实际培训 .3 考试 .4 认可的培训船经历	了解并遵循电气设备和机械的安全规定 识别并报告电气危险和不安全的设备 了解手持设备的安全电压 了解与高压设备和船上工作有关的危险
有助于电气系统和机械操作的监控	机械工程系统操作的基本知识,包括: .1 原动机,包括主推进装置 .2 机舱辅助机械 .3 操舵系统 .4 装卸货系统 .5 甲板机械 .6 生活系统	评估从下列一项或数项获取的证据: .1 认可的工作经历 .2 实际培训 .3 考试 .4 认可的培训船经历	掌握知识确保: .1 设备和系统的操作符合操作手册 .2 性能等级符合技术规范

Column 1	Column 2	Column 3	Column 4
Competence	**Knowledge, understanding and proficiency**	**Methods for demonstrating competence**	**Criteria for evaluating competence**
Contribute to monitoring the operation of electrical systems and machinery (*continued*)	*Basic knowledge of:* .1 electro-technology and electrical machines theory .2 electrical power distribution boards and electrical equipment .3 fundamentals of automation, automatic control systems and technology .4 instrumentation, alarm and monitoring systems .5 electrical drives .6 electro-hydraulic and electro-pneumatic control systems .7 coupling, load sharing and changes in electrical configuration		
Use hand tools, electrical and electronic measurement equipment for fault finding, maintenance and repair operations	Safety requirements for working on shipboard electrical systems Application of safe working practices *Basic knowledge of:* .1 construction and operational characteristics of shipboard AC and DC systems and equipment .2 use of measuring instruments, machine tools, and hand and power tools	Assessment of evidence obtained from one or more of the following: .1 approved workshop skills training .2 approved practical experience and tests	Implementation of safety procedures is satisfactory Selection and use of test equipment is appropriate and interpretation of results is accurate Selection of procedures for the conduct of repair and maintenance is in accordance with manuals and good practice

第 1 栏	第 2 栏	第 3 栏	第 4 栏
适任	**知识、理解和熟练**	**表明适任的方法**	**评价适任的标准**
有助于电气系统和机械操作的监控（续）	基本知识： .1 电子技术和电气机械理论 .2 配电屏和电气设备 .3 自动化、自动控制系统和技术的基础 .4 仪表、报警和监控系统 .5 电力驱动 .6 电子－液压和电子－气动控制系统 .7 电气装置并车、负载分配和切换		
使用手动工具、电气和电子测量设备进行故障检查、维护和修理作业	船上电气系统操作的安全要求 安全工作做法的应用 基本知识： .1 船上交流电和直流电系统和设备的构造和运行特性 .2 测量仪表、机械工具和手动与电动工具的使用	评估从下列一项或数项获取的证据： .1 认可的车间技能培训 .2 认可的实际经历和测试	安全程序的执行令人满意 正确地选择和使用测试设备，准确地解读其结果 维护和修理工作程序的选择符合手册及良好的做法

Function: Maintenance and repair at the support level

Column 1	Column 2	Column 3	Column 4
Competence	**Knowledge, understanding and proficiency**	**Methods for demonstrating competence**	**Criteria for evaluating competence**
Contribute to shipboard maintenance and repair	Ability to use lubrication and cleaning materials and equipment Knowledge of safe disposal of waste materials Ability to understand and execute routine maintenance and repair procedures Understanding manufacturer's safety guidelines and shipboard instructions	Assessment of evidence obtained from one or more of the following: .1 approved in-service experience .2 practical training .3 examination .4 approved training ship experience	Maintenance activities are carried out in accordance with technical, safety and procedural specifications Selection and use of equipment and tools is appropriate
Contribute to the maintenance and repair of electrical systems and machinery on board	*Safety and emergency procedures* Basic knowledge of electro-technical drawings and safe isolation of equipment and associated systems required before personnel are permitted to work on such plant or equipment Test, detect faults and maintain and restore electrical control equipment and machinery to operating condition Electrical and electronic equipment operating in flammable areas Basics of ship's fire-detection system Carrying out safe maintenance and repair procedures	Examination and assessment of evidence obtained from one or more of the following: .1 approved in-service experience .2 approved training ship experience .3 approved simulator training, where appropriate .4 approved laboratory equipment training	The effect of malfunctions on associated plant and systems is accurately identified, ship's technical drawings are correctly interpreted, measuring and calibrating instruments are correctly used and actions taken are justified Isolation, dismantling and reassembly of plant and equipment is in accordance with manufacturer's safety guidelines and shipboard instructions

职能:维护和修理 支持级

第 1 栏	第 2 栏	第 3 栏	第 4 栏
适任	知识、理解和熟练	表明适任的方法	评价适任的标准
有助于船上维护和修理	润滑、清洁材料和设备的使用能力 安全处置废料的知识 理解和执行日常维护及修理程序的能力 理解制造商的安全指导和船上指令	评估从下列一项或数项获取的证据: .1 认可的工作经历 .2 实际培训 .3 考试 .4 认可的培训船经历	维护行为符合技术、安全和程序的规范 正确地选择和使用设备和工具
有助于船上电气系统和机械的维护及修理	安全和应急程序 电气技术图纸的基本知识,以及允许人员维护和修理前安全隔离设备和相关系统的基本知识 电气控制设备和机械的测试、故障检查和维护并恢复运行状态 易燃区域电气和电子设备的操作 船上探火系统基础知识 执行安全维护和修理程序	考试并评估从下列一项或数项获取的证据: .1 认可的工作经历 .2 认可的培训船经历 .3 认可的模拟器培训,如适用 .4 认可的实验室设备培训	准确识别相关装置和系统的故障的影响,正确解读船舶的技术图纸,正确使用测量和校准仪表并采取正确的方法 装置和设备的隔离,拆卸和装复符合制造商的安全指导和船上指令

Column 1	Column 2	Column 3	Column 4
Competence	**Knowledge, understanding and proficiency**	**Methods for demonstrating competence**	**Criteria for evaluating competence**
Contribute to the maintenance and repair of electrical systems and machinery on board (*continued*)	Detection of machinery malfunction, location of faults and action to prevent damage Maintenance and repair of lighting fixtures and supply systems		

Function: Controlling the operation of the ship and care for persons on board at the support level

Column 1	Column 2	Column 3	Column 4
Competence	**Knowledge, understanding and proficiency**	**Methods for demonstrating competence**	**Criteria for evaluating competence**
Contribute to the handling of stores	Knowledge of procedures for safe handling, stowage and securing of stores	Assessment of evidence obtained from one or more of the following: .1 approved in-service experience .2 practical training .3 examination .4 approved training ship experience	Stores stowage operations are carried out in accordance with established safety practices and equipment operating instructions The handling of dangerous, hazardous and harmful stores complies with established safety practices Communications within the operator's area of responsibility are consistently successful
Apply precautions and contribute to the prevention of pollution of the marine environment	Knowledge of the precautions to be taken to prevent pollution of the marine environment Knowledge of use and operation of anti-pollution equipment/agents Knowledge of approved methods for disposal of marine pollutants	Assessment of evidence obtained from one or more of the following: .1 approved in-service experience .2 practical training .3 examination .4 approved training ship experience	Procedures designed to safeguard the marine environment are observed at all times

第 1 栏	第 2 栏	第 3 栏	第 4 栏
适任	知识、理解和熟练	表明适任的方法	评价适任的标准
有助于船上电气系统和机械的维护及修理(续)	机械故障及故障位置的检测和防止损坏的措施 维护和修理固定照明设备及供电系统		

职能:船舶操作控制和船上人员管理 支持级

第 1 栏	第 2 栏	第 3 栏	第 4 栏
适任	知识、理解和熟练	表明适任的方法	评价适任的标准
有助于物料管理	物料的安全管理、存放和系固程序的知识	评估从下列一项或数项获取的证据: .1 认可的工作经历 .2 实际培训 .3 考试 .4 认可的培训船经历	物料存放符合既定的安全做法和设备操作说明 危险、有毒和有害物料的处理符合既定的安全做法 操作人员职责范围内的交流持续有效
采取预防措施和有助于防止海洋环境污染	采取预防措施防止海洋环境污染的知识 防污染设备/化学药剂的使用和操作的知识 处置海洋污染物的认可方法的知识	评估从下列一项或数项获取的证据: .1 认可的工作经历 .2 实际培训 .3 考试 .4 认可的培训船经历	始终遵循旨在保护海洋环境的程序

Column 1	Column 2	Column 3	Column 4
Competence	**Knowledge, understanding and proficiency**	**Methods for demonstrating competence**	**Criteria for evaluating competence**
Apply occupational health and safety procedures	Working knowledge of safe working practices and personal shipboard safety, including: .1 electrical safety .2 lockout/tag-out .3 mechanical safety .4 permit to work systems .5 working aloft .6 working in enclosed spaces .7 lifting techniques and methods of preventing back injury .8 chemical and biohazard safety .9 personal safety equipment	Assessment of evidence obtained from one or more of the following: .1 approved in-service experience .2 practical training .3 examination .4 approved training ship experience	Procedures designed to safeguard personnel and the ship are observed at all times Safe working practices are observed and appropriate safety and protective equipment is correctly used at all times

第 1 栏	第 2 栏	第 3 栏	第 4 栏
适任	**知识、理解和熟练**	**表明适任的方法**	**评价适任的标准**
应用职业健康和安全的程序	安全工作做法和船上人身安全的实用知识,包括: .1 电气安全 .2 锁定/挂牌 .3 机械安全 .4 许可证制度 .5 高空作业 .6 封闭处所作业 .7 吊装技术和防止背部伤害的方法 .8 化学品和生物危害的安全 .9 个人安全设备	评估从下列一项或数项获取的证据: .1 认可的工作经历 .2 实际培训 .3 考试 .4 认可的培训船经历	始终遵循旨在保护人员和船舶安全的程序 始终遵循安全工作做法,始终正确使用合适的安全和防护设备

CHAPTER IV

Standards regarding radio operators

Section A-IV/1
Application

(No provisions)

Section A-IV/2
Mandatory minimum requirements for certification of GMDSS radio operators

Standard of competence

1 The minimum knowledge, understanding and proficiency required for certification of GMDSS radio operators shall be sufficient for radio operators to carry out their radio duties. The knowledge required for obtaining each type of certificate defined in the Radio Regulations shall be in accordance with those regulations. In addition, every candidate for certification of competency shall be required to demonstrate ability to undertake the tasks, duties and responsibilities listed in column 1 of table A-IV/2.

2 The knowledge, understanding and proficiency for endorsement under the Convention of certificates issued under the provisions of the Radio Regulations are listed in column 2 of table A-IV/2.

3 The level of knowledge of the subjects listed in column 2 of table A-IV/2 shall be sufficient for the candidate to carry out his duties [*].

4 Every candidate shall provide evidence of having achieved the required standard of competence through:

.1 demonstration of competence to perform the tasks and duties and to assume responsibilities listed in column 1 of table A-IV/2, in accordance with the methods for demonstrating competence and the criteria for evaluating competence tabulated in columns 3 and 4 of that table; and

.2 examination or continuous assessment as part of an approved course of training based on the material set out in column 2 of table A-IV/2.

[*] The relevant IMO Model Course(s) may be of assistance in the preparation of courses.

第 IV 章
关于无线电操作员的标准

第 A-IV/1 节
适用范围

(无条文)

第 A-IV/2 节
对全球海上遇险与安全系统(GMDSS)无线电操作员发证的强制性最低要求

适任标准

1 对 GMDSS 无线电操作员发证所要求的最低的知识、理解和熟练程度,应足以使无线电操作员履行其无线电职责。获取《无线电规则》所规定的各类证书的知识要求应符合该规则的规定。此外,每个证书申请人应按要求表明承担表 A-IV/2 第 1 栏列出的任务、职责和责任的能力。

2 根据本公约对按《无线电规则》规定签发的证书进行签证时,所要求的知识、理解和熟练程度列于表 A-IV/2 第 2 栏中。

3 表 A-IV/2 第 2 栏所列科目的知识水平,应足以使证书申请人履行其职责①。

4 每个证书申请人应通过下列各项提供已达到所要求的适任标准的证据:

.1 按照表 A-IV/2 第 3 栏和第 4 栏所列的表明适任的方法和评价适任的标准,表明承担该表第 1 栏所列的任务、职责和责任的适任能力;并且

.2 考试或连续的评估,作为基于表 A-IV/2 第 2 栏规定内容的认可的培训课程的组成部分。

① 相关 IMO 示范培训课程可有助于准备课程。

Table A-IV/2

Specification of minimum standard of competence for GMDSS radio operators

Function: Radiocommunications at the operational level

Column 1	Column 2	Column 3	Column 4
Competence	**Knowledge, understanding and proficiency**	**Methods for demonstrating competence**	**Criteria for evaluating competence**
Transmit and receive information using GMDSS subsystems and equipment and fulfilling the functional requirements of GMDSS	In addition to the requirements of the Radio Regulations, a knowledge of: .1 search and rescue radiocommunications, including procedures in the International Aeronautical and Maritime Search and Rescue (IAMSAR) Manual .2 the means to prevent the transmission of false distress alerts and the procedures to mitigate the effects of such alerts .3 ship reporting systems .4 radio medical services .5 use of the International Code of Signals and the IMO Standard Marine Communication Phrases .6 the English language, both written and spoken, for the communication of information relevant to safety of life at sea *Note*: This requirement may be reduced in the case of the Restricted Radio Operator's Certificate	Examination and assessment of evidence obtained from practical demonstration of operational procedures, using: .1 approved equipment .2 GMDSS communication simulator, where appropriate* .3 radiocommunication laboratory equipment	Transmission and reception of communications comply with international regulations and procedures and are carried out efficiently and effectively English language messages relevant to the safety of the ship, security and persons on board and protection of the marine environment are correctly handled

* See paragraph 72 of section B-I/12 of this Code.

表 A-IV/2
GMDSS 无线电操作员的最低适任标准

职能:无线电通信　操作级

第 1 栏	第 2 栏	第 3 栏	第 4 栏
适任	知识、理解和熟练	表明适任的方法	评价适任的标准
使用 GMDSS 的子系统和设备发出和接收信息,并满足 GMDSS 的功能要求	除《无线电规则》的要求外,具有下列知识: .1　搜救无线电通信,包括《国际航空和海上搜寻救助手册》中的程序 .2　防止发出误遇险报警的措施和减小此种报警影响的程序 .3　船舶报告制度 .4　无线电医疗服务 .5　使用《国际信号规则》和《IMO 标准航海通信用语》 .6　有关海上人命安全的信息沟通所用的英语书面语和口语 注:如系限用无线电操作员证书,可以降低这项要求	考试并评估从使用下列各项设备进行操作程序的实际演示中获取的证据: .1　认可的设备 .2　GMDSS 通信模拟器,如适用① .3　无线电通信实验室设备	通信的发送和接收符合国际规则和程序,并且得以充分和有效地进行 正确处理有关船舶和船上人员安全、保安以及保护海洋环境的英文信息

① 见本规则第 B-I/12 节第 72 段。

Column 1	Column 2	Column 3	Column 4
Competence	**Knowledge, understanding and proficiency**	**Methods for demonstrating competence**	**Criteria for evaluating competence**
Provide radio services in emergencies	The provision of radio services in emergencies such as: .1 abandon ship .2 fire on board ship .3 partial or full breakdown of radio installations Preventive measures for the safety of ship and personnel in connection with hazards related to radio equipment, including electrical and non-ionizing radiation hazards	Examination and assessment of evidence obtained from practical demonstration of operational procedures, using: .1 approved equipment .2 GMDSS communication simulator, where appropriate* .3 radiocommunication laboratory equipment	Response is carried out efficiently and effectively

* See paragraph 72 of section B-I/12 of this Code.

第1栏	第2栏	第3栏	第4栏
适任	知识、理解和熟练	表明适任的方法	评价适任的标准
在紧急情况下提供无线电服务	在紧急情况下提供无线电服务,如: .1 弃船 .2 船上失火 .3 无线电装置部分或全部故障 与无线电设备危害(包括电气和非电离辐射危害)有关的船舶和人员安全的预防措施	考试并评估从使用下列各项设备进行操作程序的实际演示中获取的证据: .1 认可的设备 .2 GMDSS 通信模拟器,如适用① .3 无线电通信实验室设备	快速有效地作出响应

① 见本规则第 B-I/12 节第 72 段。

CHAPTER V

Standards regarding special training requirements for personnel on certain types of ships

Section A-V/1-1
Mandatory minimum requirements for the training and qualifications of masters, officers and ratings on oil and chemical tankers

Standard of competence

1 Every candidate for certification in basic training for oil and chemical tanker cargo operations shall be required to:

.1 demonstrate the competence to undertake the tasks, duties and responsibilities listed in column 1 of table A-V/1-1-1; and

.2 provide evidence of having achieved:

.2.1 the minimum knowledge, understanding and proficiency listed in column 2 of table A-V/1-1-1, and

.2.2 the required standard of competence in accordance with the methods for demonstrating competence and the criteria for evaluating competence tabulated in columns 3 and 4 of table A-V/1-1-1.

2 Every candidate for certification in advanced training for oil tanker cargo operations shall be required to:

.1 demonstrate the competence to undertake the tasks, duties and responsibilities listed in column 1 of table A-V/1-1-2; and

.2 provide evidence of having achieved:

.2.1 the minimum knowledge, understanding and proficiency listed in column 2 of table A-V/1-1-2, and

.2.2 the required standard of competence in accordance with the methods for demonstrating competence and the criteria for evaluating competence tabulated in columns 3 and 4 of table A-V/1-1-2.

3 Every candidate for certification in advanced training for chemical tanker cargo operations shall be required to:

.1 demonstrate the competence to undertake the tasks, duties and responsibilities listed in column 1 of table A-V/1-1-3; and

第 V 章
关于特定类型船舶人员特殊培训要求的标准

第 A-V/1-1 节
对油船和化学品船船长、高级船员和普通船员的培训和资格的强制性最低要求

适任标准

1 每个申请油船和化学品船货物操作基本培训证书的申请人应:

.1 证明其具有承担表 A-V/1-1-1 第 1 栏所列的任务、职责和责任的适任能力;并且

.2 提供其已达到下列各项的证据:

.2.1 表 A-V/1-1-1 第 2 栏所列的最低的知识、理解和熟练,以及

.2.2 表 A-V/1-1-1 第 3 栏和第 4 栏所列的表明适任的方法和评估适任的标准中所要求的适任标准。

2 每个申请油船货物操作高级培训证书的申请人应:

.1 证明其具有承担表 A-V/1-1-2 第 1 栏所列的任务、职责和责任的适任能力;并且

.2 提供其已达到下列各项的证据:

.2.1 表 A-V/1-1-2 第 2 栏所列的最低的知识、理解和熟练,以及

.2.2 表 A-V/1-1-2 第 3 栏和第 4 栏所列的表明适任的方法和评估适任的标准中所要求的适任标准。

3 每个申请化学品船货物操作高级培训证书的申请人应:

.1 证明其具有承担表 A-V/1-1-3 第 1 栏所列的任务、职责和责任的适任能力;并且

.2 provide evidence of having achieved:

.2.1 the minimum knowledge, understanding and proficiency listed in column 2 of table A-V/1-1-3, and

.2.2 the required standard of competence in accordance with the methods for demonstrating competence and the criteria for evaluating competence tabulated in columns 3 and 4 of table A-V/1-1-3.

.2 提供其已达到下列各项的证据：

.2.1 表 A-V/1-1-3 第 2 栏所列的最低的知识、理解和熟练，以及

.2.2 表 A-V/1-1-3 第 3 栏和第 4 栏所列的表明适任的方法和评估适任的标准中所要求的适任标准。

Table A-V/1-1-1

Specification of minimum standard of competence in basic training for oil and chemical tanker cargo operations

Column 1	Column 2	Column 3	Column 4
Competence	**Knowledge, understanding and proficiency**	**Methods for demonstrating competence**	**Criteria for evaluating competence**
Contribute to the safe cargo operation of oil and chemical tankers	Basic knowledge of tankers: .1 types of oil and chemical tankers .2 general arrangement and construction Basic knowledge of cargo operations: .1 piping systems and valves .2 cargo pumps .3 loading and unloading .4 tank cleaning, purging, gas-freeing and inerting Basic knowledge of the physical properties of oil and chemicals: .1 pressure and temperature, including vapour pressure/temperature relationship .2 types of electrostatic charge generation .3 chemical symbols Knowledge and understanding of tanker safety culture and safety management	Examination and assessment of evidence obtained from one or more of the following: .1 approved in-service experience .2 approved training ship experience .3 approved simulator training .4 approved training programme	Communications within the area of responsibility are clear and effective Cargo operations are carried out in accordance with accepted principles and procedures to ensure safety of operations

表 A-V/1-1-1

油船和化学品船货物操作基本培训的最低适任标准

第 1 栏	第 2 栏	第 3 栏	第 4 栏
适任	**知识、理解和熟练**	**表明适任的方法**	**评价适任的标准**
有助于油船和化学品船的安全货物操作	液货船的基本知识： .1 油船和化学品船的类型 .2 总体布置和构造 货物操作的基本知识： .1 管系和阀门 .2 货泵 .3 装货和卸货 .4 洗舱、驱气、除气和惰化 油品和化学品物理性质的基本知识： .1 压力和温度，包括蒸气压力/温度关系 .2 静电电荷产生类型 .3 化学符号 液货船安全文化和安全管理的知识及理解	考试并评估从下列一项或数项获取的证据： .1 认可的工作经历 .2 认可的培训船经历 .3 认可的模拟器培训 .4 认可的培训计划	责任范围内的交流清楚、有效 货物操作符合公认的原则和程序以确保操作安全

Column 1	Column 2	Column 3	Column 4
Competence	**Knowledge, understanding and proficiency**	**Methods for demonstrating competence**	**Criteria for evaluating competence**
Take precautions to prevent hazards	Basic knowledge of the hazards associated with tanker operations, including: .1 health hazards .2 environmental hazards .3 reactivity hazards .4 corrosion hazards .5 explosion and flammability hazards .6 sources of ignition, including electrostatic hazards .7 toxicity hazards .8 vapour leaks and clouds Basic knowledge of hazard controls: .1 inerting, water padding, drying agents and monitoring techniques .2 anti-static measures .3 ventilation .4 segregation .5 cargo inhibition .6 importance of cargo compatibility .7 atmospheric control .8 gas testing Understanding of information on a Material Safety Data Sheet (MSDS)	Examination and assessment of evidence obtained from one or more of the following: .1 approved in-service experience .2 approved training ship experience .3 approved simulator training .4 approved training programme	Correctly identifies, on an MSDS, relevant cargo-related hazards to the vessel and to personnel, and takes the appropriate actions in accordance with established procedures Identification and actions on becoming aware of a hazardous situation conform to established procedures in line with best practice

第 1 栏	第 2 栏	第 3 栏	第 4 栏
适任	知识、理解和熟练	表明适任的方法	评价适任的标准
采取预防措施防止危害	有关液货船操作危害的基本知识,包括: .1 健康危害 .2 环境危害 .3 反应性危害 .4 腐蚀性危害 .5 爆炸性和易燃性危害 .6 着火源,包括静电危害 .7 毒性危害 .8 蒸气泄漏和蒸发气团 危害控制的基本知识: .1 惰化、水封、干燥剂和监测技术 .2 防静电措施 .3 通风 .4 隔离 .5 货物抑制 .6 货物兼容性的重要性 .7 舱气控制 .8 气体检测 《化学品安全说明书》(MSDS)信息的理解	考试并评估从下列一项或数项获取的证据: .1 认可的工作经历 .2 认可的培训船经历 .3 认可的模拟器培训 .4 认可的培训计划	正确识别《化学品安全说明书》(MSDS)中与货物相关的对船舶和人员的危害,并采取符合既定程序的适当行动 识别和在意识到危险局面时采取的行动符合既定程序和最佳做法

Column 1	Column 2	Column 3	Column 4
Competence	**Knowledge, understanding and proficiency**	**Methods for demonstrating competence**	**Criteria for evaluating competence**
Apply occupational health and safety precautions and measures	Function and proper use of gas-measuring instruments and similar equipment Proper use of safety equipment and protective devices, including: .1 breathing apparatus and tank-evacuating equipment .2 protective clothing and equipment .3 resuscitators .4 rescue and escape equipment Basic knowledge of safe working practices and procedures in accordance with legislation and industry guidelines and personal shipboard safety relevant to oil and chemical tankers, including: .1 precautions to be taken when entering enclosed spaces .2 precautions to be taken before and during repair and maintenance work .3 safety measures for hot and cold work .4 electrical safety .5 ship/shore safety checklist Basic knowledge of first aid with reference to a Material Safety Data Sheet (MSDS)	Examination and assessment of evidence obtained from one or more of the following: .1 approved in-service experience .2 approved training ship experience .3 approved simulator training .4 approved training programme	Procedures for entry into enclosed spaces are observed. Procedures and safe working practices designed to safeguard personnel and the ship are observed at all times Appropriate safety and protective equipment is correctly used First aid do's and don'ts

第1栏	第2栏	第3栏	第4栏
适任	**知识、理解和熟练**	**表明适任的方法**	**评价适任的标准**
应用职业健康与安全预防措施	气体测量仪器和类似设备的功能及其正确使用 安全设备和防护装置的正确使用，包括： .1 呼吸器具和货舱撤离设备 .2 防护服和装备 .3 复苏仪 .4 救助和逃生设备 符合与油船和化学品船相关的法律、行业指南及船上人员安全的安全工作做法和程序的基本知识： .1 当进入封闭处所时采取的预防措施 .2 在进行修理和维护工作之前和期间采取的预防措施 .3 热工和冷工作业的安全措施 .4 电气安全 .5 船/岸安全检查表 参照《化学品安全说明书》(MSDS)进行急救的基本知识	考试并评估从下列一项或数项获取的证据： .1 认可的工作经历 .2 认可的培训船经历 .3 认可的模拟器培训 .4 认可的培训计划	遵循进入封闭处所的程序 始终遵循旨在保护人员和船舶安全的程序和安全工作做法 正确使用适当的安全和防护设备 熟悉急救规则

Column 1	Column 2	Column 3	Column 4
Competence	**Knowledge, understanding and proficiency**	**Methods for demonstrating competence**	**Criteria for evaluating competence**
Carry out fire-fighting operations	Tanker fire response organization and action to be taken Fire hazards associated with cargo handling and transportation of hazardous and noxious liquids in bulk Fire-fighting agents used to extinguish oil and chemical fires Fixed fire-fighting foam system operations Portable fire-fighting foam operations Fixed dry chemical system operations Spill containment in relation to fire-fighting operations	Practical exercises and instruction conducted under approved and truly realistic training conditions (e.g., simulated shipboard conditions) and, whenever possible and practicable, in darkness	Initial actions and follow-up actions on becoming aware of fire on board conform with established practices and procedures Action taken on identifying muster signal is appropriate to the indicated emergency and complies with established procedures Clothing and equipment are appropriate to the nature of the fire-fighting operations The timing and sequence of individual actions are appropriate to the prevailing circumstances and conditions Extinguishment of fire is achieved using appropriate procedures, techniques and fire-fighting agents
Respond to emergencies	Basic knowledge of emergency procedures, including emergency shutdown	Examination and assessment of evidence obtained from one or more of the following: .1 approved in-service experience .2 approved training ship experience .3 approved simulator training .4 approved training programme	The type and impact of the emergency is promptly identified and the response actions conform to the emergency procedures and contingency plans

第 1 栏	第 2 栏	第 3 栏	第 4 栏
适任	知识、理解和熟练	表明适任的方法	评价适任的标准
执行消防操作	液货船火灾反应的组织和采取的行动 货物操作以及散装危险和有害液体货物运输引起的火灾危害 适用于油类和化学品火灾的灭火剂 固定式泡沫灭火系统的操作 便携式泡沫灭火器的操作 固定式干粉灭火系统的操作 与消防有关的防止溢油扩散的操作	实际演练和在认可的真实培训条件（如模拟船舶条件）下，并在可能和可行的情况下进行黑暗中训练	意识到船上火灾时采取的初始和后续行动符合既定做法和程序 识别集合信号后采取的行动适合所表明的紧急情况并符合既定程序 防护服和设备适合消防操作的性质 每个行动的时机和顺序适合当时的环境和条件 使用合适的程序、技能、灭火剂完成灭火任务
应急反应	应急程序的基本知识，包括紧急关闭	考试并评估从下列一项或数项获取的证据： .1 认可的工作经历 .2 认可的培训船经历 .3 认可的模拟器培训 .4 认可的培训计划	迅速识别紧急情况的类型和影响，并采取符合应急程序和应急计划的行动

Column 1	Column 2	Column 3	Column 4
Competence	**Knowledge, understanding and proficiency**	**Methods for demonstrating competence**	**Criteria for evaluating competence**
Take precautions to prevent pollution of the environment from the release of oil or chemicals	Basic knowledge of the effects of oil and chemical pollution on human and marine life Basic knowledge of shipboard procedures to prevent pollution Basic knowledge of measures to be taken in the event of spillage, including the need to: .1 report relevant information to the responsible persons .2 assist in implementing shipboard spill-containment procedures	Examination and assessment of evidence obtained from one or more of the following: .1 approved in-service experience .2 approved training ship experience .3 approved simulator training .4 approved training programme	Procedures designed to safeguard the environment are observed at all times

第 1 栏	第 2 栏	第 3 栏	第 4 栏
适任	**知识、理解和熟练**	**表明适任的方法**	**评价适任的标准**
采取预防措施防止油类或化学品泄漏对环境造成污染	油类和化学品污染对人类和海洋生物影响的基本知识 船上防污染程序的基本知识 发生溢漏时采取措施的基本知识,包括需要: .1 向责任人报告相关信息 .2 协助执行船上溢漏抑制的程序	考试并评估从下列一项或数项获取的证据: .1 认可的工作经历 .2 认可的培训船经历 .3 认可的模拟器培训 .4 认可的培训计划	始终遵循旨在保护环境的程序

Table A-V/1-1-2

Specification of minimum standard of competence in advanced training for oil tanker cargo operations

Column 1	Column 2	Column 3	Column 4
Competence	**Knowledge, understanding and proficiency**	**Methods for demonstrating competence**	**Criteria for evaluating competence**
Ability to safely perform and monitor all cargo operations	*Design and characteristics of an oil tanker* Knowledge of oil tanker design, systems and equipment, including: .1 general arrangement and construction .2 pumping arrangement and equipment .3 tank arrangement, pipeline system and tank venting arrangement .4 gauging systems and alarms .5 cargo heating systems .6 tank cleaning, gas-freeing and inerting systems .7 ballast system .8 cargo area venting and accommodation ventilation .9 slop arrangements .10 vapour recovery systems .11 cargo-related electrical and electronic control system .12 environmental protection equipment, including Oil Discharge Monitoring Equipment (ODME)	Examination and assessment of evidence obtained from one or more of the following: .1 approved in-service experience .2 approved training ship experience .3 approved simulator training .4 approved training programme	Communications are clear, understood and successful Cargo operations are carried out in a safe manner, taking into account oil tanker designs, systems and equipment Cargo operations are planned, risk is managed and carried out in accordance with accepted principles and procedures to ensure safety of operations and avoid pollution of the marine environment Potential non-compliance with cargo-operation-related procedures is promptly identified and rectified Proper loading, stowage and unloading of cargoes ensures that stability and stress conditions remain within safe limits at all times Actions taken and procedures followed are correctly applied and the appropriate shipboard cargo-related equipment is properly used Calibration and use of monitoring and gas-detection equipment comply with operational practices and procedures

表 A-V/1-1-2
油船货物操作高级培训的最低适任标准

第 1 栏	第 2 栏	第 3 栏	第 4 栏
适任	知识、理解和熟练	表明适任的方法	评价适任的标准
安全实施和监管所有货物操作的能力	油船的设计和特性 油船设计、系统和设备的知识,包括: .1 总体布置和构造 .2 泵系布置和设备 .3 油舱布置、管系和油舱通风的布置 .4 测量系统和报警装置 .5 货油加温系统 .6 洗舱、除气和惰化系统 .7 压载系统 .8 货舱区域通风和生活区通风 .9 污油水舱布置 .10 油气回收系统 .11 与货油相关的电气和电子控制系统 .12 环境保护设备,包括卸油监控设备(ODME)	考试并评估从下列一项或数项获取的证据: .1 认可的工作经历 .2 认可的培训船经历 .3 认可的模拟器培训 .4 认可的培训计划	交流清楚、易懂、有效 货油作业以安全方式进行,并考虑油船设计、系统和设备 货油作业有计划,有风险管理,并按公认的原则和程序进行,以确保操作安全,避免污染海洋环境 迅速识别并纠正可能不符合货油作业相关程序的做法 正确地装载、配载和卸载货油,确保船舶稳性和强度始终保持在安全界限内 采取的行动和遵循的程序正确,正确使用船上与货油相关的适当设备 监控和气体探测设备的校准与使用符合操作规程及程序

Column 1	Column 2	Column 3	Column 4
Competence	**Knowledge, understanding and proficiency**	**Methods for demonstrating competence**	**Criteria for evaluating competence**
Ability to safely perform and monitor all cargo operations (*continued*)	.13 tank coating .14 tank temperature and pressure control systems .15 fire-fighting systems Knowledge of pump theory and characteristics, including types of cargo pumps and their safe operation Proficiency in tanker safety culture and implementation of safety-management system Knowledge and understanding of monitoring and safety systems, including the emergency shutdown *Loading, unloading, care and handling of cargo* Ability to perform cargo measurements and calculations Knowledge of the effect of bulk liquid cargoes on trim, stability and structural integrity Knowledge and understanding of oil cargo-related operations, including: .1 loading and unloading plans .2 ballasting and deballasting .3 tank cleaning operations .4 inerting .5 gas-freeing		Procedures for monitoring and safety systems ensure that all alarms are detected promptly and acted upon in accordance with established emergency procedures

第 1 栏	第 2 栏	第 3 栏	第 4 栏
适任	**知识、理解和熟练**	**表明适任的方法**	**评价适任的标准**
安全实施和监管所有货物操作的能力(续)	.13 油舱涂层 .14 油舱温度和压力控制系统 .15 消防系统 泵的原理和特性的知识,包括货油泵的类型及其安全操作 精通油船安全文化和安全管理体系的实施 监控和安全系统的知识及理解,包括紧急关闭 *货物装卸、照管和作业* 进行货物测量和计算的能力 散装液体货物对船舶吃水差、稳性和结构完整性影响的知识 货油相关操作的知识和理解,包括: .1 装卸计划 .2 压载和排压载 .3 洗舱作业 .4 惰化 .5 除气		监控程序和安全系统确保迅速检测到所有报警,并按照既定的应急程序采取行动

Column 1	Column 2	Column 3	Column 4
Competence	**Knowledge, understanding and proficiency**	**Methods for demonstrating competence**	**Criteria for evaluating competence**
Ability to safely perform and monitor all cargo operations (*continued*)	.6 ship-to-ship transfers .7 load on top .8 crude oil washing Development and application of cargo-related operation plans, procedures and checklists Ability to calibrate and use monitoring and gas-detection systems, instruments and equipment Ability to manage and supervise personnel with cargo-related responsibilities		Personnel are allocated duties and informed of procedures and standards of work to be followed, in a manner appropriate to the individuals concerned and in accordance with safe operational practices
Familiarity with physical and chemical properties of oil cargoes	Knowledge and understanding of the physical and chemical properties of oil cargoes Understanding the information contained in a Material Safety Data Sheet (MSDS)	Examination and assessment of evidence obtained from one or more of the following: .1 approved in-service experience .2 approved training ship experience .3 approved simulator training .4 approved training programme	Effective use is made of information resources for identification of properties and characteristics of oil cargoes and related gases, and their impact on safety, the environment and vessel operation

第 1 栏	第 2 栏	第 3 栏	第 4 栏
适任	**知识、理解和熟练**	**表明适任的方法**	**评价适任的标准**
安全实施和监管所有货物操作的能力(续)	.6 船到船过驳 .7 顶装法 .8 原油洗舱 货物相关操作计划、程序和检查表的制定和应用 校准及使用监控与气体探测系统、仪器和设备的能力 管理和监督负有操作货物责任的人员的能力		分配人员工作,以适合相关人员的方式告知应遵循的工作程序和标准,并符合安全操作做法
熟悉货油的物理和化学性质	货油的物理和化学性质的知识和理解 理解《化学品安全说明书》(MSDS)包含的信息	考试并评估从下列一项或数项获取的证据: .1 认可的工作经历 .2 认可的培训船经历 .3 认可的模拟器培训 .4 认可的培训计划	有效使用信息源,以识别货油和相关气体的性质和特点,及其对安全、环境和船舶操作的影响

Column 1	Column 2	Column 3	Column 4
Competence	**Knowledge, understanding and proficiency**	**Methods for demonstrating competence**	**Criteria for evaluating competence**
Take precautions to prevent hazards	Knowledge and understanding of the hazards and control measures associated with oil tanker cargo operations, including: .1 toxicity .2 flammability and explosion .3 health hazards .4 inert gas composition .5 electrostatic hazards Knowledge and understanding of dangers of non-compliance with relevant rules/regulations	Examination and assessment of evidence obtained from one or more of the following: .1 approved in-service experience .2 approved training ship experience .3 approved simulator training .4 approved training programme	Relevant cargo-related hazards to the vessel and to personnel associated with oil tanker cargo operations are correctly identified, and proper control measures are taken
Apply occupational health and safety precautions	Knowledge and understanding of safe working practices, including risk assessment and personal shipboard safety relevant to oil tankers: .1 precautions to be taken when entering enclosed spaces, including correct use of different types of breathing apparatus .2 precautions to be taken before and during repair and maintenance work .3 precautions for hot and cold work .4 precautions for electrical safety .5 use of appropriate Personal Protective Equipment (PPE)	Examination and assessment of evidence obtained from one or more of the following: .1 approved in-service experience .2 approved training ship experience .3 approved simulator training .4 approved training programme	Procedures designed to safeguard personnel and the ship are observed at all times Safe working practices are observed and appropriate safety and protective equipment is correctly used Working practices are in accordance with legislative requirements, codes of practice, permits to work and environmental concerns Correct use of breathing apparatus Procedures for entry into enclosed spaces are observed

第 1 栏	第 2 栏	第 3 栏	第 4 栏
适任	知识、理解和熟练	表明适任的方法	评价适任的标准
采取预防措施防止危害	与油船货油作业相关的各类危害及控制措施的知识和理解,包括: .1 毒性 .2 易燃性和爆炸性 .3 健康危害 .4 惰性气体组成 .5 静电危害 不遵守相关规范/规则的危害的知识和理解	考试并评估从下列一项或数项获取的证据: .1 认可的工作经历 .2 认可的培训船经历 .3 认可的模拟器培训 .4 认可的培训计划	正确识别与货油相关的对船舶和参与货油作业人员的危害,并采取适当的控制措施
应用职业健康和安全预防措施	安全工作做法,包括与油船相关的风险评估和船上人员安全的知识和理解: .1 在进入封闭处所时采取的预防措施,包括不同呼吸器具的正确使用 .2 在进行维修和保养工作之前和期间采取的预防措施 .3 热工和冷工作业的预防措施 .4 电气安全预防措施 .5 使用合适的个人防护设备(PPE)	考试并评估从下列一项或数项获取的证据: .1 认可的工作经历 .2 认可的培训船经历 .3 认可的模拟器培训 .4 认可的培训计划	始终遵循旨在保护人员和船舶安全的程序 遵循安全工作做法,正确使用合适的安全和防护设备 工作做法符合法定要求、操作规程、作业许可和环保要求 正确使用呼吸器具 遵循进入封闭处所的程序

Column 1	Column 2	Column 3	Column 4
Competence	**Knowledge, understanding and proficiency**	**Methods for demonstrating competence**	**Criteria for evaluating competence**
Respond to emergencies	Knowledge and understanding of oil tanker emergency procedures, including: .1 ship emergency response plans .2 cargo operations emergency shutdown .3 actions to be taken in the event of failure of systems or services essential to cargo .4 fire-fighting on oil tankers .5 enclosed space rescue .6 use of a Material Safety Data Sheet (MSDS) Actions to be taken following collision, grounding, or spillage Knowledge of medical first aid procedures on board oil tankers	Examination and assessment of evidence obtained from one or more of the following: .1 approved in-service experience .2 approved training ship experience .3 approved simulator training .4 approved training programme	The type and impact of the emergency is promptly identified and the response actions conform with established emergency procedures and contingency plans The order of priority, and the levels and time-scales of making reports and informing personnel on board, are relevant to the nature of the emergency and reflect the urgency of the problem Evacuation, emergency shutdown and isolation procedures are appropriate to the nature of the emergency and are implemented promptly The identification of and actions taken in a medical emergency conform to current recognized first aid practice and international guidelines
Take precautions to prevent pollution of the environment	Understanding of procedures to prevent pollution of the atmosphere and the environment	Examination and assessment of evidence obtained from one or more of the following: .1 approved in-service experience .2 approved training ship experience .3 approved simulator training .4 approved training programme	Operations are conducted in accordance with accepted principles and procedures to prevent pollution of the environment

第 1 栏	第 2 栏	第 3 栏	第 4 栏
适任	知识、理解和熟练	表明适任的方法	评价适任的标准
应急反应	油船应急程序的知识和理解,包括: .1 船舶应急反应计划 .2 货油作业的紧急关闭 .3 对货油至关重要的系统或设施发生故障时应采取的行动 .4 油船消防 .5 封闭处所救助 .6 《化学品安全说明书》(MSDS)的使用 碰撞、搁浅或溢油情况下采取的行动 油船船上医疗急救程序的知识	考试并评估从下列一项或数项获取的证据: .1 认可的工作经历 .2 认可的培训船经历 .3 认可的模拟器培训 .4 认可的培训计划	迅速识别紧急情况的类型和影响,并采取符合既定应急程序和应急计划的行动 作出报告及通知船上人员的优先顺序、级别、时限与紧急事件的性质相关,并反映事态的紧急程度 撤离、紧急关闭和隔离程序适合紧急事件的性质,并迅速实施 医疗急救的情况识别及采取的做法符合当前认可的急救惯例和国际指南
采取预防措施防止环境污染	理解大气和环境的防污染程序	考试并评估从下列一项或数项获取的证据: .1 认可的工作经历 .2 认可的培训船经历 .3 认可的模拟器培训 .4 认可的培训计划	根据公认的原则和程序进行作业以防止环境污染

Column 1	Column 2	Column 3	Column 4
Competence	**Knowledge, understanding and proficiency**	**Methods for demonstrating competence**	**Criteria for evaluating competence**
Monitor and control compliance with legislative requirements	Knowledge and understanding of relevant provisions of the International Convention for the Prevention of Pollution from Ships (MARPOL), as amended, and other relevant IMO instruments, industry guidelines and port regulations as commonly applied	Examination and assessment of evidence obtained from one or more of the following: .1 approved in-service experience .2 approved training ship experience .3 approved simulator training .4 approved training programme	The handling of cargoes complies with relevant IMO instruments and established industrial standards and codes of safe working practice

第 1 栏	第 2 栏	第 3 栏	第 4 栏
适任	知识、理解和熟练	表明适任的方法	评价适任的标准
监督和控制对立法要求的遵守	经修订的《国际防止船舶造成污染公约》(MARPOL)的相关规定和其他普遍采用的相关的国际海事组织(IMO)文件、行业指南和港口规则的知识及理解	考试并评估从下列一项或数项获取的证据: .1 认可的工作经历 .2 认可的培训船经历 .3 认可的模拟器培训 .4 认可的培训计划	货油作业符合国际海事组织(IMO)相关文件、既定行业标准和安全工作做法

Table A-V/1-1-3

Specification of minimum standard of competence in advanced training for chemical tanker cargo operations

Column 1	Column 2	Column 3	Column 4
Competence	**Knowledge, understanding and proficiency**	**Methods for demonstrating competence**	**Criteria for evaluating competence**
Ability to safely perform and monitor all cargo operations	*Design and characteristics of a chemical tanker* Knowledge of chemical tanker designs, systems, and equipment, including: .1 general arrangement and construction .2 pumping arrangement and equipment .3 tank construction and arrangement .4 pipeline and drainage systems .5 tank and cargo pipeline pressure and temperature control systems and alarms .6 gauging control systems and alarms .7 gas-detecting systems .8 cargo heating and cooling systems .9 tank cleaning systems .10 cargo tank environmental control systems .11 ballast systems .12 cargo area venting and accommodation ventilation .13 vapour return/recovery systems .14 fire-fighting systems	Examination and assessment of evidence obtained from one or more of the following: .1 approved in-service experience .2 approved training ship experience .3 approved simulator training .4 approved training programme	Communications are clear, understood and successful Cargo operations are carried out in a safe manner, taking into account chemical tanker designs, systems and equipment Cargo operations are planned, risk is managed and carried out in accordance with accepted principles and procedures to ensure safety of operations and avoid pollution of the marine environment

表 A-V/1-1-3
化学品船货物操作高级培训的最低适任标准

第 1 栏	第 2 栏	第 3 栏	第 4 栏
适任	**知识、理解和熟练**	**表明适任的方法**	**评价适任的标准**
安全实施和监管所有货物操作的能力	化学品船的设计和特性 化学品船设计、系统和设备的知识,包括: .1 总体布置和构造 .2 泵系布置和设备 .3 货舱构造和布置 .4 管道和泄放系统 .5 货舱和货物管线压力及温度控制系统及报警装置 .6 测量控制系统和报警装置 .7 气体探测系统 .8 货物加温和冷却系统 .9 洗舱系统 .10 货舱环境控制系统 .11 压载系统 .12 货舱区域通风和生活区通风 .13 气体返回/回收系统 .14 消防系统	考试并评估从下列一项或数项获取的证据: .1 认可的工作经历 .2 认可的培训船经历 .3 认可的模拟器培训 .4 认可的培训计划	交流清楚、易懂、有效 货物操作以安全方式进行,并考虑化学品船的设计、系统和设备 货物操作有计划,有风险管理,并按公认的原则和程序进行,以确保操作的安全,避免污染海洋环境

Column 1	Column 2	Column 3	Column 4
Competence	**Knowledge, understanding and proficiency**	**Methods for demonstrating competence**	**Criteria for evaluating competence**
Ability to safely perform and monitor all cargo operations (*continued*)	.15 tank, pipeline and fittings' material and coatings .16 slop management Knowledge of pump theory and characteristics, including types of cargo pumps and their safe operation Proficiency in tanker safety culture and implementation of safety management system Knowledge and understanding of monitoring and safety systems, including the emergency shutdown system *Loading, unloading, care and handling of cargo* Ability to perform cargo measurements and calculations Knowledge of the effect of bulk liquid cargoes on trim and stability and structural integrity Knowledge and understanding of chemical cargo-related operations, including: .1 loading and unloading plans .2 ballasting and deballasting .3 tank cleaning operations .4 tank atmosphere control		Procedures for monitoring and safety systems ensure that all alarms are detected promptly and acted upon in accordance with established procedures Proper loading, stowage and unloading of cargoes ensures that stability and stress conditions remain within safe limits at all times Potential non-compliance with cargo-related procedures is promptly identified and rectified Actions taken and procedures followed are correctly identified and appropriate shipboard cargo-related equipment is properly used

第 1 栏	第 2 栏	第 3 栏	第 4 栏
适任	知识、理解和熟练	表明适任的方法	评价适任的标准
安全实施和监管所有货物操作的能力(续)	.15 货舱、管系和配件的材料及涂层 .16 污油水管理 泵的原理和特性的知识，包括货泵的类型及其安全操作 精通液货船安全文化和安全管理体系的实施 监控和安全系统的知识及理解，包括紧急关闭系统 货物的装卸、照管和作业 进行货物测量和计算的能力 散装液体货物对船舶吃水差、稳性和结构完整性影响的知识 化学品货物相关操作的知识和理解，包括： .1 装卸计划 .2 压载和排压载 .3 洗舱作业 .4 货舱空气控制		监控程序和安全系统确保迅速检测到所有报警，并按照既定的应急程序采取行动 正确地装货、配载和卸货，确保船舶稳性和强度始终保持在安全界限内 迅速识别并纠正可能不符合货物作业相关程序的做法 采取的行动和遵循的程序正确，正确使用船上与货物相关的适当设备

Column 1	Column 2	Column 3	Column 4
Competence	**Knowledge, understanding and proficiency**	**Methods for demonstrating competence**	**Criteria for evaluating competence**
Ability to safely perform and monitor all cargo operations (*continued*)	.5 inerting .6 gas-freeing .7 ship-to-ship transfers .8 inhibition and stabilization requirements .9 heating and cooling requirements and consequences to adjacent cargoes .10 cargo compatibility and segregation .11 high-viscosity cargoes .12 cargo residue operations .13 operational tank entry Development and application of cargo-related operation plans, procedures and checklists		
	Ability to calibrate and use monitoring and gas-detection systems, instruments and equipment		Calibration and use of monitoring and gas-detection equipment are consistent with safe operational practices and procedures
	Ability to manage and supervise personnel with cargo-related responsibilities		Personnel are allocated duties and informed of procedures and standards of work to be followed, in a manner appropriate to the individuals concerned and in accordance with safe operational practices

第 1 栏	第 2 栏	第 3 栏	第 4 栏
适任	知识、理解和熟练	表明适任的方法	评价适任的标准
安全实施和监管所有货物操作的能力(续)	.5 惰化 .6 除气 .7 船到船过驳 .8 抑制和稳定要求 .9 加温、冷却要求以及对邻近货物的影响后果 .10 货物的兼容性与隔断 .11 高黏度货物 .12 货物残渣处理 .13 可作业货舱的进入 货物相关操作计划、程序和检查表的制定和应用 监控和气体探测系统、仪器和设备的校准及使用能力 管理和监督负有操作货物责任的人员的能力		监控和气体探测设备的校准与使用符合安全操作规程及程序 分配人员工作,以适合相关人员的方式告知应遵循的工作程序和标准,并符合安全操作做法

Column 1	Column 2	Column 3	Column 4
Competence	**Knowledge, understanding and proficiency**	**Methods for demonstrating competence**	**Criteria for evaluating competence**
Familiarity with physical and chemical properties of chemical cargoes	Knowledge and understanding of the chemical and the physical properties of noxious liquid substances, including: .1 chemical cargoes categories (corrosive, toxic, flammable, explosive) .2 chemical groups and industrial usage .3 reactivity of cargoes Understanding the information contained in a Material Safety Data Sheet (MSDS)	Examination and assessment of evidence obtained from one or more of the following: .1 approved in-service experience .2 approved training ship experience .3 approved simulator training .4 approved training programme	Effective use is made of information resources for identification of properties and characteristics of noxious liquid substances and related gases, and their impact on safety, environmental protection and vessel operation
Take precautions to prevent hazards	Knowledge and understanding of the hazards and control measures associated with chemical tanker cargo operations, including: .1 flammability and explosion .2 toxicity .3 health hazards .4 inert gas composition .5 electrostatic hazards .6 reactivity .7 corrosivity .8 low-boiling-point cargoes .9 high-density cargoes .10 solidifying cargoes .11 polymerizing cargoes	Examination and assessment of evidence obtained from one or more of the following: .1 approved in-service experience .2 approved training ship experience .3 approved simulator training .4 approved training programme	Relevant cargo-related hazards to the vessel and to personnel associated with chemical tanker cargo operations are correctly identified, and proper control measures are taken

第 1 栏	第 2 栏	第 3 栏	第 4 栏
适任	知识、理解和熟练	表明适任的方法	评价适任的标准
熟悉化学品货物的物理和化学性质	有害液体物质的物理和化学性质的知识及理解,包括: .1 化学品货物类型(腐蚀性、有毒性、易燃性和易爆性) .2 化学品类别和工业用途 .3 货物间的反应性 理解《化学品安全说明书》(MSDS)包含的信息	考试并评估从下列一项或数项获取的证据: .1 认可的工作经历 .2 认可的培训船经历 .3 认可的模拟器培训 .4 认可的培训计划	有效使用信息源,以识别有毒液态物质和相关气体的性质和特点,及其对安全、环境保护和船舶操作的影响
采取预防措施防止危害	与化学品船货物作业相关的各类危害及控制措施的知识和理解,包括: .1 易燃性和爆炸性 .2 毒性 .3 健康危害 .4 惰性气体组成 .5 静电危害 .6 反应性 .7 腐蚀性 .8 低沸点货物 .9 高密度货物 .10 易凝固货物 .11 聚合货物	考试并评估从下列一项或数项获取的证据: .1 认可的工作经历 .2 认可的培训船经历 .3 认可的模拟器培训 .4 认可的培训计划	正确识别与货物相关的对船舶和参与化学品船货物作业人员的危害,并采取适当的控制措施

Column 1	Column 2	Column 3	Column 4
Competence	**Knowledge, understanding and proficiency**	**Methods for demonstrating competence**	**Criteria for evaluating competence**
Take precautions to prevent hazards *(continued)*	Knowledge and understanding of dangers of non-compliance with relevant rules/regulations		
Apply occupational health and safety precautions	Knowledge and understanding of safe working practices, including risk assessment and personal shipboard safety relevant to chemical tankers: .1 precautions to be taken when entering enclosed spaces, including correct use of different types of breathing apparatus .2 precautions to be taken before and during repair and maintenance work .3 precautions for hot and cold work .4 precautions for electrical safety .5 use of appropriate Personal Protective Equipment (PPE)	Examination and assessment of evidence obtained from one or more of the following: .1 approved in-service experience .2 approved training ship experience .3 approved simulator training .4 approved training programme	Procedures designed to safeguard personnel and the ship are observed at all times Safe working practices are observed and appropriate safety and protective equipment is correctly used Working practices are in accordance with legislative requirements, codes of practice, permits to work and environmental concerns Correct use of breathing apparatus Procedures for entry into enclosed spaces are observed

第 1 栏	第 2 栏	第 3 栏	第 4 栏
适任	**知识、理解和熟练**	**表明适任的方法**	**评价适任的标准**
采取预防措施防止危害(续)	不遵守相关规范/规则的危害的知识和理解		
应用职业健康和安全预防措施	安全工作做法,包括与化学品船相关的风险评估和船上人员安全的知识和理解: .1 进入封闭处所时采取的预防措施,包括正确使用各种呼吸器具 .2 在进行维修和保养工作之前和期间采取的预防措施 .3 热工和冷工作业的预防措施 .4 电气安全预防措施 .5 使用合适的个人防护设备(PPE)	考试并评估从下列一项或数项获取的证据: .1 认可的工作经历 .2 认可的培训船经历 .3 认可的模拟器培训 .4 认可的培训计划	始终遵循旨在保护人员和船舶安全的程序 遵循安全工作做法,正确使用合适的安全和防护装置 工作做法符合法定要求、操作规程、作业许可和环保要求 正确使用呼吸器具 遵循进入封闭处所的程序

Column 1	Column 2	Column 3	Column 4
Competence	**Knowledge, understanding and proficiency**	**Methods for demonstrating competence**	**Criteria for evaluating competence**
Respond to emergencies	Knowledge and understanding of chemical tanker emergency procedures, including: .1 ship emergency response plans .2 cargo operations emergency shutdown .3 actions to be taken in the event of failure of systems or services essential to cargo .4 fire fighting on chemical tankers .5 enclosed space rescue .6 cargo reactivity .7 jettisoning cargo .8 use of a Material Safety Data Sheet (MSDS) Actions to be taken following collision, grounding, or spillage	Examination and assessment of evidence obtained from one or more of the following: .1 approved in-service experience .2 approved training ship experience .3 approved simulator training .4 approved training programme	The type and impact of the emergency is promptly identified and the response actions conform with established emergency procedures and contingency plans The order of priority, and the levels and time-scales of making reports and informing personnel on board, are relevant to the nature of the emergency and reflect the urgency of the problem Evacuation, emergency shutdown and isolation procedures are appropriate to the nature of the emergency and are implemented promptly
	Knowledge of medical first aid procedures on board chemical tankers, with reference to the Medical First Aid Guide for Use in Accidents involving Dangerous Goods (MFAG)		The identification of and actions taken in a medical emergency conform to current recognized first aid practice and international guidelines

第 1 栏	第 2 栏	第 3 栏	第 4 栏
适任	**知识、理解和熟练**	**表明适任的方法**	**评价适任的标准**
应急反应	化学品船应急程序的知识和理解,包括: .1 船舶应急反应计划 .2 货物操作紧急关闭 .3 对货物至关重要的系统或设施发生故障时应采取的行动 .4 化学品船的消防 .5 封闭处所救助 .6 货物反应性 .7 抛弃货物 .8 《化学品安全说明书》(MSDS)的使用 碰撞、搁浅或溢漏时采取的行动 化学品船船上医疗急救程序的知识,参考《危险货物事故医疗急救指南》(MFAG)	考试并评估从下列一项或数项获取的证据: .1 认可的工作经历 .2 认可的培训船经历 .3 认可的模拟器培训 .4 认可的培训计划	迅速识别紧急情况的类型和影响,并采取符合既定应急程序和应急计划的行动 作出报告和通知船上人员的优先顺序、级别、时限与紧急事件的性质相关,并反映事态的紧急程度 撤离、紧急关闭和隔离程序适合紧急事件的性质,并迅速实施 医疗急救的情况识别及采取的做法符合当前认可的急救惯例和国际指南

Column 1	Column 2	Column 3	Column 4
Competence	**Knowledge, understanding and proficiency**	**Methods for demonstrating competence**	**Criteria for evaluating competence**
Take precautions to prevent pollution of the environment	Understanding of procedures to prevent pollution of the atmosphere and the environment	Examination and assessment of evidence obtained from one or more of the following: .1 approved in-service experience .2 approved training ship experience .3 approved simulator training .4 approved training programme	Operations are conducted in accordance with accepted principles and procedures to prevent pollution of the environment
Monitor and control compliance with legislative requirements	Knowledge and understanding of relevant provisions of the International Convention for the Prevention of Pollution from Ships (MARPOL) and other relevant IMO instruments, industry guidelines and port regulations as commonly applied Proficiency in the use of the IBC Code and related documents	Examination and assessment of evidence obtained from one or more of the following: .1 approved in-service experience .2 approved training ship experience .3 approved simulator training .4 approved training programme	The handling of cargoes complies with relevant IMO instruments and established industrial standards and codes of safe working practice

第 1 栏	第 2 栏	第 3 栏	第 4 栏
适任	**知识、理解和熟练**	**表明适任的方法**	**评价适任的标准**
采取预防措施防止环境污染	理解大气和环境的防污染程序	考试并评估从下列一项或数项获取的证据： .1 认可的工作经历 .2 认可的培训船经历 .3 认可的模拟器培训 .4 认可的培训计划	根据公认的原则和程序进行作业以防止环境污染
监督和控制对立法要求的遵守	《国际防止船舶造成污染公约》（MARPOL）的相关规定和其他普遍采用的国际海事组织（IMO）相关文件、行业指南和港口规则的知识及理解 精通《IBC 规则》和相关文件的使用	考试并评估从下列一项或数项获取的证据： .1 认可的工作经历 .2 认可的培训船经历 .3 认可的模拟器培训 .4 认可的培训计划	货物作业符合相关的国际海事组织（IMO）文件、既定的行业标准和安全工作做法

Section A-V/1-2

Mandatory minimum requirements for the training and qualifications of masters, officers and ratings on liquefied gas tankers

Standard of competence

1 Every candidate for certification in basic training for liquefied gas tanker cargo operations shall be required to:

.1 demonstrate the competence to undertake the tasks, duties and responsibilities listed in column 1 of table A-V/1-2-1; and

.2 provide evidence of having achieved:

.2.1 the minimum knowledge, understanding and proficiency listed in column 2 of table A-V/1-2-1, and

.2.2 the required standard of competence in accordance with the methods for demonstrating competence and the criteria for evaluating competence tabulated in columns 3 and 4 of table A-V/1-2-1.

2 Every candidate for certification in advanced training for liquefied gas tanker cargo operations shall be required to:

.1 demonstrate the competence to undertake the tasks, duties and responsibilities listed in column 1 of table A-V/1-2-2; and

.2 provide evidence of having achieved:

.2.1 the minimum knowledge, understanding and proficiency listed in column 2 of table A-V/1-2-2, and

.2.2 the required standard of competence in accordance with the methods for demonstrating competence and the criteria for evaluating competence tabulated in columns 3 and 4 of table A-V/1-2-2.

第 A-V/1-2 节

对液化气船船长、高级船员和普通船员的培训和资格的强制性最低要求

适任标准

1 每个申请液化气船货物操作基本培训证书的申请人应:

.1 证明其具有承担表 A-V/1-2-1 第 1 栏所列任务、职责和责任的适任能力;并且

.2 提供其已达到下列各项的证据:

.2.1 表 A-V/1-2-1 第 2 栏所列的最低的知识、理解和熟练,以及

.2.2 表 A-V/1-2-1 第 3 栏和第 4 栏所列的表明适任的方法和评估适任的标准中所要求的适任标准。

2 每个申请液化气船货物操作高级培训证书的申请人应:

.1 证明其具有承担表 A-V/1-2-2 第 1 栏所列任务、职责和责任的适任能力;并且

.2 提供其已达到下列各项的证据:

.2.1 表 A-V/1-2-2 第 2 栏所列的最低的知识、理解和熟练,以及

.2.2 表 A-V/1-2-2 第 3 栏和第 4 栏所列的表明适任的方法和评估适任的标准中所要求的适任标准。

Table A-V/1-2-1

Specification of minimum standard of competence in basic training for liquefied gas tanker cargo operations

Column 1	Column 2	Column 3	Column 4
Competence	**Knowledge, understanding and proficiency**	**Methods for demonstrating competence**	**Criteria for evaluating competence**
Contribute to the safe operation of a liquefied gas tanker	*Design and operational characteristics of liquefied gas tankers* Basic knowledge of liquefied gas tankers: .1 types of liquefied gas tankers .2 general arrangement and construction Basic knowledge of cargo operations: .1 piping systems and valves .2 cargo handling equipment .3 loading, unloading and care in transit .4 emergency shutdown (ESD) system .5 tank cleaning, purging, gas-freeing and inerting Basic knowledge of the physical properties of liquefied gases, including: .1 properties and characteristics .2 pressure and temperature, including vapour pressure/temperature relationship .3 types of electrostatic charge generation	Examination and assessment of evidence obtained from one or more of the following: .1 approved in-service experience .2 approved training ship experience .3 approved simulator training .4 approved training programme	Communications within the area of responsibility are clear and effective Cargo operations are carried out in accordance with accepted principles and procedures to ensure safety of operations

表 A-V/1-2-1

液化气船货物操作基本培训的最低适任标准

第 1 栏	第 2 栏	第 3 栏	第 4 栏
适任	**知识、理解和熟练**	**表明适任的方法**	**评价适任的标准**
有助于液化气船的安全操作	液化气船的设计和操作特性 液化气船的基本知识： .1 液化气船的类型 .2 总体布置和构造 货物操作的基本知识： .1 管系和阀门 .2 货物作业设备 .3 装货、卸货和运输中货物照管 .4 紧急关闭(ESD)系统 .5 洗舱、驱气、除气和惰化 液化气物理性质的基本知识，包括： .1 性质和特点 .2 压力和温度，包括蒸气压力/温度关系 .3 静电电荷产生的类型	考试并评估从下列一项或数项获取的证据： .1 认可的工作经历 .2 认可的培训船经历 .3 认可的模拟器培训 .4 认可的培训计划	责任范围内的交流清楚、有效 货物操作符合公认的原则和程序，以确保操作安全

Column 1	Column 2	Column 3	Column 4
Competence	**Knowledge, understanding and proficiency**	**Methods for demonstrating competence**	**Criteria for evaluating competence**
Contribute to the safe operation of a liquefied gas tanker (*continued*)	.4 chemical symbols Knowledge and understanding of tanker safety culture and safety management		
Take precautions to prevent hazards	Basic knowledge of the hazards associated with tanker operations, including: .1 health hazards .2 environmental hazards .3 reactivity hazards .4 corrosion hazards .5 explosion and flammability hazards .6 sources of ignition .7 electrostatic hazards .8 toxicity hazards .9 vapour leaks and clouds .10 extremely low temperatures .11 pressure hazards Basic knowledge of hazard controls: .1 inerting, drying and monitoring techniques .2 anti-static measures .3 ventilation .4 segregation .5 cargo inhibition .6 importance of cargo compatibility	Examination and assessment of evidence obtained from one or more of the following: .1 approved in-service experience .2 approved training ship experience .3 approved simulator training .4 approved training programme	Correctly identifies, on an MSDS, relevant cargo-related hazards to the vessel and to personnel, and takes the appropriate actions in accordance with established procedures Identification and actions on becoming aware of a hazardous situation conform to established procedures in line with best practice

第 1 栏	第 2 栏	第 3 栏	第 4 栏
适任	知识、理解和熟练	表明适任的方法	评价适任的标准
有助于液化气船的安全操作(续)	.4 化学符号 液化气船安全文化和安全管理的知识及理解		
采取预防措施防止危害	有关液化气船操作危害的基本知识,包括: .1 健康危害 .2 环境危害 .3 反应性危害 .4 腐蚀性危害 .5 爆炸及易燃性危害 .6 着火源 .7 静电危害 .8 毒性危害 .9 蒸气泄漏以及蒸发气团 .10 极低温度 .11 压力危害 危害控制的基本知识: .1 惰化、干舱和监控技术 .2 防静电措施 .3 通风 .4 隔离 .5 货物抑制 .6 货物兼容性的重要性	考试并评估从下列一项或数项获取的证据: .1 认可的工作经历 .2 认可的培训船经历 .3 认可的模拟器培训 .4 认可的培训计划	正确识别《化学品安全说明书》(MSDS)中与货物相关的对船舶和人员的危害,并采取符合既定程序的适当行动 识别和在意识到危险局面时采取的行动符合既定程序和最佳做法

Column 1	Column 2	Column 3	Column 4
Competence	**Knowledge, understanding and proficiency**	**Methods for demonstrating competence**	**Criteria for evaluating competence**
Take precautions to prevent hazards (*continued*)	.7 atmospheric control .8 gas testing Understanding of information on a Material Safety Data Sheet (MSDS)		
Apply occupational health and safety precautions and measures	Function and proper use of gas-measuring instruments and similar equipment Proper use of safety equipment and protective devices, including: .1 breathing apparatus and tank evacuating equipment .2 protective clothing and equipment .3 resuscitators .4 rescue and escape equipment Basic knowledge of safe working practices and procedures in accordance with legislation and industry guidelines and personal shipboard safety relevant to liquefied gas tankers, including: .1 precautions to be taken when entering enclosed spaces .2 precautions to be taken before and during repair and maintenance work .3 safety measures for hot and cold work .4 electrical safety .5 ship/shore safety checklist	Examination and assessment of evidence obtained from one or more of the following: .1 approved in-service experience .2 approved training ship experience .3 approved simulator training .4 approved training programme	Procedures for entry into enclosed spaces are observed Procedures and safe working practices designed to safeguard personnel and the ship are observed at all times Appropriate safety and protective equipment is correctly used

第 1 栏	第 2 栏	第 3 栏	第 4 栏
适任	知识、理解和熟练	表明适任的方法	评价适任的标准
采取预防措施防止危害(续)	.7 舱气控制 .8 气体检测 《化学品安全说明书》(MSDS)信息的理解		
应用职业健康与安全预防措施	气体测量仪器和类似设备的功能及其正确使用 安全设备和防护装置的正确使用,包括: .1 呼吸器具与货舱撤离装置 .2 防护服及装备 .3 复苏仪 .4 救助及逃生设备 符合与液化气船相关的法规、行业指南及船上人员安全的安全工作做法和程序的基本知识: .1 当进入封闭处所时采取的预防措施 .2 在进行维修和保养工作之前和期间采取的预防措施 .3 热工和冷工作业的安全措施 .4 电气安全 .5 船/岸安全检查表	考试并评估从下列一项或数项获取的证据: .1 认可的工作经历 .2 认可的培训船经历 .3 认可的模拟器培训 .4 认可的培训计划	遵守进入封闭处所的程序 始终遵循旨在保护人员和船舶安全的程序和安全工作做法 正确使用适当的安全和防护设备

Column 1	Column 2	Column 3	Column 4
Competence	**Knowledge, understanding and proficiency**	**Methods for demonstrating competence**	**Criteria for evaluating competence**
Apply occupational health and safety precautions and measures *(continued)*	Basic knowledge of first aid with reference to a Material Safety Data Sheet (MSDS)		First aid do's and don'ts
Carry out fire-fighting operations	Tanker fire organization and action to be taken Special hazards associated with cargo handling and transportation of liquefied gases in bulk Fire-fighting agents used to extinguish gas fires Fixed fire-fighting foam system operations Portable fire-fighting foam operations Fixed dry chemical system operations Basic knowledge of spill containment in relation to fire-fighting operations	Practical exercises and instruction conducted under approved and truly realistic training conditions (e.g. simulated shipboard conditions) and, whenever possible and practicable, in darkness	Initial actions and follow-up actions on becoming aware of an emergency conform with established practices and procedures Action taken on identifying muster signals is appropriate to the indicated emergency and complies with established procedures Clothing and equipment are appropriate to the nature of the fire-fighting operations The timing and sequence of individual actions are appropriate to the prevailing circumstances and conditions Extinguishment of fire is achieved using appropriate procedures, techniques and fire-fighting agents
Respond to emergencies	Basic knowledge of emergency procedures, including emergency shutdown	Examination and assessment of evidence obtained from one or more of the following: .1 approved in-service experience .2 approved training ship experience .3 approved simulator training .4 approved training programme	The type and impact of the emergency is promptly identified and the response actions conform to the emergency procedures and contingency plans

第 1 栏	第 2 栏	第 3 栏	第 4 栏
适任	**知识、理解和熟练**	**表明适任的方法**	**评价适任的标准**
应用职业健康与安全预防措施(续)	参照《化学品安全说明书》(MSDS)急救的基本知识		熟悉急救规则
执行消防操作	液化气船的消防组织及应采取的行动 与散装液化气体处理和运输相关的特殊危害 扑灭气体火灾的灭火剂 固定式泡沫灭火系统的操作 便携式泡沫灭火器的操作 固定式干粉灭火系统的操作 与消防操作有关的溢漏抑制的基本知识	实际演练和在认可的真实培训条件(如模拟船舶条件)下,并在可能和可行的情况下进行黑暗中训练	意识到紧急情况时采取的初始和后续行动符合既定做法和程序 识别集合信号后采取的行动适合所表明的紧急情况并符合既定程序 防护服和设备适合消防操作的性质 每个行动的时机和顺序适合当时的环境和条件 使用合适的程序、技能、灭火剂完成灭火任务
应急反应	应急程序的基本知识,包括紧急关闭	考试并评估从下列一项或数项获取的证据: .1 认可的工作经历 .2 认可的培训船经历 .3 认可的模拟器培训 .4 认可的培训计划	迅速识别紧急情况的类型和影响,并采取符合应急程序和应急计划的行动

Column 1	Column 2	Column 3	Column 4
Competence	**Knowledge, understanding and proficiency**	**Methods for demonstrating competence**	**Criteria for evaluating competence**
Take precautions to prevent pollution of the environment from the release of liquefied gases	Basic knowledge of the effects of pollution on human and marine life Basic knowledge of shipboard procedures to prevent pollution Basic knowledge of measures to be taken in the event of spillage, including the need to: .1 report relevant information to the responsible persons .2 assist in implementing shipboard spill-containment procedures .3 prevent brittle fracture	Examination and assessment of evidence obtained from one or more of the following: .1 approved in-service experience .2 approved training ship experience .3 approved simulator training .4 approved training programme	Procedures designed to safeguard the environment are observed at all times

第 1 栏	第 2 栏	第 3 栏	第 4 栏
适任	知识、理解和熟练	表明适任的方法	评价适任的标准
采取预防措施防止液化气泄漏造成的环境污染	污染对人类和海洋生物的影响的基本知识 船上防污染程序的基本知识 应对溢漏的措施的基本知识,包括需要: .1 向责任人报告相关信息 .2 协助执行船上溢漏抑制程序 .3 防止脆性开裂	考试并评估从下列一项或数项获取的证据: .1 认可的工作经历 .2 认可的培训船经历 .3 认可的模拟器培训 .4 认可的培训计划	始终遵循旨在保护环境的程序

Table A-V/1-2-2

Specification of minimum standard of competence in advanced training for liquefied gas tanker cargo operations

Column 1	Column 2	Column 3	Column 4
Competence	**Knowledge, understanding and proficiency**	**Methods for demonstrating competence**	**Criteria for evaluating competence**
Ability to safely perform and monitor all cargo operations	*Design and characteristics of a liquefied gas tanker* Knowledge of liquefied gas tanker design, systems, and equipment, including: .1 types of liquefied gas tankers and cargo tanks construction .2 general arrangement and construction .3 cargo containment systems, including materials of construction and insulation .4 cargo-handling equipment and instrumentation, including: .4.1 cargo pumps and pumping arrangements .4.2 cargo pipelines and valves .4.3 expansion devices .4.4 flame screens .4.5 temperature monitoring systems .4.6 cargo tank level-gauging systems .4.7 tank pressure monitoring and control systems .5 cargo temperature maintenance system	Examination and assessment of evidence obtained from one or more of the following: .1 approved in-service experience .2 approved training ship experience .3 approved simulator training .4 approved training programme	Communications are clear, understood and successful Cargo operations are carried out in a safe manner, taking into account liquefied gas tanker designs, systems and equipment Pumping operations are carried out in accordance with accepted principles and procedures and are relevant to the type of cargo Cargo operations are planned, risk is managed and carried out in accordance with accepted principles and procedures to ensure safety of operations and avoid pollution of the marine environment

表 A-V/1-2-2
液化气船货物操作高级培训的最低适任标准

第 1 栏	第 2 栏	第 3 栏	第 4 栏
适任	知识、理解和熟练	表明适任的方法	评价适任的标准
安全实施和监管所有货物操作的能力	液化气船的设计和特性 液化气船设计、系统和设备的知识，包括： .1 液化气船的种类和液货舱的结构 .2 总体布置和构造 .3 货物围护系统，包括构造和隔热材料 .4 货物作业设备和仪器，包括： .4.1 货泵和泵系布置 .4.2 货物管系和阀 .4.3 膨胀装置 .4.4 火焰防护网 .4.5 温度监控系统 .4.6 货舱液位计量系统 .4.7 货舱压力监测和控制系统 .5 货物保温系统	考试并评估从下列一项或数项获取的证据： .1 认可的工作经历 .2 认可的培训船经历 .3 认可的模拟器培训 .4 认可的培训计划	交流清楚、易懂、有效 货物操作以安全的方式进行，并考虑液化气船设计、系统和设备 按照公认的原则和程序及货物的种类进行泵系操作 货物操作有计划，有风险管理，并按公认的原则和程序进行，以确保操作安全，避免污染海洋环境

Column 1	Column 2	Column 3	Column 4
Competence	**Knowledge, understanding and proficiency**	**Methods for demonstrating competence**	**Criteria for evaluating competence**
Ability to safely perform and monitor all cargo operations (*continued*)	.6 tank atmosphere control systems (inert gas, nitrogen), including storage, generation and distribution systems .7 cofferdam heating systems .8 gas-detecting systems .9 ballast system .10 boil-off systems .11 reliquefaction systems .12 cargo Emergency Shut Down system (ESD) .13 custody transfer system Knowledge of pump theory and characteristics, including types of cargo pumps and their safe operation *Loading, unloading, care and handling of cargo* Knowledge of the effect of bulk liquid cargoes on trim and stability and structural integrity Proficiency in tanker safety culture and implementation of safety management requirements		Proper loading, stowage and unloading of liquefied gas cargoes ensures that stability and stress conditions remain within safe limits at all times Potential non-compliance with cargo-related procedures is promptly identified and rectified Actions taken and procedures followed correctly identify and make full use of appropriate shipboard equipment

第 1 栏	第 2 栏	第 3 栏	第 4 栏
适任	知识、理解和熟练	表明适任的方法	评价适任的标准
安全实施和监管所有货物操作的能力(续)	.6 舱气控制系统(惰性气体、氮气),包括储存、产生和分配系统 .7 隔离舱加温系统 .8 气体探测系统 .9 压载系统 .10 蒸发系统 .11 再液化系统 .12 货物紧急关闭系统(ESD) .13 监护驳运系统 泵的理论和特性的知识,包括货泵的种类及其安全操作 货物装卸、照管和作业 散装液体货物对船舶吃水差、稳性和结构完整性影响的知识 精通液化气船安全文化和落实安全管理要求		正确地装载、配载和卸载液化气,确保船舶稳性和强度始终保持在安全界限内 迅速识别并纠正可能不符合货物相关程序的做法 采取的行动和遵循的程序正确,充分使用船上的适当设备

Column 1	Column 2	Column 3	Column 4
Competence	**Knowledge, understanding and proficiency**	**Methods for demonstrating competence**	**Criteria for evaluating competence**
Ability to safely perform and monitor all cargo operations (*continued*)	Proficiency to apply safe preparations, procedures and checklists for all cargo operations, including: .1 post docking and loading: .1.1 tank inspection .1.2 inerting (Oxygen reduction, dewpoint reduction) .1.3 gassing-up .1.4 cooling down .1.5 loading .1.6 deballasting .1.7 sampling, including closed-loop sampling .2 sea passage: .2.1 cooling down .2.2 pressure maintenance .2.3 boil-off .2.4 inhibiting .3 unloading: .3.1 unloading .3.2 ballasting .3.3 stripping and cleaning systems .3.4 systems to make the tank liquid-free .4 pre-docking preparation: .4.1 warm-up .4.2 inerting .4.3 gas-freeing .5 ship-to-ship transfer		Calibration and use of monitoring and gas-detection equipment is consistent with safe operational practices and procedures Procedures for monitoring and safety systems ensure that all alarms are detected promptly and acted upon in accordance with established procedures

第 1 栏	第 2 栏	第 3 栏	第 4 栏
适任	知识、理解和熟练	表明适任的方法	评价适任的标准
安全实施和监管所有货物操作的能力(续)	在所有的货物操作中熟练运用安全准备工作、程序和检查表,包括: .1 靠泊后及装载时: .1.1 货舱检查 .1.2 惰化(降低氧气量、露点) .1.3 充气 .1.4 冷却 .1.5 装载 .1.6 排压载 .1.7 取样,包括闭环取样 .2 航行中: .2.1 冷却 .2.2 压力维持 .2.3 蒸发损耗 .2.4 抑制 .3 卸载: .3.1 卸载 .3.2 压载 .3.3 扫舱和洗舱系统 .3.4 干舱系统 .4 靠泊前的准备工作: .4.1 暖舱 .4.2 惰化 .4.3 除气 .5 船对船过驳		监控和气体探测设备的校准与使用符合安全工作做法及程序 监控程序和安全系统确保迅速检测到所有报警,并按照既定的程序采取行动

Column 1	Column 2	Column 3	Column 4
Competence	**Knowledge, understanding and proficiency**	**Methods for demonstrating competence**	**Criteria for evaluating competence**
Ability to safely perform and monitor all cargo operations (*continued*)	Proficiency to perform cargo measurements and calculations, including: .1 liquid phase .2 gas phase .3 On Board Quantity (OBQ) .4 Remain On Board (ROB) .5 boil-off cargo calculations Proficiency to manage and supervise personnel with cargo-related responsibilities		Personnel are allocated duties and informed of procedures and standards of work to be followed, in a manner appropriate to the individuals concerned and in accordance with safe operational practices
Familiarity with physical and chemical properties of liquefied gas cargoes	Knowledge and understanding of basic chemistry and physics and the relevant definitions related to the safe carriage of liquefied gases in bulk in ships, including: .1 the chemical structure of gases .2 the properties and characteristics of liquefied gases (including CO_2) and their vapours, including: .2.1 simple gas laws .2.2 states of matter .2.3 liquid and vapour densities .2.4 diffusion and mixing of gases .2.5 compression of gases .2.6 reliquefaction and refrigeration of gases	Examination and assessment of evidence obtained from one or more of the following: .1 approved in-service experience .2 approved training ship experience .3 approved simulator training .4 approved training programme	Effective use is made of information resources for identification of properties and characteristics of liquefied gases and their impact on safety, environmental protection and vessel operation

第 1 栏	第 2 栏	第 3 栏	第 4 栏
适任	知识、理解和熟练	表明适任的方法	评价适任的标准
安全实施和监管所有货物操作的能力(续)	熟练进行货物测量和计算,包括: .1 液态 .2 气态 .3 船上载有数量(OBQ) .4 船上剩余数量(ROB) .5 蒸发损耗货物的计算 熟练管理和监督负有操作货物责任的人员		分配人员工作,以适合相关人员的方式告知应遵循的工作程序和标准,并符合安全操作做法
熟悉液化气体货物的物理和化学性质	基础化学和物理学以及散装液化气体安全运输的相关定义的知识及理解,包括: .1 气体的化学结构 .2 液化气体(包括二氧化碳)及其蒸气的性质和特点,包括: .2.1 简单气体定律 .2.2 物质状态 .2.3 液体和蒸气密度 .2.4 气体的扩散和混合 .2.5 气体压缩 .2.6 气体再液化和冷却	考试并评估从下列一项或数项获取的证据: .1 认可的工作经历 .2 认可的培训船经历 .3 认可的模拟器培训 .4 认可的培训计划	有效使用信息源,以识别液化气的性质和特点,及其对安全、环境保护与船舶操作的影响

Column 1	Column 2	Column 3	Column 4
Competence	**Knowledge, understanding and proficiency**	**Methods for demonstrating competence**	**Criteria for evaluating competence**
Familiarity with physical and chemical properties of liquefied gas cargoes (*continued*)	.2.7 critical temperature of gases and pressure .2.8 flashpoint, upper and lower explosive limits, auto-ignition temperature .2.9 compatibility, reactivity and positive segregation of gases .2.10 polymerization .2.11 saturated vapour pressure/reference temperature .2.12 dewpoint and bubble point .2.13 lubrication of compressors .2.14 hydrate formation .3 the properties of single liquids .4 the nature and properties of solutions .5 thermodynamic units .6 basic thermodynamic laws and diagrams .7 properties of materials .8 effect of low temperature – brittle fracture Understanding the information contained in a Material Safety Data Sheet (MSDS)		

第 1 栏	第 2 栏	第 3 栏	第 4 栏
适任	知识、理解和熟练	表明适任的方法	评价适任的标准
熟悉液化气体货物的物理和化学性质(续)	.2.7 气体的临界温度和压力 .2.8 闪点、爆炸上限和下限、自燃温度 .2.9 气体的兼容性、反应性和正偏析 .2.10 聚合 .2.11 饱和蒸气压力/参考温度 .2.12 露点和始沸点 .2.13 压缩机的润滑 .2.14 水合物的形成 .3 单一液体的性质 .4 溶液的性质和特点 .5 热力单位 .6 热力学基本定律和图表 .7 材料特性 .8 低温的影响——脆性开裂 理解《化学品安全说明书》(MSDS)包含的信息		

Column 1	Column 2	Column 3	Column 4
Competence	**Knowledge, understanding and proficiency**	**Methods for demonstrating competence**	**Criteria for evaluating competence**
Take precautions to prevent hazards	Knowledge and understanding of the hazards and control measures associated with liquefied gas tanker cargo operations, including: .1 flammability .2 explosion .3 toxicity .4 reactivity .5 corrosivity .6 health hazards .7 inert gas composition .8 electrostatic hazards .9 polymerizing cargoes Proficiency to calibrate and use monitoring and gas-detection systems, instruments and equipment Knowledge and understanding of dangers of non-compliance with relevant rules/regulations	Examination and assessment of evidence obtained from one or more of the following: .1 approved in-service experience .2 approved training ship experience .3 approved simulator training .4 approved training programme	Relevant cargo-related hazards to the vessel and to personnel associated with liquefied gas tanker cargo operations are correctly identified, and proper control measures are taken Use of gas-detection devices is in accordance with manuals and good practice
Apply occupational health and safety precautions	Knowledge and understanding of safe working practices, including risk assessment and personal shipboard safety relevant to liquefied gas tankers, including: .1 precautions to be taken when entering enclosed spaces (such as compressor rooms), including the correct use of different types of breathing apparatus	Assessment of evidence obtained from one or more of the following: .1 approved in-service experience .2 approved training ship experience .3 approved simulator training .4 approved training programme	Procedures designed to safeguard personnel and the ship are observed at all times Safe working practices are observed and appropriate safety and protective equipment is correctly used Working practices are in accordance with legislative requirements, codes of practice, permits to work and environmental concerns Correct use of breathing apparatus

第1栏	第2栏	第3栏	第4栏
适任	知识、理解和熟练	表明适任的方法	评价适任的标准
采取预防措施防止危害	与液化气船货物操作有关的危害及其控制措施的知识和理解,包括: .1 易燃性 .2 爆炸性 .3 毒性 .4 反应性 .5 腐蚀性 .6 健康危害 .7 惰性气体组成 .8 静电危害 .9 聚合货物 熟练校准和使用监测及气体探测系统、仪器和装置 不遵守相关规范/规则的危害的知识及理解	考试并评估从下列一项或数项获取的证据: .1 认可的工作经历 .2 认可的培训船经历 .3 认可的模拟器培训 .4 认可的培训计划	正确识别与货物相关的对船舶和参与液化气船货物操作人员的危害,并采取适当的控制措施 气体探测设备的使用符合手册和良好做法
应用职业健康和安全预防措施	安全工作做法的知识及理解,包括与液化气船相关的风险管理和船上人员安全: .1 在进入封闭处所(如压缩机房)时采取的预防措施,包括正确使用各种呼吸器具	评估从下列一项或数项获取的证据: .1 认可的工作经历 .2 认可的培训船经历 .3 认可的模拟器培训 .4 认可的培训计划	始终遵循旨在保护人员和船舶安全的程序 遵循安全工作做法,正确使用合适的安全和防护设备 工作做法符合法定要求、操作规程、作业许可和环保要求 正确使用呼吸器具

Column 1	Column 2	Column 3	Column 4
Competence	**Knowledge, understanding and proficiency**	**Methods for demonstrating competence**	**Criteria for evaluating competence**
Apply occupational health and safety precautions *(continued)*	.2 precautions to be taken before and during repair and maintenance work, including work affecting pumping, piping, electrical and control systems .3 precautions for hot and cold work .4 precautions for electrical safety .5 use of appropriate Personal Protective Equipment (PPE) .6 precautions for cold burn and frostbite .7 proper use of personal toxicity monitoring equipment		
Respond to emergencies	Knowledge and understanding of liquefied gas tanker emergency procedures, including: .1 ship emergency response plans .2 cargo operations emergency shutdown procedure .3 emergency cargo valve operations .4 actions to be taken in the event of failure of systems or services essential to cargo operations .5 fire-fighting on liquefied gas tankers .6 jettisoning of cargo .7 enclosed space rescue	Assessment of evidence obtained from one or more of the following: .1 approved in-service experience .2 approved training ship experience .3 approved simulator training .4 approved training programme	The type and impact of emergency is promptly identified and the response actions conform with established emergency procedures and contingency plans The order of priority and the levels and timescales of making reports and informing personnel on board are relevant to the nature of the emergency and reflect the urgency of the problem Evacuation, emergency shutdown and isolation are appropriate to the nature of the emergency and implemented promptly

第 1 栏	第 2 栏	第 3 栏	第 4 栏
适任	知识、理解和熟练	表明适任的方法	评价适任的标准
应用职业健康和安全预防措施(续)	.2 在进行维修和保养工作,包括影响泵系、管系、电气和控制系统的工作之前及期间采取的预防措施 .3 热工和冷工作业的预防措施 .4 电气安全预防措施 .5 使用合适的个人防护设备(PPE) .6 冷灼伤及冻伤的预防措施 .7 个人毒性监测装置的正确使用		
应急反应	液化气船应急程序的知识和理解,包括: .1 船舶应急反应计划 .2 货物操作紧急关闭程序 .3 货阀的紧急操作 .4 对货物操作至关重要的系统或设施发生故障时应采取的行动 .5 液化气船消防 .6 货物抛弃 .7 封闭处所救助	评估从下列一项或数项获取的证据: .1 认可的工作经历 .2 认可的培训船经历 .3 认可的模拟器培训 .4 认可的培训计划	迅速识别紧急情况的类型和影响,并采取符合既定应急程序和应急计划的行动 作出报告及通知船上人员的优先顺序、级别、时限与紧急事件的性质相关,并反映事态的紧急程度 撤离、紧急关闭和隔离程序适合紧急事件的性质,并迅速实施

Column 1	Column 2	Column 3	Column 4
Competence	**Knowledge, understanding and proficiency**	**Methods for demonstrating competence**	**Criteria for evaluating competence**
Respond to emergencies (*continued*)	Actions to be taken following collision, grounding or spillage and envelopment of the ship in toxic or flammable vapour Knowledge of medical first-aid procedures and antidotes on board liquefied gas tankers, with reference to the Medical First Aid Guide for Use in Accidents involving Dangerous Goods (MFAG)		The identification of and actions taken in a medical emergency conform to current recognized first aid practice and international guidelines
Take precautions to prevent pollution of the environment	Understanding of procedures to prevent pollution of the environment	Assessment of evidence obtained from one or more of the following: .1 approved in-service experience .2 approved training ship experience .3 approved simulator training .4 approved training programme	Operations are conducted in accordance with accepted principles and procedures to prevent pollution of the environment
Monitor and control compliance with legislative requirements	Knowledge and understanding of relevant provisions of the International Convention for the Prevention of Pollution from Ships (MARPOL) and other relevant IMO instruments, industry guidelines and port regulations as commonly applied Proficiency in the use of the IBC and IGC Codes and related documents	Assessment of evidence obtained from one or more of the following: .1 approved in-service experience .2 approved training ship experience .3 approved simulator training .4 approved training programme	The handling of liquefied gas cargoes complies with relevant IMO instruments and established industrial standards and codes of safe working practices

第 1 栏	第 2 栏	第 3 栏	第 4 栏
适任	知识、理解和熟练	表明适任的方法	评价适任的标准
应急反应(续)	在发生碰撞、搁浅、泄漏及船舶被毒气或可燃气体包围的情况下采取的行动 液化气船船上急救医疗程序和解毒剂的知识，参考《危险货物事故医疗急救指南》(MFAG)		医疗急救的情况识别及采取的做法符合当前认可的急救惯例和国际指南
采取预防措施防止环境污染	理解防止环境污染的程序	评估从下列一项或数项获取的证据： .1 认可的工作经历 .2 认可的培训船经历 .3 认可的模拟器培训 .4 认可的培训计划	根据公认的原则和程序进行作业以防止环境污染
监督和控制对立法要求的遵守	《国际防止船舶造成污染公约》(MARPOL)的相关规定和其他普遍采用的相关的国际海事组织(IMO)文件、行业指南和港口规则的知识及理解 精通《IBC 规则》、《IGC 规则》和相关文件的使用	评估从下列一项或数项获取的证据： .1 认可的工作经历 .2 认可的培训船经历 .3 认可的模拟器培训 .4 认可的培训计划	液化气货物作业符合国际海事组织(IMO)的相关文件、既定的行业标准和安全工作规程

Section A-V/2

Mandatory minimum requirements for the training and qualification of masters, officers, ratings and other personnel on passenger ships

Crowd management training

1 The crowd management training required by regulation V/2, paragraph 4 for personnel designated on muster lists to assist passengers in emergency situations shall include, but not necessarily be limited to:

.1 awareness of life-saving appliance and control plans, including:

.1.1 knowledge of muster lists and emergency instructions;

.1.2 knowledge of the emergency exits; and

.1.3 restrictions on the use of elevators;

.2 the ability to assist passengers *en route* to muster and embarkation stations, including:

.2.1 the ability to give clear reassuring orders;

.2.2 the control of passengers in corridors, staircases and passageways;

.2.3 maintaining escape routes clear of obstructions;

.2.4 methods available for evacuation of disabled persons and persons needing special assistance; and

.2.5 search of accommodation spaces;

.3 mustering procedures, including:

.3.1 the importance of keeping order;

.3.2 the ability to use procedures for reducing and avoiding panic;

.3.3 the ability to use, where appropriate, passenger lists for evacuation counts; and

.3.4 the ability to ensure that the passengers are suitably clothed and have donned their lifejackets correctly.

第 A-V/2 节
对客船船长、高级船员、普通船员及其他人员的培训和资格的强制性最低要求

拥挤人群管理培训

1 规则第 V/2 条第 4 段对在应变部署表上指定的紧急情况下协助旅客的人员所要求的拥挤人群管理培训应包括,但不必限于:

.1 了解救生设备和控制计划,包括:

.1.1 应变部署表和应急指示的知识,

.1.2 紧急出口的知识,以及

.1.3 使用升降机的限制;

.2 协助旅客到达集合和登乘地点的能力,包括:

.2.1 能够下达明确的安抚指令,

.2.2 管理在走廊、楼梯和通道里的旅客,

.2.3 保持逃生通道畅通,

.2.4 撤离残障人员和需要特别协助的人员的可用方法,以及

.2.5 搜索居住舱室;

.3 集合的程序,包括:

.3.1 保持秩序的重要性,

.3.2 运用减少和避免恐慌程序的能力,

.3.3 如适合,使用旅客名单清点撤离人数的能力,以及

.3.4 确保旅客着装恰当并正确穿着救生衣的能力。

Safety training for personnel providing direct service to passengers in passenger spaces

2 The additional safety training required by regulation V/2, paragraph 5, shall at least ensure attainment of the abilities as follows:

Communication

.1 Ability to communicate with passengers during an emergency, taking into account:

.1.1 the language or languages appropriate to the principal nationalities of passengers carried on the particular route;

.1.2 the likelihood that an ability to use an elementary English vocabulary for basic instructions can provide a means of communicating with a passenger in need of assistance whether or not the passenger and crew member share a common language;

.1.3 the possible need to communicate during an emergency by some other means, such as by demonstration, or hand signals, or calling attention to the location of instructions, muster stations, life-saving devices or evacuation routes, when oral communication is impractical;

.1.4 the extent to which complete safety instructions have been provided to passengers in their native language or languages; and

.1.5 the languages in which emergency announcements may be broadcast during an emergency or drill to convey critical guidance to passengers and to facilitate crew members in assisting passengers.

Life-saving appliances

.2 Ability to demonstrate to passengers the use of personal life-saving appliances.

Embarkation procedures

.3 Embarking and disembarking passengers, with special attention to disabled persons and persons needing assistance.

Crisis management and human behaviour training

3 Masters, chief engineer officers, chief mates, second engineer officers and any person having responsibility for the safety of passengers in emergency situations shall:

.1 have successfully completed the approved crisis management and human behaviour training required by regulation V/2, paragraph 6, in accordance with their capacity, duties and responsibilities as set out in table A-V/2; and

.2 be required to provide evidence that the required standard of competence has been achieved in accordance with the methods and the criteria for evaluating competence tabulated in columns 3 and 4 of table A-V/2.

在旅客舱室为旅客提供直接服务的人员的安全培训

2 规则第 V/2 条第 5 段规定的附加安全培训，应至少确保达到以下能力：

沟通

.1 能在紧急情况下与旅客进行沟通，并考虑到：

.1.1 适合于特定航线所载旅客的主要国籍的一种或多种语言，

.1.2 使用基础英语词汇以表达基本指示的能力，为需要协助的旅客提供一种沟通手段，不管旅客和船员是否使用同一种语言，

.1.3 在紧急情况下，当采用口语交流不可行时，可能需要采用其他手段，如示范或手势或提示注意指示位置、集合地点、救生设备或逃生路线，

.1.4 尽可能用旅客的母语向其传达完整的安全指令，以及

.1.5 在紧急情况下或演习中，为向旅客传达关键指导和便于船员协助旅客，可能用于广播紧急通知的语言；

救生设备

.2 向旅客演示使用个人救生设备的能力；

登乘程序

.3 安排旅客上下，并特别注意残障人员和需要协助的旅客。

危机管理和人的行为培训

3 船长、轮机长、大副、大管轮及其他任何在紧急情况中对旅客安全负有责任的人员，应：

.1 根据表 A-V/2 所要求的能力、职责和责任，已圆满完成规则第 V/2 条第 6 段规定的认可的危机管理和人的行为培训；并且

.2 按表 A-V/2 第 3 栏和第 4 栏所列的表明适任的方法和标准，提供已达到所要求的适任标准的证据。

Passenger safety, cargo safety and hull integrity training

4 The passenger safety, cargo safety and hull integrity training required by regulation V/2, paragraph 7, for masters, chief mates, chief engineer officers, second engineer officers and persons assigned immediate responsibility for embarking and disembarking passengers, for loading, discharging or securing cargo or for closing hull openings on board ro-ro passenger ships shall at least ensure attainment of the abilities that are appropriate to their duties and responsibilities as follows:

Loading and embarkation procedures

.1 Ability to apply properly the procedures established for the ship regarding:

.1.1 loading and discharging vehicles, rail cars and other cargo transport units, including related communications;

.1.2 lowering and hoisting ramps;

.1.3 setting up and stowing retractable vehicle decks; and

.1.4 embarking and disembarking passengers, with special attention to disabled persons and persons needing assistance.

Carriage of dangerous goods

.2 Ability to apply any special safeguards, procedures and requirements regarding the carriage of dangerous goods on board ro-ro passenger ships.

Securing cargoes

.3 Ability to:

.3.1 apply correctly the provisions of the Code of Safe Practice for Cargo Stowage and Securing to the vehicles, rail cars and other cargo transport units carried; and

.3.2 use properly the cargo-securing equipment and materials provided, taking into account their limitations.

Stability, trim and stress calculations

.4 Ability to:

.4.1 make proper use of the stability and stress information provided;

.4.2 calculate stability and trim for different conditions of loading, using the stability calculators or computer programs provided;

.4.3 calculate load factors for decks; and

旅客安全、货物安全和船体完整性培训

4　规则第 V/2 条第 7 段对船长、大副、轮机长、大管轮和指定负有旅客上下船、滚装客船的货物装卸、系固或关闭船体开口直接责任的人员所要求的旅客安全、货物安全和船体完整性培训，应至少保证达到适合于其职责和责任的如下能力：

装载和登乘程序

.1　正确运用为船舶制定的有关下列各项程序的能力

　.1.1　装卸车辆、轨道车辆和其他货物运输组件，包括相关的沟通，

　.1.2　降下和升起登陆舌门，

　.1.3　放出和收回可收放的车辆甲板，以及

　.1.4　安排上下旅客，并特别注意残障人员和需要协助的人；

危险货物运输

.2　应用关于在滚装客船上运输危险货物的任何特别保护措施、程序和要求的能力；

货物系固

.3　能够：

　.3.1　正确将《货物积载和系固安全操作规则》的规定运用到所载的车辆、轨道车辆和其他货物运输组件，以及

　.3.2　正确使用所提供的货物系固设备和材料，同时考虑其局限性；

稳性、吃水差和强度计算

.4　能够：

　.4.1　正确使用所提供的稳性和强度资料，

　.4.2　运用所提供的稳性计算仪或计算机程序计算不同装载状态下的稳性和吃水差，

　.4.3　计算甲板负载系数，以及

.4.4 calculate the impact of ballast and fuel transfers on stability, trim and stress.

Opening, closing and securing hull openings

.5 Ability to:

.5.1 apply properly the procedures established for the ship regarding the opening, closing and securing of bow, stern and side doors and ramps and to correctly operate the associated systems; and

.5.2 conduct surveys on proper sealing.

Ro-ro deck atmosphere

.6 Ability to:

.6.1 use equipment, where carried, to monitor atmosphere in ro-ro spaces; and

.6.2 apply properly the procedures established for the ship for ventilation of ro-ro spaces during loading and discharging of vehicles, while on voyage and in emergencies.

.4.4 计算压载水和燃油转驳对稳性、吃水差和强度的影响;

开启、关闭和紧固船体开口

.5 能够:

.5.1 正确应用为船舶制定的有关开启、关闭和紧固船首门、船尾门、舷侧门和登陆舌门的程序,并正确操作相关系统,以及

.5.2 检查密封是否适当;

滚装甲板舱内空气

.6 能够:

.6.1 如有配备,使用设备检测滚装货舱内的空气,以及

.6.2 正确应用为船舶制定的在装卸车辆期间、在航行中和在紧急情况下,对滚装货舱进行通风的程序。

Table A-V/2

Specification of minimum standard of competence in crisis management and human behaviour

Column 1	Column 2	Column 3	Column 4
Competence	**Knowledge, understanding and proficiency**	**Methods for demonstrating competence**	**Criteria for evaluating competence**
Organize shipboard emergency procedures	Knowledge of: .1 the general design and layout of the ship .2 safety regulations .3 emergency plans and procedures The importance of the principles for the development of ship-specific emergency procedures, including: .1 the need for pre-planning and drills of shipboard emergency procedures .2 the need for all personnel to be aware of and adhere to pre-planned emergency procedures as carefully as possible in the event of an emergency situation	Assessment of evidence obtained from approved training, exercises with one or more prepared emergency plans and practical demonstration	The shipboard emergency procedures ensure a state of readiness to respond to emergency situations
Optimize the use of resources	Ability to optimize the use of resources, taking into account: .1 the possibility that resources available in an emergency may be limited .2 the need to make full use of personnel and equipment immediately available and, if necessary, to improvise Ability to organize realistic drills to maintain a state of readiness, taking into account lessons learnt from previous accidents involving passenger ships; debriefing after drills	Assessment of evidence obtained from approved training, practical demonstration and shipboard training and drills of emergency procedures	Contingency plans optimize the use of available resources Allocation of tasks and responsibilities reflects the known competence of individuals Roles and responsibilities of teams and individuals are clearly defined

表 A-V/2

危机管理和人的行为的最低适任标准

第 1 栏	第 2 栏	第 3 栏	第 4 栏
适任	**知识、理解和熟练**	**表明适任的方法**	**评价适任的标准**
组织船上应急程序	了解： .1 船舶的总体设计和布置 .2 安全规则 .3 应急计划和程序 制定船上具体应急程序原则的重要性，包括： .1 船舶应急程序的预先计划和演习的必要性 .2 在紧急情况下所有人员均注意到并尽可能认真地坚持预先计划的应急程序的必要性	评估从认可的培训、一个或多个已制定的应急计划的操练和实际演示中获取的证据	船上应急程序确保随时处于对紧急情况作出反应的准备状态
优化资源利用	优化资源利用的能力，考虑到： .1 紧急情况下可用资源也许有限的可能性 .2 需要充分利用可以立即得到的人员和设备，并在必要时临时凑成 根据从先前的客船事故中得到的教训组织现实演习以保持准备状态的能力；演习后的总结	评估从认可的培训、实际演示和船上培训及应急程序的演习中获取的证据	应急计划最好地利用了现有资源 任务和责任的分配反映了个人的已知适任能力 对团队和个人的作用和责任有明确的规定

Column 1	Column 2	Column 3	Column 4
Competence	**Knowledge, understanding and proficiency**	**Methods for demonstrating competence**	**Criteria for evaluating competence**
Control response to emergencies	Ability to make an initial assessment and provide an effective response to emergency situations in accordance with established emergency procedures *Leadership skills* Ability to lead and direct others in emergency situations, including the need: .1 to set an example during emergency situations .2 to focus decision making, given the need to act quickly in an emergency .3 to motivate, encourage and reassure passengers and other personnel *Stress handling* Ability to identify the development of symptoms of excessive personal stress and those of other members of the ship's emergency team Understanding that stress generated by emergency situations can affect the performance of individuals and their ability to act on instructions and follow procedures	Assessment of evidence obtained from approved training, practical demonstration and shipboard training and drills of emergency procedures	Procedures and actions are in accordance with established principles and plans for crisis management on board Objectives and strategy are appropriate to the nature of the emergency, take account of contingencies and make optimum use of available resources Actions of crew members contribute to maintaining order and control
Control passengers and other personnel during emergency situations	*Human behaviour and responses* Ability to control passengers and other personnel in emergency situations, including:	Assessment of evidence obtained from approved training, practical demonstration and shipboard training and drills of emergency procedures	Actions of crew members contribute to maintaining order and control

第 1 栏	第 2 栏	第 3 栏	第 4 栏
适任	**知识、理解和熟练**	**表明适任的方法**	**评价适任的标准**
控制对紧急情况的反应	按照既定的应急程序对紧急情况作出初步评估并作出有效反应的能力 *领导技能* 在紧急情况下领导和指导他人的能力,包括需要: .1 在紧急情况下作出榜样 .2 将精力放在决策工作上,因为在紧急情况下需要行动迅速 .3 激励、鼓励和安定乘客和其他人员 *紧张心理的处理* 觉察个人和船舶应急小组其他人员过度紧张心理症状发展的能力 理解紧急情况引起的紧张心理能影响各个人员的工作以及他们按指示行动和遵守程序的能力	评估从认可的培训、实际演示和应急程序的船上培训与演习中获取的证据	程序和行动符合既定的船上危机管理的原则和计划 目标和战略适合于紧急的性质,考虑到意外情况,最好地利用了现有资源 船员的行动有助于保持秩序和控制
紧急情况中对旅客和其他人员的控制	*人的行为和反应* 在紧急情况下控制旅客和其他人员的能力,包括:	评估从认可的培训、实际演示和紧急程序的船上培训与演习中获取的证据	船员的行动有助于保持秩序和控制

Column 1	Column 2	Column 3	Column 4
Competence	**Knowledge, understanding and proficiency**	**Methods for demonstrating competence**	**Criteria for evaluating competence**
Control passengers and other personnel during emergency situations (*continued*)	.1 awareness of the general reaction patterns of passengers and other personnel in emergency situations, including the possibility that: .1.1 generally it takes some time before people accept the fact that there is an emergency situation .1.2 some people may panic and not behave with a normal level of rationality, that their ability to comprehend may be impaired and they may not be as responsive to instructions as in non-emergency situations .2 awareness that passengers and other personnel may, *inter alia*: .2.1 start looking for relatives, friends and/or their belongings as a first reaction when something goes wrong .2.2 seek safety in their cabins or in other places on board where they think that they can escape danger .2.3 tend to move to the upper side when the ship is listing .3 appreciation of the possible problem of panic resulting from separating families		

第 1 栏	第 2 栏	第 3 栏	第 4 栏
适任	知识、理解和熟练	表明适任的方法	评价适任的标准
紧急情况中对旅客和其他人员的控制(续)	.1 了解在紧急情况下旅客和其他人员的一般反应方式，包括下列可能性： .1.1 一般人们要过一定时间才能接受有紧急情况的事实 .1.2 有些人可能惊慌失措，并且不以正常的理性行动；他们的理解能力可能受到损害，他们对指令的反应可能不如在非紧急情况时那样敏捷 .2 了解乘客和其他人员，除其他行动以外，可能： .2.1 在出现问题时的第一反应是开始寻找亲友和/或所有物 .2.2 躲避在其住舱或他们认为自己能避开危险的船上其他地点 .2.3 当船舶横倾时，往往移动到较高一侧 .3 了解家人失散可能会引起惊慌失措的问题		

Column 1	Column 2	Column 3	Column 4
Competence	**Knowledge, understanding and proficiency**	**Methods for demonstrating competence**	**Criteria for evaluating competence**
Establish and maintain effective communications	Ability to establish and maintain effective communications, including: .1 the importance of clear and concise instructions and reports .2 the need to encourage an exchange of information with, and feedback from, passengers and other personnel Ability to provide relevant information to passengers and other personnel during an emergency situation, to keep them apprised of the overall situation and to communicate any action required of them, taking into account: .1 the language or languages appropriate to the principal nationalities of passengers and other personnel carried on the particular route .2 the possible need to communicate during an emergency by some other means, such as by demonstration, or by hand signals or calling attention to the location of instructions, muster stations, life-saving devices or evacuation routes, when oral communication is impractical .3 the language in which emergency announcements may be broadcast during an emergency or drill to convey critical guidance to passengers and to facilitate crew members in assisting passengers	Assessment of evidence obtained from approved training, exercises and practical demonstration	Information from all available sources is obtained, evaluated and confirmed as quickly as possible and reviewed throughout the emergency Information given to individuals, emergency response teams and passengers is accurate, relevant and timely Information keeps passengers informed as to the nature of the emergency and the actions required of them

第 1 栏	第 2 栏	第 3 栏	第 4 栏
适任	**知识、理解和熟练**	**表明适任的方法**	**评价适任的标准**
建立和保持有效沟通	建立和保持有效沟通的能力，包括： .1 清楚简明的指示和报告的重要性 .2 鼓励与旅客和其他人员的信息交流，及鼓励他们提供反馈的必要性 在紧急情况下向旅客和其他人员提供有关信息，使其了解总的局势，通报要求他们采取的任何行动的能力，考虑到： .1 适合于特定航线上所载旅客和其他人员的主要国籍的一种或多种语言 .2 在紧急情况下，当采用口语交流不可行时，可能需要采用其他手段，如示范或手势或提示注意指示位置、集合地点、救生设备或逃生路线 .3 在紧急情况下或演习中，为向旅客传达关键指导和便于船员协助旅客，可能用于广播紧急通知的语言	评估从认可的培训、练习和实际演示中获取的证据	尽快地取得、评价和核实所有可用来源的信息，并在整个紧急情况期间进行审核 向个人、应急小组和旅客提供的信息是准确、相关和及时的 随时向旅客提供有关紧急情况性质以及旅客需要采取的行动的信息

CHAPTER VI

Standards regarding emergency, occupational safety, security, medical care and survival functions

Section A-VI/1

Mandatory minimum requirements for safety familiarization, basic training and instruction for all seafarers

Safety familiarization training

1 Before being assigned to shipboard duties, all persons employed or engaged on a seagoing ship, other than passengers, shall receive approved familiarization training in personal survival techniques or receive sufficient information and instruction, taking account of the guidance given in part B, to be able to:

.1 communicate with other persons on board on elementary safety matters and understand safety information symbols, signs and alarm signals;

.2 know what to do if:

.2.1 a person falls overboard,

.2.2 fire or smoke is detected, or

.2.3 the fire or abandon ship alarm is sounded;

.3 identify muster and embarkation stations and emergency escape routes;

.4 locate and don lifejackets;

.5 raise the alarm and have basic knowledge of the use of portable fire extinguishers;

.6 take immediate action upon encountering an accident or other medical emergency before seeking further medical assistance on board; and

.7 close and open the fire, weathertight and watertight doors fitted in the particular ship other than those for hull openings.

Basic training*

2 Seafarers employed or engaged in any capacity on board ship on the business of that ship as part of the ship's complement with designated safety or pollution-prevention duties in the operation of the ship shall, before being assigned to any shipboard duties:

.1 receive appropriate approved basic training or instruction in:

.1.1 personal survival techniques as set out in table A-VI/1-1,

.1.2 fire prevention and fire fighting as set out in table A-VI/1-2,

* The relevant IMO Model Course(s) may assist in the preparation of courses.

第 VI 章
关于应急、职业安全、保安、医护和求生职能的标准

第 A-VI/1 节
对所有海员的安全熟悉、基本培训和训练的强制性最低要求

安全熟悉培训

1　所有受雇或从事海船工作的人员，除旅客外，在其被指派上船任职之前，应接受认可的有关个人求生技能的熟悉培训或得到足够的资料和训练，结合考虑 B 部分给予的指导，以能够：

.1　就基本的安全事宜与船上其他人员交流，并了解安全信息的符号、标记和报警信号；

.2　了解在发生下列情况下应如何行事：

.2.1　人员落水，

.2.2　发现火情或烟雾，或

.2.3　发出火情警报或弃船警报；

.3　明确集合地点和登乘地点及紧急逃生路线；

.4　找到救生衣位置及穿着救生衣；

.5　启动报警装置并具有使用手提式灭火器的基本知识；

.6　在遇到事故或其他医疗紧急情况时，在得到船上进一步医疗救助前采取应急行动；以及

.7　关闭和开启特定船上装配的除船体开口以外的防火、风雨密和水密门。

基本培训①

2　受雇或受聘在船舶营运中担任船上任何职务的海员，作为船舶在编人员并被指派在船舶操作中负有安全或防止污染职责，在其任职之前，应：

.1　接受如下适当并认可的基本培训或训练：

.1.1　表 A-VI/1-1 所规定的个人求生技能，

.1.2　表 A-VI/1-2 所规定的防火和灭火，

① 相关 IMO 示范培训课程可有助于准备课程。

.1.3 elementary first aid as set out in table A-VI/1-3, and

.1.4 personal safety and social responsibilities as set out in table A-VI/1-4;

.2 be required to provide evidence of having achieved the required standard of competence to undertake the tasks, duties and responsibilities listed in column 1 of tables A-VI/1-1, A-VI/1-2, A-VI/1-3 and A-VI/1-4 through:

.2.1 demonstration of competence, in accordance with the methods and the criteria for evaluating competence tabulated in columns 3 and 4 of those tables, and

.2.2 examination or continuous assessment as part of an approved training programme in the subjects listed in column 2 of those tables.

3 Seafarers qualified in accordance with paragraph 2 in basic training shall be required, every five years, to provide evidence of having maintained the required standard of competence, to undertake the tasks, duties and responsibilities listed in column 1 of tables A-VI/1-1 and A-VI/1-2.

4 Parties may accept onboard training and experience for maintaining the required standard of competence in the following areas:

.1 personal survival techniques as set out in table A-VI/1-1:

.1.1 don a lifejacket;

.1.2 board a survival craft from the ship, while wearing a lifejacket;

.1.3 take initial actions on boarding a lifeboat to enhance chance of survival;

.1.4 stream a lifeboat drogue or sea-anchor;

.1.5 operate survival craft equipment; and

.1.6 operate location devices, including radio equipment;

.2 fire prevention and fire fighting as set out in table A-VI/1-2:

.2.1 use self-contained breathing apparatus; and

.2.2 effect a rescue in a smoke-filled space, using an approved smoke-generating device aboard, while wearing a breathing apparatus.

Exemptions

5 The Administration may, in respect of ships other than passenger ships of more than 500 gross tonnage engaged on international voyages and tankers, if it considers that a ship's size and the length or character of its voyage are such as to render the application of the full requirements of this section unreasonable or impracticable, exempt to that extent the seafarers on such a ship or class of ships from some of the requirements, bearing in mind the safety of people on board, the ship and property and the protection of the marine environment.

.1.3 表 A-VI/1-3 所规定的基本急救,以及

.1.4 表 A-VI/1-4 所规定的个人安全和社会责任;

.2 通过下列方法提供,已达到按表 A-VI/1-1 第 1 栏、表 A-VI/1-2 第 1 栏、表 A-VI/1-3 第 1 栏和表 A-VI/1-4 第 1 栏列出的所承担的任务、职责和责任所要求的适任标准的证据:

.2.1 按照上述各表第 3 栏和第 4 栏所列的评价适任的方法和标准,表明适任能力,以及

.2.2 考试或连续的评估,作为上述各表第 2 栏所列科目的认可的培训计划的组成部分。

3 按照基本培训第 2 段具有资格的海员应按要求每 5 年提供证据,表明其保持了所要求的适任标准,以承担表 A-VI/1-1 第 1 栏和表 A-VI/1-2 第 1 栏所列的任务、职责和责任。

4 在以下方面,缔约国可接受以船上培训和资历作为保持了所要求的适任标准:

.1 表 A-VI/1-1 中规定的个人求生技能:

.1.1 穿着救生衣;

.1.2 当穿着救生衣时,从船上登上救生艇筏;

.1.3 登艇时即采取初始行动以增加获救机会;

.1.4 抛放救生艇流锚或海锚;

.1.5 操作救生艇筏设备;以及

.1.6 操作定位仪器,包括无线电设备;

.2 表 A-VI/1-2 规定的防火和灭火:

.2.1 使用自给式呼吸器;以及

.2.2 佩戴呼吸器,使用认可的船上烟雾发生装置,在充满烟雾的处所中施行救助。

免除

5 对于除液货船和 500 总吨以上从事国际航行的客船以外的船舶,主管机关在考虑到船舶尺度和航程长短或性质,认为执行本节的全部要求不尽合理或不可行时,在充分考虑到船上人员、船舶和财产安全及保护海洋环境的情况下,可对该船或该类船舶上的海员免除部分要求。

Table A-VI/1-1

Specification of minimum standard of competence in personal survival techniques

Column 1	Column 2	Column 3	Column 4
Competence	**Knowledge, understanding and proficiency**	**Methods for demonstrating competence**	**Criteria for evaluating competence**
Survive at sea in the event of ship abandonment	Types of emergency situations which may occur, such as collision, fire, foundering Types of life-saving appliances normally carried on ships Equipment in survival craft Location of personal life-saving appliances Principles concerning survival, including: .1 value of training and drills .2 personal protective clothing and equipment .3 need to be ready for any emergency .4 actions to be taken when called to survival craft stations .5 actions to be taken when required to abandon ship .6 actions to be taken when in the water .7 actions to be taken when aboard a survival craft .8 main dangers to survivors	Assessment of evidence obtained from approved instruction or during attendance at an approved course or approved in-service experience and examination, including practical demonstration of competence to: .1 don a lifejacket .2 don and use an immersion suit .3 safely jump from a height into the water .4 right an inverted liferaft while wearing a lifejacket .5 swim while wearing a lifejacket .6 keep afloat without a lifejacket .7 board a survival craft from the ship and water while wearing a lifejacket .8 take initial actions on boarding survival craft to enhance chance of survival .9 stream a drogue or sea-anchor .10 operate survival craft equipment .11 operate location devices, including radio equipment	Action taken on identifying muster signals is appropriate to the indicated emergency and complies with established procedures The timing and sequence of individual actions are appropriate to the prevailing circumstance and conditions and minimize potential dangers and threats to survival Method of boarding survival craft is appropriate and avoids dangers to other survivors Initial actions after leaving the ship and procedures and actions in water minimize threats to survival

表 A-VI/1-1

个人求生技能的最低适任标准

第 1 栏	第 2 栏	第 3 栏	第 4 栏
适任	**知识、理解和熟练**	**表明适任的方法**	**评价适任的标准**
弃船情况下的海上求生	可能发生的紧急情况的类型,如碰撞、失火、沉没 船舶通常携带的救生设备的类型 救生艇筏内的设备 个人救生设备的位置 有关求生的原则,包括: .1 培训和演习的价值 .2 个人防护服及器具 .3 为任何紧急情况做好准备的必要性 .4 被召至救生艇筏位置时应采取的行动 .5 弃船时应采取的行动 .6 在水中时应采取的行动 .7 在救生艇筏上应采取的行动 .8 求生者的主要危险	评估从认可的训练或参加认可的课程或认可的工作经历中获取的证据和考试,包括实际演示下列适任能力: .1 穿着救生衣 .2 穿着和使用救生服 .3 安全地从高处跳入水中 .4 穿着救生衣扶正倾覆救生筏 .5 穿着救生衣游泳 .6 未穿着救生衣保持漂浮 .7 穿着救生衣从船上和水中登上救生艇筏 .8 上救生艇筏后为增加获救机会采取的初始行动 .9 抛放流锚或海锚 .10 操作救生艇筏上的设备 .11 操作定位仪器,包括无线电设备	识别紧急信号后的行动适合其所示的紧急情况并符合既定的应急程序 单个行动的时机和顺序适合于当时的环境和情况,并把潜在之危险和对求生者的威胁减小到最小程度 登救生艇筏的方法合适并避免危及其他求生者 离船后的初始行动和在水中的程序和行动把对求生者的威胁减小到最低程度

Table A-VI/1-2

Specification of minimum standard of competence in fire prevention and fire fighting

Column 1	Column 2	Column 3	Column 4
Competence	**Knowledge, understanding and proficiency**	**Methods for demonstrating competence**	**Criteria for evaluating competence**
Minimize the risk of fire and maintain a state of readiness to respond to emergency situations involving fire	Shipboard fire-fighting organization Location of fire-fighting appliances and emergency escape routes The elements of fire and explosion (the fire triangle) Types and sources of ignition Flammable materials, fire hazards and spread of fire The need for constant vigilance Actions to be taken on board ship Fire and smoke detection and automatic alarm systems Classification of fire and applicable extinguishing agents	Assessment of evidence obtained from approved instruction or attendance at an approved course	Initial actions on becoming aware of an emergency conform with accepted practices and procedures Action taken on identifying muster signals is appropriate to the indicated emergency and complies with established procedures
Fight and extinguish fires	Fire-fighting equipment and its location on board Instruction in: .1 fixed installations .2 fire-fighter's outfits .3 personal equipment .4 fire-fighting appliances and equipment .5 fire-fighting methods .6 fire-fighting agents .7 fire-fighting procedures	Assessment of evidence obtained from approved instruction or during attendance at an approved course, including practical demonstration in spaces which provide truly realistic training conditions (e.g., simulated shipboard conditions) and, whenever possible and practical, in darkness, of the ability to: .1 use various types of portable fire extinguishers .2 use self-contained breathing apparatus	Clothing and equipment are appropriate to the nature of the fire-fighting operations The timing and sequence of individual actions are appropriate to the prevailing circumstances and conditions Extinguishment of fire is achieved using appropriate procedures, techniques and fire-fighting agents Breathing apparatus procedures and techniques comply with accepted practices and procedures

表 A-VI/1-2
防火和灭火的最低适任标准

第 1 栏	第 2 栏	第 3 栏	第 4 栏
适任	**知识、理解和熟练**	**表明适任的方法**	**评价适任的标准**
最大限度地减少火灾危险并保持应对包括火灾在内的紧急局面的戒备状态	船上灭火组织 灭火器具的位置和应急逃生路线 火灾和爆炸的要素(燃烧三角形) 着火的种类和原因 可燃物质、火灾危害和火灾蔓延 日常戒备的必要性 船上应采取的措施 烟火检测系统和自动报警系统 火灾分类及可使用的灭火剂	评估从认可的训练中或参加认可的课程中获取的证据	发觉紧急情况后的初始行动符合认可的做法和程序 识别紧急集合信号后的行动适合其所示的紧急情况并符合既定的应急程序
扑灭火灾	船舶消防设备及其在船上的位置 训练: .1 固定灭火装置 .2 消防员装备 .3 个人设备 .4 消防器具和设备 .5 灭火方法 .6 灭火剂 .7 灭火程序	评估从认可的训练或参加认可的课程中获取的证据,包括在提供真实训练条件(如模拟船上条件)的地方,如可能或可行时在黑暗中实际演示下列能力: .1 使用各种类型手提式灭火器 .2 使用自给式呼吸装置	着装和装备适合灭火作业的性质 单个行动的时机和次序适合当时环境和条件 运用合适的程序、技术和灭火剂扑灭火灾 使用呼吸装置的步骤和技能符合公认的做法和程序

Column 1	**Column 2**	**Column 3**	**Column 4**
Competence	**Knowledge, understanding and proficiency**	**Methods for demonstrating competence**	**Criteria for evaluating competence**
Fight and extinguish fires (*continued*)	.8 use of breathing apparatus for fighting fires and effecting rescues	.3 extinguish smaller fires, e.g., electrical fires, oil fires, propane fires .4 extinguish extensive fires with water, using jet and spray nozzles .5 extinguish fires with foam, powder or any other suitable chemical agent .6 enter and pass through, with lifeline but without breathing apparatus, a compartment into which high-expansion foam has been injected .7 fight fire in smoke-filled enclosed spaces wearing self-contained breathing apparatus .8 extinguish fire with water fog or any other suitable fire-fighting agent in an accommodation room or simulated engine-room with fire and heavy smoke .9 extinguish oil fire with fog applicator and spray nozzles, dry chemical powder or foam applicators .10 effect a rescue in a smoke-filled space wearing breathing apparatus	

第 1 栏	第 2 栏	第 3 栏	第 4 栏
适任	知识、理解和熟练	表明适任的方法	评价适任的标准
扑灭火灾(续)	.8 灭火和实施营救时呼吸装置的使用	.3 扑灭小火,如:电气火、油火、丙烷火 .4 使用喷水枪及散射喷枪扑灭较大火灾 .5 使用泡沫、干粉或其他合适的化学剂灭火 .6 使用救生索,但不戴呼吸装置进入或通过已喷注了高膨胀泡沫的舱室 .7 佩戴自给式呼吸装置在充满烟雾的封闭处所灭火 .8 使用水雾或其他合适的灭火剂扑灭有火与浓烟的居住舱室或模拟机舱的火灾 .9 使用水雾喷头和散射喷枪、化学干粉或泡沫喷头扑救油火 .10 佩戴呼吸装置在充满烟雾的舱室实施营救	

Table A-VI/1-3

Specification of minimum standard of competence in elementary first aid

Column 1	Column 2	Column 3	Column 4
Competence	**Knowledge, understanding and proficiency**	**Methods for demonstrating competence**	**Criteria for evaluating competence**
Take immediate action upon encountering an accident or other medical emergency	Assessment of needs of casualties and threats to own safety Appreciation of body structure and functions Understanding of immediate measures to be taken in cases of emergency, including the ability to: .1 position casualty .2 apply resuscitation techniques .3 control bleeding .4 apply appropriate measures of basic shock management .5 apply appropriate measures in event of burns and scalds, including accidents caused by electric current .6 rescue and transport a casualty .7 improvise bandages and use materials in the emergency kit	Assessment of evidence obtained from approved instruction or during attendance at an approved course	The manner and timing of raising the alarm is appropriate to the circumstances of the accident or medical emergency The identification of probable cause, nature and extent of injuries is prompt and complete and the priority and sequence of actions is proportional to any potential threat to life Risk of further harm to self and casualty is minimized at all times

表 A-VI/1-3
基本急救的最低适任标准

第1栏	第2栏	第3栏	第4栏
适任	知识、理解和熟练	表明适任的方法	评价适任的标准
遇到事故或其他急症情况时立即采取应急行动	评估伤员的需要和对自身安全的威胁 了解人体构造和功能 理解在紧急情况下应采取的应急措施,包括下列能力: .1 安置伤员 .2 进行人工呼吸的技术 .3 止血 .4 采取基本的治疗休克的适当措施 .5 采取适当措施,治疗烧伤和烫伤,包括电击伤 .6 抢救运送伤员 .7 简易包扎和使用急救箱内的物品	评估从认可的训练或参加认可的课程中获取的证据	发出警报的方式和时间适合事故情况或急症情况 对受伤的可能原因、性质和范围的认定迅速充分,急救措施的先后顺序与任何对生命潜在的威胁相适应 始终把对自身和伤员的进一步危害的危险减小到最低限度

Table A-VI/1-4

Specification of minimum standard of competence in personal safety and social responsibilities

Column 1	Column 2	Column 3	Column 4
Competence	**Knowledge, understanding and proficiency**	**Methods for demonstrating competence**	**Criteria for evaluating competence**
Comply with emergency procedures	Types of emergency which may occur, such as collision, fire, foundering Knowledge of shipboard contingency plans for response to emergencies Emergency signals and specific duties allocated to crew members in the muster list; muster stations; correct use of personal safety equipment Action to take on discovering potential emergency, including fire, collision, foundering and ingress of water into the ship Action to take on hearing emergency alarm signals Value of training and drills Knowledge of escape routes and internal communication and alarm systems	Assessment of evidence obtained from approved instruction or during attendance at an approved course	Initial action on becoming aware of an emergency conforms to established emergency response procedures Information given on raising alarm is prompt, accurate, complete and clear
Take precautions to prevent pollution of the marine environment	Basic knowledge of the impact of shipping on the marine environment and the effects of operational or accidental pollution on it Basic environmental protection procedures Basic knowledge of complexity and diversity of the marine environment	Assessment of evidence obtained from approved instruction or during attendance at an approved course	Organizational procedures designed to safeguard the marine environment are observed at all times

表 A-VI/1-4

个人安全和社会责任的最低适任标准

第 1 栏	第 2 栏	第 3 栏	第 4 栏
适任	**知识、理解和熟练**	**表明适任的方法**	**评价适任的标准**
遵循应急程序	可能发生的紧急情况的类型,如碰撞、火灾、沉没 船舶各种应急计划的知识 应急部署表中的紧急信号和分配给船员的具体职责;集合位置;正确使用个人安全设备 在发现潜在紧急情况时采取的行动,包括火灾、碰撞、沉没和船舶进水 听到紧急警报信号时采取的行动 培训及演习的价值 逃生路线和船上内部通信与报警系统的知识	评估从认可的训练或参加认可的课程中获取的证据	发觉紧急情况后的最初行动符合既定的应急反应程序 报警信息迅速准确、完整、清晰
采取防止海洋环境污染的措施	航运对海洋环境的影响以及操作性或事故性污染对海洋环境危害的基本知识 环境保护的基本程序 海洋环境多样性和复杂性的基本知识	评估从认可的训练或参加认可的课程中获取的证据	始终遵守为保护海洋环境而制定的组织程序

Column 1	Column 2	Column 3	Column 4
Competence	**Knowledge, understanding and proficiency**	**Methods for demonstrating competence**	**Criteria for evaluating competence**
Observe safe working practices	Importance of adhering to safe working practices at all times Safety and protective devices available to protect against potential hazards aboard ship Precautions to be taken prior to entering enclosed spaces Familiarization with international measures concerning accident prevention and occupational health*	Assessment of evidence obtained from approved instruction or during attendance at an approved course	Safe working practices are observed and appropriate safety and protective equipment is correctly used at all times
Contribute to effective communications on board ship	Understand the principles of, and barriers to, effective communication between individuals and teams within the ship Ability to establish and maintain effective communications	Assessment of evidence obtained from approved instruction or during attendance at an approved course	Communications are clear and effective at all times
Contribute to effective human relationships on board ship	Importance of maintaining good human and working relationships aboard ship Basic teamworking principles and practice, including conflict resolution Social responsibilities; employment conditions; individual rights and obligations; dangers of drug and alcohol abuse	Assessment of evidence obtained from approved instruction or during attendance at an approved course	Expected standards of work and behaviour are observed at all times

* The ILO Code of Practice on "Accident Prevention on Board Ship at Sea and in Port" may be of assistance in the preparation of courses.

第 1 栏	第 2 栏	第 3 栏	第 4 栏
适任	知识、理解和熟练	表明适任的方法	评价适任的标准
遵守安全作业方法	任何时候都遵守安全工作做法的重要性 适用于船舶上防止潜在危害的安全和防护装置 进入封闭处所前采取的预防措施 熟悉防止事故和职业健康的国际措施①	评估从认可的训练或参加认可的课程中获取的证据	始终遵守安全作业方法并在任何时候都使用合适的安全和防护设备
有助于船上有效的交流	对船上个人和团队之间有效交流的原则和障碍的理解 建立和保持有效交流的能力	评估从认可的训练或参加认可的课程中获取的证据	在任何时候交流都清楚、有效
有助于船上有效的人际关系	保持船上良好的人际关系和工作关系的重要性 团队工作的基本原则和做法，包括冲突的解决 社会责任；雇用条件；个人权利及义务；滥用药物和酗酒的危害	评估从认可的训练或参加认可的课程中获取的证据	始终遵守所要求的工作及行为准则

① ILO《防止船舶在海上和港内发生事故的操作规则》中的规定可有助于准备课程。

Column 1	Column 2	Column 3	Column 4
Competence	**Knowledge, understanding and proficiency**	**Methods for demonstrating competence**	**Criteria for evaluating competence**
Understand and take necessary actions to control fatigue	Importance of obtaining the necessary rest Effects of sleep, schedules, and the circadian rhythm on fatigue Effects of physical stressors on seafarers Effects of environmental stressors in and outside the ship and their impact on seafarers Effects of schedule changes on seafarer fatigue	Assessment of evidence obtained from approved instruction or during attendance at an approved course	Fatigue management practices are observed and appropriate actions are used at all times

第 1 栏	第 2 栏	第 3 栏	第 4 栏
适任	知识、理解和熟练	表明适任的方法	评价适任的标准
理解并采取必要的措施控制疲劳	得到必要休息的重要性 睡眠、作息时间与生理节律对疲劳的影响 身体紧张刺激因素对海员的影响 船舶内外环境的紧张刺激因素对海员的影响及其后果 作息时间的改变对海员疲劳的影响	评估从认可的训练或参加的认可的课程获取的证据	始终遵循疲劳管理的良好做法并采取适当的措施

Section A-VI/2

Mandatory minimum requirements for the issue of certificates of proficiency in survival craft, rescue boats and fast rescue boats

PROFICIENCY IN SURVIVAL CRAFT AND RESCUE BOATS OTHER THAN FAST RESCUE BOATS

Standard of competence

1 Every candidate for a certificate of proficiency in survival craft and rescue boats other than fast rescue boats shall be required to demonstrate competence to undertake the tasks, duties and responsibilities listed in column 1 of table A-VI/2-1.

2 The level of knowledge of the subjects listed in column 2 of table A-VI/2-1 shall be sufficient to enable the candidate to launch and take charge of a survival craft or rescue boat in emergency situations*.

3 Training and experience to achieve the necessary level of theoretical knowledge, understanding and proficiency shall take account of the guidance given in part B of this Code.

4 Every candidate for certification shall be required to provide evidence of having achieved the required standard of competence through:

.1 demonstration of competence to undertake the tasks, duties and responsibilities listed in column 1 of table A-VI/2-1, in accordance with the methods for demonstrating competence and the criteria for evaluating competence tabulated in columns 3 and 4 of that table; and

.2 examination or continuous assessment as part of an approved training programme covering the material set out in column 2 of table A-VI/2-1.

5 Seafarers qualified in accordance with paragraph 4 in survival craft and rescue boats other than fast rescue boats shall be required, every five years, to provide evidence of having maintained the required standards of competence to undertake the tasks, duties and responsibilities listed in column 1 of table A-VI/2-1.

6 Parties may accept onboard training and experience for maintaining the required standard of competence of table A-VI/2-1 in the following areas:

.1 take charge of a survival craft or rescue boat during and after launch:

.1.1 interpret the markings on survival craft as to the number of persons they are intended to carry;

.1.2 give correct commands for launching and boarding survival craft, clearing the ship and handling and disembarking persons from survival craft;

.1.3 prepare and safely launch survival craft and clear the ship's side quickly; and

.1.4 safely recover survival craft and rescue boats;

* The relevant IMO Model Course(s) may be of assistance in the preparation of courses.

第 A-VI/2 节

对签发救生艇筏、救助艇和快速救助艇培训合格证书的强制性最低要求

熟练操作救生艇筏和除快速救助艇以外的救助艇

适任标准

1 每个申请救生艇筏和除快速救助艇以外的救助艇培训合格证书的申请人应表明承担表 A-VI/2-1 第 1 栏所列的任务、职责和责任的适任能力。

2 表 A-VI/2-1 第 2 栏所列科目的知识水平,应足以能使证书申请人在各种紧急情况下释放并负责救生艇筏或救助艇①。

3 为获取所需水平的理论知识、理解和熟练的培训和经历,应考虑本规则 B 部分给予的指导。

4 每个证书申请人应通过下列方法提供其已达到所要求的适任标准的证据:

.1 按表 A-VI/2-1 第 3 栏和第 4 栏所列的表明适任的方法和评价适任的标准,表明承担该表第 1 栏中所列的任务、职责和责任的适任能力;和

.2 考试或连续的评估,作为覆盖表 A-VI/2-1 第 2 栏所规定材料的认可的培训计划的组成部分。

5 根据救生艇筏和除快速救助艇以外的救助艇第 4 段具有资格的海员应按要求每 5 年提供证据,表明其保持了所要求的适任标准,以承担表 A-VI/2-1 第 1 栏所列的任务、职责和责任。

6 在以下方面,缔约国可接受以船上培训和资历作为保持了表 A-VI/2-1 所要求的适任标准:

.1 负责释放中及释放后的救生艇筏或救助艇:

.1.1 解释救生艇筏上用于表明乘员人数的标志,

.1.2 正确指挥救生艇筏的释放、登艇、驶离船舶、操作和人员下艇(筏),

.1.3 救生艇筏释放准备和安全下水,迅速驶离船舶,并且

.1.4 安全地回收救生艇筏和救助艇;

① 相关 IMO 示范培训课程可有助于准备课程。

.2 manage survivors and survival craft after abandoning ship:

.2.1 row and steer a boat and steer by compass;

.2.2 use individual items of equipment of survival crafts, except for pyrotechnics; and

.2.3 rig devices to aid location;

.3 use locating devices, including communication and signalling apparatus:

.3.1 use of portable radio equipment for survival craft; and

.4 apply first aid to survivors.

PROFICIENCY IN FAST RESCUE BOATS

Standard of competence

7 Every candidate for a certificate of proficiency in fast rescue boats shall be required to demonstrate competence to undertake the tasks, duties and responsibilities listed in column 1 of table A-VI/2-2.

8 The level of knowledge of the subjects listed in column 2 of table A-VI/2-2 shall be sufficient to enable the candidate to launch and take charge of a fast rescue boat in emergency situations*.

9 Training and experience to achieve the necessary level of theoretical knowledge, understanding and proficiency shall take account of the guidance given in part B of this Code.

10 Every candidate for certification shall be required to provide evidence of having achieved the required standard of competence through:

.1 demonstration of competence to undertake the tasks, duties and responsibilities listed in column 1 of table A-VI/2-2, in accordance with the methods for demonstrating competence and the criteria for evaluating competence tabulated in columns 3 and 4 of that table; and

.2 examination or continuous assessment as part of an approved training programme covering the material set out in column 2 of table A-VI/2-2.

11 Seafarers qualified in accordance with paragraph 10 in fast rescue boats shall be required, every five years, to provide evidence of having maintained the required standards of competence to undertake the tasks, duties and responsibilities listed in column 1 of table A-VI/2-2.

* The relevant IMO Model Course(s) may be of assistance in the preparation of courses.

.2 弃船后对求生人员和救生艇筏的管理:

.2.1 划桨和驾艇以及运用罗经驾艇,

.2.2 使用救生艇筏各项设备,烟火除外,并且

.2.3 安设装置以助定位;

.3 使用定位设备,包括通信和信号设备:

.3.1 使用救生艇筏的便携式无线电设备;并且

.4 对求生人员进行急救。

熟练操作快速救助艇

适任标准

7 每个申请快速救助艇培训合格证书的申请人应表明其承担表 A-VI/2-2 第1栏所列的任务、职责和责任的适任能力。

8 表 A-VI/2-2 第2栏所列科目的知识水平,应足以能使证书申请人在各种紧急情况下释放并负责快速救助艇①。

9 为获取所需水平的理论知识、理解和熟练的培训和经验,应考虑本规则 B 部分给予的指导。

10 每个证书申请人应通过下列方法提供其已达到所要求的适任标准的证据:

.1 按表 A-VI/2-2 第3栏和第4栏中所列的表明适任的方法和评价适任的标准,表明承担该表第1栏所列的任务、职责和责任的适任能力;和

.2 考试或连续的评估,作为覆盖表 A-VI/2-2 第2栏所规定材料的认可的培训计划的组成部分。

11 根据快速救助艇第10段具有资格的海员应按要求每5年提供证据,表明其保持了所要求的适任标准,以承担表 A-VI/2-2 第1栏所列的任务、职责和责任。

① 相关 IMO 示范培训课程可有助于准备课程。

12 Parties may accept onboard training and experience for maintaining the required standard of competence of table A-VI/2-2, in the following areas:

.1 Take charge of a fast rescue boat during and after launch:

.1.1 control safe launching and recovery of a fast rescue boat;

.1.2 handle a fast rescue boat in prevailing weather and sea conditions;

.1.3 use communications and signalling equipment between the fast rescue boat and a helicopter and a ship;

.1.4 use the emergency equipment carried; and

.1.5 carry out search patterns, taking account of environmental factors.

12　在以下方面,缔约国可接受以船上培训和资历作为保持了表 A-VI/2-2 所要求的适任标准:

.1　负责释放中和释放后的快速救助艇:

.1.1　控制快速救助艇的安全释放和回收;

.1.2　在当时的天气和海况下操纵快速救助艇;

.1.3　在快速救助艇与直升机和船舶之间使用通信和信号设备;

.1.4　使用所携带的应急设备;并且

.1.5　结合环境因素实施搜救方式。

Table A-VI/2-1

Specification of the minimum standard of competence in survival craft and rescue boats other than fast rescue boats

Column 1	Column 2	Column 3	Column 4
Competence	**Knowledge, understanding and proficiency**	**Methods for demonstrating competence**	**Criteria for evaluating competence**
Take charge of a survival craft or rescue boat during and after launch	Construction and outfit of survival craft and rescue boats and individual items of their equipment Particular characteristics and facilities of survival craft and rescue boats Various types of device used for launching survival craft and rescue boats Methods of launching survival craft into a rough sea Methods of recovering survival craft Action to be taken after leaving the ship Methods of launching and recovering rescue boats in a rough sea Dangers associated with use of on-load release devices Knowledge of maintenance procedures	Assessment of evidence obtained from practical demonstration of ability to: .1 right an inverted liferaft while wearing a lifejacket .2 interpret the markings on survival craft as to the number of persons they are intended to carry .3 give correct commands for launching and boarding survival craft, clearing the ship and handling and disembarking persons from survival craft .4 prepare and safely launch survival craft and clear the ship's side quickly and operate off-load and on-load release devices .5 safely recover survival craft and rescue boats, including the proper resetting of both off-load and on-load release devices using: inflatable liferaft and open or enclosed lifeboat with inboard engine or approved simulator training, where appropriate	Preparation, boarding and launching of survival craft are within equipment limitations and enable survival craft to clear the ship safely Initial actions on leaving the ship minimize threat to survival Recovery of survival craft and rescue boats is within equipment limitations Equipment is operated in accordance with manufacturers' instructions for release and resetting
Operate a survival craft engine	Methods of starting and operating a survival craft engine and its accessories together with the use of the fire extinguisher provided	Assessment of evidence obtained from practical demonstration of ability to start and operate an inboard engine fitted in an open or enclosed lifeboat	Propulsion is available and maintained as required for manoeuvring

表 A-VI/2-1

救生艇筏和除快速救助艇以外的救助艇的最低适任标准

第 1 栏	第 2 栏	第 3 栏	第 4 栏
适任	**知识、理解和熟练**	**表明适任的方法**	**评价适任的标准**
在释放期间和之后负责救生艇筏或救助艇	救生艇筏和救助艇的结构和属具及其各项设备 救生艇筏和救助艇的特性和设施 救生艇筏和救助艇的各种释放装置 在恶劣海况下释放救生艇筏的方法 回收救生艇筏的方法 离船后采取的行动 在恶劣海况下释放和回收救助艇的方法 与使用承载释放装置有关的危险 维护保养程序的知识	评估从实际演示下列能力中获取的证据: .1 穿着救生衣扶正倾覆的救生筏 .2 解释救生艇筏用于表明乘载人员数目的标志 .3 正确指挥救生艇筏的释放和登艇、驶离船舶、操纵及人员下艇(筏) .4 救生艇筏释放准备和安全下水,迅速驶离船舶,并操作空载和承载释放装置 .5 安全回收救生艇筏和救助艇,包括对空载和承载释放装置的正确复位 使用气胀式救生筏和带内装机器的开敞式或封闭式救生艇或认可的模拟器培训,如适用	在设备限定的条件下完成释放艇筏的准备、人员上艇和释放艇筏,并能使艇筏安全离船 离船时所采取的最初行动能最大限度地减少对求生者的威胁 在设备限定的条件下完成救生艇筏和救助艇的回收 按照制造商关于释放和复位的使用说明操作设备
操作救生艇的机器	启动、操作救生艇机器及其附属机具和使用所备灭火器的方法	评估从实际演示启动和操作开敞式或封闭式救生艇的机器的能力中获取的证据	按操纵要求提供并保持推进动力

Column 1	Column 2	Column 3	Column 4
Competence	**Knowledge, understanding and proficiency**	**Methods for demonstrating competence**	**Criteria for evaluating competence**
Manage survivors and survival craft after abandoning ship	Handling survival craft in rough weather Use of painter, sea-anchor and all other equipment Apportionment of food and water in survival craft Action taken to maximize detectability and location of survival craft Method of helicopter rescue Effects of hypothermia and its prevention; use of protective covers and garments, including immersion suits and thermal protective aids Use of rescue boats and motor lifeboats for marshalling liferafts and rescue of survivors and persons in the sea Beaching survival craft	Assessment of evidence obtained from practical demonstration of ability to: .1 row and steer a boat and steer by compass .2 use individual items of equipment of survival craft .3 rig devices to aid location	Survival management is appropriate to prevailing circumstances and conditions
Use locating devices, including communication and signalling apparatus and pyrotechnics	Radio life-saving appliances carried in survival craft, including satellite EPIRBs and SARTs Pyrotechnic distress signals	Assessment of evidence obtained from practical demonstration of ability to: .1 use portable radio equipment for survival craft .2 use signalling equipment, including pyrotechnics	Use and choice of communication and signalling apparatus is appropriate to prevailing circumstances and conditions

第 1 栏	第 2 栏	第 3 栏	第 4 栏
适任	知识、理解和熟练	表明适任的方法	评价适任的标准
弃船后对求生者和救生艇筏管理	在恶劣天气下操纵救生艇筏 使用艇首缆、海锚及所有其他设备 救生艇筏上食物和淡水的分配 为最大可能地使救生艇筏被发现和定位应采取的行动 直升机营救的方法 低温效应及其预防;包括救生服和保温器具在内的防护遮盖物和服装的使用 使用救助艇和机动救生艇集结救生筏,并营救求生者和落水者 救生艇筏抢滩	评估从实际演示下列能力中获取的证据: .1 划桨和驾艇以及运用罗经驾艇 .2 使用救生艇筏的各项设备 .3 安设装置以助定位	求生管理适于当时的环境和条件
使用定位设备,包括通信设备、信号设备及烟火信号	救生艇筏上的无线电救生设备,包括卫星应急无线电示位标(EPIRBs)和搜救应答器(SARTs) 烟火遇险信号	评估从实际演示下列能力中获取的证据: .1 使用救生艇筏的便携式无线电设备 .2 使用包括烟火信号在内的信号设备	对通信和信号设备的使用和选择适于当时环境和条件

Column 1	Column 2	Column 3	Column 4
Competence	**Knowledge, understanding and proficiency**	**Methods for demonstrating competence**	**Criteria for evaluating competence**
Apply first aid to survivors	Use of the first-aid kit and resuscitation techniques Management of injured persons, including control of bleeding and shock	Assessment of evidence obtained from practical demonstration of ability to deal with injured persons both during and after abandonment, using first-aid kit and resuscitation techniques	Identification of the probable cause, nature and extent of injuries or condition is prompt and accurate Priority and sequence of treatment minimizes any threat to life

第 1 栏	第 2 栏	第 3 栏	第 4 栏
适任	知识、理解和熟练	表明适任的方法	评价适任的标准
对求生者进行急救	使用急救箱和复苏技能 伤员处置,包括止血和控制休克	评估从实际演示在弃船时或弃船后,使用急救箱及复苏技能抢救伤员的能力中获取的证据	对伤势的可能原因、性质和受伤程度能迅速和准确的认定 治疗的先后次序能最大限度地减少对人命的威胁

Table A-VI/2-2

Specification of the minimum standard of competence in fast rescue boats

Column 1	Column 2	Column 3	Column 4
Competence	**Knowledge, understanding and proficiency**	**Methods for demonstrating competence**	**Criteria for evaluating competence**
Understand the construction, maintenance, repair and outfitting of fast rescue boats	Construction and outfitting of fast rescue boats and individual items of their equipment Knowledge of the maintenance and emergency repairs of fast rescue boats and the normal inflation and deflation of buoyancy compartments of inflated fast rescue boats	Assessment of evidence obtained from practical instruction	The method of carrying out routine maintenance and emergency repairs Identify components and required equipment for fast rescue boats
Take charge of the launching equipment and appliance as commonly fitted, during launching and recovery	Assessment of the readiness of launching equipment and launching appliance of fast rescue boats for immediate launching and operation Understand the operation and limitations of the winch, brakes, falls, painters, motion-compensation and other equipment as commonly fitted Safety precautions during launching and recovery of a fast rescue boat Launching and recovery of a fast rescue boat in prevailing and adverse weather and sea conditions	Assessment of evidence obtained from practical demonstration of ability to control safe launching and recovery of a fast rescue boat, with equipment as fitted	Ability to prepare and take charge of the launching equipment and appliance during launching and recovery of a fast rescue boat
Take charge of a fast rescue boat as commonly fitted, during launching and recovery	Assessment of the readiness of fast rescue boats and related equipment for immediate launching and operation Safety precautions during launching and recovery of a fast rescue boat Launching and recovery of a fast rescue boat in prevailing and adverse weather and sea conditions	Assessment of evidence obtained from practical demonstration of ability to conduct safe launching and recovery of a fast rescue boat, with equipment as fitted	Ability to take charge of a fast rescue boat during launching and recovery

表 A-VI/2-2
快速救助艇的最低适任标准

第 1 栏	第 2 栏	第 3 栏	第 4 栏
适任	**知识、理解和熟练**	**表明适任的方法**	**评价适任的标准**
理解快速救助艇的构造、维护、修理和属具	快速救助艇的构造和属具及其各项设备 快速救助艇的维护和紧急修理、气胀式快速救助艇气室的正常充气和放气的知识	评估从实际训练中获取的证据	采取日常维护和紧急修理的的方法 识别快速救助艇的部件及所需的设备
负责在释放和回收期间通常装备的释放设备和设施	评估快速救助艇的释放设备和释放装置为立即释放和操作所做的准备 理解绞车、刹车、吊艇索、艇首缆、运动补偿和其他通常所配设备的操作及其局限性 在释放和回收快速救助艇期间的安全预防措施 在通常和恶劣的天气和海况条件下释放和回收快速救助艇	评估从利用所配设备控制快速救助艇安全释放和回收的能力实际演示中获取的证据	在释放和回收快速救助艇期间准备和负责释放设备和设施的能力
负责在释放和回收期间通常装备的快速救助艇	评估释放设备和释放装置为立即释放和操作快速救助艇所做的准备程度 释放和回收快速救助艇期间的安全预防措施 在通常和恶劣的天气和海况条件下释放和回收快速救助艇	评估从利用所配设备执行快速救助艇安全释放和回收行动的能力实际演示中获取的证据	在释放和回收期间负责快速救助艇的能力

Column 1	Column 2	Column 3	Column 4
Competence	**Knowledge, understanding and proficiency**	**Methods for demonstrating competence**	**Criteria for evaluating competence**
Take charge of a fast rescue boat after launching	Particular characteristics, facilities and limitations of fast rescue boats Procedures for the righting of a capsized fast rescue boat How to handle a fast rescue boat in prevailing and adverse weather and sea conditions Navigational and safety equipment available in a fast rescue boat Search patterns and environmental factors affecting their execution	Assessment of evidence obtained from practical demonstration of ability to: .1 right a capsized fast rescue boat .2 handle a fast rescue boat in prevailing weather and sea conditions .3 swim in special equipment .4 use communications and signalling equipment between the fast rescue boat and a helicopter and a ship .5 use the emergency equipment carried .6 recover a casualty from the water and transfer a casualty to a rescue helicopter or to a ship or to a place of safety .7 carry out search patterns, taking account of environmental factors	Demonstration of operation of fast rescue boats within equipment limitations in prevailing weather conditions
Operate a fast rescue boat engine	Methods of starting and operating a fast rescue boat engine and its accessories	Assessment of evidence obtained from practical demonstration of ability to start and operate a fast rescue boat engine	Engine is started and operated as required for manoeuvring

第 1 栏	第 2 栏	第 3 栏	第 4 栏
适任	**知识、理解和熟练**	**表明适任的方法**	**评价适任的标准**
在释放后负责快速救助艇	快速救助艇的特性、设施及其局限性 扶正倾覆的快速救助艇的程序 在通常和恶劣的天气和海况条件下如何操纵快速救助艇 快速救助艇内可用的助航仪器和安全设备 搜救方式及影响其实施的环境因素	评估从实际演示下列能力中获得的证据： .1 扶正倾覆的快速救助艇 .2 在普通的天气和海况条件下操纵快速救助艇 .3 佩戴特别装置游泳 .4 在快速救助艇与直升机和船舶之间使用通信与信号设备 .5 使用所配备的应急设备 .6 从水中营救伤员及把伤员运送至营救直升机、船舶或安全地点 .7 结合环境因素实施搜寻方式	在通常的天气条件下，快速救助艇的操作演示是在设备的限度以内进行的
操作快速救助艇的机器	启动并操作快速救助艇的机器及其附属机具的方法	评估从实际演示启动并操纵快速救助艇机器的能力中获取的证据	按操纵要求启动和操作机器

Section A-VI/3
Mandatory minimum training in advanced fire fighting

Standard of competence

1 Seafarers designated to control fire-fighting operations shall have successfully completed advanced training in techniques for fighting fire, with particular emphasis on organization, tactics and command, and shall be required to demonstrate competence to undertake the tasks, duties and responsibilities listed in column 1 of table A-VI/3.

2 The level of knowledge and understanding of the subjects listed in column 2 of table A-VI/3 shall be sufficient for the effective control of fire-fighting operations on board ship*.

3 Training and experience to achieve the necessary level of theoretical knowledge, understanding and proficiency shall take account of the guidance given in part B of this Code.

4 Every candidate for certification shall be required to provide evidence of having achieved the required standard of competence, in accordance with the methods for demonstrating competence and the criteria for evaluating competence tabulated in columns 3 and 4 of table A-VI/3.

5 Seafarers qualified in accordance with paragraph 4 in advanced fire fighting shall be required, every five years, to provide evidence of having maintained the required standards of competence to undertake the tasks, duties and responsibilities listed in column 1 of table A-VI/3.

6 Parties may accept onboard training and experience for maintaining the required standard of competence of table A-VI/3, in the following areas:

.1 Control fire-fighting operations aboard ships;

.1.1 fire-fighting procedures at sea and in port, with particular emphasis on organization, tactics and command;

.1.2 communication and coordination during fire-fighting operations;

.1.3 ventilation control, including smoke extraction;

.1.4 control of fuel and electrical systems;

.1.5 fire-fighting process hazards (dry distillation, chemical reactions, boiler uptake, fires);

.1.6 fire precautions and hazards associated with the storage and handling of materials;

.1.7 management and control of injured persons; and

.1.8 procedures for coordination with shore-based fire fighters.

* The relevant IMO Model Course(s) may be of assistance in the preparation of courses.

第 A-VI/3 节

高级消防培训的强制性最低要求

适任标准

1 被指定控制消防作业的海员应圆满完成着重于消防组织、战术和指挥方面的消防技术的高级培训，并应表明承担表 A-VI/3 第 1 栏所列的任务、职责和责任的适任能力。

2 表 A-VI/3 第 2 栏所列科目的知识和理解水平，应足以有效地控制船上的消防作业①。

3 为获得所需水平的理论知识、理解和熟练的培训和经历，应考虑本规则 B 部分给予的指导。

4 每个证书申请人，应按表 A-VI/3 第 3 栏和第 4 栏所列的表明适任的方法和评价适任的标准，提供已达到所要求的适任标准的证据。

5 按照高级消防培训第 4 段具有资格的海员应按要求每 5 年提供证据，表明其保持了所要求的适任标准，以承担表 A-VI/3 第 1 栏所列的任务、职责和责任。

6 在以下方面，缔约国可接受以船上培训和资历作为保持了表 A-VI/3 所要求的适任标准：

.1 控制船舶消防作业：

.1.1 以消防组织、战术和指挥为重点的海上和港内船舶消防程序，

.1.2 灭火作业中的通信和协调，

.1.3 通风控制，包括排烟，

.1.4 燃油和电气系统的控制，

.1.5 灭火过程中的危险（干馏、化学反应、锅炉烟道），

.1.6 与储存和处置物料有关的火灾预防和危害，

.1.7 对伤员的管理和控制，以及

.1.8 与岸上消防队员协调的程序。

① 相关 IMO 示范培训课程可有助于准备课程。

Table A-VI/3

Specification of minimum standard of competence in advanced fire fighting

Column 1	Column 2	Column 3	Column 4
Competence	**Knowledge, understanding and proficiency**	**Methods for demonstrating competence**	**Criteria for evaluating competence**
Control fire-fighting operations aboard ships	Fire-fighting procedures at sea and in port, with particular emphasis on organization, tactics and command Use of water for fire-extinguishing, the effect on ship stability, precautions and corrective procedures Communication and coordination during fire-fighting operations Ventilation control, including smoke extraction Control of fuel and electrical systems Fire-fighting process hazards (dry distillation, chemical reactions, boiler uptake fires, etc.) Fire fighting involving dangerous goods Fire precautions and hazards associated with the storage and handling of materials (paints, etc.) Management and control of injured persons Procedures for coordination with shore-based fire fighters	Practical exercises and instruction conducted under approved and truly realistic training conditions (e.g., simulated shipboard conditions) and, whenever possible and practicable, in darkness	Actions taken to control fires are based on a full and accurate assessment of the incident, using all available sources of information The order of priority, timing and sequence of actions are appropriate to the overall requirements of the incident and to minimize damage and potential damage to the ship, injuries to personnel and impairment of the operational effectiveness of the ship Transmission of information is prompt, accurate, complete and clear Personal safety during fire control activities is safeguarded at all times
Organize and train fire parties	Preparation of contingency plans Composition and allocation of personnel to fire parties Strategies and tactics for control of fires in various parts of the ship	Practical exercises and instruction conducted under approved and truly realistic training conditions, e.g., simulated shipboard conditions	Composition and organization of fire control parties ensure the prompt and effective implementation of emergency plans and procedures

表 A-VI/3
高级消防的最低适任标准

第 1 栏	第 2 栏	第 3 栏	第 4 栏
适任	**知识、理解和熟练**	**表明适任的方法**	**评价适任的标准**
控制船舶消防作业	以消防组织、战术和指挥为重点的海上和港内船舶消防程序 用水灭火,对船舶稳性的影响,预防和纠正程序 灭火作业中的通信和协调 通风控制,包括排烟 燃油和电气系统的控制 灭火过程中的危险(干馏、化学反应、锅炉烟道失火等) 扑灭涉及危险货物的火灾 与储存和处置物料(如油漆等)有关的火灾预防和危害 对伤员的管理和控制 与岸上消防人员协调的程序	在认可的真实的培训条件(如模拟船上条件)下和可能和可行时,在黑暗中进行实际练习和训练	所采取的控制火势的行动是以运用所有可利用的信息对事故进行全面准确的估计为基础的 采取行动命令的先后次序和时间适合事故的全面需求,并能最大限度减少船舶损害或潜在损害、人员伤害及对船舶操作的有效性的影响 信息传递迅速、准确、完整、清楚 在灭火控制活动中,始终保护人员安全
消防队的组织和训练	应急计划的准备 消防队组成和人员的调配 控制船舶各部位火灾的战略和战术	在认可的真实培训条件(如模拟船上条件)下进行的实际练习和训练	消防队的组成和组织能确保迅速有效地实施应急计划和程序

Column 1	Column 2	Column 3	Column 4
Competence	**Knowledge, understanding and proficiency**	**Methods for demonstrating competence**	**Criteria for evaluating competence**
Inspect and service fire-detection and fire-extinguishing systems and equipment	Fire-detection systems; fixed fire-extinguishing systems; portable and mobile fire-extinguishing equipment, including appliances, pumps and rescue, salvage, life-support, personal protective and communication equipment Requirements for statutory and classification surveys	Practical exercises, using approved equipment and systems in a realistic training environment	Operational effectiveness of all fire-detection and fire-extinguishing systems and equipment is maintained at all times in accordance with performance specifications and legislative requirements
Investigate and compile reports on incidents involving fire	Assessment of cause of incidents involving fire	Practical exercises in a realistic training environment	Causes of fire are identified and the effectiveness of countermeasures is evaluated

第 1 栏	第 2 栏	第 3 栏	第 4 栏
适任	知识、理解和熟练	表明适任的方法	评价适任的标准
检查和保养烟火探测和灭火系统及设备	烟火探测系统;固定灭火系统;便携式和移动式灭火设备,包括各种器械、泵以及救助、生命支持、人员保护和通信设备 法定检验和船级检验的要求	使用认可的设备和系统在真实的培训环境下进行实际练习	按照功能规格和法定要求,始终保证所有烟火探测和消防系统和设备的操作有效性
调查和编写涉及火灾的事故报告	对火灾事故原因进行评估	在真实培训环境下实际练习	确定火灾原因,评价措施的有效性

Section A-VI/4

Mandatory minimum requirements related to medical first aid and medical care

Standard of competence for seafarers designated to provide medical first aid on board ship

1 Every seafarer who is designated to provide medical first aid on board ship shall be required to demonstrate the competence to undertake the tasks, duties and responsibilities listed in column 1 of table A-VI/4-1.

2 The level of knowledge of the subjects listed in column 2 of table A-VI/4-1 shall be sufficient to enable the designated seafarer to take immediate effective action in the case of accidents or illness likely to occur on board ship*.

3 Every candidate for certification under the provisions of regulation VI/4, paragraph 1 shall be required to provide evidence that the required standard of competence has been achieved in accordance with the methods for demonstrating competence and the criteria for evaluating competence tabulated in columns 3 and 4 of table A-VI/4-1.

Standard of competence for seafarers designated to take charge of medical care on board ship

4 Every seafarer who is designated to take charge of medical care on board ship shall be required to demonstrate the competence to undertake the tasks, duties and responsibilities listed in column 1 of table A-VI/4-2.

5 The level of knowledge of the subjects listed in column 2 of table A-VI/4-2 shall be sufficient to enable the designated seafarer to take immediate effective action in the case of accidents or illness likely to occur on board ship*.

6 Every candidate for certification under the provisions of regulation VI/4, paragraph 2 shall be required to provide evidence that the required standard of competence has been achieved in accordance with the methods for demonstrating competence and the criteria for evaluating competence tabulated in columns 3 and 4 of table A-VI/4-2.

* The relevant IMO Model Course(s) may assist in the preparation of courses.

第 A-VI/4 节

医疗急救和医护的强制性最低要求

被指定在船上提供医疗急救的海员的适任标准

1 每个指定在船上提供医疗急救的海员，应表明承担表 A-VI/4-1 第 1 栏所列的任务、职责和责任的适任能力。

2 表 A-VI/4-1 第 2 栏所列科目的知识水平，应足以能使指定的海员在船上一旦发生可能的事故或疾病时立即采取有效的行动[①]。

3 规则第 VI/4 条第 1 段规定的每个证书申请人，应按照表 A-VI/4-1 第 3 栏和第 4 栏所列的表明适任的方法和评价适任的标准，提供已达到所要求适任标准的证据。

被指定在船上负责医护的海员的适任标准

4 每个指定在船上负责医护的海员，应表明承担表 A-VI/4-2 第 1 栏所列的任务、职责和责任的适任能力。

5 表 A-VI/4-2 第 2 栏所列科目的知识水平，应足以能使指定的海员在船上一旦发生意外事故或疾病时立即采取有效的行动[①]。

6 规则第 VI/4 条第 2 段规定的每个证书申请人，应按照表 A-VI/4-2 第 3 栏和第 4 栏所列的表明适任的方法和评价适任的标准，提供已达到所要求的适任标准的证据。

---

① 相关 IMO 示范培训课程可有助于准备课程。

Table A-VI/4-1

Specification of minimum standard of competence in medical first aid

Column 1	Column 2	Column 3	Column 4
Competence	**Knowledge, understanding and proficiency**	**Methods for demonstrating competence**	**Criteria for evaluating competence**
Apply immediate first aid in the event of accident or illness on board	First-aid kit Body structure and function Toxicological hazards on board, including use of the Medical First Aid Guide for Use in Accidents Involving Dangerous Goods (MFAG) or its national equivalent Examination of casualty or patient Spinal injuries Burns, scalds and effects of heat and cold Fractures, dislocations and muscular injuries Medical care of rescued persons Radio medical advice Pharmacology Sterilization Cardiac arrest, drowning and asphyxia	Assessment of evidence obtained from practical instruction	The identification of probable cause, nature and extent of injuries is prompt, complete and conforms to current first-aid practice Risk of harm to self and to others is minimized at all times Treatment of injuries and the patient's condition is appropriate and conforms to recognized first-aid practice and international guidelines

表 A-VI/4-1

医疗急救的最低适任标准

第 1 栏	第 2 栏	第 3 栏	第 4 栏
适任	**知识、理解和熟练**	**表明适任的方法**	**评价适任的标准**
船上一旦发生意外事故或疾病时立即实施急救	急救箱 人体的构造和功能 船上有毒物的危害,包括《危险货物事故医疗急救指南》(MFAG)或其国家的等效规则的应用 伤病员的检查 脊椎损伤 烧伤、烫伤和热与冷的影响 骨折、脱臼和肌肉损伤 被救人员的护理 无线电医疗建议 药理学 消毒 心脏停跳、溺水和窒息	评估从实际训练中获取的证据	对损伤的可能原因、性质和程度的判断是迅速的、充分的,并与通常急救做法相符 始终将对自身和他人的危险降到最低 对伤病员处理是适当的并与公认的急救做法和国际指南相符

Table A-VI/4-2

Specification of minimum standard of competence in medical care

Column 1	**Column 2**	**Column 3**	**Column 4**
Competence	**Knowledge, understanding and proficiency**	**Methods for demonstrating competence**	**Criteria for evaluating competence**
Provide medical care to the sick and injured while they remain on board	Care of casualty involving: .1 head and spinal injuries .2 injuries of ear, nose, throat and eyes .3 external and internal bleeding .4 burns, scalds and frostbite .5 fractures, dislocations and muscular injuries .6 wounds, wound healing and infection .7 pain relief .8 techniques of sewing and clamping .9 management of acute abdominal conditions .10 minor surgical treatment .11 dressing and bandaging Aspects of nursing: .1 general principles .2 nursing care Diseases, including: .1 medical conditions and emergencies .2 sexually transmitted diseases .3 tropical and infectious diseases Alcohol and drug abuse	Assessment of evidence obtained from practical instruction and demonstration Where practicable, approved practical experience at a hospital or similar establishment	Identification of symptoms is based on the concepts of clinical examination and medical history Protection against infection and spread of diseases is complete and effective Personal attitude is calm, confident and reassuring Treatment of injury or condition is appropriate and conforms to accepted medical practice and relevant national and international medical guides The dosage and application of drugs and medication complies with manufacturers' recommendations and accepted medical practice The significance of changes in patient's condition is promptly recognized

表 A-VI/4-2
医护最低适任标准

第1栏	第2栏	第3栏	第4栏
适任	知识、理解和熟练	表明适任的方法	评价适任的标准
为船上的伤病员提供医护	对伤病员的医护涉及： .1 头部和脊椎损伤 .2 耳、鼻、喉和眼睛的损伤 .3 外出血和内出血 .4 烧伤、烫伤和冻伤 .5 骨折、脱臼和肌肉损伤 .6 伤口、伤口的愈合和感染 .7 止痛 .8 缝合和夹板技术 .9 腹部急性炎症的处理 .10 外科小手术 .11 包扎和使用绷带 护理方面： .1 一般原则 .2 护理业务 疾病，包括： .1 急病和急症 .2 性传染疾病 .3 热带病和传染性疾病 酗酒和滥用药物	评估从实际训练和演示中获取的证据 如可行，在医院或类似机构中认可的实际经验	症状的判断基于临床诊断和病史 预防传染和疾病蔓延是充分和有效的 个人态度温和、有信心并让人放心 对伤、病情的处理是适当的，并与公认的医疗做法和有关的国家与国际医疗指南相符 内、外用药的剂量和用法，符合制造商的建议及认可的医疗做法 迅速认识病情变化的意义

Column 1	Column 2	Column 3	Column 4
Competence	**Knowledge, understanding and proficiency**	**Methods for demonstrating competence**	**Criteria for evaluating competence**
Provide medical care to the sick and injured while they remain on board (*continued*)	Dental care Gynaecology, pregnancy and childbirth Medical care of rescued persons Death at sea Hygiene Disease prevention, including: .1 disinfection, disinfestation, de-ratting .2 vaccinations Keeping records and copies of applicable regulations: .1 keeping medical records .2 international and national maritime medical regulations		
Participate in coordinated schemes for medical assistance to ships	External assistance, including: .1 radio medical advice .2 transportation of the ill and injured, including helicopter evacuation .3 medical care of sick seafarers involving cooperation with port health authorities or out-patient wards in port		Clinical examination procedures are complete and comply with instructions received The method and preparation for evacuation is in accordance with recognized procedures and is designed to maximize the welfare of the patient Procedures for seeking radio medical advice conform to established practice and recommendations

第 1 栏	第 2 栏	第 3 栏	第 4 栏
适任	知识、理解和熟练	表明适任的方法	评价适任的标准
为船上的伤病员提供医护(续)	牙科护理 妇科、怀孕和分娩 对获救者的医护 海上死亡 船上卫生 疾病预防,包括: .1 预防传染、杀虫、灭鼠 .2 预防接种 保持医疗记录和有关规定的副本: .1 保持医疗记录 .2 国际和国内的海上医疗规定		
参加对船舶医疗援助的协调计划	外部援助,包括: .1 无线电医疗咨询 .2 伤病员的运送,包括直升机运送 .3 伤病海员医疗,包括与港口医疗当局或港口诊所的协调		临床检查程序是完整的并符合收到的指导 运送伤病员的方法和准备工作符合认可的程序,并最大限度地为病员着想 寻求无线电医疗咨询的程序符合既定做法和建议

Section A-VI/5

Mandatory minimum requirements for the issue of certificates of proficiency for ship security officers

Standard of competence

1 Every candidate for a certificate of proficiency as a ship security officer shall be required to demonstrate competence to undertake the tasks, duties and responsibilities listed in column 1 of table A-VI/5.

2 The level of knowledge of the subjects listed in column 2 of table A-VI/5 shall be sufficient to enable the candidate to act as the designated ship security officer.

3 Training and experience to achieve the necessary level of theoretical knowledge, understanding and proficiency shall take into account the guidance in section B-VI/5 of this Code.

4 Every candidate for certification shall be required to provide evidence of having achieved the required standard of competence in accordance with the methods for demonstrating competence and the criteria for evaluating competence tabulated in columns 3 and 4 of table A-VI/5.

第 A-VI/5 节

签发船舶保安员培训合格证书的强制性最低要求

适任标准

1 每个申请船舶保安员证书的申请人,应表明承担表 A-VI/5 第 1 栏所列的任务、职责和责任的适任能力。

2 表 A-VI/5 第 2 栏所列科目的知识水平,应足以能使申请人作为指定的船舶保安员。

3 为获得所需水平的理论知识、理解和熟练的培训和经验,应考虑本规则第 B-VI/5 节的指导。

4 每个证书申请人,应依照表 A-VI/5 第 3 栏和第 4 栏所列的表明适任的方法和评价适任的标准,提供已达到所要求的适任标准的证据。

Table A-VI/5

Specifications of minimum standard of competence for ship security officers

Column 1	Column 2	Column 3	Column 4
Competence	**Knowledge, understanding and proficiency**	**Methods for demonstrating competence**	**Criteria for evaluating competence**
Maintain and supervise the implementation of a ship security plan	Knowledge of international maritime security policy and responsibilities of Governments, companies and designated persons, including elements that may relate to piracy and armed robbery Knowledge of the purpose for and the elements that make up a ship security plan, related procedures and maintenance of records, including those that may relate to piracy and armed robbery Knowledge of procedures to be employed in implementing a ship security plan and reporting of security incidents Knowledge of maritime security levels and the consequential security measures and procedures aboard ship and in the port facility environment Knowledge of the requirements and procedures for conducting internal audits, on-scene inspections, control and monitoring of security activities specified in a ship security plan Knowledge of the requirements and procedures for reporting to the company security officer any deficiencies and non-conformities identified during internal audits, periodic reviews, and security inspections	Assessment of evidence obtained from approved training or examination	Procedures and actions are in accordance with the principles established by the ISPS Code and the SOLAS, 1974, as amended Legislative requirements relating to security are correctly identified Procedures achieve a state of readiness to respond to changes in maritime security levels Communications within the ship security officer's area of responsibility are clear and understood

表 A-VI/5

船舶保安员的最低适任标准

第1栏	第2栏	第3栏	第4栏
适任	**知识、理解和熟练**	**表明适任的方法**	**评价适任的标准**
维持并监督船舶保安计划的实施	国际海上保安方针和政府、公司指定人员责任的知识,包括可能与海盗及武装抢劫有关的要素 制定船舶保安计划、相关程序和维持记录的目的和要素的知识,包括可能与海盗及武装抢劫有关的内容 实施船舶保安计划和报告保安事故所采用的程序的知识 海上保安等级以及在船上和在港口设施环境下相应保安措施和程序的知识 船舶保安计划规定的内部审核、现场检查、保安活动的要求和程序的知识 向公司保安员报告内部审核、定期审核和保安检查期间发现的任何缺陷和不符合项的要求和程序的知识	评估从认可的培训或考试中获取的证据	程序和行动符合《国际船舶和港口设施保安规则》和经修正的《1974 年国际海上人命安全公约》所确定的原则 正确识别有关保安的法定要求 程序达到应对海上保安等级的变化的准备状态 在船舶保安员责任范围区内的交流清楚、易懂

Column 1	Column 2	Column 3	Column 4
Competence	**Knowledge, understanding and proficiency**	**Methods for demonstrating competence**	**Criteria for evaluating competence**
Maintain and supervise the implementation of a ship security plan (*continued*)	Knowledge of the methods and procedures used to modify the ship security plan Knowledge of security-related contingency plans and the procedures for responding to security threats or breaches of security, including provisions for maintaining critical operations of the ship/port interface, including also elements that may relate to piracy and armed robbery Working knowledge of maritime security terms and definitions, including elements that may relate to piracy and armed robbery		
Assess security risk, threat, and vulnerability	Knowledge of risk assessment and assessment tools Knowledge of security assessment documentation, including the Declaration of Security Knowledge of techniques used to circumvent security measures, including those used by pirates and armed robbers Knowledge enabling recognition, on a non-discriminatory basis, of persons posing potential security risks Knowledge enabling recognition of weapons, dangerous substances and devices and awareness of the damage they can cause Knowledge of crowd management and control techniques, where appropriate	Assessment of evidence obtained from approved training, or approved experience and examination, including practical demonstration of competence to: .1 conduct physical searches .2 conduct non-intrusive inspections	Procedures and actions are in accordance with the principles established by the ISPS Code and the SOLAS, 1974, as amended Procedures achieve a state of readiness to respond to changes in the maritime security levels Communications within the ship security officer's area of responsibility are clear and understood

第 1 栏	第 2 栏	第 3 栏	第 4 栏
适任	知识、理解和熟练	表明适任的方法	评价适任的标准
维持并监督船舶保安计划的实施（续）	修改船舶保安计划所用的方法和程序的知识 与保安有关的应急计划和应对保安威胁或保安违规的反应程序的知识，包括保持船/港界面关键操作的规定，还包括可能与海盗及武装抢劫有关的要素 海上保安术语和定义的实用知识，包括可能与海盗及武装抢劫有关的术语和定义		
评估保安风险、威胁和弱点	风险评估和评估工具的知识 保安评估文件（包括保安声明）的知识 用于躲避保安措施的技术的知识，包括海盗及武装抢劫分子使用的技术 能在非歧视的基础上识别对保安有潜在风险的人员的知识 能够识别武器、危险品和危险装置的知识并清楚其可能造成的损害 拥挤人群管理和控制技术的知识，如适用	评估从认可的培训或认可的经验和考试中获取的证据，包括展示以下方面的能力的实际演示： .1 进行搜身 .2 进行非侵入性检查	程序和行动符合《国际船舶和港口设施保安规则》和经修正的《1974 年国际海上人命安全公约》确定的原则 为达到准备状态的程序适应于海上保安等级的变化 在船舶保安员责任范围区内的交流清楚、易懂

Column 1	Column 2	Column 3	Column 4
Competence	**Knowledge, understanding and proficiency**	**Methods for demonstrating competence**	**Criteria for evaluating competence**
Assess security risk, threat, and vulnerability (*continued*)	Knowledge in handling sensitive security-related information and security-related communications Knowledge of implementing and co-ordinating searches Knowledge of the methods for physical searches and non-intrusive inspections		
Undertake regular inspections of the ship to ensure that appropriate security measures are implemented and maintained	Knowledge of the requirements for designating and monitoring restricted areas Knowledge of controlling access to the ship and to restricted areas on board ship Knowledge of methods for effective monitoring of deck areas and areas surrounding the ship Knowledge of security aspects relating to the handling of cargo and ship's stores with other shipboard personnel and relevant port facility security officers Knowledge of methods for controlling the embarkation, disembarkation and access while on board of persons and their effects	Assessment of evidence obtained from approved training or examination	Procedures and actions are in accordance with the principles established by the ISPS Code and the SOLAS,1974, as amended Procedures achieve a state of readiness to respond to changes in the maritime security levels Communications within the ship security officer's area of responsibility are clear and understood
Ensure that security equipment and systems, if any, are properly operated, tested and calibrated	Knowledge of the various types of security equipment and systems and their limitations, including those that could be used in case of attacks by pirates and armed robbers Knowledge of the procedures, instructions and guidance on the use of ship security alert systems	Assessment of evidence obtained from approved training or examination	Procedures and actions are in accordance with the principles established by the ISPS Code and the SOLAS, 1974, as amended

第1栏	第2栏	第3栏	第4栏
适任	知识、理解和熟练	表明适任的方法	评价适任的标准
评估保安风险、威胁和弱点(续)	处理保安相关敏感信息和进行保安相关交流的知识 实施和协调搜寻的知识 搜身和非侵入式检查方法的知识		
执行定期的船舶检查以确保适当的保安措施已经实施并得已维持	确定和监控受控区域的要求的知识 控制进入船舶和船上受限制区域的知识 监控甲板区域和船舶周围区域的有效方法的知识 在与其他船上人员及相关的港口设施保安人员处理货物与船舶物料方面的保安方面的知识 控制船上人员上船、下船和在船活动范围及其携带物品的方法的知识	评估从认可的培训或考试中获取的证据	程序和行动符合《国际船舶和港口设施保安规则》和经修正的《1974 年国际海上人命安全公约》所确定的原则 为达到准备状态的程序适应于海上保安等级的变化 在船舶保安员责任范围区内的交流清楚、易懂
确保保安设备和系统(如有)正规操作、测试和校准	各种保安设备和系统及其局限性的知识,包括在发生海盗及武装抢劫事件时可以使用的设备和系统 使用船舶保安报警系统的程序、说明和指南的知识	评估从认可的培训或考试中获取的证据	程序和行动符合《国际船舶和港口设施保安规则》和经修正的《1974 年国际海上人命安全公约》所确定的原则

Column 1	Column 2	Column 3	Column 4
Competence	**Knowledge, understanding and proficiency**	**Methods for demonstrating competence**	**Criteria for evaluating competence**
Ensure that security equipment and systems, if any, are properly operated, tested and calibrated *(continued)*	Knowledge of the methods for testing, calibrating, and maintaining security systems and equipment, particularly whilst at sea		
Encourage security awareness and vigilance	Knowledge of training, drill and exercise requirements under relevant conventions, codes and IMO circulars, including those relevant to anti-piracy and anti-armed robbery Knowledge of the methods for enhancing security awareness and vigilance on board Knowledge of the methods for assessing the effectiveness of drills and exercises	Assessment of evidence obtained from approved training or examination	Procedures and actions are in accordance with the principles established by the ISPS Code and the SOLAS, 1974, as amended Communications within the ship security officer's area of responsibility are clear and understood

第 1 栏	第 2 栏	第 3 栏	第 4 栏
适任	知识、理解和熟练	表明适任的方法	评价适任的标准
确保保安设备和系统(如有)正规操作、测试和校准(续)	测试、校准和维护保安系统和设备的方法(尤其是在海上)的知识		
鼓励保安意识和警惕性	有关公约、规则及 IMO 通函中包括有关防海盗及武装抢劫要求的培训、演习和操练的知识 加强保安意识和船上警惕性的的知识 评估演习和操作有效性的方法的知识	评估从认可的培训或考试中获取的证据	程序和行动符合《国际船舶和港口设施保安规则》和经修正的《1974 年国际海上人命安全公约》所确定的原则 在船舶保安员责任范围区内的交流清楚、易懂

Section A-VI/6
Mandatory minimum requirements for security-related training and instruction for all seafarers

Standard of competence for security-related familiarization training

1 Before being assigned to shipboard duties, all persons employed or engaged on a seagoing ship which is required to comply with the provisions of the ISPS Code, other than passengers, shall receive approved security-related familiarization training, taking account of the guidance given in part B, to be able to:

.1 report a security incident, including a piracy or armed robbery threat or attack;

.2 know the procedures to follow when they recognize a security threat; and

.3 take part in security-related emergency and contingency procedures.

2 Seafarers with designated security duties engaged or employed on a seagoing ship shall, before being assigned such duties, receive security-related familiarization training in their assigned duties and responsibilities, taking into account the guidance given in part B.

3 The security-related familiarization training shall be conducted by the ship security officer or an equally qualified person.

Standard of competence for security-awareness training

4 Seafarers employed or engaged in any capacity on board a ship which is required to comply with the provisions of the ISPS Code on the business of that ship as part of the ship's complement without designated security duties shall, before being assigned to any shipboard duties:

.1 receive appropriate approved training or instruction in security awareness as set out in table A-VI/6-1;

.2 be required to provide evidence of having achieved the required standard of competence to undertake the tasks, duties and responsibilities listed in column 1 of table A-VI/6-1:

.2.1 by demonstration of competence, in accordance with the methods and the criteria for evaluating competence tabulated in columns 3 and 4 of table A-VI/6-1; and

.2.2 by examination or continuous assessment as part of an approved training programme in the subjects listed in column 2 of table A-VI/6-1.

Transitional provisions

5 Until 1 January 2014, seafarers who commenced an approved seagoing service prior to the date of entry into force of this section shall be able to establish that they meet the requirements of paragraph 4 by:

.1 approved seagoing service as shipboard personnel, for a period of at least six months in total during the preceding three years; or

第 A-VI/6 节

对所有海员与保安有关的培训和训练的强制性最低要求

与保安有关的熟悉培训的适任标准

1 在按要求应遵守《ISPS 规则》的海船上,除旅客外,所有受雇或受聘人员,在被指派船上职责之前应接受认可的与保安有关的熟悉培训,并考虑 B 部分给予的指导,以便能够:

.1 报告保安事件,包括海盗或武装抢劫的威胁或袭击;

.2 当确认存在保安威胁时,了解应遵循的程序;并

.3 参加与保安有关的应急和紧急程序。

2 受聘或受雇于海船上承担指定保安职责的海员,在被指派该职责之前,应接受与其职责和责任相关的保安熟悉培训,并考虑 B 部分给予的指导。

3 与保安有关的熟悉培训应由船舶保安员或具有同等资格的人员实施。

保安意识培训的适任标准

4 受雇或受聘于应遵守《ISPS 规则》规定的船舶担任船上任何职务的海员,在船舶营运中作为无指定保安职责的在编人员,在其任职之前,应:

.1 接受适当的认可的表 A-VI/6-1 规定的保安意识培训或训练;

.2 提供已经达到按表 A-VI/6-1 第 1 栏列出所承担的任务、职责和责任所要求的适任标准的证据:

.2.1 通过适任能力的演示,达到表 A-VI/6-1 第 3 栏和第 4 栏所列的表明适任的方法和评价适任的标准,并且

.2.2 通过考试或连续评估,作为表 A-VI/6-1 第 2 栏所列科目的认可的培训计划的组成部分。

过渡规定

5 截至 2014 年 1 月 1 日,在本节生效前已经开始了认可的海上服务的海员应能够通过下列各项确定他们符合第 4 段的要求:

.1 在之前 3 年内至少有 6 个月的时间以船上人员的身份从事经认可的海上服务;或

.2 having performed security functions considered to be equivalent to the seagoing service required in paragraph 5.1; or

.3 passing an approved test; or

.4 successfully completing approved training.

Standard of competence for seafarers with designated security duties

6 Every seafarer who is designated to perform security duties, including anti-piracy and anti-armed-robbery-related activities, shall be required to demonstrate competence to undertake the tasks, duties and responsibilities listed in column 1 of table A-VI/6-2.

7 The level of knowledge of the subjects in column 2 of table A-VI/6-2 shall be sufficient to enable every candidate to perform on board designated security duties, including anti-piracy and anti-armed-robbery-related activities.

8 Every candidate for certification shall be required to provide evidence of having achieved the required standard of competence through:

.1 demonstration of competence to undertake the tasks, duties and responsibilities listed in column 1 of table A-VI/6-2, in accordance with the methods for demonstrating competence and the criteria for evaluating competence tabulated in columns 3 and 4 of that table; and

.2 examination or continuous assessment as part of an approved training programme covering the material set out in column 2 of table A-VI/6-2.

Transitional provisions

9 Until 1 January 2014, seafarers with designated security duties who commenced an approved seagoing service prior to the date of entry into force of this section shall be able to demonstrate competence to undertake the tasks, duties and responsibilities listed in column 1 of table A-VI/6-2 by:

.1 approved seagoing service as shipboard personnel with designated security duties, for a period of at least six months in total during the preceding three years; or

.2 having performed security functions considered to be equivalent to the seagoing service required in paragraph 9.1; or

.3 passing an approved test; or

.4 successfully completing approved training.

.2 已履行被认为等效于第 5.1 段所要求的海上服务的保安职能;或

.3 通过认可的测试;或

.4 成功地完成认可的培训。

承担指定保安职责的海员的适任标准

6 每个被指定履行包括防海盗和防武装抢劫相关活动的保安职责的海员,应表明承担表 A-VI/6-2 第 1 栏所列的任务、职责和责任的适任能力。

7 表 A-VI/6-2 第 2 栏所列明的科目的知识水平,应足以使每个证书申请人能够履行船上指定的保安职责,包括防海盗和防武装抢劫相关的活动。

8 每个证书申请人应依据下列各项提供已经达到所要求的适任标准的证据:

.1 按表 A-VI/6-2 第 3 栏和第 4 栏所列表明适任的方法和评估适任的标准,表明具有执行该表第 1 栏所列的任务、职责和责任的适任能力;并且

.2 考试或连续的评估,作为覆盖表 A-VI/6-2 第 2 栏所规定材料的认可的培训项目的组成部分。

过渡规定

9 截至 2014 年 1 月 1 日,在本节生效前已经开始了认可的海上服务的负有指定保安职责的海员应能够通过下列各项表明承担表 A-VI/6-2 第 1 栏所列的任务、职责和责任的适任能力:

.1 在之前 3 年内至少有 6 个月的时间以船上人员的身份从事经认可的海上服务;或

.2 已履行被认为等效于第 9.1 段所要求的海上服务的保安职能;或

.3 通过认可的测试;或

.4 成功地完成认可的培训。

Table A-VI/6-1

Specification of minimum standard of competence in security awareness

Column 1	Column 2	Column 3	Column 4
Competence	**Knowledge, understanding and proficiency**	**Methods for demonstrating competence**	**Criteria for evaluating competence**
Contribute to the enhancement of maritime security through heightened awareness	Basic working knowledge of maritime security terms and definitions, including elements that may relate to piracy and armed robbery Basic knowledge of international maritime security policy and responsibilities of Governments, companies and persons Basic knowledge of maritime security levels and their impact on security measures and procedures aboard ship and in port facilities Basic knowledge of security reporting procedures Basic knowledge of security-related contingency plans	Assessment of evidence obtained from approved instruction or during attendance at an approved course	Requirements relating to enhanced maritime security are correctly identified
Recognition of security threats	Basic knowledge of techniques used to circumvent security measures Basic knowledge enabling recognition of potential security threats, including elements that may relate to piracy and armed robbery Basic knowledge enabling recognition of weapons, dangerous substances and devices and awareness of the damage they can cause Basic knowledge in handling security-related information and security-related communications	Assessment of evidence obtained from approved instruction or during attendance at an approved course	Maritime security threats are correctly identified

表 A-VI/6-1
保安意识的最低适任标准

第 1 栏	第 2 栏	第 3 栏	第 4 栏
适任	**知识、理解和熟练**	**表明适任的方法**	**评价适任的标准**
有助于通过增强意识来加强海上保安	包括可能与海盗和武装抢劫有关的海上保安术语和定义的基本的实用知识 国际海上保安方针和政府、公司及个人责任的基本知识 海上保安等级及其对船上和港口实施保安措施和程序影响的基本知识 保安报告程序的基本知识 与保安相关的应急计划的基本知识	评估从认可的训练或参加认可的课程中获取的证据	正确地确认有关增强海上保安的要求
保安威胁的确认	用于规避保安措施的技术的基本知识 能够确认包括可能与海盗和武装抢劫有关的事项在内的潜在保安威胁的基本知识 能够识别武器、危险物质和装置的基本知识，并清楚它们能够引起的损害 处理保安相关信息和保安相关通信的基本知识	评估从认可的训练或参加认可的课程中获取的证据	正确地识别海上保安威胁

Column 1	Column 2	Column 3	Column 4
Competence	**Knowledge, understanding and proficiency**	**Methods for demonstrating competence**	**Criteria for evaluating competence**
Understanding of the need for and methods of maintaining security awareness and vigilance	Basic knowledge of training, drill and exercise requirements under relevant conventions, codes and IMO circulars, including those relevant for anti-piracy and anti-armed robbery	Assessment of evidence obtained from approved instruction or during attendance at an approved course	Requirements relating to enhanced maritime security are correctly identified

第 1 栏	第 2 栏	第 3 栏	第 4 栏
适任	**知识、理解和熟练**	**表明适任的方法**	**评价适任的标准**
理解保持保安意识和警惕性的必要性和方法	有关的公约、规则和 IMO 通函中关于培训、演习和练习要求的基本知识,包括与防海盗和防武装抢劫有关的知识	评估从认可的训练或参加认可的课程中获取的证据	正确地确认有关增强海上保安的要求

Table A-VI/6-2

Specifications of minimum standard of competence for seafarers with designated security duties

Column 1	Column 2	Column 3	Column 4
Competence	**Knowledge, understanding and proficiency**	**Methods for demonstrating competence**	**Criteria for evaluating competence**
Maintain the conditions set out in a ship security plan	Working knowledge of maritime security terms and definitions, including elements that may relate to piracy and armed robbery Knowledge of international maritime security policy and responsibilities of Governments, companies and persons, including working knowledge of elements that may relate to piracy and armed robbery Knowledge of maritime security levels and their impact on security measures and procedures aboard ship and in the port facilities Knowledge of security reporting procedures Knowledge of procedures and requirements for drills and exercises under relevant conventions, codes and IMO circulars, including working knowledge of those that may relate to piracy and armed robbery Knowledge of the procedures for conducting inspections and surveys and for the control and monitoring of security activities specified in a ship security plan	Assessment of evidence obtained from approved instruction or during attendance at an approved course	Procedures and actions are in accordance with the principles established by the ISPS Code and the SOLAS, 1974, as amended Legislative requirements relating to security are correctly identified Communications within the area of responsibility are clear and understood

表 A-VI/6-2
负有指定保安职责海员的最低适任标准

第 1 栏	第 2 栏	第 3 栏	第 4 栏
适任	**知识、理解和熟练**	**表明适任的方法**	**评价适任的标准**
保持船舶保安计划所设定的状态	海上保安术语和定义的实用知识,包括可能与海盗和武装抢劫有关的要素 国际海上保安方针和政府、公司及个人的职责的知识,包括可能与海盗和武装抢劫有关的部分的实用知识 海上保安级别及其对船舶和港口设施安全措施和程序的影响的知识 保安报告程序的知识 有关公约、规则和 IMO 通函要求的演习和练习程序的知识,包括可能与防海盗和防武装抢劫等有关的实用知识 执行检查和检验、控制并监控船舶保安计划列明的保安活动的程序的知识	评估从认可的训练或参加认可的课程中获取的证据	程序和措施符合《国际船舶和港口设施保安规则》和经修正的《1974 年国际海上人命安全公约》所确定的原则 正确识别与保安相关的法定要求 职责范围内的交流清楚易懂

Column 1	Column 2	Column 3	Column 4
Competence	**Knowledge, understanding and proficiency**	**Methods for demonstrating competence**	**Criteria for evaluating competence**
Maintain the conditions set forth in a ship security plan *(continued)*	Knowledge of security-related contingency plans and the procedures for responding to security threats or breaches of security, including provisions for maintaining critical operations of the ship/port interface, and including also working knowledge of those that may relate to piracy and armed robbery		
Recognition of security risks and threats	Knowledge of security documentation, including the Declaration of Security Knowledge of techniques used to circumvent security measures, including those used by pirates and armed robbers Knowledge enabling recognition of potential security threats Knowledge enabling recognition of weapons, dangerous substances and devices and awareness of the damage they can cause Knowledge of crowd management and control techniques, where appropriate Knowledge in handling security-related information and security-related communications Knowledge of the methods for physical searches and non-intrusive inspections	Assessment of evidence obtained from approved instruction or during attendance at an approved course	Procedures and actions are in accordance with the principles established by the ISPS Code and the SOLAS, 1974, as amended

第 1 栏	第 2 栏	第 3 栏	第 4 栏
适任	**知识、理解和熟练**	**表明适任的方法**	**评价适任的标准**
保持船舶保安计划所设定的状态（续）	保安相关的应急计划和应对保安威胁或违反保安规定的反应程序的知识，包括保持船/港界面关键操作的规定，也包括可能与海盗和武装抢劫有关的实用知识		
识别安全风险和威胁	保安文件知识，包括《保安声明》 用于躲避保安措施技术的知识，包括海盗和武装抢劫分子使用的技术 能够识别潜在保安危险的知识 能够识别武器、危险品和危险装置的知识，并清楚其能够造成的损害 拥挤人群管理和控制技术的知识，如适用 处理与保安相关的信息和保安通信的知识 搜身和非侵入式检查的方法的知识	评估从认可的训练或参加认可的课程中获取的证据	程序和行动符合《国际船舶和港口设施保安规则》和经修正的《1974 年国际海上人命安全公约》所确定的原则

Column 1	Column 2	Column 3	Column 4
Competence	**Knowledge, understanding and proficiency**	**Methods for demonstrating competence**	**Criteria for evaluating competence**
Undertake regular security inspections of the ship	Knowledge of the techniques for monitoring restricted areas Knowledge of controlling access to the ship and to restricted areas on board ship Knowledge of methods for effective monitoring of deck areas and areas surrounding the ship Knowledge of inspection methods relating to the cargo and ship's stores Knowledge of methods for controlling the embarkation, disembarkation and access while on board of persons and their effects	Assessment of evidence obtained from approved instruction or during attendance at an approved course	Procedures and actions are in accordance with the principles established by the ISPS Code and the SOLAS Convention, as amended
Proper usage of security equipment and systems, if any	General knowledge of various types of security equipment and systems, including those that could be used in case of attacks by pirates and armed robbers, including their limitations Knowledge of the need for testing, calibrating, and maintaining security systems and equipment, particularly whilst at sea	Assessment of evidence obtained from approved instruction or during attendance at an approved course	Equipment and systems operations are carried out in accordance with established equipment operating instructions and taking into account the limitations of the equipment and systems Procedures and actions are in accordance with the principles established by the ISPS Code and the SOLAS, 1974, as amended

第 1 栏	第 2 栏	第 3 栏	第 4 栏
适任	知识、理解和熟练	表明适任的方法	评价适任的标准
对船舶进行定期的保安检查	监视限制区域的技术的知识 控制上船和进入船上限制区域的知识 有效监视甲板区域和船舶周围环境的方法的知识 与货物和船舶物料相关的检查方法的知识 控制船上人员上船、下船和在船活动范围及其携带物品的方法的知识	评估从认可的训练或参加认可的课程中获取的证据	程序和行动符合《国际船舶和港口设施保安规则》和经修正的《1974 年国际海上人命安全公约》所确定的原则
正确使用保安设备和系统,如有	包括发生海盗和武装劫匪攻击时可使用的各种保安设备和系统及其局限性的一般知识 测试、校准和维护保安系统和设备的必要性的知识,特别是在海上	评估从认可的训练或参加认可的课程中获取的证据	按照既定的设备操作规程操作设备和系统并考虑其局限性 程序和行动符合《国际船舶和港口设施保安规则》和经修正的《1974 年国际海上人命安全公约》所确定的原则

CHAPTER VII

Standards regarding alternative certification

Section A-VII/1
Issue of alternative certificates

1 Every candidate for certification at the operational level under the provisions of chapter VII of the annex to the Convention shall be required to complete relevant education and training and meet the standard of competence for all the functions prescribed in either table A-II/1 or table A-III/1. Functions specified in table A-II/1 or A-III/1 respectively may be added provided the candidate completes, as appropriate, additional relevant education and training and meets the standards of competence prescribed in those tables for the functions concerned.

2 Every candidate for certification at the management level as the person having command of a ship of 500 gross tonnage or more, or the person upon whom the command of such a ship will fall in the event of the incapacity of the person in command, shall be required, in addition to compliance with the standard of competence specified in table A-II/1, to complete relevant education and training and meet the standard of competence for all of the functions prescribed in table A-II/2. Functions specified in the tables of chapter III of this part may be added provided the candidate completes, as appropriate, additional relevant education and training and meets the standards of competence prescribed in those tables for the functions concerned.

3 Every candidate for certification at the management level as the person responsible for the mechanical propulsion of a ship powered by main propulsion machinery of 750 kW or more, or the person upon whom such responsibility will fall in the event of the incapacity of the person responsible for the mechanical propulsion of the ship, shall be required, in addition to compliance with the standard of competence specified in table A-III/1, to complete relevant education and training and meet the standard of competence for all of the functions prescribed in table A-III/2, as appropriate. Functions specified in the tables of chapter II of this part may be added provided the candidate completes, as appropriate, additional relevant education and training and meets the standards of competence prescribed in those tables for the functions concerned.

4 Every candidate for certification at the support level:

.1 in navigation or marine engineering shall be required to complete relevant training and meet the standard of competence for the function prescribed in either table A-II/4 or table A-III/4. Functions specified in table A-III/4 or A-II/4 respectively may be added provided the candidate completes, as appropriate, additional relevant training and meets the standards of competence prescribed in those tables for the function concerned;

.2 as able seafarer deck shall be required, in addition to compliance with the standard of competence specified in table A-II/4, to complete relevant training and meet the standard of competence for all of the functions prescribed in table A-II/5. Functions specified in table A-III/4 or A-III/5 may be added provided the candidate completes, as appropriate, additional relevant training and meets the standard of competence prescribed in that (those) table(s) for the function(s) concerned; and

.3 as able seafarer engine shall be required, in addition to compliance with the standard of competence specified in table A-III/4, to complete relevant training and meet

第 VII 章
关于可供选择的发证的标准

第 A-VII/1 节
可供选择的证书的签发

1 每个申请本公约附则第 VII 章规定的操作级证书的申请人,应完成相应的教育和培训,并达到表 A-II/1 或表 A-III/1 中规定的所有职能的适任标准。只要申请人相应地完成附加的有关教育和培训,并达到表中所规定的有关职能的适任标准,可以分别增加表 A-II/1 或表 A-III/1 规定的职能。

2 每个申请作为指挥 500 总吨或以上船舶,或一旦指挥者不能履行职责时将代其指挥船舶的管理级证书的申请人,除应符合表 A-II/1 规定的适任标准要求外,还应完成相应的教育和培训,并达到表 A-II/2 规定的所有职能的适任标准。只要证书申请人相应地完成附加的有关教育和培训,并达到本部分第 III 章表中规定的有关职能的适任标准,可以增加相应表中规定的职能。

3 每个申请负责主推进装置为 750 千瓦或以上的船舶动力装置管理级证书的申请人,或一旦负责推进机器的人不能履行职责时将代其履行此职责的管理级证书的申请人,除应达到表 A-III/1 规定的适任标准外,还应完成适当和相应的教育和培训,并达到表 A-III/2 规定的所有职能的适任标准。只要证书申请人完成适当和相应的附加教育和培训,并达到本部分第 II 章表中规定的有关职能的适任标准,可以增加相应表中所规定的职能。

4 每个支持级证书的申请人:

.1 申请航行或轮机工程支持级证书,应完成相应的培训并达到表 A-II/4 或表A-III/4规定的相关职能的适任标准,如申请人完成适当和相应的附加培训,并达到表 A-III/4 或表 A-II/4 分别规定的职能的适任标准,可增加相应表中所规定的职能;

.2 申请高级值班水手证书,除符合表 A-II/4 规定的适任标准外,还应完成相关培训并达到表 A-II/5 规定的所有职能的适任标准,如申请人完成适当和相应的附加培训,并达到表 A-III/4 或表 A-III/5 规定的相关职能的适任标准,可增加相应表中所规定的职能;以及

.3 申请高级值班机工证书,除符合表 A-III/4 规定的适任标准外,还应完成相关培训并达到表 A-III/5 规定的所有职能的适任标准,如申请人完成适当和相应的附加培训,并达到表 A-II/4 或表 A-II/5 规定的职能的适任标准,可增加相应表中所规定的职能。

the standard of competence for all of the functions prescribed in table A-III/5. Functions specified in table A-II/4 or A-II/5 may be added provided the candidate completes, as appropriate, additional relevant training and meets the standards of competence prescribed in that (those) table(s) for the function(s) concerned.

Section A-VII/2
Certification of seafarers

1 In accordance with the requirements of regulation VII/1, paragraph 1.3, every candidate for certification under the provisions of chapter VII at the operational level in functions specified in tables A-II/1 and A-III/1 shall:

.1 have approved seagoing service of not less than 12 months, which service shall include a period of at least six months performing engine-room duties under the supervision of a qualified engineer officer and, where the function of navigation is required, a period of at least six months performing bridge watchkeeping duties under the supervision of a qualified bridge watchkeeping officer; and

.2 have completed, during this service, onboard training programmes approved as meeting the relevant requirements of sections A-II/1 and A-III/1 and documented in an approved training record book.

2 Every candidate for certification under the provisions of chapter VII at the management level in a combination of functions specified in tables A-II/2 and A-III/2 shall have approved seagoing service related to the functions to be shown in the endorsement to the certificate as follows:

.1 *for persons other than those having command or responsibility for the mechanical propulsion of a ship* – 12 months performing duties at the operational level related to regulation III/2 or III/3 as appropriate and, where the function of navigation at the management level is required, at least 12 months performing bridge watchkeeping duties at the operational level;

.2 *for those having command or the responsibility for the mechanical propulsion of a ship* – not less than 48 months, including the provisions in paragraph 2.1 of this section, performing, as a certificated officer, duties related to the functions to be shown in the endorsement to the certificate, of which 24 months shall be served performing functions set out in table A-III/1 and 24 months shall be served performing functions set out in tables A-III/1 and A-III/2.

3 In accordance with the requirements of regulation VII/1, paragraph 1.3, every candidate for certification under the provisions of chapter VII at support level in functions specified in tables A-II/4 and A-III/4 shall have completed:

.1 approved seagoing service including not less than 12 months experience, made up of:

.1.1 not less than 6 months associated with navigational watchkeeping duties; and

.1.2 not less than 6 months associated with engine-room duties; or

第 A-VII/2 节

对海员的发证

1　根据规则第 VII/1 条第 1.3 段的要求，每个根据第 VII 章规定申请表 A-II/1 和表 A-III/1 规定的操作级职能证书的申请人应：

.1　具有不少于 12 个月的认可的海上服务资历，该资历应包括在合格的轮机部高级船员监督下至少 6 个月的机舱值班，如果要求航行职能，则应包括在合格的驾驶台值班高级船员监督下至少 6 个月的驾驶台值班资历；并且

.2　在此服务期间，完成了认可的符合第 A-II/1 节和第 A-III/1 节有关要求的船上培训计划，并在认可的培训记录簿中记载。

2　每个根据第 VII 章规定申请表 A-II/2 和表 A-III/2 规定的组合职能的管理级证书的申请人，应具有以下与证书签证上载明的职能有关的认可的海上服务资历：

.1　对于指挥船舶或负责船舶机械推进人员以外的人员——履行与规则第 III/2 条或规则第 III/3条有关的相应操作级职责 12 个月，如要求有管理级的航行职能，则要有至少 12 个月履行操作级的驾驶台值班职责；

.2　对于指挥船舶和负责船舶机械推进的人员——作为持证高级船员履行包括本节第 2.1 段的规定在内的与证书签证上载明的职能有关的职责不少于 48 个月，其中 24 个月应履行表 A-III/1规定的职能，24 个月应履行表 A-III/1 和表A-III/2规定的职能。

3　根据规则第 VII/1 条第 1.3 段的要求，每个根据第 VII 章规定申请表 A-II/4 和表 A-III/4 规定的支持级职能证书的申请人应完成：

.1　不少于 12 个月的认可的海上服务资历，其中包括：

.1.1　不少于 6 个月的与航行值班职责相关的资历，和

.1.2　不少于 6 个月的与机舱职责相关的资历；或

.2 special training, either pre-sea or on board ship, including an approved period of seagoing service which shall not be less than 4 months, made up of:

.2.1 not less than 2 months associated with navigational watchkeeping duties; and

.2.2 not less than 2 months associated with engine-room duties;

.3 the seagoing service, training and experience required by paragraph 3.1 or 3.2 shall be carried out under the direct supervision of an appropriately qualified officer or rating.

4 In accordance with the requirements of regulation VII/1, paragraph 1.3, every candidate for certification under the provisions of chapter VII at the support level in functions specified in tables A-II/5 and A-III/5 shall, while qualified to serve as a rating forming part of a navigational and engine-room watch, meet the standards of competence specified in sections A-II/5 and A-III/5 of the STCW Code and have completed:

.1 approved seagoing service of not less than 30 months, made up of:

.1.1 not less than 18 months associated with able seafarer deck duties, and

.1.2 not less than 12 months associated with able seafarer engine duties; or

.2 an approved training programme and not less than 18 months of approved seagoing service, made up of:

.2.1 not less than 12 months associated with able seafarer deck duties, and

.2.2 not less than 6 months associated with able seafarer engine duties; or

.3 an approved special integrated deck and engine training programme, including not less than 12 months' approved seagoing service in an integrated deck and engine department, made up of:

.3.1 not less than 6 months associated with able seafarer deck duties, and

.3.2 not less than 6 months associated with able seafarer engine duties.

Section A-VII/3

Principles governing the issue of alternative certificates

(No provisions)

.2　在上船前或在船上的特定培训，并具有不少于 4 个月的认可的海上服务资历，其中包括：

.2.1　不少于 2 个月的与航行值班职责相关的资历，和

.2.2　不少于 2 个月的与机舱职责相关的资历；

.3　第 3.1 段或第 3.2 段要求的海上服务、培训和资历应在具有相应资格的高级船员或普通船员的直接监督下进行。

4　根据规则第 VII/1 条第 1.3 段的要求，每个根据第 VII 章规定申请表 A-II/5 和表 A-III/5 规定的支持级职能证书的申请人，在具有组成航行值班和机舱值班部分的普通船员资格的同时，还应达到《STCW 规则》第 A-II/5 节和第 A-III/5 节规定的适任标准，并已完成：

.1　不少于 30 个月的认可的海上服务资历，其中包括：

.1.1　不少于 18 个月的与高级值班水手职责相关的资历，和

.1.2　不少于 12 个月的与高级值班机工职责相关的资历；或

.2　认可的培训计划，并具有不少于 18 个月的认可的海上服务资历，其中包括：

.2.1　不少于 12 个月的与高级值班水手职责相关的资历，和

.2.2　不少于 6 个月的与高级值班机工职责相关的资历，或

.3　认可的特定甲板和机舱组合培训计划，包括在甲板机舱综合部门不少于 12 个月的认可的海上服务资历，其中包括：

.3.1　不少于 6 个月的与高级值班水手职责相关的资历，和

.3.2　不少于 6 个月的与高级值班机工职责相关的资历。

第 A-VII/3 节

关于签发可供选择的证书的原则

（无条文）

CHAPTER VIII

Standards regarding watchkeeping

Section A-VIII/1
Fitness for duty

1 Administrations shall take account of the danger posed by fatigue of seafarers, especially those whose duties involve the safe and secure operation of a ship.

2 All persons who are assigned duty as officer in charge of a watch or as a rating forming part of a watch and those whose duties involve designated safety, prevention of pollution and security duties shall be provided with a rest period of not less than:

.1 a minimum of 10 hours of rest in any 24-hour period; and

.2 77 hours in any 7-day period.

3 The hours of rest may be divided into no more than two periods, one of which shall be at least 6 hours in length, and the intervals between consecutive periods of rest shall not exceed 14 hours.

4 The requirements for rest periods laid down in paragraphs 2 and 3 need not be maintained in the case of an emergency or in other overriding operational conditions. Musters, fire-fighting and lifeboat drills, and drills prescribed by national laws and regulations and by international instruments, shall be conducted in a manner that minimizes the disturbance of rest periods and does not induce fatigue.

5 Administrations shall require that watch schedules be posted where they are easily accessible. The schedules shall be established in a standardized format* in the working language or languages of the ship and in English.

6 When a seafarer is on call, such as when a machinery space is unattended, the seafarer shall have an adequate compensatory rest period if the normal period of rest is disturbed by call-outs to work.

7 Administrations shall require that records of daily hours of rest of seafarers be maintained in a standardized format*, in the working language or languages of the ship and in English, to allow monitoring and verification of compliance with the provisions of this section. The seafarers shall receive a copy of the records pertaining to them, which shall be endorsed by the master or by a person authorized by the master and by the seafarers.

8 Nothing in this section shall be deemed to impair the right of the master of a ship to require a seafarer to perform any hours of work necessary for the immediate safety of the ship, persons on board or cargo, or for the purpose of giving assistance to other ships or persons in distress at sea. Accordingly, the master may suspend the schedule of hours of rest and require a seafarer to perform any hours of work necessary until the normal situation has been restored. As soon as practicable after the normal situation has been restored, the master shall ensure that

* The *IMO/ILO Guidelines for the development of tables of seafarers' shipboard working arrangements and formats of records of seafarers' hours of work or hours of rest* may be used.

第 VIII 章
关于值班的标准

第 A-VIII/1 节
适于值班

1 主管机关应考虑海员,特别是涉及船舶安全和保安工作职责的海员,由于疲劳所引发的危险。

2 为所有负责值班的高级船员或参与值班的普通船员以及涉及指定的安全、防污染和保安职责的人员提供的休息时间应不少于:

.1 任何 24 小时内最少 10 小时;以及

.2 任何 7 天内 77 小时。

3 休息时间可以分为不超过 2 个时间段,其中一个时间段至少要求有 6 小时,连续休息时间段之间的间隔不应超过 14 小时。

4 在紧急或在其他超常工作情况下不必要保持第 2 段和第 3 段规定的关于休息时间的要求。紧急集合演习、消防和救生艇演习,以及国家法律与规则和国际文件规定的演习,应以对休息时间的干扰最小且不导致船员疲劳的形式进行。

5 主管机关应要求将值班安排表张贴在易显见处。该值班安排表应按照标准格式①使用船上工作语言和英语编制。

6 在海员处于待命情况下,例如机舱处于无人看守时,如该海员因被召去工作而打扰了正常的休息时间,则应给与充分的补休。

7 主管机关应要求使用船上工作语言和英语按照标准格式①保持对船员每天休息时间的记录,以监督和核实是否符合本节的规定。海员应得到一份由船长或船长授权的人员和海员签注的有关其休息情况的记录。

8 本节任何规定并不妨碍船长因船舶、船上人员或货物出现紧急安全需要,或出于帮助海上遇险的其他船舶或人员的目的,而要求海员从事长时间工作的权利。为此,船长可暂停执行休息时间制度,要求海员从事必要的长时间工作,直至情况恢复正常。一旦情况恢复正常,只要可行,船长就应确保在原定休息时间内完成工作的任何海员获得充足的休息时间。

① 可以使用《IMO/ILO 编制船员船上工作安排表和船员工作时间或休息时间记录格式指南》。

any seafarers who have performed work in a scheduled rest period are provided with an adequate period of rest.

9 Parties may allow exceptions from the required hours of rest in paragraphs 2.2 and 3 above provided that the rest period is not less than 70 hours in any 7-day period.

Exceptions from the weekly rest period provided for in paragraph 2.2 shall not be allowed for more than two consecutive weeks. The intervals between two periods of exceptions on board shall not be less than twice the duration of the exception.

The hours of rest provided for in paragraph 2.1 may be divided into no more than three periods, one of which shall be at least 6 hours in length and neither of the other two periods shall be less than one hour in length. The intervals between consecutive periods of rest shall not exceed 14 hours. Exceptions shall not extend beyond two 24-hour periods in any 7-day period.

Exceptions shall, as far as possible, take into account the guidance regarding prevention of fatigue in section B-VIII/1.

10 Each Administration shall establish, for the purpose of preventing alcohol abuse, a limit of not greater than 0.05% blood alcohol level (BAC) or 0.25 mg/*l* alcohol in the breath or a quantity of alcohol leading to such alcohol concentration for masters, officers and other seafarers while performing designated safety, security and marine environmental duties.

Section A-VIII/2

Watchkeeping arrangements and principles to be observed

PART 1 – CERTIFICATION

1 The officer in charge of the navigational or deck watch shall be duly qualified in accordance with the provisions of chapter II or chapter VII appropriate to the duties related to navigational or deck watchkeeping.

2 The officer in charge of the engineering watch shall be duly qualified in accordance with the provisions of chapter III or chapter VII appropriate to the duties related to engineering watchkeeping.

PART 2 – VOYAGE PLANNING

General requirements

3 The intended voyage shall be planned in advance, taking into consideration all pertinent information, and any course laid down shall be checked before the voyage commences.

4 The chief engineer officer shall, in consultation with the master, determine in advance the needs of the intended voyage, taking into consideration the requirements for fuel, water, lubricants, chemicals, expendable and other spare parts, tools, supplies and any other requirements.

Planning prior to each voyage

5 Prior to each voyage, the master of every ship shall ensure that the intended route from the port of departure to the first port of call is planned using adequate and appropriate charts and other nautical publications necessary for the intended voyage, containing accurate, complete and

9 缔约国可以允许对上文第 2.2 段和第 3 段中所规定的休息时间有例外,但在任何 7 天内的休息时间不得少于 70 小时。

第 2.2 段规定的每周休息时间的例外,不应超过连续两个星期。在船上连续两次例外时间的间隔不应少于该例外持续时间的两倍。

第 2.1 段规定的休息时间可以分成为不超过 3 个时间段,其中之一至少为 6 个小时,而另外两个时间段均不应少于 1 个小时。连续休息时间段间隔不得超过 14 个小时。例外在任何 7 天时间内不得超过两个 24 小时时间段。

例外应尽可能考虑到在 B-VIII/1 节里关于防止疲劳的指导。

10 为防止酗酒,主管机关应对正在履行安全、保安和海洋环境职责的船长、高级船员和其他海员设定血液酒精浓度(BAC)不高于 0.05% 或呼吸中酒精浓度不高于 0.25 mg/L,或可导致该酒精浓度的酒精量的限制。

第 A-VIII/2 节

值班安排和应遵循的原则

第 1 部分　发证

1 负责航行或甲板值班的高级船员的资格应完全符合第 II 章或第 VII 章有关航行或甲板值班职责的相应规定。

2 负责轮机值班的高级船员的资格应完全符和第 III 章或第 VII 章有关轮机值班职责的相应规定。

第 2 部分　航次计划

一般要求

3 对预定的航次,应在研究所有有关资料后事先作出计划,并应在航次开始前对设定的任何航线进行核实。

4 轮机长应与船长协商,预先确定计划航次的需要,并考虑对燃料、淡水、润滑油、化学品、消耗品和其他备件、工具、供应品的需要以及任何其他需要。

每一航次前的计划

5 每一航次前,各船船长应保证充分并恰当地运用本航次所必需的海图和其他航海出版物,对自出发港至第一停靠港的预定航线作出计划,所述海图和航海出版物应包含永久性的或可预测的以及涉及船舶航行安全的航行限制和危险的准确、完整和最新的资料。

up-to-date information regarding those navigational limitations and hazards which are of a permanent or predictable nature and which are relevant to the safe navigation of the ship.

Verification and display of planned route

6 When the route planning is verified, taking into consideration all pertinent information, the planned route shall be clearly displayed on appropriate charts and shall be continuously available to the officer in charge of the watch, who shall verify each course to be followed prior to using it during the voyage.

Deviation from planned route

7 If a decision is made, during a voyage, to change the next port of call of the planned route, or if it is necessary for the ship to deviate substantially from the planned route for other reasons, then an amended route shall be planned prior to deviating substantially from the route originally planned.

PART 3 – WATCHKEEPING PRINCIPLES IN GENERAL

8 Watches shall be carried out based on the following bridge and engine-room resource management principles:

.1 proper arrangements for watchkeeping personnel shall be ensured in accordance with the situations;

.2 any limitation in qualifications or fitness of individuals shall be taken into account when deploying watchkeeping personnel;

.3 understanding of watchkeeping personnel regarding their individual roles, responsibility and team roles shall be established;

.4 the master, chief engineer officer and officer in charge of watch duties shall maintain a proper watch, making the most effective use of the resources available, such as information, installations/equipment and other personnel;

.5 watchkeepingpersonnel shall understand functions and operation of installations/equipment, and be familiar with handling them;

.6 watchkeeping personnel shall understand information and how to respond to information from each station/installation/equipment;

.7 information from the stations/installations/equipment shall be appropriately shared by all the watchkeeping personnel;

.8 watchkeepingpersonnel shall maintain an exchangeof appropriate communication in any situation; and

.9 watchkeeping personnel shall notify the master/chief engineer officer/officer in charge of watch duties without any hesitation when in any doubt as to what action to take in the interest of safety.

计划航线的核实和标绘

6 在考虑了所有有关信息并核实了航线设计后，计划航线应清晰地标绘在相应的海图上，并在航行期间供值班高级船员随时使用，他应在使用之前核实将采用的每一航线。

偏离计划航线

7 如果在航行期间决定改变计划航线的下一停靠港，或者因其他原因船舶需要大幅度地偏离计划航线，那么，应在大幅度地偏离原计划航线之前计划出经修改的航线。

第 3 部分 值班的一般原则

8 值班应基于下列驾驶台和机舱的资源管理原则：

.1 应确保根据情况合理地安排值班人员；

.2 在安排值班人员时应考虑人员的资格或适合能力的局限性；

.3 应使值班人员理解其个人角色、责任和团队角色；

.4 船长、轮机长和负责值班的高级船员应保持适当的值班，并最有效地使用可用资源，如信息、装置/设备和其他人员；

.5 值班人员应理解装置/设备的功能和操作，并熟练使用；

.6 值班人员应理解信息及如何回应来自每一工作站/装置/设备的信息；

.7 所有值班人员应适当地共享来自工作站/装置/设备的信息；

.8 值班人员在任何情况下应保持适当的相互交流；并且

.9 对为安全而采取的行动产生任何怀疑时，值班人员应毫不犹豫地通知船长/轮机长/负责值班的高级船员。

PART 4 – WATCHKEEPING AT SEA Principles applying to watchkeeping generally

9 Parties shall direct the attention of companies, masters, chief engineer officers and watchkeeping personnel to the following principles, which shall be observed to ensure that safe watches are maintained at all times.

10 The master of every ship is bound to ensure that watchkeeping arrangements are adequate for maintaining a safe navigational or cargo watch. Under the master's general direction, the officers of the navigational watch are responsible for navigating the ship safely during their periods of duty, when they will be particularly concerned with avoiding collision and stranding.

11 The chief engineer officer of every ship is bound, in consultation with the master, to ensure that watchkeeping arrangements are adequate to maintain a safe engineering watch.

Protection of marine environment

12 The master, officers and ratings shall be aware of the serious effects of operational or accidental pollution of the marine environment and shall take all possible precautions to prevent such pollution, particularly within the framework of relevant international and port regulations.

Part 4-1 – Principles to be observed in keeping a navigational watch

13 The officer in charge of the navigational watch is the master's representative and is primarily responsible at all times for the safe navigation of the ship and for complying with the International Regulations for Preventing Collisions at Sea, 1972, as amended.

Lookout

14 A proper lookout shall be maintained at all times in compliance with rule 5 of the International Regulations for Preventing Collisions at Sea, 1972, as amended and shall serve the purpose of:

.1 maintaining a continuous state of vigilance by sight and hearing, as well as by all other available means, with regard to any significant change in the operating environment;

.2 fully appraising the situation and the risk of collision, stranding and other dangers to navigation; and

.3 detecting ships or aircraft in distress, shipwrecked persons, wrecks, debris and other hazards to safe navigation.

15 The lookout must be able to give full attention to the keeping of a proper lookout and no other duties shall be undertaken or assigned which could interfere with that task.

16 The duties of the lookout and helmsperson are separate and the helmsperson shall not be considered to be the lookout while steering, except in small ships where an unobstructed all-round view is provided at the steering position and there is no impairment of night vision or

第 4 部分　海上值班

适用于值班的一般原则

9　缔约国应指示公司、船长、轮机长和值班人员注意遵守下列原则，以确保能始终保持安全值班。

10　各船船长必须确保值班的安排足以保持安全航行值班或货物值班。在船长的统一指挥下，航行值班的高级船员在他们的值班期间，特别是他们在涉及避免碰撞和搁浅时，负责船舶的安全航行。

11　各船轮机长必须与船长协商，确保值班的安排足以保持安全的轮机值班。

保护海洋环境

12　船长、高级船员和普通船员应了解操作性或事故性的海洋环境污染的严重后果，并应采取一切可能的预防措施防止这类污染，特别是有关国际规则和港口规章规定范围内的污染。

第 4-1 部分　航行值班中应遵循的原则

13　负责航行值班的高级船员是船长的代表，并在任何时候，主要负责船舶的安全航行和遵守经修订的《1972 年国际海上避碰规则》。

瞭望

14　应遵照经修订的《1972 年国际海上避碰规则》第 5 条随时保持正规的瞭望，并应达到下列目的：

.1　针对操作环境中发生的任何重大变化，利用视觉和听觉以及所有其他可用的手段保持连续戒备状态；

.2　全面评估碰撞、搁浅和其他航行危险的局面和风险；以及

.3　探明遇险的船舶或飞机、遇难船舶人员、沉船、残骸和其他航行危险物。

15　瞭望人员必须全神贯注地保持正规瞭望，不得从事或分派给会影响瞭望的其他工作。

16　瞭望人员和舵工的职责是分开的，舵工在操舵时不应视为瞭望人员，除非在某些小船上，操舵位置具有四周无遮挡的视野并且没有夜视障碍或其他保持正规瞭望的妨碍。在下列情况下，负责航行值班的高级船员在白天可以是唯一的瞭望人员：

other impediment to the keeping of a proper lookout. The officer in charge of the navigational watch may be the sole lookout in daylight provided that, on each such occasion:

.1 the situation has been carefully assessed and it has been established without doubt that it is safe to do so;

.2 full account has been taken of all relevant factors, including, but not limited to:

- state of weather;
- visibility;
- traffic density;
- proximity of dangers to navigation; and
- the attention necessary when navigating in or near traffic separation schemes; and

.3 assistance is immediately available to be summoned to the bridge when any change in the situation so requires.

17 In determining that the composition of the navigational watch is adequate to ensure that a proper lookout can continuously be maintained, the master shall take into account all relevant factors, including those described in this section of the Code, as well as the following factors:

.1 visibility, state of weather and sea;

.2 traffic density, and other activities occurring in the area in which the vessel is navigating;

.3 the attention necessary when navigating in or near traffic separation schemes or other routeing measures;

.4 the additional workload caused by the nature of the ship's functions, immediate operating requirements and anticipated manoeuvres;

.5 the fitness for duty of any crew members on call who are assigned as members of the watch;

.6 knowledge of, and confidence in, the professional competence of the ship's officers and crew;

.7 the experience of each officer of the navigational watch, and the familiarity of that officer with the ship's equipment, procedures, and manoeuvring capability;

.8 activities taking place on board the ship at any particular time, including radiocommunication activities, and the availability of assistance to be summoned immediately to the bridge when necessary;

.9 the operational status of bridge instrumentation and controls, including alarm systems;

.10 rudder and propeller control and ship manoeuvring characteristics;

.11 the size of the ship and the field of vision available from the conning position;

.1 对局面作了充分估计,确信无疑这样做是安全的;

.2 充分考虑了包括但不限于下列一切相关因素:

- 天气情况,
- 能见度,
- 通航密度,
- 邻近的航行危险物,和
- 航行在分道通航制内或附近时必要的注意;以及

.3 当局面发生任何变化而需要时,能立即召唤人员到驾驶台协助。

17 在判断航行值班的组成是否足以保证能连续保持正规瞭望时,船长应考虑所有的相关因素,其中包括本规则本节所述的因素和以下因素:

.1 能见度、天气状况和海况;

.2 通航密度,以及发生在船舶航行区域内的其他活动;

.3 当航行在分道通航制或其他定线制水域内或附近时必要的注意;

.4 由船舶功能的性质、即时操纵要求和预期操纵所引起的额外工作量;

.5 应召并被指定为值班人员的任何船员适于值班的情况;

.6 对船舶高级船员和普通船员专业适任能力的了解和信心;

.7 每个负责航行值班的高级船员的经验和对船舶设备、程序和操纵能力的熟悉程度;

.8 任何特定时刻船上发生的活动,包括无线电通信活动,和必要时召唤人员立即到驾驶台给予协助的可能性;

.9 驾驶台的仪器和操纵装置(包括报警系统)的工作状况;

.10 舵和推进器的控制以及船舶操纵特性;

.11 船舶尺度和指挥位置的视野;

.12 the configuration of the bridge, to the extent such configuration might inhibit a member of the watch from detecting by sight or hearing any external development; and

.13 any other relevant standard, procedure or guidance relating to watchkeeping arrangements and fitness for duty which has been adopted by the Organization.

Watch arrangements

18 When deciding the composition of the watch on the bridge, which may include appropriately qualified ratings, the following factors, *inter alia*, shall be taken into account:

.1 at no time shall the bridge be left unattended;

.2 weather conditions, visibility and whether there is daylight or darkness;

.3 proximity of navigational hazards which may make it necessary for the officer in charge of the watch to carry out additional navigational duties;

.4 use and operational condition of navigational aids such as ECDIS, radar or electronic position-indicating devices and any other equipment affecting the safe navigation of the ship;

.5 whether the ship is fitted with automatic steering;

.6 whether there are radio duties to be performed;

.7 unmanned machinery space (UMS) controls, alarms and indicators provided on the bridge, procedures for their use and their limitations; and

.8 any unusual demands on the navigational watch that may arise as a result of special operational circumstances.

Taking over the watch

19 The officer in charge of the navigational watch shall not hand over the watch to the relieving officer if there is reason to believe that the latter is not capable of carrying out the watchkeeping duties effectively, in which case the master shall be notified.

20 The relieving officer shall ensure that the members of the relieving watch are fully capable of performing their duties, particularly as regards their adjustment to night vision. Relieving officers shall not take over the watch until their vision is fully adjusted to the light conditions.

21 Prior to taking over the watch, relieving officers shall satisfy themselves as to the ship's estimated or true position and confirm its intended track, course and speed, and UMS controls as appropriate and shall note any dangers to navigation expected to be encountered during their watch.

.12 驾驶台的结构，这种结构可能对值班人员利用视觉或听觉探测外部情况所造成的妨碍程度；以及

.13 本组织通过的涉及值班安排和适于值班的任何其他有关标准、程序或指南。

值班安排

18 在决定可能包括合格的普通船员在内的驾驶台值班组成时，应特别考虑下列因素：

.1 在任何时候，驾驶台不许无人值守；

.2 天气情况、能见度以及是否白天或黑夜；

.3 接近航行危险物可能需要负责航行值班的高级船员执行额外的航行职责；

.4 助航仪器，如电子海图显示与信息系统（ECDIS）、雷达或电子定位仪以及任何其他影响船舶安全航行的设备的使用和工作状态；

.5 船上是否装有自动操舵装置；

.6 是否履行无线电职责；

.7 装备在驾驶台上的无人机舱（UMS）控制装置、警报和指示器及其使用程序和局限性；以及

.8 特殊的操作环境可能导致对航行值班的出乎寻常的任何要求。

交接班

19 负责航行值班的高级船员，如果有理由相信来接班的高级船员不能有效地履行其职责，则不应向其交班，在这种情况下应通知船长。

20 接班的高级船员应确保本班人员完全能履行他们的职责，特别是他们夜视的适应性。接班的高级船员在其视力未完全调节到适应光线条件以前，不应该接班。

21 接班的高级船员在接班前，应彻底搞清本船的推算船位或真船位，并核实本船的计划航线、航向和航速以及无人机舱控制装置（如有的话），还应注意在他们值班期间预计可能遇到的任何航行危险。

22 Relieving officers shall personally satisfy themselves regarding the:

.1 standing orders and other special instructions of the master relating to navigation of the ship;

.2 position, course, speed and draught of the ship;

.3 prevailing and predicted tides, currents, weather, visibility and the effect of these factors upon course and speed;

.4 procedures for the use of main engines to manoeuvre when the main engines are on bridge control; and

.5 navigational situation, including, but not limited to:

.5.1 the operational condition of all navigational and safety equipment being used or likely to be used during the watch;

.5.2 the errors of gyro- and magnetic compasses;

.5.3 the presence and movement of ships in sight or known to be in the vicinity;

.5.4 the conditions and hazards likely to be encountered during the watch; and

.5.5 the possible effects of heel, trim, water density and squat on under-keel clearance.

23 If, at any time, the officer in charge of the navigational watch is to be relieved when a manoeuvre or other action to avoid any hazard is taking place, the relief of that officer shall be deferred until such action has been completed.

Performing the navigational watch

24 The officer in charge of the navigational watch shall:

.1 keep the watch on the bridge;

.2 in no circumstances leave the bridge until properly relieved; and

.3 continue to be responsible for the safe navigation of the ship, despite the presence of the master on the bridge, until informed specifically that the master has assumed that responsibility and this is mutually understood.

25 During the watch, the course steered, position and speed shall be checked at sufficiently frequent intervals, using any available navigational aids necessary, to ensure that the ship follows the planned course.

26 The officer in charge of the navigational watch shall have full knowledge of the location and operation of all safety and navigational equipment on board the ship and shall be aware and take account of the operating limitations of such equipment.

22 接班的高级船员应亲自搞清以下有关情况：

.1 船长对船舶航行有关的常规命令和其他特别指示；

.2 船位、航向、航速和船舶吃水；

.3 当时和预报的潮汐、潮流、气象和能见度以及这些因素对航向和航速的影响；

.4 当在驾驶台控制主机时操纵主机的程序；以及

.5 航行局面，包括但不限于：

.5.1 正在使用或在值班期间有可能使用的所有航行和安全设备的工作状况，

.5.2 陀螺罗经和磁罗经的误差，

.5.3 看到或知道附近船舶的位置及动态，

.5.4 在值班期间可能会遇到的有关情况和危险，以及

.5.5 船舶横倾、纵倾、水的密度及船体下坐而可能对龙骨下富余水深的影响。

23 负责航行值班的高级船员交班时，如果正在进行船舶操纵或其他避免危险的行动，则该高级船员的交班应推迟到这种操纵完成之后再进行。

履行航行值班

24 负责航行值班的高级船员应：

.1 在驾驶台保持值班；

.2 在正式交班之前，任何情况下均不得离开驾驶台；

.3 即使船长在驾驶台，继续对船舶安全航行负责，直至被明确告知船长已承担此责任并且彼此领会为止。

25 在值班期间，应使用任何可用的、必要的助航仪器，以足够频繁的时间间隔对所航行的航向、船位和航速进行核对，以确保本船沿着计划航线航行。

26 负责航行值班的高级船员应充分了解船上所有安全和航行设备的放置地点和操作方法，并应知道和考虑这些设备在操作上的局限性。

27 The officer in charge of the navigational watch shall not be assigned or undertake any duties which would interfere with the safe navigation of the ship.

28 When using radar, the officer in charge of the navigational watch shall bear in mind the necessity to comply at all times with the provisions on the use of radar contained in the International Regulations for Preventing Collisions at Sea, 1972, as amended in force.

29 In cases of need, the officer in charge of the navigational watch shall not hesitate to use the helm, engines and sound signalling apparatus. However, timely notice of intended variations of engine speed shall be given where possible or effective use shall be made of UMS engine controls provided on the bridge in accordance with the applicable procedures.

30 Officers of the navigational watch shall know the handling characteristics of their ship, including its stopping distances, and should appreciate that other ships may have different handling characteristics.

31 A proper record shall be kept during the watch of the movements and activities relating to the navigation of the ship.

32 It is of special importance that at all times the officer in charge of the navigational watch ensures that a proper lookout is maintained. In a ship with a separate chartroom, the officer in charge of the navigational watch may visit the chartroom, when essential, for a short period for the necessary performance of navigational duties, but shall first ensure that it is safe to do so and that proper lookout is maintained.

33 Operational tests of shipboard navigational equipment shall be carried out at sea as frequently as practicable and as circumstances permit, in particular before hazardous conditions affecting navigation are expected. Whenever appropriate, these tests shall be recorded. Such tests shall also be carried out prior to port arrival and departure.

34 The officer in charge of the navigational watch shall make regular checks to ensure that:

.1 the person steering the ship or the automatic pilot is steering the correct course;

.2 the standard compass error is determined at least once a watch and, when possible, after any major alteration of course; the standard and gyro-compasses are frequently compared and repeaters are synchronized with their master compass;

.3 the automatic pilot is tested manually at least once a watch;

.4 the navigation and signal lights and other navigational equipment are functioning properly;

.5 the radio equipment is functioning properly in accordance with paragraph 86 of this section; and

.6 the UMS controls, alarms and indicators are functioning properly.

27　负责航行值班的高级船员，不应被分派或担负任何妨碍船舶安全航行的职责。

28　在使用雷达时，负责航行值班的高级船员应切记，有必要在任何时候均应遵守经修订的有效的《1972 年国际海上避碰规则》载明的对使用雷达的规定。

29　在需要时，负责航行值班的高级船员应毫不犹豫地使用舵、主机和音响信号装置，但如有可能，应及时通知拟进行主机变速，或者按照适用的程序有效地使用装配在驾驶台的无人机舱主机控制装置。

30　航行值班的高级船员应知晓包括冲程在内的本船操纵性能，并应意识到其他船舶可能具有不同的操纵性能。

31　值班期间应保持对与航行有关的动态和活动的正规记录。

32　特别重要的是，负责航行值班的高级船员要确保随时保持正规瞭望。在具有单独海图室的船上，必要时，为了履行必需的航行职责，该负责航行值班的高级船员可以短时间进入海图室。但是，他应首先确信这样做是安全的，并保持正规瞭望。

33　在条件允许和可行的情况下，特别是在危险状况预计影响航行之前，应对船上的航行设备在海上进行频繁的操作性测试。适当时应对这些测试作好记录。这种测试还应在到港前和出港前进行。

34　负责航行值班的高级船员应作定期检查，以确保：

.1　舵工或自动舵正操作在正确的航向上；

.2　标准罗经误差每班至少测定一次，如可能，在任何大幅度改向后也测定，标准罗经和陀螺罗经经常核对，罗经复示仪与主罗经同步；

.3　自动舵至少每班手动测试一次；

.4　航行灯和信号灯及其他航行设备正常工作；

.5　无线电设备按照本节第 86 段规定正常工作；以及

.6　无人机舱（UMS）控制装置、报警和指示器工作正常。

35 The officer in charge of the navigational watch shall bear in mind the necessity to comply at all times with the requirements in force of the International Convention for the Safety of Life at Sea (SOLAS), 1974*. The officer of the navigational watch shall take into account:

.1 the need to station a person to steer the ship and to put the steering into manual control in good time to allow any potentially hazardous situation to be dealt with in a safe manner; and

.2 that, with a ship under automatic steering, it is highly dangerous to allow a situation to develop to the point where the officer in charge of the navigational watch is without assistance and has to break the continuity of the lookout in order to take emergency action.

36 Officers of the navigational watch shall be thoroughly familiar with the use of all electronic navigational aids carried, including their capabilities and limitations, and shall use each of these aids when appropriate and shall bear in mind that the echo-sounder is a valuable navigational aid.

37 The officer in charge of the navigational watch shall use the radar whenever restricted visibility is encountered or expected, and at all times in congested waters, having due regard to its limitations.

38 The officer in charge of the navigational watch shall ensure that the range scales employed are changed at sufficiently frequent intervals so that echoes are detected as early as possible. It shall be borne in mind that small or poor echoes may escape detection.

39 Whenever radar is in use, the officer in charge of the navigational watch shall select an appropriate range scale and observe the display carefully, and shall ensure that plotting or systematic analysis is commenced in ample time.

40 The officer in charge of the navigational watch shall notify the master immediately:

.1 if restricted visibility is encountered or expected;

.2 if the traffic conditions or the movements of other ships are causing concern;

.3 if difficulty is experienced in maintaining course;

.4 on failure to sight land, or a navigation mark or to obtain soundings by the expected time;

.5 if, unexpectedly, land or a navigation mark is sighted or a change in soundings occurs;

.6 on breakdown of the engines, propulsion machinery remote control, steering gear or any essential navigational equipment, alarm or indicator;

.7 if the radio equipment malfunctions;

* See SOLAS regulations V/24, V/25 and V/26.

35 负责航行值班的高级船员应切记始终遵守《1974 年国际海上人命安全公约》①中有效要求的必要性。航行值班的高级船员应考虑到：

.1 使舵工就位并及时改为手动操舵以使潜在的危险局面转危为安的必要性；以及

.2 使用自动舵的船舶，如让局面发展到使负责航行值班的高级船员得不到帮助以致不得不中断瞭望而采取紧急措施是非常危险的。

36 航行值班的高级船员应完全熟悉所装备的所有电子助航仪器的使用方法，其中包括其性能及局限性。适当时，应使用每一种助航仪器并应切记回声测深仪是一种很有价值的助航仪器。

37 遇到或预料到能见度不良时，以及在拥挤水域的全部时间里，负责航行值班的高级船员应使用雷达，并注意其局限性。

38 负责航行值班的高级船员应确保所使用的量程以足够频繁的时间间隔进行转换，以便能及早地发现回波，应切记小的或微弱的回波有可能探测不到。

39 每当使用雷达时，负责航行值班的高级船员应选择适当的量程，仔细观察显示器，并应确保有充分的时间进行标绘或进行系统的分析。

40 在下列情况下，负责航行值班的高级船员应立即通知船长：

.1 遇到或预料到能见度不良时；

.2 对交通状况或他船的动态产生疑虑时；

.3 对保持航向感到困难时；

.4 到预定时间未能看到陆地、航行标志或测不到水深时；

.5 意外地看到陆地、航行标志或水深突然发生变化时；

.6 主机，推进机械的遥控装置，舵机或者任何重要的航行设备、警报或指示仪发生故障时；

.7 无线电设备发生故障时；

① 参见 SOLAS 公约 V/24 条、第/25 条和 V/26 条。

.8 in heavy weather, if in any doubt about the possibility of weather damage;

.9 if the ship meets any hazard to navigation, such as ice or a derelict; and

.10 in any other emergency or if in any doubt.

41 Despite the requirement to notify the master immediately in the foregoing circumstances, the officer in charge of the navigational watch shall, in addition, not hesitate to take immediate action for the safety of the ship, where circumstances so require.

42 The officer in charge of the navigational watch shall give watchkeeping personnel all appropriate instructions and information which will ensure the keeping of a safe watch, including a proper lookout.

Watchkeeping under different conditions and in different areas

Clear weather

43 The officer in charge of the navigational watch shall take frequent and accurate compass bearings of approaching ships as a means of early detection of risk of collision and shall bear in mind that such risk may sometimes exist even when an appreciable bearing change is evident, particularly when approaching a very large ship or a tow or when approaching a ship at close range. The officer in charge of the navigational watch shall also take early and positive action in compliance with the applicable International Regulations for Preventing Collisions at Sea, 1972, as amended and subsequently check that such action is having the desired effect.

44 In clear weather, whenever possible, the officer in charge of the navigational watch shall carry out radar practice.

Restricted visibility

45 When restricted visibility is encountered or expected, the first responsibility of the officer in charge of the navigational watch is to comply with the relevant rules of the International Regulations for Preventing Collisions at Sea, 1972, as amended with particular regard to the sounding of fog signals, proceeding at a safe speed and having the engines ready for immediate manoeuvre. In addition, the officer in charge of the navigational watch shall:

.1 inform the master;

.2 post a proper lookout;

.3 exhibit navigation lights; and

.4 operate and use the radar.

In hours of darkness

46 The master and the officer in charge of the navigational watch, when arranging lookout duty, shall have due regard to the bridge equipment and navigational aids available for use, their limitations, procedures and safeguards implemented.

.8 在恶劣天气中,怀疑可能有天气危害时;

.9 船舶遇到任何航行危险时,诸如冰或海上弃船;以及

.10 其他紧急情况或感到怀疑时。

41 尽管在上述情况下要求立即通知船长,但在情况需要时,负责航行值班的高级船员为了船舶安全,应毫不犹豫地采取果断行动。

42 负责航行值班的高级船员应给予全体值班人员一切适当的指示和信息,以确保包括正规瞭望在内的安全值班得以保持。

在不同条件下和不同水域内的值班

良好天气

43 负责航行值班的高级船员应频繁地测定驶近船舶的精确罗经方位作为及早发现碰撞危险的方法,并应切记有时方位变化明显但碰撞危险依然存在,特别是在驶近大型船舶或拖带船队时或是在近距离接近他船时,负责航行值班的高级船员还应按适用的经修订的《1972年国际海上避碰规则》及早采取积极的行动,随后还应检查此种避碰行动是否取得预期的效果。

44 天气良好时,只要有可能,负责航行值班的高级船员应进行雷达操练。

能见度不良

45 遇到或预料到能见度不良时,负责航行值班的高级船员的首要职责是遵守经修订的《1972 年国际海上避碰规则》的相应条款,特别是有关鸣放雾号、以安全航速航行并使主机处于立即可操作的准备状态的条款。此外,负责航行值班的高级船员还应:

.1 通知船长;

.2 布置正规的瞭望;

.3 显示航行灯;并且

.4 操作和使用雷达。

黑暗期间

46 船长和负责航行值班的高级船员在安排瞭望职责时应充分考虑到可供使用的驾驶台设备和助航仪器及其局限性、程序和所实施的安全措施。

Coastal and congested waters

47 The largest scale chart on board, suitable for the area and corrected with the latest available information, shall be used. Fixes shall be taken at frequent intervals, and shall be carried out by more than one method whenever circumstances allow. When using ECDIS, appropriate usage code (scale) electronic navigational charts shall be used and the ship's position shall be checked by an independent means of position fixing at appropriate intervals.

48 The officer in charge of the navigational watch shall positively identify all relevant navigation marks.

Navigation with pilot on board

49 Despite the duties and obligations of pilots, their presence on board does not relieve the master or the officer in charge of the navigational watch from their duties and obligations for the safety of the ship. The master and the pilot shall exchange information regarding navigation procedures, local conditions and the ship's characteristics. The master and/or the officer in charge of the navigational watch shall co-operate closely with the pilot and maintain an accurate check on the ship's position and movement.

50 If in any doubt as to the pilot's actions or intentions, the officer in charge of the navigational watch shall seek clarification from the pilot and, if doubt still exists, shall notify the master immediately and take whatever action is necessary before the master arrives.

Ship at anchor

51 If the master considers it necessary, a continuous navigational watch shall be maintained at anchor. While at anchor, the officer in charge of the navigational watch shall:

.1 determine and plot the ship's position on the appropriate chart as soon as practicable;

.2 when circumstances permit, check at sufficiently frequent intervals whether the ship is remaining securely at anchor by taking bearings of fixed navigation marks or readily identifiable shore objects;

.3 ensure that proper lookout is maintained;

.4 ensure that inspection rounds of the ship are made periodically;

.5 observe meteorological and tidal conditions and the state of the sea;

.6 notify the master and undertake all necessary measures if the ship drags anchor;

.7 ensure that the state of readiness of the main engines and other machinery is in accordance with the master's instructions;

.8 if visibility deteriorates, notify the master;

.9 ensure that the ship exhibits the appropriate lights and shapes and that appropriate sound signals are made in accordance with all applicable regulations; and

沿海和拥挤水域

47　应使用船上适合于该地区并依据最新资料改正过的最大比例尺海图，应以频繁的时间间隔测定船位，环境许可时应采取多种方法定位。使用电子海图显示与信息系统（ECDIS），应选择适当使用码（比例尺）的电子海图，并以适当的时间间隔通过独立的定位方法对船位进行核查。

48　负责航行值班的高级船员应确切地辨认所有相关的航行标志。

有引航员在船时的航行

49　尽管引航员有其职责和义务，但他们在船上引航时并不解除船长或负责航行值班的高级船员对船舶安全所负的职责和义务。船长和引航员应交换有关航行程序、当地情况和船舶性能等信息。船长和/或负责航行值班的高级船员应与引航员密切配合，并保持对船舶的位置和动态进行准确的核对。

50　如果负责航行值班的高级船员对引航员的行动或意图有所怀疑，他应要求引航员予以澄清，如仍有怀疑，应立即报告船长，并在船长到达之前采取必要的行动。

船在锚泊

51　如果船长认为必要，船舶在锚泊情况下也应保持连续的航行值班。船在锚泊时，负责航行值班的高级船员应：

.1　尽快地测定船位并标绘在相应的海图上；

.2　条件允许时，以足够频繁的时间间隔，利用固定航标或岸上容易辨认的物标测定方位，以校核船舶是否安全地保持在锚位上；

.3　确保保持正规的瞭望；

.4　确保定时巡视船舶；

.5　观察气象和潮汐情况以及海况；

.6　如船舶走锚，通知船长并采取一切必要措施；

.7　确保主机和其他机器按照船长指示处于准备状态；

.8　如果能见度恶化，通知船长；

.9　确保船舶按照所有适用的规定显示相应号灯、号型并鸣放相应的声号；并且

.10 take measures to protect the environment from pollution by the ship and comply with applicable pollution regulations.

Part 4-2 – Principles to be observed in keeping an engineering watch

52 The term *engineering watch* as used in parts 4-2, 5-2 and 5-4 of this section means either a person or a group of personnel comprising the watch or a period of responsibility for an officer during which the physical presence in machinery spaces of that officer may or may not be required.

53 The *officer in charge of the engineering watch* is the chief engineer officer's representative and is primarily responsible, at all times, for the safe and efficient operation and upkeep of machinery affecting the safety of the ship and is responsible for the inspection, operation and testing, as required, of all machinery and equipment under the responsibility of the engineering watch.

Watch arrangements

54 The composition of the engineering watch shall, at all times, be adequate to ensure the safe operation of all machinery affecting the operation of the ship, in either automated or manual mode, and be appropriate to the prevailing circumstances and conditions.

55 When deciding the composition of the engineering watch, which may include appropriately qualified ratings, the following criteria, *inter alia*, shall be taken into account:

.1 the type of ship and the type and condition of the machinery;

.2 the adequate supervision, at all times, of machinery affecting the safe operation of the ship;

.3 any special modes of operation dictated by conditions such as weather, ice, contaminated water, shallow water, emergency conditions, damage containment or pollution abatement;

.4 the qualifications and experience of the engineering watch;

.5 the safety of life, ship, cargo and port, and protection of the environment;

.6 the observance of international, national and local regulations; and

.7 maintaining the normal operations of the ship.

Taking over the watch

56 The officer in charge of the engineering watch shall not hand over the watch to the relieving officer if there is reason to believe that the latter is obviously not capable of carrying out the watchkeeping duties effectively, in which case the chief engineer officer shall be notified.

57 The relieving officer of the engineering watch shall ensure that the members of the relieving engineering watch are apparently fully capable of performing their duties effectively.

.10 采取措施防止船舶污染环境,并遵守适用的防止污染规则。

第 4-2 部分 轮机值班中应遵循的原则

52 本节中第 4-2 部分、第 5-2 部分和第 5-4 部分所使用的“轮机值班”一词,系指一个人或组成值班的一组人,或一个高级船员的责任时间段,在此时间段内,可以要求也可以不要求该高级船员亲临机舱。

53 负责轮机值班的高级船员是轮机长的代表,在任何时候,主要负责对影响船舶安全的机械设备进行安全有效的操作和保养,并按要求负责轮机值班责任范围内的一切机械和设备的检查、操作和测试。

值班安排

54 在任何时候,轮机值班的组成足以确保影响船舶运行的所有机器,无论是自动还是手动方式均能安全运转,并适于当时的环境和条件。

55 在决定可能包括合格的普通船员在内的轮机值班的组成时,下列准则应特别予以考虑:

.1 船舶类型以及机器类型和状况;

.2 始终对影响船舶安全运行的机器予以有效的监管;

.3 由于天气、冰、被污染水域、浅水、各种紧急情况、损害的控制或污染的减轻等情况而采用的任何特殊操作方式;

.4 轮机值班人员的资格和经历;

.5 人命、船舶、货物和港口的安全以及环境保护;

.6 遵守国际、国家和当地的规章;以及

.7 保持船舶的正常营运。

交接班

56 负责轮机值班的高级船员,如有理由认为接班的高级船员显然不能有效地履行其值班职责,不应向其交班,在这种情况下应通知轮机长。

57 轮机值班接班的高级船员应确保本班人员显然完全能有效地履行其职责。

58 Prior to taking over the engineering watch, relieving officers shall satisfy themselves regarding at least the following:

.1 the standing orders and special instructions of the chief engineer officer relating to the operation of the ship's systems and machinery;

.2 the nature of all work being performed on machinery and systems, the personnel involved and potential hazards;

.3 the level and, where applicable, the condition of water or residues in bilges, ballast tanks, slop tanks, reserve tanks, fresh water tanks, sewage tanks and any special requirements for use or disposal of the contents thereof;

.4 the condition and level of fuel in the reserve tanks, settling tank, day tank and other fuel storage facilities;

.5 any special requirements relating to sanitary system disposals;

.6 condition and mode of operation of the various main and auxiliary systems, including the electrical power distribution system;

.7 where applicable, the condition of monitoring and control console equipment, and which equipment is being operated manually;

.8 where applicable, the condition and mode of operation of automatic boiler controls such as flame safeguard control systems, limit control systems, combustion control systems, fuel-supply control systems and other equipment related to the operation of steam boilers;

.9 any potentially adverse conditions resulting from bad weather, ice, or contaminated or shallow water;

.10 any special modes of operation dictated by equipment failure or adverse ship conditions;

.11 the reports of engine-room ratings relating to their assigned duties;

.12 the availability of fire-fighting appliances; and

.13 the state of completion of the engine-room log.

Performing the engineering watch

59 The officer in charge of the engineering watch shall ensure that the established watchkeeping arrangements are maintained and that, under direction, engine-room ratings, if forming part of the engineering watch, assist in the safe and efficient operation of the propulsion machinery and auxiliary equipment.

60 The officer in charge of the engineering watch shall continue to be responsible for machinery-space operations, despite the presence of the chief engineer officer in the machinery spaces, until specifically informed that the chief engineer officer has assumed that responsibility and this is mutually understood.

58 轮机值班接班的高级船员在接班之前,应至少就以下各项使自己满意:

.1 轮机长对船舶有关系统和机器操作的常规命令和特别指示;

.2 对机器和各系统进行的一切工作的性质和参与人员以及潜在的危险;

.3 舱底水、压载舱、污油舱、备用舱、淡水柜、粪便柜中的水或残渣的液位和状况(如适用),以及对其中贮存物的使用或处理的任何特殊要求;

.4 备用舱、沉淀柜、日用柜和其他燃油贮存设施中的燃油液位和状况;

.5 有关卫生系统处理的特殊要求;

.6 各种主、辅系统包括配电系统的状况和操作模式;

.7 如适用,监视和控制台设备及其手动操作设备的状况;

.8 如适用,自动锅炉控制装置诸如火焰安全控制系统、限位控制系统、燃烧控制系统、燃油供给控制系统和其他与蒸汽锅炉操作有关的设备的状况和操作模式;

.9 由于恶劣天气、冰、被污染的水或浅水引起的任何潜在不利条件;

.10 由于设备故障或不利的船舶条件而采取的特殊操作模式;

.11 机舱普通船员涉及其所指定职责的报告;

.12 消防设备的可用性;以及

.13 轮机日志的填写情况。

履行轮机值班

59 负责轮机值班的高级船员应确保保持既定的值班安排,并应确保组成机舱值班部分的普通船员根据指示在推进机械和辅助设备安全与有效操作方面给予协助。

60 尽管轮机长在机舱,负责轮机值班的高级船员仍应继续对机舱工作负责,直至被明确告知轮机长已承担此责任并且双方都已彼此领会为止。

61 All members of the engineering watch shall be familiar with their assigned watchkeeping duties. In addition, every member shall, with respect to the ship they are serving in, have knowledge of:

.1 the use of appropriate internal communication systems;

.2 the escape routes from machinery spaces;

.3 the engine-room alarm systems and be able to distinguish between the various alarms, with special reference to the fire-extinguishing media alarm; and

.4 the number, location and types of fire-fighting equipment and damage-control gear in the machinery spaces, together with their use and the various safety precautions to be observed.

62 Any machinery not functioning properly, expected to malfunction or requiring special service shall be noted along with any action already taken. Plans shall be made for any further action if required.

63 When the machinery spaces are in the manned condition, the officer in charge of the engineering watch shall at all times be readily capable of operating the propulsion equipment in response to needs for changes in direction or speed.

64 When the machinery spaces are in the periodic unmanned condition, the designated duty officer in charge of the engineering watch shall be immediately available and on call to attend the machinery spaces.

65 All bridge orders shall be promptly executed. Changes in direction or speed of the main propulsion units shall be recorded, except where an Administration has determined that the size or characteristics of a particular ship make such recording impracticable. The officer in charge of the engineering watch shall ensure that the main propulsion unit controls, when in the manual mode of operation, are continuously attended under stand-by or manoeuvring conditions.

66 Due attention shall be paid to the ongoing maintenance and support of all machinery, including mechanical, electrical, electronic, hydraulic and pneumatic systems, their control apparatus and associated safety equipment, all accommodation service systems equipment and the recording of stores and spare gear usage.

67 The chief engineer officer shall ensure that the officer in charge of the engineering watch is informed of all preventive maintenance, damage control, or repair operations to be performed during the engineering watch. The officer in charge of the engineering watch shall be responsible for the isolation, bypassing and adjustment of all machinery under the responsibility of the engineering watch that is to be worked on, and shall record all work carried out.

68 When the engine-room is put in a stand-by condition, the officer in charge of the engineering watch shall ensure that all machinery and equipment which may be used during manoeuvring is in a state of immediate readiness and that an adequate reserve of power is available for steering gear and other requirements.

69 Officers in charge of an engineering watch shall not be assigned or undertake any duties which would interfere with their supervisory duties in respect of the main propulsion system and

61　轮机值班的所有成员都应熟悉所指派的值班职责。此外，每个成员对其服务的船舶应具有下列知识：

.1　适当内部通信系统的使用；

.2　从机器处所逃生的路线；

.3　机舱报警系统和辨别各种报警装置的能力，特别是灭火介质警报；以及

.4　机舱的消防设备和损害控制装置的数量、位置和种类，以及它们的使用方法和应遵守的各种安全预防措施。

62　对任何运转失常、预料将发生故障或需特殊维护的机器，连同已经采取的措施应作好记录。如果需要，应对进一步采取的措施作出计划。

63　当机器处所处于有人值守状态时，负责轮机值班的高级船员应始终能立即操作推进设备以应对换向或变速的需要。

64　当机器处所处于周期性无人值守状态时，被指定负责轮机值班的高级船员应能够立即就备并随时待命到达机器处所。

65　驾驶台的所有命令应迅速执行。对主推进装置的换向和变速应作好记录，除非主管机关认为特定船舶的尺度或特性使这种记录不可行。在备车或机动操纵状态下，当使用手动操作时，负责轮机值班的高级船员应确保主推进装置的操纵装置不间断地有人值守。

66　对所有机器的日常保养和维护应给予足够的注意，其中包括机械、电气、电子、液压和气动系统，它们的控制装置和相关的安全设备，所有居住舱室的服务系统设备，以及物料和备用品的使用情况记录。

67　轮机长应确保将值班时拟进行的所有预防性保养、损害控制或修理工作等通知负责轮机值班的高级船员。对于拟处理的并属于轮机值班责任内的所有机器，负责轮机值班的高级船员应负责其隔离、旁通和调整，并将已进行的所有工作作好记录。

68　当机舱处于准备状态时，负责轮机值班的高级船员应确保使所有在操作时可能用到的机器和设备处于随时可用状态，并使电力有充足的富余量，以用于舵机和其他需要。

69　负责轮机值班的高级船员不应被分派或承担任何可能妨碍他监管主推进系统及附属设备职责的任务。他们应使主推进装置和辅助系统处于不间断的监管之下，直至正式交班为止，并应定时检查其负责的机器。他们还应确保在机舱和舵机间进行足够的巡视，以便观察和报告设备的故障和损坏，履行或指导日常调整、要求的保养和任何其他必要的工作。

ancillary equipment. They shall keep the main propulsion plant and auxiliary systems under constant supervision until properly relieved, and shall periodically inspect the machinery in their charge. They shall also ensure that adequate rounds of the machinery and steering-gear spaces are made for the purpose of observing and reporting equipment malfunctions or breakdowns, performing or directing routine adjustments, required upkeep and any other necessary tasks.

70 Officers in charge of an engineering watch shall direct any other member of the engineering watch to inform them of potentially hazardous conditions which may adversely affect the machinery or jeopardize the safety of life or of the ship.

71 The officer in charge of the engineering watch shall ensure that the machinery space watch is supervised, and shall arrange for substitute personnel in the event of the incapacity of any engineering watch personnel. The engineering watch shall not leave the machinery spaces unsupervised in a manner that would prevent the manual operation of the engine-room plant or throttles.

72 The officer in charge of the engineering watch shall take the action necessary to contain the effects of damage resulting from equipment breakdown, fire, flooding, rupture, collision, stranding, or other cause.

73 Before going off duty, the officer in charge of the engineering watch shall ensure that all events related to the main and auxiliary machinery which have occurred during the engineering watch are suitably recorded.

74 The officer in charge of the engineering watch shall cooperate with any engineer in charge of maintenance work during all preventive maintenance, damage control or repairs. This shall include, but not necessarily be limited to:

.1 isolating and bypassing machinery to be worked on;

.2 adjusting the remaining plant to function adequately and safely during the maintenance period;

.3 recording, in the engine-room log or other suitable document, the equipment worked on and the personnel involved, and which safety steps have been taken and by whom, for the benefit of relieving officers and for record purposes; and

.4 testing and putting into service, when necessary, the repaired machinery or equipment.

75 The officer in charge of the engineering watch shall ensure that any engine-room ratings who perform maintenance duties are available to assist in the manual operation of machinery in the event of automatic equipment failure.

76 The officer in charge of the engineering watch shall bear in mind that changes in speed, resulting from machinery malfunction, or any loss of steering may imperil the safety of the ship and life at sea. The bridge shall be immediately notified in the event of fire and of any impending action in machinery spaces that may cause reduction in the ship's speed, imminent steering failure, stoppage of the ship's propulsion system or any alteration in the generation of electric power or similar threat to safety. This notification, where possible, shall be accomplished before changes are made, in order to afford the bridge the maximum available time to take whatever action is possible to avoid a potential marine casualty.

70 负责轮机值班的高级船员应指导任何其他的轮机值班人员，告知他们有关对机器会造成不利影响或危及人命或船舶安全的潜在危险情况。

71 负责轮机值班的高级船员应确保机器处所的值班处于监管之下，一旦值班人员丧失值班能力，应安排替代人员。轮机值班不能使机器处所无人监管，否则将妨碍机舱装置或操纵阀的手动操作。

72 负责轮机值班的高级船员应采取必要措施，以遏制由于设备损坏、失火、进水、破裂、碰撞、搁浅和其他原因所引起损害的影响。

73 在下班前，负责轮机值班的高级船员应确保在本轮机值班期间发生的有关主机和辅机的事件都有适当的记录。

74 在进行所有预防性保养、损害控制或维修工作时，负责轮机值班的高级船员应与负责维修工作的高级船员配合。这种配合应包括但不必限于如下内容：

.1 对要进行处理的机器加以隔离和旁通；

.2 在维修期间，将未维修的设备调节至充分和安全地发挥功能的状态；

.3 为了便于接班的高级船员工作和作好记录，在轮机日志或其他适当的文件上记载维修保养的设备、参加人员以及何人采取何种安全措施；以及

.4 必要时对修理过的机器或设备进行测试，并将其投入使用。

75 负责轮机值班的高级船员应确保，一旦自动设备失灵时，从事维修工作的机舱普通船员，可协助对机器进行手动操作。

76 负责轮机值班的高级船员应切记，由于机器故障引起的速度变化，或任何操舵失效，可能会危及船舶和海上人命安全。万一机舱发生火灾，采取紧急行动，可能导致船速下降、舵机瞬间失灵、船舶推进系统停止运转，或发电机发生任何变化或类似威胁安全的情况，应立即通知驾驶台。这种通知，如可能，应在发生变化之前完成，以便使驾驶台有最充分的时间采取一切可能的行动以避免潜在的海上事故。

77 The officer in charge of the engineering watch shall notify the chief engineer officer without delay:

.1 when engine damage or a malfunction occurs which may be such as to endanger the safe operation of the ship;

.2 when any malfunction occurs which, it is believed, may cause damage or breakdown of propulsion machinery, auxiliary machinery or monitoring and governing systems; and

.3 in any emergency or if in any doubt as to what decision or measures to take.

78 Despite the requirement to notify the chief engineer officer in the foregoing circumstances, the officer in charge of the engineering watch shall not hesitate to take immediate action for the safety of the ship, its machinery and crew where circumstances require.

79 The officer in charge of the engineering watch shall give the watchkeeping personnel all appropriate instructions and information which will ensure the keeping of a safe engineering watch. Routine machinery upkeep, performed as incidental tasks as a part of keeping a safe watch, shall be set up as an integral part of the watch routine. Detailed repair maintenance involving repairs to electrical, mechanical, hydraulic, pneumatic or applicable electronic equipment throughout the ship shall be performed with the cognizance of the officer in charge of the engineering watch and chief engineer officer. These repairs shall be recorded.

Engineering watchkeeping under different conditions and in different areas

Restricted visibility

80 The officer in charge of the engineering watch shall ensure that permanent air or steam pressure is available for sound signals and that at all times bridge orders relating to changes in speed or direction of operation are immediately implemented and, in addition, that auxiliary machinery used for manoeuvring is readily available.

Coastal and congested waters

81 The officer in charge of the engineering watch shall ensure that all machinery involved with the manoeuvring of the ship can immediately be placed in the manual mode of operation when notified that the ship is in congested waters. The officer in charge of the engineering watch shall also ensure that an adequate reserve of power is available for steering and other manoeuvring requirements. Emergency steering and other auxiliary equipment shall be ready for immediate operation.

Ship at anchor

82 At an unsheltered anchorage the chief engineer officer shall consult with the master whether or not to maintain the same engineering watch as when under way.

77 若发生以下情况，负责轮机值班的高级船员应立即通知轮机长：

.1 当机器发生故障或损坏，可能会危及船舶的安全营运时；

.2 发生任何故障时，而确认这些故障可能会导致推进机械、辅机或监控和调节系统的损坏或破坏；以及

.3 发生紧急情况或对于采取何种措施或决定无把握时。

78 除在上述情况下需要报告轮机长以外，为了船舶、机器和船员的安全，负责轮机值班的高级船员应视情况需要，立即毫不犹豫地采取措施。

79 负责轮机值班的高级船员应将保证安全轮机值班的一切适当的指示和信息告知值班人员。作为保持安全值班一部分的附带任务来完成的机器日常保养工作应纳入值班的日常工作之内。详细的维修工作，包括对全船的电气、机械、液压、气动或适用的电子设备的修理，应在负责轮机值班的高级船员和轮机长知道的情况下进行，对这些修理应作好记录。

在不同条件下和不同水域内的轮机值班

能见度不良

80 负责轮机值班的高级船员应确保提供鸣放声号所使用的持久的空气或蒸汽压力，并随时执行驾驶台的有关变速或换向的任何命令。此外，还应保证操纵用的辅机随时可用。

沿海和拥挤水域

81 负责轮机值班的高级船员，当发觉船舶位于拥挤水域时，应确保所有涉及船舶操纵的机器能即刻置于手动操作模式。负责轮机值班的高级船员还应确保有足够的备用电力用于操舵和满足其他操纵要求。应急操舵和其他辅助设备应处于随时可用状态。

船在锚泊

82 在开敞锚地，轮机长应与船长协商是否仍保持与在航时同样的轮机值班。

83 When a ship is at anchor in an open roadstead or any other virtually "at-sea" condition, the engineer officer in charge of the engineering watch shall ensure that:

.1 an efficient engineering watch is kept;

.2 periodic inspection is made of all operating and stand-by machinery;

.3 main and auxiliary machinery is maintained in a state of readiness in accordance with orders from the bridge;

.4 measures are taken to protect the environment from pollution by the ship, and that applicable pollution-prevention regulations are complied with; and

.5 all damage-control and fire-fighting systems are in readiness.

Part 4-3 – Principles to be observed in keeping a radio watch

General provisions

84 Administrations shall direct the attention of companies, masters and radio watchkeeping personnel to comply with the following provisions to ensure that an adequate safety radio watch is maintained while a ship is at sea. In complying with this Code, account shall be taken of the Radio Regulations.

Watch arrangements

85 In deciding the arrangements for the radio watch, the master of every seagoing ship shall:

.1 ensure that the radio watch is maintained in accordance with the relevant provisions of the Radio Regulations and the SOLAS Convention;

.2 ensure that the primary duties for radio watchkeeping are not adversely affected by attending to radio traffic not relevant to the safe movement of the ship and safety of navigation; and

.3 take into account the radio equipment fitted on board and its operational status.

Performing the radio watch

86 The radio operator performing radio watchkeeping duties shall:

.1 ensure that watch is maintained on the frequencies specified in the Radio Regulations and the SOLAS Convention; and

.2 while on duty, regularly check the operation of the radio equipment and its sources of energy and report to the master any observed failure of this equipment.

87 The requirements of the Radio Regulations and the SOLAS Convention on keeping a radiotelegraph or radio log, as appropriate, shall be complied with.

88 The maintenance of radio records, in compliance with the requirements of the Radio Regulations and the SOLAS Convention, is the responsibility of the radio operator designated as having primary responsibility for radiocommunications during distress incidents.The following shall be recorded, together with the times at which they occur:

83　当船舶在开敞的港外锚地或任何其他的实际上是"在海上"锚泊的情况下，负责轮机值班的高级船员应确保：

.1　保持有效的轮机值班；

.2　定时检查所有正在运行和处于准备状态的机器；

.3　按驾驶台命令使主机和辅机保持准备状态；

.4　采取措施，防止本船污染环境并遵守适用的防污染规则；以及

.5　所有损害控制和消防系统均处于准备状态。

第 4-3 部分　无线电值班中应遵循的原则

总则

84　主管机关应指示公司、船长和无线电值班人员注意遵守下列规定，以确保船舶在海上时，保持足够的无线电安全值班。在执行本规则时，应考虑《无线电规则》。

值班安排

85　在决定无线电值班安排时，各海船船长应：

.1　保证按照《无线电规则》和《SOLAS 公约》的有关规定来保持无线电值班；

.2　保证无线电值班的首要职责不会因处理与船舶安全移动和安全航行无关的无线电通信而受到不利影响；并且

.3　考虑到船上安装的无线电设备及其工作状态。

履行无线电值班

86　履行无线电值班职责的无线电操作员应：

.1　保证在《无线电规则》和《SOLAS 公约》规定的频率上保持值守；并且

.2　在值班时，定时检查无线电设备工作状况及其电源，并且在发现设备故障时报告船长。

87　如适当，应遵守《无线电规则》及《SOLAS 公约》有关无线电报或无线电日志的要求。

88　在发生遇险事件时，按照《无线电规则》和《SOLAS 公约》保持无线电记录是指定担负无线电通信首要职责的无线电操作员的责任。下列事项及其发生时间应予以记录：

.1 a summary of distress, urgency and safety radiocommunications;

.2 important incidents relating to the radio service;

.3 where appropriate, the position of the ship at least once per day; and

.4 a summary of the condition of the radio equipment, including its sources of energy.

89 The radio records shall be kept at the distress communications operating position, and shall be made available:

.1 for inspection by the master; and

.2 for inspection by any authorized official of the Administration and by any duly authorized officer exercising control under article X of the Convention.

PART 5 – WATCHKEEPING IN PORT

Principles applying to all watchkeeping

General

90 On any ship safely moored or safely at anchor under normal circumstances in port, the master shall arrange for an appropriate and effective watch to be maintained for the purpose of safety. Special requirements may be necessary for special types of ships' propulsion systems or ancillary equipment and for ships carrying hazardous, dangerous, toxic or highly flammable materials or other special types of cargo.

Watch arrangements

91 Arrangements for keeping a deck watch when the ship is in port shall at all times be adequate to:

.1 ensure the safety of life, of the ship, the port and the environment, and the safe operation of all machinery related to cargo operation;

.2 observe international, national and local rules; and

.3 maintain order and the normal routine of the ship.

92 The master shall decide the composition and duration of the deck watch depending on the conditions of mooring, type of the ship and character of duties.

93 If the master considers it necessary, a qualified officer shall be in charge of the deck watch.

94 The necessary equipment shall be so arranged as to provide for efficient watchkeeping.

.1 遇险、紧急和安全无线电通信概要；

.2 与无线电服务有关的重要事件；

.3 视情况，每天一次船位；以及

.4 无线电装置包括电源状况的概要。

89 无线电记录应保留在遇险通信工作地点，并应使其可供：

.1 船长检查；和

.2 主管机关任何授权官员和根据本公约第 X 条实施监督的任何正式授权官员检查。

第 5 部分 港内值班

所有值班应遵循的原则

总则

90 正常情况下，在港内安全系泊或锚泊的任何船上，为了安全目的，船长应安排保持适当而有效的值班。对于具有特殊类型推进系统或辅助设备的船舶以及对于载有有害的、危险的、有毒的或高度易燃物质或其他特种货物的船舶，可有必要予以特殊要求。

值班安排

91 船舶在港内时，保持甲板值班的安排应始终足以：

.1 确保人命、船舶、港口和环境的安全以及所有与货物作业有关的机械的安全操作；

.2 遵守国际、国内及当地的规章；以及

.3 保持船上秩序和日常工作。

92 船长应根据系泊情况、船舶种类和值班特点决定甲板值班人员的组成和值班的持续时间。

93 如船长认为必要，应安排一名合格的高级船员负责甲板值班。

94 为了有效的值班，应安排必要的设备。

95 The chief engineer officer, in consultation with the master, shall ensure that engineering watchkeeping arrangements are adequate to maintain a safe engineering watch while in port. When deciding the composition of the engineering watch, which may include appropriate engine-room ratings, the following points are among those to be taken into account:

.1 on all ships of 3,000 kW propulsion power and over there shall always be an officer in charge of the engineering watch;

.2 on ships of less than 3,000 kW propulsion power there may be, at the master's discretion and in consultation with the chief engineer officer, no officer in charge of the engineering watch; and

.3 officers, while in charge of an engineering watch, shall not be assigned or undertake any task or duty which would interfere with their supervisory duty in respect of the ship's machinery system.

Taking over the watch

96 Officers in charge of the deck or engineering watch shall not hand over the watch to their relieving officer if they have any reason to believe that the latter is obviously not capable of carrying out watchkeeping duties effectively, in which case the master or chief engineer shall be notified accordingly. Relieving officers of the deck or engineering watch shall ensure that all members of their watch are apparently fully capable of performing their duties effectively.

97 If, at the moment of handing over the deck or engineering watch, an important operation is being performed, it shall be concluded by the officer being relieved, except when ordered otherwise by the master or chief engineer officer.

Part 5-1 – Taking over the deck watch

98 Prior to taking over the deck watch, the relieving officer shall be informed by the officer in charge of the deck watch as to the following:

.1 the depth of the water at the berth, the ship's draught, the level and time of high and low waters; the securing of the moorings, the arrangement of anchors and the scope of the anchor chain, and other mooring features important to the safety of the ship; the state of main engines and their availability for emergency use;

.2 all work to be performed on board the ship; the nature, amount and disposition of cargo loaded or remaining, and any residue on board after unloading the ship;

.3 the level of water in bilges and ballast tanks;

.4 the signals or lights being exhibited or sounded;

.5 the number of crew members required to be on board and the presence of any other persons on board;

.6 the state of fire-fighting appliances;

.7 any special port regulations;

95　轮机长经与船长协商，应确保轮机值班的安排足以保持安全的在港轮机值班。在决定轮机值班人员的组成（可能包括相应的机舱普通船员在内）时，应考虑下列各点：

.1　在所有推进功率为 3 000 kW 及以上的船舶上，应始终有一名负责轮机值班的高级船员；

.2　在推进功率为 3 000 kW 以下的船舶上，船长酌情考虑并与轮机长协商后，可不设高级船员负责轮机值班；以及

.3　高级船员在负责轮机值班期间不应被指派或承担任何会妨碍其监控船上机械系统职责的任务或职责。

交接班

96　负责甲板或轮机值班的高级船员如有任何理由认为接班的高级船员显然不能有效地履行其值班职责，则不应向其交班，在这种情况下应据情通知船长或轮机长。接班的高级船员应确保本班人员显然完全能有效地履行他们的职责。

97　在进行甲板或轮机值班的交接班时，如正在进行重要操作，除非船长或轮机长另有指令，该操作应由交班的高级船员完成。

第 5-1 部分　甲板值班的交接班

98　在交班前，负责甲板值班的高级船员应告知接班的高级船员下列事项：

.1　泊位水深、船舶吃水、高潮和低潮的水位和时间、系缆情况、抛锚和抛出的锚链情况以及对船舶安全至关重要的其他系泊情况；主机情况和应急使用的可行性；

.2　船上拟进行的所有工作，已装货物或余留货物以及卸后船上残存物的性质、数量及其配置状况；

.3　舱底和压载舱中的水位；

.4　正在显示或鸣放的信号、灯号或声号；

.5　要求在船的船员人数和其他人员的在船情况；

.6　消防设备的情况；

.7　任何特殊的港口规定；

.8 the master's standing and special orders;

.9 the lines of communication available between the ship and shore personnel, including port authorities, in the event of an emergency arising or assistance being required;

.10 any other circumstances of importance to the safety of the ship, its crew, cargo or protection of the environment from pollution; and

.11 the procedures for notifying the appropriate authority of any environmental pollution resulting from ship activities.

99 Relieving officers, before assuming charge of the deck watch, shall verify that:

.1 the securing of moorings and anchor chain is adequate;

.2 the appropriate signals or lights are properly exhibited or sounded;

.3 safety measures and fire-protection regulations are being maintained;

.4 they are aware of the nature of any hazardous or dangerous cargo being loaded or discharged and the appropriate action to be taken in the event of any spillage or fire; and

.5 no external conditions or circumstances imperil the ship and that it does not imperil others.

Part 5-2 – Taking over the engineering watch

100 Prior to taking over the engineering watch, the relieving officer shall be informed by the officer in charge of the engineering watch as to:

.1 the standing orders of the day, any special orders relating to the ship operations, maintenance functions, repairs to the ship's machinery or control equipment;

.2 the nature of all work being performed on machinery and systems on board ship, personnel involved and potential hazards;

.3 the level and condition, where applicable, of water or residue in bilges, ballast tanks, slop tanks, sewage tanks, reserve tanks and special requirements for the use or disposal of the contents thereof;

.4 any special requirements relating to sanitary system disposals;

.5 the condition and state of readiness of portable fire-extinguishing equipment and fixed fire-extinguishing installations and fire-detection systems;

.6 authorized repair personnel on board engaged in engineering activities, their work locations and repair functions and other authorized persons on board and the required crew;

.8 船长的常规命令和特殊命令；

.9 在发生紧急情况或需要援助时，船舶与岸方人员包括与港口当局之间可供使用的通信线路；

.10 有关船舶、船员、货物的安全或防止环境污染的任何其他重要情况；以及

.11 向有关当局报告由于船舶行为造成环境污染的程序。

99 接班的高级船员在承担甲板值班任务前应核实：

.1 系泊缆绳或锚链是恰当的；

.2 显示的信号和灯号以及鸣放的声号是正确的；

.3 安全措施和防火规定是维持着的；

.4 已知道正在装卸的有害或危险货物的性质，和在发生溢漏或火灾时应采取的相应措施；以及

.5 外界情况或环境没有危及本船，本船也不危及其他船舶。

第 5-2 部分 轮机值班的交接班

100 在交接班前，负责轮机值班的高级船员应告知接班的高级船员下列事项：

.1 当日的常规命令，任何有关船舶操作、船舶机械或控制设备的功能维护以及修理的特殊命令；

.2 对船舶机械和系统进行的所有修理工作的性质，参与人员和潜在的危险；

.3 舱底、压载舱、污油舱、粪便柜、备用柜内的水或残渣的液位及状态（如适用），以及对其中贮存物的使用或处理的特殊要求；

.4 有关卫生系统处理的任何特殊要求；

.5 移动式灭火设备和固定式灭火装置以及火情探测系统的状况和准备状态；

.6 获准在船上从事机器修理的人员，其工作地点和修理项目，以及其他获准上船的人员和所需要的船员；

.7 any port regulations pertaining to ship effluents, fire-fighting requirements and ship readiness, particularly during potential bad weather conditions;

.8 the lines of communication available between the ship and shore personnel, including port authorities, in the event of an emergency arising or assistance being required;

.9 any other circumstance of importance to the safety of the ship, its crew, cargo or the protection of the environment from pollution; and

.10 the procedures for notifying the appropriate authority of environmental pollution resulting from engineering activities.

101 Relieving officers, before assuming charge of the engineering watch, shall satisfy themselves that they are fully informed by the officer being relieved, as outlined above; and:

.1 be familiar with existing and potential sources of power, heat and lighting and their distribution;

.2 know the availability and condition of ship's fuel, lubricants and all water supplies; and

.3 be ready to prepare the ship and its machinery, as far as is possible, for stand-by or emergency conditions as required.

Part 5-3 – Performing the deck watch

102 The officer in charge of the deck watch shall:

.1 make rounds to inspect the ship at appropriate intervals;

.2 pay particular attention to:

.2.1 the condition and securing of the gangway, anchor chain and moorings, especially at the turn of the tide and in berths with a large rise and fall, if necessary, taking measures to ensure that they are in normal working condition;

.2.2 the draught, under-keel clearance and the general state of the ship, to avoid dangerous listing or trim during cargo handling or ballasting;

.2.3 the weather and sea state;

.2.4 the observance of all regulations concerning safety and fire protection;

.2.5 the water level in bilges and tanks;

.2.6 all persons on board and their location, especially those in remote or enclosed spaces; and

.2.7 the exhibition and sounding, where appropriate, of lights and signals;

.7 任何港口有关船舶排出物、消防要求以及船舶防备的规章，特别是出现潜在的恶劣天气期间；

.8 在发生紧急情况或需要援助时，船舶与岸方人员包括与港口当局之间可供使用的通信线路；

.9 有关船舶、船员、货物的安全或防止环境污染的任何其他重要情况；以及

.10 向有关当局报告由于轮机部的活动造成环境污染的程序。

101 接班的高级船员在承担轮机值班任务前，应彻底搞清交班高级船员充分告知的上述事项，同时还应：

.1 熟悉现有的和可用的电、热和照明来源及其分配情况；

.2 了解船上的燃油、润滑油及所有淡水供给的可用性和有关情况；并且

.3 尽可能将船舶和机器准备妥，以便在需要时备车或应付紧急状况。

第 5-3 部分 履行甲板值班

102 负责甲板值班的高级船员应：

.1 以适当的时间间隔巡查全船；

.2 特别要注意：

.2.1 舷梯、锚链或系泊缆绳的状况和固定情况，特别是在转潮时和在有较大潮差的泊位上，必要时采取措施以确保它们处于正常工作状态，

.2.2 船舶吃水、龙骨下富裕水深和船舶的一般状态，在装卸货或压载时防止发生危险的横倾和纵倾，

.2.3 天气情况和海况，

.2.4 遵守所有有关安全和防火方面的规定，

.2.5 舱底和液舱中的水位，

.2.6 所有在船人员及其所在地点，特别是那些在远处或封闭处所内的人员，以及

.2.7 视情况显示的信号、灯号和鸣放的声号；

.3 in bad weather, or on receiving a storm warning, take the necessary measures to protect the ship, persons on board and cargo;

.4 take every precaution to prevent pollution of the environment by the ship;

.5 in an emergency threatening the safety of the ship, raise the alarm, inform the master, take all possible measures to prevent any damage to the ship, its cargo and persons on board, and, if necessary, request assistance from the shore authorities or neighbouring ships;

.6 be aware of the ship's stability condition so that, in the event of fire, the shore fire-fighting authority may be advised of the approximate quantity of water that can be pumped on board without endangering the ship;

.7 offer assistance to ships or persons in distress;

.8 take necessary precautions to prevent accidents or damage when propellers are to be turned; and

.9 enter, in the appropriate log-book, all important events affecting the ship.

Part 5-4 – Performing the engineering watch

103 Officers in charge of the engineering watch shall pay particular attention to:

.1 the observance of all orders, special operating procedures and regulations concerning hazardous conditions and their prevention in all areas in their charge;

.2 the instrumentation and control systems, monitoring of all power supplies, components and systems in operation;

.3 the techniques, methods and procedures necessary to prevent violation of the pollution regulations of the local authorities; and

.4 the state of the bilges.

104 Officers in charge of the engineering watch shall:

.1 in emergencies, raise the alarm when, in their opinion, the situation so demands, and take all possible measures to prevent damage to the ship, persons on board and cargo;

.2 be aware of the deck officer's needs relating to the equipment required in the loading or unloading of the cargo and the additional requirements of the ballast and other ship stability control systems;

.3 make frequent rounds of inspection to determine possible equipment malfunction or failure, and take immediate remedial action to ensure the safety of the ship, of cargo operations, of the port and the environment;

.3 在坏天气或收到风暴警报时，采取必要措施以保护船舶、船上人员和货物；

.4 采取各种预防措施以防止船舶对环境的污染；

.5 在危及船舶安全的紧急情况下，鸣放警报，通知船长，采取一切可能的措施以防止对船舶、其货物和船上人员造成损害，如有必要，要求岸上当局或附近船舶给予援助；

.6 掌握船舶的稳性情况，以便在失火时能建议岸上消防当局向船上喷水的大致数量而不致危及船舶；

.7 向遇险的船舶或人员提供援助；

.8 当拟转动推进器时，采取必要的预防措施以防止发生事故或损坏；并且

.9 将对船舶有影响的所有重要事项记入相应的日志。

第 5-4 部分　履行轮机值班

103　负责轮机值班的高级船员应特别注意：

.1 遵守在他值班范围内的一切命令、特殊操作程序和关于各种危险情况及其防范措施的规定；

.2 仪表和控制系统，对运行中的所有电力供应、部件和系统的监测；

.3 为防止违反地方当局有关防污染规定而采用的技术、方法和程序；以及

.4 污水的情况。

104　负责轮机值班的高级船员应：

.1 在紧急情况下，当他认为情况需要时，鸣放警报并采取一切可能的措施以防止对船舶、船上人员和货物造成损害；

.2 了解甲板部高级船员在装卸货物时对必要设备的需求情况，以及对压载和其他船舶稳性控制系统的附加要求；

.3 经常巡查以判定可能发生的设备故障或损坏，并立即采取补救措施以确保船舶、货物作业、港口和周围环境的安全；

.4 ensure that the necessary precautions are taken, within their area of responsibility, to prevent accidents or damage to the various electrical, electronic, hydraulic, pneumatic and mechanical systems of the ship; and

.5 ensure that all important events affecting the operation, adjustment or repair of the ship's machinery are satisfactorily recorded.

Part 5-5 – Watch in port on ships carrying hazardous cargo

General

105 The master of every ship carrying cargo that is hazardous, whether explosive, flammable, toxic, health-threatening or environment-polluting, shall ensure that safe watchkeeping arrangements are maintained. On ships carrying hazardous cargo in bulk, this will be achieved by the ready availability on board of a duly qualified officer or officers, and ratings where appropriate, even when the ship is safely moored or safely at anchor in port.

106 On ships carrying hazardous cargo other than in bulk, the master shall take full account of the nature, quantity, packing and stowage of the hazardous cargo and of any special conditions on board, afloat and ashore.

Part 5-6 – Cargo watch

107 Officers with responsibility for the planning and conduct of cargo operations shall ensure that such operations are conducted safely through the control of the specific risks, including when non-ship's personnel are involved.

.4 保证在其职责范围内采取必要的预防措施,以避免发生事故或对船上的各种电气、电子、液压、气动和机械系统造成损坏;以及

.5 保证将影响船上机械运转、调节或修理的所有重要事项做好记录。

第 5-5 部分　载运危险货物船舶的在港值班

总则

105　载运危险货物船舶的船长,不论货物是否是易爆的、易燃的、有毒的、危害健康的或是污染环境的,均应确保保持安全值班安排。对载运散装危险货物的船舶,这种值班应由船上的一个或几个合格的高级船员,需要时,还包括普通船员来承担,即使当船舶安全地在港系泊或锚泊也是如此。

106　对于载运非散装危险货物的船舶,船长应充分注意这些危险货物的性质、数量、包装和积载以及船上、水上和岸上的任何特殊情况。

第 5-6 部分　货物作业值班

107　负责计划和实施货物作业的高级船员应通过对特定风险的控制,包括涉及非船上人员时,确保该作业的安全实施。

2 The part B of the Seafarers' Training, Certification and Watchkeeping (STCW) Code is replaced by the following:

PART B

Recommended guidance regarding provisions of the STCW Convention and its annex

Introduction

1 This part of the STCW Code contains recommended guidance intended to assist Parties to the STCW Convention and those involved in implementing, applying or enforcing its measures to give the Convention full and complete effect in a uniform manner.

2 The measures suggested are not mandatory and the examples given are only intended to illustrate how certain Convention requirements may be complied with. However, the recommendations in general represent an approach to the matters concerned which has been harmonized through discussion within IMO involving, where appropriate, consultation with the International Labour Organization, the International Telecommunication Union and the World Health Organization.

3 Observance of the recommendations contained in this part will assist the Organization in achieving its goal of maintaining the highest practicable standards of competence in respect of crews of all nationalities and ships of all flags.

4 Guidance is provided in this part in respect of certain articles of the Convention, in addition to guidance on certain regulations in its annex. The numbering of the sections of this part therefore corresponds with that of the articles and the regulations of the Convention. As in part A, the text of each section may be divided into numbered parts and paragraphs, but such numbering is unique to that text alone.

2 《海员培训、发证和值班规则》(《STCW 规则》)的 B 部分由以下内容代替:

B 部分
关于《STCW 公约》及其附则条款的建议性指导

引言

1 《STCW 规则》本部分所包括的建议性指导,旨在协助《STCW 公约》缔约国和涉及实施、应用或采取措施的各方以统一的方式使公约得以充分和完全实施。

2 所建议的措施是非强制性的,所举出的例证仅为说明如何满足公约的某些要求,但这些建议总体上代表了对有关问题的解决方法,这些方法是在国际海事组织内部通过讨论进行了统一并视情况与国际劳工组织、国际电信联盟和世界卫生组织进行过协商。

3 遵守本部分的建议将有助于本组织实现其所有船旗国的船舶和所有国籍的船员保持最实际可行的适任标准的目标。

4 除了对本公约附则中的某些规则提供指导外,本部分还对公约某些条款提供指导。因此,本部分各章节的编号同公约的条款和规则的编号是相对应的。如同在 A 部分,每节的文本可能分为若干带编号的部分和段落,但这些编号仅用于该文本。

GUIDANCE REGARDING PROVISIONS OF THE ARTICLES

Section B-I
Guidance regarding general obligations under the Convention

(No provisions)

Section B-II
Guidance regarding definitions and clarifications

1 The definitions contained in article II of the Convention, and the definitions and clarifications contained in regulation I/1 of its annex, apply equally to the terms used in parts A and B of this Code. Supplementary definitions which apply only to the provisions of this Code are contained in section A-I/1.

2 The definition of *certificate* appearing in article II (c) provides for three possibilities:

.1 the Administration may issue the certificate;

.2 the Administration may have the certificate issued under its authority; or

.3 the Administration may recognize a certificate issued by another Party, as provided for in regulation I/10.

Section B-III
Guidance regarding the application of the Convention

1 While the definition of *fishing vessel* contained in article II, paragraph (h) excludes vessels used for catching fish, whales, seals, walrus or other living resources of the sea from application of the Convention, vessels not engaged in the catching activity cannot enjoy such exclusion.

2 The Convention excludes all wooden ships of primitive build, including junks.

Section B-IV
Guidance regarding the communication of information

1 In paragraph (1)(b) of article IV, the words "where appropriate" are intended to include:

.1 the recognition of a certificate issued by another Party; or

.2 the issue of the Administration's own certificate, where applicable, on the basis of recognition of a certificate issued by another Party.

Section B-V
Guidance regarding other treaties and interpretation

The word "arrangements" in paragraph (1) of article V is intended to include provisions previously established between States for the reciprocal recognition of certificates.

关于《STCW 公约》条款的指导

第 B-I 节
关于公约的一般义务的指导

(无条款)

第 B-II 节
关于定义和说明的指导

1　本公约第 II 条中的定义以及其附则规则第 I/1 条中的定义和说明同样适用于本规则 A 部分和 B 部分所使用的术语。仅适用于本规则条款的补充定义包括在第 A-I/1 节中。

2　公约第 II 条第(c)段中所出现的证书的定义规定了三种可能性:

.1　主管机关可签发证书;

.2　主管机关可授权签发证书;或

.3　主管机关可按规则第 I/10 条承认另一缔约国所签发的证书。

第 B-III 节
关于公约适用范围的指导

1　按公约第 II 条第(h)段中关于渔船的定义,本公约不适用于从事捕捞鱼、鲸、海豹、海象或其他海洋生物资源的船舶,但不从事捕捞活动的船舶不能享受这一免除。

2　本公约不适用于一切构造简单的木船,包括木帆船。

第 B-IV 节
关于资料交流的指导

1　第 IV 条第(1)(b)段中的"如适用"一词意在包括:

.1　承认另一缔约国所签发的证书;或

.2　如可行,在承认另一缔约国所签发的证书的基础上,签发主管机关自己的证书。

第 B-V 节
关于其他条约和解释的指导

第 V 条第(1)段中"协定"一词意在包括国家间以前所签订的有关相互承认证书的规定。

Section B-VI
Guidance regarding certificates

See the guidance given in sections B-I/2 and B-II.

A policy statement and an outline of the procedures to be followed should be published for the information of companies operating ships under the flag of the Administration.

Section B-VII
Guidance regarding transitional provisions

Certificates issued for service in one capacity which are currently recognized by a Party as an adequate qualification for service in another capacity, e.g., chief mate certificates recognized for service as master, should continue to be accepted as valid for such service under article VII. This acceptance also applies to such certificates issued under the provisions of paragraph (2) of article VII.

Section B-VIII
Guidance regarding dispensations

A policy statement and an outline of the procedures to be followed should be published for the information of companies operating ships under the flag of the Administration. Guidance should be provided to those officials authorized by the Administration to issue dispensations. Information on action taken should be summarized in the initial report communicated to the Secretary-General in accordance with the requirements of section A-I/7.

Section B-IX
Guidance regarding equivalents

Naval certificates may continue to be accepted and certificates of service may continue to be issued to naval officers as equivalents under article IX, provided that the requirements of the Convention are met.

Section B-X
Guidance regarding control

(No provisions – see section B-I/4.)

Section B-XI
Guidance regarding the promotion of technical co-operation

1 Governments should provide, or arrange to provide, in collaboration with IMO, assistance to States which have difficulty in meeting the requirements of the Convention and which request such assistance.

2 The importance of adequate training for masters and other personnel serving on board oil, chemical and liquefied gas tankers and ro-ro passenger ships is stressed, and it is recognized that in some cases there may be limited facilities for obtaining the required experience and providing specialized training programmes, particularly in developing countries.

第 B-VI 节
关于证书的指导

见第 B-I/2 节和第 B-II 节给出的指导。
应公布一份政策声明和一份应遵循的程序概要，使经营悬挂主管机关国旗的船舶的公司知晓。

第 B-VII 节
关于过渡规定的指导

对担任一种职务所签发的证书，如一缔约国目前承认其具有担任另一职务的任职资格，例如大副证书被认可担任船长职务，对此情况，应按照第 VII 条规定继续承认这种任职资格有效。这种承认也适用于按照第 VII 条第(2)段规定所签发的证书。

第 B-VIII 节
关于特免证明的指导

应公布一份政策声明和一份应遵循的程序概要，使经营悬挂主管机关国旗的船舶的公司知晓。应对主管机关授权签发特免证明的官员提供有关指导。关于采取措施的信息，应按第 A-I/7 节的要求，概略地包括在提交给秘书长的最初报告中。

第 B-IX 节
关于等效的指导

在满足本公约要求的条件下，海军证书可继续予以承认，服务证书可继续签发给海军官员，作为公约第 IX 条所规定的等效物。

第 B-X 节
关于监督的指导

(无条款——见第 B-I/4 节。)

第 B-XI 节
关于促进技术合作的指导

1　各政府应与国际海事组织合作，向在满足本公约要求方面有困难并请求帮助的国家提供或安排提供此种帮助。
2　应强调对油船、化学品船、液化气船和滚装客船上任职的船长和其他人员进行足够培训的重要性，并且认识到在某些情况下用于获取所要求的经验和提供特殊培训计划的设施可能有限，尤其在发展中国家。

Examination database

3 Parties with maritime training academies or examination centres serving several countries and wishing to establish a database of examination questions and answers are encouraged to do so, on the basis of bilateral co-operation with a country or countries which already have such a database.

Availability of maritime training simulators

4 The IMO Secretariat maintains a list of maritime training simulators, as a source of information for Parties and others on the availability of different types of simulators for training seafarers, in particular where such training facilities may not be available to them nationally.

5 Parties are urged* to provide information on their national maritime training simulators to the IMO Secretariat and to update the information whenever any change or addition is made to their maritime training simulator facilities.

Information on technical co-operation

6 Information on technical advisory services, access to international training institutions affiliated with IMO, and information on fellowships and other technical co-operation which may be provided by or through IMO may be obtained by contacting the Secretary-General at 4 Albert Embankment, London SE1 7SR, United Kingdom.

(No guidance is provided regarding articles XII to XVII.)

* See MSC.1/Circ.1209 on simulators available for maritime training.

考试数据库

3　鼓励拥有海事培训院校或考试中心、为数个国家提供服务并有愿望建立考试试题和答案数据库的缔约国，在与已经建立此类数据库的一个或数个国家开展双边合作的基础上建立此类数据库。

航海培训模拟器的提供

4　国际海事组织秘书处保存一份航海培训模拟器清单，作为向缔约国和其他各方，特别是那些本国可能不具备这类培训设施的国家，提供目前可用的培训海员用的各种模拟器的信息源。

5　敦请各缔约国①向国际海事组织秘书处提供有关他们国家航海培训模拟器的资料，并且在改变和增加模拟器设施时予以更新。

关于技术合作的资料

6　有关技术咨询服务的资料和利用隶属于国际海事组织的国际培训机构的资料，以及有关团体和可能由国际海事组织提供或通过国际海事组织提供的技术合作的资料，可向秘书长联系索取，地址：4 Albert Embankment, London SE1 7SR, United Kingdom.

（对第 XII 至 XVII 条无指导。）

① 参见关于航海培训可用的模拟器的 MSC. 1/Circ. 1209 号通函。

GUIDANCE REGARDING PROVISIONS OF THE ANNEX TO THE STCW CONVENTION

CHAPTER I

Guidance regarding general provisions

Section B-I/1
Guidance regarding definitions and clarifications

1 The definitions contained in article II of the Convention, and the definitions and interpretations contained in regulation I/1 of its annex, apply equally to the terms used in parts A and B of this Code. Supplementary definitions which apply only to the provisions of this Code are contained in section A-I/1.

2 Officers with capacities covered under the provisions of chapter VII may be designated as "polyvalent officer", "dual-purpose officer" or other designations as approved by the Administration, in accordance with the terminology used in the applicable safe manning requirements.

3 Ratings qualified to serve in capacities covered under the provisions of chapter VII may be designated as "polyvalent ratings" or other designations as approved by the Administration, in accordance with the terminology used in the applicable safe manning requirements.

Section B-I/2
Guidance regarding certificates and endorsements

1 Where an endorsement is integrated in the format of a certificate as provided by section A-I/2, paragraph 1, the relevant information should be inserted in the certificate in the manner explained hereunder, except for the omission of the space numbered .2. Otherwise, in preparing endorsements attesting the issue of a certificate, the spaces numbered .1 to .17 in the form which follows the text hereunder should be completed as follows:

.1 Enter the name of the issuing State.

.2 Enter the number assigned to the certificate by the Administration.

.3 Enter the full name of the seafarer to whom the certificate is issued. The name should be the same as that appearing in the seafarer's passport, seafarer's identity certificate and other official documents issued by the Administration.

.4 The number or numbers of the STCW Convention regulation or regulations under which the seafarer has been found qualified should be entered here, for example:

.4.1 "Regulation II/1", if the seafarer has been found qualified to fill the capacity of officer in charge of a navigational watch;

.4.2 "Regulation III/1", if the seafarer has been found qualified to act as engineer officer in charge of a watch in a manned engine-room, or as designated duty engineer officer in a periodically unmanned engine-room;

关于《STCW 公约》附则条款的指导

第 I 章
关于总则的指导

第 B-I/1 节
关于定义和说明的指导

1 本公约第 II 条所包括的定义和其附则规则第 I/1 条所包括的定义和说明，同样适用于本规则 A 部分和 B 部分所使用的术语。仅适用于本规则条款的补充定义包括在第 A-I/1 节中。

2 具有第 VII 章规定的能力的高级船员，按照适用的安全配员要求中所采用的术语，可命名为“多能高级船员”、“双职高级船员”或主管机关认可的其他名称。

3 有资格担任第 VII 章规定的职务的普通船员，按照适用的安全配员要求中所采用的术语，可命名为“多能普通船员”或主管机关认可的其他名称。

第 B-I/2 节
关于证书和签证的指导

1 如按第 A-I/2 节第 1 段规定将签证综合在证书格式中，则除了省略编号为.2 的空格外，有关的资料应按以下说明的方法填入证书中。否则，在制作证明签发证书的签证时，本段文字后面的表格中编号为.1 至.17 的空格处应按以下说明填写：

.1 填入签发国名称。

.2 填入主管机关对证书所分配的编号。

.3 填入被签发证书的船员的全名，姓名应与船员的护照、身份证件及主管机关签发的其他官方文书上的姓名一致。

.4 应填入确认船员具备资格所依据的《STCW 公约》的某一条或数条规则的编号，例如：

.4.1 如果该船员被确认为有资格担任负责航行值班的高级船员职务，填入“II/1”；

.4.2 如果该船员被确认为有资格担任有人值班机舱负责值班的轮机部高级船员或周期性无人值班机舱指派值班的轮机部高级船员职务，填入“III/1”；

.4.3 "Regulation IV/2", if the seafarer has been found qualified to fill the capacity of radio operator;

.4.4 "Regulation VII/1", if the certificate is a functional certificate and the seafarer has been found qualified to perform functions specified in part A of the Code, for example, the function of marine engineering at the management level; and

.4.5 "Regulations III/1 and V/1", if found qualified to act as the engineer officer in charge of a watch in a manned engine-room, or as designated duty engineer officer in a periodically unmanned engine-room in tankers. (See limitations in paragraphs .8 and .10 below.)

.5 Enter the date of expiry of the endorsement. This date should not be later than the date of expiry, if any, of the certificate in respect of which the endorsement is issued, nor later than five years after the date of issue of the endorsement.

.6 In this column should be entered each of the functions specified in part A of the Code which the seafarer is qualified to perform. Functions and their associated levels of responsibility are specified in the tables of competence set out in chapters II, III and IV of part A of the Code, and are also listed for convenient reference in the introduction to part A. When reference is made under .4 above to regulations in chapter II, III or IV it is not necessary to list specific functions.

.7 In this column should be entered the levels of responsibility at which the seafarer is qualified to perform each of the functions entered in column .6. These levels are specified in the tables of competence set out in chapters II, III and IV of part A of the Code, and are also listed, for convenient reference, in the introduction to part A.

.8 A general limitation, such as the requirement to wear corrective lenses when performing duties, should be entered prominently at the top of this limitations column. Limitations applying to the functions listed in column .6 should be entered on the appropriate line against the function concerned, for example:

.8.1 "Not valid for service in tankers" if not qualified under chapter V;

.8.2 "Not valid for service in tankers other than oil tankers" if qualified under chapter V for service only in oil tankers;

.8.3 "Not valid for service in ships in which steam boilers form part of the ship's machinery" if the related knowledge has been omitted in accordance with STCW Code provisions; and

.8.4 "Valid only on near-coastal voyages" if the related knowledge has been omitted in accordance with STCW Code provisions.

Note: Tonnage and power limitations need not be shown here if they are already indicated in the title of the certificate and in the capacity entered in column .9.

.4.3 如果该船员被确认为有资格担任无线电操作员职务，填入“IV/2”；

.4.4 如果证书为职能证书，并且该船员被确认有资格履行本规则 A 部分所规定的职能，如管理级的轮机工程职能，填入“VII/1”；以及

.4.5 如果该船员被确认为有资格担任液货船的有人值班机舱负责值班的轮机部高级船员或周期性无人值班机舱指定值班的轮机部高级船员职务（见下面第.8 段和第.10 段的限制），填入“III/1 和 V/1”。

.5 填入签证的失效日期。此日期不应超过加以签证的证书的失效日期（如有），也不应超过自签证日期起的 5 年时间。

.6 本栏中应填入本规则 A 部分规定的、该船员有资格履行的各项职能。各项职能及与其相关的责任级别已在本规则 A 部分第 II 章、第 III 章和第 IV 章的适任表中规定。为便于参照，也列于 A 部分的引言中。如按照上述第.4 段已填写第 II 章、第 III 章或第 IV 章的规则，则无必要列出具体的职能。

.7 本栏中应填入该海员有资格履行的、第.6 栏所注明的各项职能的责任级别。这些责任级别已在本规则 A 部分第 II 章、第 III 章和第 IV 章的适任表中规定。为便于参照，也列于 A 部分的引言中。

.8 在限制条件栏上部的明显处应填入一般性的限制条件，例如履行职责时应佩戴矫正眼镜的要求。在与有关职能对应的适当行中，应填入适用于第.6 栏所列职能的限制条件，例如：

.8.1 如果按照第 V 章规定是不合格的，填入“在液货船上服务无效”；

.8.2 如果按照第 V 章规定仅有资格在油船上服务，填入“在非油船的液货船上服务无效”；

.8.3 如果有关的知识已按照《STCW 规则》的规定进行了删除，填入“在蒸汽锅炉构成船舶机器一部分的船上服务无效”；以及

.8.4 如果有关知识已按照《STCW 规则》的规定进行了删除，填入“仅对近岸航行有效”。

注：如果在第.9 栏所填的职务中和证书的名称中已注明对吨位和功率的限制，则此处无必要再写明。

.9 The capacity or capacities entered in this column should be those specified in the title to the STCW regulation or regulations concerned in the case of certificates issued under chapter II or III, or should be as specified in the applicable safe manning requirements of the Administration, as appropriate.

.10 A general limitation, such as the requirement to wear corrective lenses when performing duties, should be entered prominently at the top of this limitations column also. The limitations entered in column .10 should be the same as those shown in column .8 for the functions performed in each capacity entered.

.11 The number entered in this space should be that of the certificate, so that both certificate and endorsement have the same unique number for reference and for location in the register of certificates and/or endorsements, etc.

.12 The date of original issue of the endorsement should be entered here; it may be the same as, or differ from, the date of issue of the certificate, in accordance with the circumstances.

.13 The name of the official authorized to issue the endorsement should be shown here in block letters below the official's signature.

.14 The date of birth shown should be the date confirmed from Administration records or as otherwise verified.

.15 The endorsement should be signed by the seafarer in the presence of an official, or may be incorporated from the seafarer's application form duly completed and verified.

.16 The photograph should be a standard black and white or colour passport-type head and shoulders photograph, supplied in duplicate by the seafarer so that one may be kept in or associated with the register of certificates.

.17 If the blocks for revalidation are shown as part of the endorsement form (see section A-I/2, paragraph 1), the Administration may revalidate the endorsement by completing the block after the seafarer has demonstrated continuing proficiency as required by regulation I/11.

.9 如果证书是依据第 II 章或第 III 章签发的,此栏所填入的一种或几种职位应是《STCW 公约》某一条或数条规则标题中所规定的职位,或是主管机关签发的安全配员要求中所规定的职位,视情况确定。

.10 在限制条件栏上部的明显处还应填入一般性的限制项目,例如履行职责时应配戴矫正眼镜的要求。对于填入的每一职位所履行的职能,第.10 栏内填入限制条件应与第.8 栏内显示的限制条件相一致。

.11 此处空格所填入的编号应与证书上的编号相一致,以便证书和签证都具有同一专用编号供参考,并在证书和/或签证登记簿中定位。

.12 此处应填入最初签证的日期;根据具体情况,此日期可与签发证书的日期相同,也可以不同。

.13 此处应在官员签字的下方以印刷体字填入被授权签发签证官员的姓名。

.14 所填的出生日期应与主管机关记录所确认的或以其他方法核实的日期相一致。

.15 签证应在一名官员在场时由海员本人签字,或可由正式填写并经核实的海员申请表并入。

.16 照片应是显示头部和肩部的黑白或彩色的护照规格标准照片,由海员提供,一式两张,其中一张存入或附于证书登记簿。

.17 如果再有效的空格作为签证格式的一部分(见第 A-I/2 节第 1 段),主管机关可在海员已表明规则第 I/11 条所要求的持续熟练水平后填写该空格,使签证再有效。

(Official Seal)

(COUNTRY)

ENDORSEMENT ATTESTING THE ISSUE OF A CERTIFICATE UNDER THE PROVISIONS OF THE INTERNATIONAL CONVENTION ON STANDARDS OF TRAINING, CERTIFICATION AND WATCHKEEPING FOR SEAFARERS, 1978, AS AMENDED

The Government of .... .1 .... certifies that Certificate No. ..... .2 ...... has been issued to .... .3 .... who has been found duly qualified in accordance with the provisions of regulation .... .4 .... of the above Convention, as amended, and has been found competent to perform the following functions, at the levels specified, subject to any limitations indicated until .... .5 .... or until the date of expiry of any extension of the validity of this endorsement as may be shown overleaf:

.6 FUNCTION	.7 LEVEL	.8 LIMITATIONS APPLYING (IF ANY)

The lawful holder of this endorsement may serve in the following capacity or capacities specified in the applicable safe manning requirements of the Administration:

.9 CAPACITY	.10 LIMITATIONS APPLYING (IF ANY)

Endorsement No .... .11 .... issued on .... .12 ....

(Official Seal)

....
Signature of duly authorized official

.... .13 ....
Name of duly authorized official

The original of this endorsement must be kept available in accordance with regulation I/2, paragraph 11 of the Convention while its holder is serving on a ship.

Date of birth of the holder of the certificate .... .14 ....

Signature of the holder of the certificate .... .15 ....

Photograph of the holder of the certificate

.16

（公章）

（国家名称）

证明根据经修正的《1978 年海员培训、发证和值班标准国际公约》的规定签发证书的签证

.... .1 .... 政府证明编号为 .... .2 .... 的证书已签发给 .... .3 .... 该持证人按照经修正的上述公约的规则 .... .4 .... 的规定完全合格，有资格履行规定级别的下列职能，但受载明的任何限制的制约，有效期至 .... .5 .... 或至可能在背面载明的此签证有效期的任何延期届满之日止：

.6 职能	.7 等级	.8 适用的限制（如有）

本签证的合法持有人可担任主管机关在相应的安全配员要求中规定的下列一种或几种职位：

.9 职位	.10 适用的限制（如有）

签证编号 .... .11 .... 签发日期 .... .12 ....

（公章）

....

经正式授权的官员签名

.... .13 ....

经正式授权的官员姓名

按照本公约规则第 I/2 条第 11 段规定，当在船上服务时，本签证原件必须保持随时可用。

持证人出生日期 .... .14 ....

持证人签名 .... .15 ....

持证人照片

.16

The validity of this endorsement is hereby extended until ....

(Official Seal) ....
Signature of duly authorized official

....
Date of revalidation .... .17 *Name of duly authorized official*

The validity of this endorsement is hereby extended until ....

(Official Seal) ....
Signature of the authorized official

....
Date of revalidation .... .17 *Name of duly authorized official*

2 An endorsement attesting the recognition of a certificate may be attached to and form part of the certificate endorsed, or may be issued as a separate document (see STCW regulation I/2, paragraph 8). All entries made in the form are required to be in Roman characters and Arabic figures (see STCW regulation I/2, paragraph 10). The spaces numbered .1 to .17 in the form which follows the text hereunder are intended to be completed as indicated in paragraph 1 above, except in respect of the following spaces:

.2 where the number assigned by the Party which issued the certificate being recognized should be entered;

.3 where the name entered should be the same as that appearing in the certificate being recognized;

.4 where the name of the Party which issued the certificate being recognized should be entered;

.9 where the capacity or capacities entered should be selected, as appropriate, from those specified in the safe applicable manning requirements of the Administration which is recognizing the certificate;

.11 where the number entered should be unique to the endorsement both for reference and for location in the register of endorsements; and

.12 where the date of original issue of the endorsement should be entered.

本签证的有效期特此延至..	
（公章）	....
	经正式授权的官员签名
	....
再有效日期...17	经正式授权的官员姓名
本签证的有效期特此延至..	
（公章）	....
	经正式授权的官员签名
	....
再有效日期...17	经正式授权的官员姓名

2　证明承认证书的签证可以附于证书并成为所签注的证书的一部分,也可以作为一份单独的文件签发(见《STCW 公约》规则第 I/2 条第 8 段)。表格中所有条目均要求使用罗马字母和阿拉伯数字(见《STCW 公约》规则第 I/2 第 10 段)。文字后的表格中编号为.1 至.17 的空格可按上述第 1 段的说明填写,但下列空格除外:

.2　此处应填入签发承认证书的缔约国分配给该证书的编号;

.3　此处所填的姓名应同被承认的证书上的姓名相一致;

.4　此处应填入签发承认证书的缔约国的名称;

.9　此处所填入的职位应从承认该证书的主管机关的安全配员要求中所规定的职位中适当选择;

.11　此处填入的编号应为唯一编号,用于参考和在签证登记簿中定位;并且

.12　此处应填入最初签证日期。

(Official Seal)

(COUNTRY)

ENDORSEMENT ATTESTING THE RECOGNITION OF A CERTIFICATE UNDER THE PROVISIONS OF THE INTERNATIONAL CONVENTION ON STANDARDS OF TRAINING, CERTIFICATION AND WATCHKEEPING FOR SEAFARERS, 1978, AS AMENDED

The Government of .... .1 .... certifies that Certificate No. .... .2 .... issued to .... .3 ....by or on behalf of the Government of .... .4 ...... is duly recognized in accordance with the provisions of regulation I/10 of the above Convention, as amended, and the lawful holder is authorized to perform the following functions, at the levels specified, subject to any limitations indicated until .... .5 ....or until the date of expiry of any extension of the validity of this endorsement as may be shown overleaf:

.6 FUNCTION	.7 LEVEL	.8 LIMITATIONS APPLYING (IF ANY)

The lawful holder of this endorsement may serve in the following capacity or capacities specified in the applicable safe manning requirements of the Administration:

.9 CAPACITY	.10 LIMITATIONS APPLYING (IF ANY)

Endorsement No .... .11 .... issued on .... .12 ....

(Official Seal)

....

Signature of duly authorized official

.... .13 ....

Name of duly authorized official

The original of this endorsement must be kept available in accordance with regulation I/2, paragraph 11 of the Convention while its holder is serving on a ship.

Date of birth of the holder of the certificate .... .14 ....

Signature of the holder of the certificate .... .15 ....

Photograph of the holder of the certificate

.16

（公章）

（国家名称）

证明根据经修正的《1978 年海员培训、发证和值班标准国际公约》的规定承认证书的签证

.... .1 ....政府证明，对由或者代表............ .4 ....政府签发给............ .3 ....的编号为............ .2 的证书，按照经修正的上述公约规则第 I/10 条的规定予以正式承认，并且准许合法持证人履行规定级别的下列职能，但受载明的任何限制的制约，有效期至............ .5 ....或至可能在背面载明的此签证有效期的任何延期届满之日止：

.6 职能	.7 等级	.8 适用的限制(如有)

本签证的合法持有人可担任主管机关在相应的安全配员要求中规定的下列一种或几种职位：

.9 职位	.10 适用的限制(如有)

签证编号............ .11 ....签发日期............ .12 ....

（公章）

....

经正式授权的官员签名

.... .13 ....

经正式授权的官员姓名

按本公约规则第 I/2 条第 11 段规定，当在船上服务时，本签证原件必须保持随时可用。

持证人出生日期............ .14 ....

持证人签名............ .15 ....

持证人照片

.16

The validity of this endorsement is hereby extended until	
(Official Seal)	.... *Signature of duly authorized official*
Date of revalidation .... .17	.... *Name of duly authorized official*
The validity of this endorsement is hereby extended until	
(Official Seal)	.... *Signature of the authorized official*
Date of revalidation .... .17	.... *Name of duly authorized official*

3 When replacing a certificate or endorsement which has been lost or destroyed, Parties should issue the replacement under a new number, to avoid confusion with the document to be replaced.

4 If an application for revalidation is made within six months before the expiry of an endorsement, the endorsement referred to in paragraphs 5, 6 and 7 of regulation I/2 may be revalidated until:

.1 the fifth anniversary of the date of validity, or extension of the validity, of the endorsement; or

.2 the date the certificate endorsed expires, whichever is earlier.

5 Where a Certificate of Proficiency is issued, it should contain at least the following information:

.1 names of the issuing Party and authority;

.2 number assigned to the certificate by the issuing authority;

.3 full name and date of birth of the seafarer to whom the certificate is issued. The name and birthdate should be the same as that appearing in the seafarer's passport or seafarer's identification document;

.4 title of the certificate. For example, if the certificate is issued in relation to regulation VI/3, paragraph 2, the title used should be "advanced fire fighting" and if it is issued in relation to regulation VI/5, paragraph 1, the title used should be "ship security officer";

本签证的有效期特此延至..	
（公章）	.... 经正式授权的官员签名
再有效日期..............................17	.... 经正式授权的官员姓名
本签证的有效期特此延至..	
（公章）	.... 经正式授权的官员签名
再有效日期..............................17	.... 经正式授权的官员姓名

3　证书或签证因丢失或损坏需要更换时，缔约国应以一个新的编号签发更换的证书，以防止与被更换的证书相混淆。

4　如果在签证到期前6个月内申请再有效，规则 I/2 条中的第5段、第6段和第7段所提及的签证可再有效至：

.1　签证有效期或者延期到期日的第5个周年日；或者

.2　已签证的证书失效的日期，以较早者为准。

5　签发的培训合格证书应至少包括如下信息：

.1　发证的缔约国和机构的名称；

.2　发证机构分配给该证书的编号；

.3　持证船员的全名和出生日期，此处所填的姓名和出生日期应与此船员护照或身份证明文件上的 ·致；

.4　证书名称，例如，如果签发的证书涉及规则第 VI/3 条第2段，证书名称应为“高级消防”，如果签发的证书涉及规则第 VI/5 条第1段，名称应为“船舶保安员”；

.5 number, or numbers, of the Convention regulation(s) or of the STCW Code section under which the seafarer has been found qualified;

.6 dates of issue and expiry of the certificate. If the validity of the certificate is unlimited, then, for the benefit of clarification, the "unlimited" term should be entered in front of the date of expiry;

.7 if applicable, limitations, either general limitation (such as the requirement to wear corrective lenses), ship's type limitation (such as "valid only for service on ships of GT<500") or, voyage limitation (such as "valid only on near-coastal voyages");

.8 name and signature of the authorized person who issues the certificate;

.9 photograph of the seafarer. The photograph should be a standard black and white or colour passport-type head and shoulders photograph;

.10 if the certificate is intended to be revalidated, then the date of revalidation, extension of the validity, name and signature of the authorized person; and

.11 the contact details of the issuing Authority.

.5 证明船员合格所依据的本公约规则或《STCW 规则》章节的编号；

.6 证书签发日期和失效日期，如果证书的有效期是无限制的，为清楚起见，术语“无限制”应填写在失效日期之前；

.7 如适用，应填入限制，无论是一般的限制（如要求戴矫正眼镜）、船舶类型限制（如“只对在小于 500 总吨的船舶上服务有效”），或航程限制（如“只在近岸航区有效”）；

.8 被授权签发证书者的姓名和签名；

.9 船员的照片，此照片应是显示头部和肩部的黑白或彩色的护照规格标准照片；

.10 如果证书需要再有效，应填入再有效日期、有效期的延期时间，被授权者的姓名和签名；以及

.11 签发机构的详细联系方式。

Table B-I/2

List of certificates or documentary evidence required under the STCW Convention

The list below identifies all certificates or documentary evidence described in the Convention which authorize the holder to serve in certain functions on board ships. The certificates are subject to the requirements of regulation I/2 regarding language and their availability in original form.

The list also references the relevant regulations and the requirements for endorsement, registration and revalidation.

Regulations	Type of certificate and brief description	Endorsement attesting recognition of a certificate[1]	Registration required[2]	Revalidation of certificate[3]
II/1, II/2, II/3, III/1, III/2, III/3, III/6,IV/2, VII/2	Certificate of Competency – For masters, officers and GMDSS radio operators	Yes	Yes	Yes
II/4, III/4, VII/2	Certificate of Proficiency – For ratings duly certified to be a part of a navigational or engine-room watch	No	Yes	No
II/5, III/5, III/7, VII/2	Certificate of Proficiency – For ratings duly certified as able seafarer deck, able seafarer engine or electro-technical rating	No	Yes	No
V/1-1, V/1-2	Certificate of Proficiency or endorsement to a Certificate of Competency – For masters and officers on oil, chemical or liquefied gas tankers	Yes	Yes	Yes
V/1-1, V/1-2	Certificate of Proficiency – For ratings on oil, chemical or liquefied gas tankers	No	Yes	No
V/2	Documentary evidence – Training for masters, officers, ratings and other personnel serving on passenger ships	No	No	No[4]
VI/1	Certificate of Proficiency[5] – Basic training	No	Yes	Yes[6]
VI/2	Certificate of Proficiency[5] – Survival craft, rescue boats and fast rescue boats	No	Yes	Yes[6]
VI/3	Certificate of Proficiency[5] – Advanced fire fighting	No	Yes	Yes[6]
VI/4	Certificate of Proficiency[5] – Medical first aid and medical care	No	Yes	No
VI/5	Certificate of Proficiency – Ship security officer	No	Yes	No
VI/6	Certificate of Proficiency[7] – Security awareness training or security training for seafarers with designated security duties	No	Yes	No

表 B-I/2
《STCW 公约》所要求的证书或书面证明

下表给出了本公约中授权持证人在船舶上履行某种职能的所有证书或书面证明。这些证书应符合规则第 I/2 条中关于语言和证书原始格式可用性的要求。

下表也参考了签证登记和再有效的相关规则和要求。

规则	证书类型和简单描述	证明承认证书的签证[1]	要求登记[2]	证书的再有效[3]
II/1，II/2，II/3，III/1，III/2，III/3，III/6，IV/2，VII/2	适任证书——对船长、高级船员和 GMDSS 无线电操作员	是	是	是
II/4，III/4，VII/2	培训合格证书——对具有适当资质的、参与航行和机舱值班的普通船员	否	是	否
II/5，III/5，III/7，VII/2	培训合格证书——对具有高级值班水手、高级值班机工或电子技工适当资质的普通船员	否	是	否
V/1-1，V/1-2	培训合格证书或适任证书的签证——对油船、化学品船和液化气船的船长和高级船员	是	是	是
V/1-1，V/1-2	培训合格证书——对油船、化学品船和液化气船的普通船员	否	是	否
V/2	书面证明——对客船的船长、高级船员、普通船员和其他人员的培训	否	否	否[4]
VI/1	培训合格证书[5]——基本培训	否	是	是[6]
VI/2	培训合格证书[5]——救生艇筏、救助艇和快速救助艇	否	是	是[6]
VI/3	培训合格证书[5]——高级消防	否	是	是[6]
VI/4	培训合格证书[5]——医疗急救和医护	否	是	否
VI/5	培训合格证书——船舶保安员	否	是	否
VI/6	培训合格证书[7]——保安意识培训或者负有指定保安职责船员的保安培训	否	是	否

Notes:

1 *Endorsement attesting recognition of a certificate* means endorsement in accordance with regulation I/2, paragraph 7.

2 *Registration required* means as part of register or registers in accordance with regulation I/2, paragraph 14.

3 *Revalidation of a certificate* means establishing continued professional competence in accordance with regulation I/11 or maintaining the required standards of competence in accordance with sections A-VI/1 to A-VI/3, as applicable.

4 As required by regulation V/2, paragraph 3 seafarers who have completed training in "crowd management", "crisis management and human behaviour" or "passenger safety, cargo safety and hull integrity" shall at intervals not exceeding five years, undertake appropriate refresher training or to provide evidence of having achieved the required standards of competence within the previous five years.

5 The certificates of competency issued in accordance with regulations II/1, II/2, II/3, III/1, III/2, III/3, III/6 and VII/2 include the proficiency requirements in "basic training", "survival craft and rescue boats other than fast rescue boats", "advanced fire fighting" and "medical first aid" therefore, holders of mentioned certificates of competency are not required to carry Certificates of Proficiency in respect of those competences of chapter VI.

6 In accordance with sections A-VI/1, A-VI/2 and A-VI/3, seafarers shall provide evidence of having maintained the required standards of competence every five years.

7 Where security awareness training or training in designated security duties is not included in the qualification for the certificate to be issued.

注：

1　证明承认证书的签证系指依据规则第 I/2 条第 7 段的签证。

2　要求登记系指依据规则第 I/2 条第 14 段成为登记的一部分。

3　证书的再有效系根据规则第 I/11 条确定持续的专业适任能力，或者，如适用，根据第 A-VI/1节至第 A-VI/3 节保持所需的适任标准。

4　根据规则第 V/2 条第 3 段的要求，完成"拥挤人群管理"、"危机管理和人的行为"或"旅客安全、货物安全和船体完整性"培训的船员应在不超过 5 年的间隔内完成适当的更新培训，或者提供在之前 5 年内达到所需适任标准的证明。

5　根据规则第 II/1 条、第 II/2 条、第 II/3 条、第 III/1 条、第 III/2 条、第 III/3 条、第 III/6 条和第 VII/2 条签发的适任证书包含了"基本培训"、"除快速救助艇以外的救生艇筏和救助艇"、"高级消防"和"医疗急救"的技能要求，则上述适任证书的持有人不需要根据第 VI 章的适任要求持有相应的培训合格证书。

6　根据第 A-VI/1 节、第 A-VI/2 节和第 A-VI/3 节的要求，船员每 5 年应提供保持了所需适任标准的证据。

7　此处保安意识培训或者负有指定保安职责船员的培训没有包含在签发证书的条件中。

Section B-I/3
Guidance regarding near-coastal voyages

Coastal States may adopt regional "near-coastal voyage limits" through bilateral or multilateral arrangements. Details of such arrangements shall be reported to the Secretary-General, who shall circulate such particulars to all Parties.

Section B-I/4
*Guidance regarding control procedures**

Introduction

1 The purpose of the control procedures of regulation I/4 is to enable officers duly authorized by port States to ensure that the seafarers on board have sufficient competence to ensure safe, secure and pollution-free operation of the ship.

2 This provision is no different in principle from the need to make checks on ships' structures and equipment. Indeed, it builds on these inspections to make an appraisal of the total system of onboard safety, security and pollution prevention.

Assessment

3 By restricting assessment as indicated in section A-I/4, the subjectivity which is an unavoidable element in all control procedures is reduced to a minimum, no more than would be evident in other types of control inspection.

4 The clear grounds given in regulation I/4, paragraph 1.3 will usually be sufficient to direct the inspector's attention to specific areas of competency, which could then be followed up by seeking evidence of training in the skills in question. If this evidence is inadequate or unconvincing, the authorized officer may ask to observe a demonstration of the relevant skill.

5 It will be a matter for the professional judgement of the inspector when on board, either following an incident as outlined in regulation I/4 or for the purposes of a routine inspection, whether the ship is operated in a manner likely to pose a danger to persons, property or the environment**.

Section B-I/5
Guidance regarding national provisions

(No provisions)

---

* The relevant IMO Model Course(s) may be of assistance in the preparation of courses.

** See the Code of International Standards and Recommended Practices for a Safety Investigation into a marine casualty or marine incident (Casualty Investigation Code).

第 B-I/3 节
关于近岸航行的指导

1　沿岸国可通过双边或多边安排采取区域性“近岸航行限制”。这种安排的详情应报告给秘书长，秘书长应将此规定告知所有缔约国。

第 B-I/4 节
关于监督程序的指导①

引言

1　规则第 I/4 条的监督程序的目的是使港口国正式授权的官员能够确保船上的海员充分适任，以保证船舶操作的安全、无污染。
2　此项规定在原则上与对船舶结构和设备所要求的检查并无差别。实际上，就是通过这些检查对船上安全、保安和防止污染的整个体系进行评估。

评估

3　通过第 A-I/4 节所述的有限制的评估，各种监督程序中不可避免的主观性可减少到最低限度，且不会比其他种类的监督检查中的主观性更加明显。
4　规则第 I/4 条第 1.3 段所述的明显理由通常足以指导检查官员注意具体适任范围，继而可查找有疑问的技能培训的证据。如果证据不充分或不可信，被授权的官员可以要求观看有关技能的演示。
5　无论是在发生了规则第 I/4 条所述的事件之后，还是为了例行检查，登船的检查官员都要对船舶是否以可能对人身、财产或环境构成危险的方式操作作出专业判断②。

第 B-I/5 节
关于国家规定的指导

（无条款）

① 相关 IMO 示范培训课程可有助于准备课程。
② 参见《海难和海上事件安全调查国际标准和推荐做法》（海上事故调查规则）。

Section B-I/6
Guidance regarding training and assessment

Qualifications of instructors and assessors

1 Each Party should ensure that instructors and assessors are appropriately qualified and experienced for the particular types and levels of training or assessment of competence of seafarers, as required under the Convention, in accordance with the guidelines in this section.

In-service training and assessment

2 Any person, on board or ashore, conducting in-service training of a seafarer intended to be used in qualifying for certification under the Convention should have received appropriate guidance in instructional techniques*.

3 Any person responsible for the supervision of in-service training of a seafarer intended to be used in qualifying for certification under the Convention should have appropriate knowledge of instructional techniques and of training methods and practice.

4 Any person, on board or ashore, conducting an in-service assessment of the competence of a seafarer intended to be used in qualifying for certification under the Convention should have:

.1 received appropriate guidance in assessment methods and practice*; and

.2 gained practical assessment experience under the supervision and to the satisfaction of an experienced assessor.

5 Any person responsible for the supervision of the in-service assessment of competence of a seafarer intended to be used in qualifying for certification under the Convention should have a full understanding of the assessment system, assessment methods and practice*.

Use of distance learning and e-learning

6 Parties may allow the training of seafarers by distance learning and e-learning in accordance with the standards of training and assessment set out in section A-I/6 and the guidance given below.

Guidance for training by distance learning and e-learning

7 Each Party should ensure that any distance learning and e-learning programme:

.1 is provided by an entity that is approved by the Party;

.2 is suitable for the selected objectives and training tasks to meet the competence level for the subject covered;

.3 has clear and unambiguous instructions for the trainees to understand how the programme operates;

.4 provides learning outcomes that meet all the requirements to provide the underpinning knowledge and proficiency of the subject;

* The relevant IMO Model Course(s) may be of assistance in the preparation of courses.

第 B-I/6 节

关于培训和评估的指导

教员和评估人员的资格

1 各缔约国应确保教员和评估人员具有适当的资格和经验，按照本公约的要求，根据本节的指导，对特定种类和等级的培训或对海员适任能评估。

在职培训和评估

2 无论在船上还是岸上，任何对按照本公约要求欲取得发证资格的海员进行在职培训的人员，都应接受过适当的教学技术指导①。

3 任何对按照本公约要求欲取得发证资格的海员的在职培训负责监督的人员，都应具有适当的教学技术、培训方法和培训实践方面的知识。

4 无论在船上还是岸上，任何对按照本公约要求欲取得发证资格的海员进行在职适任评估的人员都应：

.1 接受过有关评估方法和实践方面的适当指导①；并且

.2 在有经验的评估人员监督下获得了实际评估经验并使其满意。

5 任何对按照本公约要求欲取得发证资格的海员的在职适任评估负责监督的人员，都应对评估制度、评估方法和实践有全面的理解①。

远程教学和电子教学的使用

6 缔约国可允许依据第 A-I/6 节和如下指导中规定的培训和评估标准，采用远程教学和电子教学方式对船员进行培训。

对远程教学和电子教学的指导

7 各缔约国应确保任何远程教学和电子教学课程：

.1 由缔约国认可的机构提供；

.2 适合于选定的目标和训练任务以达到所涵盖科目的适任水平；

.3 对学员清晰无误地指导，使学员理解课程如何进行；

.4 给出符合对提供该科目基本知识和熟练的所有要求的学习结果；

① 相关 IMO 示范培训课程可有助于准备课程。

.5 is structured in a way that enables the trainee to systematically reflect on what has been learnt through both self assessment and tutor-marked assignments; and

.6 provides professional tutorial support through telephone, facsimile or e-mail communications.

8 Companies should ensure that a safe learning environment is provided and that there has been sufficient time provided to enable the trainee to study.

9 Where e-learning is provided, common information formats such as XML (Extensible Markup Language), which is a flexible way to share both the format and the data on the World Wide Web, intranets, and elsewhere, should be used.

10 The e-learning system should be secured from tampering and attempts to hack into the system.

Guidance for assessing a trainee's progress and achievements by training by distance learning and e-learning

11 Each Party should ensure that approved assessment procedures are provided for any distance learning and e-learning programme, including:

.1 clear information to the trainees on the way that tests and examinations are conducted and how the results are communicated;

.2 have test questions that are comprehensive and will adequately assess a trainee's competence and are appropriate to the level being examined;

.3 procedures in place to ensure questions are kept up to date;

.4 the conditions where the examinations can take place and the procedures for invigilation to be conducted;

.5 secure procedures for the examination system so that it will prevent cheating; and

.6 secure validation procedures to record results for the benefit of the Party.

Register of approved training providers, courses and programmes

12 Each Party should ensure that a register or registers of approved training providers, courses and programmes are maintained and made available to companies and other Parties on request.

Section B-I/7
Guidance regarding communication of information

Reports of difficulties encountered

1 Parties are encouraged, when communicating information in accordance with article IV and regulation I/7 of the Convention, to include an index specifically locating the required information as follows:

.5 指导的方式是通过学员自我评估和教员批改作业并用，使学员系统地思考所学的知识；以及

.6 通过电话、传真或电子邮件等通信方式提供专业的辅导支持。

8 公司应保证提供安全的学习环境并且使学员有充足的时间学习。

9 当提供电子教学时，应使用公共信息格式，如 XML（可扩展标志语言），这是一种在万维网和内联网及其他地方分享格式和数据的灵活方式。

10 应保证电子教学系统不被破坏和非法侵入。

对接受远程教学和电子教学的学员的学业成绩进行评估的指导

11 各缔约国应确保对任何远程教学和电子教学课程都提供认可的评估程序，包括：

.1 向学员提供进行测验和考试以及通报结果的方式的明确信息；

.2 具有全面且能综合评估学员适任能力并且适合于考试级别的试题；

.3 确保试题保持更新的程序；

.4 可进行考试的条件和监考程序；

.5 防止作弊的考试系统安全程序；以及

.6 有利于缔约国的记录考试结果的安全认证程序。

认可的培训机构、课程和计划的登记

12 各缔约国应保证确保对认可的培训机构、课程和计划的登记，并且在公司和其他缔约国请求时能予以提供。

第 B-I/7 节

关于资料交流的指导

报告遇到的困难

1 鼓励缔约国在根据本公约第 IV 条和规则第 I/7 条交流资料时包括一份专门指明以下所要求的资料的位置的索引：

Index of materials submitted in accordance with article IV and regulation I/7 of the STCW Convention

	Article IV of the STCW Convention	Location
1	Text of laws, decrees, orders, regulations and instruments	(article IV(1)(a))
2	Details on study courses	(article IV(1)(b))
3	National examination and other requirements	(article IV(1)(b))
4	Specimen certificates	(article IV(1)(c))

	Section A-I/7 part 1 of the STCW Code	Location
5	Information on Governmental organization	(section A-I/7, paragraph 2.1)
6	Explanation of legal and administrative measures	(section A-I/7, paragraph 2.2)
7	Statement of the education, training, examination, assessment and certification policies	(section A-I/7, paragraph 2.3)
8	Summary of the courses, training programmes, examinations and assessments by certificate	(section A-I/7, paragraph 2.4)
9	Outline of the procedures and conditions for authorizations, accreditations and approvals	(section A-I/7, paragraph 2.5)
10	List of authorizations, accreditations and approvals granted	(section A-I/7, paragraph 2.5)
11	Summary of procedures for dispensations	(section A-I/7, paragraph 2.6)
12	Comparison carried out pursuant to regulation I/11	(section A-I/7, paragraph 2.7)
13	Outline of refresher and upgrading training mandated	(section A-I/7, paragraph 2.7)

根据《STCW 公约》第 IV 条和规则第 I/7 条提交的材料的索引

《STCW 公约》第 IV 条	位置
1 法律、法令、命令、规则和其他文件的文本	(第 IV 条第(1)段(a)项)
2 学习课程的详细情况	(第 IV 条第(1)段(b)项)
3 国家的考试及其他要求	(第 IV 条第(1)段(b)项)
4 证书样本	(第 IV 条第(1)段(c)项)

《STCW 规则》第 A-I/7 节第 1 部分	位置
5 政府组织机构的资料	(第 A-I/7 节第 2.1 段)
6 法律和行政管理措施的介绍	(第 A-I/7 节第 2.2 段)
7 教育、培训、考试、评估和发证政策的证明	(第 A-I/7 节第 2.3 段)
8 对发证的课程、培训计划、考试和评估的总结	(第 A-I/7 节第 2.4 段)
9 对授权、认可和批准的程序和条件的概述	(第 A-I/7 节第 2.5 段)
10 授权、认可和批准清单	(第 A-I/7 节第 2.5 段)
11 对特免证书程序的总结	(第 A-I/7 节第 2.6 段)
12 按照规则第 I/11 条所作的比较	(第 A-I/7 节第 2.7 段)
13 强制性知识更新培训概述	(第 A-I/7 节第 2.7 段)

Section A-I/7, part 2, paragraph 3 of the STCW Code		**Location**
14	Description of equivalency arrangements adopted pursuant to article IX	(section A-I/7, paragraph 3.1)
15	Summary of measures taken to ensure compliance with regulation I/10	(section A-I/7, paragraph 3.2)
16	Specimen copy of safe manning documents issued to ships employing seafarers holding alternative certificates under regulation VII/1	(section A-I/7, paragraph 3.3)

Section A-I/7, part 2, paragraph 4 of the STCW Code		**Location**
17	Report of results of independent evaluations carried out pursuant to regulation I/8 covering:	
	.1 Terms of reference of evaluators for the independent evaluation	
	.2 Qualifications and experience of evaluators	
	.3 Date and scope of evaluation	
	.4 Non-conformities found	
	.5 Corrective measures recommended	
	.6 Corrective measures carried out	
	.7 List of training institutions/centres covered by the independent evaluation	

Section A-I/7, part 2, paragraph 6 of the STCW Code		**Location**
18	Explanation of legal and administrative measures	(section A-I/7, paragraph 6.1)
19	Statement of the education, training, examination, assessment and certification policies	(section A-I/7, paragraph 6.2)
20	Summary of the courses, training programmes, examinations and assessments by certificate	(section A-I/7, paragraph 6.3)
21	Outline of refresher and upgrading training mandated	(section A-I/7, paragraph 6.4)
22	Comparison carried out pursuant to regulation I/11	(section A-I/7, paragraph 6.5)

《STCW 规则》第 A-I/7 节第 2 部分第 3 段	位置
14　对根据公约第 IX 条所采取的等效安排的说明	（第 A-I/7 节第 3.1 段）
15　对确保遵守规则第 I/10 条所采取的措施的总结	（第 A-I/7 节第 3.2 段）
16　签发给雇用持有规则第 VII/1 条可供选择证书的海员的船舶的安全配员证书的样本	（第 A-I/7 节第 3.3 段）

《STCW 规则》第 A-I/7 节第 2 部分第 4 段	位置
17　按照规则第 I/8 条对独立评价结果的报告，包括：	
.1　评价人员对独立评价的职责范围	
.2　评价人员的资格和经历	
.3　评价日期与范围	
.4　不符合项	
.5　推荐的纠正措施	
.6　已采取的纠正措施	
.7　独立评价涵盖的培训机构/中心名单	

《STCW 规则》第 A-I/7 节第 2 部分第 6 段	位置
18　对法律和行政措施的说明	（第 A-I/7 节第 6.1 段）
19　对教育、培训、考试、评估和发证政策的陈述	（第 A-I/7 节第 6.2 段）
20　认证的课程、培训计划、考试和评估的总结	（第 A-I/7 节第 6.3 段）
21　规定的知识更新培训概述	（第 A-I/7 节第 6.4 段）
22　按照规则第 I/11 条进行的比较	（第 A-I/7 节第 6.5 段）

2 Parties are requested to include, in the reports required by regulation I/7, an indication of any relevant guidance contained in part B of this Code, the observance of which has been found to be impracticable.

Section B-I/8
Guidance regarding quality standards

1 In applying quality standards under the provisions of regulation I/8 and section A-I/8 to the administration of its certification system, each Party should take account of existing national or international models, and incorporate the following key elements:

.1 an expressed policy regarding quality and the means by which such policy is to be implemented;

.2 a quality system incorporating the organizational structure, responsibilities, procedures, processes and resources necessary for quality management;

.3 the operational techniques and activities to ensure quality control;

.4 systematic monitoring arrangements, including internal quality-assurance evaluations, to ensure that all defined objectives are being achieved; and

.5 arrangements for periodic external quality evaluations as described in the following paragraphs.

2 In establishing such quality standards for the administration of their national certification system, Administrations should seek to ensure that the arrangements adopted:

.1 are sufficiently flexible to enable the certification system to take account of the varying needs of the industry, and that they facilitate and encourage the application of new technology;

.2 cover all the administrative matters that give effect to the various provisions of the Convention, in particular regulations I/2 to I/15 and other provisions which enable the Administration to grant certificates of service and dispensations and to withdraw, cancel and suspend certificates;

.3 encompass the Administration's responsibilities for approving training and assessment at all levels, from undergraduate-type courses and updating courses for certificates of competency to short courses of vocational training; and

.4 incorporate arrangements for the internal quality-assurance reviews under paragraph 1.4 involving a comprehensive self-study of the administrative procedures, at all levels, in order to measure achievement of defined objectives and to provide the basis for the independent external evaluation required under section A-I/8, paragraph 3.

2　要求缔约国在规则第 I/7 条所要求的报告中指出《STCW 规则》B 部分中无法遵行的有关指导。

第 B-I/8 节

关于质量标准的指导

1　为了将规则第 I/8 条和第 A-I/8 节规定的质量标准应用于其发证体系的管理中，各缔约国应考虑到现有的国内和国际的模式，并将下列要素包括在内：

.1　明确的质量方针及实施这一方针的方法；

.2　质量体系，包括为实施质量管理所必需的组织结构、责任、程序、过程和资源；

.3　保证质量控制的操作技术和活动；

.4　为确保达到所有既定目标的系统的监控安排，包括内部质量保证评价；以及

.5　以下段落所述的定期外部质量评价安排。

2　在为国家发证体系的管理确立质量标准时，主管机关应力求确保所采取的安排：

.1　具有足够的灵活性，以便能使发证体系考虑到行业的不同需要并且便于和鼓励新技术的应用；

.2　覆盖实施本公约各条款的所有行政事项，特别是实施规则第 I/2 条至第 I/15 条以及能使主管机关签发服务证书和特免证明以及撤销、注销、暂扣证书的其他规定；

.3　包含主管机关认可各级别培训和评估的责任，从本科课程和适任证书更新课程到短期职业培训课程；并且

.4　包含按照第 1.4 段的要求进行内部质量保证评审的安排，它包括在各级别上对管理程序的全面自查，以便检测既定目标是否达到，并为第 A-I/8 节第 3 段所要求的独立的外部评价奠定基础。

Quality standards model for assessment of knowledge, understanding, skills and competence

3 The quality standards model for assessment of knowledge, understanding, skills and competence should incorporate the recommendations of this section within the general framework of either:

.1 a national scheme for education and training accreditation or quality standards; or

.2 an alternative quality-standards model acceptable to the Organization.

4 The above quality-standards model should incorporate:

.1 a quality policy, including a commitment by the training institution or unit to the achievement of its stated aims and objectives and to the consequential recognition by the relevant accrediting or quality-standards authority;

.2 those quality-management functions that determine and implement the quality policy, relating to aspects of the work which impinge on the quality of what is provided, including provisions for determining progression within a course or programme;

.3 quality system coverage, where appropriate, of the academic and administrative organizational structure, responsibilities, procedures, processes and the resources of staff and equipment;

.4 the quality-control functions to be applied at all levels to the teaching, training, examination and assessment activities, and to their organization and implementation, in order to ensure their fitness for their purpose and the achievement of their defined objectives;

.5 the internal quality-assurance processes and reviews which monitor the extent to which the institution, or training unit, is achieving the objectives of the programmes it delivers, and is effectively monitoring the quality-control procedures which it employs; and

.6 the arrangements made for periodic external quality evaluations required under regulation I/8, paragraph 2 and described in the following paragraphs, for which the outcome of the quality-assurance reviews forms the basis and starting point.

5 In establishing quality standards for education, training and assessment programmes, the organizations responsible for implementing these programmes should take account of the following:

.1 Where provisions exist for established national accreditation, or education quality standards, such provisions should be utilized for courses incorporating the knowledge and understanding requirements of the Convention. The quality standards should be applied to both management and operational levels of the activity, and should take account of how it is managed, organized, undertaken and evaluated, in order to ensure that the identified goals are achieved.

.2 Where acquisition of a particular skill or accomplishment of a designated task is the primary objective, the quality standards should take account of whether real or simulated equipment is utilized for this purpose, and of the appropriateness of the qualifications and experience of the assessors, in order to ensure achievement of the set standards.

评估知识、理解、技能和适任的质量标准模式

3 评估知识、理解、技能和适任的质量标准模式应将本节的建议纳入以下任一总体框架内：

.1 国家教育和培训的鉴定制度和质量标准制度；或

.2 本组织接受的可供选择的质量标准模式。

4 上述质量标准模式应包含：

.1 质量方针，包括培训机构或单位对达到其既定目的和目标，以及最后获得有关鉴定或质量标准当局的承认所做的承诺；

.2 确定和执行质量方针的质量管理功能，它涉及与所提供的服务质量紧密相关的工作的诸方面，包括有关确定课程和计划进度的规定；

.3 质量体系范围，如适当，包括教学和管理的组织结构、责任、程序、过程以及人员和设备资源；

.4 应用于各级别的教学、培训、考试和评估活动及其组织和实施的质量管理功能，以保证适合其目的并达到既定目标；

.5 内部质量保证过程和评审，它用于监督教育机构或培训单位达到其提出的计划目标的程度，并对其所采用的质量管理程序进行有效的监控；以及

.6 为规则第 I/8 条第 2 段要求的和下列各段所述的外部定期质量评价所作的安排，质量保证评审的结果是此项安排的基础和起点。

5 在确立教育、培训和评估计划的质量标准时，负责实施这些计划的组织机构应考虑以下几点：

.1 如已存在国家鉴定或教育质量标准的既有规定，应将这种规定结合本公约的知识和理解要求运用于课程中。应将质量标准运用于管理和操作两个级别的活动中，并且应考虑到如何对其进行管理、组织、实施和评价，以保证达到确定目标。

.2 如果主要目的是获得某一特定技能或完成某一指定任务，则质量标准应考虑是否为此目的使用真实设备或模拟设备，并应考虑评估人员的资格和经验是否合适，以确保达到既定标准。

.3 The internal quality-assurance evaluations should involve a comprehensive self-study of the programme, at all levels, to monitor achievement of defined objectives through the application of quality standards. These quality-assurance reviews should address the planning, design, presentation and evaluation of programmes as well as the teaching, learning and communication activities. The outcome provides the basis for the independent evaluation required under section A-I/8, paragraph 3.

The independent evaluation

6 Each independent evaluation should include a systematic and independent examination of all quality activities, but should not evaluate the validity of the defined objectives. The evaluation team should:

.1 carry out the evaluation in accordance with documented procedures;

.2 ensure that the results of each evaluation are documented and brought to the attention of those responsible for the area evaluated; and

.3 check that timely action is taken to correct any deficiencies.

7 The purpose of the evaluation is to provide an independent assessment of the effectiveness of the quality-standard arrangements at all levels. In the case of an education or training establishment, a recognized academic accreditation or quality-standards body or Government agency should be used. The evaluation team should be provided with sufficient advance information to give an overview of the tasks in hand. In the case of a major training institution or programme, the following items are indicative of the information to be provided:

.1 the mission statement of the institution;

.2 details of academic and training strategies in use;

.3 an organization chart and information on the composition of committees and advisory bodies;

.4 staff and student information;

.5 a description of training facilities and equipment; and

.6 an outline of the policies and procedures on:

.6.1 student admission;

.6.2 the development of new courses and review of existing courses;

.6.3 the examination system, including appeals and resits;

.6.4 staff recruitment, training, development, appraisal and promotion;

.6.5 feedback from students and from industry; and

.6.6 staff involvement in research and development.

.3 内部质量保证评价应包括对计划进行各个层次的综合性自查,以便通过对质量标准的应用来监督其达到既定目标。这些质量保证评审应针对课程的策划、设计、进行和评价以及教、学和交流活动。评审结果将作为第 A-I/8 节第 3 段所要求的独立评价的基础。

独立的评价

6 每个独立的评价应包括对所有质量活动的系统而独立的检查,但无须对既定目标的有效性进行评价。评价组应:

.1 按文件规定的程序进行评价;

.2 确保每次评价的结果记入文件并提请被评价单位负责人注意;并且

.3 核实是否已及时采取措施纠正缺陷。

7 评价的目的是对各级质量标准安排的有效性进行独立的评估。如果评价的是教育或培训机构,则应动用认可的学术鉴定或质量标准机构或政府机构。应向评价组提供足够的先期资料,使其对所承担的任务有概括的了解。就较大的培训机构或计划而言,所应提供的资料应包括以下项目:

.1 培训机构的任务说明;

.2 采用的教学和培训策略的细节;

.3 组织结构图以及各委员会和咨询机构组成的资料;

.4 教职员和学员的资料;

.5 培训设施和设备的说明;以及

.6 对以下各项政策和程序的概要:

.6.1 招生,

.6.2 新课程的制定和对现有课程的评审,

.6.3 考试制度,包括申诉和重考,

.6.4 教职员的招聘、培训、发展、鉴定和晋升,

.6.5 来自学员和行业的反馈,以及

.6.6 教职员在研究和开发方面的参与。

The report

8 Before submitting a final report, the evaluation team should forward an interim report to the management, seeking their comments on their findings. Upon receiving their comments, the evaluators should submit their final report, which should:

.1 include brief background information about the institution or training programme;

.2 be full, fair and accurate;

.3 highlight the strengths and weaknesses of the institution;

.4 describe the evaluation procedure followed;

.5 cover the various elements identified in paragraph 4;

.6 indicate the extent of compliance or non-compliance with the requirements of the Convention and the effectiveness of the quality standards in ensuring achievement of defined aims and objectives; and

.7 spell out clearly the areas found to be deficient, offer suggestions for improvement and provide any other comments the evaluators consider relevant.

Section B-I/9
Guidance regarding medical standards

MEDICAL EXAMINATION AND CERTIFICATION

1 Parties, in establishing seafarer medical fitness standards and provisions, should take into account the minimum physical abilities set out in table B-I/9 and the guidance given within this section, bearing in mind the different duties of seafarers.

2 Parties, in establishing seafarer medical fitness standards and provisions, should follow the guidance contained in the ILO/WHO publication *Guidelines for Conducting Pre-sea and Periodic Medical Fitness Examinations for Seafarers*, including any subsequent versions, and any other applicable international guidelines published by the International Labour Organization, the International Maritime Organization or the World Health Organization.

3 Appropriate qualifications and experience for medical practitioners conducting medical fitness examinations of seafarers may include occupational health or maritime health qualifications, experience of working as a ship's doctor or a shipping company doctor or working under the supervision of someone with the aforementioned qualifications or experience.

4 The premises where medical fitness examinations are carried out should have the facilities and equipment required to carry out medical fitness examination of seafarers.

5 Administrations should ensure that recognized medical practitioners enjoy full professional independence in exercising their medical judgement when undertaking medical examination procedures.

6 Persons applying for a medical certificate should present to the recognized medical practitioner appropriate identity documentation to establish their identity. They should also surrender their previous medical certificate.

报告

8　评价小组在提交最终报告前，应先向管理部门递交一份中期报告以征求对其结论的看法。在收到他们的意见后，评价人员应提交最终报告。该报告应：

.1　包括培训机构或培训计划的简要背景资料；

.2　完整、公平和准确；

.3　重点说明培训机构的强项和弱点；

.4　说明所遵循的评价程序；

.5　论及第 4 段中所明确的各个要素；

.6　指出符合或不符合本公约要求的程度，以及质量标准在保证达到既定目的和目标方面的有效性；并且

.7　清楚地指出已发现缺陷的地方，提出改进建议，并且提供评价人员认为相关的任何其他意见。

第 B-I/9 节

关于健康标准的指导

健康检查和发证

1　缔约国在制定海员健康标准和规定时，应考虑到表 B-I/9 中的最低体能要求和本部分中的指导，并考虑海员的不同职责。

2　缔约国在建立海员健康标准和规定时，应遵从国际劳工组织/世界卫生组织出版物《海员上船前和定期健康检查指南》的指导，包括任何后续版本和其他任何由国际劳工组织、国际海事组织或世界卫生组织出版的适用的国际指南。

3　对海员进行健康检查的从业医生的适当资格和经历可以包括职业健康或海上健康检查资格，作为船医或航运公司医生的工作经验或在具有上述资格和经历的人员监督下的工作经验。

4　进行健康检查的场所应具备对海员进行健康检查的必要设施和设备。

5　主管机关应确保认可的从业医生在进行健康检查程序中作出医学判断时享有完全的独立决策权。

6　申请健康证明的人员应向已认可的从业医生出示适当的身份证明文件以表明其身份，并应交出先前的健康证明。

7 Each Administration has the discretionary authority to grant a variance or waiver of any of the standards set out in table B-I/9 hereunder, based on an assessment of a medical evaluation and any other relevant information concerning an individual's adjustment to the condition and proven ability to satisfactorily perform assigned shipboard functions.

8 The medical fitness standards should, so far as possible, define objective criteria with regard to fitness for sea service, taking into account access to medical facilities and medical expertise on board ship. They should, in particular, specify the conditions under which seafarers suffering from potentially life-threatening medical conditions that are controlled by medication may be allowed to continue to serve at sea.

9 The medical standards should also identify particular medical conditions, such as colour blindness, which might preclude seafarers holding particular positions on board ship.

10 The minimum in-service eyesight standards in each eye for unaided distance vision should be at least 0.1*.

11 Persons requiring the use of spectacles or contact lenses to perform duties should have a spare pair or pairs, as required, conveniently available on board the ship. Any need to wear visual aids to meet the required standards should be recorded on the medical fitness certificate issued.

12 Colour vision testing should be in accordance with the *International Recommendation for Colour Vision Requirements for Transport*, published by the Commission Internationale de l'Eclairage (CIE 143-2001 including any subsequent versions) or equivalent test methods.

* Value given in Snellen decimal notation.

7 基于对体检报告以及对个人身体情况调整和证实能够令人满意地履行船上指定职能的任何其他信息的评估，每一个主管机关都有权改变或放弃表 B-I/9 中设定的任何标准。

8 考虑到船上可获得医疗设施和医疗专业知识的情况，健康标准应尽可能界定与海上服务的健康相关的客观标准。这些标准应特别规定在何种条件下，海员出现用药物可控制的潜在威胁生命的健康问题仍能获准继续海上服务。

9 医疗标准也应规定特定的医疗状况，如色盲，因为这会妨碍海员在船上担任某种职务。

10 在职视力最低标准为每只眼睛非矫正远距视力应至少为 0.1①。

11 需要配戴眼镜或隐形眼镜来履行职责的人，应在船上方便可取处备有一副或多副备用眼镜。任何需要借助矫正手段达到所要求标准的情况，均应记录在其签发的健康证书中。

12 辨色力测试应以国际照明委员会公布的《运输辨色力要求的国际建议》(CIE 143-2001，包括其后续版本)或等效的测试方法为依据。

① 数值在 Snellen 视力表中给出。

Table B-I/9

Assessment of minimum entry level and in-service physical abilities for seafarers[3]

Shipboard task, function, event or condition[3]	**Related physical ability**	**A medical examiner should be satisfied that the candidate[4]**
Routine movement around vessel: - on moving deck - between levels - between compartments *Note 1 applies to this row*	Maintain balance and move with agility Climb up and down vertical ladders and stairways Step over coamings (e.g., Load Line Convention requires coamings to be 600 mm high) Open and close watertight doors	Has no disturbance in sense of balance Does not have any impairment or disease that prevents relevant movements and physical activities Is, without assistance[5], able to: - climb vertical ladders and stairways - step over high sills - manipulate door closing systems
Routine tasks on board: - Use of hand tools - Movement of ship's stores - Overhead work - Valve operation - Standing a four-hour watch - Working in confined spaces - Responding to alarms, warnings and instructions - Verbal communication *Note 1 applies to this row*	Strength, dexterity and stamina to manipulate mechanical devices Lift, pull and carry a load (e.g., 18 kg) Reach upwards Stand, walk and remain alert for an extended period Work in constricted spaces and move through restricted openings (e.g., SOLAS requires minimum openings in cargo spaces and emergency escapes to have the minimum dimensions of 600 mm × 600 mm – SOLAS regulation 3.6.5.1) Visually distinguish objects, shapes and signals Hear warnings and instructions Give a clear spoken description	Does not have a defined impairment or diagnosed medical condition that reduces ability to perform routine duties essential to the safe operation of the vessel Has ability to: - work with arms raised - stand and walk for an extended period - enter confined space - fulfil eyesight standards (table A-I/9) - fulfil hearing standards set by competent authority or take account of international guidelines - hold normal conversation

表 B-I/9

对海员准入体能和在职体能的评估[3]

船上任务、职能或条件[3]	相关的体能	证书申请人应使体检人员满意[4]
船上日常活动： ——在活动的甲板上 ——在不同层面间 ——在舱室之间 注释 1 适用于本行	保持平衡及行动敏捷 上下直梯和阶梯 登上舱口围板（如载重线公约要求的围板高度为 600 mm） 开启和关闭水密门	平衡感无障碍 无妨碍相关运动和体力活动的任何损伤或疾病 能够不需协助地[5]： ——爬上直梯和阶梯 ——跨越高的门槛 ——操作关门系统
船上的日常任务： ——使用手动工具 ——移动船舶物料 ——头顶上方的作业 ——阀门操作 ——站立值班 4 小时 ——在空间有限的场所工作 ——对警报、警告及指示的反应 ——口头交流 注释 1 适用于本行	操作机械设备所需的力量、机敏和耐力 提起、拉动和承担负载（如 18 kg） 摸高 保持更长时间的站立、行走和警惕 在受限区域工作和穿过受限制的开口（如 SOLAS 所要求的货物处所和应急逃生通道的最小开口的尺寸为 600 mm × 600 mm —— SOLAS 规则 3.6.5.1） 视觉识别出物体、形状和信号 听得到警告和指令 作出清楚的口头描述	无降低其履行船舶安全操作的基本日常职责能力的明显损伤或确诊的健康问题 能够： ——举起胳膊工作 ——站立和行走更长时间 ——进入受限区域 ——达到视力标准（表 A-I/9） ——达到主管当局规定的听力标准，或考虑国际指南 ——正常会话

Shipboard task, function, event or condition[3]	**Related physical ability**	**A medical examiner should be satisfied that the candidate**[4]
Emergency duties [6] on board: - Escape - Fire-fighting - Evacuation *Note 2 applies to this row*	Don a lifejacket or immersion suit Escape from smoke-filled spaces Take part in fire-fighting duties, including use of breathing apparatus Take part in vessel evacuation procedures	Does not have a defined impairment or diagnosed medical condition that reduces ability to perform emergency duties essential to the safe operation of the vessel Has ability to: - don lifejacket or immersion suit - crawl - feel for differences in temperature - handle fire-fighting equipment - wear breathing apparatus (where required as part of duties)

Notes:

1 Rows 1 and 2 of the above table describe (a) ordinary shipboard tasks, functions, events and conditions, (b) the corresponding physical abilities which may be considered necessary for the safety of a seafarer, other crew members and the ship, and (c) high-level criteria for use by medical practitioners assessing medical fitness, bearing in mind the different duties of seafarers and the nature of shipboard work for which they will be employed.

2 Row 3 of the above table describes (a) ordinary shipboard tasks, functions, events and conditions, (b) the corresponding physical abilities which should be considered necessary for the safety of a seafarer, other crew members and the ship, and (c) high-level criteria for use by medical practitioners assessing medical fitness, bearing in mind the different duties of seafarers and the nature of shipboard work for which they will be employed.

3 This table is not intended to address all possible shipboard conditions or potentially disqualifying medical conditions. Parties should specify physical abilities applicable to the category of seafarers (such as "Deck officer" and "Engine rating"). The special circumstances of individuals and for those who have specialized or limited duties should receive due consideration.

4 If in doubt, the medical practitioner should quantify the degree or severity of any relevant impairment by means of objective tests, whenever appropriate tests are available, or by referring the candidate for further assessment.

5 The term "assistance" means the use of another person to accomplish the task.

6 The term "emergency duties" is used to cover all standard emergency response situations such as abandon ship or fire fighting as well as the procedures to be followed by each seafarer to secure personal survival.

船上任务、职能或条件[3]	相关的身体能力	证书申请人应使体检人员满意[4]
船上的应急职责[6]： ——逃生 ——灭火 ——疏散 注释 2 适用于本行	穿救生衣或救生服 逃离充满烟雾的场所 参与灭火职责，包括使用呼吸器 参与船舶疏散程序	无降低其履行船舶安全操作的基本应急职责能力的明显损伤或确诊的健康问题 能够： ——穿救生衣或救生服 ——爬行 ——感觉温度变化 ——使用灭火设备 ——佩戴呼吸器（若职责需要）

注：

1. 上述表格第 1、2 行说明：(a)通常的船上任务、职能、事件和条件，(b)为了海员、其他船员以及船舶的安全而必须考虑的相应体能，以及(c)从业医生在使用高标准进行体检时，应考虑海员的不同职责及其被雇用在船上工作的性质。
2. 上述表格第 3 行说明：(a)通常的船上任务、职能、事件和条件，(b)为了海员、其他船员以及船舶的安全而应考虑的相应体能，以及(c)从业医生在使用高标准进行体检时，应考虑海员的不同职责及其被雇用在船上工作的性质。
3. 该表并不试图给出所有可能的船上条件或潜在不合格的健康问题。缔约国应明确适用不同类别的海员（如“甲板部高级船员”、“轮机部普通船员”）的体能。对个人特殊状况以及那些被指定或限定职责的人应予以适当考虑。
4. 如有怀疑，只要能作适当检查，从业医生应通过客观测试手段或通过嘱咐申请者作进一步检查来量化任何相关损伤的程度或严重性。
5. “协助”一词意指使用另一个人来完成任务。
6. 该表中“应急职责”一词用以涵盖所有标准的应急反应情况，诸如弃船或灭火以及每个海员为求生所遵循的程序。

Section B-I/10

Guidance regarding the recognition of certificates

1 Training carried out under the STCW Convention which does not lead to the issue of a certificate of competency and on which information provided by a Party is found by the Maritime Safety Committee to give full and complete effect to the Convention in accordance with regulation I/7, paragraph 2 may be accepted by other Parties to the Convention as meeting the relevant training requirements thereof.

2 Contacted Administrations should issue the documentary proof referred to in regulation I/10, paragraph 5 to enable port State control authorities to accept the same in lieu of endorsement of a certificate issued by another Party for a period of three months from the date of issue, providing the information listed below:

.1 seafarer's name
.2 date of birth
.3 number of the original Certificate of Competency
.4 capacity
.5 limitations
.6 contact details of the Administration
.7 dates of issue and expiry.

3 Such documentary proof may be made available by electronic means.

Section B-I/11

Guidance regarding the revalidation of certificates

1 The courses required by regulation I/11 should include relevant changes in marine legislation, technology and recommendations concerning the safety of life at sea, security and the protection of the marine environment.

2 A test may take the form of written or oral examination, the use of a simulator or other appropriate means.

3 Approved seagoing service stated in section A-I/11, paragraph 1 may be served in an appropriate lower officer rank than that stated in the certificate held.

4 If an application for revalidation of a certificate referred to in paragraph 1 of regulation I/11 is made within six months before expiry of the certificate, the certificate may be revalidated until the fifth anniversary of the date of validity, or extension of the validity, of the certificate.

Section B-I/12

Guidance regarding the use of simulators

1 When simulators are being used for training or assessment of competency, the following guidelines should be taken into consideration in conducting any such training or assessment.

第 B-I/10 节

关于承认证书的指导

1　根据《STCW 公约》进行的但无须签发适当证书的培训及缔约国提交的有关该培训的资料，若被海上安全委员会认为是遵照规则第 I/7 条第 2 段使本公约充分和完全实施，则可被该公约的其他缔约国接受为满足了相关的培训要求。

2　被联络的主管机关应签发规则第 I/10 条第 5 段提及的为期三个月的证明文件，替代另一缔约国所签发证书的签证，使港口国监督机构接受该证明文件；该证明文件载明以下信息：

.1　海员姓名

.2　出生日期

.3　原适任证书号码

.4　职位

.5　限制

.6　主管机关联系方式

.7　签发日和过期日。

3　上述文件证明可以电子的方式提供。

第 B-I/11 节

关于证书再有效的指导

1　规则第 I/11 条要求的课程应该包括有关涉及海上人命安全、保安和海洋环境保护等方面的海事法规、技术和建议的相关变化。

2　测试可以采用书面或口头、模拟器的操作或其他适当的方式。

3　第 A-I/11 节第 1 段所述的认可的海上服务资历可通过任职于适当低于所持证书职位而获得。

4　如果规则第 I/11 条第 1 段所涉及证书在到期日前 6 个月申请再有效，证书可以再有效至有效期或延期到期日的第 5 年。

第 B-I/12 节

关于模拟器使用的指导

1　如果使用模拟器进行培训或适任评估，在进行这种培训或评估时，应考虑以下指南。

TRAINING AND ASSESSMENT IN RADAR OBSERVATION AND PLOTTING*

2 Training and assessment in radar observation and plotting should:

.1 incorporate the use of radar simulation equipment; and

.2 conform to standards not inferior to those given in paragraphs 3 to 17 below.

3 Demonstrations of and practice in radar observation should be undertaken, where appropriate, on live marine radar equipment, including the use of simulators. Plotting exercises should preferably be undertaken in real time, in order to increase trainees' awareness of the hazards of the improper use of radar data and improve their plotting techniques to a standard of radar plotting commensurate with that necessary for the safe execution of collision-avoidance manoeuvring under actual seagoing conditions.

General

Factors affecting performance and accuracy

4 An elementary understanding should be attained of the principles of radar, together with a full practical knowledge of:

.1 range and bearing measurement, characteristics of the radar set which determine the quality of the radar display, radar antennae, polar diagrams, the effects of power radiated in directions outside the main beam, a non-technical description of the radar system, including variations in the features encountered in different types of radar set, performance monitors and equipment factors which affect maximum and minimum detection ranges and accuracy of information;

.2 the current marine radar performance specification adopted by the Organization**;

.3 the effects of the siting of the radar antenna, shadow sectors and arcs of reduced sensitivity, false echoes, effects of antenna height on detection ranges and of siting radar units and storing spares near magnetic compasses, including magnetic safe distances; and

.4 radiation hazards and safety precautions to be taken in the vicinity of antennae and open waveguides.

Detection of misrepresentation of information, including false echoes and sea returns

5 A knowledge of the limitations to target detection is essential, to enable the observer to estimate the dangers of failure to detect targets. The following factors should be emphasized:

.1 performance standard of the equipment;

.2 brilliance, gain and video processor control settings;

.3 radar horizon;

* The relevant IMO Model Course(s) may be of assistance in the preparation of courses.

** See relevant/appropriate performance standards adopted by the Organization.

雷达观测和标绘的培训和评估①

2 雷达观测和标绘的培训和评估应：

.1 结合雷达模拟设备的使用；并且

.2 达到不低于以下第 3 段至第 17 段所述的培训标准。

3 雷达观测的演示和练习应在真实的船用雷达上进行，如合适，包括使用模拟器。最好进行实时标绘练习，使学员更加意识到不正确使用雷达数据所产生的危险，并且提高他们的标绘技术，达到相当于海上航行实际条件下安全执行避碰操作所必需的雷达标绘标准。

一般要求

影响性能和精度的因素

4 应基本了解雷达的原理和以下全面的实践知识：

.1 距离和方位的测量，决定雷达显示质量的雷达特性、雷达天线、极坐标图、主波束以外各方向辐射功率的影响、雷达系统的非技术性说明，包括不同类型雷达所具备的不同特点、性能监视器以及影响最大和最小探测距离和信息准确性的设备因素；

.2 目前本组织采纳的船用雷达性能规范②；

.3 雷达天线位置的影响、阴影扇形区和灵敏度降低弧、假回波、天线高度对于探测距离的影响、雷达装置安装位置的影响以及将备件存放在磁罗经附近的影响，包括磁性安全距离；以及

.4 在天线和开敞波导附近的辐射伤害和应采取的预防措施。

探查包括假回波和海浪回波在内的信息误显示

5 了解目标探测的局限性对于观测人员估计探测不到目标的危险是至关重要的。应强调以下因素：

.1 设备的性能标准；

.2 亮度、增益和视频处理器控制的设定；

.3 雷达作用距离；

① 相关 IMO 示范培训课程可有助于准备课程。

② 见国际海事组织采纳的相关/适当的性能标准。

.4 size, shape, aspect and composition of targets;

.5 effects of the motion of the ship in a seaway;

.6 propagation conditions;

.7 meteorological conditions; sea clutter and rain clutter;

.8 anti-clutter control settings;

.9 shadow sectors; and

.10 radar-to-radar interference.

6 A knowledge should be attained of factors which might lead to faulty interpretation, including false echoes, effects of nearby pylons and large structures, effects of power lines crossing rivers and estuaries, echoes from distant targets occurring on second or later traces.

7 A knowledge should be attained of aids to interpretation, including corner reflectors and radar beacons; detection and recognition of land targets; the effects of topographical features; effects of pulse length and beam width; radar-conspicuous and -inconspicuous targets; factors which affect the echo strength from targets.

Practice

Setting up and maintaining displays

8 A knowledge should be attained of:

.1 the various types of radar display mode; unstabilized ship's-head-up relative motion; ship's-head-up, course-up and north-up stabilized relative motion and true motion;

.2 the effects of errors on the accuracy of information displayed; effects of transmitting compass errors on stabilized and true-motion displays; effects of transmitting log errors on a true-motion display; and the effects of inaccurate manual speed settings on a true-motion display;

.3 methods of detecting inaccurate speed settings on true-motion controls; the effects of receiver noise limiting the ability to display weak echo returns, and the effects of saturation by receiver noise, etc.; the adjustment of operational controls; criteria which indicate optimum points of adjustment; the importance of proper adjustment sequence, and the effects of maladjusted controls; the detection of maladjustments and corrections of:

.3.1 controls affecting detection ranges; and

.3.2 controls affecting accuracy;

.4 the dangers of using radar equipment with maladjusted controls; and

.4 目标的尺寸、形状、外观和组成；

.5 船舶在海上运动的影响；

.6 电波传播条件；

.7 气象条件，海上杂波和雨杂波；

.8 抗杂波控制设定；

.9 阴影扇形区；以及

.10 雷达与雷达间的干扰。

6 应了解有可能导致错误分析的种种因素，其中包括假回波，附近铁塔和高大建筑的影响，跨河跨湾电线的影响，在第二次和其后扫描中来自远方目标的回波。

7 应了解有助于分析的装置，包括角反射器和雷达信标，陆地目标的探测和辨认，地貌的影响，脉冲长度和射束宽度的影响，显著和不显著的雷达目标，影响目标回波强度的因素。

练习

显示的设置和保持

8 应知晓以下内容：

.1 各种类型的雷达显示模式，不稳定的船首线向上相对运动，船首线向上、航向向上及真北向上的稳定相对运动和真运动；

.2 误差对所显示信息的精度的影响，罗经传送误差对稳定真运动显示的影响；计程仪传送误差对真运动显示的影响，以及不准确的人工速度设定对真运动显示的影响；

.3 真运动控钮上不准确速度设定的探测方法，限制弱反射回波显示能力的接收机噪声的影响以及接收机噪声饱和的影响等，操作控钮的调整，指示最佳调整点的标准，正确的调整顺序的重要性以及控钮误调的影响，检测下列误调和校正：

.3.1 影响探测距离的控钮，和

.3.2 影响精度的控钮；

.4 使用控钮调节不当的雷达设备的危险性；以及

.5 the need for frequent regular checking of performance, and the relationship of the performance indicator to the range performance of the radar set.

Range and bearing

9 A knowledge should be attained of:

.1 the methods of measuring ranges; fixed range markers and variable range markers;

.2 the accuracy of each method and the relative accuracy of the different methods;

.3 how range data are displayed; ranges at stated intervals, digital counter and graduated scale;

.4 the methods of measuring bearings; rotatable cursor on transparent disc covering the display, electronic bearing cursor and other methods;

.5 bearing accuracy and inaccuracies caused by parallax, heading marker displacement, centre maladjustment;

.6 how bearing data are displayed; graduated scale and digital counter; and

.7 the need for regular checking of the accuracy of ranges and bearings, methods of checking for inaccuracies and correcting or allowing for inaccuracies.

Plotting techniques and relative-motion concepts

10 Practice should be provided in manual plotting techniques, including the use of reflection plotters, with the objective of establishing a thorough understanding of the interrelated motion between own ship and other ships, including the effects of manoeuvring to avoid collision. At the preliminary stages of this training, simple plotting exercises should be designed to establish a sound appreciation of plotting geometry and relative-motion concepts. The degree of complexity of exercises should increase throughout the training course until the trainee has mastered all aspects of the subject. Competence can best be enhanced by exposing the trainee to real-time exercises performed on a simulator or using other effective means.

Identification of critical echoes

11 A thorough understanding should be attained of:

.1 position fixing by radar from land targets and sea marks;

.2 the accuracy of position fixing by ranges and by bearings;

.3 the importance of cross-checking the accuracy of radar against other navigational aids; and

.4 the value of recording ranges and bearings at frequent, regular intervals when using radar as an aid to collision avoidance.

.5 经常地定期进行雷达性能检查的必要性，及雷达性能指示器与量程性能的关系。

距离和方位

9 应知晓以下内容：

.1 测量距离的方法，固定量程标尺及可变量程标尺；

.2 每种方法的精度及不同方法的相对精度；

.3 量程数据的显示方法，标尺间隔的量程、数字计数器以及比例尺；

.4 测量方位的方法，显示器透明盘上的可转动游标、电子方位游标及其他方法；

.5 方位精度和由于视差、船首标志位移、中心失调造成的误差；

.6 方位数据的显示方法，刻度尺和数字计数器；以及

.7 定时检查距离和方位精度的必要性，检查误差和纠正或修正误差的方法。

标绘技术和相对运动概念

10 应提供人工标绘技术的练习，包括使用反射标绘仪，其目的是透彻地理解本船和他船间的相对运动，包括避碰操作的作用。在此种培训的最初阶段，应设计一些简单的标绘练习，来建立对标绘几何学和相对运动概念的全面认识。应在培训课程的进行中不断加深练习的复杂程度，直至学员完全掌握这一科目的各个方面。通过使用模拟器或其他有效手段让学员进行实时练习，可以大大增强其适任能力。

关键回波的识别

11 应透彻地理解：

.1 利用岸上或海上目标进行雷达定位；

.2 用距离和方位定位的精度；

.3 对照其他航标对雷达精度进行相互核对的重要性；以及

.4 在使用雷达作为避碰设备时，频繁和定时记录距离和方位的价值。

Course and speed of other ships

12 A thorough understanding should be attained of:

.1 the different methods by which course and speed of other ships can be obtained from recorded ranges and bearings, including:

.1.1 the unstabilized relative plot;

.1.2 the stabilized relative plot; and

.1.3 the true plot; and

.2 the relationship between visual and radar observations, including detail and the accuracy of estimates of course and speed of other ships, and the detection of changes in movements of other ships.

Time and distance of closest approach of crossing, meeting or overtaking ships

13 A thorough understanding should be attained of:

.1 the use of recorded data to obtain:

.1.1 measurement of closest approach distance and bearing;

.1.2 time to closest approach; and

.2 the importance of frequent, regular observations.

Detecting course and speed changes of other ships

14 A thorough understanding should be attained of:

.1 the effects of changes of course and/or speed by other ships on their tracks across the display;

.2 the delay between change of course or speed and detection of that change; and

.3 the hazards of small changes as compared with substantial changes of course or speed in relation to rate and accuracy of detection.

Effects of changes in own ship's course or speed or both

15 A thorough understanding of the effects on a relative-motion display of own ship's movements, and the effects of other ships' movements and the advantages of compass stabilization of a relative display.

他船的航向和航速

12　应透彻地理解：

.1　从所记录的他船的距离和方位来求得其航向和航速的不同方法，包括：

.1.1　不稳定的相对运动标绘，

.1.2　稳定的相对运动标绘，和

.1.3　真运动标绘；以及

.2　目测和雷达观测的关系，包括估计他船航向和航速的细节和精度，以及对他船运动变化的探测。

船舶交叉相遇、对遇或追越时到达最接近点的时间和距离

13　应透彻地理解：

.1　用所记录的数据求得：

.1.1　到最接近点的距离和方位的计算，和

.1.2　到最接近点的时间；以及

.2　频繁和定时观测的重要性。

对他船航向、航速变化的探测

14　应透彻地理解：

.1　他船航向或航速的变化对其在显示器上的航迹的影响；

.2　航向或航速变化与察觉这一变化的时间延迟；以及

.3　航向或航速的微小变化与明显变化相比，在探测率和探测精度上的危险性。

本船航向或航速的变化或两者都变化的影响

15　应透彻地理解本船运动和他船运动对相对运动显示的影响，以及相对运动显示中罗经稳定的好处。

16 In respect of true-motion displays, a thorough understanding should be attained of:

.1 the effects of inaccuracies of:

.1.1 speed and course settings; and

.1.2 compass stabilization data driving a stabilized relative-motion display;

.2 the effects of changes in course or speed or both by own ship on tracks of other ships on the display; and

.3 the relationship of speed to frequency of observations.

Application of the International Regulations for Preventing Collisions at Sea, 1972, as amended

17 A thorough understanding should be attained of the relationship of the International Regulations for Preventing Collisions at Sea, 1972, as amended to the use of radar, including:

.1 action to avoid collision, dangers of assumptions made on inadequate information and the hazards of small alterations of course or speed;

.2 the advantages of safe speed when using radar to avoid collision;

.3 the relationship of speed to closest approach distance and time and to the manoeuvring characteristics of various types of ships;

.4 the importance of radar observation reports and radar reporting procedures being well defined;

.5 the use of radar in clear weather, to obtain an appreciation of its capabilities and limitations, compare radar and visual observations and obtain an assessment of the relative accuracy of information;

.6 the need for early use of radar in clear weather at night and when there are indications that visibility may deteriorate;

.7 comparison of features displayed by radar with charted features; and

.8 comparison of the effects of differences between range scales.

TRAINING AND ASSESSMENT IN THE OPERATIONAL USE OF AUTOMATIC RADAR PLOTTING AIDS (ARPA)

18 Training and assessment in the operational use of automatic radar plotting aids (ARPA) should:

.1 require prior completion of the training in radar observation and plotting or combine that training with the training given in paragraphs 19 to 35 below;*

* The relevant IMO Model Course(s) and resolution MSC.64(67), as amended, may be of assistance in the preparation of courses.

16 对于真运动显示，应透彻地理解：

.1 以下误差的影响：

.1.1 速度和航向的设定，和

.1.2 驱动稳定的相对运动显示的罗经稳定数据；

.2 本船航向或航速的变化或两者都变化对他船在显示器上的航迹的影响；以及

.3 航速与观测频率的关系。

《1972 年国际海上避碰规则》的应用

17 应透彻理解经修订的《1972 年国际海上避碰规则》与使用雷达的关系，包括：

.1 避碰行动，依赖不充分的信息做出推断的危险性以及航向和航速微小变化的危险性；

.2 使用雷达避碰时，安全航速的好处；

.3 航速与最接近点的距离和时间以及与不同类型船舶操纵特性的关系；

.4 明确规定的雷达观测报告和雷达报告程序的重要性；

.5 在天气晴朗时使用雷达以了解其性能和局限性，比较雷达观测和目测并对信息的相对准确性予以评估；

.6 在天气晴朗的夜间和有迹象表明能见度会下降时及早使用雷达的必要性；

.7 比较雷达显示的岸形和海图上的岸形；以及

.8 比较各量程标尺的不同影响。

自动雷达标绘仪（ARPA）操作使用的培训和评估

18 自动雷达标绘仪（ARPA）操作使用的培训和评估应：

.1 要求先完成雷达观测和标绘的培训，或将该培训与以下第 19 段至第 35 段所述的培训相结合；①

① 相关 IMO 示范培训课程和经修正的海安会决议 MSC.64(67)可有助于准备课程。

.2 incorporate the use of ARPA simulation equipment; and

.3 conform to standards not inferior to those given in paragraphs 19 to 35 below.

19 Where ARPA training is provided as part of the general training under the 1978 STCW Convention, masters, chief mates and officers in charge of a navigational watch should understand the factors involved in decision-making based on the information supplied by ARPA in association with other navigational data inputs, having a similar appreciation of the operational aspects and of system errors of modern electronic navigational systems, including ECDIS. This training should be progressive in nature, commensurate with the responsibilities of the individual and the certificates issued by Parties under the 1978 STCW Convention.

Theory and demonstration

Possible risks of over-reliance on ARPA

20 Appreciation that ARPA is only a navigational aid and:

.1 that its limitations, including those of its sensors, make over-reliance on ARPA dangerous, in particular for keeping a look-out; and

.2 the need to observe at all times the Principles to be observed in keeping a navigational watch and the Guidance on keeping a navigational watch.

Principal types of ARPA systems and their display characteristics

21 Knowledge of the principal types of ARPA systems in use; their various display characteristics and an understanding of when to use ground- or sea-stabilized modes and north-up, course-up or head-up presentations.

IMO performance standards for ARPA

22 An appreciation of the IMO performance standards for ARPA, in particular the standards relating to accuracy.*

Factors affecting system performance and accuracy

23 Knowledge of ARPA sensor input performance parameters radar, compass and speed inputs and the effects of sensor malfunction on the accuracy of ARPA data.

24 Knowledge of:

.1 the effects of the limitations of radar range and bearing discrimination and accuracy and the limitations of compass and speed input accuracies on the accuracy of ARPA data; and

.2 factors which influence vector accuracy.

* See relevant/appropriate performance standards adopted by the Organization.

.2 结合 ARPA 模拟设备的使用;并且

.3 达到不低于以下第 19 段至第 35 段给出的标准。

19 当 ARPA 培训作为《1978 年 STCW 公约》要求的一般培训的一部分时,船长、大副和负责航行值班的高级船员应理解根据 APRA 所提供的信息连同其他航行数据的输入而做出决策所涉及的各种因素,对于操纵方面和包括电子海图显示与信息系统(ECDIS)在内的现代电子航行系统的系统误差有同样的认识。此种培训应是渐进的,并与个人责任和根据《1978 年 STCW 公约》由缔约国签发的证书相适应。

理论和演示

过分依赖 ARPA 可能产生的危险

20 认识到 ARPA 仅是一种助航设备,以及:

.1 ARPA 的局限性,包括其传感器的局限性,使得过分依赖 ARPA 是危险的,特别是用于瞭望值班更是如此;和

.2 在任何时候都遵守航行值班中应遵循的基本原则和保持航行值班的导则的必要性。

ARPA 系统的主要类型及其显示特点

21 了解现用的 ARPA 系统的主要类型、它们的各种显示特点,并且理解何时使用对地或对海稳定模式以及真北向上、航向向上或船首向上显示。

国际海事组织的 ARPA 性能标准

22 认识国际海事组织的 ARPA 性能标准,特别是关于精度的标准。①

影响系统性能和精度的因素

23 了解 ARPA 传感器输入性能参数——雷达、罗经和航速输入以及传感器故障对 ARPA 数据精度的影响。

24 了解:

.1 雷达的距离、方位分辨力和精度局限性以及罗经和航速输入精度局限性对 ARPA 数据精度的影响;以及

.2 影响矢量精度的因素。

① 见国际海事组织采纳的相关/适当的性能标准。

Tracking capabilities and limitations

25 Knowledge of:

.1 the criteria for the selection of targets by automatic acquisition;

.2 the factors leading to the correct choice of targets for manual acquisition;

.3 the effects on tracking of "lost" targets and target fading; and

.4 the circumstances causing "target swap" and its effects on displayed data.

Processing delays

26 Knowledge of the delays inherent in the display of processed ARPA information, particularly on acquisition and re-acquisition or when a tracked target manoeuvres.

Operational warnings, their benefits and limitations

27 Appreciation of the uses, benefits and limitations of ARPA operational warnings and their correct setting, where applicable, to avoid spurious interference.

System operational tests

28 Knowledge of:

.1 methods of testing for malfunctions of ARPA systems, including functional self-testing; and

.2 precautions to be taken after a malfunction occurs.

Manual and automatic acquisition of targets and their respective limitations

29 Knowledge of the limits imposed on both types of acquisition in multi-target scenarios, and the effects on acquisition of target fading and target swap.

True and relative vectors and typical graphic representation of target information and danger areas

30 Thorough knowledge of true and relative vectors; derivation of targets' true courses and speeds, including:

.1 threat assessment, derivation of predicted closest point of approach and predicted time to closest point of approach from forward extrapolation of vectors, the use of graphic representation of danger areas;

.2 the effects of alterations of course and/or speed of own ship and/or targets on predicted closest point of approach and predicted time to closest point of approach and danger areas;

跟踪能力和局限性

25 了解：

.1 用自动录取方式选择目标的标准；

.2 导致采用手动录取方式正确选择目标的因素；

.3 对跟踪“丢失”目标和正在消失目标的影响；以及

.4 造成“目标交换”的环境及其对显示数据的影响。

处理延迟

26 了解在显示经处理的 ARPA 信息时所固有的延迟，特别是对录取和再录取，或当被跟踪目标处于操纵状态时。

操作性报警，其好处和局限性

27 认识 ARPA 操作性报警的使用、好处和局限性及其正确设定，如适用，以防止杂散干扰。

系统的操作性测试

28 了解：

.1 对 ARPA 系统故障的测试方法，包括功能自测；以及

.2 故障出现后应采取的措施。

手动和自动录取目标及其各自的局限性

29 了解在多目标情况下，两种录取方式的局限性以及对录取正在消失的目标和目标交换的影响。

真运动矢量和相对运动矢量以及目标信息和危险区域的典型图示

30 透彻了解真运动矢量和相对运动矢量，目标的真航向和航速的推导，包括：

.1 威胁评估，根据矢量外推对预计最接近点和到达最接近点的时间的推导，危险区域图示的应用；

.2 本船和/或他船的航向和/或航速的改变对预计最接近点和到达最接近点的时间及危险区域的影响；

.3 the effects of incorrect vectors and danger areas; and

.4 the benefit of switching between true and relative vectors.

Information on past positions of targets being tracked

31 Knowledge of the derivation of past positions of targets being tracked, recognition of historic data as a means of indicating recent manoeuvring of targets and as a method of checking the validity of the ARPA's tracking.

Practice

Setting up and maintaining displays

32 Ability to demonstrate:

.1 the correct starting procedure to obtain the optimum display of ARPA information;

.2 the selection of display presentation; stabilized relative-motion displays and true-motion displays;

.3 the correct adjustment of all variable radar display controls for optimum display of data;

.4 the selection, as appropriate, of required speed input to ARPA;

.5 the selection of ARPA plotting controls, manual/automatic acquisition, vector/graphic display of data;

.6 the selection of the timescale of vectors/graphics;

.7 the use of exclusion areas when automatic acquisition is employed by ARPA; and

.8 performance checks of radar, compass, speed input sensors and ARPA.

System operational tests

33 Ability to perform system checks and determine data accuracy of ARPA, including the trial manoeuvre facility, by checking against basic radar plot.

Obtaining information from the ARPA display

34 Demonstrate the ability to obtain information in both relative- and true-motion modes of display, including:

.1 the identification of critical echoes;

.2 the speed and direction of target's relative movement;

.3 the time to, and predicted range at, target's closest point of approach;

.3 不正确的矢量和危险区域的影响;以及
.4 真运动矢量和相对运动矢量间进行转换的好处。

被跟踪目标过去位置的信息

31 了解被跟踪目标过去位置的推导,认识历史数据可用以说明目标当前的操纵运动,并可用以检查 ARPA 跟踪的有效性。

练习

显示的设定和保持

32 能够演示:
.1 为获得最佳 ARPA 信息显示的正确启动程序;
.2 选择显示方式,稳定的相对运动显示和真运动显示;
.3 为获得最佳的数据显示,正确调整雷达各可调显示控钮;
.4 视情况有选择地向 ARPA 输入所需的航速;
.5 选择 ARPA 标绘控钮,手动/自动录取,数据的矢量/图形显示;
.6 选择矢量/图形的时间比例;
.7 当 ARPA 使用自动录取时,排除区域的运用;以及
.8 雷达、罗经、航速输入传感器和 ARPA 的性能检测。

系统操作性测试

33 通过对照基本的雷达标绘进行核查,能够执行系统的核查并确定 ARPA 的数据精度,包括试操纵装置。

从 ARPA 显示中获得信息

34 表明从相对运动和真运动显示模式中获得信息的能力,包括:
.1 对关键回波的识别;
.2 目标相对运动的速度和方向;
.3 到达目标的最接近点的时间和预测距离;

.4 the courses and speeds of targets;

.5 detecting course and speed changes of targets and the limitations of such information;

.6 the effect of changes in own ship's course or speed or both; and

.7 the operation of the trial manoeuvre facility.

Application of the International Regulations for Preventing Collisions at Sea, 1972, as amended

35 Analysis of potential collision situations from displayed information, determination and execution of action to avoid close-quarters situations in accordance with the International Regulations for Preventing Collisions at Sea, 1972, as amended, in force.

TRAINING AND ASSESSMENT IN THE OPERATIONAL USE OF ELECTRONIC CHART DISPLAY AND INFORMATION SYSTEMS (ECDIS)

Introduction

36 When simulators are being used for training or assessment in the operational use of Electronic Chart Display and Information Systems (ECDIS), the following interim guidance should be taken into consideration in any such training or assessment.

37 Training and assessment in the operational use of the ECDIS should:

.1 incorporate the use of ECDIS simulation equipment; and

.2 conform to standards not inferior to those given in paragraphs 38 to 65 below.

38 ECDIS simulation equipment should, in addition to meeting all applicable performance standards set out in section A-I/12 of the STCW Code, as amended, be capable of simulating navigational equipment and bridge operational controls which meet all applicable performance standards adopted by the Organization, incorporate facilities to generate soundings and:

.1 create a real-time operating environment, including navigation control and communications instruments and equipment appropriate to the navigation and watchkeeping tasks to be carried out and the manoeuvring skills to be assessed; and

.2 realistically simulate "own ship" characteristics in open-water conditions, as well as the effects of weather, tidal stream and currents.

39 Demonstrations of, and practice in, ECDIS use should be undertaken, where appropriate, through the use of simulators. Training exercises should preferably be undertaken in real time, in order to increase trainees' awareness of the hazards of the improper use of ECDIS. Accelerated timescale may be used only for demonstrations.

.4 目标的航向和航速；

.5 对目标航向和航速变化的探测以及这种信息的局限性；

.6 本船航向或航速变化或两者都变化的影响；以及

.7 对试操纵装置的操作。

经修订的《1972 年国际海上避碰规则》的应用

35 用显示的信息分析潜在碰撞形势，按照现行的经修订的《1972 年国际海上避碰规则》决定和执行避免紧迫局面的行动。

电子海图显示和信息系统(ECDIS)操作使用的培训和评估

前言

36 在模拟器用于 ECDIS 操作使用的培训和评估时，应考虑下列暂行性指导。

37 ECDIS 操作使用的培训和评估应：

.1 同时使用 ECDIS 模拟器设备；并且

.2 达到不低于以下第 38 段到第 65 段给出的标准。

38 ECDIS 模拟设备除了达到经修正的《STCW 规则》中第 A-I/12 节规定的所有适用的性能标准外，还应能够模拟达到本组织通过的所有适用的性能标准的导航设备和驾驶台操作控制，包括测深设备，以及：

.1 产生实时操作环境，包括适于完成航行和值班任务和评估操纵技能的航行控制和通信仪器设备；以及

.2 真实模拟“本船”在开阔水域条件下的特性，以及天气、潮流和水流的影响。

39 ECDIS 使用的演示和实操在适当情况下应使用模拟器。培训练习最好采取实时模式以增强学员对不正确使用 ECDIS 的危害的认识。加速模式仅用于演示。

General

Goals of an ECDIS training programme

40 The ECDIS trainee should be able to:

.1 operate the ECDIS equipment, use the navigational functions of ECDIS, select and assess all relevant information and take proper action in the case of a malfunction;

.2 state the potential errors of displayed data and the usual errors of interpretation; and

.3 explain why ECDIS should not be relied upon as the sole reliable aid to navigation.

Theory and demonstration

41 As the safe use of ECDIS requires knowledge and understanding of the basic principles governing ECDIS data and their presentation rules as well as potential errors in displayed data and ECDIS-related limitations and potential dangers, a number of lectures covering the theoretical explanation should be provided. As far as possible, such lessons should be presented within a familiar context and make use of practical examples. They should be reinforced during simulator exercises.

42 For safe operation of ECDIS equipment and ECDIS-related information (use of the navigational functions of ECDIS, selection and assessment of all relevant information, becoming familiar with ECDIS man–machine interfacing), practical exercises and training on the ECDIS simulators should constitute the main content of the course.

43 For the definition of training objectives, a structure of activities should be defined. A detailed specification of learning objectives should be developed for each topic of this structure.

Simulator exercises

44 Exercises should be carried out on individual ECDIS simulators, or full-mission navigation simulators including ECDIS, to enable trainees to acquire the necessary practical skills. For real-time navigation exercises, navigation simulators are recommended to cover the complex navigation situation. The exercises should provide training in the use of the various scales, navigational modes, and display modes which are available, so that the trainees will be able to adapt the use of the equipment to the particular situation concerned.

45 The choice of exercises and scenarios is governed by the simulator facilities available. If one or more ECDIS workstations and a full-mission simulator are available, the workstations may primarily be used for basic exercises in the use of ECDIS facilities and for passage-planning exercises, whereas full-mission simulators may primarily be used for exercises related to passage-monitoring functions in real time, as realistic as possible in connection with the total workload of a navigational watch. The degree of complexity of exercises should increase throughout the training programme until the trainee has mastered all aspects of the learning subject.

46 Exercises should produce the greatest impression of realism. To achieve this, the scenarios should be located in a fictitious sea area. Situations, functions and actions for different

一般要求

ECDIS 培训项目的目标

40 ECDIS 的学员应能：

.1 操作 ECDIS 设备，使用 ECDIS 的导航功能，选择和评估所有的相关信息并在设备发生故障时采取适当措施；

.2 说明显示数据的潜在误差和解读常见误差；以及

.3 解释 ECDIS 不能作为唯一可靠的助航手段的原因。

理论和演示

41 鉴于安全使用 ECDIS 需了解和掌握其数据管理的基本原理、显示规则和显示数据的可能误差以及 ECDIS 相关限制和潜在危险，应开设多门课讲解理论知识，并且此类课程应尽可能在熟悉环境下进行实例教学。课程知识应在模拟器练习过程中予以强化。

42 为安全操作 ECDIS 设备和相关信息（使用 ECDIS 的导航功能、选择和评估所有相关信息、熟悉其人机交互），该门课程主要内容应是 ECDIS 模拟器的实操和训练。

43 为明确培训目标，应定义一个行动架构，架构中每个子标题的学习目标应详细描述。

模拟器练习

44 练习应在单独的 ECDIS 模拟器或在包括 ECDIS 功能在内的全功能航海模拟器上进行，使学员获得必要的实操技能。推荐使用航海模拟器进行复杂航海情况的实时航海练习。练习应提供在可用的不同比例尺、导航模式和显示方式下的训练，以使学员能够将设备运用于有关的特定局面。

45 练习和场景选择受可用模拟器设备制约。如能提供一个或多个 ECDIS 工作站和一个全功能模拟器，工作站应作为使用 ECDIS 装置的基础练习和航线设计练习的首选；实时航行监控功能相关的练习则首选全功能模拟器，并尽可能真实地接入航行值班的整个工作负荷。在整个训练计划中，练习的复杂程度应递增，直至学员掌握所学科目的全部知识。

46 练习应最大可能地体现真实感。为此，场景应设定为假设的某海区。可以将为不同训练目标设计的在不同海区发生的各种情景、功能和行动整合在一个练习中，并以实时的方式体验。

learning objectives which occur in different sea areas can be integrated into one exercise and experienced in real time.

47 The main objective of simulator exercises is to ensure that trainees understand their responsibilities in the operational use of ECDIS in all safety-relevant aspects and are thoroughly familiar with the system and equipment used.

Principal types of ECDIS systems and their display characteristics

48 The trainee should gain knowledge of the principal types of ECDIS in use; their various display characteristics, data structure and an understanding of:

.1 differences between vector and raster charts;

.2 differences between ECDIS and ECS;

.3 differences between ECDIS and RCDS*;

.4 characteristics of ECDIS and their different solutions; and

.5 characteristics of systems for special purposes (unusual situations/emergencies).

Risks of over-reliance on ECDIS

49 The training in ECDIS operational use should address:

.1 the limitations of ECDIS as a navigational tool;

.2 potential risk of improper functioning of the system;

.3 system limitations, including those of its sensors;

.4 hydrographic data inaccuracy; limitations of vector and raster electronic charts (ECDIS *vs* RCDS and ENC *vs* RNC); and

.5 potential risk of human errors.

Emphasis should be placed on the need to keep a proper look-out and to perform periodical checking, especially of the ship's position, by ECDIS-independent methods.

Detection of misrepresentation of information

50 Knowledge of the limitations of the equipment and detection of misrepresentation of information is essential for the safe use of ECDIS. The following factors should be emphasized during training:

.1 performance standards of the equipment;

.2 radar data representation on an electronic chart, elimination of discrepancy between the radar image and the electronic chart;

* SN/Circ.207/Rev.1 – Differences between RCDS and ECDIS.

47 模拟器练习的主要目的是确保学员理解所有安全相关方面操作使用 ECDIS 的责任并且完全熟悉所使用的系统和设备。

ECDIS 主要类型和显示性能

48 学员应掌握现用 ECDIS 主要类型、显示特性和数据结构,并理解:

.1 矢量海图和光栅海图的区别;

.2 ECDIS 与电子海图系统的区别;

.3 ECDIS 与光栅海图显示系统的区别①;

.4 ECDIS 的特性及不同操作方式;以及

.5 用于特殊目的(非正常情况/应急情况)的系统特性。

过度依赖 ECDIS 的风险

49 在 ECDIS 操作使用培训中应注意:

.1 ECDIS 作为导航工具的局限性;

.2 系统故障的潜在风险;

.3 系统包括传感器在内的局限性;

.4 水文数据不精确性,矢量型和光栅型电子海图系统(ECDIS 和 RCDS, ENC 和 RNC)的局限性;以及

.5 人为失误的潜在风险。

应强调保持正规瞭望和进行定期检查的必要性,特别是船位核查方式,应独立于 ECDIS。

探测信息的错误显示

50 掌握设备的局限性和探测信息的错误显示对安全使用 ECDIS 至关重要。在培训中应强调下列因素:

.1 设备的性能标准;

.2 在电子海图上显示雷达数据,减小雷达图像和电子海图之间的差异;

① SN/Circ. 207/Rev. 1—“电子海图显示和信息系统”和“光栅海图显示系统”的区别。

.3 possible projection discrepancies between an electronic and paper charts;

.4 possible scale discrepancies (overscaling and underscaling) in displaying an electronic chart and its original scale;

.5 effects of using different reference systems for positioning;

.6 effects of using different horizontal and vertical datums;

.7 effects of the motion of the ship in a seaway;

.8 ECDIS limitations in raster chart display mode;

.9 potential errors in the display of:

.9.1 the own ship's position;

.9.2 radar data and ARPA and AIS information;

.9.3 different geodetic coordinate systems; and

.10 verification of the results of manual or automatic data correction:

.10.1 comparison of chart data and radar picture; and

.10.2 checking the own ship's position by using the other independent position-fixing systems.

51 False interpretation of the data and proper action taken to avoid errors of interpretation should be explained. The implications of the following should be emphasized:

.1 ignoring overscaling of the display;

.2 uncritical acceptance of the own ship's position;

.3 confusion of display mode;

.4 confusion of chart scale;

.5 confusion of reference systems;

.6 different modes of presentation;

.7 different modes of vector stabilization;

.8 differences between true north and gyro north (radar);

.9 using the same data reference system;

.10 using the appropriate chart scale;

.11 using the best-suited sensor to the given situation and circumstances;

.3 电子海图和纸质海图可能出现的投影差异；

.4 在电子海图显示的比例尺和原比例尺之间可能的差异(过大或过小)；

.5 使用不同参照系对定位的影响；

.6 使用不同水平和垂直基准面的影响；

.7 船舶在航路上运动的影响；

.8 ECDIS 采用光栅海图显示模式的局限性；

.9 显示下列信息时的潜在误差：

.9.1 本船位置，

.9.2 雷达数据和 ARPA 以及自动识别系统(AIS)信息，

.9.3 不同大地坐标系；以及

.10 验证手动或自动数据修正的结果：

.10.1 比较海图数据和雷达图像，以及

.10.2 使用其他独立定位系统核查本船位置。

51 应就错误解读数据和避免此类错误解读应该采取的正确措施作出解释。为此应重视下列因素的影响：

.1 忽视显示的比例尺过大；

.2 对本船位置不加鉴别地接收；

.3 显示模式混淆；

.4 海图比例尺混淆；

.5 参照系混淆；

.6 显示模式不同；

.7 矢量稳定模式不同；

.8 真北和陀螺北(雷达)的差别；

.9 使用相同的数据参照系；

.10 使用合适的海图比例尺；

.11 使用最适合指定的情况和环境的传感器；

.12 entering the correct values of safety data:

.12.1 the own ship's safety contour,

.12.2 safety depth (safe water), and

.12.3 events; and

.13 proper use of all available data.

52 Appreciation that RCDS is only a navigational aid and that, when operating in the RCDS mode, the ECDIS equipment should be used together with an appropriate portfolio of up-to-date paper charts:

.1 appreciation of the differences in operation of RCDS mode as described in SN.1/Circ.207/Rev.1 "Differences between RCDS and ECDIS"; and

.2 ECDIS, in any mode, should be used in training with an appropriate portfolio of up-to-date charts.

Factors affecting system performance and accuracy

53 An elementary understanding should be attained of the principles of ECDIS, together with a full practical knowledge of:

.1 starting and setting up ECDIS; connecting data sensors: satellite and radio navigation system receivers, radar, gyro-compass, log, echo-sounder; accuracy and limitations of these sensors, including effects of measurement errors and ship's position accuracy, manoeuvring on the accuracy of course indicator's performance, compass error on the accuracy of course indication, shallow water on the accuracy of log performance, log correction on the accuracy of speed calculation, disturbance (sea state) on the accuracy of an echo-sounder performance; and

.2 the current performance standards for electronic chart display and information systems adopted by the Organization*.

Practice

Setting up and maintaining display

54 Knowledge and skills should be attained in:

.1 the correct starting procedure to obtain the optimum display of ECDIS information;

.2 the selection of display presentation (standard display, display base, all other information displayed individually on demand);

* See relevant/appropriate performance standards adopted by the Organization.

.12 输入安全数据的正确值：

.12.1 本船的安全等深线，

.12.2 安全水深（安全水域），及

.12.3 事件；以及

.13 正确使用所有可用的数据。

52 理解光栅海图显示系统仅仅是一种助航设备，当使用光栅海图显示系统模式时，电子海图与显示系统设备应与相应的最新纸质海图一起使用：

.1 理解光栅海图显示系统操作模式的差别，如通函 SN. 1/Circ. 207/Rev. 1“光栅海图显示系统与 ECDIS 的差别”所述；及

.2 培训中，无论 ECDIS 处于何种模式，均应与相应的最新海图并用。

影响系统性能和精确性的因素

53 应基本理解 ECDIS 原理，并有下列全面的实际知识：

.1 启动并设定 ECDIS，连接数据传感器：卫星和无线电导航系统接收机、雷达、陀螺罗经、计程仪、回声测深仪，这些传感器的精度和局限性，包括测量误差和船位精度的影响、操纵对航向指示器精度的影响、罗经误差对航向指示精度的影响、浅水对计程仪精度的影响、计程仪校正对速度计算精度的影响、干扰（海况）对回声测深仪精度的影响；以及

.2 本组织采纳的现行 ECDIS 性能标准①。

实践

显示的设定和保持

54 应掌握下列的知识和技能：

.1 为获得最佳 ECDIS 信息显示的正确启动程序；

.2 显示方式（标准显示、显示背景、所有其他按要求单独显示的信息）的选择；

① 见国际海事组织采纳的相关/适当的性能标准。

.3 the correct adjustment of all variable radar/ARPA display controls for optimum display of data;

.4 the selection of convenient configuration;

.5 the selection, as appropriate, of required speed input to ECDIS;

.6 the selection of the timescale of vectors; and

.7 performance checks of position, radar/ARPA, compass, speed input sensors and ECDIS.

Operational use of electronic charts

55 Knowledge and skills should be attained in:

.1 the main characteristics of the display of ECDIS data and selecting proper information for navigational tasks;

.2 the automatic functions required for monitoring ship's safety, such as display of position, heading/gyro course, speed, safety values and time;

.3 the manual functions (by the cursor, electronic bearing line, range rings);

.4 selecting and modification of electronic chart content;

.5 scaling (including underscaling and overscaling);

.6 zooming;

.7 setting of the own ship's safety data;

.8 using a daytime or night-time display mode;

.9 reading all chart symbols and abbreviations;

.10 using different kinds of cursors and electronic bars for obtaining navigational data;

.11 viewing an area in different directions and returning to the ship's position;

.12 finding the necessary area, using geographical coordinates;

.13 displaying indispensable data layers appropriate to a navigational situation;

.14 selecting appropriate and unambiguous data (position, course, speed, etc.);

.15 entering the mariner's notes;

.16 using north-up orientation presentation and other kinds of orientation; and

.17 using true- and relative-motion modes.

.3 为获得最佳的数据显示,正确调整雷达/ARPA 各可调显示控钮;
.4 选择便利的配置;
.5 如适用,选择所需的速度输入 ECDIS;
.6 选择矢量的时间尺度;以及
.7 船位、雷达/ARPA、罗经、速度输入传感器和 ECDIS 的性能检测。

电子海图的操作使用

55 应掌握下列知识和技能:
.1 ECDIS 数据显示的主要特性和正确选择航行任务信息;
.2 监测船舶安全需要的自动功能,诸如显示船位、船首向/陀螺航向、速度、安全值和时间;
.3 手动功能(使用光标、电子方位线、距离圈);
.4 选择和调整电子海图内容;
.5 比例尺(包括过小或过大);
.6 缩小或放大;
.7 设定本船安全数据;
.8 使用日视和夜视显示模式;
.9 识读所有海图符号和缩写;
.10 使用各种光标和电子标志获得航行数据;
.11 从不同方向观察某一区域并返回本船位置;
.12 使用地理坐标寻找所需水域;
.13 显示适合于航行状况的必不可少的数据层;
.14 选择适当和明了的数据(位置、航向、航速等);
.15 输入航行记录;
.16 使用北向上显示模式和其他方向显示模式;及
.17 使用真运动和相对运动模式。

Route planning

56 Knowledge and skills should be attained in:

.1 loading the ship's characteristics into ECDIS;

.2 selection of a sea area for route planning:

.2.1 reviewing required waters for the sea passage, and

.2.2 changing over of chart scale;

.3 verifying that proper and updated charts are available;

.4 route planning on a display by means of ECDIS, using the graphic editor, taking into consideration rhumb line and great-circle sailing:

.4.1 using the ECDIS database for obtaining navigational, hydro-meteorological and other data;

.4.2 taking into consideration turning radius and wheel-over points/lines when they are expressed on chart scale;

.4.3 marking dangerous depths and areas and exhibiting guarding depth contours;

.4.4 marking waypoints with the crossing depth contours and critical cross-track deviations, as well as by adding, replacing and erasing of waypoints;

.4.5 taking into consideration safe speed;

.4.6 checking pre-planned route for navigational safety; and

.4.7 generating alarms and warnings;

.5 route planning with calculation in the table format, including:

.5.1 waypoints selection;

.5.2 recalling the waypoints list;

.5.3 planning notes;

.5.4 adjustment of a planned route;

.5.5 checking a pre-planned route for navigational safety;

.5.6 alternative route planning;

.5.7 saving planned routes, loading and unloading or deleting routes;

.5.8 making a graphic copy of the monitor screen and printing a route;

航线设计

56 应掌握下列知识和技能：

.1 将船舶特性数据输入 ECDIS；

.2 选择航线设计的海区：

.2.1 检查海上航路所需水域，及

.2.2 变更海图比例尺；

.3 核查是否有相应的最新海图；

.4 在 ECDIS 上使用图形编辑器进行航线设计，并考虑恒向线和大圆航线航法：

.4.1 使用 ECDIS 数据库获取导航、水文气象和其他数据，

.4.2 考虑旋回半径和施舵点/线时应注意海图比例尺，

.4.3 标示危险深度和海区及警戒等深线，

.4.4 用横向等深线和航迹偏差临界值标示转向点，以及添加、取代、清除转向点，

.4.5 考虑安全航速，

.4.6 为航行安全检查预定航线，以及

.4.7 产生警报和警告；

.5 航线设计计算采用表格形式，包括：

.5.1 选择转向点，

.5.2 召回转向点列表，

.5.3 说明计划，

.5.4 调整计划航线，

.5.5 为安全航行检查预定航线，

.5.6 替代的计划航线，

.5.7 存储计划航线，下载、卸载或删除航线，

.5.8 监视屏图形备份及打印航线，

.5.9 editing and modification of the planned route;

.5.10 setting of safety values according to the size and manoeuvring parameters of the vessel;

.5.11 back-route planning; and

.5.12 connecting several routes.

Route monitoring

57 Knowledge and skills should be attained in:

.1 using independent data to control ship's position or using alternative systems within ECDIS;

.2 using the look-ahead function:

.2.1 changing charts and their scales;

.2.2 reviewing navigational charts;

.2.3 vector time selecting;

.2.4 predicting the ship's position for some time interval;

.2.5 changing the pre-planned route (route modification);

.2.6 entering independent data for the calculation of wind drift and current allowance;

.2.7 reacting properly to the alarm;

.2.8 entering corrections for discrepancies of the geodetic datum;

.2.9 displaying time markers on a ship's route;

.2.10 entering ship's position manually; and

.2.11 measuring coordinates, course, bearings and distances on a chart.

Alarm handling

58 Knowledge and ability to interpret and react properly to all kinds of systems, such as navigational sensors, indicators, data and charts alarms and indicator warnings, including, switching the sound and visual alarm signalling system, should be attained in case of:

.1 absence of the next chart in the ECDIS database;

.2 crossing a safety contour;

.3 exceeding cross-track limits;

.4 deviation from planned route;

.5.9 编辑和修改计划航线，
.5.10 根据船舶尺度和操纵参数设定安全值，
.5.11 返回航线设计，及
.5.12 连接几段航线。

航线监控

57 应掌握下列知识和技能：
.1 使用独立数据控制船位或使用 ECDIS 内可替代系统；
.2 使用预测功能：
.2.1 更换海图和比例尺，
.2.2 审查导航图，
.2.3 选择矢量时间，
.2.4 以一定时间间隔预测船位，
.2.5 改变预定航线（航线修正），
.2.6 输入独立数据以计算风流压差，
.2.7 正确应对报警，
.2.8 输入大地基准面偏差的修正，
.2.9 显示船舶航线上的时间标志，
.2.10 手动输入船位，及
.2.11 在海图上测量坐标、航向、方位和距离。

报警处理

58 在下列情况下，应具有正确解释和响应各种系统（包括切换声光报警信号系统）的知识和能力，这些系统包括航行传感器、指示器、数据和海图警报和指示器报警：
.1 ECDIS 数据库中下一张海图缺失；
.2 穿越安全等深线；
.3 超过计划航迹带边界；
.4 偏离预定航线；

.5 approaching a waypoint;

.6 approaching a critical point;

.7 discrepancy between calculated and actual time of arrival to a waypoint;

.8 information on under-scaling or over-scaling;

.9 approaching an isolated navigational danger or danger area;

.10 crossing a specified area;

.11 selecting a different geodetic datum;

.12 approaching other ships;

.13 watch termination;

.14 switching timer;

.15 system test failure;

.16 malfunctioning of the positioning system used in ECDIS;

.17 failure of dead-reckoning; and

.18 inability to fix vessel's position using the navigational system.

Manual correction of a ship's position and motion parameters

59 Knowledge and skills should be attained in manually correcting:

.1 the ship's position in dead-reckoning mode, when the satellite and radio navigation system receiver is switched off;

.2 the ship's position, when automatically obtained coordinates are inaccurate; and

.3 course and speed values.

Records in the ship's log

60 Knowledge and skills should be attained in:

.1 automatic voyage recording;

.2 reconstruction of past track, taking into account:

.2.1 recording media;

.2.2 recording intervals;

.2.3 verification of database in use;

.5 接近转向点；

.6 接近临界点；

.7 抵达转向点计算时间和实际时间的差异；

.8 比例尺过小或过大的信息；

.9 接近孤立航行危险物或危险区；

.10 穿越特定区域；

.11 选择不同大地基准面；

.12 接近他船；

.13 值班结束；

.14 开关定时器；

.15 系统测试故障；

.16 ECDIS 使用的定位系统故障；

.17 推算船位故障；以及

.18 无法使用导航系统定位。

手动校正船位和运动参数

59 应掌握手动校正下列各项的知识和技能：

.1 在卫星和无线电导航系统接收机关闭时推算模式下的船位；

.2 在自动获得坐标不精确时的船位；以及

.3 航向和航速数据。

船舶日志的记录

60 应掌握下列知识和技能：

.1 自动航行记录；

.2 重现历史航迹时应考虑：

.2.1 记录媒介，

.2.2 记录间隔，

.2.3 验证使用中的数据库；

.3 viewing records in the electronic ship's log;

.4 instant recording in the electronic ship's log;

.5 changing ship's time;

.6 entering the additional data;

.7 printing the content of the electronic ship's log;

.8 setting up the automatic record time intervals;

.9 composition of voyage data and reporting; and

.10 interface with a voyage data recorder (VDR).

Chart updating

61 Knowledge and skills should be attained in:

.1 performing manual updating of electronic charts. Special attention should be paid to reference-ellipsoid conformity and to conformity of the measurement units used on a chart and in the correction text;

.2 performing semi-automatic updating of electronic charts, using the data obtained on electronic media in the electronic chart format; and

.3 performing automatic updating of electronic charts, using update files obtained via electronic data communication lines.

In the scenarios where non-updated data are employed to create a critical situation, trainees should be required to perform *ad hoc* updating of the chart.

Operational use of ECDIS where radar/ARPA is connected

62 Knowledge and skills should be attained in:

.1 connecting ARPA to ECDIS;

.2 indicating target's speed vectors;

.3 indicating target's tracks;

.4 archiving target's tracks;

.5 viewing the table of the targets;

.6 checking alignment of radar overlay with charted geographic features;

.7 simulating one or more manoeuvres;

.8 corrections to own ship's position, using a reference point captured by ARPA; and

.9 corrections using the ARPA's cursor and electronic bar.

See also section B-I/12, Guidance regarding the use of simulators (pertaining to radar and ARPA), especially paragraphs 17 to 19 and 36 to 38.

.3 回放电子船舶日志记录；
.4 电子船舶日志即时记录；
.5 变更船舶时间；
.6 输入附加数据；
.7 打印电子船舶日志内容；
.8 设定自动记录时间间隔；
.9 编制航次数据和报告；以及
.10 与航行数据记录仪（VDR）的接口。

海图更新

61 应掌握下列知识和技能：
.1 手动更新电子海图，应特别注意参考椭圆体的一致性以及海图上和更正文本里所用的计量单位的一致性；
.2 使用电子海图格式在电子媒介上获得的数据实现电子海图半自动更新；以及
.3 使用通过电子数据通信线路获得的更新文件实现电子海图的自动更新。
在使用未更新的海图数据建立一个危急情况的场景时，应要求学员进行临时的海图更新。

连接雷达/ARPA 时 ECDIS 的操作使用

62 应掌握下列知识和技能：
.1 连接 ARPA 和 ECDIS；
.2 显示目标速度矢量；
.3 显示目标航迹；
.4 保存目标航迹；
.5 查看目标表格；
.6 检查图示的地理特征与雷达图像叠加的一致性；
.7 模拟一个或多个操纵；
.8 采用 ARPA 捕获的参照点修正本船船位；以及
.9 使用 ARPA 光标和电子标志进行修正。
也应参见第 B-I/12 节——关于模拟器使用（有关雷达和 ARPA）的指导，特别是第 17 段到第 19 段、第 36 段到第 38 段。

Operational use of ECDIS where AIS is connected

63 Knowledge and skills should be attained in:

.1 interface with AIS;

.2 interpretation of AIS data;

.3 indicating target's speed vectors;

.4 indicating target's tracks; and

.5 archiving target's tracks.

Operational warnings, their benefits and limitations

64 Trainees should gain an appreciation of the uses, benefits and limitations of ECDIS operational warnings and their correct setting, where applicable, to avoid spurious interference.

System operational tests

65 Knowledge and skills should be attained in:

.1 methods of testing for malfunctions of ECDIS, including functional self-testing;

.2 precautions to be taken after a malfunction occurs; and

.3 adequate back-up arrangements (take over and navigate using the back-up system).

Debriefing exercise

66 The instructor should analyze the results of all exercises completed by all trainees and print them out. The time spent on the debriefing should occupy between 10% and 15% of the total time used for simulator exercises.

RECOMMENDED PERFORMANCE STANDARDS FOR NON-MANDATORY TYPES OF SIMULATION

67 Performance standards for non-mandatory simulation equipment used for training and/or assessment of competence or demonstration of skills are set out hereunder. Such forms of simulation include, but are not limited to, the following types:

.1 navigation and watchkeeping;

.2 ship handling and manoeuvring;

.3 cargo handling and stowage;

.4 reporting and radiocommunications; and

.5 main and auxiliary machinery operation.

连接 AIS 时 ECDIS 的操作使用

63 应掌握下列知识和技能：

.1 与 AIS 的接口；

.2 解释 AIS 数据；

.3 显示目标速度矢量；

.4 显示目标航迹；以及

.5 保存目标航迹。

操作性警告及其益处和局限

64 学员应理解 ECDIS 操作性警告的用途、益处及其局限性，如适用，进行正确设置，以避免杂散干扰。

系统操作性测试

65 应掌握下列知识和技能：

.1 ECDIS 故障测试方法，包括功能自检；

.2 故障出现后采取的预防措施；以及

.3 足够的备份安排（切换并使用备份系统航行）。

练习总结

66 教员应当分析和打印学员完成所有练习的结果。总结用时应占模拟器练习总用时的 10% 到 15%。

非强制性模拟的建议的性能标准

67 用于培训和/或适任评估或技能演示的非强制性模拟设备的性能标准如下规定。此种模拟的形式包括但不限于以下类型：

.1 航行与值班；

.2 船舶操作和操纵；

.3 货物装卸和积载；

.4 报告和无线电通信；以及

.5 主机和辅机操作。

Navigation and watchkeeping simulation

68 Navigation and watchkeeping simulation equipment should, in addition to meeting all applicable performance standards set out in section A-I/12, be capable of simulating navigational equipment and bridge operational controls which meet all applicable performance standards adopted by the Organization,* incorporate facilities to generate soundings and:

.1 create a real-time operating environment, including navigation control and communications instruments and equipment appropriate to the navigation and watchkeeping tasks to be carried out and the manoeuvring skills to be assessed;

.2 provide a realistic visual scenario by day or by night, including variable visibility, or by night only as seen from the bridge, with a minimum horizontal field of view available to the trainee in viewing sectors appropriate to the navigation and watchkeeping tasks and objectives;

.3 realistically simulate "own ship" dynamics in open-water conditions, including the effects of weather, tidal stream, currents and interaction with other ships; and

.4 realistically simulate VTS communication procedures between ship and shore.

Ship handling and manoeuvring simulation

69 In addition to meeting the performance standards set out in paragraph 37, ship handling simulation equipment should:

.1 provide a realistic visual scenario as seen from the bridge, by day and by night, with variable visibility throughout a minimum horizontal field of view available to the trainee in viewing sectors appropriate to the ship handling and manoeuvring training tasks and objectives;** and

.2 realistically simulate "own ship" dynamics in restricted waterways, including shallow-water and bank effects.

70 Where manned scale models are used to provide ship handling and manoeuvring simulation, in addition to the performance standards set out in paragraphs 68.3 and 69.2, such equipment should:

.1 incorporate scaling factors which present accurately the dimensions, areas, volume and displacement, speed, time and rate of turn of a real ship; and

.2 incorporate controls for the rudder and engines, to the correct timescale.

Cargo handling and stowage simulation

71 Cargo handling simulation equipment should be capable of simulating cargo handling and control equipment which meets all applicable performance standards adopted by the Organization*** and incorporate facilities to:

* See relevant/appropriate performance standards adopted by the Organization.

** The relevant IMO Model Course(s) may be of assistance in the preparation of courses.

*** No standards have as yet been adopted by the Organization.

航行与值班模拟

68　航行和值班模拟设备，除应满足第 A-I/12 节规定的所有适用的性能标准外，还应能够模拟达到本组织采纳的所有适用的性能标准的航行设备和驾驶台操作性控制装置，①并装有测深装置，还应：

.1　创造一个实时操作环境，包括与所执行的航行和值班任务和所评估的操纵技能相适应的航行控制、通信仪器和设备；

.2　提供一个真实的白天或夜间的视景，包括各种能见度，或仅在夜间从驾驶台观察，提供给受培训者的最小水平视野适于航行和值班任务和目的；

.3　真实地模拟"本船"在开阔水域条件下的动态特性，包括天气、潮流、海流的影响和与他船的相互作用；并且

.4　真实地模拟船岸之间的船舶交通管理（VTS）通信程序。

船舶操作和操纵模拟

69　除满足第 37 段所规定的性能标准外，船舶操作模拟设备应：

.1　提供各种能见度的白天和夜间从驾驶台看到的真实视景，提供给受培训者的最小水平视野适于操作和操纵培训任务和目的；②并且

.2　真实地模拟出"本船"在受限制的水域中的动态特性，包括浅水效应和岸壁效应。

70　当使用人工操纵船模进行船舶操作和操纵模拟时，除满足第 68.3 段和第 69.2 段所规定的性能标准外，该设备还应：

.1　包含比例因数，以精确地表示出真实船舶的尺度、面积、体积、排水量、速度、时间和旋回速率；并且

.2　包含舵和机器的控制以反映正确的时间比例。

货物装卸和积载模拟

71　货物装卸和积载模拟设备应能够模拟达到本组织通过的所有适用的性能标准③的货物装卸和控制设备，并包含有关设施，以便：

---

① 参见国际海事组织采纳的相关/适当的性能标准。

② 相关 IMO 示范培训课程可有助于准备课程。

③ 本组织还没有已采纳的标准。

.1 create an effective operational environment, including a cargo-control station with such instrumentation as may be appropriate to the particular type of cargo system modelled;

.2 model loading and unloading functions and stability and stress data appropriate to the cargo-handling tasks to be carried out and the skills to be assessed; and

.3 simulate loading, unloading, ballasting and deballasting operations and appropriate associated calculations for stability, trim, list, longitudinal strength, torsional stress and damage stability*.

GMDSS communication simulation

72 GMDSS communication simulation equipment should be capable of simulating GMDSS communication equipment which meets all applicable performance standards adopted by the Organization** and incorporate facilities to:

.1 simulate the operation of VHF, VHF-DSC, NAVTEX, EPIRB and watch receiver equipment as required for the Restricted Operator's Certificate (ROC);

.2 simulate the operation of INMARSAT-A, -B and -C ship earth stations, MF/HF NBDP, MF/HF-DSC, VHF, VHF-DSC, NAVTEX, EPIRB and watch receiver equipment as required for the General Operator's Certificate (GOC);

.3 provide voice communication with background noise;

.4 provide a printed text communication facility; and

.5 create a real-time operating environment, consisting of an integrated system, incorporating at least one instructor/assessor station and at least two GMDSS ship or shore stations.

Main and auxiliary machinery operation simulation

73 Engine-room simulation equipment should be capable of simulating a main and auxiliary machinery system and incorporate facilities to:

.1 create a real-time environment for seagoing and harbour operations, with communication devices and simulation of appropriate main and auxiliary propulsion machinery equipment and control panels;

.2 simulate relevant sub-systems that should include, but not be restricted to, boiler, steering gear, electrical power general and distribution systems, including emergency power supplies, and fuel, cooling water, refrigeration, bilge and ballast systems;

.3 monitor and evaluate engine performance and remote sensing systems;

.4 simulate machinery malfunctions;

---

* The relevant IMO Model Course(s) may be of assistance in the preparation of courses.

** See relevant/appropriate performance standards adopted by the Organization.

.1 创造一个有效的操作环境,包括具备可能适于所模拟的特定类型货物系统仪器的货物控制站;
.2 模仿与所执行的货物装卸任务和所评估的技能相适应的装卸功能和稳性及强度数据;
.3 模拟装货、卸货、压载和排放压载操作,以及对稳性、纵倾、横倾、纵向强度、扭应力和破舱稳性的有关计算①。

GMDSS 通信模拟

72 GMDSS 通信模拟设备应能够模拟达到本组织通过的所有适用的性能标准②的 GMDSS 通信设备,并纳入有关设施,以便:
.1 模拟对限用操作员证书(ROC)要求的 VHF、VHF-DSC、NAVTEX、EPIRB 和值班接收设备的操作;
.2 模拟对通用操作员证书(GOC)要求的 INMARSAT-A 和-B 和-C 船舶地球站、MF/HF NBDP、MF/HF-DSC、VHF、VHF-DSC、NAVTEX、EPIRB 和值班接收设备的操作;
.3 提供带有背景噪声的通话;
.4 提供打印文本通信设备;以及
.5 创造由一个完整系统组成的实时操作环境,其中包括至少一个教员/评估员站和至少两个 GMDSS 船站或岸站。

主机和辅机的操作模拟

73 机舱模拟设备应能够模拟主机和辅机系统,并包含有关设施,以便:
.1 创造一个海上航行和港口操作的实时环境,具有通信装置,模拟相应的主、辅推进机器装置和控制台;
.2 模拟有关的分系统,分系统应包括但不局限于锅炉、舵机、发电机和配电系统,其中包括应急电源和燃料、冷却水、制冷、舱底水和压载系统;
.3 监控和评价机器性能和遥感系统;
.4 模拟机器故障;

① 相关的国际海事组织示范培训课程可有助于准备课程。
② 参见国际海事组织采纳的相关/适当的性能标准。

.5 allow for the variable external conditions to be changed so as to influence the simulated operations: weather, ship's draught, seawater and air temperatures;

.6 allow for instructor-controlled external conditions to be changed: deck steam, accommodation steam, deck air, ice conditions, deck cranes, heavy power, bow thrust, ship load;

.7 allow for instructor-controlled simulator dynamics to be changed: emergency run, process responses, ship responses; and

.8 provide a facility to isolate certain processes, such as speed, electrical system, diesel oil system, lubricating oil system, heavy oil system, seawater system, steam system, exhaust boiler and turbo generator, for performing specific training tasks.*

Section B-I/13
Guidance regarding the conduct of trials

(No provisions)

Section B-I/14
Guidance regarding responsibilities of companies and recommended responsibilities of masters and crew members

Companies

1 Companies should provide ship-specific introductory programmes aimed at assisting newly employed seafarers to familiarize themselves with all procedures and equipment relating to their areas of responsibility. Companies should also ensure that:

.1 all seafarers on a ship fitted with free-fall lifeboats should receive familiarization training in boarding and launching procedures for such lifeboats;

.2 prior to joining a ship, seafarers assigned as operating crew of free-fall lifeboats should have undergone appropriate training in boarding, launching and recovering of such lifeboats, including participation on at least one occasion in a free-fall launch; and

.3 personnel who may be required to operate the GMDSS equipment receive GMDSS familiarization training, on joining the ship and at appropriate intervals thereafter.

2 The familiarization training required by paragraph 3 of section A-I/14 should at least ensure attainment of the abilities that are appropriate to the capacity to be filled and the duties and responsibilities to be taken up, as follows:

Design and operational limitations

.1 Ability to properly understand and observe any operational limitations imposed on the ship, and to understand and apply performance restrictions, including speed limitations in adverse weather, which are intended to maintain the safety of life, ship and cargo.

* The relevant IMO Model Course(s) may be of assistance in the preparation of courses.

.5 允许改变可变的外部条件以影响所模拟的操作,如天气、船舶吃水、海水和空气温度;

.6 允许由教员控制改变外部条件,如甲板蒸汽、居住处所蒸汽、甲板空气、冰况、甲板克令吊、重载起重机、船首推进和船舶负荷;

.7 允许由教员控制改变模拟器动态特点,如应急操作、过程反应、船舶反应;并且

.8 提供一个装置能使某些过程脱离,如速度、电气系统、轻油系统、润滑油系统、重油系统、海水系统、蒸汽系统、废气锅炉和透平发电机来执行特定的培训任务。①

第 B-I/13 节

关于实施试验的指导

(无条文)

第 B-I/14 节

关于公司责任以及船长和船员建议责任的指导

公司

1 公司应向船舶提供旨在帮助新雇用的海员熟悉其责任范围内的所有程序和设备的针对具体船舶的介绍性培训计划。公司还应确保:

.1 在配备自由降落式救生艇的船上的所有海员应接受该种救生艇登艇和释放程序的熟悉培训;

.2 被指定操作自由降落式救生艇的海员在上船前应接受过登艇、释放和回收该种救生艇的适当培训,包括至少参加过一次自由降落式释放;并且

.3 可能被要求操作 GMDSS 设备的人员在上船时以及随后适当时间间隔内接受 GMDSS 的熟悉训练。

2 第 A-I/14 节第 3 段要求的熟悉培训应确保至少获得适合于要担任的职位以及要承担的职责和责任的能力,表述如下:

设计和操作性限制

.1 旨在保护人命、船舶和货物安全,适当理解和遵循对船舶的任何操作性限制以及理解和应用性能限制包括恶劣天气下的速度限制的能力。

① 相关的国际海事组织示范培训课程可有助于准备课程。

Procedures for opening, closing and securing hull openings

.2 Ability to apply properly the procedures established for the ship regarding the opening, closing and securing of bow, stern, and side doors and ramps and to correctly operate the related systems.

Legislation, codes and agreements affecting ro-ro passenger ships

.3 Ability to understand and apply international and national requirements for ro-ro passenger ships relevant to the ship concerned and the duties to be performed.

Stability and stress requirements and limitations

.4 Ability to take proper account of stress limitations for sensitive parts of the ship, such as bow doors and other closing devices that maintain watertight integrity, and of special stability considerations which may affect the safety of ro-ro passenger ships.

Procedures for the maintenance of special equipment on ro-ro passenger ships

.5 Ability to apply properly the shipboard procedures for maintenance of equipment peculiar to ro-ro passenger ships such as bow, stern and side doors and ramps, scuppers and associated systems.

Loading and cargo securing manuals and calculators

.6 Ability to make proper use of the loading and securing manuals in respect of all types of vehicles and rail cars where applicable, and to calculate and apply stress limitations for vehicle decks.

Dangerous cargo areas

.7 Ability to ensure proper observance of special precautions and limitations applying to designated dangerous cargo areas.

Emergency procedures

.8 Ability to ensure proper application of any special procedures to:

.8.1 prevent or reduce the ingress of water on vehicle decks;

.8.2 remove water from vehicle decks; and

.8.3 minimize effects of water on vehicle decks.

Master

3 The master should take all steps necessary to implement any company instructions issued in accordance with section A-I/14. Such steps should include:

.1 identifying all seafarers who are newly employed on board the ship before they are assigned to any duties;

开关和紧固船体开口的程序

.2 正确运用为船舶制定的有关开关和紧固船首门、船尾门、船舷门及登陆舌门的程序，并能正确操作相应系统的能力。

有关滚装客船的法规、规则和协议

.3 理解并运用国际、国内对滚装客船涉及有关船舶及其应履行职责的要求的能力。

稳性和强度要求和限制

.4 适当考虑船舶敏感部位强度限制，诸如船首门和其他关闭装置保持水密完整性的能力，以及特别考虑影响滚装客船安全的稳性的能力。

维护滚装客船特殊设备的程序

.5 正确运用滚装客船特有的船上设备，如船首门、船尾门、船舷门、登陆舌门、排水孔以及相应系统的维护程序的能力。

装载和货物系固手册以及货物积载仪

.6 如可行，正确使用有关各种车型和有轨车辆装载和系固手册，以及计算和运用车辆甲板的强度限制的能力。

危险品区域

.7 确保正确遵守适用于指定危险品区域的特别注意事项和限制的能力。

应急程序

.8 确保正确运用任何特殊程序的能力，以：
  8.1 防止或减少车辆甲板进水；
  8.2 排除车辆甲板积水；
  8.3 减少车辆甲板积水的影响。

船长

3 船长应采取一切必要步骤来执行公司按照第 A-I/14 节要求所发布的任何指令。此种步骤应包括：

.1 在分派职责以前，认清所有新雇用上船的海员；

.2 providing the opportunity for all newly arrived seafarers to:

.2.1 visit the spaces in which their primary duties will be performed;

.2.2 get acquainted with the location, controls and display features of equipment they will be operating or using;

.2.3 activate the equipment when possible, and perform functions, using the controls on the equipment; and

.2.4 observe and ask questions of someone who is already familiar with the equipment, procedures and other arrangements, and who can communicate information in a language which the seafarer understands; and

.3 providing for a suitable period of supervision when there is any doubt that a newly employed seafarer is familiar with the shipboard equipment, operating procedures and other arrangements needed for the proper performance of his or her duties.

Crew members

4 Seafarers who are newly assigned to a ship should take full advantage of every opportunity provided to become familiar with the shipboard equipment, operating procedures and other arrangements needed for the proper performance of their duties. Immediately upon arriving on board for the first time, each seafarer has the responsibility to become acquainted with the ship's working environment, particularly with respect to new or unfamiliar equipment, procedures or arrangements.

5 Seafarers who do not promptly attain the level of familiarity required for performing their duties have the obligation to bring this fact to the attention of their supervisor or to the attention of the crew member designated in accordance with section A-I/14, paragraph 2.2, and to identify any equipment, procedure or arrangement which remains unfamiliar.

Section B-I/15
Guidance regarding transitional provisions

(No provisions)

.2 为所有新来的海员提供以下机会：

.2.1 参观其将要履行主要职责的处所，

.2.2 使其了解他们将要使用和操作的设备的位置、控钮和显示特点，

.2.3 如可能，启动设备并使用设备的控钮执行职能，并且

.2.4 观察并向已熟悉设备、程序和其他安排以及能够以海员明白的语言进行信息交流的人提问；以及

.3 在对新雇用的海员是否已熟悉其正确履行职责所需的设备、操作程序和其他安排尚有怀疑时，规定一定的接受监督的期限。

船员

4 新分配到船上工作的海员应充分利用所提供的一切机会来熟悉船上的设备、操作程序和正确履行职责所需的其他安排。第一次登船的每一海员有责任熟悉船上的工作环境，特别是对有关新的或不熟悉的设备、程序和安排的情况。

5 未按时达到履行职责所必需的熟悉水平的海员，有责任将此情况报告其监督人，或按第 A-I/14 节第 2.2 段所指定的船员，并应说明仍不熟悉的设备、程序或安排。

第 B-I/15 节

关于过渡条款的指导

（无条文）

CHAPTER II

Guidance regarding the master and the deck department

Section B-II/1
Guidance regarding the certification of officers in charge of a navigational watch on ships of 500 gross tonnage or more

Training

1 Every candidate for certification as officer in charge of a navigational watch should have completed a planned and structured programme of training designed to assist a prospective officer to achieve the standard of competence in accordance with table A-II/1.

2 The structure of the programme of training should be set out in a training plan which clearly expresses, for all parties involved, the objectives of each stage of training on board and ashore. It is important that the prospective officer, tutors, ships' staff and company personnel are clear about the competences which are to be achieved at the end of the programme and how they are to be achieved through a combination of education, training and practical experience on board and ashore.

3 The mandatory periods of seagoing service are of prime importance in learning the job of being a ship's officer and in achieving the overall standard of competence required. Properly planned and structured, the periods of seagoing service will enable prospective officers to acquire and practice skills and will offer opportunities for competences achieved to be demonstrated and assessed.

4 Where the seagoing service forms part of an approved training programme, the following principles should be observed:

.1 The programme of onboard training should be an integral part of the overall training plan.

.2 The programme of onboard training should be managed and coordinated by the company which manages the ship on which the seagoing service is to be performed.

.3 The prospective officer should be provided with a training record book* to enable a comprehensive record of practical training and experience at sea to be maintained. The training record book should be laid out in such a way that it can provide detailed information about the tasks and duties which should be undertaken and the progress towards their completion. Duly completed, the record book will provide unique evidence that a structured programme of onboard training has been completed which can be taken into account in the process of evaluating competence for the issue of a certificate.

.4 At all times, the prospective officer should be aware of two identifiable individuals who are immediately responsible for the management of the programme of onboard training. The first of these is a qualified seagoing officer,

* The relevant IMO Model Course(s) and a similar document produced by the International Shipping Federation may be of assistance in the preparation of training record books.

第 II 章
关于船长和甲板部的指导

第 B-II/1 节
对 500 总吨或以上船舶负责航行值班的高级船员发证的指导

培训

1　每个申请负责航行值班的高级船员证书的申请人，应完成旨在协助未来的甲板部高级船员按照表 A-II/1 达到适任标准的经规划和组织的培训计划。

2　培训计划的结构应在培训规划中规定，该培训规划要向所涉及的各方清楚地表达船上和岸上培训的每一阶段的目标。重要的是，未来的甲板部高级船员、教员、船上全体船员和公司人员要弄清楚在培训结束时欲达到的适任标准，以及如何通过船上和岸上的教育、培训和实践经验相结合来达到适任标准。

3　强制要求的海上服务资历，在学会担当船舶甲板部高级船员的工作和达到所要求的全部适任标准方面，尤其重要。经过适当规划和组织，海上服务资历能使未来的甲板部高级船员获取并锻炼技能，以及为表明和评估所达到的适任提供机会。

4　当海上服务资历组成经认可的培训计划的一部分时，应遵循以下原则：

.1　船上培训计划应成为整个培训规划的一个组成部分。

.2　船上培训计划应由经营船舶的公司进行管理和协调，因海上服务将在其船上进行。

.3　应向未来的甲板部高级船员提供培训记录簿①，以便对海上实际培训和资历保持全面的记录。培训记录簿应如此编排，即能提供应执行任务和职责的具体信息以及完成任务和职责的进度。在正式完成记录后，该记录簿将提供完成有组织的船上培训计划的唯一证据，并在为签发证书而进行的适任评价过程中加以考虑。

.4　在任何时候，未来的甲板部高级船员应知晓有两位确定的人员直接对船上培训计划的管理负责。其一是称之为“船上培训师”的合格的海船高级船员，他应在船长的授权之下组织和监管各航次的培训计划。其二是公司提名的人员，称之为“公司培训师”，他应对培训计划以及与院校和培训机构的协调负完全责任。

① 相关 IMO 示范培训课程和国际航运联合会所制定的类似文件可有助于编制培训记录簿。

referred to as the "shipboard training officer", who, under the authority of the master, should organize and supervise the programme of training for the duration of each voyage. The second should be a person nominated by the company, referred to as the "company training officer", who should have an overall responsibility for the training programme and for coordination with colleges and training institutions.

.5 The company should ensure that appropriate periods are set aside for completion of the programme of onboard training within the normal operational requirements of the ship.

Roles and responsibilities

5 The following section summarizes the roles and responsibilities of those individuals involved in organizing and conducting onboard training:

.1 The company training officer should be responsible for:

.1.1 overall administration of the programme of training;

.1.2 monitoring the progress of the prospective officer throughout; and

.1.3 issuing guidance as required and ensuring that all concerned with the training programme play their parts.

.2 The shipboard training officer should be responsible for:

.2.1 organizing the programme of practical training at sea;

.2.2 ensuring, in a supervisory capacity, that the training record book is properly maintained and that all other requirements are fulfilled; and

.2.3 making sure, so far as is practicable, that the time the prospective officer spends on board is as useful as possible in terms of training and experience, and is consistent with the objectives of the training programme, the progress of training and the operational constraints of the ship.

.3 The master's responsibilities should be to:

.3.1 provide the link between the shipboard training officer and the company training officer ashore;

.3.2 fulfil the role of continuity if the shipboard training officer is relieved during the voyage; and

.3.3 ensure that all concerned are effectively carrying out the onboard training programme.

.4 The prospective officer's responsibilities should be to:

.4.1 follow diligently the programme of training as laid down;

.5　公司应确保，在船上的正常工作要求之内安排相应的时间来完成船上培训计划。

作用和责任

5　下列各节概括了组织和实施船上培训的有关人员的作用和责任：

.1　公司培训师应负责：

.1.1　培训计划的全面管理；

.1.2　监测未来甲板部高级船员整个进程；以及

.1.3　按要求给予指导，并确保与培训计划有关的各个方面发挥其作用。

.2　船上培训师应负责：

.2.1　组织海上的实际培训计划；

.2.2　在监管职位上保证培训记录簿的正规记录并满足所有其他要求；以及

.2.3　尽实际可能，确保未来甲板部高级船员在海上度过的时间尽可能用于培训和实践，并符合培训计划的目标、培训进度和船舶的操作限制。

.3　船长的责任是：

.3.1　在船上培训师和岸上的公司培训师之间进行联络；

.3.2　在航行中船上培训师交班后，保持工作的连续性；以及

.3.3　确保各有关方面有效地实施船上培训计划。

.4　未来甲板部高级船员的责任是：

.4.1　努力完成规定的培训计划；

.4.2 make the most of the opportunities presented, be they in or outside working hours; and

.4.3 keep the training record book up to date and ensure that it is available at all times for scrutiny.

Induction

6 At the beginning of the programme and at the start of each voyage on a different ship, prospective officers should be given full information and guidance as to what is expected of them and how the training programme is to be organized. Induction presents the opportunity to brief prospective officers about important aspects of the tasks they will be undertaking, with particular regard to safe working practices and protection of the marine environment.

Shipboard programme of training

7 The training record book should contain, amongst other things, a number of training tasks or duties which should be undertaken as part of the approved programme of onboard training. Such tasks and duties should relate to at least the following areas:

.1 steering systems;

.2 general seamanship;

.3 mooring, anchoring and port operations;

.4 life-saving and fire-fighting appliances;

.5 systems and equipment;

.6 cargo work;

.7 bridge work and watchkeeping; and

.8 engine-room familiarization.

8 It is extremely important that the prospective officer is given adequate opportunity for supervised bridge watchkeeping experience, particularly in the later stages of the onboard training programme.

9 The performance of the prospective officers in each of the tasks and duties itemized in the training record book should be initialled by a qualified officer when, in the opinion of the officer concerned, a prospective officer has achieved a satisfactory standard of proficiency. It is important to appreciate that a prospective officer may need to demonstrate ability on several occasions before a qualified officer is confident that a satisfactory standard has been achieved.

Monitoring and reviewing

10 Guidance and reviewing are essential to ensure that prospective officers are fully aware of the progress they are making and to enable them to join in decisions about their future programme. To be effective, reviews should be linked to information gained through the training record book and other sources as appropriate. The training record book should be scrutinized and

.4.2 在工作时间之内或之外,充分利用所提供的机会;以及

.4.3 保持在培训记录簿上不断记录,并确保随时提供检查。

引导

6 在培训计划开始时以及在不同船上的每个航次开始时,应向未来的甲板部高级船员提供关于对他们有何期望和培训计划如何组织的全部信息和指导。这种引导提供一个机会向未来的甲板部高级船员简要介绍他们将执行任务的重要方面,特别是安全工作做法和海洋环境的保护。

船上培训计划

7 培训记录簿应首先包含一些应承担的并作为认可的船上培训计划一部分的培训任务或职责。这些任务和职责应至少与以下各方面有关:

.1 操舵系统;

.2 通用船艺;

.3 系泊、锚泊和港口操作;

.4 救生和消防设备;

.5 系统和设备;

.6 货物作业;

.7 驾驶台工作和值班;以及

.8 熟悉机舱。

8 极其重要的是给予未来的甲板部高级船员以足够的有监督下的驾驶台值班的机会,特别是在船上培训计划的后阶段。

9 未来的甲板部高级船员执行培训记录簿中所列的每一任务和职责的表现,应由合格的甲板部高级船员当他认为未来的甲板部高级船员已满意地达到业务能力的标准时签字。重要的是要意识到在合格的驾驶员确认未来的甲板部高级船员已满意地达到标准之前,未来的甲板部高级船员可能需要在几个场合中表明其能力。

监督和审查

10 指导和审查重在确保未来的甲板部高级船员全面了解他们正在取得的进步,并能使他们就其未来的计划参与决策。为取得效果,审查应与通过培训记录簿和其他适当的来源获得的信息相联系。培训记录簿应由船长和船上培训师在每一航次的开始、中间和结束时仔细检查和正式签注。记录簿还应由公司培训师在两个航次之间予以查验和签注。

endorsed formally by the master and the shipboard training officer at the beginning, during and at the end of each voyage. The training record book should also be examined and endorsed by the company training officer between voyages.

Assessment of abilities and skills in navigational watchkeeping

11 A candidate for certification who is required to have received special training and assessment of abilities and skills in navigational watchkeeping duties should be required to provide evidence, through demonstration either on a simulator or on board ship as part of an approved programme of shipboard training, that the skills and ability to perform as officer in charge of a navigational watch in at least the following areas have been acquired, namely to:

.1 prepare for and conduct a passage, including:

.1.1 interpreting and applying information obtained from charts;

.1.2 fixing position in coastal waters;

.1.3 applying basic information obtained from tide tables and other nautical publications;

.1.4 checking and operating bridge equipment;

.1.5 checking magnetic and gyro-compasses;

.1.6 assessing available meteorological information;

.1.7 using celestial bodies to fix position;

.1.8 determining the compass error by celestial and terrestrial means; and

.1.9 performing calculations for sailings of up to 24 hours;

.2 operate and apply information obtained from electronic navigation systems;

.3 operate radar, ARPA and ECDIS and apply radar information for navigation and collision avoidance;

.4 operate propulsion and steering systems to control heading and speed;

.5 implement navigational watch routines and procedures;

.6 implement the manoeuvres required for rescue of persons overboard;

.7 initiate action to be taken in the event of an imminent emergency situation (e.g., fire, collision, stranding) and action in the immediate aftermath of an emergency;

.8 initiate action to be taken in event of malfunction or failure of major items of equipment or plant (e.g., steering gear, power, navigation systems);

评估航行值班的能力和技能

11 按要求接受特殊培训和航行值班能力与技能评估的证书申请人，应通过模拟器或作为认可的船上培训计划一部分的船上培训，获得表明其至少在下列各方面已具有作为负责航行值班的高级船员的技能和能力的证据，即

.1 准备和引导航行，包括：

.1.1 解释和运用从海图上获得的信息，

.1.2 在沿海水域中定位，

.1.3 运用从潮汐表与其他航海出版物中获得的基本信息，

.1.4 检查和操作驾驶台设备，

.1.5 检查磁罗经和陀螺罗经，

.1.6 评估获得的气象信息，

.1.7 运用天体定位，

.1.8 通过天文和地文方法测定罗经差，以及

.1.9 进行长达 24 小时的航行计算；

.2 操作并应用从电子导航系统中获得的信息；

.3 操作雷达、ARPA 和 ECDIS，并将雷达信息运用于航行和避碰；

.4 操作推进和操舵系统以控制船首向和航速；

.5 执行航行值班日常工作和程序；

.6 进行救助落水人员所需的操纵；

.7 一旦出现应急情况（如失火、碰撞、搁浅）时应采取的行动和在应急情况出现之后立即采取的行动；

.8 设备和装置（如舵机、动力装置、导航系统）的主要部件一旦出现故障时应采取的行动；

.9 conduct radiocommunications and visual and sound signalling in normal and emergency situations; and

.10 monitor and operate safety and alarm systems, including internal communications.

12 Assessment of abilities and skills in navigational watchkeeping should:

.1 be made against the criteria for evaluating competence for the function of navigation set out in table A-II/1;

.2 ensure that the candidate performs navigational watchkeeping duties in accordance with the Principles to be observed in keeping a safe navigational watch (section A-VIII/2, part 4-1) and the Guidance on keeping a navigational watch (section B-VIII/2, part 4-1).

Evaluation of competence

13 The standard of competence to be achieved for certification as officer in charge of a navigational watch is set out in table A-II/1. The standard specifies the knowledge and skill required and the application of that knowledge and skill to the standard of performance required on board ship.

14 Scope of knowledge is implicit in the concept of competence. Assessment of competence should, therefore, encompass more than the immediate technical requirements of the job, the skills and tasks to be performed, and should reflect the broader aspects needed to meet the full expectations of competent performance as a ship's officer. This includes relevant knowledge, theory, principles and cognitive skills which, to varying degrees, underpin all levels of competence. It also encompasses proficiency in what to do, how and when to do it, and why it should be done. Properly applied, this will help to ensure that a candidate can:

.1 work competently in different ships and across a range of circumstances;

.2 anticipate, prepare for and deal with contingencies; and

.3 adapt to new and changing requirements.

15 The criteria for evaluating competence (column 4 of table A-II/1) identify, primarily in outcome terms, the essential aspects of competent performance. They are expressed so that assessment of a candidate's performance can be made against them and should be adequately documented in the training record book.

16 Evaluation of competence is the process of:

.1 collecting sufficient valid and reliable evidence about the candidate's knowledge, understanding and proficiency to accomplish the tasks, duties and responsibilities listed in column 1 of table A-II/1; and

.2 judging that evidence against the criteria specified in the standard.

17 The arrangements for evaluating competence should be designed to take account of different methods of assessment which can provide different types of evidence about candidates' competence, e.g.:

.9　在正常和应急情况下进行无线电通信以及视觉和声响信号通信；以及

.10　监测和操作安全报警系统，包括船舶内部通信。

12　对航行值班能力和技能的评估应：

.1　按照表 A-II/1 规定的评价航行职能的适任标准进行；

.2　保证申请人按照安全航行值班中应遵循的基本原则（第 A-VIII/2 节，第 4-1 部分）与关于保持航行值班的指导（第 B-VIII/2 节，第 4-1 部分）履行航行值班职责。

适任评价

13　申请负责航行值班的高级船员证书应达到的适任标准见表 A-II/1。该标准规定了所要求的知识和技能以及将这些知识和技能运用到船上要求的工作标准上。

14　知识的范围隐含在适任能力的概念中。因此，对适任能力的评估应不仅仅围绕对工作、技能和所执行的任务的直接技术要求，还应反映符合作为船舶高级船员胜任工作的全面要求的更广泛内容。这包括相关的知识、理论、原则和认识能力，它们在不同程度上支撑着各个级别的适任能力。这也围绕着业务能力，即做什么，怎么做，什么时候做和为什么需要做。如果能正确应用，这将有助于确保申请人能够：

.1　在不同的船上和不同的环境中胜任工作；

.2　预测、防备和处理意外情况；并且

.3　适于新的和变化着的要求。

15　评价适任的标准（表 A-II/1 第 4 栏）主要以结果的方式说明适任操作的基本方面。采用这种表达方式可以有助于对照这些标准来评估申请人的表现，并应在培训记录簿中充分记载。

16　评价适任是一个包括下列内容的过程：

.1　搜集足够的、有效的、可信的有关申请人完成表 A-II/1 第 1 栏所列的任务、职责和责任的知识、理解和熟练程度的证据；以及

.2　对照适任标准中规定的标准判断证据。

17　评价适任的安排应旨在考虑不同方式的评估，即能对申请人的适任能力提供不同类型的证据，例如：

.1 direct observation of work activities (including seagoing service);

.2 skills/proficiency/competency tests;

.3 projects and assignments;

.4 evidence from previous experience; and

.5 written, oral and computer-based questioning techniques*.

18 One or more of the first four methods listed should almost invariably be used to provide evidence of ability, in addition to appropriate questioning techniques to provide evidence of supporting knowledge and understanding.

Training in celestial navigation

19 The following areas summarize the recommended training in celestial navigation:

.1 correctly adjust sextant for adjustable errors;

.2 determine corrected reading of the sextant altitude of celestial bodies;

.3 accurate sight reduction computation, using a preferred method;

.4 calculate the time of meridian altitude of the sun;

.5 calculate latitude by Polaris or by meridian altitude of the sun;

.6 accurate plotting of position line(s) and position fixing;

.7 determine time of visible rising/setting sun by a preferred method;

.8 identify and select the most suitable celestial bodies in the twilight period;

.9 determine compass error by azimuth or by amplitude, using a preferred method;

.10 nautical astronomy as required to support the required competence in paragraphs 19.1 to 19.9 above.

20 Training in celestial navigation may include the use of electronic nautical almanac and celestial navigation calculation software.

Section B-II/2
Guidance regarding the certification of masters and chief mates on ships of 500 gross tonnage or more

(See section B-II/1 for guidance.)

* The relevant IMO Model Course(s) may be of assistance in the preparation of courses.

.1　对工作活动（包括海上服务资历）的直接观察；
.2　技能/熟练程度/适任测试；
.3　安排项目并分配任务；
.4　取自以往经历的证据；以及
.5　书面的、口头的和基于计算机的询问技术①。

18　应一直采用上述前四种方法中的一种或多种提供能力方面的证据，还可采用适当的询问技术以提供辅助性的知识和理解的证据。

天文航海培训

19　以下方面概括了推荐的天文航海培训：
.1　正确校准六分仪的可校正误差；
.2　确定修正的六分仪天体高度读数；
.3　使用优选的方法进行准确测天计算；
.4　计算太阳中天高度的时间；
.5　利用北极星或太阳中天高度计算纬度；
.6　准确标绘位置线和定位；
.7　使用优选的方法确定太阳视出/没的时间；
.8　在晨昏朦影期间辨认和选择最适合的天体；
.9　使用优选的方法通过天体方位角或出没方位角测定罗经差；
.10　支撑上述第 19.1 至 19.9 段要求的适任能力所要求的航海天文学。

20　天文航海培训可以包括电子航海天文历和天文航海计算软件的使用。

第 B-II/2 节

对 500 总吨或以上船舶的船长和大副发证的指导

（参见第 B-II/1 节的指导。）

① 相关 IMO 示范培训课程可有助于准备课程。

Section B-II/3
Guidance regarding the certification of officers in charge of a navigational watch and of masters on ships of less than 500 gross tonnage

(See section B-II/1 for guidance.)

Section B-II/4
Guidance regarding the training and certification of ratings forming part of a navigational watch

1 In addition to the requirements stated in table A-II/4 of this Code, Parties are encouraged, for safety reasons, to include the following subjects in the training of ratings forming part of a navigational watch:

.1 a basic knowledge of the International Regulations for Preventing Collisions at Sea, 1972, as amended;

.2 rigging a pilot ladder;

.3 an understanding of wheel orders given by pilots in English;

.4 training for proficiency in survival craft and rescue boats;

.5 support duties when berthing and unberthing and during towing operations;

.6 a basic knowledge of anchoring;

.7 a basic knowledge of dangerous cargoes;

.8 a basic knowledge of stowage procedures and arrangements for bringing stores on board; and

.9 a basic knowledge of deck maintenance and of tools used on deck.

Section B-II/5
Guidance regarding the certification of ratings as able seafarer deck

Onboard training should be documented in an approved training record book.

第 B-II/3 节

对未满 500 总吨船舶的船长和负责航行值班的高级船员发证的指导

(参见第 B-II/1 节的指导。)

第 B-II/4 节

对组成航行值班部分的普通船员培训和发证的指导

1 除本规则表 A-II/4 规定的要求外,鼓励缔约国为安全起见在对组成航行值班部分的普通船员的培训中包括下列各项:

.1 经修订的《1972 年国际海上避碰规则》的基本知识;

.2 安置引航梯;

.3 理解引航员用英语发出的舵令;

.4 培训对救生艇筏和救助艇的熟练操作;

.5 靠、离泊和拖带作业中的辅助性工作;

.6 抛锚的基本知识;

.7 危险货物的基本知识;

.8 积载程序和安排物料上船的基本知识;以及

.9 保养甲板和甲板上所用工具的基本知识。

第 B-II/5 节

对作为高级值班水手的普通船员发证的指导

船上培训应在认可的培训记录簿中予以记载。

CHAPTER III

Guidance regarding the engine department

Section B-III/1

Guidance regarding the certification of officers in charge of an engineering watch in a manned engine-room or as designated duty engineers in a periodically unmanned engine-room

1 In table A-III/1, the tools referred to should include hand tools, common measuring equipment, centre lathes, drilling machines, welding equipment and milling machines as appropriate.

2 Training in workshop skills ashore can be carried out in a training institution or approved workshop.

3 Onboard training should be adequately documented in the training record book by qualified assessors.

Section B-III/2

Guidance regarding the certification of chief engineer officers and second engineer officers of ships powered by main propulsion machinery of 3,000 kW propulsion power or more

(No provisions)

Guidance regarding training of engineering personnel having management responsibilities for the operation and safety of electrical power plant above 1,000 volts

1 Training of engineering personnel having management responsibilities for the operation and safety of electrical power plant of more than 1,000 V should at least include:

.1 the functional, operational and safety requirements for a marine high-voltage system;

.2 assignment of suitably qualified personnel to carry out maintenance and repair of high-voltage switchgear of various types;

.3 taking remedial action necessary during faults in a high-voltage system;

.4 producing a switching strategy for isolating components of a high-voltage system;

.5 selecting suitable apparatus for isolation and testing of high-voltage equipment;

.6 carrying out a switching and isolation procedure on a marine high-voltage system, complete with safety documentation; and

.7 performing tests of insulation resistance and polarization index on high-voltage equipment.

第 III 章
关于轮机部的指导

第 B-III/1 节
对有人值班机舱负责轮机值班高级船员或周期性无人值班机舱指定值班的轮机员发证的指导

1　表 A-III/1 中提及的工具，应包括手工工具、普通测量设备、普通车床、钻床、焊接设备，视情况还可包括铣床。

2　岸上的车间技能培训可以在培训机构或认可的车间进行。

3　船上培训应由合格的评估人员在培训记录簿中充分记载。

第 B-III/2 节
对主推进装置为 3 000 kW 或以上船舶轮机长和大管轮发证的指导

（无条文）

对负责管理 1 000 V 以上电站操作和安全的轮机部人员的培训指导

1　对负责管理 1 000 V 以上电站操作和安全的轮机部人员的培训至少应包括：

.1　船舶高压系统的功能、操作和安全要求；

.2　指派有适当资质的人员对各种高压开关进行维护和修理；

.3　高压系统出故障时采取必要的补救措施；

.4　制定高压系统部件隔离的切换方案；

.5　选择适当的设备进行高压设备的隔离和检查；

.6　按照安全操作文件的要求，执行船舶高压系统切换和隔离程序；以及

.7　进行高压设备绝缘电阻和极化指数检测。

Section B-III/3

Guidance regarding the certification of chief engineer officers and second engineer officers of ships powered by main propulsion machinery between 750 kW and 3,000 kW propulsion power

(No provisions)

Section B-III/4

Guidance regarding the training and certification of ratings forming part of a watch in a manned engine-room or designated to perform duties in a periodically unmanned engine-room

1 In addition to the requirements stated in section A-III/4 of this Code, Parties are encouraged, for safety reasons, to include the following items in the training of ratings forming part of an engineering watch:

.1 a basic knowledge of routine pumping operations, such as bilge, ballast and cargo pumping systems;

.2 a basic knowledge of electrical installations and the associated dangers;

.3 a basic knowledge of maintenance and repair of machinery and tools used in the engine-room; and

.4 a basic knowledge of stowage and arrangements for bringing stores on board.

Section B-III/5

Guidance regarding the certification of ratings as able seafarer engine

Onboard training should be documented in an approved training record book.

Section B-III/6

Guidance regarding training and certification for electro-technical officers

In addition to the requirements stated in table A-III/6 of this Code, Parties are encouraged to take into account resolution A.702(17) concerning radio maintenance guidelines for the Global Maritime Distress and Safety System (GMDSS) within their training programmes.

Section B-III/7

Guidance regarding training and certification for electro-technical ratings

(No provisions)

第 B-III/3 节

对主推进装置为 750 kW 至 3 000 kW 船舶轮机长和大管轮发证的指导

(无条文)

第 B-III/4 节

对有人值班机舱组成值班部分或指定在周期性无人值班机舱履行职责的普通船员培训和发证的指导

1 除本规则第 A-III/4 节规定的要求外,鼓励缔约国为安全起见在对组成轮机值班部分的普通船员的培训中包括下列各项:

.1 泵的日常操作,诸如污水、压载水和液货泵系统,的基本知识;

.2 电气装置及其危险性的基本知识;

.3 维护和修理机械设备及机舱中使用的工具的基本知识;和

.4 安排物料上船及其存放的基本知识。

第 B-III/5 节

对高级值班机工发证的指导

船上培训应在认可的培训记录簿中记载。

第 B-III/6 节

对电子员培训和发证的指导

除本规则表 A-III/6 规定的要求外,鼓励缔约国在其培训计划中考虑决议 A.702(17)关于全球海上遇险与安全系统的无线电维护指南。

第 B-III/7 节

对电子技工培训和发证的指导

(无条文)

CHAPTER IV

Guidance regarding radiocommunication and radio operators

Section B-IV/1
Guidance regarding the application of chapter IV

(No provisions)

Section B-IV/2
Guidance regarding training and certification of GMDSS radio operators

TRAINING RELATED TO THE FIRST-CLASS RADIOELECTRONIC CERTIFICATE

General

1 The requirements of medical fitness, especially as to hearing, eyesight and speech, should be met by the candidate before training is commenced.

2 The training should be relevant to the provisions of the STCW Convention, the provisions of the Radio Regulations annexed to the International Telecommunication Convention (Radio Regulations) and the provisions of the International Convention for the Safety of Life at Sea (SOLAS Convention) currently in force, with particular attention given to provisions for the global maritime distress and safety system (GMDSS). In developing training requirements, account should be taken of at least the knowledge and training given in paragraphs 3 to 14 hereunder.

Theory

3 Knowledge of the general principles and basic factors necessary for safe and efficient use of all sub-systems and equipment required in the GMDSS, sufficient to support the practical training provisions given in paragraph 13.

4 Knowledge of the use, operation and service areas of GMDSS sub-systems, including satellite system characteristics, navigational and meteorological warning systems and selection of appropriate communication circuits.

5 Knowledge of the principles of electricity and the theory of radio and electronics sufficient to meet the provisions given in paragraphs 6 to 10 below.

6 Theoretical knowledge of GMDSS radiocommunication equipment, including narrow-band direct-printing telegraphy and radiotelephone transmitters and receivers, digital selective calling equipment, ship earth stations, emergency position-indicating radio beacons (EPIRBs), marine antenna systems, radio equipment for survival craft together with all auxiliary items, including power supplies, as well as general knowledge of the principles of other equipment generally used for radionavigation, with particular reference to maintaining the equipment in service.

7 Knowledge of factors that affect system reliability, availability, maintenance procedures and proper use of test equipment.

8 Knowledge of microprocessors and fault diagnosis in systems using microprocessors.

9 Knowledge of control systems in the GMDSS radio equipment, including testing and analysis.

第 IV 章
关于无线电通信和无线电操作员的指导

第 B-IV/1 节
关于第 IV 章适用范围的指导

(无条文)

第 B-IV/2 节
关于 GMDSS 无线电操作员培训和发证的指导

关于一级无线电电子证书的培训

一般要求

1 在开始培训前,申请人应符合健康要求,特别是听力、视力和语言表达能力方面的要求。

2 培训应参照《STCW 公约》的规定、《国际电信公约》附则中的《无线电规则》(无线电规则)的规定和现行有效的《国际海上人命安全公约》(SOLAS 公约)的规定进行,特别要注意对全球海上遇险与安全系统(GMDSS)的规定。在制定培训要求时,至少应考虑到以下第 3 段至第 14 段所述的知识和培训。

理论

3 安全和有效地使用 CMDSS 中所要求的全部子系统和设备所必需的、足以支持第 13 段实际培训规定的一般原理和基本要素的知识。

4 GMDSS 子系统的使用、操作和服务区域的知识,包括卫星系统特性、航行和气象警告系统以及选择适当通信线路的知识。

5 电学原理和无线电及电子学理论的知识足以符合以下第 6 段至第 10 段的规定。

6 GMDSS 无线电通信设备的理论知识,包括窄带直接印字电报和无线电话发射机和接收机、数字选择呼叫设备、船舶地球站、应急无线电示位标(EPIRBs)、船舶天线系统、救生艇筏无线电设备及其所有辅助设备,包括电源以及通常用于无线电导航的其他设备原理的一般知识,特别是关于保持设备处于可使用状态的知识。

7 影响系统可靠性、可用性、保养程序和正确使用测试设备的因素的知识。

8 微处理机和使用微处理机判断系统故障的知识。

9 GMDSS 无线电设备控制系统的知识,包括测试和分析。

10 Knowledge of the use of computer software for the GMDSS radio equipment and methods for correcting faults caused by loss of software control of the equipment.

Regulations and documentation

11 Knowledge of:

.1 the SOLAS Convention and the Radio Regulations, with particular emphasis on:

.1.1 distress, urgency and safety radiocommunications;

.1.2 avoiding harmful interference, particularly with distress and safety traffic; and

.1.3 prevention of unauthorized transmissions;

.2 other documents relating to operational and communication procedures for distress, safety and public correspondence services, including charges, navigational warnings, and weather broadcasts in the Maritime Mobile Service and the Maritime Mobile Satellite Service; and

.3 use of the International Code of Signals and the IMO Standard Marine Communication Phrases.

Watchkeeping and procedures

12 Knowledge of and training in:

.1 communication procedures and discipline to prevent harmful interference in GMDSS sub-systems;

.2 procedures for using propagation-prediction information to establish optimum frequencies for communications;

.3 radiocommunication watchkeeping relevant to all GMDSS sub-systems, exchange of radiocommunication traffic, particularly concerning distress, urgency and safety procedures, and radio records;

.4 use of the international phonetic alphabet;

.5 monitoring a distress frequency while simultaneously monitoring or working on at least one other frequency;

.6 ship reporting systems and procedures;

.7 radiocommunication procedures of the International Aeronautical and Maritime Search and Rescue (IAMSAR) Manual;

.8 radio medical systems and procedures; and

.9 causes of false distress alerts and means to avoid them.*

* See COM/Circ.127 – Guidelines for avoiding false distress alerts.

10 使用 GMDSS 无线电设备的计算机软件的知识和排除因设备软件控制丧失所造成故障的方法的知识。

规则和文件

11 了解：

.1 《SOLAS 公约》和《无线电规则》，重点是：

.1.1 遇险、紧急和安全无线电通信，

.1.2 避免有害干扰，特别是对遇险和安全通信的干扰，和

.1.3 防止未经授权的发射；

.2 有关遇险、安全和公众通信业务的操作和通信程序的其他文件，包括海上移动业务和海上移动卫星业务的收费、航行警告和天气预报；以及

.3 使用《国际信号规则》和《IMO 标准航海通信用语》。

值班和程序

12 了解并培训：

.1 在 GMDSS 子系统中防止有害干扰的通信程序和纪律；

.2 使用传播预报信息来确定最佳通信频率的程序；

.3 有关所有 GMDSS 子系统的无线电通信值班，无线电通信通报的交换，特别是关于遇险、紧急和安全程序，以及无线电记录；

.4 使用国际标音字母；

.5 在监听或使用至少另一频率的同时监听遇险频率；

.6 船舶报告制度和程序；

.7 《国际航空和海上搜寻救助手册》的无线电通信程序；

.8 无线电医疗系统和程序；以及

.9 误遇险报警的原因及其防止手段。①

① 见 COM/Circ.127 号通函——关于防止误遇险报警的指南。

Practical

13 Practical training, supported by appropriate laboratory work, should be given in:

.1 correct and efficient operation of all GMDSS sub-systems and equipment under normal propagation conditions and under typical interference conditions;

.2 safe operation of all the GMDSS communication equipment and ancillary devices, including safety precautions;

.3 adequate and accurate keyboard skills for the satisfactory exchange of communications;

.4 operational techniques for:

.4.1 receiver and transmitter adjustment for the appropriate mode of operation, including digital selective calling and direct-printing telegraphy;

.4.2 antenna adjustment and realignment, as appropriate;

.4.3 use of radio life-saving appliances; and

.4.4 use of emergency position-indicating radio beacons (EPIRBs);

.5 antenna rigging, repair and maintenance, as appropriate;

.6 reading and understanding pictorial, logic and circuit diagrams;

.7 use and care of those tools and test instruments necessary to carry out at-sea electronic maintenance;

.8 manual soldering and desoldering techniques, including those involving semi-conductor devices and modern circuits, and the ability to distinguish whether the circuit is suitable to be manually soldered or desoldered;

.9 tracing and repair of faults to component level, where practicable, and to board/module level in other cases;

.10 recognition and correction of conditions contributing to the fault occurring;

.11 maintenance procedures, both preventive and corrective, for all GMDSS communication equipment and radionavigation equipment; and

.12 methods of alleviating electrical and electromagnetic interference such as bonding, shielding and bypassing.

Miscellaneous

14 Knowledge of and/or training in:

.1 the English language, both written and spoken, for the satisfactory exchange of communications relevant to the safety of life at sea;

实践

13 应在以下方面进行由适当的实验室工作支持的实际培训：

.1 在正常传播条件下和在典型干扰条件下，所有 GMDSS 子系统和设备的正确和有效操作；

.2 所有 GMDSS 通信设备和辅助装置的安全操作，包括安全预防措施；

.3 进行令人满意的信息交换所需的足够和准确的键盘输入技能；

.4 下列操作技术：

.4.1 对接收机和发射机进行调节以获得适当的工作模式，包括数字选择呼叫和直接印字电报，

.4.2 视情况对天线进行调整和重新校准，

.4.3 使用无线电救生设备，和

.4.4 使用应急无线电示位标（EPIRBs）；

.5 视情况对天线进行安装、修理和保养；

.6 阅读和理解有关示意图、逻辑图和电路图；

.7 使用和保养海上电子维修所需的工具和测试仪器；

.8 手工焊接和去焊技术，包括对半导体装置和新型电路的焊接和去焊以及分辨电路是否适合于手工焊接和去焊的能力；

.9 查找和修理元件故障，如可行，在其他情况下查找和修理电路板/模块的故障；

.10 判明和更正导致发生故障的条件；

.11 所有 GMDSS 通信设备和无线电导航设备的保养程序，包括预防和更正；以及

.12 减轻电气和电磁干扰的方法，如接地、屏蔽和旁路。

其他

14 了解和/或培训：

.1 英语，在书面和口语上均能令人满意地进行有关海上人命安全信息的沟通；

.2 world geography, especially the principal shipping routes, services of rescue coordination centres (RCCs) and related communication routes;

.3 survival at sea, the operation of lifeboats, rescue boats, liferafts, buoyant apparatus and their equipment, with special reference to radio life-saving appliances;

.4 fire prevention and fire fighting, with particular reference to the radio installation;

.5 preventive measures for the safety of ship and personnel in connection with hazards related to radio equipment, including electrical, radiation, chemical and mechanical hazards;

.6 first aid, including heart-respiration revival techniques; and

.7 coordinated universal time (UTC), global time zones and the international date line.

TRAINING RELATED TO THE SECOND-CLASS RADIOELECTRONIC CERTIFICATE

General

15 The requirements of medical fitness, especially as to hearing, eyesight and speech, should be met by the candidate before training is commenced.

16 The training should be relevant to the provisions of the STCW Convention and the SOLAS Convention currently in force, with particular attention given to provisions for the global maritime distress and safety system (GMDSS). In developing training requirements, account should be taken of at least the knowledge and training given in paragraphs 17 to 28 hereunder*.

Theory

17 Knowledge of the general principles and basic factors necessary for safe and efficient use of all sub-systems and equipment required in the GMDSS, sufficient to support the practical training provisions given in paragraph 27 below.

18 Knowledge of the use, operation and service areas of GMDSS sub-systems, including satellite system characteristics, navigational and meteorological warning systems and selection of appropriate communication circuits.

19 Knowledge of the principles of electricity and the theory of radio and electronics sufficient to meet the provisions given in paragraphs 20 to 24 below.

20 General theoretical knowledge of GMDSS radiocommunication equipment, including narrow-band direct-printing telegraphy and radiotelephone transmitters and receivers, digital selective calling equipment, ship earth stations, emergency position-indicating radio beacons (EPIRBs), marine antenna systems, radio equipment for survival craft together with all auxiliary items, including power supplies, as well as general knowledge of other equipment generally used for radionavigation, with particular reference to maintaining the equipment in service.

21 General knowledge of factors that affect system reliability, availability, maintenance procedures and proper use of test equipment.

* The relevant IMO Model Course(s) may be of assistance in the preparation of courses.

.2 世界地理，特别是主要航线、救助协调中心（RCCs）的服务和有关通信线路；

.3 海上求生，救生艇、救助船、救生筏、浮力器具及其设备（特别是无线电救生设备）的操作；

.4 防火和灭火，特别是对无线电设备的防火和灭火；

.5 与无线电设备危害（包括电气、放射性、化学和机械危害）有关的船舶和人员安全预防措施；

.6 急救，包括心肺复苏技术；以及

.7 世界协调时（UTC）、全球时区和国际日期变更线。

关于二级无线电电子证书的培训

一般要求

15 在开始培训前，申请人应符合健康要求，特别是听力、视力和语言表达能力方面的要求。

16 培训应参照现行有效的《STCW 公约》和《SOLAS 公约》的规定，特别要注意对全球海上遇险与安全系统（GMDSS）的规定。在制定培训要求时，至少应考虑到以下第 17 段至第 28 段所述的知识和培训①。

理论

17 安全和有效地使用 GMDSS 中所要求的全部子系统和设备所必需的，足以支持以下第 27 段实际培训规定的一般原理和基本要素的知识。

18 GMDSS 子系统的使用、操作和服务区域的知识，包括卫星系统特性、航行和气象警告系统以及选择适当的通信线路的知识。

19 电学原理和无线电及电子学理论的知识足以符合以下第 20 段至第 24 段的规定。

20 GMDSS 无线电通信设备的一般理论知识，包括窄带直接印字电报和无线电话发射机和接收机、数字选择呼叫设备、船舶地球站、应急无线电示位标（EPIRBs）、船舶天线系统、救生艇筏无线电设备及其所有辅助设备，包括电源以及通常用于无线电导航的其他设备原理的一般知识，特别是关于保养使用中的设备的知识。

21 影响系统可靠性、可用性、保养程序和正确使用测试设备的因素的一般知识。

① 相关 IMO 示范培训课程可有助于准备课程。

22 General knowledge of microprocessors and fault diagnosis in systems using microprocessors.

23 General knowledge of control systems in the GMDSS radio equipment, including testing and analysis.

24 Knowledge of the use of computer software for the GMDSS radio equipment and methods for correcting faults caused by loss of software control of the equipment.

Regulations and documentation

25 Knowledge of:

.1 the SOLAS Convention and the Radio Regulations, with particular emphasis on:

.1.1 distress, urgency and safety radiocommunications;

.1.2 avoiding harmful interference, particularly with distress and safety traffic; and

.1.3 the prevention of unauthorized transmissions;

.2 other documents relating to operational and communication procedures for distress, safety and public correspondence services,including charges, navigational warnings, and weather broadcasts in the Maritime Mobile Service and the Maritime Mobile Satellite Service; and

.3 the use of the International Code of Signals and the IMO Standard Marine Communication Phrases.

Watchkeeping and procedures

26 Training should be given in:

.1 communication procedures and discipline to prevent harmful interference in GMDSS sub-systems;

.2 procedures for using propagation-prediction information to establish optimum frequencies for communications;

.3 radiocommunication watchkeeping relevant to all GMDSS sub-systems, exchange of radiocommunication traffic, particularly concerning distress, urgency and safety procedures, and radio records;

.4 use of the international phonetic alphabet;

.5 monitoring a distress frequency while simultaneously monitoring or working on at least one other frequency;

.6 ship reporting systems and procedures;

.7 radiocommunication procedures of the International Aeronautical and Maritime Search and Rescue (IAMSAR) Manual;

22　微处理机和使用微处理机判断系统故障的一般知识。

23　GMDSS 无线电设备控制系统的一般知识，包括测试和分析。

24　使用 GMDSS 无线电设备的计算机软件的知识和排除因设备软件控制丧失所造成故障的方法的知识。

规则和文件

25　了解：

.1　《SOLAS 公约》和《无线电规则》，重点是：

.1.1　遇险、紧急和安全无线电通信，

.1.2　避免有害干扰，特别是对遇险和安全通信的干扰，和

.1.3　防止未经授权的发射；

.2　有关遇险、安全和公众通信业务的操作和通信程序的其他文件，包括海上移动业务和海上移动卫星业务的收费、航行警告和天气预报；以及

.3　使用《国际信号规则》和《IMO 标准航海通信用语》。

值班和程序

26　应给予以下培训：

.1　在 GMDSS 子系统中防止有害干扰的通信程序和纪律；

.2　使用传播预报信息来确定最佳通信频率的程序；

.3　有关所有 GMDSS 子系统的无线电通信值班，无线电通信通报的交换，特别是关于遇险、紧急和安全程序，以及无线电记录；

.4　使用国际标音字母；

.5　在监听或使用至少另一频率的同时监听遇险频率；

.6　船舶报告制度和程序；

.7　《国际航空和海上搜寻救助手册》的无线电通信程序；

.8 radio medical systems and procedures; and

.9 causes of false distress alerts and means to avoid them.*

Practical

27 Practical training, supported by appropriate laboratory work, should be given in:

.1 correct and efficient operation of all GMDSS sub-systems and equipment under normal propagation conditions and under typical interference conditions;

.2 safe operation of all the GMDSS communication equipment and ancillary devices, including safety precautions;

.3 adequate and accurate keyboard skills for the satisfactory exchange of communications;

.4 operational techniques for:

.4.1 receiver and transmitter adjustment for the appropriate mode of operation, including digital selective calling and direct-printing telegraphy;

.4.2 antenna adjustment and realignment, as appropriate;

.4.3 use of radio life-saving appliances; and

.4.4 use of emergency position-indicating radio beacons (EPIRBs);

.5 antenna rigging, repair and maintenance, as appropriate;

.6 reading and understanding pictorial, logic and module interconnection diagrams;

.7 use and care of those tools and test instruments necessary to carry out at-sea electronic maintenance at the level of replacement of a unit or module;

.8 basic manual soldering and desoldering techniques and their limitations;

.9 tracing and repair of faults to board/module level;

.10 recognition and correction of conditions contributing to the fault occurring;

.11 basic maintenance procedures, both preventive and corrective, for all the GMDSS communication equipment and radionavigation equipment; and

.12 methods of alleviating electrical and electromagnetic interference, such as bonding, shielding and bypassing.

* See .COM/Circ.127 and IMO Assembly resolution A.814 (19) —Guidelines for avoiding false distress alerts.

.8 无线电医疗系统和程序；以及

.9 误遇险报警的原因及其防止手段。①

实践

27 应在以下方面进行由适当的实验室工作支持的实际培训：

.1 在正常传播条件下和在典型干扰条件下，所有 GMDSS 子系统和设备的正确和有效操作；

.2 所有 GMDSS 通信设备和辅助装置的安全操作，包括安全预防措施；

.3 进行令人满意的信息交换所需的足够和准确的键盘输入技能；

.4 下列操作技术：

.4.1 对接收机和发射机进行调节以获得适当的工作模式，包括数字选择呼叫和直接印字电报，

.4.2 视情况对天线进行调整和重新校准，

.4.3 使用无线电救生设备，和

.4.4 使用应急无线电示位标（EPIRBs）；

.5 视情况对天线进行安装、修理和保养；

.6 阅读和理解有关示意图、逻辑图和电路图；

.7 使用及保养用于替换某个单元或模块的海上电子维修所需的工具和测试仪器；

.8 基本手工焊接和去焊技术及其局限性；

.9 查找和修理电路板/模块的故障；

.10 判明和更正导致发生故障的条件；

.11 所有 GMDSS 通信设备和无线电导航设备的基本保养程序，包括预防和更正；以及

.12 减轻电气和电磁干扰的方法，如接地、屏蔽和旁路。

① 见 COM/Circ. 127 号通函和 IMO 第 A. 814(19)号大会决议——关于防止误遇险报警的指南。

Miscellaneous

28 Knowledge of, and/or training in:

.1 the English language, both written and spoken, for the satisfactory exchange of communications relevant to the safety of life at sea;

.2 world geography, especially the principal shipping routes, services of rescue coordination centres (RCCs) and related communication routes;

.3 survival at sea, the operation of lifeboats, rescue boats, liferafts, buoyant apparatus and their equipment, with special reference to radio life-saving appliances;

.4 fire prevention and fire fighting, with particular reference to the radio installation;

.5 preventive measures for the safety of ship and personnel in connection with hazards related to radio equipment, including electrical, radiation, chemical and mechanical hazards;

.6 first aid, including heart-respiration revival techniques; and

.7 coordinated universal time (UTC), global time zones and the international date line.

TRAINING RELATED TO THE GENERAL OPERATOR'S CERTIFICATE

General

29 The requirements of medical fitness, especially as to hearing, eyesight and speech, should be met by the candidate before training is commenced.

30 The training should be relevant to the provisions of the STCW Convention, the Radio Regulations and the SOLAS Convention currently in force, with particular attention given to provisions for the global maritime distress and safety system (GMDSS). In developing training requirements, account should be taken of at least the knowledge and training given in paragraphs 31 to 36 hereunder*.

Theory

31 Knowledge of the general principles and basic factors necessary for safe and efficient use of all sub-systems and equipment required in the GMDSS sufficient to support the practical training provisions given in paragraph 35 below.

32 Knowledge of the use, operation and service areas of GMDSS sub-systems, including satellite system characteristics, navigational and meteorological warning systems and selection of appropriate communication circuits.

---

* The relevant IMO Model Course(s) may be of assistance in the preparation of courses.

其他

28 了解和/或培训：

.1 英语，在书面和口语上均能令人满意地进行有关海上人命安全信息的沟通；

.2 世界地理，特别是主要航线、救助协调中心（RCCs）的服务和有关通信线路；

.3 海上求生，救生艇、救助船、救生筏、浮力器具及其设备（特别是无线电救生设备）的操作；

.4 防火和灭火，特别是对无线电设备的防火和灭火；

.5 与无线电设备危害（包括电气、放射性、化学和机械危害）有关的船舶和人员安全预防措施；

.6 急救，包括心肺复苏技术；以及

.7 世界协调时（UTC）、全球时区和国际日期变更线。

关于通用操作员证书的培训

一般要求

29 在开始培训前，申请人应符合健康要求，特别是听力、视力和语言表达能力方面的要求。

30 培训应参照现行有效的《STCW 公约》和《无线电规则》和《SOLAS 公约》的规定，特别要注意对全球海上遇险与安全系统（GMDSS）的规定。在制定培训要求时，至少应考虑到以下第 31 段至第 36 段所述的知识和培训①。

理论

31 安全和有效地使用 GMDSS 中所要求的全部子系统和设备所必需的、足以支持以下第 35 段实际培训规定的一般原理和基本要素的知识。

32 GMDSS 子系统的使用、操作和服务区域的知识，包括卫星系统特性、航行和气象警告系统以及选择适当通信线路的知识。

① 相关 IMO 示范培训课程可有助于准备课程。

Regulations and documentation

33 Knowledge of:

.1 the SOLAS Convention and the Radio Regulations, with particular emphasis on:

.1.1 distress, urgency and safety radiocommunications;

.1.2 avoiding harmful interference, particularly with distress and safety traffic; and

.1.3 prevention of unauthorized transmissions;

.2 other documents relating to operational and communication procedures for distress, safety and public correspondence services, including charges, navigational warnings, and weather broadcasts in the Maritime Mobile Service and the Maritime Mobile Satellite Service; and

.3 use of the International Code of Signals and the IMO Standard Marine Communication Phrases.

Watchkeeping and procedures

34 Training should be given in:

.1 communication procedures and discipline to prevent harmful interference in GMDSS sub-systems;

.2 procedures for using propagation-prediction information to establish optimum frequencies for communications;

.3 radiocommunication watchkeeping relevant to all GMDSS sub-systems, exchange of radiocommunication traffic, particularly concerning distress, urgency and safety procedures, and radio records;

.4 use of the international phonetic alphabet;

.5 monitoring a distress frequency while simultaneously monitoring or working on at least one other frequency;

.6 ship reporting systems and procedures;

.7 radiocommunication procedures of the International Aeronautical and Maritime Search and Rescue (IAMSAR) Manual;

.8 radio medical systems and procedures; and

.9 causes of false distress alerts and means to avoid them.*

* See COM/Circ.127 and IMO Assembly resolution A.814 (19) – Guidelines for avoiding false distress alerts.

规则和文件

33 了解：

.1 《SOLAS 公约》和《无线电规则》，重点是：

.1.1 遇险、紧急和安全无线电通信，

.1.2 避免有害干扰，特别是对遇险和安全通信的干扰，和

.1.3 防止未经授权的发射；

.2 有关遇险、安全和公众通信业务的操作和通信程序的其他文件，包括海上移动业务和海上移动卫星业务的收费、航行警告和天气预报；以及

.3 使用《国际信号规则》和《IMO 标准航海通信用语》。

值班和程序

34 应给予以下培训：

.1 在 GMDSS 子系统中防止有害干扰的通信程序和纪律；

.2 使用传播预报信息来确定最佳通信频率的程序；

.3 有关所有 GMDSS 子系统的无线电通信值班，无线电通信通报的交换，特别是关于遇险、紧急和安全程序，以及无线电记录；

.4 使用国际标音字母；

.5 在监听或使用至少另一频率的同时监听遇险频率；

.6 船舶报告制度和程序；

.7 《国际航空和海上搜寻救助手册》的无线电通信程序；

.8 无线电医疗系统和程序；以及

.9 误遇险报警的原因及其防止手段。①

① 见 COM/Circ.127 号通函和 IMO 第 A.814(19)号大会决议——关于防止误遇险报警的指南。

Practical

35 Practical training should be given in:

.1 correct and efficient operation of all GMDSS sub-systems and equipment under normal propagation conditions and under typical interference conditions;

.2 safe operation of all the GMDSS communications equipment and ancillary devices, including safety precautions;

.3 accurate and adequate keyboard skills for the satisfactory exchange of communications; and

.4 operational techniques for:

.4.1 receiver and transmitter adjustment for the appropriate mode of operation, including digital selective calling and direct-printing telegraphy;

.4.2 antenna adjustment and realignment as appropriate;

.4.3 use of radio life-saving appliances; and

.4.4 use of emergency position-indicating radio beacons (EPIRBs).

Miscellaneous

36 Knowledge of, and/or training in:

.1 the English language, both written and spoken, for the satisfactory exchange of communications relevant to the safety of life at sea;

.2 world geography, especially the principal shipping routes, services of rescue coordination centres (RCCs) and related communication routes;

.3 survival at sea, the operation of lifeboats, rescue boats, liferafts, buoyant apparatus and their equipment, with special reference to radio life-saving appliances;

.4 fire prevention and fire-fighting, with particular reference to the radio installation;

.5 preventive measures for the safety of ship and personnel in connection with hazards related to radio equipment, including electrical, radiation, chemical and mechanical hazards;

.6 first aid, including heart-respiration revival techniques; and

.7 coordinated universal time (UTC), global time zones and the international date line.

实践

35 应给予以下实际培训：

.1 在正常传播条件下和在典型干扰条件下，所有 GMDSS 子系统和设备的正确和有效操作；

.2 所有 GMDSS 通信设备和辅助装置的安全操作，包括安全预防措施；

.3 进行令人满意的信息交换所需的足够和准确的键盘输入技能；以及

.4 下列操作技术：

.4.1 对接收机和发射机进行调节以获得适当的工作模式，包括数字选择呼叫和直接印字电报，

.4.2 视情况对天线进行调整和重新校准，

.4.3 使用无线电救生设备，和

.4.4 使用应急无线电示位标(EPIRBs)。

其他

36 了解和/或培训：

.1 英语，在书面和口语上均能令人满意地进行有关海上人命安全信息的交流；

.2 世界地理，特别是主要航线、救助协调中心(RCCs)的服务和有关通信线路；

.3 海上求生，救生艇、救助艇、救生筏、浮力器具及其设备(特别是无线电救生设备)的操作；

.4 防火和灭火，特别是对无线电设备的防火和灭火；

.5 与无线电设备危害(包括电气、放射性、化学和机械危害)有关的船舶和人员安全预防措施；

.6 急救，包括心肺复苏技术；以及

.7 世界协调时(UTC)、全球时区和国际日期变更线。

TRAINING RELATED TO THE RESTRICTED OPERATOR'S CERTIFICATE

General

37 The requirements of medical fitness, especially as to hearing, eyesight and speech, should be met by the candidate before training is commenced.

38 The training should be relevant to the provisions of the STCW Convention, the Radio Regulations and the SOLAS Convention currently in force, with particular attention given to provisions for the global maritime distress and safety system (GMDSS). In developing training guidance, account should be taken of at least the knowledge and training given in paragraphs 39 to 44 hereunder*.

Theory

39 Knowledge of the general principles and basic factors, including VHF range limitation and antenna height effect necessary for safe and efficient use of all sub-systems and equipment required in GMDSS in sea area A1, sufficient to support the training given in paragraph 43 below.

40 Knowledge of the use, operation and service areas of GMDSS sea area A1 sub-systems, e.g., navigational and meteorological warning systems and the appropriate communication circuits.

Regulations and documentation

41 Knowledge of:

.1 those parts of the SOLAS Convention and the Radio Regulations relevant to sea area A1, with particular emphasis on:

.1.1 distress, urgency and safety radiocommunications;

.1.2 avoiding harmful interference, particularly with distress and safety traffic; and

.1.3 prevention of unauthorized transmissions;

.2 other documents relating to operational and communication procedures for distress, safety and public correspondence service including charges, navigational warnings and weather broadcasts in the Maritime Mobile Service in sea area A1; and

.3 use of the International Code of Signals and the IMO Standard Marine Communication Phrases.

Watchkeeping and procedures

42 Training should be given in:

.1 communication procedures and discipline to prevent harmful interference in GMDSS sub-systems used in sea area A1;

* The relevant IMO Model Course(s) may be of assistance in the preparation of courses.

关于限用操作员证书的培训

总则

37 在开始培训前,申请人应符合健康要求,特别是听力、视力和语言表达能力方面的要求。

38 培训应参照现行有效的《STCW 公约》和《无线电规则》和《SOLAS 公约》的规定,特别要注意对全球海上遇险与安全系统(GMDSS)的规定。在制定培训要求时,至少应考虑到以下第 39 段至第 44 段所述的知识和培训①。

理论

39 安全有效地使用 GMDSS A1 海区所要求的全部子系统和设备所必需的、足以支持以下第 43 段所述培训的一般原理和基本要素的知识,包括 VHF 限制距离和天线高度的影响。

40 对 GMDSS A1 海区的子系统的使用、操作和服务区域的知识,例如航行和气象警告系统以及选择适当的通信电路。

规则和文件

41 了解:

.1 《SOLAS 公约》和《无线电规则》中与 A1 海区有关的部分,重点是:

.1.1 遇险、紧急和安全无线电通信,

.1.2 避免有害干扰,特别是对遇险和安全通信的干扰,和

.1.3 防止未经授权的发射;

.2 有关遇险、安全和公众通信业务的操作和通信程序的其他文件,包括 A1 海区海上移动业务的收费、航行警告和天气预报;以及

.3 使用《国际信号规则》和《IMO 标准航海通信用语》。

值班和程序

42 应给予以下培训:

.1 在 A1 海区使用的在 GMDSS 子系统中防止有害干扰的通信程序和纪律;

① 相关 IMO 示范培训课程可有助于准备课程。

.2 VHF communication procedures for:

.2.1 radiocommunication watchkeeping, exchange of radiocommunication traffic, particularly concerning distress, urgency and safety procedures, and radio records;

.2.2 monitoring a distress frequency while simultaneously monitoring or working on at least one other frequency; and

.2.3 the digital selective calling system;

.3 use of the international phonetic alphabet;

.4 ship reporting systems and procedures;

.5 VHF radiocommunication procedures of the International Aeronautical and Maritime Search and Rescue (IAMSAR) Manual;

.6 radio medical systems and procedures; and

.7 causes of false distress alerts and means to avoid them.*

Practical

43 Practical training should be given in:

.1 correct and efficient operation of the GMDSS sub-systems and equipment prescribed for ships operating in sea area A1 under normal propagation conditions and under typical interference conditions;

.2 safe operation of relevant GMDSS communication equipment and ancillary devices, including safety precautions; and

.3 operational techniques for use of:

.3.1 VHF, including channel, squelch, and mode adjustment, as appropriate;

.3.2 radio life-saving appliances;

.3.3 emergency position-indicating radio beacons (EPIRBs); and

.3.4 NAVTEX receivers.

Miscellaneous

44 Knowledge of, and/or training in:

.1 the English language, both written and spoken, for the satisfactory exchange of communications relevant to the safety of life at sea;

.2 services of rescue coordination centres (RCCs) and related communication routes;

* See .COM/Circ.127 and IMO Assembly resolution A.814 (19) —Guidelines for avoiding false distress alerts.

.2 对以下项目的 VHF 通信程序：

.2.1 无线电通信值班，无线电通信通报的交换，特别是关于遇险、紧急和安全程序，以及无线电记录，

.2.2 在监听或使用至少另一频率的同时监听遇险频率，和

.2.3 数字选择呼叫系统；

.3 使用国际标音字母；

.4 船舶报告制度和程序；

.5 《国际航空和海上搜寻救助(IAMSAR)手册》的 VHF 无线电通信程序；

.6 无线电医疗系统和程序；以及

.7 误遇险报警的原因及其防止手段。①

实践

43 应给予以下实际培训：

.1 在正常传播条件下和在典型干扰条件下，为在 A1 海区操纵的船舶规定的 GMDSS 子系统和设备的正确和有效操作；

.2 有关 GMDSS 通信设备和辅助装置的安全操作，包括安全预防措施；以及

.3 使用以下设备的操作技术：

.3.1 VHF，视情况包括频道、噪声抑制和模式调整，

.3.2 无线电救生设备，

.3.3 应急无线电示位标(EPIRBs)，和

.3.4 航海电传(NAVTEX)接收机。

其他

44 了解和/或培训：

.1 英语，在书面和口语上均能令人满意地进行有关海上人命安全信息的交流；

.2 救助协调中心(RCCs)的服务和有关通信线路；

① 见 COM/Circ.127 号通函和 IMO 第 A.814(19)号大会决议——关于防止误遇险报警的指南。

.3 survival at sea, the operation of lifeboats, rescue boats, liferafts, buoyant apparatus and their equipment, with special reference to radio life-saving appliances;

.4 fire prevention and fire fighting, with particular reference to the radio installation;

.5 preventive measures for the safety of ship and personnel in connection with hazards related to radio equipment, including electrical, radiation, chemical and mechanical hazards; and

.6 first aid, including heart-respiration revival techniques.

TRAINING RELATED TO MAINTENANCE OF GMDSS INSTALLATIONS ON BOARD SHIPS

General

45 Reference is made to the maintenance requirements of SOLAS Convention regulation IV/15, and to IMO resolution A.702(17) on Radio maintenance guidelines for the GMDSS related to sea areas A3 and A4, which includes in its annex the following provision:

> "4.2 The person designated to perform functions for at-sea electronic maintenance should either hold an appropriate certificate as specified by the Radio Regulations, as required, or have equivalent at-sea electronic maintenance qualifications, as may be approved by the Administration, taking into account the recommendations of the Organization on the training of such personnel."

46 The following guidance on equivalent electronic maintenance qualifications is provided for use by Administrations as appropriate.

47 Training as recommended below does not qualify any person to be an operator of GMDSS radio equipment who does not hold an appropriate Radio Operator's Certificate.

Maintenance training equivalent to the First-Class Radioelectronic Certificate

48 In determining training equivalent to the elements of the listed First-Class Radioelectronic Certificate:

.1 the theory content should cover at least the subjects given in paragraphs 3 to 10;

.2 the practical content should cover at least the subjects given in paragraph 13; and

.3 the miscellaneous knowledge included should cover at least the subjects given in paragraph 14.

Maintenance training equivalent to the Second-Class Radioelectronic Certificate

49 In determining training equivalent to the maintenance elements of the Second-Class Radioelectronic Certificate:

.1 the theory content should cover at least the subjects given in paragraphs 17 to 24;

.2 the practical content should cover at least the subjects given in paragraph 27; and

.3 the miscellaneous knowledge included should cover at least the subjects given in paragraph 28.

.3 海上求生,救生艇、救助艇、救生筏、浮力器具及其设备(特别是无线电救生设备)的操作;

.4 防火和灭火,特别是对无线电设备的防火和灭火;

.5 与无线电设备危害(包括电气、放射性、化学和机械危害)有关的船舶和人员安全预防措施;以及

.6 急救,包括心肺复苏技术。

关于对船上 GMDSS 设备进行维修的培训

总则

45 参阅《SOLAS 公约》规则第 IV/15 条的有关维修要求,和关于 A3 和 A4 海区 GMDSS 无线电维护指南的 IMO 第 A.702(17)号决议,该决议的附件中包括以下规定:

> “4.2 指定履行海上电子维修职能的人员应按要求持有《无线电规则》规定的适当证书或具有主管机关可能认可的等效的海上电子维修资格,并考虑本组织关于对此类人员进行培训的建议。”

46 以下关于等效的电子维修资格的指导供主管机关在适当情况下使用。

47 以下建议的培训并不能使不持有适当的无线电操作员证书的任何人员有资格担任 GMDSS 无线电设备的操作人员。

与一级无线电电子证书等效的维护培训

48 在确定与所列一级无线电电子证书的要素等效的培训时:

.1 理论内容应至少包括第 3 段至第 10 段所列的科目;

.2 实践内容应至少包括第 13 段所列的科目;以及

.3 其他知识应至少包括第 14 段所列的科目。

与二级无线电电子证书等效的维护培训

49 在确定与二级无线电电子证书的维护要素等效的培训时:

.1 理论内容应至少包括第 17 段至第 24 段所列的科目;

.2 实践内容应至少包括第 27 段所列的科目;以及

.3 其他知识应至少包括第 28 段所列的科目。

CHAPTER V

Guidance regarding special training requirements for personnel on certain types of ships

Section B-V/1
Guidance regarding the training and qualifications of tanker personnel

Person with immediate responsibility

1 The term "person with immediate responsibility" as used in paragraphs 3 and 5 of regulation V/1-1 and paragraph 3 of regulation V/1-2 means a person being in a decision-making capacity with respect to loading, discharging, care in transit, handling of cargo, tank cleaning or other cargo-related operations.

FAMILIARIZATION TRAINING FOR ALL TANKER PERSONNEL

2 All tanker personnel should undergo familiarization training on board and, where appropriate, ashore before being assigned to shipboard duties, which should be given by qualified personnel experienced in the handling and characteristics of oil, chemical or liquefied gas cargoes, as appropriate, and the safety procedures involved. The training should at least cover the matters set out in paragraphs 3 to 8 below.

Regulations

3 Knowledge of the ship's rules and regulations governing the safety of personnel on board a tanker in port and at sea.

Health hazards and precautions to be taken

4 Dangers of skin contact; inhalation and accidental swallowing of cargo; the harmful properties of the cargoes carried, personnel accidents and associated first aid; lists of do's and don'ts.

Fire prevention and fire fighting

5 Control of smoking and cooking restrictions; sources of ignition; fire and explosion prevention; methods of fire fighting; portable fire extinguishers and fixed installations.

Pollution prevention

6 Procedures to be followed to prevent air and water pollution and measures which will be taken in the event of spillage.

Safety equipment and its use

7 The proper use of protective clothing and equipment, resuscitators, escape and rescue equipment.

Emergency procedures

8 Familiarization with the emergency plan procedures.

第 V 章
关于特定类型船舶人员特殊培训要求的指导

第 B-V/1 节
关于对液货船人员培训和资格的指导

承担直接责任的人员

1　规则第 V/1-1 条第 3 段和第 5 段及规则第 V/1-2 条第 3 段中的术语“承担直接责任的人员”指在装货、卸货、运输中照管货物、货物作业、洗舱或其他货物相关操作中具有决策职责的人。

所有液货船人员熟悉培训

2　所有液货船船员在被指派承担船上职责之前均应在船上和岸上（如适合）进行熟悉培训，该培训应由在油类、化学品或液化气体货物（如适合）的操作和特性以及有关的安全程序方面具有经验的合格人员实施。该培训应至少包括以下第 3 段至第 8 段中规定的内容。

规则

3　液货船在港内和海上时管理有关船上人员安全的船舶规章的知识。

健康危害和应采取的预防措施

4　皮肤接触的危害；吸入或意外吞咽货物；所载运货物的有害性质，人员的意外事故和有关的急救；注意事项一览表。

防火和灭火

5　吸烟控制和炊事限制；着火源；防止着火和爆炸；灭火方法；便携式灭火器和固定式灭火装置。

防止污染

6　应遵循的防止空气和水域污染的程序和发生溢漏时应采取的措施。

安全设备及其使用

7　防护服和设备、复苏仪、逃生和救助设备的正确使用。

应急程序

8　熟悉应急计划的程序。

PROOF OF QUALIFICATION

9 The master of every oil, chemical and liquefied gas tanker should ensure that the officer or the person primarily responsible for the cargo possesses the appropriate certificate, issued or endorsed or validated as required by regulation V/1-1, paragraph 3; regulation V/1-1, paragraph 5 or regulation V/1-2, paragraph 3, as appropriate, and has had adequate recent practical experience on board an appropriate type of tanker to permit that officer or person to safely perform the duties assigned.

GUIDANCE REGARDING APPROVED ONBOARD TRAINING

General

10 The purpose of qualifying shipboard service is to provide training and knowledge for the safe carriage of specific tanker cargoes.

11 To satisfy the experience appropriate to their duties on the type of tanker on which they serve referred to in regulation V/1-1, paragraph 4.2.2, regulation V/1-1, paragraph 6.2.2 and regulation V/1-2, paragraph 4.2.2, onboard training should:

.1 emphasize practical "hands on experience" and be related to the employment of the seafarer, i.e. the training of deck and engineering departments may be different;

.2 be under the supervision of personnel qualified and experienced in the handling, characteristics and safety procedures of the cargoes being carried by the vessel;

.3 be on board the tanker carrying products relative to the tanker Certificate of Proficiency/Endorsement being sought and should be such that the specialist equipment is brought into operation but may be on a ballast passage between cargoes for part of that period;

.4 take part in at least three loading and discharge operations*; and

.5 at least cover the matters set out in "Onboard training criteria" in paragraph 19.

12 The onboard training programme must in no way affect the safe running or the seaworthiness of the vessel.

Onboard training programme

13 The trainee should be carried in a supernumerary capacity (i.e. the trainee will have no other duties than that of undertaking the training programme and emergency duties).

* A loading or discharging operation is considered to be the loading or discharge of more than 60% of the total cargo tank capacity of the vessel. Loading/discharges of less than this quantity may be summed together to be equivalent to this quantity.

资格证明

9　每个油船、化学品船和液化气船船长应确保，高级船员或对货物负有主要责任的人员持有按照规则第 V/1-1 条第 3 段、规则第 V/1-1 条第 5 段或规则第 V/1-2 条第 3 段（如适合）的要求签发、签注或生效的相应证书，并已具备在适当类型的液货船上的足够的近期实际经验，以使该高级船员或人员能安全地履行指定的职责。

关于对认可的船上培训的指导

总则

10　取得合格船上服务资历的目的是为特定液货船货物的安全运输提供培训和知识。

11　为满足规则第 V/1-1 条第 4.2.2 段、规则第 V/1-1 条第 6.2.2 段和规则第 V/1-2 条第 4.2.2 段提及的适合船员在其所服务类型的液货船职责的经历，船上培训应：

.1　注重实际的"实操经历"并与海员受雇岗位，即甲板部和轮机部的培训可以有所不同；

.2　受到对船舶所运输的货物作业、特性和安全程序有资格和有经验的人员的监督；

.3　在载有与所申请液货船培训合格证书/签证相关的货物的液货船上进行，并且专用设备应处于使用状态，但可在一段时间内处于不同货物运输间的空载航行中；

.4　参加至少 3 次装货和卸货操作①；并且

.5　至少涵盖第 19 段中"船上培训标准"规定的事项。

12　船上培训计划不得影响船舶安全航行或适航性。

船上培训计划

13　学员应为编外人员，即学员除了执行培训计划和承担应急职责外没有其他职责。

① 一次装货或卸货操作系指装货或卸货超过船舶货舱总容积的 60%。装/卸量低于此数量的，可相加累计达到此数量。

14 The programme of onboard training should be managed and coordinated by the company which manages the ship on which the seagoing service is to be performed and be a vessel nominated by the company as a training vessel.*

15 At all times, the trainee should be aware of two identifiable individuals who are immediately responsible for the management of the programme of onboard training. The first of these is a qualified seagoing officer, referred to as the "shipboard training officer", who, under the authority of the master, should organize and supervise the programme of training. The second should be a person nominated by the company, referred to as the "company training officer", who should have an overall responsibility for the training programme and for coordination with training organizations.

16 The trainee should be provided with an approved training record book to enable a comprehensive record of practical training and experience at sea to be maintained. The approved training record book should be laid out in such a way that it can provide detailed information about the tasks and duties which should be undertaken and the progress towards their completion. Duly completed and countersigned by the master, the approved record book will provide unique evidence that a structured programme of onboard training has been completed leading towards the issue of a relevant Certificate in Advanced Training for Tanker Cargo Operations.

17 During the approved onboard training programme the trainee should be instructed in the loading, discharging, care in transit, handling of cargo, tank cleaning or other cargo-related operations of the tanker to ensure that the experience gained is at least equal to that which would be obtained in three months' normal service.

18 If the three-loading and three-unloading criteria cannot be achieved within the one-month onboard training period, then the period of onboard training should be extended until these criteria have been satisfactorily achieved.

Onboard training criteria

19 The onboard training should at least provide knowledge and experience, relevant to the applicable tanker type, of the following:

.1 Safety

.1.1 All tanker types

.1.1.1 Ship's safety-management system
.1.1.2 Cargo-specific fire-fighting equipment and procedures
.1.1.3 Cargo-specific first-aid procedures, including the Medical First Aid Guide for Use in Accidents involving Dangerous Goods (MFAG)
.1.1.4 Ship-/cargo-specific hazards, including smoking regulations, oxygen-depleted atmospheres, cargo hydrocarbon narcosis and toxicity
.1.1.5 Risk assessment systems

* A nominated training vessel is a trading vessel named by the company that is suitable for the purpose of this guidance, as applicable.

14　船上培训计划应由管理获取海上服务资历的船舶的公司管理和协调,并且该船舶为公司指定的培训船。①

15　学员在任何时候都应知道对船上培训计划管理负直接责任的两个身份明确的人员。一个是有资格的高级船员,称为“船上培训师”,应在船长的领导下组织和管理培训计划。另一个是公司指定的人员,称为“公司培训师”,应对培训计划和培训机构的协调工作负全面责任。

16　应向学员提供一份认可的培训记录薄,以便对海上的实际培训和经历作出全面记录。认可的培训记录薄应以能提供所从事的任务、职责及完成的进展情况的详细信息的方式填写。经正式填写和船长会签,认可的记录薄将作为已完成了系统的船上培训计划的唯一证据,并作为签发相关液货船货物操作高级培训证书的依据。

17　在认可的船上培训计划实施期间,应在装货、卸货、运输中照管货物、货物作业、洗舱或其他货物相关的操作中对学员进行指导,以确保其所获得的经历至少等同于 3 个月的正常服务。

18　如果在一个月船上培训期间不能达到 3 次装货和 3 次卸货标准,则船上培训期应该延期到满意达到此标准为止。

船上培训标准

19　船上培训应至少提供如下与适用的液货船类型相关的知识和经历:

.1　安全

.1.1　所有液货船类型

.1.1.1　船舶安全管理体系

.1.1.2　与货物相关的消防设备和程序

.1.1.3　与货物相关的急救程序,包括《危险货物事故医疗急救指南》(MFAG)

.1.1.4　与船舶/货物相关的危害,包括吸烟规则、氧耗、货物烃麻醉性和毒性

.1.1.5　风险评估体系

① 指定的培训船是由适合本指导目的的公司指定的营运船舶,如适用。

.1.1.6 Permit to work, including hot work and enclosed spaces entry procedures
.1.1.7 Use of personal protective equipment

.1.2 Additional for liquefied gas tankers

.1.2.1 Dangers and precautions related to handling and storage of cargoes at cryogenic temperatures

.2 Construction, cargo, cargo tanks and pipelines

.2.1 All tanker types

.2.1.1 Hull/tank construction and limitations
.2.1.2 Cargo connections
.2.1.3 Properties and hazards associated with the types of cargo being carried, including use of Material Safety Data Sheets
.2.1.4 The risks that cargo operations (such as purging/gas-freeing/tank cleaning) may have on the accommodation ventilation systems and actions to mitigate these risks
.2.1.5 Configuration of cargo and ballast system
.2.1.6 Pumps and associated equipment
.2.1.7 Specialist equipment associated with the cargo operations
.2.1.8 Particulars of the tanker's construction and how this affects the cargo operations

.2.2 Additional for liquefied gas tankers

.2.2.1 Use of segregation, separation and airlocks to maintain gas-safe areas
.2.2.2 Cargo tank, inter-barrier, insulation spaces, and pipeline relief valves and vapour venting systems
.2.2.3 Cargo vapour compressors and associated equipment

.3 Trim and stability

.3.1 All tanker types

.3.1.1 Tanker's stability information and calculating equipment
.3.1.2 Importance of maintaining stress levels within acceptable limits
.3.1.3 Dangers of free surface effect and "sloshing" effect

.4 Cargo operations

.4.1 All tanker types

.4.1.1 Pre-planning of loading/in-transit care, discharge/ballast operations
.4.1.2 Record keeping
.4.1.3 Start up/stopping procedures, including emergency shutdown
.4.1.4 Attention required for mooring arrangements during cargo operations
.4.1.5 Purging and inerting requirements and associated hazards
.4.1.6 Loading cargo, including topping-off operations

.1.1.6　作业许可,包括热工作业和进入封闭处所程序

.1.1.7　个人防护设备的使用

.1.2　液化气船的附加要求

.1.2.1　与低温货物作业和储藏相关的危险和预防措施

.2　结构、货物、货舱和管系

.2.1　所有液货船类型

.2.1.1　船体/液舱的结构和局限性

.2.1.2　货物连接

.2.1.3　与所载运货物类型相关的性质和危害,包括使用《化学品安全说明书》

.2.1.4　货物操作(如驱气/除气/洗舱)可能对生活区通风系统造成的风险,以及降低这些风险的措施

.2.1.5　货物和压载系统的配置

.2.1.6　泵及相关设备

.2.1.7　与货物操作相关的专用设备

.2.1.8　液货船构造细节及其对货物操作的影响

.2.2　液化气船的附加要求

.2.2.1　使用隔离、分隔和气锁来保持气体安全区域

.2.2.2　货舱、舱内分隔装置、隔离舱室及管线泄压阀和蒸气排气系统

.2.2.3　货物蒸气压缩机及相关设备

.3　吃水差和稳性

.3.1　所有液货船类型

.3.1.1　液货船稳性资料和计算设备

.3.1.2　维持可接受限度的强度水平的重要性

.3.1.3　自由液面效应和“晃动”效应的危险

.4　货物操作

.4.1　所有液货船类型

.4.1.1　装货/运输中照管货物、卸货/压载操作的预先计划

.4.1.2　记录的保持

.4.1.3　启动/停止程序,包括紧急关闭

.4.1.4　在货物操作期间系泊安排要求的注意事项

.4.1.5　驱气和惰化要求及相关危害

.4.1.6　装货,包括平舱操作

.4.1.7 Discharging cargo, including draining and stripping operations
.4.1.8 Monitoring of cargo during loading/discharging operations, including sampling where applicable
.4.1.9 Tank gauging and alarm systems
.4.1.10 Dangers from electrostatic discharge and its prevention
.4.1.11 Ballasting and deballasting operations
.4.1.12 Maintenance requirements, including coating inspections

.4.2 Additional for chemical tankers

.4.2.1 Polymerization, cargo compatibility, tank coating compatibility and other reactions
.4.2.2 Functions of inhibitors and catalysts
.4.2.3 Vapour/gas dispersion

.4.3 Additional for liquefied gas tankers

.4.3.1 Polymerization, cargo compatibility, tank coating compatibility and other reactions
.4.3.2 Functions of inhibitors and catalysts
.4.3.3 Causes of backpressure and pressure surge effects
.4.3.4 Use of boil-off gas as a fuel
.4.3.5 Vapour/gas dispersion
.4.3.6 Purging and cool-down operations
.4.3.7 Operation and maintenance of re-liquefaction equipment
.4.3.8 Understanding and use of the custody transfer system

.4.4 Additional for oil tankers

.4.4.1 Crude oil washing systems

.5 Tank washing/cleaning

.5.1 All tanker types

.5.1.1 Tank cleaning systems and equipment fitted on the tanker
.5.1.2 Pre-planning of tank washing/cleaning operations
.5.1.3 Tank washing procedures, including purging and inerting
.5.1.4 Control of slops/waste product
.5.1.5 Electro-static hazards
.5.1.6 Cleanliness requirements
.5.1.7 Maintenance requirements

.5.2 Additional for chemical tankers

.5.2.1 Removal of inhibitors and residues
.5.2.2 Use of absorption, cleaning agents and detergents

.5.3 Additional for liquefied gas tankers

.5.3.1 Hot-gassing/boil-off of liquid residues and regassification process

.4.1.7 卸货,包括排残和扫舱操作
.4.1.8 装载/卸载操作时货物的监管,如可行,包括取样
.4.1.9 货舱计量和报警系统
.4.1.10 静电危害及其预防
.4.1.11 压载和排压载操作
.4.1.12 保养要求,包括涂层检查

.4.2 化学品船的附加要求
.4.2.1 聚合、货物兼容性、货舱涂层兼容性和其他反应
.4.2.2 抑制剂和催化剂的功能
.4.2.3 蒸气/气体扩散

.4.3 液化气船的附加要求
.4.3.1 聚合、货物兼容性、货舱涂层兼容性和其他反应
.4.3.2 抑制剂和催化剂的功能
.4.3.3 背压原因和压力剧增效应
.4.3.4 蒸发气体作为燃料的使用
.4.3.5 蒸气/气体扩散
.4.3.6 驱气和冷却操作
.4.3.7 再液化设备的操作和保养
.4.3.8 监护驳运系统的理解和使用

.4.4 油船的附加要求
.4.4.1 原油洗舱系统

.5 洗舱/清洗

.5.1 所有液货船类型
.5.1.1 安装于液货船上的洗舱系统和设备
.5.1.2 洗舱/清洗操作的预先计划
.5.1.3 洗舱程序,包括驱气和惰化
.5.1.4 污油水/废液控制
.5.1.5 静电危害
.5.1.6 清洁要求
.5.1.7 保养要求

.5.2 化学品船的附加要求
.5.2.1 去除抑制剂和残留物
.5.2.2 使用吸收剂、清洁剂和洗涤剂

.5.3 液化气船的附加要求
.5.3.1 加热/蒸发液体残留物和重新气化过程

.6 Inert gas systems

.6.1 All tanker types

.6.1.1 Inerting system(s) and equipment fitted to the tanker
.6.1.2 Hazards associated with inerting of spaces, with particular reference to safe entry into tanks
.6.1.3 Purging, maintaining inert atmosphere and gas-freeing operations
.6.1.4 Maintenance requirements

.7 Pollution prevention and control

.7.1 All tanker types

.7.1.1 International, flag State and company regulations, documentation and plans
.7.1.2 Operation of the tanker's pollution-prevention systems and equipment, including discharge monitoring
.7.1.3 Operation of the tanker's pollution-containment equipment

.8 Gas-detection equipment and instruments

.8.1 All tanker types

.8.1.1 Use and calibration of personal, portable and fixed gas analysers, with particular reference to oxygen and hydrocarbon monitoring equipment
.8.1.2 Operation, maintenance and limitation of cargo tank level measuring, level alarm and temperature-measuring systems

.8.2 Additional for liquefied gas tankers

.8.2.1 Operation and maintenance of hull temperature measurement

.9 Publications

.9.1 All tanker types

.9.1.1 International, flag State and company publications relevant to the operation of the tanker, including SOLAS, MARPOL and applicable guidance manuals
.9.1.2 Operating and maintenance manuals specific to the equipment on board
.9.1.3 Established industrial standards and code of safe working practice (e.g., ICS, OCIMF, SIGTTO)

.6 惰气系统

.6.1 所有液货船类型

.6.1.1 安装于液货船上的惰气系统和设备

.6.1.2 与惰化区特别是与安全进入液货舱相关的危害

.6.1.3 驱气、保持惰性环境和除气操作

.6.1.4 保养要求

.7 污染预防与控制

.7.1 所有液货船类型

.7.1.1 国际的、船旗国的和船公司的规则、文件和计划

.7.1.2 液货船防污染系统和设备的操作,包括卸货监管

.7.1.3 液货船污染围护设备的操作

.8 气体探测设备和仪器

.8.1 所有液货船类型

.8.1.1 个人、便携式和固定式气体分析仪的使用和校准,特别是涉及氧气和烃类气体的监测设备

.8.1.2 货舱液位测量、液位报警和温度测量系统的操作、维护和局限性

.8.2 液化气船的附加要求

.8.2.1 船体温度测量的操作和维护

.9 出版物

.9.1 所有液货船类型

.9.1.1 与液货船操作有关的国际的、船旗国的和船公司的出版物,包括《SOLAS 公约》、《MARPOL 公约》和适用的指导手册

.9.1.2 船上设备的操作和维护手册

.9.1.3 既定的行业标准和安全工作做法的规则(例如 ICS、OCIMF 和 SIGTTO)

Section B-V/1-1

Guidance regarding training and qualifications of masters, officers and ratings on oil and chemical tankers

OIL TANKER TRAINING

20 The training required by paragraphs 2.2 and 4.3 of regulation V/1-1 in respect of oil tankers should be set out in a training plan which clearly expresses, for all parties involved, the objectives of the training. Training may be given on board or ashore, where appropriate. It should be supplemented by practical instruction on board and, where appropriate, in a suitable shore-based installation. All training and instruction should be given by properly qualified and suitably experienced personnel*.

21 As much use as possible should be made of shipboard operation and equipment manuals, films and suitable visual aids, and the opportunity should be taken to introduce discussion of the part to be played by the safety organization on board ship and the role of safety officers and safety committees.

CHEMICAL TANKER TRAINING

22 The training required by paragraphs 2.2 and 6.3 of regulation V/1-1 in respect of chemical tankers should be set out in a training plan which clearly expresses, for all parties involved, the objectives of the training. Training may be given on board or ashore, where appropriate. It should be supplemented by practical instruction on board and, where appropriate, in a suitable shore-based installation. All training and instruction should be given by properly qualified and suitably experienced personnel*.

23 As much use as possible should be made of shipboard operation and equipment manuals, films and suitable visual aids, and the opportunity should be taken to introduce discussion of the part to be played by the safety organization on board ship and the role of safety officers and safety committees.

Section B-V/1-2

Guidance regarding training and qualifications of masters, officers and ratings on liquefied gas tankers

24 The training required by paragraphs 2.2 and 4.3 of regulation V/1-2 in respect of liquefied gas tankers should be set out in a training plan which clearly expresses, for all parties involved, the objectives of the training. Training may be given on board or ashore, where appropriate. It should be supplemented by practical instruction on board and, where appropriate, in a suitable shore-based installation. All training and instruction should be given by properly qualified and suitably experienced personnel*.

25 As much use as possible should be made of shipboard operation and equipment manuals, films and suitable visual aids, and the opportunity should be taken to introduce discussion of the part to be played by the safety organization on board ship and the role of safety officers and safety committees.

* The relevant IMO Model Course(s) may be of assistance in the preparation of courses.

第 B-V/1-1 节
关于对油船和化学品船船长、高级船员和普通船员培训和资格的指导

油船培训

20 规则第 V/1-1 条第 2.2 段和第 4.3 段要求的油船培训应在培训计划中规定，该计划向相关各方清楚地表明培训目的。培训可在船上或岸上（如适当）进行，并且应由船上的实际训练和视情况合适的岸基设施的实际训练作为补充。所有的培训和训练均应由有适当资格和经验的人员负责实施①。

21 应尽可能地采用船上操作和设备手册、影片和适当的视觉辅助材料，并利用时机对船上的安全组织所起的作用和安全官员与安全委员会的作用进行讨论。

化学品船培训

22 规则第 V/1-1 条第 2.2 段和第 6.3 段要求的化学品船培训应在培训计划中规定，该计划向相关各方清楚地表明培训目的。培训可在船上或岸上（如适当）进行，并且应由船上的实际训练和视情况合适的岸基设施的实际训练作为补充。所有的培训和训练均应由有适当资格和经验的人员负责实施①。

23 应尽可能地采用船上操作和设备手册、影片和适当的视觉辅助材料，并利用时机对船上安全组织所起的作用和安全官员与安全委员会的作用进行讨论。

第 B-V/1-2 节
关于对液化气船船长、高级船员和普通船员培训和资格的指导

24 规则第 V/1-2 条第 2.2 段和第 4.3 段要求的液化气船培训应在培训计划中规定，该计划向相关各方清楚地表明培训目的。培训可在船上或岸上（如适当）进行，并且应由船上的实际训练和视情况合适的岸基设施的实际训练作为补充。所有的培训和训练均应由有适当资格和经验的人员负责实施①。

25 应尽可能采用船上操作和设备手册、影片和适当的视觉辅助材料，并利用时机对船上安全组织所起的作用和安全官员与安全委员会的作用进行讨论。

① 相关 IMO 示范培训课程可有助于准备课程。

Section B-V/2
Guidance regarding training of seafarers on passenger ships

ENHANCED FIRE FIGHTING

1 For officers and crew on passenger ships, additional training should be provided highlighting the difficulties of fighting fires, including access to confined spaces and prevention of the spread of fire to adjoining spaces.

DAMAGE CONTROL

2 In developing standards of competency given in sections A-II/1, A-II/2 and A-III/2 to achieve the necessary level of theoretical knowledge, understanding and proficiency in damage control and watertight integrity, companies and training institutions should take into account the minimum knowledge, understanding and proficiency for damage control and watertight integrity as given below:

Competence

Minimize the risk of flooding and maintain a state of readiness to respond to emergency situations involving damage to the watertight integrity of the ship.

Knowledge, understanding and proficiency

Shipboard damage control plans and organization.

Damage control systems, equipment (lockers) and emergency escape routes

The key elements in maintaining stability and watertight integrity.

Importance of securing flooding and maintaining watertight boundaries.

Actions to be taken aboard a ship in the event of an explosion, grounding, collision, or fire

Damage control techniques consistent with equipment found on board including the ship bilge systems and pumps.

Section B-V/a*
Guidance regarding additional training for masters and chief mates of large ships and ships with unusual manoeuvring characteristics

1 It is important that masters and chief mates should have had relevant experience and training before assuming the duties of master or chief mate of large ships or ships having unusual manoeuvring and handling characteristics significantly different from those in which they have recently served. Such characteristics will generally be found in ships which are of considerable deadweight or length or of special design or of high speed.

* Note there are no corresponding regulations in the Convention or sections in part A of the Code for Section B-V/a, B-V/b, B-V/c, B-V/d, B-V/e, B-V/f and B-V/g.

第 B-V/2 节

关于对客船船员培训的指导

消防强化培训

1　对客船的高级船员和一般船员，应提供附加培训以突出消防的困难，其中包括进入受限舱室、防止火灾蔓延到相邻舱室。

破损控制

2　在制定为达到第 A-II/1 节、第 A-II/2 节和 第 A-III/2 节中给出的有关破损控制和水密完整性的理论知识、理解和熟练所需水平的适任标准时，公司和培训机构应考虑如下的关于破损控制和水密完整性的最低的知识、理解和熟练：

适任

将进水的风险减至最小，并对涉及船舶水密完整性损害的紧急情况保持戒备状态。

知识、理解和熟练

船舶破损控制计划和组织。

破损控制系统、设备(锁闭装置)和紧急逃生路线

保持稳性和水密完整性的关键因素。

防止进水和维持水密边界的重要性。

发生爆炸、搁浅、碰撞或火灾时船上应采取的行动

与船上设备(包括舱底污水系统和泵)相应的破损控制技术。

第 B-V/a 节①

关于对大型船舶和特殊操纵性能船舶的船长和大副附加培训的指导

1　船长或大副在大型船舶上任职之前，或在明显不同于他们最近服务的并具有特殊操纵和操作性能的船舶上任职之前，应具有相应的经验和培训，这是十分重要的。这种特殊操纵性能通常属于具有相当大的载重吨或长度或特殊设计的或高速的船舶。

① 公约或规则 A 部分的节中没有关于第 B-V/a, B-V/b, B-V/c, B-V/d, B-V/e, B-V/f 和 B-V/g 节的相应规定。

2 Prior to their appointment to such a ship, masters and chief mates should:

.1 be informed of the ship's handling characteristics by the company, particularly in relation to the knowledge, understanding and proficiency listed under ship manoeuvring and handling in column 2 of table A-II/2 Specification of the minimum standard of competence for masters and chief mates on ships of 500 gross tonnage or more; and

.2 be made thoroughly familiar with the use of all navigational and manoeuvring aids fitted in the ship concerned, including their capabilities and limitations.

3 Before initially assuming command of one of the ships referred to above, the prospective master should have sufficient and appropriate general experience as master or chief mate, and either:

.1 have sufficient and appropriate experience manoeuvring the same ship under supervision or in manoeuvring a ship having similar manoeuvring characteristics; or

.2 have attended an approved ship handling simulator course on an installation capable of simulating the manoeuvring characteristics of such a ship.*

4 The additional training and qualifications of masters and chief mates of dynamically supported and high-speed craft should be in accordance with the relevant guidelines of the IMO Code of Safety for Dynamically Supported Craft and the IMO International Codes of Safety for High-Speed Craft (1994 HSC Code and 2000 HSC Code), as appropriate.

Section B-V/b**

Guidance regarding training of officers and ratings responsible for cargo handling on ships carrying dangerous and hazardous substances in solid form in bulk

1 Training should be divided into two parts, a general part on the principles involved and a part on the application of such principles to ship operation. All training and instruction should be given by properly qualified and suitably experienced personnel and cover at least the subjects given in paragraphs 2 to 14 hereunder.

PRINCIPLES

Characteristics and properties

2 The important physical characteristics and chemical properties of dangerous and hazardous substances, sufficient to give a basic understanding of the intrinsic hazards and risks involved.

Classification of materials possessing chemical hazards

3 IMO dangerous goods classes 4 to 9 and the hazards associated with each class; and materials hazardous only in bulk (MHB) outlined in the International Maritime Solid Bulk Cargoes (IMSBC) Code.

* The relevant IMO Model Course(s) may be of assistance in the preparation of courses.

** Note there are no corresponding regulations in the Convention or sections in part A of the Code for Section B-V/a, B-V/b, B-V/c, B-V/d, B-V/e, B-V/f and B-V/g.

2　在被选派到这种船上任职之前，船长和大副应：

.1　由公司告知其船舶操作特性，尤其是关于表 A-II/2（500 总吨或以上船舶的船长和大副的最低适任标准）第 2 栏列出的船舶操纵和操作的知识、理解和熟练的内容；并且

.2　使其完全熟知在相关船上装设的所有助航设备和操纵设备的使用，包括其性能和局限性。

3　在上述某一船舶上初次担任指挥之前，未来的船长应具有足够的和相应的作为船长或大副的一般经验，并且：

.1　具有在监督之下操纵相同船舶或操纵具有相似操纵特性船舶的足够和相应的经验；或

.2　已在能模拟这种船舶操纵特性的装置上参加了认可的船舶操作模拟器课程。①

4　动力支撑和高速船艇的船长和大副的附加培训和资格，应视情况符合 IMO《动力支撑船艇安全规则》及 IMO《国际高速船（HSC）安全规则》（1994 HSC 规则和 2000 HSC 规则）的有关指南。

第 B-V/b 节②

关于对在载运散装固体危险和有害物质的船上负责货物作业的高级船员和普通船员培训的指导

1　培训应分成两个部分，即有关原理的基础部分和这些原理在船舶操作上的应用部分。所有的培训和训练均应由有适当资格和经验的人员进行，并且至少包括以下第 2 段至第 14 段列出的科目。

原理

特性和性质

2　危险和有害物质的重要物理特性和化学性质，对其固有危害和有关危险有足够的基本的理解。

具有化学危害性的物质的分类

3　IMO 第 4 类至第 9 类危险货物及与各类有关的危害性和列于《国际海运固体散装货物（IMSBC）规则》中的仅在散装时有危害的物质（MHB）。

① 相关 IMO 示范培训课程可有助于准备课程。

② 公约或规则 A 部分的节中没有关于第 B-V/a，B-V/b，B-V/c，B-V/d，B-V/e，B-V/f 和 B-V/g 节的相应规定。

Health hazards

4 Dangers from skin contact, inhalation, ingestion and radiation.

Conventions, regulations and recommendations

5 General familiarization with the relevant requirements of chapters II-2 and VII of the 1974 SOLAS Convention, as amended.

6 General use of and familiarization with the International Maritime Solid Bulk Cargoes (IMSBC) Code, with particular reference to:

.1 safety of personnel, including safety equipment, measuring instruments, their use and practical application and interpretation of results;

.2 hazards from cargoes which have a tendency to shift; and

.3 materials possessing chemical hazards.

SHIPBOARD APPLICATION

Class 4.1 Flammable solids
Class 4.2 Substances liable to spontaneous combustion
Class 4.3 Substances which, in contact with water, emit flammable gases

7 Carriage, stowage and control of temperature to prevent decomposition and possible explosion; stowage categories; general stowage precautions, including those applicable to self-reactive and related substances; segregation requirements to prevent heating and ignition; the emission of poisonous or flammable gases and the formation of explosive mixtures.

Class 5.1 Oxidizing substances

8 Carriage, stowage and control of temperature to prevent decomposition and possible explosion; stowage categories; general stowage precautions and segregation requirements to ensure separation from combustible material, from acids and heat sources to prevent fire, explosion and the formation of toxic gases.

Class 6.1 Toxic substances

9 Contamination of foodstuffs, working areas and living accommodation and ventilation.

Class 7 Radioactive material

10 Transport index; types of ores and concentrates; stowage and segregation from persons, undeveloped photographic film and plates and foodstuffs; stowage categories; general stowage requirements; special stowage requirements; segregation requirements and separation distances; segregation from other dangerous goods.

Class 8 Corrosive substances

11 Dangers from wetted substances.

健康危害

4　皮肤接触、吸入、摄入和放射性产生的危险。

公约、规则及建议

5　基本熟悉经修正的《1974 年 SOLAS 公约》中第 II-2 章和第 VII 章的有关要求。

6　一般熟悉和基本应用《国际海运固体散装货物(IMSBC)规则》,特别关于:

.1　人员的安全,包括安全设备、测量仪器及其使用、实际应用及对结果的解释:

.2　具有移动倾向的货物的危害;以及

.3　具有化学危害性的物质。

船上应用

第 4.1 类——易燃固体

第 4.2 类——易自燃物质

第 4.3 类——与水接触放出易燃气体的物质

7　载运、积载和控制温度以防止分解和可能引起的爆炸;积载类;包括那些适用于自行反应和相关物质在内的一般积载的预防措施;为防止发热和着火的隔离要求;有毒或易燃气体的散发和爆炸混合物的形成。

第 5.1 类——氧化物质

8　载运、积载和温度控制以防止分解和可能引起的爆炸;积载类;一般积载的预防措施和隔离要求以确保与可燃物质、酸和热源隔离,目的是防止着火、爆炸和毒性气体的形成。

第 6.1 类——有毒物质

9　对食物、工作区和居住处所的污染及通风。

第 7 类——放射性物质

10　运输指数;矿砂和精矿种类;积载和与人、未经显影的胶片及底片以及食品的隔离;积载类;一般积载要求;特殊积载要求;隔离要求和分隔距离;与其他危险货物的隔离。

第 8 类——腐蚀性物质

11　受潮物质引起的危险。

Class 9 Miscellaneous dangerous substances and articles

12 Examples and associated hazards; the hazards of materials hazardous only in bulk (IMSBC Code); general and specific stowage precautions; working and transport precautions; segregation requirements.

Safety precautions and emergency procedures

13 Electrical safety in cargo spaces; precautions to be taken for entry into enclosed spaces that may contain oxygen-depleted, poisonous or flammable atmospheres; the possible effects of fire in shipments of substances of each class; use of the Emergency Response Procedures for Ships Carrying Dangerous Goods; emergency plans and procedures to be followed in case of incidents involving dangerous and hazardous substances and the use of individual entries in the International Maritime Solid Bulk Cargoes (IMSBC) Code, as appropriate, in this respect.

Medical first aid

14 The IMO Medical First Aid Guide for Use in Accidents Involving Dangerous Goods (MFAG) and its use and application in association with other guides and medical advice by radio.

Section B-V/c*

Guidance regarding training of officers and ratings responsible for cargo handling on ships carrying dangerous and hazardous substances in packaged form

1 Training should be divided into two parts, a general part on the principles involved and a part on the application of such principles to ship operation. All training and instruction should be given by properly qualified and suitably experienced personnel and cover at least the subjects given in paragraphs 2 to 19 hereunder.

PRINCIPLES

Characteristics and properties

2 The important physical characteristics and chemical properties of dangerous and hazardous substances, sufficient to give a basic understanding of the intrinsic hazards and risks involved.

Classification of dangerous and hazardous substances and materials possessing chemical hazards

3 IMO dangerous goods classes 1 to 9 and the hazards associated with each class.

Health hazards

4 Dangers from skin contact, inhalation, ingestion and radiation.

---

* Note there are no corresponding regulations in the Convention or sections in part A of the Code for sections B-V/a, B-V/b, B-V/c, B-V/d, B-V/e, B-V/f and B-V/g.

第 9 类——杂项危险物质和物品

12 实例和相关危害;仅在散装时有危险物质(IMSBC 规则)的危害;一般和特殊积载的预防措施;工作和运输的预防措施;隔离要求。

安全预防措施和应急程序

13 货物处所内的电气安全;进入可能包括缺氧、有毒或易燃舱气在内的封闭处所应采取的预防措施;船舶载运各类物质时火灾可能引起的后果;船舶《载运危险货物应急反应措施》的应用;危险和有害物质发生意外事故时应遵循的应急计划和程序,以及《国际海运散装固体货物(IMSBC)规则》个别条文在这方面的应用,如适用。

医疗急救

14 IMO《危险货物事故医疗急救指南》(MFAG)及其应用,以及结合其他指南和无线电医疗咨询的运用。

第 B-V/c 节①

关于对在载运包装危险和有害物质的船上负责货物作业的高级船员和普通船员培训的指导

1 培训应分成两个部分,即有关原理的基础部分和这些原理在船舶操作上的应用部分。所有的培训和训练均应由有适当资格和经验的人员进行,并且至少包括以下第 2 段至第 19 段列出的科目。

原理

特性和性质

2 危险和有害物质的重要物理特性和化学性质;对其固有危害和有关危险有足够的基本的理解。

危险和有害物质及具有化学危害性的物质的分类

3 IMO 第 1 类至第 9 类危险货物以及与各类有关的危害性。

健康危害

4 皮肤接触、吸入、摄入和放射性的产生危险。

① 公约或规则 A 部分的节中没有关于第 B-V/a, B-V/b, B-V/c, B-V/d, B-V/e, B-V/f 和 B-V/g 节的相应规定。

Conventions, regulations and recommendations

5 General familiarization with the relevant requirements of chapters II-2 and VII of the 1974 SOLAS Convention and of Annex III of MARPOL 73/78, including its implementation through the IMDG Code.

Use of and familiarization with the International Maritime Dangerous Goods (IMDG) Code

6 General knowledge of the requirements of the IMDG Code concerning declaration, documentation, packing, labelling and placarding; freight container and vehicle packing; portable tanks, tank containers and road tank vehicles, and other transport units used for dangerous substances.

7 Knowledge of identification, marking and labelling for stowage, securing, separation a segregation in different ship types mentioned in the IMDG Code.

8 Safety of personnel, including safety equipment, measuring instruments, their use a practical application and the interpretation of results.

SHIPBOARD APPLICATION

Class 1 Explosives

9 The six hazard divisions and 13 compatibility groups; packagings and magazines used for carriage of explosives; structural serviceability of freight containers and vehicles; stowage provisions, including specific arrangements for on-deck and under-deck stowage; segregation from dangerous goods of other classes within class 1 and from non-dangerous goods; transport and stowage on passenger ships; suitability of cargo spaces; security precautions; precautions to be taken during loading and unloading.

Class 2 Gases (compressed, liquefied, or dissolved under pressure), flammable, non-flammable, non-toxic and toxic

10 Types of pressure vessels and portable tanks, including relief and closing devices used; stowage categories; general stowage precautions, including those for flammable and poisonous gases and gases which are marine pollutants.

Class 3 Flammable liquids

11 Packagings, tank containers, portable tanks and road tank vehicles; stowage categories, including the specific requirements for plastics receptacles; general stowage precautions, including those for marine pollutants; segregation requirements; precautions to be taken when carrying flammable liquids at elevated temperatures.

Class 4.1 Flammable solids
Class 4.2 Substances liable to spontaneous combustion
Class 4.3 Substances which, in contact with water, emit flammable gases

12 Types of packagings; carriage and stowage under controlled temperatures to prevent decomposition and possible explosion; stowage categories; general stowage precautions,including those applicable to self-reactive and related substances, desensitized explosives and marine pollutants; segregation requirements to prevent heating and ignition, the emission of poisonous or flammable gases and the formation of explosive mixtures.

公约、规则和建议

5　基本熟悉《1974 年 SOLAS 公约》第 II-2 章和第 VII 章以及 MARPOL 73/78 附则 III 的有关要求，包括通过《IMDG 规则》对其的执行。

熟悉和运用《国际海运危险货物(IMDG)规则》

6　《IMDG 规则》的有关申报、单证、包装、标志和标牌等要求的基本知识；货物集装箱和车辆装载；可移动罐柜、罐式箱、公路罐车以及用于运输危险物质的其他组件。
7　《IMDG 规则》中提及的不同类型船舶的积载、系固、分隔和隔离的识别、标记和标志的知识。
8　人员安全，包括安全设备、测量仪器及其使用、实际应用以及对结果的解释。

船上的应用

第 1 类——爆炸品

9　6 种危险类别和 13 种配装类；载运爆炸品用的包装和弹药舱；货物集装箱和货车的结构适用性；包括舱面和舱内积载的特殊布置在内的积载规定；与第 1 类内其他类别危险货物以及与非危险货物的隔离；在客船上运输和积载；装货处所的适用性；安全预防措施；在装卸期间应采取的预防措施。

第 2 类——气体(压缩、液化或压力下溶解的)，易燃、非易燃、无毒和有毒

10　压力容器和可移动罐柜的类型，包括其所用的安全释放装置和关闭装置；积载类；包括那些易燃和有毒气体以及属于海洋污染物的气体在内的一般积载预防措施。

第 3 类——易燃液体

11　包装、罐式箱、可移动罐柜和公路罐车；积载类，包括对塑料容器的特殊要求；包括海洋污染物在内的一般积载预防措施；隔离要求；在高温下载运易燃液体时应采取的预防措施。

第 4.1 类——易燃固体
第 4.2 类——易自燃物质
第 4.3 类——与水接触放出易燃气体的物质

12　包装类型；为防止分解和可能的爆炸而在控制温度下的运输和积载；积载类；包括适用于自行反应和相关物质、不敏感爆炸品和海洋污染物在内的一般积载预防措施；为防止发热和着火、有毒或可燃气体的散发和爆炸混合物的形成的隔离要求。

Class 5.1 Oxidizing substances
Class 5.2 Organic peroxides

13 Types of packagings; carriage and stowage under controlled temperatures to prevent decomposition and possible explosion; stowage categories; general stowage precautions, including those applicable to marine pollutants; segregation requirements to ensure separation from combustible material, from acids and heat sources to prevent fire, explosion and the formation of toxic gases; precautions to minimize friction and impact which can initiate decomposition.

Class 6.1 Toxic substances
Class 6.2 Infectious substances

14 Types of packagings; stowage categories; general stowage precautions, including those applicable to toxic, flammable liquids and marine pollutants; segregation requirements, especially considering that the characteristic common to these substances is their ability to cause death or serious injury to human health; decontamination measures in the event of spillage.

Class 7 Radioactive material

15 Types of packagings; transport index in relation to stowage and segregation; stowage and segregation from persons, undeveloped photographic film and plates and foodstuffs; stowage categories; general stowage requirements; segregation requirements and separation distances; segregation from other dangerous goods.

Class 8 Corrosive substances

16 Types of packagings; stowage categories; general stowage precautions, including those applicable to corrosive, flammable liquids and marine pollutants; segregation requirements, especially considering that the characteristic common to these substances is their ability to cause severe damage to living tissue.

Class 9 Miscellaneous dangerous substances and articles

17 Examples of hazards, including marine pollution.

Safety precautions and emergency procedures

18 Electrical safety in cargo spaces; precautions to be taken for entry into enclosed spaces that may contain oxygen-depleted, poisonous or flammable atmospheres; the possible effects of spillage or fire in shipments of substances of each class; consideration of events on deck or below deck; use of the IMO Emergency Response Procedures for Ships Carrying Dangerous Goods; emergency plans and procedures to be followed in case of incidents involving dangerous substances.

Medical first aid

19 The IMO Medical First Aid Guide for Use in Accidents Involving Dangerous Goods (MFAG) and its use and application in association with other guides and medical advice by radio.

第 5.1 类——氧化物质
第 5.2 类——有机过氧化物

13　包装类型；为防止分解和可能的爆炸而在控制温度下的运输和积载；积载类；包括适用于海洋污染物在内的一般积载预防措施；为确保与可燃物质、酸和热源隔离，防止着火、爆炸和有毒气体形成的隔离要求；减少能产生分解的摩擦和撞击的措施。

第 6.1 类——有毒物质
第 6.2 类——感染性物质

14　包装类型；积载类；包括适用于有毒、易燃液体和海洋污染物在内的一般积载预防措施；隔离要求，特别要考虑这些物质的共性是能够引起死亡或严重损害人类健康；在溢漏时清除污染的措施。

第 7 类——放射性物质

15　包装类型；与积载和隔离有关的运输指数；积载和与人员、未经显影的胶片及底片以及食品的隔离；积载类；一般积载要求；隔离要求和分隔距离；与其他危险货物的隔离。

第 8 类——腐蚀性物质

16　包装类型；积载类；包括适用于腐蚀性、易燃液体和海洋污染物在内的一般积载预防措施；隔离要求，特别要考虑这些物质的共性是能够对活体组织引起严重损害。

第 9 类——杂项危险物质和物品

17　包括海洋污染物在内的危害性举例。

安全预防措施和应急程序

18　货物处所内的电气安全；进入可能包括缺氧、有毒或有易燃舱气在内的封闭处所应采取的预防措施；船舶载运各类物质时溢漏或火灾可能引起的后果；对舱面和舱内发生有关情况的考虑；IMO《船舶载运危险货物应急反应措施》的应用；一旦发生涉及危险物质的事故时应遵循的应急计划和程序。

医疗急救

19　IMO《危险货物事故医疗急救指南》（MFAG）及其应用，以及结合其他指南和无线电医疗咨询的运用。

Section B-V/d*

Guidance on application of the provisions of the STCW Convention to mobile offshore units (MOUs)

1 The provisions of the STCW Convention apply to the maritime personnel of self-propelled MOUs proceeding on voyages.

2 The provisions of the STCW Convention do not apply to non-self-propelled MOUs or to MOUs on station.

3 When considering appropriate standards of training and certification when an MOU is on station, the country of registry should take account of relevant IMO recommendations. In particular, all maritime crew members on self-propelled MOUs and, where required, on other units should meet the requirements of the STCW Convention, as amended.

4 Self-propelled MOUs proceeding on international voyages are required to carry safe manning documents.

5 MOUs on station are subject to the national legislation of the coastal State in whose Exclusive Economic Zone (EEZ) they are operating. Such coastal States should also take account of relevant IMO recommendations and should not prescribe higher standards for MOUs registered in other countries than the standards applied to MOUs registered in that coastal State.

6 All special personnel employed on board MOUs (whether or not self-propelled) should be provided with appropriate familiarization and basic training in accordance with relevant IMO recommendations.

Section B-V/e*

Guidance regarding training and qualifications of masters and officers in charge of a navigational watch on board offshore supply vessels

1 It is important that masters and officers involved in offshore supply operations should have relevant experience or training before assuming their duties on offshore supply vessels. The focus should be on onboard operational experience or a combination of operational experience and simulator training.

2 Masters and officers should understand the unique manoeuvring and handling characteristics common to offshore supply vessels.

3 Prior to performing offshore supply operations, the master and officers should:

.1 have knowledge of the offshore industry and the terms used in the various operations;

.2 understand the importance of maintaining a safe working distance at all times when working in an offshore location/installation;

.3 have knowledge of vessel manoeuvring and station-keeping under various weather conditions;

* Note there are no corresponding regulations in the Convention or sections in part A of the Code for sections B-V/a, B-V/b, B-V/c, B-V/d, B-V/e, B-V/f and B-V/g.

第 B-V/d 节[①]

关于对《STCW 公约》的规定适用于海上移动平台(MOUs)的指导

1 《STCW 公约》的规定适用于航行期间的自推进式海上移动平台上的海上人员。

2 《STCW 公约》的规定不适用于非自推进式海上移动平台或就位后的海上移动平台。

3 当考虑海上移动平台就位后的培训和发证的适当标准时,登记国应参考 IMO 的相关建议。特别是,工作于自推进式海上移动平台,或有此要求的其他平台上的所有海员,应符合经修正的《STCW 公约》的要求。

4 自推进式海上移动平台在国际航线航行时要求备有安全配员证书。

5 就位后的海上移动平台若在沿岸国专属经济区域作业,则应遵守沿岸国的法律。此沿岸国应参考 IMO 的相关建议,并且对在其他国家登记的海上移动平台规定的标准不得高于其本国登记的海上移动平台适用的标准。

6 在海上移动平台(无论是否自推进式)上的所有专业人员应接受符合 IMO 相关建议的适当的熟悉和基本安全培训。

第 B-V/e 节[①]

关于对近海供应船舶船长和负责航行值班的高级船员的培训和资格的指导

1 重要的是,参与近海供应作业的船长和高级船员在履行船上职责前,应具有相关的经历或培训。重点应放在船上操作经历,或船上操作经历与模拟器培训的结合上。

2 船长和高级船员应该理解对近海供应船通用的独特操纵性和操作特点。

3 执行近海供应作业之前,船长和高级船员应:

.1 具有近海工业和不同作业所使用的术语的知识;

.2 在近海地点/设施工作时,理解始终保持安全作业距离的重要性;

.3 具有在各种天气条件下船舶操纵和船位保持的知识;

① 公约或规则 A 部分的节中没有关于第 B-V/a, B-V/b, B-V/c, B-V/d, B-V/e, B-V/f 和 B-V/g 节的相应规定。

.4 understand the specific design parameters of the vessels; and

.5 understand the need to have unrestricted oversight and views of work areas.

4 While on board an offshore supply vessel, the master and officers should:

.1 have knowledge of the handling characteristics and behaviour of vessels fitted with various propulsion arrangements; and

.2 be capable of operating the offshore supply vessel in close proximity to an offshore installation and other vessels.

5 Masters should understand the need for other personnel on board who are involved in performing offshore supply operations to be familiarized with their duties.

Offshore supply vessels performing anchor-handling operations

6 It is important that masters and officers in charge of a navigational watch on board offshore supply vessels involved in anchor-handling operations have relevant experience and training.

7 Prior to performing anchor-handling operations, masters and officers in charge of a navigational watch should:

.1 be well informed of the ship's handling characteristics in relation to anchor-handling, including, but not limited to:

.1.1 navigation and position-holding;

.1.2 ship-handling;

.1.3 thorough knowledge of the stability of offshore supply vessels, in particular the combination of low GZ_{max}, low open deck and large external forces. Use of loading calculators and the conflict between a rigid and stiff ship and good work environment on deck. Potential reduction of stability from use of anti-rolling devices; and

.1.4 operations in hazardous oil-field areas, including locating any pipelines or other structures on the seabed in the area where anchors or other mooring equipment is likely to be used; and

.2 be made thoroughly familiar with the use of all instruments and systems fitted in the ship concerned and involved in anchor-handling, including their capabilities and limitations, including, but not limited to:

.2.1 use of various thrusters, conventional or azimuth propulsion;

.2.2 pickup, handling, heavy lifting, towing out, anchor-handling and laying of anchors for offshore rigs, barges and installations;

.2.3 towing of rigs, barges and other vessels;

.4 理解船舶的具体设计参数;并且

.5 理解无障碍地监视作业区域的必要性。

4 当在近海供应船上时,船长及高级船员应:

.1 具有配备各种推进装置的船舶操作特点及表现的知识;并且

.2 能够操纵近海供应船靠近近海设施和其他船舶。

5 船长应理解让执行近海供应作业的船上其他人员熟悉其职责的必要性。

执行操锚作业的近海供应船

6 重要的是,负责有关操锚作业的供应船船长和负责航行值班的高级船员应具有相关的经历和培训。

7 在执行操锚作业之前,船长和负责航行值班的高级船员应:

.1 充分了解船舶有关操锚的作业特点,包括但不限于:

.1.1 航行和船位保持;

.1.2 船舶操作;

.1.3 近海供应船稳性的充足知识,特别是低 GZ_{max}、低开敞甲板和大外力三种情况结合时,使用装载计算仪,以及复原性强和"硬性"船舶与甲板上良好的工作环境间的矛盾,使用减摇设备造成的潜在的稳性降低;以及

.1.4 在危险的采油区域的作业,包括在可能用于抛锚或其他系泊设备的海床上安放任何管线或其他建造物; 并且

.2 能够完全熟练掌握船舶操锚作业所使用的安装于船上的各种仪器和系统,包括其性能和局限性,包括但不限于:

.2.1 各种推进器、传统型或全回转式推进装置的使用;

.2.2 为近海装置、驳船和其他设施的收起、操作、吊起、拖出、操锚和布锚;

.2.3 装置、驳船和其他船舶的拖带;

.2.4 operation of lifting and towing winches with up to 600 metric tons bollard pull;

.2.5 detailed thorough knowledge of the basis of operation of towing- and anchor-handling winches; in particular, functions of load-limiting devices and release systems and associated equipment as towing pins and stoppers; and

.2.6 the significant difference between emergency release of towing hooks and winches.

8 Masters and officers in charge of a navigational watch when in charge of anchor-handling should have sufficient and appropriate training and experience by having been supervised during a number of Rig-moves, as deemed appropriate by the Administration. Training may be supplemented by appropriate simulator training.

Section B-V/f*

Guidance on the training and experience for personnel operating dynamic positioning systems

1 Dynamic positioning is defined as the system whereby a self-propelled vessel's position and heading is automatically controlled by using its own propulsion units.

2 Personnel engaged in operating a Dynamic Positioning (DP) system should receive relevant training and practical experience. Theoretical elements of this training should enable Dynamic Positioning Operators (DPOs) to understand the operation of the DP system and its components. Knowledge, understanding and experience gained should enable personnel to operate vessels safely in DP, with due regard for safety of life at sea and protection of the marine environment.

3 The content of training and experience should include coverage of the following components of a DP system:

.1 DP control station;

.2 power generation and management;

.3 propulsion units;

.4 position reference systems;

.5 heading reference systems;

.6 environmental reference systems; and

.7 external force reference systems, such as hawser tension gauges.

4 Training and experience should cover the range of routine DP operations, as well as the handling of DP faults, failures, incidents and emergencies, to ensure that operations are continued or terminated safely. Training should not be limited to DPOs and DP masters only;

* Note there are no corresponding regulations in the Convention or sections in part A of the Code for sections B-V/a, B-V/b, B-V/c, B-V/d, B-V/e, B-V/f and B-V/g.

.2.4 达到600公吨拉力的吊装和牵引绞车的操作；

.2.5 详细、全面的牵引和操锚绞车操作的基本知识，特别是对负荷限制设备和释放系统以及相关设备如拖带销和制动器等的功能；以及

.2.6 拖钩和绞车的紧急释放操作之间的重大区别。

8 船长和负责航行值班的高级船员，如负责操锚作业，应具有充分和适当的培训和资历，通过数次有督导的设施移动实现，并被主管机关认定为合适。培训可以通过适当的模拟器训练来补充。

第 B-V/f 节①

关于对动力定位系统操作人员的培训和资历的指导

1 动力定位指自推进船舶的位置和船首向由其自身推进装置自动控制的系统。

2 从事动力定位（DP）系统操作的人员应接受相关培训并具有实际经验。该培训的理论部分应能够使动力定位的操作员（DPOs）理解 DP 系统及其组成部分的操作。知识、理解和获得的经验应能使人员使用 DP 系统安全操作船舶，并充分考虑海上人命安全和海洋环境保护。

3 培训的内容和经验应涵盖 DP 系统的下列组成部分：

.1 DP 控制站；

.2 发电和管理；

.3 推进装置；

.4 位置参考系统；

.5 船首向参考系统；

.6 环境参考系统；和

.7 外力参考系统，例如缆索张力计。

4 培训和经验应涵盖 DP 的常规操作，以及对 DP 故障、失效、事故和紧急情况的处理，确保操作安全持续或终止。培训对象不应仅限于 DPOs 和 DP 船长；船上的其他人员，例如电子员和轮机部高级船员，可要求附加培训和经验以确保他们能在 DP 船舶上履行其职责。应考虑将适当的 DP 演习作为船上培训和经验的一部分。DPOs 应了解与 DP 操作相关的文件（例如操作手册、故障模式和后果分析和控位能力）的种类和目的。

---

① 公约或规则 A 部分的节中没有关于第 B-V/a，B-V/b，B-V/c，B-V/d，B-V/e，B-V/f 和 B-V/g 节的相应规定。

other personnel on board, such as electro-technical and engineer officers, may require additional training and experience to ensure that they are able to carry out their duties on a DP vessel. Consideration should be given to conducting appropriate DP drills as a part of onboard training and experience. DPOs should be knowledgeable of the type and purpose of documentation associated with DP operations, such as operational manuals, Failure Modes and Effects Analysis (FMEAs) and capability plots.

5 All training should be given by properly qualified and suitably experienced personnel.

6 Upon appointment to a vessel operating in DP mode, the master, DPOs and other DP-trained personnel should be familiarized with the specific equipment fitted on and the characteristics of the vessel. Particular consideration should be given to the nature of the work of the vessel and the importance of the DP system to this work.

Section B-V/g*

*Guidance regarding training of masters and officers for ships operating in polar waters***

1 It is important that masters, officers in charge of a navigational watch and officers in charge of an engineering watch on board ships operating in polar waters should have relevant experience and training, as follows:

.1 Prior to being assigned duties on board such ships:

.1.1 For masters and officers in charge of a navigational watch, the training should provide basic knowledge on at least the subjects given in paragraphs 2 to 11 hereunder; and

.1.2 For officers in charge of an engineering watch, the training should provide basic knowledge on at least the subjects given in paragraphs 3, 6, 10 and 11 hereunder.

.2 Masters and Chief Engineer Officers should have sufficient and appropriate experience in operating ships in polar waters.

Ice characteristics – ice areas

2 Interpretation of different ice-charts and awareness of limitations in meteorology and oceanography data, ice physics, formation, growth, ageing and stage of melt; ice types and concentrations; ice pressure; friction from snow-covered ice; implications of spray-icing and icing up; precautions against icing up and mitigation of consequences; ice regimes in different regions and different seasons, including the differences between the Arctic and the Antarctic; recognition of consequences of rapid change in ice and weather conditions; movement of icebergs and pack ice.

---

* Note there are no corresponding regulations in the Convention or sections in part A of the Code for sections B-V/a, B-V/b, B-V/c, B-V/d, B-V/e, B-V/f and B-V/g.

** Refer to IMO Assembly resolution A.1024(26) on Guidelines for ships operating in polar waters.

5　所有的培训都应由具有适当资格和合适经验的人员实施。

6　在 DP 操作模式的船舶任职时，船长、DPOs 和其他接受过 DP 培训的人员应熟悉船载特定设备及该船的特性。应特别考虑该船工作的性质和 DP 系统对此项工作的重要性。

第 B-V/g 节①

关于对在极地水域操作的船舶船长和高级船员培训的指导②

1　重要的是，在极地水域操作的船舶的船长、负责航行值班的高级船员和负责轮机值班的高级船员应有如下相关经验和培训：

.1　在该类船舶上任职前：

.1.1　对于船长和负责航行值班的高级船员，培训应至少提供以下第 2 段至第 11 段所列科目的基本知识；以及

.1.2　对于负责轮机值班的高级船员，培训应至少提供以下第 3 段、第 6 段、第 10 段和第 11 段所列科目的基本知识。

.2　船长和轮机长应具有充足和适当的极地水域操作船舶的经验。

冰的特性——冰区

2　解释各种冰况图并意识到气象学和海洋学数据的局限性，冰的物理特性、形成、增长、老化和融化阶段；冰的类型和密集度；冰压力；积雪覆盖的冰的摩擦力；飞溅浪花结冰和积冰的后果；防止积冰的措施和缓解后果；不同地区和不同季节的冰情，包括北极和南极冰的区别；识别冰情和天气条件快速变化的后果；冰山和浮冰群的移动。

① 公约或规则 A 部分的节中没有关于第 B-V/a，B-V/b，B-V/c，B-V/d，B-V/e，B-V/f 和 B-V/g 节的相应规定。

② 参考 IMO 大会决议 A.1024(26) 关于在极地水域操作的船舶的导则。

Ship's performance in ice and cold climate

3 Vessel characteristics; vessel types, hull designs; ice-strengthening requirements; ice-class of different classification societies – polar class and local regulations; limitations of ice-classes; winterization and preparedness of vessel; low-temperature system performance.

Voyage and passage planning for a ship in ice*

4 Development of safe routeing and passage planning to avoid ice where possible, including interpreting various forms of ice imagery and data to assist in the preparation of a strategic passage planning; entering ice from open water to avoid icebergs and dangerous ice conditions; navigation, determining when it is safe or not safe to enter areas containing ice or icebergs due to darkness, swell, fog or pressure ice.

Operating and handling a ship in ice

5 Preparations and risk assessment before approaching ice-infested waters; unassisted operation of vessels with different ice-class in different ice-types; safe speed in the presence of ice and icebergs; communications with an icebreaker and other vessels; navigation in various ice concentrations and coverage; awareness of the increase in energy of movement; use of icebergs for shelter and access through packed ice.

6 Use of different type of propulsion system and rudder, including awareness of system strength and capacity limitations; use of heeling and trim systems, engine loads and cooling problems.

Regulations and recommendations

7 Local requirements for entering different regions, including the Antarctic Treaty; international regulations and recommendations.

Equipment limitations

8 Use of and hazards associated with terrestrial navigational aids in polar waters; high-latitude compass errors; discrimination of radar targets and ice-features in ice-clutter; limitations of electronic positioning systems at high latitude; limitations in nautical charts and pilot descriptions; limitations in communication systems.

Safety precautions and emergency procedures

9 Availability of hydrographic data sufficient for safe navigation; precautions when navigating in poorly charted waters; limitations of search and rescue readiness and responsibility, including GMDSS area A4 and its SAR communication facility limitation; awareness of contingency planning; knowledge of towing procedures; value of contact with other ships and local SAR organization; recognizing dangers when crews are exposed to low temperatures; procedures and techniques for abandoning the ship and survival on the ice; crew-fatigue problems due to noise and vibrations; carriage of additional resources such as bunkers, food and extra clothing; awareness of the additional severity of consequences of incidents in polar waters.

---

* Refer to IMO Assembly resolution A.999(25) on Guidelines on voyage planning for passenger ships operating in remote areas.

冰冻和严寒气候中的船舶性能

3　船舶特性;船舶类型、船体设计;抗冰加强要求;不同船级社的抗冰等级—极地船级和地方性规定;抗冰等级的限制;船舶的过冬防寒准备;低温系统性能。

船舶在冰区的航次和航路计划①

4　制定安全的航次和航路计划以避开可能遭遇的冰情,包括解释不同形式的冰像和数据以协助制定策略的航行计划;从开阔水域进入冰区以避开冰山和危险冰况;航行,并判明由于夜间、涌浪、雾或冰压在何时进入存在浮冰、冰山的区域是安全的或是不安全的。

在冰区操作和操纵船舶

5　驶近浮冰大量出现的水域前的准备和风险评估;船舶在不同冰级和不同冰型下无协助的操作;在冰和冰山出现时的安全航速;与破冰船及其他船舶的通信;在各种冰密集度和覆盖量下的航行;意识到动能的增加;利用冰山掩护通过积冰。

6　使用不同类型的推进系统和舵,包括意识到系统强度和能力的局限性;使用横倾和纵倾系统并考虑机器负荷和冷却问题。

规则和建议

7　进入不同地区时的当地要求,包括《南极条约》;国际规则和建议。

设备的限制性

8　极地水域陆地助航标志的使用及相关的危险;高纬度罗经差;在冰杂波中分辨雷达目标和浮冰特征;电子定位系统在高纬度的局限性;海图和引航指南的局限性;通信系统的局限性。

安全预防措施和应急程序

9　满足安全航行所需的水文数据的可用性;在海图资料不充分的水域中航行时的预防措施;搜救准备和责任的局限性,包括 GMDSS A4 区及其搜救通信设施的局限性;对应急计划的意识;拖带程序的知识;与其他船舶和当地搜救组织联络的价值;认识到船员暴露在低温下的危险;弃船及冰区求生的程序和技术;噪声和振动导致的船员疲劳问题;诸如燃料、食品和多余衣物的额外资源的携带;对极地水域事故后果格外严重。

① 参考 IMO 大会决议 A.999(25) 关于在偏远地区操作的客船制定航次计划的导则。

10 Establishing safe working procedures; awareness of the most common hull and equipment damages and how to avoid them; fire-fighting systems limitations.

Environmental considerations

11 Sensitive sea areas regarding discharge; areas where shipping is prohibited or should be avoided; Special Areas in MARPOL; oil-spill equipment limitations; plan for coping with increased volumes of garbage, bilge water, sludge, sewage, etc.; consequences of pollution in a cold climate.

10　制定安全工作程序；意识到最常见的船体和设备损坏以及如何预防；灭火系统的局限性。

环保考虑

11　敏感海域的有关排放；禁航和避航区域；《MARPOL 公约》规定的特殊区域；防溢油设备的局限性；应对垃圾、舱底水、污泥和污水等数量增加的计划；严寒气候下的污染后果。

CHAPTER VI

Guidance regarding emergency, occupational safety, security, medical care and survival functions

Section B-VI/1

Guidance regarding mandatory requirements for safety familiarization and basic training and instruction for all seafarers

FIRE PREVENTION AND FIRE FIGHTING

1 The training in fire prevention and fire fighting required by section A-VI/1 should include at least the theoretical and practical elements itemized in paragraphs 2 to 4 hereunder.*

Theoretical training

2 The theoretical training should cover:

.1 the three elements of fire and explosion (the fire triangle): fuel; source of ignition; oxygen;

.2 ignition sources: chemical; biological; physical;

.3 flammable materials: flammability; ignition point; burning temperature; burning speed; thermal value; lower flammable limit (LFL); upper flammable limit (UFL); flammable range; inerting; static electricity; flashpoint; auto-ignition;

.4 fire hazard and spread of fire by radiation, convection and conduction;

.5 reactivity;

.6 classification of fires and applicable extinguishing agents;

.7 main causes of fire on board ships: oil leakage in engine-room; cigarettes; overheating (bearings); galley appliances (stoves, flues, fryers, hotplates, etc.); spontaneous ignition (cargo, wastes, etc.); hot work (welding, cutting, etc.); electrical apparatus (short circuit, non-professional repairs); reaction, self-heating and auto-ignition; arson; static electricity;

.8 fire prevention;

.9 fire- and smoke-detection systems; automatic fire alarms;

.10 fire-fighting equipment, including:

.10.1 fixed installations on board and their locations; fire mains, hydrants; international shore connection; smothering installations, carbon dioxide (CO_2), foam; pressure water spray system in special category spaces, etc.;

---

* The relevant IMO Model Course(s) may be of assistance in the preparation of courses.

第 VI 章
关于应急、职业安全、保安、医护和救生职能的指导

第 B-VI/1 节
关于对所有海员的安全熟悉和基本培训和训练的强制性要求的指导

防火和灭火

1 第 A-VI/1 节中所要求的防火和灭火的培训应至少包括以下第 2 段至第 4 段所列的理论和实践内容。①

理论培训

2 理论培训应包括：

.1 燃烧和爆炸三要素（燃烧三角形）：燃料，火源，氧气；

.2 着火源：化学的，生物的，物理的；

.3 易燃物质：可燃性，燃点，燃烧温度，燃烧速度，热值，燃烧下限（LFL），燃烧上限（UFL），燃烧范围，惰化，静电，闪点，自燃；

.4 火灾的危害和由辐射、对流和传导引起的火势蔓延；

.5 反应性；

.6 火灾分类和适用的灭火剂；

.7 船舶火灾的主要原因：机舱漏油，香烟，（轴承的）过热，厨房设备（炉灶、烟道、炒锅、热平底锅等），自燃（货物、废棉纱等），热工作业（电焊、切割等），电气设备（短路、非专业性修理），反应、自热和自燃，放火，静电；

.8 火灾预防；

.9 烟火探测系统，自动烟火报警装置；

.10 灭火设备包括：

.10.1 船上固定设备及其位置，消防总管、消火栓，国际通岸接头，窒息灭火装置、二氧化碳、泡沫，特殊空间的压力喷水系统等，自动洒水装置，应急消防泵，应急发电机，化学干粉装置，要求配置的和可用的移动设备概要，高压水雾装置，高膨胀泡沫，新发展与新设备；

.10.2 消防员装备、个人装备，呼吸面具，人工呼吸器，防毒面具及头盔，防火救生绳及索具，及其船上的安置地点；以及

.10.3 通用设备，包括消防水龙，喷枪，接头，消防斧，便携式灭火器，消防毯；

① 相关 IMO 示范培训课程可有助于准备课程。

automatic sprinkler system; emergency fire pump; emergency generator; chemical powder applicants; general outline of required and available mobile apparatus; high-pressure fog system; high-expansion foam; new developments and equipment;

.10.2 firefighter's outfit, personal equipment; breathing apparatus; resuscitation apparatus; smoke helmet or mask; fireproof lifeline and harness; and their location on board; and

.10.3 general equipment, including fire hoses, nozzles, connections, fire axes; portable fire extinguishers; fire blankets;

.11 construction and arrangements, including escape routes; means for gas-freeing tanks; Class A, B and C divisions; inert gas systems;

.12 ship fire-fighting organization, including general alarm; fire control plans, muster stations and duties of individuals; communications, including ship–shore when in port; personnel safety procedures; periodic shipboard drills; patrol systems;

.13 practical knowledge of resuscitation methods;

.14 fire-fighting methods, including sounding the alarm; locating and isolating; jettisoning; inhibiting; cooling; smothering; extinguishing; reflash watch; smoke extraction; and

.15 fire-fighting agents, including water, solid jet, spray, fog, flooding; high-, medium- and low-expansion foam; carbon dioxide (CO_2); aqueous-film-forming foam (AFFF); dry chemical powder; new developments and equipment.

Practical training

3 The practical training given below should take place in spaces which provide truly realistic training conditions (e.g., simulated shipboard conditions), and whenever possible and practical should also be carried out in darkness as well as by daylight and should allow the trainees to acquire the ability to:

.1 use various types of portable fire extinguishers;

.2 use self-contained breathing apparatus;

.3 extinguish smaller fires, e.g., electrical fires, oil fires and propane fires;

.4 extinguish extensive fires with water (jet and spray nozzles);

.5 extinguish fires with either foam, powder or any other suitable chemical agent;

.6 enter and pass through, with lifeline but without breathing apparatus, a compartment into which high-expansion foam has been injected;

.7 fight fire in smoke-filled enclosed spaces, wearing self-contained breathing apparatus;

.11 结构和布置,包括逃生路线,舱室除气方法,A、B、C 类分隔,惰性气体系统;

.12 船舶消防组织,包括一般警报,防火控制图、人员集合地点及各自的职责,通信(包括在港时的船对岸通信),人员安全程序,定期船上演习,巡查制度;

.13 复苏方法的实际知识;

.14 灭火方法,包括警报鸣放,确定位置和隔离,弃货,抑制法,冷却法,窒息法,灭火,防再燃值守,排烟;以及

.15 灭火剂,包括水、固体喷射物、喷水、水雾、水淹、泡沫(高、中、低膨胀),二氧化碳(CO_2),水帘状泡沫(AFFF),化学干粉,新发展和新设备。

实际培训

3 下列各项实际培训应在能提供真实培训条件(如模拟的船上条件)的场所进行,可行时还应进行黑暗和光亮环境中训练,使受培训者能掌握以下技能:

.1 使用各种手提式灭火器;

.2 使用自供式呼吸装置;

.3 扑灭小火,如电气火、油火和丙烷火;

.4 使用水扑灭较大火灾(喷射和散射喷枪);

.5 使用泡沫、干粉或其他合适的化学灭火剂灭火;

.6 使用救生索但不戴呼吸器进入或通过已喷注了高膨胀泡沫的舱室;

.7 佩戴上自供式呼吸器在充满烟雾的封闭处所灭火;

.8 extinguish fire with water fog or any other suitable fire-fighting agent in an accommodation room or simulated engine-room with fire and heavy smoke;

.9 extinguish an oil fire with fog applicator and spray nozzles; dry chemical powder or foam applicators; and

.10 effect a rescue in a smoke-filled space, wearing breathing apparatus.

General

4 Trainees should also be made aware of the necessity of maintaining a state of readiness on board.

ELEMENTARY FIRST AID*

5 The training in elementary first aid required by regulation VI/1 as part of the basic training should be given at an early stage in vocational training, preferably during pre-sea training, to enable seafarers to take immediate action upon encountering an accident or other medical emergency until the arrival of a person with first-aid skills or the person in charge of medical care on board.

PERSONAL SAFETY AND SOCIAL RESPONSIBILITIES*

6 Administrations should bear in mind the significance of communication and language skills in maintaining safety of life and property at sea and in preventing marine pollution. Given the international character of the maritime industry, the reliance on voice communications from ship to ship and from ship-to-shore, the increasing use of multinational crews, and the concern that crew members should be able to communicate with passengers in an emergency, adoption of a common language for maritime communications would promote safe practice by reducing the risk of human error in communicating essential information.

7 Although not universal, by common practice English is rapidly becoming the standard language of communication for maritime safety purposes, partly as a result of the use of the IMO Standard Marine Communication Phrases.

8 Administrations should consider the benefits of ensuring that seafarers have an ability to use at least an elementary English vocabulary, with an emphasis on nautical terms and situations.

Section B-VI/2
Guidance regarding certification for proficiency in survival craft, rescue boats and fast rescue boats

1 Before training is commenced, the requirement of medical fitness, particularly regarding eyesight and hearing, should be met by the candidate.

2 The training should be relevant to the provisions of the International Convention for the Safety of Life at Sea (SOLAS), as amended.

3 Parties may also accept onboard training and experience (such as participation in drills) for maintaining the required standard of competence of table A-VI/2-1, in the areas outlined in

* The relevant IMO Model Course(s) may be of assistance in the preparation of courses.

.8 使用水雾或其他合适的灭火剂扑灭有浓烟火的居舱或模拟机舱内的火灾;

.9 使用水雾喷枪和散射喷枪、化学干粉或泡沫喷头扑灭油火;

.10 佩戴呼吸器在充满烟雾的处所进行救生。

一般要求

4 还应使受培训者认识到在船期间保持戒备状态的必要性。

基本急救①

5 在职业培训的早期,最好在海上培训之前,应对海员进行规则第 VI/1 条所要求的基本急救的培训,并作为基本培训的一个部分,使海员能在面临事故或其他医疗紧急情况下,在具有急救技能的人员或在船上负责医护的人员到达之前,采取急救行动。

个人安全与社会责任①

6 主管机关应切记信息交流和语言技能在保持海上人命与财产安全和防止海上污染方面的重要性。由于航运业的国际化特点,船对船、船对岸通信中都依靠口语通信,多国船员同船现象增多,以及对船员在紧急情况下有无与旅客沟通能力的关注,所以海事通信采用一种通用语言以减少在交流重要信息中的人为错误,促进安全操作。

7 英语,虽非全球性语言,但正在迅速地在实践中成为海上安全通信的标准语言,其部分原因是使用了 IMO《标准航海通信用语》。

8 主管机关应考虑到保证海员至少具有运用以航海术语和航海情景为重点的基础英语词汇能力的好处。

第 B-VI/2 节

关于对签发救生艇筏救助艇和快速救助艇培训合格证书的指导

1 培训开始前,证书申请人应符合健康要求,特别是有关视力和听力的要求。

2 培训应符合经修正的《国际海上人命安全公约》(SOLAS)的有关规定。

3 缔约国还可接受第 A-VI/2 节第 6.1.2 段、第 6.1.3 段、第 6.1.4 段、第 6.2.1 段和第 12.1.5段列明的船上培训和资历(例如参加演习),以维持表 A-VI/2-1 中要求的适任标准。主管机关应切记上述船上培训项目仅在良好天气条件和港口规则允许的情况下才能进行。

① 相关 IMO 示范培训课程可有助于准备课程。

section A-VI/2, paragraphs 6.1.2, 6.1.3, 6.1.4, 6.2.1, and 12.1.5. Administrations should bear in mind that onboard training in these areas can only be carried out under good weather conditions and port regulations permitting.

Section B-VI/3
Guidance regarding training in advanced fire fighting

(No provisions)

Section B-VI/4
Guidance regarding requirements in medical first aid and medical care

Training programmes for seafarers designated to undertake the tasks, duties and responsibilities listed in column 1 of table A-VI/4-1 to provide medical first aid on board ship should take into account guidance in the revised International Medical Guide for Ships, as appropriate.

Section B-VI/5
Guidance regarding training and certification for ship security officers

1 The training should be relevant to the provisions of the ISPS Code and the SOLAS Convention, as amended*.

2 On completion of training, a ship security officer should have adequate knowledge of the English language to correctly interpret and communicate messages relevant to ship or port facility security.

3 In circumstances of exceptional necessity, when a person holding a certificate of proficiency as a ship security officer is temporarily unavailable, the Administration may permit a seafarer having specific security duties and responsibilities and an understanding of the ship security plan to serve as ship security officer and to execute all duties and responsibilities of the ship security officer until the next port of call or for a period not exceeding 30 days, whichever is greater. The company should, as soon as possible, inform the competent authorities of the next port(s) of call of the arrangements in place.

Section B-VI/6
Guidance regarding mandatory minimum requirements for security-related training and instruction for all seafarers

Familiarization and security-awareness

1 Seafarers and shipboard personnel are not security experts and it is not the aim of the provisions of the Convention or this Code to convert them into security specialists.

2 Seafarers and shipboard personnel should receive adequate security-related training or instruction and familiarization training so as to acquire the required knowledge and understanding to perform their assigned duties and to collectively contribute to the enhancement of maritime security.

* The relevant IMO Model Course(s) may be of assistance in the preparation of courses.

第 B-VI/3 节
关于对高级消防培训的指导

（无条文）

第 B-VI/4 节
关于对医疗急救和医护要求的指导

指定承担表 A-VI/4-1 第 1 栏所列的任务、职责和责任以提供船上急救的海员应接受的培训项目，应考虑适用的经修订的《国际船舶医疗指南》的指导。

第 B-VI/5
关于对船舶保安员培训和发证的指导

1　培训应与《ISPS 规则》和经修正的《SOLAS 公约》的规定相关①。

2　在完成培训后，船舶保安员应有足够的英语知识以正确解释和交流与船舶或港口设施保安有关的消息。

3　在特别必要的情况下，当暂时没有可用的持有船舶保安员培训合格证书的船员，主管机关可允许具有专门保安职责和责任且理解船舶保安计划的海员担任船舶保安员，在抵达下一停靠港前或不超过 30 天内（取时间较长者），担负船舶保安员的所有职责和责任。公司应尽快将现有安排通知下一停靠港的主管当局。

第 B-VI/6 节
关于对所有海员与保安有关的培训和训练的强制性最低要求的指导

熟悉和保安意识

1　海员和船上人员不是保安专家，因此本公约或本规则规定的目的不在于使其成为保安专家。

2　海员和船上人员应接受足够的与保安相关的培训或训练和熟悉培训，以使其获得履行其指派职责和有助于共同增强海上保安所要求的知识和理解。

① 相关 IMO 示范培训课程可有助于准备课程。

3 Seafarers without designated security duties should complete the security awareness training or instruction set out in section A-VI/6 at least one time in their career. There is no need for refreshment or revalidation of this training if the seafarer or the shipboard personnel concerned meet the security-related familiarization requirements of regulation VI/6 and participate in the drills and exercises required by the ISPS Code.

Seafarers with designated security duties

4 The expression "with designated security duties" in section A-VI/6 denotes those having specific security duties and responsibilities in accordance with the ship security plan.

5 Seafarers with designated security duties should complete the training as set out in section A-VI/6 at least one time in their career. There is no need for refreshment or revalidation of this training if the seafarer or the shipboard personnel concerned meet the security-related familiarization requirements of regulation VI/6 and participate in the drills and exercises required by the ISPS Code.

6 Those providing "security-related familiarization training" in accordance with section A-VI/6 should not be required to meet the requirements of either regulation I/6 or of section A-I/6.

7 In circumstances of exceptional necessity, when the shipboard security-related duties are required to be undertaken by a person qualified to perform designated security-related duties and such a person is temporarily unavailable, the Administration may permit a seafarer without designated security duties to perform such duties provided such a person has an understanding of the ship security plan, until the next port of call or for a period not exceeding 30 days, whichever is greater.

3　没有指定保安职责的海员，在其职业生涯中应至少完成一次第 A-VI/6 节规定的保安意识培训或训练。如果有关的海员或船上人员满足了规则第 VI/6 条规定的与保安有关的熟悉要求，并参加了《ISPS 规则》要求的演习和练习，则没有必要对这项培训进行更新或再有效。

承担指定保安职责的海员

4　第 A-VI/6 节中的"承担指定保安职责"的表述指根据船上保安计划负有特定保安职责和责任的人员。

5　负有指定保安职责的海员，在其职业生涯中应至少完成一次第 A-VI/6 节中规定的培训。如果有关的海员或船上人员满足了规则第 VI/6 条规定的与保安有关的熟悉要求，并参加了《ISPS 规则》要求的演习和练习，则没有必要对这项培训进行更新或再有效。

6　按照第 A-VI/6 节提供"与保安有关熟悉培训"的那些人员无须满足规则第 I/6 条或第 A-I/6节的要求。

7　在特别必要的情况下，当要求由具有履行指定的与保安有关的职责资格的人员承担船上与保安有关的职责，而暂时没有这样可用的人员时，主管机关可以允许没有承担指定保安职责但理解船舶保安计划的海员，在抵达下一停靠港前或不超过 30 天内（取时间较长者），担任这一职责。

CHAPTER VII

Guidance regarding alternative certification

Section B-VII/1
Guidance regarding the issue of alternative certificates

(No provisions)

Section B-VII/2
Guidance regarding special integrated deck and engine training programmes

1 Each Party should ensure that any special integrated deck and engine training programme:

.1 is provided by means of an approved training programme;

.2 takes place ashore within maritime training institutions and/or on board approved training ships; and

.3 is documented in an approved training record book.

Section B-VII/3
Guidance regarding principles governing the issue of alternative certificates

(No provisions)

第 VII 章
关于可供选择的发证的指导

第 B-VII/1 节
关于可供选择的发证的指导

（无条文）

第 B-VII/2 节
关于特定的甲板和机舱组合培训计划的指导

1 每个缔约国应确保任何特定的甲板和机舱组合培训计划：

.1 以认可的方式实施；

.2 在岸上航海培训机构实施和/或在认可的培训船上实施；和

.3 在认可的培训记录簿中记载。

第 B-VII/3 节
关于控制签发可供选择的证书的原则指导

（无条文）

CHAPTER VIII

Guidance regarding watchkeeping

Section B-VIII/1
Guidance regarding fitness for duty

Prevention of fatigue

1 In observing the rest period requirements, "overriding operational conditions" should be construed to mean only essential shipboard work which cannot be delayed for safety, security or environmental reasons or which could not reasonably have been anticipated at the commencement of the voyage.

2 Although there is no universally accepted technical definition of fatigue, everyone involved in ship operations should be alert to the factors which can contribute to fatigue, including, but not limited to, those identified by the Organization*, and take them into account when making decisions on ship operations.

3 In applying regulation VIII/1, the following should be taken into account:

.1 provisions made to prevent fatigue should ensure that excessive or unreasonable overall working hours are not undertaken. In particular, the minimum rest periods specified in section A-VIII/1 should not be interpreted as implying that all other hours may be devoted to watchkeeping or other duties;

.2 the frequency and length of leave periods, and the granting of compensatory leave, are material factors in preventing fatigue from building up over a period of time; and

.3 the provisions may be varied for ships on short sea voyages, provided special safety arrangements are put in place.

4 Exceptions provided for in section A-VIII/1, paragraph 9, should be construed to mean the exceptions laid down by the ILO Convention on Seafarers' Hours of Work and the Manning of Ships, 1996 (No.180) or the Maritime Labour Convention, 2006, when it enters into force. The circumstances under which such exceptions are applied should be defined by the Parties.

5 Based on information received as a result of investigating maritime casualties, Administrations should keep their provisions on prevention of fatigue under review.

Prevention of drug and alcohol abuse

6 Drug and alcohol abuse directly affect the fitness and ability of a seafarer to perform watchkeeping duties or duties that involve designated safety, prevention of pollution and security duties. Seafarers found to be under the influence of drugs or alcohol should not be permitted to perform watchkeeping duties or duties that involve designated safety, prevention of pollution and security duties, until they are no longer impaired in their ability to perform those duties.

* See the annex to IMO Assembly resolution A.772(18) on Fatigue factor in manning and safety, paragraphs 2 to 4.4.1 and MSC/Circ.1014. on Guidance on fatigue mitigation and management.

第 VIII 章
关于值班的指导

第 B-VIII/1 节
关于适于值班的指导

防止疲劳

1 在遵守休息时间的要求时,“超常工作情况”应解释为仅指由于安全或防止污染原因而不能延误的或在航次开始时不能合理预料的至关重要的船上工作。

2 虽然疲劳尚没有普遍接受的技术性定义,但每一个参与船舶工作的人应警惕能导致疲劳的因素,其中包括但不仅限于那些本组织①已明确的因素,并应在决定船舶工作时加以考虑。

3 在运用规则第 VIII/1 条时,应考虑以下各项:

.1 所制定的防止疲劳的规定应确保不采取过多的和不合理的整段工作时间,特别是第 A-VIII/1 节规定的最少休息时间不应解释为暗示所有其他时间可用于值班或履行其他职责;

.2 休息时段的次数和长短以及准予的补休是一段时间内防止疲劳的关键因素;以及

.3 对短航次的船舶,只要作出特殊的安全方面的安排,可以有不同的规定。

4 第 A-VIII/1 节第 9 段所列的例外规定应解释为系指国际劳工组织 1996 年(第 180 号)《海员工作时间和船舶配员公约》或生效后的《2006 年海事劳工公约》所列的例外规定。适用该例外规定的情况应由缔约国确定。

5 主管机关应以从海上事故调查结果所获得的信息为基础,对其防止疲劳的规定进行审核。

防止滥用药物和酗酒

6 滥用药物和酗酒直接影响到船员履行值班职责或有关安全、防污染和保安值班职责的健康和能力。当船员被发现受到药物或酒精的影响时,应不允许其履行值班职责或有关安全、防污染和保安值班职责,直至他们履行这些职责的能力不再受到影响为止。

① 参见 IMO A.772(18)号决议关于配员和安全中的疲劳因素的附件第 2 段至第 4.4.1 段海安会 1014 号通函关于疲劳缓解与管理的指导。

7 Administrations should ensure that adequate measures are taken to prevent alcohol and drugs from impairing the ability of watchkeeping personnel and those whose duties involve designated safety, prevention of pollution and security duties, and should establish screening programmes as necessary which:

.1 identify drug and alcohol abuse;

.2 respect the dignity, privacy, confidentiality and fundamental legal rights of the individuals concerned; and

.3 take into account relevant international guidelines.

8 Companies should consider the implementation of a clearly written policy of drug and alcohol abuse prevention, including prohibition to consume alcohol within four hours prior to serving as a member of a watch either by inclusion in the company's quality-management system or by means of providing adequate information and education to the seafarers.

9 Those involved in establishing drug and alcohol abuse prevention programmes should take into account the guidance contained in the ILO publication *Drug and Alcohol Prevention Programmes in the Maritime Industry (A Manual for Planners)*[*], as may be amended.

Section B-VIII/2
Guidance regarding watchkeeping arrangements and principles to be observed

The following operational guidance should be taken into account by companies, masters and watchkeeping officers.

PART 1 – GUIDANCE ON CERTIFICATION

(No provisions)

PART 2 – GUIDANCE ON VOYAGE PLANNING

(No provisions)

PART 3 – WATCHKEEPING PRINCIPLES IN GENERAL

(No provisions)

[*] Annex III of this manual includes "Guiding Principles on Drug and Alcohol Testing procedures for Worldwide Application in the Maritime Industry". These guiding principles were adopted by the Joint ILO/WHO Committee on the Health of Seafarers (May 1993).

7 主管机关应确保采取适当措施以防止药物或酒精影响值班人员或履行安全、防污染和保安值班职责人员的能力，并应根据需要制定甄别计划：

.1 鉴别滥用药物和酗酒；

.2 尊重有关个人的尊严、隐私、秘密和基本的法定权利；以及

.3 考虑相关的国际指南。

8 公司应考虑通过纳入公司质量管理体系或向船员提供足够的信息和教育的方法，实施明文规定的防止滥用药物和酗酒的政策，包括禁止值班人员在值班前 4 小时内饮酒。

9 参与制定防止滥用药物和酗酒方案的人员应考虑 ILO 出版的可能会被修正的《海运业防止滥用药物和酗酒方案（设计人员手册）》①中的指南。

第 B-VIII/2 节

关于值班安排和应遵循的原则的指导

公司、船长和值班的高级船员应考虑以下操作性指导。

第 1 部分　关于发证的指导

（无条文）

第 2 部分　关于航次计划的指导

（无条文）

第 3 部分　关于值班的一般原则

（无条文）

① 本手册附则 III 包括“关于全球适用的海运业药物及酒精测试程序的指导原则”。该指导原则已由国际劳工组织/世界卫生组织海员健康联合委员会通过（1993 年 5 月）。

PART 4 – GUIDANCE ON WATCHKEEPING AT SEA

Part 4-1 – Guidance on keeping a navigational watch **Introduction**

2 Particular guidance may be necessary for special types of ships as well as for ships carrying hazardous, dangerous, toxic or highly flammable cargoes. The master should provide this operational guidance as appropriate.

3 It is essential that officers in charge of the navigational watch appreciate that the efficient performance of their duties is necessary in the interests of the safety of life, security and property at sea and of preventing pollution of the marine environment.

Anchor watch

4 The master of every ship at an unsheltered anchorage, at an open roadstead or any other virtually "at sea" conditions in accordance with chapter VIII, section A-VIII/2, part 4-1, paragraph 51 of the STCW Code, should ensure that watchkeeping arrangements are adequate for maintaining a safe watch at all times. A deck officer should at all times maintain responsibility for a safe anchor watch.

5 In determining the watchkeeping arrangements, and commensurate with maintaining the ship's safety and security and the protection of the marine environment, the master should take into account all pertinent circumstances and conditions such as:

.1 maintaining a continuous state of vigilance by sight and hearing as well as by all other available means;

.2 ship-to-ship and ship-to-shore communication requirements;

.3 the prevailing weather, sea, ice and current conditions;

.4 the need to continuously monitor the ship's position;

.5 the nature, size and characteristics of anchorage;

.6 traffic conditions;

.7 situations which might affect the security of the ship;

.8 loading and discharging operations;

.9 the designation of stand-by crew members; and

.10 the procedure to alert the master and maintain engine readiness.

第 4 部分　关于海上值班的指导

第 4-1 部分　关于保持航行值班的指导

引言

2　对特殊类型的船舶以及载运有害、危险、有毒或高度易燃性货物的船舶，可能需要特别的指导。船长应根据情况提供操作性指导。

3　重要的是，负责航行值班的高级船员要认识到有效地履行其职责对海上人命和财产安全、保安以及防止海洋环境污染的必要性。

锚泊值班

4　在非遮蔽锚地、开敞的港外锚地或任何其他实际“在海上”锚泊情况下，依据《STCW 规则》第 VIII 章第 A-VIII/2 节第 4-1 部分第 51 段的规定，每一船舶的船长应确保足以保持所有锚泊时间安全的值班安排。甲板部高级船员应始终负有锚泊安全值班的责任。

5　在确定值班安排时，为统筹维持船舶安全、保安和海洋环境保护，船长应考虑所有相关的环境和条件，如：

.1　通过视觉、听觉以及其他一切可用手段保持连续的警戒状态；

.2　船与船、船与岸的通信要求；

.3　当时的天气、海浪、冰和海流的状况；

.4　连续监测船位的需要；

.5　锚地的性质、大小和特征；

.6　交通状况；

.7　可能影响船舶保安的情况；

.8　装卸作业；

.9　待命船员的指定；以及

.10　向船长报警和保持主机备用状态的程序。

Part 4-2 – Guidance on keeping an engineering watch

6 Particular guidance may be necessary for special types of propulsion systems or ancillary equipment and for ships carrying hazardous, dangerous, toxic or highly flammable materials or other special types of cargo. The chief engineer officer should provide this operational guidance as appropriate.

7 It is essential that officers in charge of the engineering watch appreciate that the efficient performance of engineering watchkeeping duties is necessary in the interest of the safety of life and property at sea and of preventing pollution of the marine environment.

8 The relieving officer, before assuming charge of the engineering watch, should:

.1 be familiar with the location and use of the equipment provided for the safety of life in a hazardous or toxic environment;

.2 ascertain that materials for the administration of emergency medical first aid are readily available, particularly those required for the treatment of burns and scalds; and

.3 when in port, safely anchored or moored, be aware of:

.3.1 cargo activities, the status of maintenance and repair functions and all other operations affecting the watch, and

.3.2 the auxiliary machinery in use for passenger or crew accommodation services, cargo operations, operational water supplies and exhaust systems.

Part 4-3 – Guidance on keeping a radio watch

General

9 Among other things, the Radio Regulations require that each ship radio station is licensed, is under the ultimate authority of the master or other person responsible for the ship and is only operated under the control of adequately qualified personnel. The Radio Regulations also require that a distress alert shall only be sent on the authority of the master or other person responsible for the ship.

10 The master should bear in mind that all personnel assigned responsibility for sending a distress alert must be instructed with regard to, be knowledgeable of, and be able to operate properly all radio equipment on the ship, as required by regulation I/14, paragraph 1.5. This should be recorded in the deck or radio log-book.

Watchkeeping

11 In addition to the requirements concerning radio watchkeeping, the master of every seagoing ship should ensure that:

.1 the ship's radio station is adequately manned for the purpose of exchanging general communications – in particular public correspondence, taking into account the constraints imposed by the duties of those authorized to operate it; and

第 4-2 部分　关于保持轮机值班的指导

6　对特殊类型的推进系统或辅助设备以及载运有害、危险、有毒或高度易燃性货物或其他特种货物的船舶，可能需要特别的指导。轮机长应根据情况提供操作性指导。

7　重要的是，负责轮机值班的高级船员要认识到有效地履行其职责对海上人命和财产安全以及防止海洋环境污染的必要性。

8　接班的高级船员在承担轮机值班职责前应：

.1　熟悉为在危险或有毒环境中的人命安全提供的设备的位置和使用方法；

.2　确认紧急医疗急救工作所用的物品备妥可用，特别是那些处理烧伤、烫伤用的物品；并且

.3　当在港内安全系泊或锚泊时，要了解：

.3.1　货物作业活动、维护和修理状况及所有其他影响值班的作业，以及

.3.2　正在用于旅客或船员舱室服务、货物作业、操作性供水和排气系统的辅机。

第 4-3 部分　关于保持无线电值班的指导

一般要求

9　除其他规定外，《无线电规则》要求每艘船的电台要有执照，并且在船长或船舶其他负责人的最终授权下，只能由完全合格的人员进行操作和管理。《无线电规则》还要求，遇险警报只能在船长或船舶其他负责人批准后拍发。

10　船长应切记所有指定负责拍发遇险警报的人员必须按照规则第 I/14 条第 1.5 段的要求，对船上一切无线电设备都接受过训练和具有知识并能准确操作，对此，应在甲板日志或无线电日志上记载。

值班

11　除关于无线电值班的要求外，每一海船船长还应确保：

.1　为了交换一般通信，特别是公众通信，船舶无线电台应适当配员，并考虑到被批准操作船舶无线电台人员的职责所带来的限制；并且

.2 the radio equipment provided on board and, where fitted, the reserve sources of energy are maintained in an efficient working condition.

12 Necessary instruction and information on use of radio equipment and procedures for distress and safety purposes should be given periodically to all relevant crew members by the person designated in the muster list to have primary responsibility for radiocommunications during distress incidents. This should be recorded in the radio log.

13 The master of every ship not subject to the SOLAS, 1974 should require that radio watchkeeping is adequately maintained as determined by the Administration, taking into account the Radio Regulations.

Operational

14 Prior to sailing, the radio operator designated as having primary responsibility for radiocommunications during distress incidents should ensure that:

.1 all distress and safety radio equipment and the reserve source of energy are in an efficient working condition, and that this is recorded in the radio log;

.2 all documents required by international agreement, notices to ship radio stations and additional documents required by the Administration are available and are corrected in accordance with the latest supplements, and that any discrepancy is reported to the master;

.3 the radio clock is correctly set against standard time signals;

.4 antennae are correctly positioned, undamaged and properly connected; and

.5 to the extent practicable, routine weather and navigational warning messages for the area in which the ship will be navigating are updated together with those for other areas requested by the master, and that such messages are passed to the master.

5 On sailing and opening the station, the radio operator on watch should:

.1 listen on the appropriate distress frequencies for any possible existing distress situation; and

.2 send a traffic report (name, position and destination, etc.) to the local coast station and any other appropriate coast station from which general communications may be expected.

6 While the station is open, the radio operator on watch should:

.1 check the radio clock against standard time signals at least once a day;

.2 send a traffic report when entering and on leaving the service area of a coast station from which general communications might be expected; and

.3 transmit reports to ship reporting systems in accordance with the instructions of the master.

.2 船上备有无线电设备以及备用电源(如有的话)保持有效的工作状态。

12 应变部署表中指定在遇险事件中负有无线电通信主要职责者,应定期向所有有关船员提供无线电设备的使用和遇险与安全程序方面必要的介绍和信息,这些活动应记入无线电日志。

13 不受《1974 年 SOLAS 公约》约束的每一船舶的船长应考虑《无线电规则》,要求按主管机关的决定充分保持无线电值班。

操作性要求

14 开航前,指定在遇险事件中负有无线电通信主要职责的无线电操作员应确保:

.1 所有遇险和安全方面的无线电设备和备用电源处于有效的工作状态并将其记入无线电日志;

.2 备妥国际协定要求的所有文书、船舶电台通告以及主管机关要求的其他附加文书,并根据最新的增补进行改正,如有不符,报告船长;

.3 无线电时钟按标准时间信号予以正确设定;

.4 天线已正确就位,无损坏并已妥善连接;并且

.5 按实际,尽可能更新船舶将要航行区域(包括船长要求的其他区域)的常规气象报告和航行警告的信文,并将这些信文传递给船长。

15 航行并开启电台后,值班无线电操作员应:

.1 在适当的遇险频率上守听可能存在的遇险情况;并且

.2 向当地海岸电台和其他任何合适的、可能进行一般通信的海岸电台发一通报(船名、位置和目的地等)。

16 当电台开通时,值班的无线电操作员应:

.1 以标准时间信号校对无线电时钟,至少每天一次;

.2 在进入和离开某一进行一般通信的海岸电台的服务区域时,向该海岸电台发一通报;并且

.3 按照船长指示向船舶报告系统发报。

17 While at sea, the radio operator designated as having primary responsibility for radiocommunications during distress incidents should ensure the proper functioning of:

.1 the digital selective calling (DSC) distress and safety radio equipment by means of a test call at least once each week; and

.2 the distress and safety radio equipment by means of a test at least once each day but without radiating any signal.

The results of these tests should be recorded in the radio log.

18 The radio operator designated to handle general communications should ensure that an effective watch is maintained on those frequencies on which communications are likely to be exchanged, having regard to the position of the ship in relation to those coast stations and to coast earth stations from which traffic may be expected. When exchanging traffic, radio operators should follow the relevant ITU recommendations.

19 When closing the station on arrival at a port, the radio operator on watch should advise the local coast station and other coast stations with which contact has been maintained of the ship's arrival and of the closing of the station.

20 When closing the radio station, the radio operator designated as having primary responsibility for radiocommunications during distress incidents should:

.1 ensure that transmitting antennae are earthed; and

.2 check that the reserve sources of energy are sufficiently charged.

Distress alerts and procedures

21 The distress alert or distress call has absolute priority over all other transmissions. All stations which receive such signals are required by the Radio Regulations to immediately cease all transmissions capable of interfering with distress communications.

22 In the case of a distress affecting own ship, the radio operator designated as having primary responsibility for radiocommunications during distress incidents should immediately assume responsibility for following the procedures of the Radio Regulations and relevant ITU-R Recommendations.

23 On receiving a distress alert:

.1 the radio operator on watch should alert the master and, if appropriate, the radio operator designated as having primary responsibility for radiocommunications during distress incidents; and

.2 the radio operator designated as having primary responsibility for radiocommunications during distress incidents should evaluate the situation and immediately assume responsibility for following the procedures of the Radio Regulations and relevant ITU-R Recommendations.

17　当在海上时,指定在遇险事件中负有无线电通信主要职责的无线电操作员应保证以下设备正常工作:

.1　每周至少一次,用试验呼叫方法测试数字选择性呼叫(DSC)遇险和安全无线电设备;以及

.2　每天至少一次,测试遇险和安全无线电设备,但不发射任何信号。

测试结果应记入无线电日志。

18　指定处理一般通信的无线电操作员应考虑到本船船位与那些可能要进行通信业务的海岸电台和海岸地球站的相对位置,保证在可能交换通信的频率上保持有效值班。在交换通信业务时,无线电操作员应遵守国际电信联盟(ITU)的有关建议。

19　在抵达港口而关闭电台时,值班的无线电操作员应将抵港并关闭电台一事通知当地海岸电台和其他保持过联系的海岸电台。

20　在关闭电台时,指定在遇险事件中负有无线电通信主要职责的无线电操作员应:

.1　保证发射天线接地;并且

.2　检查备用电源是否已经充满。

遇险报警和程序

21　遇险报警或遇险呼叫绝对优先于一切其他发射。《无线电规则》规定,所有收到这种信号的电台应立即停止可能影响遇险通信的一切发射。

22　如果是本船遇险,指定在遇险事件中负有无线电通信主要职责的无线电操作员应立即按《无线电规则》的程序并有关 ITU-R 建议承担起责任。

23　在收到遇险报警时:

.1　值班的无线电操作员应立即向船长报警,如果合适,还应向指定在遇险事件中负有无线电通信主要职责的无线电操作员报警;并且

.2　指定在遇险事件中负有无线电通信主要职责的无线电操作员应评价局势,并立即按照《无线电规则》的程序和有关的 ITU-R 建议承担起责任。

Urgency messages

24 In cases of urgency affecting own ship, the radio operator designated as having responsibility for radiocommunications during distress incidents should immediately assume responsibility for following the procedures of the Radio Regulations and relevant ITU-R Recommendations.

25 In cases of communications relating to medical advice, the radio operator designated as having primary responsibility for radiocommunications during distress incidents should follow the procedures of the Radio Regulations and adhere to the conditions as published in the relevant international documentation (see paragraph 14.2) or as specified by the satellite service provider.

26 In cases of communications relating to medical transports, as defined in the Protocol additional to the Geneva Conventions of 12 August 1949, and relating to the protection of victims of international armed conflicts (Protocol I), the radio operator designated as having primary responsibility for radiocommunication during distress incidents should follow the procedures of the Radio Regulations.

27 On receiving an urgency message, the radio operator on watch should alert the master and, if appropriate, the radio operator designated as having primary responsibility for radiocommunications during distress incidents.

Safety messages

28 When a safety message is to be transmitted, the master and the radio operator on watch should follow the procedures of the Radio Regulations.

29 On receiving a safety message, the radio operator on watch should note its content and act in accordance with the master's instructions.

30 Bridge-to-bridge communications should be exchanged on VHF channel 13. Bridge-to-bridge communications are described as "Intership Navigation Safety Communications" in the Radio Regulations.

Radio records

31 Additional entries in the radio log should be made in accordance with paragraphs 10, 12, 14, 17 and 33.

32 Unauthorized transmissions and incidents of harmful interference should, if possible, be identified, recorded in the radio log and brought to the attention of the Administration in compliance with the Radio Regulations, together with an appropriate extract from the radio log.

Battery maintenance

33 Batteries providing a source of energy for any part of the radio installation, including those associated with uninterrupted power supplies, are the responsibility of the radio operator designated as having primary responsibility for radiocommunications during distress incidents and should be:

.1 tested on-load and off-load daily and, where necessary, brought up to the fully charged condition;

紧急信文

24　一旦本船发生紧急事件，指定在遇险事件中负有无线电通信主要职责的无线电操作员应按照《无线电规则》的程序和有关的 ITU-R 建议承担起责任。

25　在进行有关医疗建议的通信时，指定在遇险事件中负有无线电通信主要职责的无线电操作员应遵循《无线电规则》的程序并根据有关的国际性文件（见第 14.2 段）或卫星业务提供人所指明的条件办理。

26　在进行有关 1949 年 8 月 12 日日内瓦公约的补充议定书（议定书 I）所称的医疗运输事件的通信和关于保护国际武装冲突中受害者的通信时，指定在遇险事件中负有无线电通信主要职责的无线电操作员应遵照《无线电规则》的程序办理。

27　在收到紧急信文时，值班的无线电操作员应向船长报警，如果合适，还应向指定在遇险事件中负有无线电通信主要职责的无线电操作员报警。

安全信文

28　当发送安全信文时，船长和值班的无线电操作员应遵照《无线电规则》办理。

29　在收到安全信文时，值班的无线电操作员应记录其内容并按船长指示处理。

30　驾驶台与驾驶台之间的通信应在 VHF13 频道上进行。驾驶台与驾驶台之间的通信详见《无线电规则》中的“船舶间航行安全通信”。

无线电记录

31　应按照第 10 段、第 12 段、第 14 段、第 17 段和第 33 段在无线电日志上作附加记录。

32　如可能，对未经许可的发射和有害的干扰事件，应辨认清楚并记入无线电日志，同时根据《无线电规则》，连同一份相应的无线电日志摘抄提请主管机关注意。

蓄电池的保养

33　为无线电装置（包括带有不间断电源的无线电装置）各个部分提供电源的蓄电池是由指定在遇险事件中负有无线电通信主要职责的无线电操作员负责的，对蓄电池应：

.1　每天进行带负荷和不带负荷的测试，并且在必要时使之处于充满的状态；

.2 tested once per week by means of a hydrometer where practicable, or, where a hydrometer cannot be used, by a suitable load test; and

.3 checked once per month for the security of each battery and its connections and the condition of the batteries and their compartment or compartments.

The results of these tests should be recorded in the radio log.

PART 5 – GUIDANCE ON WATCHKEEPING IN PORT

(No provisions)

.2 如可行,每周用液体比重计测试一次,如比重计不能使用,可用合适的负载试验;并且

.3 每月检查一次每个蓄电池及其接点的可靠性以及蓄电池的状态和它们的分隔室。

测试结果应记入无线电日志。

第 5 部分　关于在港值班的指导

(无条文)

Attachment 3 to the Final Act of the Conference

Resolution 3

Expression of appreciation to the host Government

THE 2010 MANILA CONFERENCE,

NOTING with appreciation the kind invitation of the Government of the Philippines to the International Maritime Organization to hold the International Conference to adopt amendments to the International Convention on Standards of Training, Certification and Watchkeeping for Seafarers, 1978 and the Seafarers Training, Certification and Watchkeeping Code,

ACKNOWLEDGING the generous financial and in-kind contribution and excellent arrangements made by the Government of the Philippines for the Conference, as well as the hospitality, courtesies and other amenities bestowed on the Participants to the Conference,

1. EXPRESSES its profound gratitude and thanks to the Government and the People of the Philippines for their valuable contribution to the success of the Conference;

2. DECIDES, in grateful recognition of this contribution, to designate the amendments adopted by the Conference as:

> **"THE MANILA AMENDMENTS TO THE INTERNATIONAL CONVENTION ON STANDARDS OF TRAINING, CERTIFICATION AND WATCHKEEPING FOR SEAFARERS, 1978"**

大会最终文件附件 3

决议 3
对主办国政府表示感谢

2010 年马尼拉大会，

注意到应对菲律宾政府邀请国际海事组织在马尼拉举办外交大会以通过《1978 年海员培训、发证和值班标准国际公约》修正案表示感谢，

承认菲律宾政府对本次大会给予慷慨的财政支持、实物捐助、周到的安排，以及对与会者热情、礼貌的招待及其他礼遇，

1. 对菲律宾政府及人民为此次大会的圆满成功所作的一切宝贵的贡献**表示**深深感谢；

2. 为认可菲律宾政府做出的贡献，**决定**将大会通过的修正案冠名为：

“1978 **年海员培训、发证和值班标准国际公约马尼拉修正案**”。

Resolution 4

Transitional provisions and early implementation

THE 2010 MANILA CONFERENCE,

HAVING ADOPTED the Manila amendments to the International Convention on Standards of Training, Certification and Watchkeeping for Seafarers, 1978 and to the Seafarers' Training, Certification and Watchkeeping Code, as amended (STCW Convention and Code),

HAVING AGREED to include regulation I/15 on Transitional provisions, which allows for an interval of five years, or until the time of the next revalidation of certificate(s) of competency after the amendments have entered into force, whichever is later, before Parties will be required to issue, recognize and endorse certificates in accordance with the amendments adopted by the Conference,

RECOGNIZING that, in order to achieve full compliance by 1 January 2017, it is necessary for Parties to promptly begin taking appropriate measures to implement the STCW Convention and Code in their national training, certification and administration systems,

BEING CONCERNED that difficulties, which may arise in connection with the implementation of the requirements of the STCW Convention and Code, could undermine the objective of introducing the highest practicable standards of competence at the earliest possible time,

1. URGES each Party to keep the Maritime Safety Committee of the International Maritime Organization informed of progress made in respect of the transitional provisions of regulation I/15 under its national system to implement the requirements of the amendments to the STCW Convention and Code, adopted by the Conference, as well as any difficulties encountered in this regard;

2. FURTHER URGES each Party to take appropriate steps for early implementation of the amendments to the STCW Convention and Code adopted by the Conference;

3. INVITES the Maritime Safety Committee of the International Maritime Organization, in order to promote the introduction of the highest practicable standards of competence as soon as possible, to monitor progress toward implementation of the STCW Convention and Code by all Parties, with the aim of encouraging an orderly transition and anticipating complications, which could otherwise undermine full and effective implementation.

决议 4
过渡规定和及早实施

2010 年马尼拉大会，

已通过《1978 年海员培训、发证和值班标准国际公约》和经修订的《海员培训、发证和值班规则》(STCW 公约和 STCW 规则)的马尼拉修正案，

已同意纳入关于过渡规定的规则 I/15，在要求各方按照大会通过的修正案签发、认可和签注适任证书之前，该条规则允许 5 年的时间间隔，或直到修正案生效后的下一次适任证书再有效时，以较迟者为准，

认识到为在 2017 年 1 月 1 日取得完全一致，需要各方开始迅速采取适当措施在其国内培训、发证和管理系统实施经修正的 STCW 公约和 STCW 规则，

意识到履行 STCW 公约和 STCW 规则的要求可能出现的困难会削弱尽早引入最高可行适任标准的目标，

1. **敦促**各方在规则第 I/15 条规定的过渡期内向国际海事组织海上安全委员会进行通报，内容包括其国内体系在执行大会通过的 STCW 公约和 STCW 规则修正案要求方面取得的进展和遇到的困难，

2. **进一步敦促**各方采取适当步骤及早实施大会通过的 STCW 公约和 STCW 规则修正案，

3. 为推进早日引入最高可行适任标准，**敦请**海上安全委员会监督所有缔约国在实施经修订的 STCW 公约和 STCW 规则方面的进展，旨在鼓励有序过渡和预估其他方面可能存在的不利于全面有效履约的复杂状况。

Resolution 5

Verification of certificates of competency and endorsements

THE 2010 MANILA CONFERENCE,

HAVING ADOPTED the Manila amendments to the International Convention on Standards of Training, Certification and Watchkeeping for Seafarers, 1978, and to the Seafarers' Training, Certification and Watchkeeping Code, as amended,

RECOGNIZING the importance of adequate education and training for, and experience acquired by, all seafarers,

RECOGNIZING ALSO the need for all ships to be manned and operated by properly trained and certified seafarers,

RECOGNIZING FURTHER that the verification of certificates of competency and endorsements issued to seafarers is essential also from the point of view of preventing unlawful practices associated with the issuance of such certificates as well as to supporting port State control activities,

RECOMMENDS that Administrations take appropriate steps to:

.1 establish electronic databases to assist in verifying the authenticity and validity of certificates of competency and endorsements they issue; and

.2 respond appropriately and in a timely manner to any request from other Administrations for verification of the authenticity and validity of certificates of competency and endorsements.

决议 5
适任证书和签证的核实

2010 年马尼拉大会，

已通过《1978 年海员培训、发证和值班标准国际公约》和经修订的《海员培训、发证和值班规则》(STCW 公约和 STCW 规则)的马尼拉修正案，

认识到接受适当的教育、培训和获得经验对所有海员的重要性，

也认识到由适当培训和持证的海员配备和操纵船舶的必要性，

进一步认识到从防止发生与适任证书签发有关的非法行为的角度出发，也为了支持港口国监督检查工作，对核实签发给海员的适任证书和签证的重要性，

建议主管机关采取适当步骤：

.1 建立电子数据库，以便核实其签发的适任证书和签证的真实性和有效性；

.2 适当、及时地回应其他主管机关任何关于核实适任证书和签证的真实性和有效性的请求。

Resolution 6

Standards of training and certification and ships' manning levels

THE 2010 MANILA CONFERENCE,

HAVING ADOPTED the Manila amendments to the International Convention on Standards of Training, Certification and Watchkeeping for Seafarers, 1978, and to the Seafarers' Training, Certification and Watchkeeping Code, as amended (STCW Convention and Code),

RECOGNIZING the importance of adequate education and training for, and experience acquired by, all seafarers,

RECOGNIZING ALSO the need for all ships to be manned and operated by properly trained and certified seafarers,

NOTING that the STCW Convention and Code establish standards of training, certification and watchkeeping for seafarers,

1. REAFFIRMS that the STCW Convention and Code are instruments concerned with standards of training and certification and do not determine ships' manning levels;

2. REAFFIRMS ALSO that any decision relating to ships' manning levels is the responsibility of the Administrations and shipowners concerned taking into account the principles of safe manning* adopted by the International Maritime Organization.

* Refers to resolution A.890(21), as amended on Principles of safe manning, adopted by the Assembly of the International Maritime Organization on 25 November 1999.

决议 6
培训、发证标准和船舶配员水平

2010 年马尼拉大会，

已通过《1978 年海员培训、发证和值班标准国际公约》和经修订的《海员培训、发证和值班规则》(STCW 公约和 STCW 规则)的马尼拉修正案，

认识到接受适当的教育、培训和获得经验对所有海员的重要性，

也认识到所有船舶的配员和操作都应由接受过适当培训的持证海员完成，

注意到 STCW 公约和 STCW 规则为海员的培训、发证和值班建立了标准，

1. **重申** STCW 公约和 STCW 规则是关于培训和发证标准的文件，不决定船舶的配员水平；

2. **并重申**由主管机关和有关船东负责制定船舶配员标准，并考虑国际海事组织通过的安全配员原则①。

① 见经修订的关于安全配员原则的 A. 890(21)号决议，IMO 大会于 1999 年 11 月 25 日通过。

Resolution 7

Promotion of technical knowledge, skills and professionalism of seafarers

THE 2010 MANILA CONFERENCE,

HAVING ADOPTED the Manila amendments to the International Convention on Standards of Training, Certification and Watchkeeping for Seafarers, 1978 and to the Seafarers' Training, Certification and Watchkeeping Code, as amended (STCW Convention and Code),

NOTING with concern the reported and anticipated shortage of qualified officers to effectively man and operate ships engaged in international trade,

APPRECIATING that the overall effectiveness of selection, training and certification processes can only be evaluated through the skills, abilities and competence exhibited by seafarers during the course of their service on board ship,

RECOMMENDS that Administrations make arrangements to ensure that shipping companies:

.1 establish criteria and processes for the selection of seafarers exhibiting the highest practicable standards of technical knowledge, skills and professionalism;

.2 monitor the standards exhibited by ships' personnel in the performance of their duties;

.3 encourage all officers serving on their ships to participate actively in the training of junior personnel;

.4 monitor carefully and review frequently the progress made by junior personnel in the acquisition of knowledge and skills during their service on board ship;

.5 provide refresher and updating training at suitable intervals, as may be required; and

.6 take all appropriate measures to instil pride in the maritime profession and encourage the creation of a safety culture and environmental conscience among all those who serve on their ships.

决议 7
提升海员的知识、技能和职业化水平

2010 年马尼拉大会，

已通过《1978 年海员培训、发证和值班标准国际公约》和经修订的《海员培训、发证和值班规则》（STCW 公约和 STCW 规则）的马尼拉修正案，

注意到报导关注和预期用于有效配备和操作从事国际贸易的船舶的合格高级船员的短缺，

充分意识到遴选、培训和发证程序是否有效，只能通过船员在船上服务期间呈现的技能和适任能力进行评估，

建议主管机关应作出安排以确保公司：

.1 为遴选能表现出最高可行的知识、技能和职业化水平的海员建立标准和程序；

.2 监督船上人员在履职过程中呈现出的标准；

.3 鼓励高级船员积极参与对低级别海员的的培训；

.4 密切关注并经常评估低级别海员在船期间知识和技能方面取得的进展；

.5 按要求并适当排期，提供知识更新培训；并且

.6 采取所有适当措施，培养所有在船服务人员的职业自豪感，鼓励创建安全文化和环境意识。

Resolution 8

Development of guidelines to implement international standards of medical fitness for seafarers

THE 2010 MANILA CONFERENCE,

HAVING ADOPTED the Manila amendments to the International Convention on Standards of Training, Certification and Watchkeeping for Seafarers, 1978 and to the Seafarers' Training, Certification and Watchkeeping Code, as amended (STCW Convention and Code),

RECOGNIZING the importance of the overall medical fitness of masters and ships' crews to the safety of life and property at sea and the protection of the marine environment,

TAKING COGNIZANCE OF the international standards of medical fitness for seafarers included in the STCW Convention and Code and the Maritime Labour Convention, 2006,

INVITES the International Maritime Organization, in co-operation with the International Labour Organization and the World Health Organization, to develop guidelines to implement the aforementioned standards.

决议 8
起草实施国际海员健康标准指南

2010 年马尼拉大会，

已通过《1978 年海员培训、发证和值班标准国际公约》和经修订的《海员培训、发证和值班规则》(STCW 公约和 STCW 规则)的马尼拉修正案，

认识到船长和船员的全面健康对海上人命和财产安全和海洋环境保护的重要性，

注意到 STCW 公约和 STCW 规则以及《2006 年海事劳工公约》中的国际海员健康标准，

敦请国际海事组织与国际劳工组织、世界卫生组织合作，共同起草实施上述标准的指南。

Resolution 9

Revision of existing model courses published by the International Maritime Organization and development of new model courses

THE 2010 MANILA CONFERENCE,

HAVING ADOPTED the Manila amendments to the International Convention on Standards of Training, Certification and Watchkeeping for Seafarers, 1978 and to the Seafarers' Training, Certification and Watchkeeping Code, as amended (STCW Convention and Code),

RECOGNIZING the significant contribution made to seafarers' training and certification through model courses, validated and published by the International Maritime Organization (IMO), providing core curricula based on the minimum requirements of the STCW Convention and Code,

APPRECIATING that the aforementioned model courses have assisted many training institutions to improve the quality of the training they provide and have been used to improve procedures for assessing competency,

DESIRING to achieve greater uniformity in the application of the training and assessment provisions of the STCW Convention and Code,

INVITES:

.1 IMO to take steps to revise and update existing model courses and develop new model courses, which provide guidance on the implementation of the training and assessment provisions of the STCW Convention and Code; and

.2 Governments and international organizations to provide funding for, and otherwise assist in, the revision, updating of existing model courses and development of new model courses.

决议 9
修订国际海事组织出版的现有示范培训课程并制定新的示范培训课程

2010 年马尼拉大会，

已通过《1978 年海员培训、发证和值班标准国际公约》和经修订的《海员培训、发证和值班规则》(STCW 公约和 STCW 规则)的马尼拉修正案，

认识到通过国际海事组织进行有效发布的示范培训课程，是基于 STCW 公约和 STCW 规则最低要求设计的核心课程为海员的培训和发证工作作出了卓著的贡献，

充分意识到上述示范培训课程已协助众多培训机构提高了培训质量和改进了适任评估程序，

希望使 STCW 公约和 STCW 规则中关于培训和评估的规定得到更广泛一致的应用，

敦请：

.1 国际海事组织采取措施修订和更新现有的示范培训课程，开发新的示范培训课程，为实施 STCW 公约和 STCW 规则的培训和评估规定提供指导；和

.2 政府和国际组织提供资金，或协助，用于修订和更新现有的示范培训课程，开发新的示范培训课程。

Resolution 10

Promotion of technical co-operation

THE 2010 MANILA CONFERENCE,

HAVING ADOPTED the Manila amendments to the International Convention on Standards of Training, Certification and Watchkeeping for Seafarers, 1978 and to the Seafarers' Training, Certification and Watchkeeping Code, as amended (STCW Convention and Code),

RECALLING IMO Assembly resolution A.998(25) on Need for capacity building for the development and implementation of new, and amendments to existing instruments,

RECOGNIZING the importance of adequate education and training for, and experience acquired by, all seafarers,

RECOGNIZING FURTHER that, in some cases, there may be limited facilities for providing specialized training programmes and obtaining the required experience, particularly in developing countries,

BELIEVING that the promotion of technical co-operation will assist countries lacking adequate expertise or facilities in providing proper training and experience to implement the STCW Convention and Code,

1. STRONGLY URGES Parties to provide, or arrange to provide, in co-operation with the International Maritime Organization (IMO), assistance to those States, which have difficulty in meeting the revised requirements of the STCW Convention and Code and which request such assistance;

2. INVITES IMO to intensify its endeavours to provide States with the assistance they may require and to make adequate provision for that purpose within its technical co-operation programme.

决议 10
促进技术合作

2010 年马尼拉大会，

已通过《1978 年海员培训、发证和值班标准国际公约》和经修订的《海员培训、发证和值班规则》（STCW 公约和 STCW 规则）的马尼拉修正案，

忆及国际海事组织 A.998(25) 号大会决议，提及需要进行能力建设，以制定和实施新文件、对现有文件进行修正，

认识到适当的教育、培训和获得经验对所有海员的重要性，

进一步认识到某些情况下，特别是在发展中国家，提供专业培训计划和获取所需经验的设施不足，

相信促进技术合作可以协助那些在提供培训和经验方面缺乏适当专门技术或培训设施的国家实施 STCW 公约和 STCW 规则，

.1 **强烈敦促**各方与国际海事组织合作，为那些对满足经修正的 STCW 公约和 STCW 规则要求有困难并提出协助请求的国家提供协助，或作出提供协助的安排；

.2 **敦请**国际海事组织尽最大努力为那些提出请求的国家提供协助，并在其技术合作计划里作出适当的规定。

Resolution 11

Measures to ensure the competency of masters and officers of ships operating in polar waters

THE 2010 MANILA CONFERENCE,

HAVING ADOPTED the Manila amendments to the International Convention on Standards of Training, Certification and Watchkeeping for Seafarers, 1978, and to the Seafarers' Training, Certification and Watchkeeping Code, as amended (STCW Convention and Code),

NOTING that, as a result of the increase in maritime traffic in polar waters, several accidents have occurred there in recent years,

NOTING FURTHER the remoteness and the singular hydrographic, oceanographic, meteorological and glaciological characteristics of polar waters, to the extent that search and rescue, care and evacuation of persons and addressing the consequences of pollution entail considerable operational and logistical problems,

RECOGNIZING that the operation of ships sailing in polar waters calls for specific education, training, experience and related qualifications for masters and officers on board such ships,

RECOGNIZING ALSO the efforts made by governments to train masters and officers through courses dedicated to this particular class of navigation,

RECOGNIZING FURTHER both the *Guidelines for ships operating in polar waters*[*] and the need for mandatory training requirements when the Polar Code under development by the International Maritime Organization is adopted,

RECOMMENDS that governments adopt measures conducive to ensuring that masters and officers of ships, which operate in polar waters, have appropriate training and experience, so that they are able to:

.1 plan voyages to polar waters, taking into account glaciological, hydrographic, oceanographic and meteorological factors;

.2 navigate safely in polar waters, in particular in restricted ice-covered areas under adverse conditions of wind and visibility; and

.3 supervise and ensure compliance with the requirements deriving from intergovernmental agreements and with those relating to safety of life at sea and protection of the marine environment.

---

[*] Refer to resolution A.1024(26) – Guidelines for ships operating in polar waters, adopted by the Assembly of the International Maritime Organization on 2 December 2009.

决议 11
确保在极区水域操作船舶的船长和高级船员适任的措施

2010 年马尼拉大会,

已通过《1978 年海员培训、发证和值班标准国际公约》和经修订的《海员培训、发证和值班规则》(STCW 公约和 STCW 规则)的马尼拉修正案,

注意到随着极区水域航运业的发展,近年来已发生数起海上事故,

进一步注意到由于极区水域地理位置偏远,水文、海洋、气象、冰河现象独特,在搜救、援助和疏散人员时和处理环境污染问题时会遇到严重的操作困难和后勤保障困难,

认识到在极区水域操作船舶,船长和高级船员需要特定教育、培训、经验和相关资格,

还认识到一些政府已作出努力通过专门用于这类特定航行的课程培训船长和高级船员,

进一步认识到现有的国际海事组织《极区水域船舶操作指南》①和《极区规则》通过后的强制性培训需求,

建议政府采取可行措施,确保在极区水域操作船舶的船长和高级船员接受专门培训和获得经验,以便他们有能力:

.1 制定驶往极区水域的航次计划,考虑在极区水域航行时的冰河、水文、海洋和气象因素;

.2 在极区水域安全航行,特别是在受限制的冰覆盖水域内风向和能见度均不利时;并且

.3 监控并确保遵守源自政府间协议的要求以及海上人命安全和海洋环境保护的规定。

① 见关于极区水域船舶操作指南的 A.1024(26)号决议,IMO 大会于 2009 年 12 月 2 日通过。

Resolution 12

Attracting new entrants to, and retaining seafarers in, the maritime profession

THE 2010 MANILA CONFERENCE,

HAVING ADOPTED the Manila amendments to the International Convention on Standards of Training, Certification and Watchkeeping for Seafarers, 1978, and to the Seafarers' Training, Certification and Watchkeeping Code, as amended (STCW Convention and Code),

BEING AWARE that more than 90% of world trade is carried by sea and that the shipping industry operates safely, securely, efficiently and in an environmentally-sound manner,

RECOGNIZING the vital service seafarers provide to shipping, an industry that contributes significantly to global and sustainable development and prosperity,

RECOGNIZING ALSO the need for today's increasingly sophisticated ships to be entrusted to seafarers who are competent in all respects to operate them in a safe, secure, efficient and environmentally-sound manner,

RECOGNIZING FURTHER that any discriminative legislation adopted and practices enacted have the potential to discourage young people from joining the profession and serving seafarers from remaining in it,

NOTING with concern the reported and anticipated shortage of qualified officers to effectively man and operate ships,

NOTING ALSO with appreciation the "Go to Sea!" campaign launched, in November 2008, by the Secretary-General of the International Maritime Organization, in co-operation with the International Labour Organization, BIMCO, International Chamber of Shipping, International Shipping Federation, INTERCARGO, INTERTANKO and the International Transport Workers' Federation,

APPRECIATING the overall efforts of the shipping industry to promote among young persons a career at sea,

RECOMMENDS that Administrations, shipping companies, shipowner, ship manager and seafarer organizations and any other entities concerned do their utmost to promote among young persons a career at sea and to retain existing seafarers within the industry by:

.1 engendering a more favourable public perception, in particular among young people, of the maritime industry;

.2 promoting a greater awareness and knowledge among young people of the opportunities offered by a career at sea;

决议 12
吸引新人加入海员职业，留住现有海员

2010 年马尼拉大会，

已通过《1978 年海员培训、发证和值班标准国际公约》和经修订的《海员培训、发证和值班规则》（STCW 公约和 STCW 规则）的马尼拉修正案，

意识到世界贸易 90% 的运输量是从海上进行运输，国际航运业的运作方式安全、保安、有效且环保，

认识到在航运业为全球化、可持续发展和经济繁荣方面作出卓越贡献的过程中，海员提供至关重要的服务，

也认识到当今日益复杂的船舶必须倚赖各方面都适任的海员，才能以安全、保安、环保并有效的方式进行操作，

进一步认识到采用区别对待的立法和实践，可能阻碍年轻人加入这个职业和无法留住在职海员，

关切地注意到已有报道并预期可用于有效配备和操作船舶的合格高级船员的短缺，

也注意到 2008 年国际海事组织秘书长与国际劳工组织、波罗地海国际海事委员会、国际航运公会、国际航运联合会、国际干货船船东协会、国际独立油轮船东协会和国际运输工人联合会共同发起“出海去！”的倡议活动，

意识到这一行业正共同努力鼓励年轻人从事海上职业，

建议主管机关、船公司、船东、船舶经理人与海员组织和其他相关机构正尽力通过以下措施鼓励年轻人从事海上职业并留住现有海员：

.1 特别是在年轻人中，养成公众对海运业的正面认识；

.2 提升年轻人对海上职业所提供的机遇的认识和了解；

.3 improving the quality of life at sea by bringing it more closely in line with the career alternatives available ashore and by enhancing the facilities provided on board ships, including accessing the Internet;

.4 encouraging all officers serving on their ships to participate actively in the training and mentoring of junior personnel during their service on board ship;

.5 encouraging the provision of adequate accommodation for trainees on new buildings; and

.6 taking all appropriate measures to instil pride in the maritime profession and encourage the creation of a safety culture and environmental conscience among all those who serve on their ships.

.3 提高海上生活质量,使之更接近岸上可从事行业的水平,提高船上配备给海员的设施水准,例如接入因特网;

.4 鼓励在船服务的所有高级船员积极参与对船上低级别船员的培训和辅导;

.5 鼓励新造船舶上为受训人员提供适当的膳宿安排;并且

.6 采取所有适当措施,培养所有在船服务人员的职业自豪感,鼓励创建安全文化和环境意识。

Resolution 13

Accommodation for trainees

THE 2010 MANILA CONFERENCE,

HAVING ADOPTED the Manila amendments to the International Convention on Standards of Training, Certification and Watchkeeping for Seafarers, 1978 and to the Seafarers' Training, Certification and Watchkeeping Code, as amended (STCW Convention and Code),

NOTING with concern the reported and anticipated shortage of qualified officers to effectively man and operate ships engaged in international trade,

RECOGNIZING the need for today's increasingly sophisticated ships to be entrusted to seafarers who are competent in all respects to operate them in a safe, secure, efficient and environmentally-sound manner,

RECOGNIZING ALSO that minimum mandatory seagoing service forms part of the requirements prescribed in the STCW Convention and Code for operational level and support level certification,

RECOGNIZING FURTHER that the lack of adequate accommodation for trainees on board ships constitutes a significant impediment to properly training them and subsequently retaining them at sea, thus adding to the aforementioned shortage,

URGES shipowners, ship managers and shipping companies to provide suitable accommodation for trainees on board their ships both existing and new.

决议 13
受训人员住宿

2010 年马尼拉大会，

已通过《1978 年海员培训、发证和值班标准国际公约》和经修订的《海员培训、发证和值班规则》（STCW 公约和 STCW 规则）的马尼拉修正案，

关切地注意到报道并预期可用于有效配备和操作从事国际贸易船舶的合格高级船员的短缺，

认识到当今日益复杂的船舶必须倚赖各方面都适任的海员，才能以安全、环保并有效的方式进行操作，

也认识到海上服务资历是 STCW 公约和 STCW 规则规定中对操作级和支持级发证的强制性最低要求的一部分，

进一步认识到船上缺乏适当的受训人员住宿安排，是提供船员培训过程中的主要障碍，也导致无法留住船员继续服务，从而使船员短缺现象更严重，

敦促船东、管理人和船公司在现有和新造船舶上为受训人员提供适当的住宿安排。

Resolution 14

Promotion of the participation of women in the maritime industry

THE 2010 MANILA CONFERENCE,

HAVING ADOPTED the Manila amendments to the International Convention on Standards of Training, Certification and Watchkeeping for Seafarers, 1978 and to the Seafarers' Training, Certification and Watchkeeping Code, as amended,

NOTING the Long- and Medium-Term Plans for the Integration of Women in the Maritime Sector developed by the International Maritime Organization,

NOTING ALSO the resolution concerning the promotion of opportunities for women seafarers adopted by the International Labour Conference of the International Labour Organization on 22 February 2006,

EXPRESSING SUPPORT for the latter's aims to promote the training of women in the maritime sector,

CONSIDERING HIGHLY DESIRABLE that both men and women have equal access opportunities to maritime training and to employment on board ship,

1. INVITES Governments:

   .1 to give special consideration to securing equal access by men and women in all sectors of the maritime industry; and

   .2 to highlight the role of women in the seafaring profession and to promote their greater participation in maritime training and at all levels in the maritime industry;

2. FURTHER INVITES Governments and the industry:

   .1 to endeavour considering ways to identify and overcome, at international level, the existing constraints, such as the lack of facilities for women on board training vessels, so that women can participate fully and without hindrance in seafaring activities in order to facilitate effectively the achievement of Millennium Development Goals (MDG) 3 (Promote gender equality and empower women);

   .2 to support the provision of on-the-job-training opportunities so that women may acquire the appropriate level of practical experience required to enhance professional maritime skills.

决议 14
鼓励女性进入航海行业

2010 年马尼拉大会，

已通过《1978 年海员培训、发证和值班标准国际公约》和经修订的《海员培训、发证和值班规则》（STCW 公约和 STCW 规则）的马尼拉修正案，

注意到国际海事组织的中长期规划鼓励女性加入航海领域，

还注意到国际劳工大会 2006 年 2 月 22 日通过的有关提高女性海员就业机会的决议，

明确支持该目标，促进女性在航海领域的培训，

认为非常有必要让女性和男性在接受航海教育和在船上就业方面具有同等机会，

1. **敦请**各国政府：

   .1 在保障女性和男性在海事行业各领域中机会均等方面予以特别考虑；并且

   .2 突出女性在海员职业的作用，促进其在航海培训和航海行业的各个层次更广泛地参与。

2. **进一步敦请**政府和业界：

   .1 以国际视野认真考虑如何识别和突破目前的局限，如培训船上缺少供女性使用的设施等，以便女性可以无阻碍地全面参与航海活动，以便有效促进实现联合国千年目标 3（促进两性平等并赋予妇女权力）；

   .2 支持提供在职培训的机会，以便女性可以获得适当的实际经验，以提升其航海职业技能。

Resolution 15

Future amendments and review of the STCW Convention and Code

THE 2010 MANILA CONFERENCE,

HAVING ADOPTED the Manila amendments to the International Convention on Standards of Training, Certification and Watchkeeping for Seafarers, 1978 and to the Seafarers' Training, Certification and Watchkeeping Code, as amended (STCW Convention and Code),

NOTING that rapidly evolving technology and training methodologies require a consistent approach towards reviewing, amending and updating the STCW Convention and Code,

NOTING FURTHER, however, that frequent amendments to the STCW Convention and Code may be problematic to Maritime Administrations, shipowners, maritime training and education institutions and/or seafarers and should, therefore, be avoided,

1. RECOMMENDS that significant and extensive amendments to the STCW Convention and Code should, as far as possible, be developed and adopted on a five-yearly cycle basis;

2. RECOMMENDS FURTHER that a comprehensive review of the STCW Convention and Code should, as far as possible, be carried out every ten years to address any inconsistencies identified in the interim; and to ensure that they are up to date with emerging technologies.

决议 15
对 STCW 公约和 STCW 规则的后续修正和回顾

2010 年马尼拉大会，

已通过《1978 年海员培训、发证和值班标准国际公约》和经修订的《海员培训、发证和值班规则》(STCW 公约和 STCW 规则)的马尼拉修正案，

注意到科技和培训方法的日异月新，需要在今后对 STCW 公约和 STCW 规则进行回顾、修正和更新时采取一致的方法，

进一步注意到频繁修正 STCW 公约和 STCW 规则既不利于海事主管机关、船东、航海培训和教育机构，也不利于海员，应尽量避免，

1. **建议**对 STCW 公约和 STCW 规则的显著的和大范围的修正应尽量在以每 5 年为一周期的基础上进行；

2. **进一步建议**对 STCW 公约和 STCW 规则的全面回顾应每 10 年进行一次，以便对期间已确定为不一致的内容作出调整，并与新兴科技保持同步。

Resolution 16

Contribution of the International Labour Organization

THE 2010 MANILA CONFERENCE,

HAVING ADOPTED the Manila amendments to the International Convention on Standards of Training, Certification and Watchkeeping for Seafarers, 1978 and to the Seafarers' Training, Certification and Watchkeeping Code, as amended (STCW Convention and Code),

RECOGNIZING the role, competence and expertise of the International Labour Organization (ILO) on matters relating to the occupational safety and health of seafarers,

RECOGNIZING ALSO the significant benefit to the achievement of the objective of the International Maritime Organization and the shipping industry from the Maritime Labour Convention, 2006 (MLC 2006), once in force and implemented,

1. EXPRESSES its appreciation for the contribution made by ILO during the development of the aforementioned amendments to the STCW Convention and Code;

2. STRONGLY RECOMMENDS to Governments, which have not yet done so, to promptly ratify the MLC 2006 to enable its expeditious entry into force and, thereafter, to ensure its wide and effective implementation.

决议 16
国际劳工组织的贡献

2010 年马尼拉大会，

已通过《1978 年海员培训、发证和值班标准国际公约》和经修订的《海员培训、发证和值班规则》(STCW 公约和 STCW 规则)的马尼拉修正案，

认识到国际劳工组织在职业安全和海员健康方面担负的作用、能力和专门知识，

也认识到在《2006 年海事劳工公约》一旦生效和实施后，将对国际海事组织和航运业实现其目标有显著效益，

1. **表达**对国际劳工组织在 STCW 公约和 STCW 规则修正过程中作出贡献的感谢；

2. **强烈建议**尚未批准《2006 年海事劳工公约》的各国政府迅速采取行动，使公约早日生效，并确保其得到广泛而有效的实施。

Resolution 17

Role of the World Maritime University, the IMO International Maritime Law Institute and the International Maritime Safety, Security and Environment Academy (IMSSEA) in promoting enhanced maritime standards

THE 2010 MANILA CONFERENCE,

HAVING ADOPTED the Manila amendments to the International Convention on Standards of Training, Certification and Watchkeeping for Seafarers, 1978 and to the Seafarers' Training, Certification and Watchkeeping Code, as amended (STCW Convention and Code),

BEING AWARE of the difficulties of countries, in particular developing countries, in achieving the standards of training and assessment required by the STCW Convention and Code,

RECOGNIZING the significant contribution made by graduates of the World Maritime University (WMU) and the IMO International Maritime Law Institute (IMLI) and the International Maritime Safety, Security and Environment Academy (IMSSEA) to the global and uniform implementation of standards incorporated in maritime safety and pollution prevention-related instruments adopted by the International Maritime Organization (IMO), including the STCW Convention and Code,

RECOGNIZING ALSO the need to maintain the required level of competence of personnel in the international maritime field in order to achieve the objectives of the Organization for safer, secure and efficient shipping in an environmentally sound manner worldwide,

RECOGNIZING FURTHER the leading role played by WMU, IMLI and IMSSEA in maritime education, training and research and the transfer of knowledge through their activities,

RECOGNIZING FURTHER the desirability of common and coordinated approaches in maritime education and training programmes of academic organizations and institutions in line with those of WMU, IMLI and IMSSEA for global implementation of the enhanced standards of the STCW Convention and Code,

APPRECIATING the generous contribution of various entities and donors (in particular, the Governments of China, Italy, Malta, Sweden and the Nippon Foundation of Japan), which have, over many years, been providing financial support and fellowships to candidates from developing countries enrolled in courses at WMU, IMLI and IMSSEA,

1. URGES IMO to continue promoting the role of WMU, IMLI and IMSSEA in maritime education, training and research in the context of the global implementation of IMO instruments, including the enhanced standards of the STCW Convention and Code;

2. RECOMMENDS STRONGLY that Governments, international organizations and shipping industry maintain and further develop their support to WMU, IMLI and IMSSEA to enable them both to continue to make available highly qualified maritime lecturers, administrators and lawyers; and to continue to provide maritime education, training and research to the benefit of maritime industry, especially candidates from developing countries;

决议 17
世界海事大学(WMU),IMO 国际海商法学院(IMLI)以及国际海上安全、保安及环境学会(IMSSEA)在倡议提高海事标准方面的作用

2010 年马尼拉大会,

已通过《1978 年海员培训、发证和值班标准国际公约》及经修订的《海员培训、发证和值班规则》(STCW 公约和 STCW 规则)的马尼拉修正案,

注意到各国,特别是发展中国家,在达到 STCW 公约及 STCW 规则所要求的关于培训和评估的标准时遇到的困难,

认识到世界海事大学、IMO 国际海商法学院以及国际海上安全、保安及环境学会(IMSSEA)毕业生对在全球统一执行 IMO 颁布的海上安全和防污染标准相关的公约(包括 STCW 公约及 STCW 规则)方面所作的贡献,

还认识到需要保持国际海事行业从业人员所必备的适任水平以实现该组织在世界范围内"更加安全、保安、高效及环保的航运业"的目标,

进一步认识到 WMU、IMLI 和 IMSSEA 在海事教育、培训与研究以及通过活动传播知识等方面的主导作用,

进一步认识到希望学术组织和机构采用的海事教育与培训计划中的共同和普遍方法与 WMU、IMLI 和 IMSSEA 相一致,以便在全球执行提高标准的 STCW 公约和 STCW 规则;

意识到给予慷慨捐助的各个实体和捐赠人(特别是中国、意大利、马耳他、瑞典政府和日本财团),多年来对发展中国家学员进入 WMU、IMLI 和 IMSSEA 学习给予的财政支持和奖学金资助,

1. **敦促** IMO,在 IMO 公约(包括提高标准的 STCW 公约和 STCW 规则)全球履约的大背景下,继续提升 WMU、IMLI 和 IMSSEA 在海事教育、培训及研究方面的作用;

2. **强烈建议**成员国政府、国际组织及航运业保持并进一步加大对 WMU、IMLI 和 IMSSEA 的支持,使它们能够继续聘用高质量的教师、管理人员以及律师,继续为海事行业特别是为来自发展中国家的学员提供海事教育、培训和研究;

3. COMMENDS the staff (both academic and administrative) of WMU, IMLI and IMSSEA for their dedication and commitment to their duties and their contribution to the attainment of the objectives of the institutions.

3. **赞扬** WMU、IMLI 和 IMSSEA(从事教育和管理)的人员对职责的付出和奉献,以及为了达到机构目标作出的贡献。

Resolution 18

Year of the Seafarer

THE 2010 MANILA CONFERENCE,

HAVING ADOPTED the Manila amendments to the International Convention on Standards of Training, Certification and Watchkeeping for Seafarers, 1978 and to the Seafarers' Training, Certification and Watchkeeping Code, as amended,

BEING AWARE of the decision of the International Maritime Organization (IMO) to name 2010 as the "Year of the Seafarer",

BEING EQUALLY AWARE of the contribution seafarers from all over the world make to international seaborne trade, the world economy and civil society as a whole,

RECOGNIZING FULLY the enormous risks seafarers shoulder in the execution of their daily tasks and duties in an often hostile environment,

MINDFUL of the deprivations to which seafarers are subject through spending long periods of their professional life at sea away from their families and friends,

BEING CONCERNED at reported instances in which seafarers were unfairly treated when their ships were involved in accidents; were abandoned in foreign ports; were refused shore leave for security purposes; and were subjected to serious risks while their ships were sailing through piracy-infested areas and to potentially harmful treatment while in the hands of pirates,

DESIRING to join in the celebrations of IMO and the maritime community to pay due tribute to seafarers for the contribution referred to above,

1. EXPRESSES DEEP APPRECIATION to IMO for its timely and appropriate decision to dedicate the current year to the Seafarer;

2. EXPRESSES ALSO DEEP APPRECIATION AND GRATITUDE to seafarers from all over the world for their unique contribution to international seaborne trade, the world economy and civil society as a whole;

3. EQUALLY EXPRESSES DEEP APPRECIATION to maritime pilots, VTS operators, seafarer welfare organizations and all others who contribute to assisting ships and seafarers to enter, stay at, or leave ports and offshore terminals and to navigate through hazardous waters safely and with due care for the marine environment;

4. URGES Governments, shipping organizations and companies and all other parties concerned to take appropriate action to recognize the contribution of seafarers as highlighted above, including by working together, under the auspices of IMO and the International Labour Organization (ILO), to promote seafaring as a career choice for young persons and encourage those already in the profession to continue serving the industry;

决议 18
海员年

2010 年马尼拉大会，

已通过《1978 年海员培训、发证和值班标准国际公约》和经修订的《海员培训、发证和值班规则》（STCW 公约和 STCW 规则）的马尼拉修正案，

意识到国际海事组织将 2010 年命名为“海员年”，

同样意识到全球海员对国际海运贸易、世界经济和公民社会连为一体作出的贡献，

全面认识到海员在履行其职责时，因常处于恶劣环境而承担着巨大风险，

牢记海员因长时间在海上度过其职业生涯，被迫远离家人和朋友，

关注有报道海员由于其服务的船舶发生事故而受到不公平待遇，在国外港口遭遗弃，以安全为理由拒绝海员上岸休假，船舶航行于海盗猖獗地区时海员面临严重风险，以及一旦被海盗劫持可能受到伤害，

希望与国际海事组织和海事界一起，共同向海员致敬，感谢他们的奉献：

1. 对国际海事组织作出了及时而适当的决定——将今年敬献给海员，**表示高度赞赏**；

2. 对全球海员作出独到的贡献使国际海运贸易、世界经济和公民社会连为一体**同样表示高度赞赏和衷心感谢**；

3. 对海上引航员、VTS 操作员、海员福利组织，以及协助船舶和海员进入、暂留或离开港口和近岸码头，充分考虑保护海洋环境的需要并引导船舶和海员安全通过危险水域的其他人员，**表示同等高度的赞赏**；

4. **敦促**政府、航运组织和船公司及其他有关方面对海员作出的上述显著贡献采取适当措施予以承认，包括在国际海事组织和国际劳工组织支持下，共同努力推动年轻人将海员作为职业选择，鼓励那些已经从业的海员继续在业内服务；

5. URGES ALSO Governments, shipping organizations and companies and all other parties concerned, working together under the auspices of IMO and ILO, to take appropriate action to promote and implement, as widely and effectively as possible:

.1 the IMO/ILO Guidelines on the fair treatment of seafarers in the event of a maritime accident;

.2 the IMO/ILO Guidelines on provision of financial security in case of abandonment of seafarers; and

.3 the IMO/ILO Guidelines on shipowners' responsibilities in respect of contractual claims for personal injury to, or death of, seafarers.

6. URGES FURTHER Governments and the shipping industry to take appropriate action to implement:

.1 the International Ship and Port Facility Security (ISPS) Code;

.2 the Guidelines adopted and promulgated by IMO to prevent and suppress acts of piracy and robbery against ships; and

.3 the Convention for the Suppression of Unlawful Acts Against the Safety of Maritime Navigation, 1988 (1988 SUA Convention) and the Protocol for the Suppression of Unlawful Acts Against the Safety of Fixed Platforms Located on the Continental Shelf, 1988 (1988 SUA Protocol), as amended by the 2005 Protocol to the 1988 SUA Convention and the 2005 Protocol to the 1988 SUA Protocol,

in a manner that, while ensuring that maximum protection is afforded to seafarers, does not subject them to any unfair treatment and unnecessary inconvenience;

7. URGES ALSO Governments to ratify, accept, approve or accede to, and thereafter effectively implement, the Maritime Labour Convention, 2006;

8. INVITES IMO, ILO and industry organizations to intensify their efforts to deliver the Year of the Seafarer Action Plan to the full and in the best interests of the seafarers.

5. **同样敦促**政府、航运组织及船公司和其他所有相关方面,在国际海事组织和国际劳工组织支持下,采取适当措施,尽可能广泛而有效地宣传和实施:

.1 国际海事组织和国际劳工组织关于在发生海上事故时公平对待海员的指南;和

.2 国际海事组织和国际劳工组织关于提供海员遭到遗弃时的财务保障的指南;

.3 国际海事组织和国际劳工组织关于船东在海员遭受人身伤亡时按合同赔偿的责任的指南。

6. **进一步敦促**政府和航运业采取适当措施实施:

.1 国际船舶与港口设施保安规则(ISPS Code);

.2 国际海事组织通过和颁布的防止和制止海盗行为和抢劫船舶的指南;和

.3 经 2005 年议定书修订的《1988 年制止危及海上航行安全非法行为公约》(1988 SUA 公约)和《1988 年制止危及大陆架固定平台安全非法行为议定书》(1988 SUA 议定书),

采取保证给予海员最大程度的保护的方式实施上述规定,使海员免于任何不公平的对待和不必要的麻烦;

7. **同样敦促**政府批准、接受、认可或加入《2006 年海事劳工公约》,并有效实施;

8. **敦请**国际海事组织和国际劳工组织及行业组织加大努力,全面考虑和关注海员的利益,将海员年行动计划付诸实施。

Resolution 19

Day of the Seafarer

THE 2010 MANILA CONFERENCE,

HAVING ADOPTED the Manila amendments to the International Convention on Standards of Training, Certification and Watchkeeping for Seafarers (STCW), 1978 and to the Seafarers' Training, Certification and Watchkeeping Code, as amended,

RECOGNIZING FULLY the unique contribution seafarers from all over the world make to international seaborne trade, the world economy and civil society as a whole,

RECOGNIZING EQUALLY the considerable risks seafarers shoulder in the execution of their daily tasks and duties in an often hostile environment,

MINDFUL of the deprivations to which seafarers are subject through spending long periods of their professional life at sea away from their families and friends,

DEEPLY APPRECIATIVE that, in recognition of the above, the International Maritime Organization has named 2010 as the "Year of the Seafarer" in order for it and the maritime community as a whole to pay due tribute to seafarers in recognition of the above,

DESIRING to ensure the continued expression of this deep appreciation and gratitude to seafarers from all over the world for the reasons explained above on an annual basis,

RECOGNIZING that the adoption of the aforementioned amendments to the STCW Convention and Code on this, the 25th June 2010, makes this a very significant day for the maritime community and those who serve it on board ships,

1. RESOLVES to nominate the 25th June of each year hereafter as the "**Day of the Seafarer**";

2. ENCOURAGES Governments, shipping organizations, companies, shipowners and all other parties concerned to duly and appropriately promote the Day of the Seafarer and take action to celebrate it meaningfully;

3. INVITES the Secretary-General of the International Maritime Organization to bring this resolution to the attention of the IMO Assembly for endorsement and for any other appropriate action it may deem necessary to promote the letter and spirit of the Day.

决议 19
海员日

2010 年马尼拉大会,

已通过《1978 年海员培训、发证和值班标准国际公约》和经修订的《海员培训、发证和值班规则》(STCW 公约和 STCW 规则)的马尼拉修正案,

充分认识到全球海员对国际海运贸易、世界经济和公民社会连为一体作出了独到的贡献,

同样认识到海员在履行其职责时因常处于恶劣环境面临的巨大风险,

牢记海员因长时间在海上度过其职业生涯,被迫远离家人和朋友,

高度赞赏国际海事组织因认同以上所述,将 2010 年命名为“海员年”,与海事界共同向海员致敬,感谢他们的奉献,

希望能基于以上原因,持续每年都对全球海员表达这种高度赞赏和衷心感谢,

认识到 2010 年 6 月 25 日通过 STCW 公约与 STCW 规则修正案的这一天,对海事界和在船上服务的人员是个非常有意义的日子,

1. **决定**命名今后每年的 6 月 25 日为“海员日”;

2. **鼓励**政府、航运组织、船公司、船东和所有相关方面对海员日给予充分而适当的宣传,并采取措施组织有意义的庆祝活动;

3. **敦请**国际海事组织秘书长将本决议呈送国际海事组织成员国大会批准,并采取任何必要的适当措施对海员日无论在形式上和实际上都予以大力宣传。